Diego Rivera

The exhibition **Diego Rivera: A Retrospective** is presented by the Founders Society Detroit Institute of Arts and the Instituto Nacional de Bellas Artes, Secretaría de Educación Pública, and the Secretaría de Relaciones Exteriores of Mexico. The international presentation of the exhibition has been made possible through the collaboration and support of the Ford Motor Company Fund, with assistance from the National Endowment for the Arts, a Federal Agency of the United States of America.

Diego Rivera
A Retrospective

Founders Society Detroit Institute of Arts

Hayward Gallery, South Bank Centre, London

In Association with

W. W. Norton & Company

New York London

The schedule for the exhibition is as follows:

Detroit Institute of Arts, February 10, 1986–April 27, 1986

Philadelphia Museum of Art, June 2, 1986–August 10, 1986

At the Philadelphia Museum of Art,
the presentation of the exhibition is supported
by a grant from The Pew Memorial Trust.

Museo del Palacio de Bellas Artes, Mexico, D.F.,
September 29, 1986–January 4, 1987

Salas Pablo Ruiz Picasso, Madrid, February 17, 1987–April 26, 1987

Staatliche Kunsthalle Berlin, West Berlin,
July 23, 1987–September 15, 1987

Hayward Gallery, South Bank Centre, London,
October 29, 1987–January 10, 1988

Editor: Cynthia Newman Helms

Cover: Diego Rivera, *Flower Day*, 1925, encaustic on canvas, 147.4 x 120.6 cm. Los Angeles County Museum of Art, L.A. County Funds (25.7.1).

Back cover: Diego Rivera, *Self-Portrait*, 1941, oil on canvas, 61 × 43 cm. Northampton, Massachusetts, Smith College Museum of Art, Gift of Mrs. Irene Rich Clifford, 1977.

The text of this book is composed in Syntax
Composition by Trufont Typographers
Manufacturing by Balding & Mansell Ltd.

Printed in Great Britain

This edition published for the South Bank Centre, 1987

ISBN 0-393-02275-7

W. W. Norton & Co. Inc., 500 Fifth Avenue, New York, N.Y. 10110

W. W. Norton & Co. Ltd., 37 Great Russell Street, London WC1B 3NU

3 4 5 6 7 8 9 0

On September 19 and 20, 1985, Mexico experienced the worst earthquakes in its recent history. This book and the exhibition are dedicated to the memory of those who lost their lives and to the indomitable spirit and creative genius of the Mexican people.

Organizing Curators

Linda Downs, Curator of Education
The Detroit Institute of Arts

Ellen Sharp, Curator of Graphic Arts
The Detroit Institute of Arts

Honorary Consultants

Dolores Olmedo, Director
Museo Frida Kahlo and Museo Diego Rivera—Anahuacalli

Fernando Gamboa, Director
Banamex Collection

Xavier Moyssén
Instituto de Investigaciones Estéticas
Universidad Nacional Autónoma de México

Javier Barros Valero, Director
Instituto Nacional de Bellas Artes, México

Anne d'Harnoncourt, Director
Philadelphia Museum of Art

Samuel Sachs II, Director
The Detroit Institute of Arts

Michael Kan, Deputy Director
The Detroit Institute of Arts

Curatorial Consultants

Alicia Azuela
Instituto de Investigaciones Estéticas
Universidad Nacional Autónoma de México

Stanton L. Catlin
Professor Emeritus, Museum Studies and Art History
Syracuse University, New York

Mildred Constantine
Retired Associate Curator of Design
Museum of Modern Art, New York

Ramón Favela
Professor, Departments of Art History and Chicano Studies
University of California, Santa Barbara

Contents

Lenders

Amherst, Massachusetts
Amherst College, Mead Art Museum

Amsterdam
Stedelijk Museum

Armonk, New York
IBM Corporation

Baltimore
Baltimore Museum of Art

Baton Rouge, Louisiana
Louisiana State University, Anglo-American Museum

Columbus, Ohio
Columbus Museum of Art

Detroit
The Detroit Institute of Arts

Exeter, New Hampshire
Phillips Exeter Academy, The Lamont Gallery

Grosse Pointe, Michigan
Edsel and Eleanor Ford House

Leeds
Leeds City Art Galleries

Little Rock, Arkansas
Arkansas Arts Center Foundation Collection

Los Angeles
Los Angeles County Museum of Art

Mexico City
Galerías A. Cristóbal
Instituto Nacional de Bellas Artes (INBA)
  Museo de Arte Alvar y Carmen T. Carrillo Gil
  Museo de Arte Moderno
  Museo Diego Rivera (Guanajuato)
  Museo Nacional de Arte
Museo Franz Mayer
Secretaría de Hacienda y Crédito Público
Universidad Autónoma de México (UNAM)
  Escuela Nacional de Artes Plásticas
  Museo Universitario de Ciencias y Arte

Minneapolis, Minnesota
Minneapolis Institute of Arts

New York
The Museum of Modern Art

Northampton, Massachusetts
Smith College Museum of Art

Palm Springs, California
B. Lewin Galleries

Philadelphia
Philadelphia Museum of Art

Phoenix, Arizona
Phoenix Art Museum

Poughkeepsie, New York
Vassar College Gallery of Art

San Antonio, Texas
San Antonio Museum of Art

San Francisco
California Palace of the Legion of Honor
Regents of the University of California
San Francisco Museum of Modern Art

São Paulo
Museu de Arte de São Paulo

Mr. and Mrs. Fred H. Altshuler
The Placido Arango Collection
Mrs. Jean Charlot
Rafael Coronel
The Family of Osceola Heard Davenport
Emilia Guzzy de Gálvez
Mr. and Mrs. Kenneth E. Hill
Burt B. Holmes
Rafael and Dora Mareyna
Mr. and Mrs. Marcos Micha Levy
Dolores Olmedo
Guadalupe Rivera de Iturbe
Dr. and Mrs. David R. Sacks
Frances de Santos
The Sollins Family
Madeleine Blanche Vallier
Daniel Yankelewitz B.

Foreword

It is a double privilege for the Instituto Nacional de Bellas Artes de México to present, in conjunction with the Detroit Institute of Arts, this great retrospective of the work of Diego Rivera: this collaboration makes it possible to exhibit the most extensive group of artworks by this notable Mexican painter that has been shown to date, and it allows us the opportunity for significant participation in the celebration of the centennial of the founding of the Detroit Institute of Arts.

The talent, energy, knowledge, and dedication of many people, both in Detroit and in Mexico, provided the basis for the concept and the organization of this exceptional exhibition, the definitive internationalization of the art of Rivera. This is particularly important, since in 1986 Mexico will celebrate the centennial of the artist's birth. The happy coincidence that allows the joint celebration of both anniversaries has been pointed out in exemplary fashion by Samuel Sachs II, Director of the Detroit Institute of Arts, to whom we extend our gratitude for his collaboration and support, a gratitude that we also extend to all the enthusiastic individuals who have collaborated on this exhibition.

Diego Rivera's work is a clear example of how eclecticism in the formation of an artist can provide the necessary variety of elements to achieve a body of work of great quality. Rivera experienced and then rejected traditional training, incorporated many diverse influences into his work, assimilated what he considered useful, and participated in the most relevant contemporary currents and aesthetic movements.

After a ten-year stay in Europe, where his art underwent a lengthy and arduous process of development, Rivera returned to Mexico. There, as a result of his encounter with the propitious political and social conditions of the moment, Rivera's brilliant personal style reached maturity. The triumph of the Mexican Revolution and the implementation of the humanist ideals of the new minister of education, José Vasconcelos, allowed Rivera to give complete expression to his concerns and opened the way to his participation in the birth and development of a profoundly innovative art: Mexican muralism.

Rivera achieved, simultaneously, a rigorous knowledge of traditional art and a skillful management of contemporary plastic language. With these, he created a body of work that is both a profound revelation of the past and a critical description of his present. In this way, Rivera was able to reveal his complete, though utopian, certainty of a better and more just future and to transmit his strong conviction of the creative and transforming role of man and society.

It is noteworthy that Diego Rivera was able to paint murals both within Mexico and outside his native country and that he was able to give permanent expression and an imposing presence to his political ideals. Through these murals, Rivera continues to communicate his ideas and concepts with dazzling force and beauty, through images, colors, and truly masterful composition; his aspirations, his beliefs, and his affections are seen in works that are, without a doubt, among the greatest monuments of the art of this century.

This great exhibition will surely be a landmark in the history of art of our time, and once again we express our gratitude to all those who have made it possible.

Javier Barros Valero
Director
Instituto Nacional de Bellas Artes
December 1985

In the spring of 1979, thirteen monumental drawings, long thought to be lost, were discovered in an obscure storage area in the Detroit Institute of Arts and unrolled for the first time in forty-seven years. These drawings had been created in 1932 as part of Diego Rivera's preparation for the *Detroit Industry* frescoes in the museum's Garden Court. The centerpiece of the museum collections, and the finest modern monumental work devoted to industry in the United States, this fresco cycle holds special meaning for Detroit as a representation of the technological and industrial soul of the city. The discovery of these drawings was thus a major event in the museum's history and ultimately provided the impetus for this exhibition, the first major retrospective in the United States to be devoted to the Mexican muralist's career.

In 1983 a special partnership between the Detroit Institute of Arts and the Instituto Nacional de Bellas Artes (INBA), the Mexican government agency responsible for the arts, was established to develop this exhibition. Since the majority of Rivera's works are held in Mexican collections, both public and private, and the Mexican government officially recognizes his work as a national treasure, it was critical to gain the approval of INBA. As a magnanimous demonstration of INBA's complete support, Javier Barros Valero, Director of the Instituto Nacional de Bellas Artes, graciously offered to lend 70 percent of the Mexican museums' holdings of Rivera's works as well as to cosponsor the exhibition. Señor Barros, Marinela Barrios, former Director of International Relations, INBA, and Teresa del Conde, Director, Artes Plasticas, INBA, as well as numerous INBA officials, museum directors, conservators, and curators, devoted enormous energy to the development of the exhibition. Two other individuals in Mexico, Dolores Olmedo and Fernando Gamboa, provided crucial assistance in developing the concept of the exhibition and in the initial selection and location of works. Over the past forty years, they have made enormous contributions on an international scale to the promotion and understanding of Rivera's work. We are indebted to them for their continuous guidance.

The successful realization of this exhibition is due in great part to the talent and devotion of the two organizing curators, Linda Downs, Curator of Education, and Ellen Sharp, Curator of Graphic Arts, at the Detroit Institute of Arts. We would like to give special thanks to them for their continuing efforts over the past several years.

This exhibition would not have been possible without the generous support of the Ford Motor Company, whose grant, awarded in January 1985 at the direction of retiring president Philip Caldwell, is the largest ever received by the museum for an exhibition. It is extremely fitting that this award, the culmination of over sixty years of museum patronage by the Ford family and the Ford Motor Company, should be in support of the Rivera exhibition. The Ford family's interest in the museum began with Edsel Ford, son of Henry Ford and the first president of the Ford Motor Company, who became president of the Arts Commission of the City of Detroit (the governing board of the museum) in 1925 and who, in 1931, underwrote the *Detroit Industry* fresco commission (in which he himself appears). Over the years, the Ford family has made generous gifts of works of art, provided funds for acquisitions, publications, educational programs, and capital projects, and made two important bequests, those of Edsel himself and of his wife, Eleanor Clay Ford. In recent years, the Ford Motor Company has been a generous contributor, not only through yearly corporate gifts but also through its sponsorship of the 1978 exhibition "The Rouge: The Image of Industry in the Art of Charles Sheeler and Diego Rivera," in commemoration of the company's seventy-fifth anniversary.

The *Detroit Industry* fresco cycle has been a source of enjoyment for the Detroit public for over fifty years, and it is most appropriate that we celebrate both the museum's centennial and the one hundredth anniversary of Diego Rivera's birth with this exhibition. We are very pleased that this international tribute to the great Mexican muralist will give many people in the United States and Europe their first opportunity to see and enjoy the work of this modern master.

Samuel Sachs II
Director
The Detroit Institute of Arts
December 1985

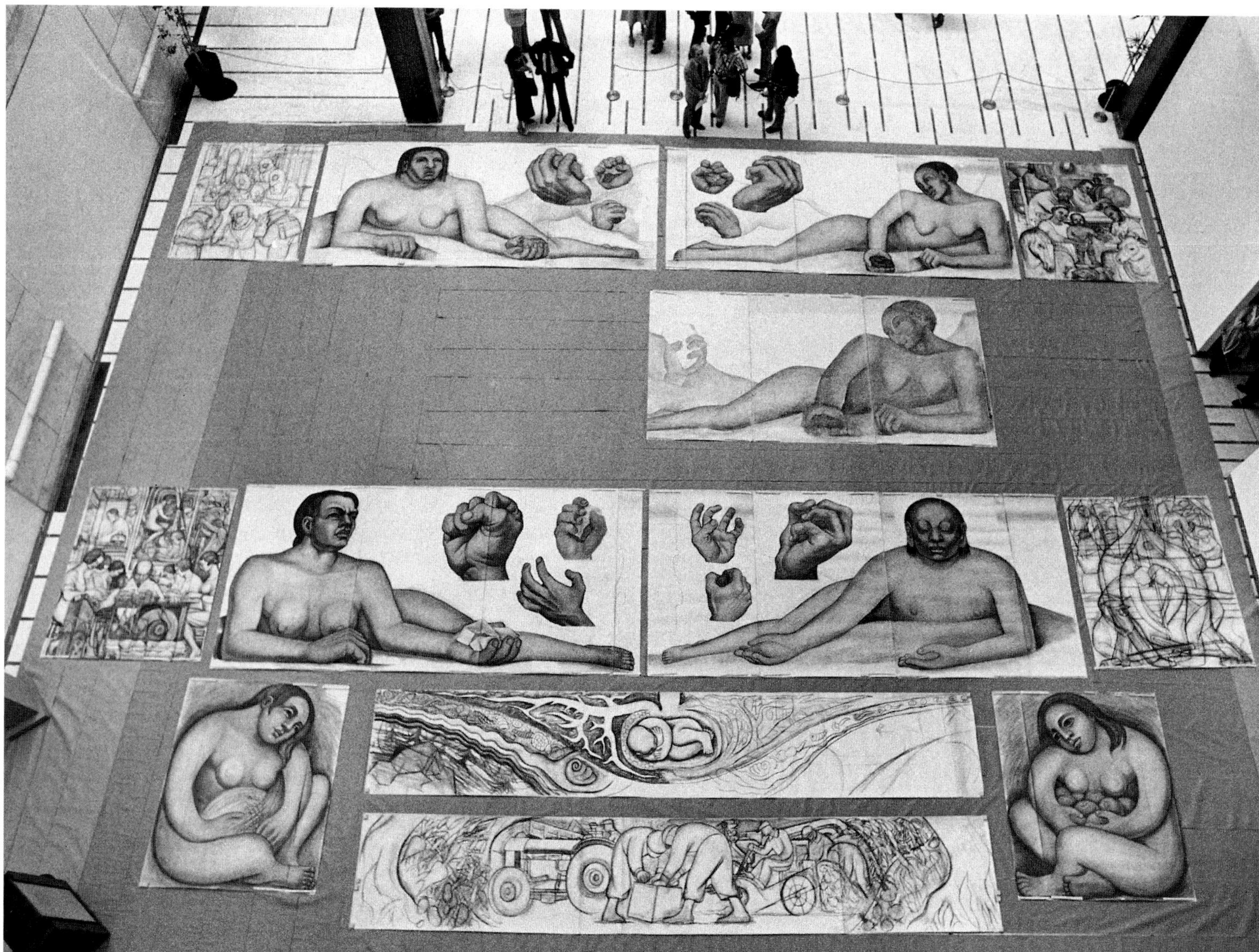

Preface and Acknowledgments

Linda Downs and Ellen Sharp

Cartoons for *Detroit Industry,* Detroit Institute of Arts.

In 1978, the Detroit Institute of Arts organized "The Rouge: The Image of Industry in the Art of Charles Sheeler and Diego Rivera," the first exhibition in Detroit to be devoted to Rivera's work since the unveiling of the *Detroit Industry* frescoes nearly fifty years earlier. In the course of the research for this show, an enormous amount of unpublished material documenting Rivera's activity in Detroit during 1931–32 was discovered at the Ford Archives, Henry Ford Museum; the Archives of American Art, Smithsonian Institution; the Ford Motor Company; and the Detroit Institute of Arts. Included in this material were over three hundred photographs comprising an almost daily record of the murals' creation. One of the most tantalizing aspects of these photographs was the fact that full-size preliminary drawings, or cartoons, for the upper registers of the frescoes were depicted. Correspondence in the museum files indicated that these drawings were intended as a gift to the Institute, but had apparently been lost. Less than six months later, as a result of a search for the original architectural drawings for the museum, the drawings were found in the back of a dimly lit storage room, and in an atmosphere of great excitement, they were unrolled and displayed on the floor of the museum's north court. Discussions began immediately as to how and when to exhibit them, and soon plans for a retrospective exhibition of Rivera's drawings and a monograph on the *Detroit Industry* fresco cycle were underway.

In the fall of 1980, we attended the International Conference of Museums in Mexico City. We were graciously received by Fernando Gamboa, then the Director of the Museo de Arte Moderno. The founding director of the Museo Tamayo and a contemporary and colleague of Rivera who had organized two great retrospectives of the artist's work in 1949 and 1978 in Mexico, he was fascinated by our information about the Detroit drawings and encouraged us to meet with Dolores Olmedo, Director of the Museo Frida Kahlo and the Museo Diego Rivera–Anahuacalli and the major private collector of Rivera's work.

Señora Olmedo was intensely interested in the Detroit drawings and announced that they should be shown as part of a major retrospective exhibition that would be organized by the Detroit Institute of Arts, with her total support, and would be held in 1986 in commemoration of the one hundredth anniversary of Rivera's birth. The idea was staggering but enormously appealing. Not since the exhibition at the Museum of Modern Art, New York, in 1931 had there been a major retrospective of Rivera's work in the United States.

Thus inspired, we enthusiastically continued our research on Rivera, but an exhibition could not be scheduled until the drawings could receive the necessary conservation attention. In 1981 the National Endowment for the Arts awarded funds for this purpose. Under the direction of Valerie Baas, Paper Conservator at the Detroit Institute of Arts, it took over three years of intensive work to clean, repair, and create special mounts for the drawings.

In March 1983 the idea of mounting a major retrospective received further impetus when a symposium was held in Detroit to celebrate the fiftieth anniversary of the completion of the *Detroit Industry* frescoes. Its overwhelmingly enthusiastic reception made it clear that there was intense interest in Rivera among both scholars and the public alike.

With the idea of a major show now paramount, we enlisted the support of the Instituto Nacional de Bellas Artes (INBA), the government agency that oversees the arts in Mexico. José Bremer, then Subsecretario de Educación, and Javier Barros Valero, Director, INBA, graciously offered to cosponsor such an exhibition. They felt, furthermore, that it should circulate not only in North America, but to European sites as well, since Rivera had lived in Paris and had also traveled and worked in Berlin, Spain, London, Italy, the U.S.S.R., Poland, and Czechoslovakia. With INBA's cooperation assured, we could now turn our attention to the exhibition itself.

Presenting a retrospective of an artist whose major works are permanently a part of buildings in Mexico City, San Francisco, and Detroit posed a major problem. How could we convey the scale, the complexity, and the relationship of the murals to their architectural spaces? After reviewing various options, we decided to create a film about the murals and make it an integral part of the exhibition. Produced by Michael Camerini and Stanton L. Catlin, the film provides a complement to the painting and drawing sections, creating a complete overview of Rivera's sixty-year career. The final section of the exhibition contains photographs, many of them vintage prints by such photographers as Manuel Alvarez Bravo, Edward Weston, and Tina Modotti. Developed by Mildred Constantine, this section is intended to familiarize the public in the United States and Europe with Rivera's Mexico and his extraordinary circle of friends.

The catalogue for the exhibition is the first comprehensive presentation on Rivera's life and work to appear in the United States since Bertram D. Wolfe's *The Fabulous Life of Diego Rivera* was published in 1963. In Mexico many insightful studies have been published, such as Antonio Rodríguez's *Diego Rivera* (1948), Luís Cardoza y Aragon's *Los frescos en la Secretaría de Educación Pública* (1980), as well as comprehensive exhibition catalogues such as the *Diego Rivera: 50 años de su labor artística* (1951), and *Exposicion nacional de homenaje a Diego Rivera* (1977). We hope that these publications and those in progress in Mexico will be made available to other countries through translation and distribution.

Our task in developing this catalogue as a comprehensive book on Rivera's life and work was both to provide a comprehensive overview for those readers unfamiliar with Rivera's oeuvre and at the same time to address major issues of interest to Mexican, European, and United States scholars. The first section of the catalogue, the illustrated chronology prepared by Laurance P. Hurlburt, with the assistance of Alicia Azuela, Mildred Constantine, Nancy Jones, Fernando Gamboa, Dolores Olmedo, and Teresa del Conde, presents Rivera's artistic career within the context of the major events of his life. The mural census prepared by Stanton Catlin is the first attempt to systematically record, describe, and provide diagrams and measurements of each mural project.

The ten essays treat more specifically various aspects of the career of this 20th-century "renaissance man." Rivera was a draftsman, painter, printmaker, sculptor, book illustrator, costume and set designer, and architect, as well as one of the first collectors of pre-Colombian art and a political activist. His encyclopedic interests and studies led him into such diverse fields as science; medicine; archaeology; social, cultural, and political history; philosophy; mythology; and industrial technology. Essays by Francis O'Connor and Betty Ann Brown analyze his explorations in various fields as well as his applied understanding of his discoveries and identify many of his seminal sources. The essay by Jorge Hernández Campos addresses Rivera's early philosophical and stylistic development, which prompted his diverse interests and formed the basis for his mature work, while those of Ellen Sharp, Xavier Moyssén, and Rita Eder use the artist's graphic works, his portraits, and self-portraits as points of departure in illuminating the broad range of his activity.

Of critical importance to an understanding of Rivera's work, and particularly his murals, is the relationship of Rivera's aesthetic to Marxist political theory. While acknowledging the use of Marxist theory in the development of the subjects, themes, and composition of his murals, his biographers Bertram Wolfe and Loló de la Torriente claim that he never read Marx. They particularly point out that Rivera had little tolerance for dogma of any kind. Ida Rodríguez-Prampolini analyzes Rivera's attempt to visualize the Marxist dialectic in his Mexican murals and Alicia Azuela examines the expression of political ideology in his United States murals.

Rivera's influence on artists in the United States is beginning to be explored as a result of the recent scholarly interest in the mural project of the Depression-era Works Progress Administration, and an essay by Francis O'Connor more fully explores that influence. Finally, Luís Cardoza y Aragón discusses Rivera's unique contribution to modern art.

This exhibition could not have been realized without the assistance, collaboration and expertise of the many people whose names are listed in the acknowledgments. Here we would like to give special recognition to several individuals to whom we owe an enormous debt of gratitude: Dolores Olmedo, for inspiring the concept of the exhibition, for her dedicated guidance of its development, and for the generous loan of a large portion of her own collection; Fernando Gamboa, whose insight and counsel were invaluable and who helped to locate many key works; Javier Barros Valero, Director, Instituto Nacional de Bellas Artes, and Teresa del Conde, Director, Artes Plasticas, Instituto Nacional de Bellas Artes, who ensured the participation of the Mexican art museums and whose support on all aspects of the exhibition was indispensable; curatorial consultants Mildred Constantine, Stanton L. Catlin, Alicia Azuela, and Ramón Favela, whose knowledge, insight, and counsel helped to shape the exhibition and with whom it was a great pleasure to work; Nancy Jones, whose work as translator, international messenger, and coordinator of educational programs was invaluable; and Cynthia Newman Helms, editor of the catalogue, Dirk Bakker, the museum's Chief Photographer, his staff, and the Mexican photographer Bob Schalkwijk, all of whose admirable work is evident here.

The exhibition and catalogue required the assistance of innumerable scholars and dealers in both the United States and Mexico. Many of the scholars whose essays appear here graciously accepted the challenge of working outside of their usual fields. Two dealers, Mary-Anne Martin and Armando Colina, deserve special recognition for their tireless efforts in locating works and acting as intermediaries with collectors.

Various departments of the Detroit Institute of Arts contributed greatly to the realization of the exhibition—Publications, Photography, Conservation, Exhibitions, Development, Registrar, Building and Grounds, Marketing, Public Relations, Performing Arts, Data Processing/D.A.R.I.S., and Education. We would like especially to thank the members of the Education and Graphic Arts departments for assuming additional responsibilities while we focused on the exhibition. Laurel Sicklesteel, Secretary to the Curator of Education, carried out the majority of the extensive paperwork for the exhibition, and we are greatly appreciative of her outstanding work.

We are also wholly indebted to the lenders, who by graciously consenting to part with their works for the duration of the tour, have made this exhibition possible. They are listed on pages 8 and 9.

We would like to thank Frederick J. Cummings, former Director of the Detroit Institute of Arts, for his support and guidance during the initial stages of this project, and Michael Kan, Deputy Director, whose diplomatic skills were invaluable in keeping the project on course. We are also grateful to Samuel Sachs II, Director; William Peck, Chief Curator; and Joseph P. Bianco, Jr., Executive Vice-President and Chief Operating Officer of the Founders Society, for their encouragement, support, and enthusiasm.

Acknowledgments

Secretaría de Educación Pública, México
Miguel González Avelar, Secretario
Leonel Durán, Subsecretario de Cultura
Juan José Bremer, former Subsecretario de Cultura

Secretaría de Relaciones Exteriores, México
Bernardo Sepúlveda Amor, Secretario
Ricardo Valero Becerra, Subsecretario de Cooperación Internacional
Jorge Alberto Lozoya, Director en Jefe de Cooperación Internacional
Luz del Amo, Directora General de Cultura

Instituto Nacional de Bellas Artes, México
Javier Barros Valero, Director
Marinela Barrios
Estela Duarte
Francisco Serrano
Tomás Zurián

Artes Plasticas
Teresa del Conde, Directora
Luz Elena Daños
Antonio Luque
Enrique Mariño
Xavier Villagomez

Museo del Palacio Nacional de Bellas Artes
Mariam Kaiser, Directora

Museo Nacional de Arte
Jorge Hernández Campos, Director
Christina Galvez, Subdirectora

Museo de Arte Alvar y Carmen T. Carrillo Gil
Sylvia Pandolfi, Directora

Museo de Arte Moderno
Oscar Urrutia, Director

Museo Diego Rivera, Guanajuato
Herlinda Martinez de Villegas, Encargada Curadora

Museo Frida Kahlo and Museo Diego Rivera–Anahuacalli, Mexico
Dolores Olmedo, Directora

Museo Tamayo, Mexico
Robert R. Littman, Director
Francoise Reynaud, Former Director
Miriam Minkow, Registrar
Ana Zagury, Exhibitions Coordinator

Instituto de Investigaciones Estéticas, Mexico City
Beatriz de la Fuente, Directora
Jorge Alberto Manrique, former Director
Alicia Azuela
Rita Eder
Xavier Moyssén
Ida Rodríguez-Prampolini

Mexican Embassy, Washington, D.C.
Jorge Espinosa de los Reyes, Ambassador to the United States

United States Embassy, Mexico City
John Gavin, Ambassador to Mexico
Sidney Hamolsky, Cultural Attaché

Philadelphia Museum of Art
Anne d'Harnoncourt, Director
Darrell Sewell, Curator of American Art
Susan Wells, Registrar
Ann Percy, Curator of Drawings
Martha Shahroudi, Curator of Photography

Neue Gesellschaft für bildende Kunst, Berlin
Ulrich Roloff-Momin, President
Suzanne von Falkenhausen, Executive Secretary
Olav Münzberg
Michael Nungesser
Otto Schily
Jürgen Egert
Manfred Schleiss
Josephine Geier
Gisela Gnoff
Irene Meyer-Schoop

Staatliche Kunsthalle, Berlin
Dieter Ruckhaberle, Director

Ministry of Culture, Madrid
Carmen Gimenez, Minister
Catherine Coleman

Mexican Consulate, Detroit
Robert J. Gonzales, Consul
Elda Paz, Assistant Consul

Programs for Alternative Creative Education, Detroit
John Aldrich, Director
James Tatum, Chairman
The Detroit Institute of Arts
Samuel Sachs II, Director
Michael Kan, Deputy Director
William H. Peck, Chief Curator
Joseph P. Bianco, Jr., Executive Vice-President, Founders Society
Joseph L. Hudson, Jr., President, Arts Commission
Walter B. Ford II, President, Founders Society Board of Trustees
Carol S. Campbell, Mayor's Liaison to the Detroit Institute of Arts

Education Department, Patience Young, Nancy Jones, Laurel Sicklesteel, Diana Pagotto, Michael Jones, Dolores Slowinski, Deborah Lubera, Gina Alexander, Jean Mira, Lynne Alvarez; *Graphic Arts,* Diana Bulka, Douglas Bulka, Kathleen Erwin, Michael Jackson, Dianne Johnston, Margaret Lewis, Christine Swenson; *Publications,* Julia Henshaw, Cynthia Newman Helms, Cynthia Jo Fogliatti, A. D. Miller, Nathan Guequierre, Opal D. Suddeth-Hodge; *Conservation,* Barbara Heller, Valerie Baas, Abraham Joel, Jerri Reynolds, Christopher Foster, Uziel Sason, Elizabeth Buschor; *Photography,* Dirk Bakker, Marianne Letasi, Robert Hensleigh, Timothy Thayer, David Krieger; *Exhibitions,* Lou Gauci, Barbara Lee; *Registrar's Office,* Karen Serota, Mary Gast, Michele Peplin; *Marketing and Public Relations,* Lisa J. Steele, Margaret DeGrace; *Development,* Michael Fahlund, Marianne DePalma, Margaret Tallet, Eve Cockburn; *African, Oceanic, and New World Cultures,* David Penney, Vada Dunifer; *Ancient Art,* David Caccioli; European Paintings, J. Patrice Marandel

Don Beatty, Betty Boon, Lola Álvarez Bravo, Manuel Álvarez Bravo, Ronald W. Brenne, Luís Cardoza y Aragón, Michael Camerini, Stanton L. Catlin, Miguel Cervantes, Zomah Charlot, John Charlot, Nicola Colegy, Armando Colina, Mildred Constantine, Karen Cordero, Rafael Coronel, Juan Coronel, Lucienne Bloch Dimitroff, Stephen Dimitroff, Timothy Downs, Alan Fern, Fernando Gamboa, Alfonso Gobela, Susan Hakim, Guadalupe Rivera de Iturbe, James Jensen, Irene Phillips de José, José Júarez, John Kraniauskas, James L. Mairs, María Teresa Mariscal, Mary-Anne Martin, Javier Becerril Mecalco, Garnett McCoy, Charles McGee, Peter Morse, Christiana Olsen, Emmy Lou Packard, Lisa Palmer, Bob Schalkwijk, Sharon Schultz, Durdica Segota, Virginia Stern, Laura Sueoka, Jeremy Townsend, Eleazar Lopez Zamora, and Martha Zamora.

Detroit, December 1985

London Acknowledgements

The London showing of this exhibition, not envisaged at the outset, has been made possible by exceptional generosity on the part of the lenders, both public and private, and by a willingness on the part of the organisers in Detroit and in Mexico to share their magnificent exhibition with the British public.

The regrettably few exhibitions of Mexican art which have taken place here in recent years—exhibitions devoted to José Clemente Orozco, Frida Kahlo, and the photographer Manuel Alvarez Bravo—have each served to increase our understanding of a country with which we have long been fascinated, as the "Mexican" novels of D.H. Lawrence, Malcolm Lowry, and Graham Greene testify. Our hope is that the Rivera exhibition at the Hayward Gallery will focus and encourage this interest. The programme of events associated with the exhibition—films, lectures, seminars, readings and parallel exhibitions—has been arranged with this aim in mind.

Acknowledgement is made in other texts prefacing this book to those involved in the organisation of the exhibition. Inevitably repeating these expressions of gratitude, the British organisers would like to make special acknowledgement of the central role of the Mexican authorities: the Secretaría de Relaciones Exteriores and its Minister, His Excellency Bernardo Sepúlveda; the Instituto Nacional de Bellas Artes and its Director, Lic. Manuel de la Cera; His Excellency the Ambassador to the United Kingdom, Sr. Jorge Eduardo Navarrete, Minister Dr. Margo Glantz, and their staff at the Embassy in London who have been unfailingly helpful with the arrangements for the London showing. We are also greatly indebted to the Director of the Detroit Institute of Arts, Samuel Sachs II, and to the Executive Vice-President of the Institute's Founders Society, Joseph P. Bianco, Jr., as well as to the two curators who conceived and formed the exhibition, Linda Downs and Ellen Sharp, and the team at the Institute who have taken care of all the practical arrangements. Lastly, we would like to thank the sponsors, the Ford Motor Company, whose generous support has made the international tour of the exhibition possible.

Joanna Drew
Director
Hayward Exhibitions

July 1987

Introduction

Linda Downs

The public persona of Diego Rivera and the heroic status bestowed upon him in Mexico was such that the artist became the subject of myth in his own lifetime. His own memories, as recorded in his various autobiographies, have contributed to his image as a precocious child of exotic parentage, a young firebrand who fought in the Mexican Revolution, and a visionary who completely repudiated his participation in the European avant-garde to follow a predestined course as the leader of Mexico's art revolution.

The facts are more prosaic. The product of a middle-class family, the young artist completed an academic course of training at the prestigious Academy of San Carlos before leaving Mexico for the traditional period of European study. During his first stay abroad, like many other young painters, he came under a variety of influences, including Post-Impressionism and Symbolism. As for participating in the early battles of the Mexican Revolution, recent research would seem to indicate that he did not. Although he was in Mexico for a time in late 1910–early 1911, his tales of fighting with the Zapatistas cannot be substantiated.[1]

From the summer of 1911 until the winter of 1920, Rivera lived in Paris. This period of his career has been brilliantly illuminated by Ramón Favela in the 1984–85 exhibition "Diego Rivera: The Cubist Years." The work of these years, which will be even more carefully documented in Favela's forthcoming catalogue raisonné, reveals diverse influences, from the art of El Greco and new applications of mathematical principles, in which Rivera had been well schooled at San Carlos, to subject matter and techniques that reflect the discussions on the role of art in the service of revolution that preoccupied the community of emigré artists in Montparnasse.

By 1917, Rivera had begun to turn away from Cubism, and by 1918 his rejection of Cubist style, if not all the tenets of Cubism, was complete. The reasons for this rejection have not been completely determined, but certainly the inspiration of the Russian Revolution and the general return to realism among European artists were factors that contributed. In 1920, Rivera went to Italy. There, in the murals of the Italian painters of the quattrocento, he found the inspiration for a new and revolutionary public art capable of furthering the ideals of the ongoing revolution in his native land.

Rivera returned to Mexico in 1921 and soon became one of a number of Mexican and foreign artists who received commissions for murals in public buildings from the new government. By 1923, the completion of the first of his monumental series at the Secretaría de Educación Pública and his assumption of control over the decoration of the entire building had established his preeminence in the movement now known as the Mexican Mural Renaissance.

In his work at the Secretaría, which would occupy him for another four years, and in the chapel at the former Escuela de Agricultura at Chapingo, Rivera brought to full development his classical figure style and his epic approach to historical painting, which focused on subjects that promoted revolutionary ideals and celebrated the indigenous cultural heritage of Mexico.

In the period following World War I, the literary, artistic, and intellectual vitality of postrevolutionary Mexico, in which the mural movement played an integral role, created a cultural "mecca" that drew young artists from the United States, Europe, and Latin America. As a result, by the late 1920s, Rivera's murals, and those of José Clemente Orozco and David Alfaro Siqueiros, were well known in the United States. In the early 1930s, Rivera became one of the most sought-after artists in this country. In addition to numerous commissions for easel paintings, he received commissions for three murals in San Francisco and was given a one-person exhibition at the Museum of Modern Art. Also, his costume and set designs were used in the ballet *H. P. (Horsepower),* which premiered in Philadelphia; he decorated the central court of the Detroit Institute of Arts; he was invited by General Motors to create murals at the Chicago World's Fair; and he painted murals at Rockefeller Center and the New Workers School in New York.

Rivera's sojourns in the United States were pivotal to his work. For the first time in his career as a muralist, he was separated from the rich cultural history upon which he drew for his subjects and was under no compulsion to confine himself to themes in promotion of Mexican nationalist ideals. He was also able, at least temporarily, to escape from the turmoil of his precarious political position in Mexico, where the Mexican Communist Party, of which he had been a member between 1922 and 1929, disapproved of his growing ties to Mexico's government. Finally, he was at last able to indulge his deep fascination with technology, which was evident in a highly developed form in the industrial society of the United States.

Rivera's period of work in the United States enabled him to explore an industrial society, to analyze the role of the artist within it, to postulate its link to the universal order by analogy with earlier societies such as that of the Aztecs, and finally to present his own concept of a new society based on science and technology. The murals in the United States served to clarify his understanding of his native Mexico and expanded his personal philosophy. They were the source of inspiration for many of his later works, including the late murals at the Palacio Nacional and those at the Golden Gate Exposition in San Francisco, the Lerma waterworks, and the Hospital de la Raza.

Rivera's activities in the United States were marked by controversy. In Detroit, he was accused of using sacrilegious and even pornographic subject matter, his politics were questioned, and he was criticized for causing dreaded industry to invade the museum. The safety of the murals was even threatened until Edsel Ford made a public statement in their defense. Rivera, who believed that the *Detroit Industry* fresco cycle was his greatest artistic achievement, was dismayed by these attacks.

An even larger and more bitter controversy erupted at Rockefeller Center in New York when Rivera included a portrait of Lenin in his representation of the new society. Asked to remove it, Rivera refused and the mural was ultimately destroyed, one of the great scandals of art history. When Rivera returned to Mexico in December 1933, he was one of the most highly publicized artists in United States history, hailed by the intellectual left and the art community and scorned by conservatives and the corporate patrons who had once sought him out.

Rivera's influence on American artists continued throughout the 1930s through the agency of the mural section of the Federal Art Project of the Works Progress Administration. This project, which owed its very creation to the example of the Mexican government's commissioning of works for public buildings, distributed to participating artists a handbook outlining Rivera's fresco technique.

Rivera's popularity with the American public continued into the 1940s, but his reputation among art critics and scholars diminished as realism and emphasis on social content fell into disfavor in the face of a growing interest in the styles of Cubism, Dada, and Surrealism, then being brought to this country by European artists fleeing Hitler.

It is perhaps understandable that Rivera's work became inextricably linked with social realism. His trip to the U.S.S.R. in 1927–28 brought him into contact with many young Russian artists who later carried out government mural commissions, and his works were well known in Moscow through the publication of newspaper and magazine articles. The artists, such as Ben Shahn, with whom Rivera associated during his two stays in New York were politically active individuals who, like their Russian counterparts, admired Rivera as the great revolutionary who had put into practice what they still hoped to achieve. Rivera's political philosophy and the subjects of his murals did create a common bond between his work and that of the social realists. However, his mural style, indeed his overall aesthetic, modeled as it was on his studies of Italian Renaissance frescoes, classical proportions, pre-Colombian sculptural forms, Cubist space, and Futurist conventions of movement, bears little relationship to social realism.

Over the past forty years, critical opinion in the United States has remained virtually unchanged: Rivera's work and the Mexican mural movement as a whole have been characterized as politically motivated, stylistically retrograde, and historically isolated. Furthermore, Mexican scholars have traditionally emphasized the overt revolutionary ideals and didactic content of Rivera's murals in Mexico, thus extolling the very aspects of his work that have carried a negative connotation in the United States. In Mexico Rivera's work is synonymous with the institutionalized ideals of the Mexican Revolution, which promoted indigenous culture to the exclusion of foreign influence. As a consequence, in Mexico the vast body of published literature on Rivera has concentrated on his Mexican murals (considered his mature work), while little attention has been given to his work in the United States and Europe or to his easel paintings and drawings.

Rivera's own statements support this view of his art as a unique and indigenous effort in service of revolutionary ideals. In his autobiography, *My Art, My Life,* his Paris years and his sojourn in Italy are acknowledged as preparation for the creation of the new revolutionary murals, but he characterized the formation of his mural style as spontaneously generated from indigenous Mexican culture:

My homecoming produced an aesthetic exhilaration which it is impossible to describe. It was as if I were being born anew, born in a new world. . . . I was in the very center of the plastic world, where forms and colors existed in absolute purity. In everything I saw a potential masterpiece—the crowds, the markets, the festivals, the marching battalions, the workingmen in the shop and in the fields—in every glowing face, in every luminous child. . . . My style was born as children are born, in a moment, except that this birth had come after a torturous pregnancy of thirty-five years.[2]

Limited but significant European scholarly attention, particularly from Germany, has been devoted to Rivera. Hans F. Secker's *Diego Rivera*, published the year of Rivera's death, was the first major publication to present a comprehensive study of the artist's work to the European public. Recent exhibitions such as *Kunst de Mexikanischen Revolution: Legende und Wirklichkeit* (West Berlin, Neue Gesellschaft für bildende Kunst, 1974) and *Wand Bild Mexico* (West Berlin, National Galerie, 1982) have followed the Mexican critical perspective, focusing on the importance of social content in the Mexican muralists' work and their role in the context of the Mexican Revolution. Recently, scholarly interest in the WPA/FAP mural project and the documentation of community mural projects in the United States as well as other recent revolutionary murals have served to shed new light on Rivera's influence in the 1930s and in the civil rights era of the 1960s as well as his continuing influence in Latin America. The renewed interest in realism and social content in art has led others to trace the heritage of these trends in the social realist and Mexican mural movements. The reception of the recent biography of Frida Kahlo by Hayden Herrera and the exhibition of Kahlo's work, which originated in London and circulated through the United States and Mexico, demonstrates the public's passionate interest in this amazing couple.

The first publication in Mexico to be devoted exclusively to Rivera's work in Europe *Diego de Montparnasse* (1979), by Olivier Debroise, and the previously mentioned exhibition of his Cubist works, organized by Ramón Favela, presented a wealth of information and a carefully documented analysis of this little-known period of the artist's life and work.

While it is clear that the major accomplishments of Rivera's career were his vast mural programs in Mexico and the United States, the tendency of scholars and critics to limit their perspective and focus only on those works has served to overshadow his overall accomplishments as an artist.

Rivera's life was filled with contradictions—a pioneer of Cubism who promoted art for art's sake, he became one of the leaders of the Mexican Mural Renaissance; a Marxist/Communist, he received mural commissions from the United States corporate establishment; a champion of the worker, he had a deep fascination with the form and function of machines and pronounced engineers America's greatest artists; a great revolutionary artist, he also painted society portraits.

Part of the challenge in organizing this exhibition has been the attempt to separate fact from fiction. Gladys March, who wrote *My Art, My Life* with Rivera, commented on his mythologizing:

Rivera, who . . . was to transform the history of Mexico into one of the great myths of our century, could not, in recalling his own life to me, suppress his colossal fancy. He had already converted certain events, particularly of his early years, into legends.[3]

Fact and fiction become one with Rivera. His biographers, Bertram D. Wolfe, Ernestine Evans, Florence Arquin, Luis Suárez, Gladys March, and Loló de la Torriente, all attempted to deal with this problem while remaining true to the spirit of the man.

Rivera's philosophy of art and life correspond to no specific dogma. He had an extraordinarily well developed intuitive sense that shaped his understanding of the world and his humanistic understanding of the role of the artist and the role of art in society. His ability to masterfully present universal images and ideas in his art continues to captivate the viewer today.

As Jean Charlot stated in the conclusion of his book *The Mexican Mural Renaissance*:

A re-estimate of Rivera may be next, as the anecdotes he so dutifully wove into his murals lose in topical value and, therefore, in interest. When looking at Lorenzetti's frescoes, few care who were the villains and who the heroes in Sienese politics five hundred years ago. Yet Lorenzetti is alive as ever. Rivera's work, as it is drained of its journalistic meaning, may acquire added stylistic meaning and dignity for generations to come. . . .[4]

This exhibition and catalogue are one step toward the reevaluation of Rivera's work. We hope that they will bring enjoyment and a greater understanding as well as prompt continued scholarly study.

Notes

1. Phoenix 1984, 29 (III).
2. March 1960, 124 (I).
3. Ibid., 12.
4. Charlot 1962a, 316 (IV).

In general titles of artworks are given in English, and the names of institutions, buildings, etc., in the original language. Height precedes width in all dimensions, which provide only the maximum measurements.

Citations for works included in the six-part bibliography at the back of this book are given throughout in a shortened form that generally gives the author's or editor's name and the date of publication (when no author or editor is known, a partial title or the name of the periodical is substituted). The Roman numerals at the ends of these short forms indicate the section of the bibliography in which the full citation may be found.

Throughout the text are parenthetical cross-references to the Secretaría de Educación Pública section of the mural census. These consist of the abbreviation SEP, followed by a series of numbers keyed to the census diagrams.

Diego Rivera

Diego Rivera (1886–1957): A Chronology of His Art, Life, and Times

I.
Childhood and Early Artistic Training

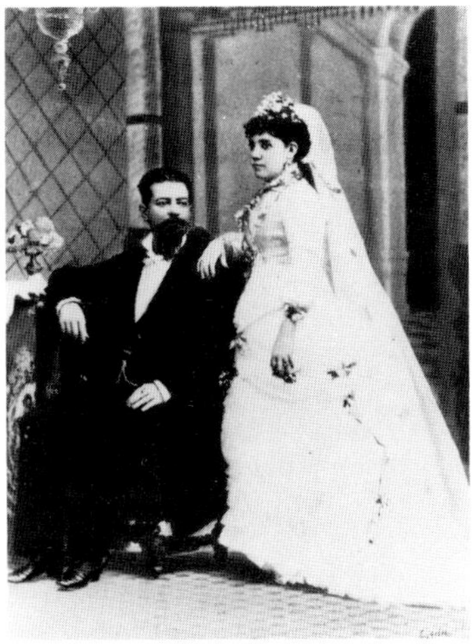

Figure 1
Rivera's parents on their wedding day, 1882.

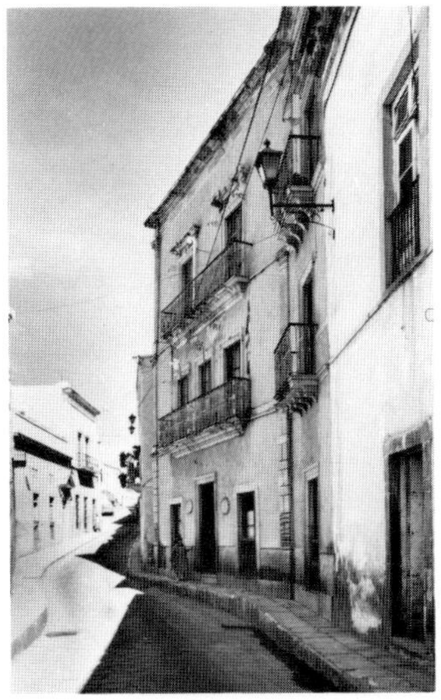

Figure 2
The Rivera family home in Guanajuato.

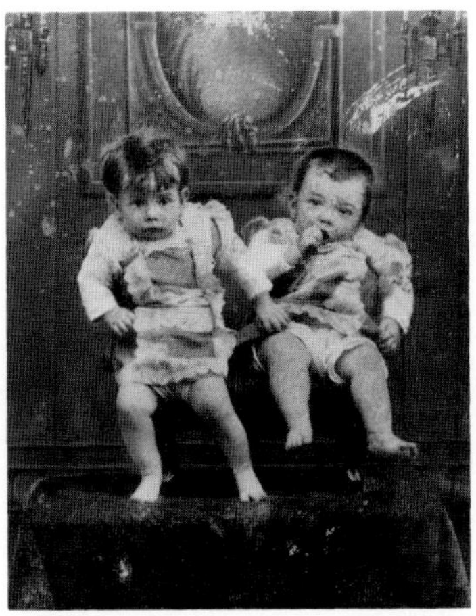

Figure 3
Rivera and his twin brother, ca. 1887.

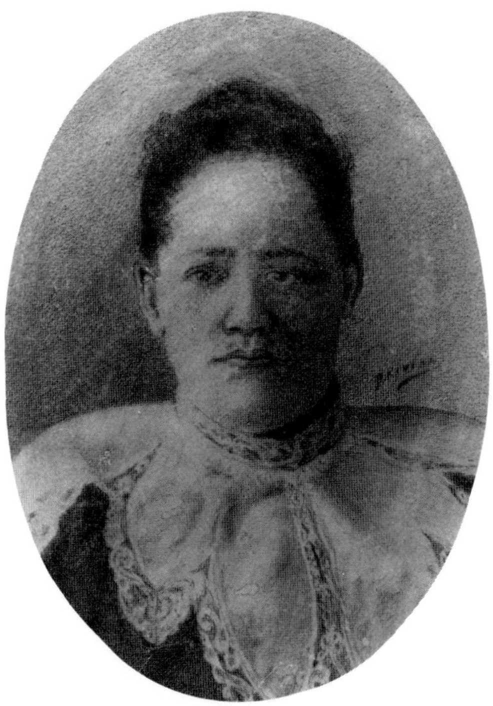

Figure 4
Portrait of Maria Barrientos de Rivera, 1896, pencil, 31 × 22 cm. Collection of Dolores Olmedo.

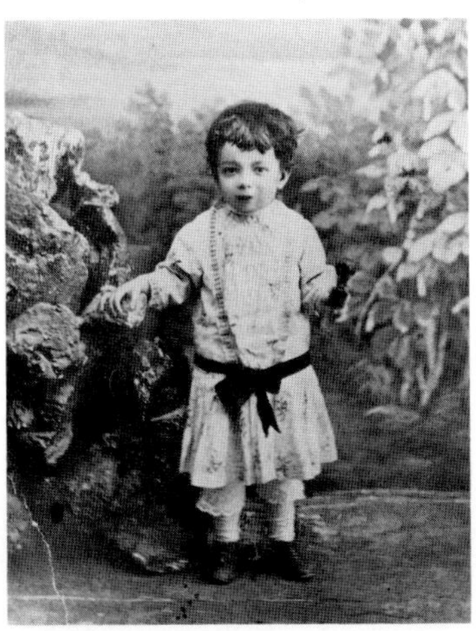

Figure 5
Rivera at about age four, ca. 1890.

1886

December 13: born José Diego María Rivera (twin brother José Carlos María Rivera), in Guanajuato, Mexico, to Diego Rivera, a schoolteacher with liberal political views whose father was a mine owner, and María Barrientos de Rivera, also a teacher.[1]

Second period of the "Porfiriato" (1876–80; 1884–1910). Porfirio Díaz, a military leader during the War of French Intervention, had seized the presidency in 1876. Upon his reelection in 1884, having quelled all resistance, Díaz gathers around him a group of advisers known as "*los científicos*" (the scientists). Their influence results in the adoption of the positivist philosophy of Auguste Comte as the administration's official ideology. The Porfiriato is characterized by large-scale foreign investment in Mexico, the creation of huge self-ruling *haciendas* (estates) from seized land, and the establishment of a rural police force, the *Guardia Rural*, to enforce Díaz's policies.

1888

José Carlos dies at age one and a half, and Rivera's mother undertakes the study of medicine as therapy; she becomes a practicing midwife.

1889

Begins to draw at age three.

1890

Father teaches Rivera to read.

José Clemente Orozco, age seven, moves to Mexico City with his family from his birthplace in Guadalajara.

1891

Sister, María Rivera Barrientos, born.

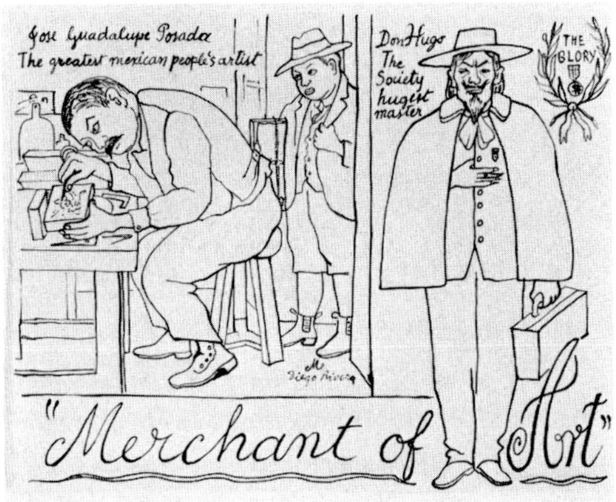

Figure 6
Merchant of Art, ca. 1944, pen and black ink, 20.9 × 26.7 cm. Collection of Leah Brenner. This illustration for Leah Brenner's book *An Artist Grows Up in Mexico* echoes Rivera's contention that he first encountered the popular graphic art of José Guadalupe Posada during his early years at San Carlos. In fact, his student work shows no concern for the sociopolitical themes of Posada, and Rivera's first mention of Posada's influence occurred in 1928.

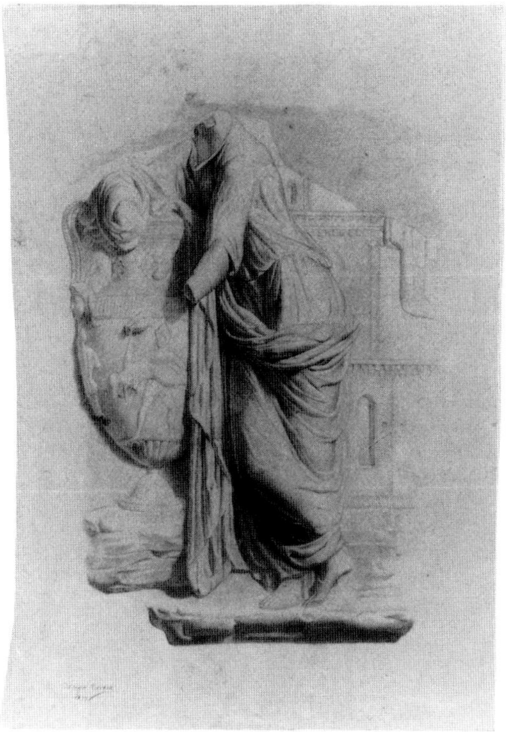

Figure 7
Classical Standing Figure Leaning on an Urn, 1898, pencil, 50.7 × 35.2 cm. Mexico City, UNAM, Escuela Nacional de Artes Plásticas.

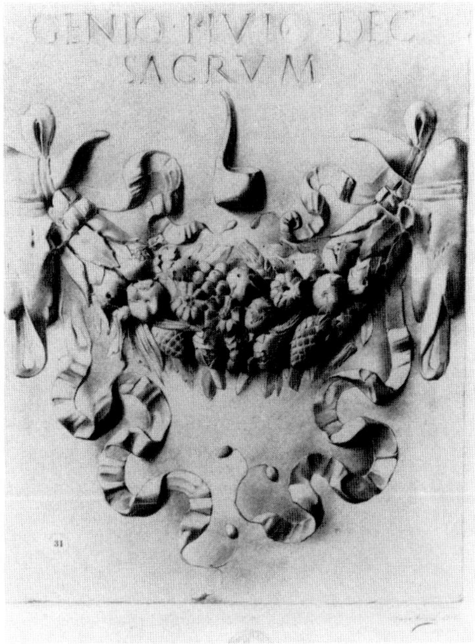

Figure 8
Swag, 1900, pencil on gray paper, 60.6 × 44.1 cm. Mexico City, UNAM, Escuela Nacional de Artes Plásticas.

1892
Acquires the nickname "the engineer" because of his interest in mechanical objects, especially trains and mining machinery.

His father's advocacy of radical ideas in the semiweekly liberal newspaper *El democrata* results in political enmity toward the family, and they move to Mexico City.

Unhappy in the city, Rivera develops, in succession, scarlet fever, typhoid, and diphtheria.

Enthralled by his first exposure to Mexican popular art in the collection of a great aunt.

1894
Attends school for the first time: three months at the Colegio Católico Carpantier (a religious school chosen by his mother, a devout Catholic). Chief interests are military history and making mechanical toys.

1896
December: as a student at the Liceo Católico Hispano-Mexicano, wins third-year examination prize.

December 29: birth of David Alfaro Siqueiros.

Enters evening art course at the Academy of San Carlos.

1898
Father appointed to position of inspector in the Department of Public Health; in this post he is required to travel throughout the republic. At this time he may have brought his son's artistic talent to the attention of the benevolent and cultured governor of the state of Veracruz, Teodoro A. Dehesa, who would later become Rivera's patron.

Completes elementary education and passes qualifying examination for the Escuela Nacional Preparatoria.

At his father's insistence enrolls in a military college, but after only two weeks, repelled by the prospect of regimented training, he is permitted to enroll in regular classes at San Carlos when awarded a scholarship.

During his years at San Carlos (1898–1905), absorbs a strictly ordered program of studies that emphasizes technical expertise as well as the positivistic ideals of study from nature and rational investigation. His teachers at the academy include Félix Parra, who introduces him to the beauty of pre-Colombian art, José María Velasco, from whom he gains his understanding of the laws of perspective and his love for the Mexican landscape, and Santiago Rebull, a student of Ingres, who will have a profound influence on his treatment of the figure and his use of the golden section as the foundation for his compositions. In the text for Velasco's perspective course, *Foundations: Compendium of Linear and Aerial Perspective, Shadows, Reflections, and Refractions with the Necessary Rudiments of Geometry,* Rivera encounters a work that will prove critical in developing his inclination toward a rationally ordered art.

1902
Receives a monthly scholarship from Governor Dehesa.

In addition to studio work begins to draw and paint in the open air.

Gerardo Murillo (later known as Dr. Atl) returns from Europe and greatly impresses the younger students with his account of contemporary European art.

1903
Santiago Rebull dies. The new subdirector of the academy, the Catalonian painter Antonio Fabrés Costa, introduces the Pillet method of drawing (based on the teachings of the French academician Jules-Jean Désiré Pillet, this method emphasized drawing from direct observation and photographs instead of from master drawings and prints).

1904
Paints both figure studies and landscapes in the manner of Velasco, including *La era* (fig. 13) and *La Casteñada* (fig. 14).

Wins the medal for Fabrés's painting class.

Díaz reelected for fourth time.

December: Rivera's work is included in the annual exhibition held by pupils at the academy.

1905
January: wins a government pension of twenty pesos per month.

1906
Loses government pension but receives a modest four-year scholarship for European study from Governor Dehesa (three-hundred francs per month).

Included in an exhibition at San Carlos of twelve artists either pensioned to travel to Europe or already working there. Exhibits some fifteen landscapes in various media, including the paintings *The Mixcoac Ravine* (fig. 17) and *Citlaltépetl.* Through the efforts of Murillo, enough works are sold to pay for Rivera's passage to Europe.

Becomes part of *Savia Moderna,* a promodernist group of young artists, architects, writers, and intellectuals, which publishes a magazine of the same title. Several members of this group will later be associated with Rivera in Madrid and Paris.

May: participates in an exhibition organized for *Savia Moderna* by Murillo, which emphasizes the modern European styles Impressionism, Symbolism, and Art Nouveau.

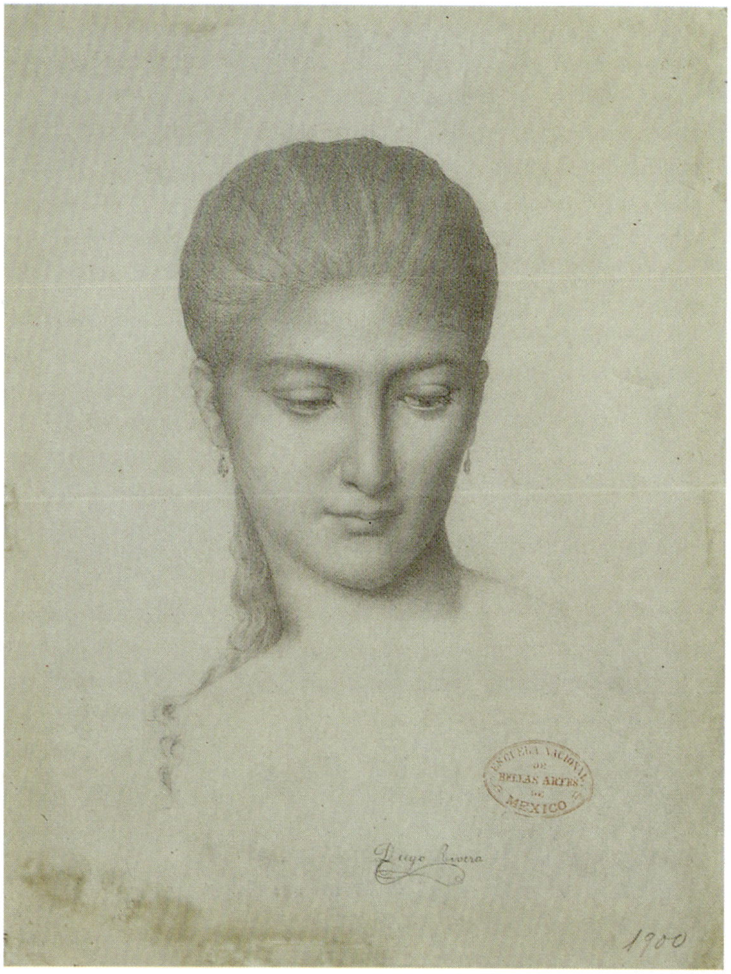

Figure 9
Head of a Woman, 1898, pencil on greenish blue paper, 36.2 × 28.3 cm. Mexico City, UNAM, Escuela Nacional de Artes Plásticas.

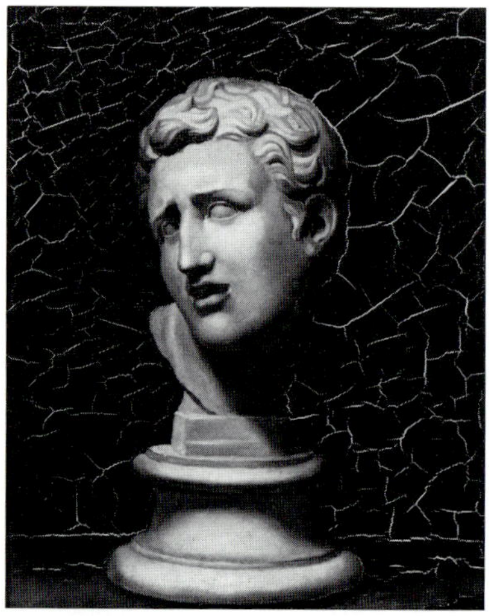

Figure 10
Classical Head, 1902, oil on canvas, 48.5 × 39.2 cm. Guanajuato, Museo Diego Rivera (INBA). This student work reflects Rivera's training at the Academy of San Carlos, where students were required to follow a traditional European-style academic curriculum that included rendering classical sculpture.

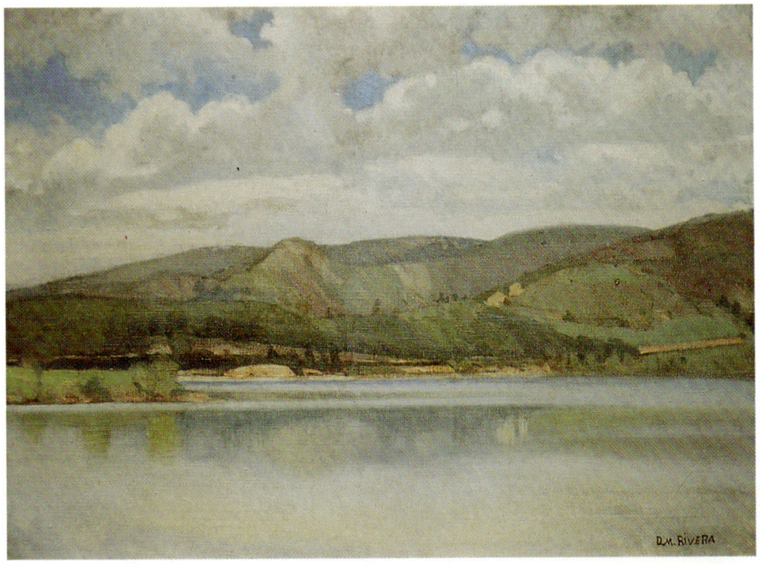

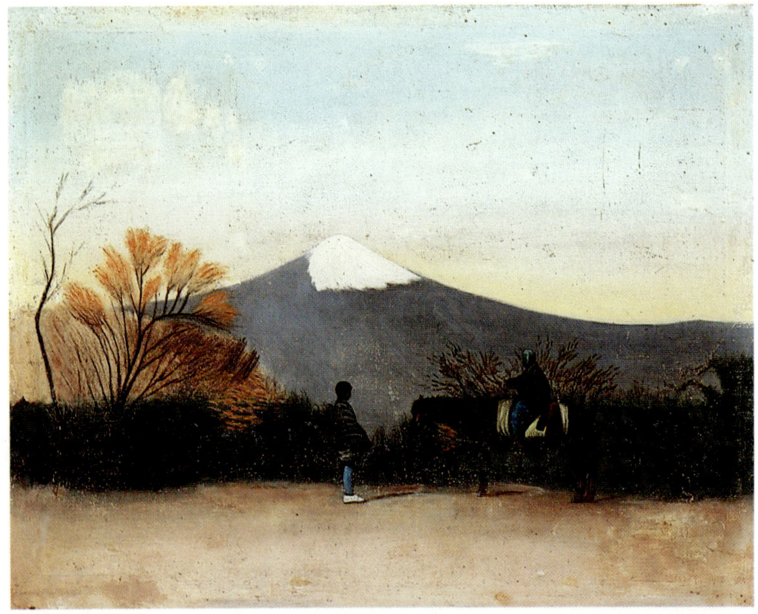

Figure 11
Landscape with Lake, ca. 1900, oil on canvas, 53 × 73 cm. Collection of Daniel Yankelewitz B., Costa Rica. Reflections on water are the subject of several of Rivera's early landscapes, which were probably the result of exercises designed to teach students to calculate the angles of light refraction.

Figure 12
Landscape, 1896/97, oil on canvas, 70 × 55 cm. Collection of Guadalupe Rivera de Iturbe.

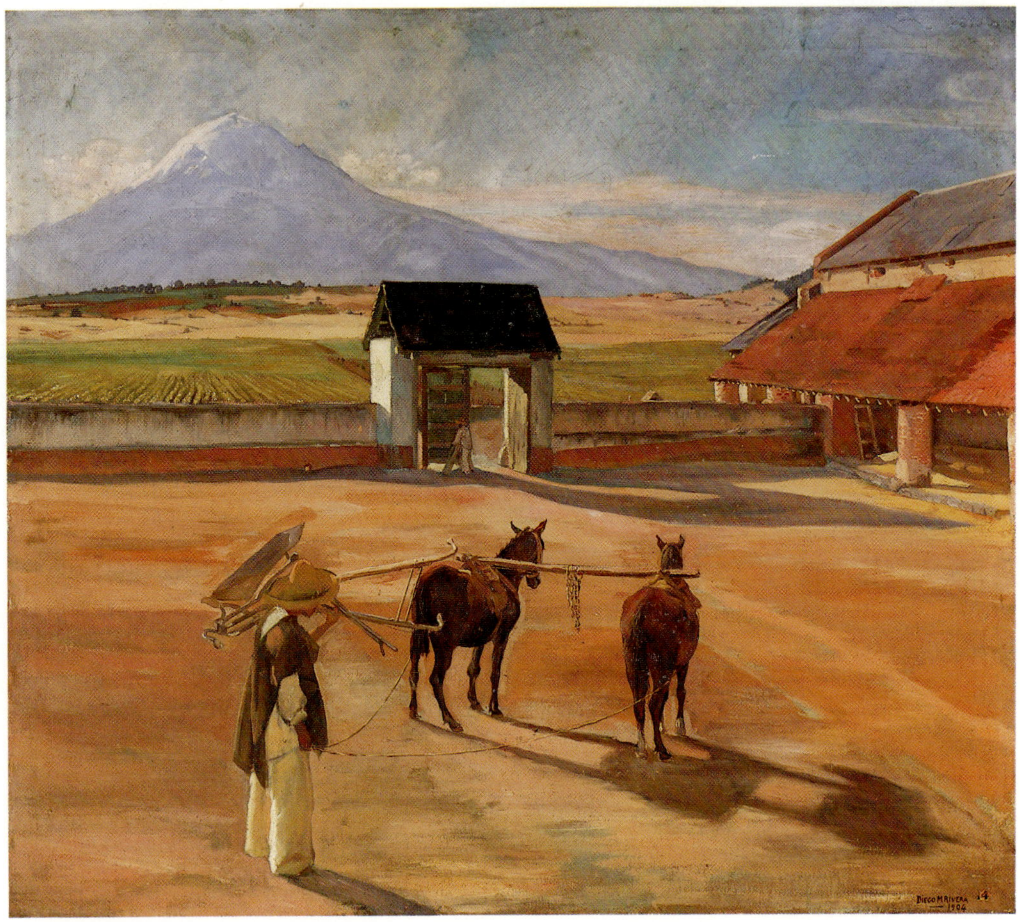

Figure 13
La era, 1904, oil on canvas, 100 × 114.6 cm. Guanajuato, Museo Diego Rivera, Marte R. Gómez Collection (INBA). The influence of his teacher, José María Velasco, is evident in Rivera's depiction of a man preparing a team of horses on the vast plain at the foot of the volcano Popocatepetl. Like Velasco, the young artist devoted his energies to capturing the specific tonalities and atmosphere of a typical Mexican landscape.

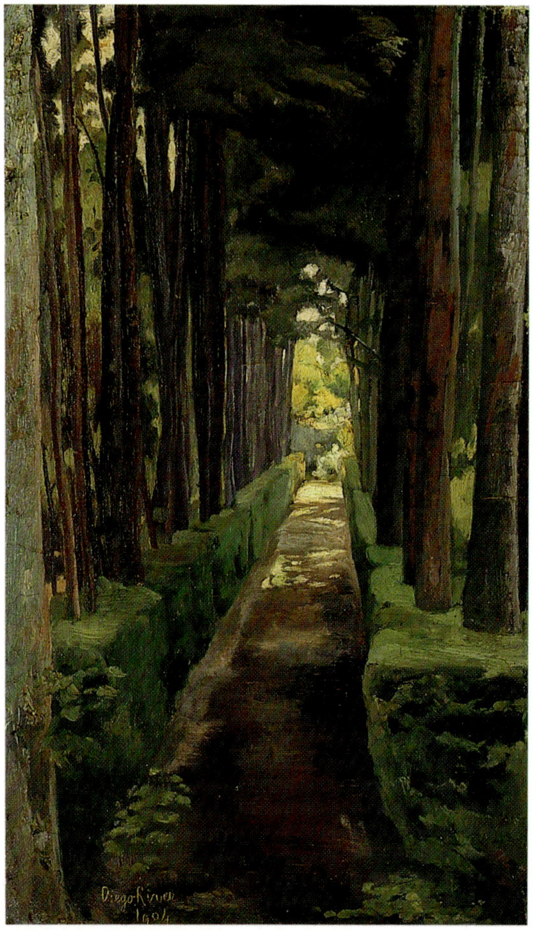

Figure 14
La Casteñada, also known as *Paseo de los melancólicos,* 1904, oil on canvas, 85 × 50 cm. Mexico City, Museo Franz Mayer. This scene shows the grounds of La Casteñada, Mexico City's mental asylum. *Los melancólicos* is the common Mexican term for an asylum's inmates.

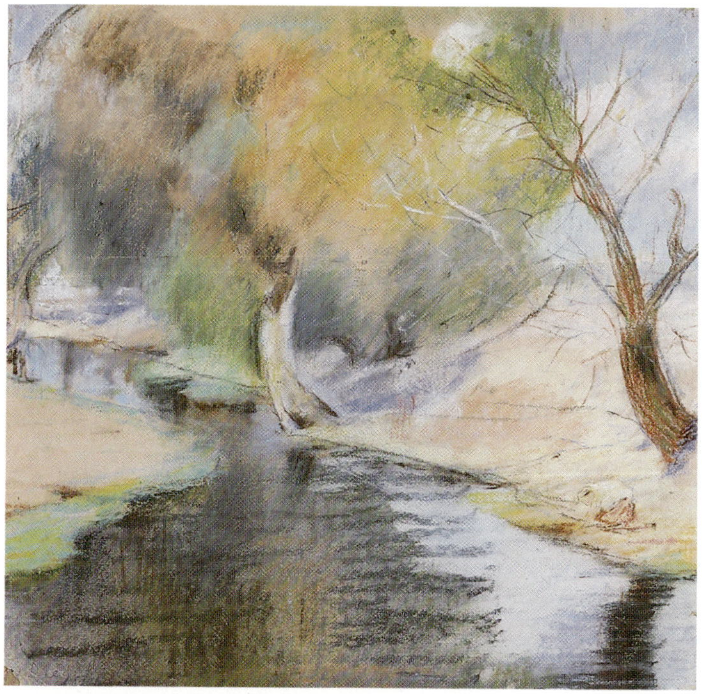

Figure 15
Confluence of the Streams, 1906, pastel, 31 × 32 cm. Mexico City, Banamex.

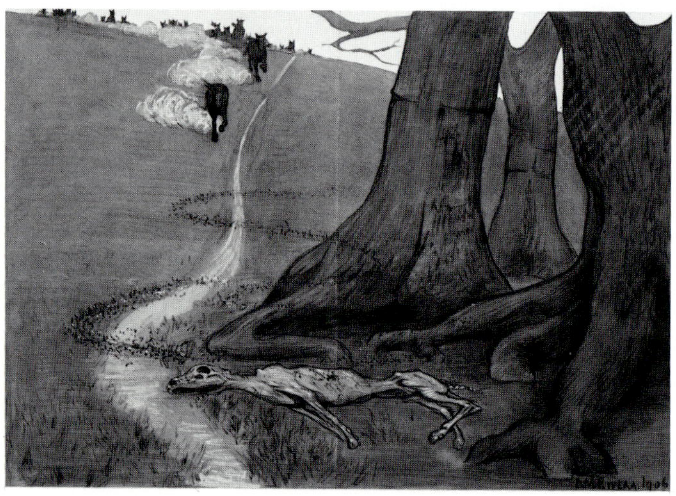

Figure 16
Dead Horse, 1906, charcoal, gouache, and brush in black ink on greige paper, 32.6 × 39.7 cm. New York, The Museum of Modern Art, New York Inter-American Fund (1586.68).

Figure 17
The Mixcoac Ravine, also known as *Mixcoac House,* 1906, oil on canvas, 71 × 106.8 cm. Property of the State of Veracruz. This carefully rendered landscape reflects Rivera's rigorous academic training, but his choice of subject—the Mixcoac ravine is the site of a small pre-Hispanic settlement on the outskirts of Mexico City—relates it to the renewed interest in indigenous Mexican subjects promoted by Dr. Atl.

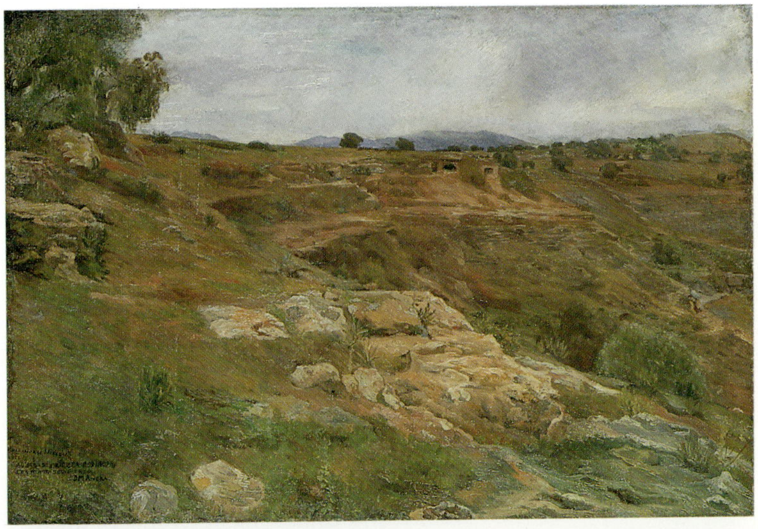

Figure 18
Cerro de las campanas, Querétaro, 1906, gouache, 31.2 × 48.2 cm. Collection of Mrs. Matilda Gray Stream. This drawing depicts the "hill of the bells" near Magdalena, Querétaro, where Maximilian, emperor of Mexico, 1864–1867, was captured and executed.

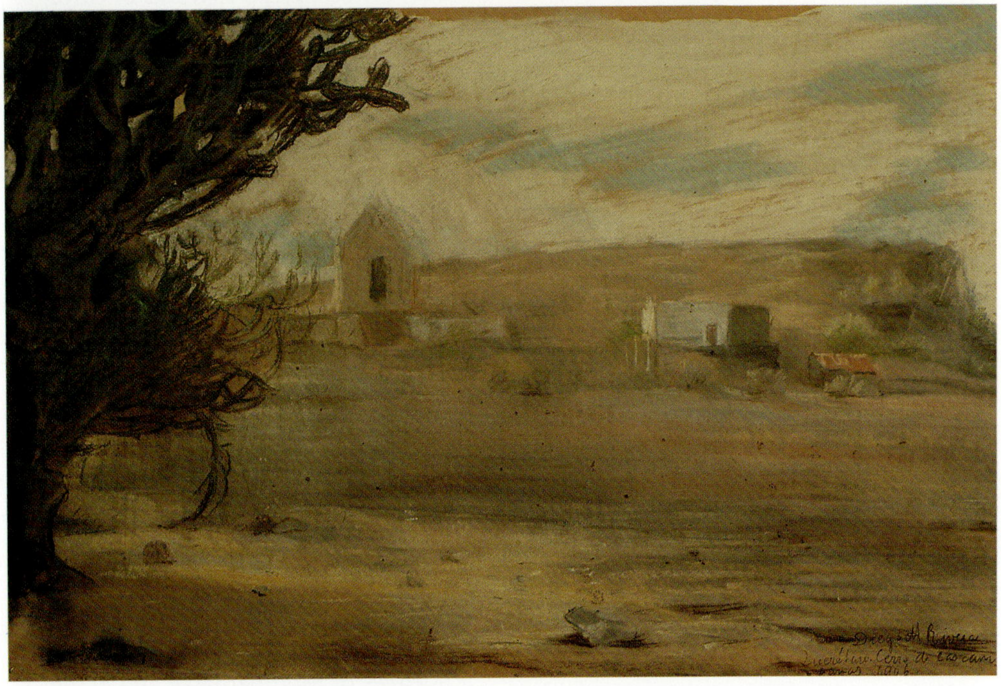

II.
Europe:
An Artistic Apprenticeship

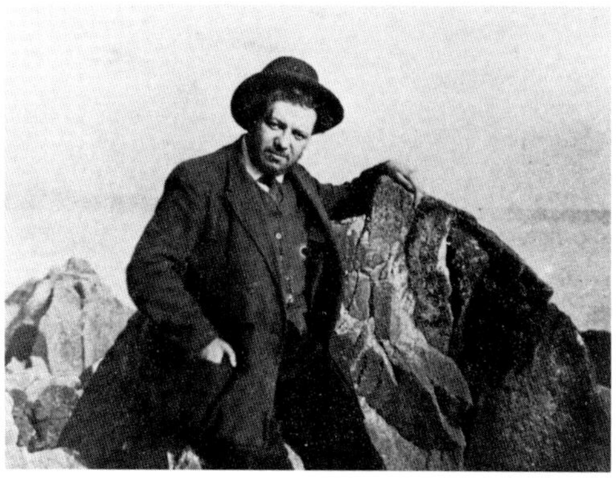

Figure 19
Rivera in Spain, ca. 1907.

1907

January 6: Rivera arrives in Spain, weighing three-hundred pounds and well over six feet tall. The only condition of the Dehesa grant is that Rivera must send the governor a painting every six months to demonstrate his progress.

Gerardo Murillo has provided a letter of introduction to the fashionable Spanish realist Eduardo Chicharro y Agüera, who takes Rivera on as a student and after six months calls his progress astonishing.

1907–08

Studies and copies masterworks in the Prado; attracted by the works of Goya, especially the late "black" paintings, El Greco, Velázquez, Brueghel, Cranach, and Bosch.

Forms friendships with leading members of the Spanish avant-garde, including the writers Ramón Gómez de la Serna and Ramón del Valle-Inclan and the painter María Gutiérrez Blanchard.

Paints *Church of Lequeito, The Picador,* and *La calle de Ávila* (fig. 21), which are included in an exhibition of the work of Chicharro and his students in Madrid.

1909

March: arrives in Paris, where he lives at the Hôtel du Suisse in the Latin Quarter. Studies museum collections, attends exhibitions and lectures, works in the free academies of Montparnasse and in the open air along the Seine.

Summer: visits Bruges, where he begins *House on the Bridge* (fig. 23) and through Blanchard meets a young Russian artist, Angeline Beloff, who will later become his common-law wife.

Goes to London, where he visits museums, studies Turner, Blake, and Hogarth, and sketches the industrial environment and the slums.

November: returns to Paris.

1910

Studies Dutch artists and 19th-century French artists in the Louvre; also studies with the academic painter Victor-Octave Guillonet.

Travels to Brittany; paintings include *Head of a Breton Woman* and *Breton Girl* (fig. 27).

Completes and exhibits *House on the Bridge* as well as several other paintings in the 1910 exhibition of the *Société des Artistes Indépendants*.

April: the Anti-Reelectionist Party nominates Francisco I. Madero as their presidential candidate. He is subsequently forced into exile in the United States, and Díaz is once again reelected.

June: Rivera travels to Madrid to prepare for the forthcoming exhibition of his European paintings at the Academy of San Carlos as part of Mexico's Centennial of Independence celebrations.

October 2: Rivera arrives back in Mexico.

Madero launches the Mexican Revolution with his "Plan of San Luís Potosí," in which

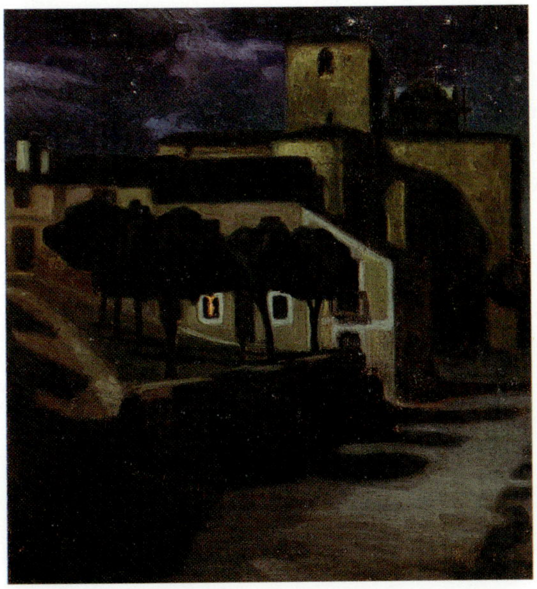

Figure 20
Night in Ávila, 1907, oil on burlap, 97 × 90.5 cm. Collection of Dolores Olmedo. This nocturnal landscape has an atmosphere of mystery and nostalgia that derives from its languid, sensuous lines, cold colors, and the play of light against shadow—elements Rivera adopted from the work of Spain's Catalonian modernists.

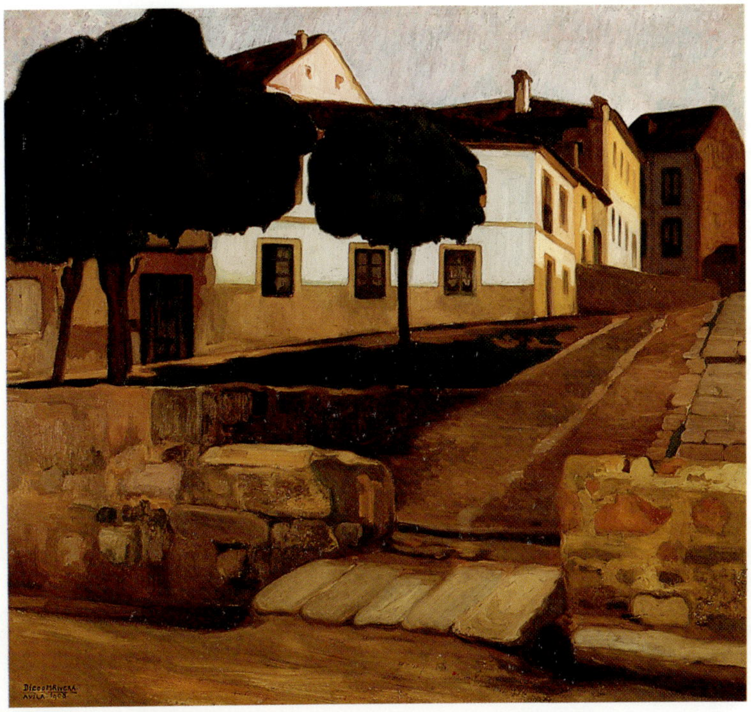

Figure 21
La calle de Ávila, 1908, oil on canvas, 129 × 141 cm. Mexico City, Museo Nacional de Arte (INBA). Rivera often experimented with different artistic styles within a single work, as is evident here in the contrast between the geometric volume of the buildings and the impressionistic treatment of the sky.

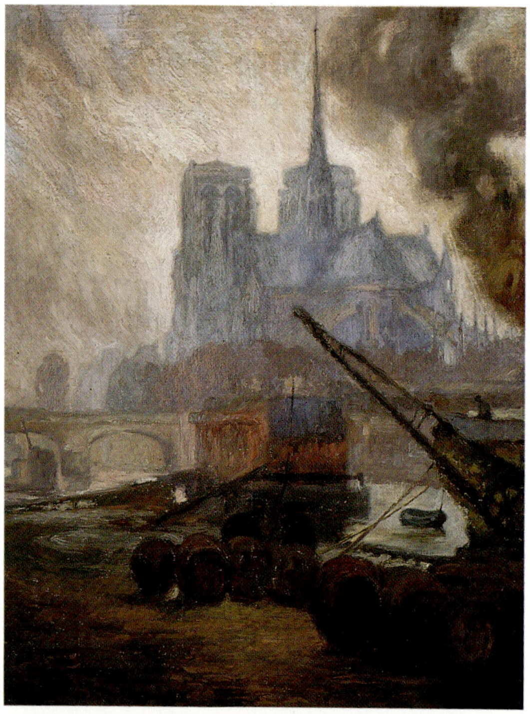

Figure 22
Nôtre Dame de Paris, 1909, oil on canvas, 144 × 113 cm. Mexico City, Museo Nacional de Arte (INBA). The influence of Claude Monet's late work can be seen both in the theme of this painting, a monumental edifice the solidity of which is dissolved by the mist, and in its surface texture, a thick impasto built up of diagonal brushstrokes.

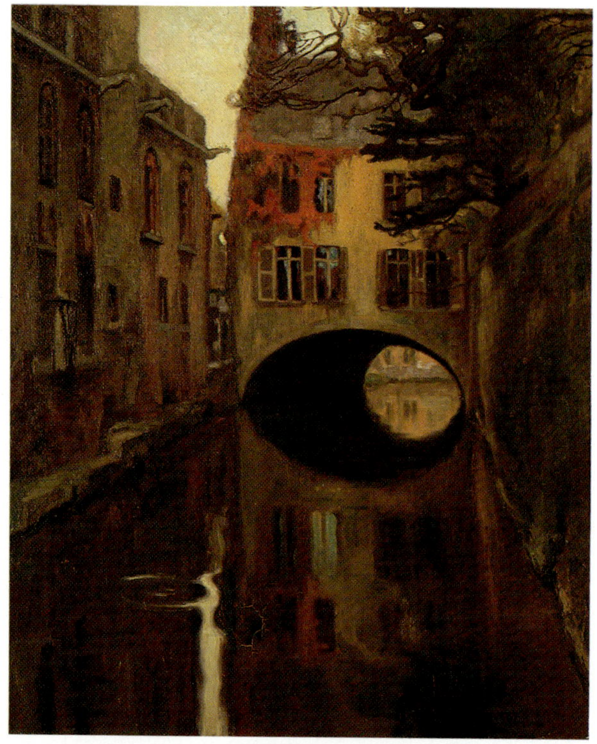

Figure 23
House on the Bridge, 1909, oil on canvas, 146 × 140 cm. Mexico City, Museo Nacional de Arte (INBA). The city of Bruges was an important center for the Symbolists, and this work, painted in that city, is typically Symbolist in its central motif; the ambiguous reflections on the water, which allude to the multiple levels of reality.

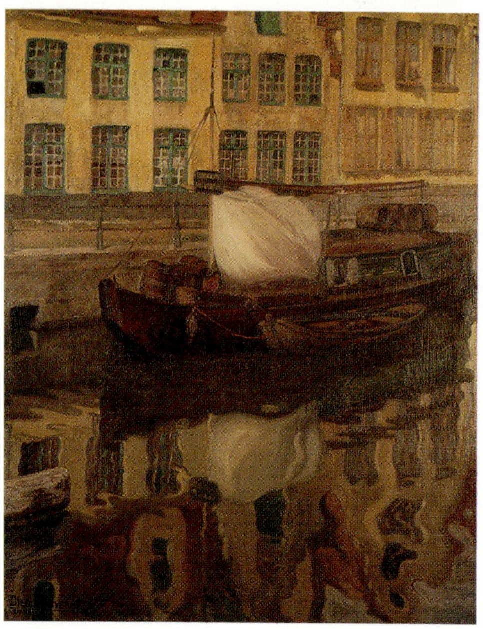

Figure 24
Reflections, 1909, oil on canvas, 81.3 × 100.3 cm. Collection of Mrs. Matilda Gray Stream.

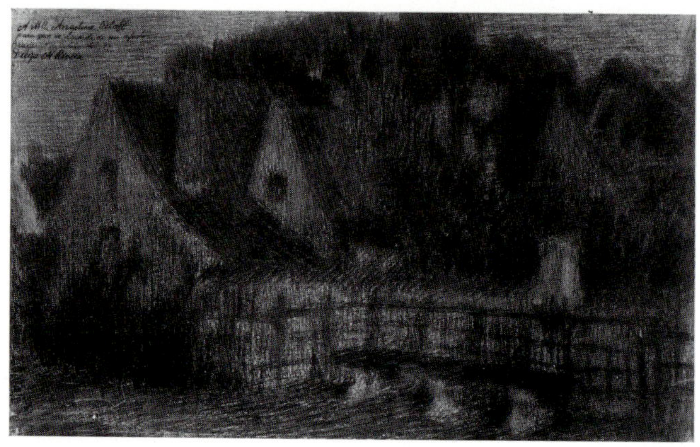

Figure 25
Béguinage à Bruges, also known as *Night Scene,* 1909, charcoal, 27.8 × 46 cm. Guanajuato, Museo Diego Rivera (INBA).

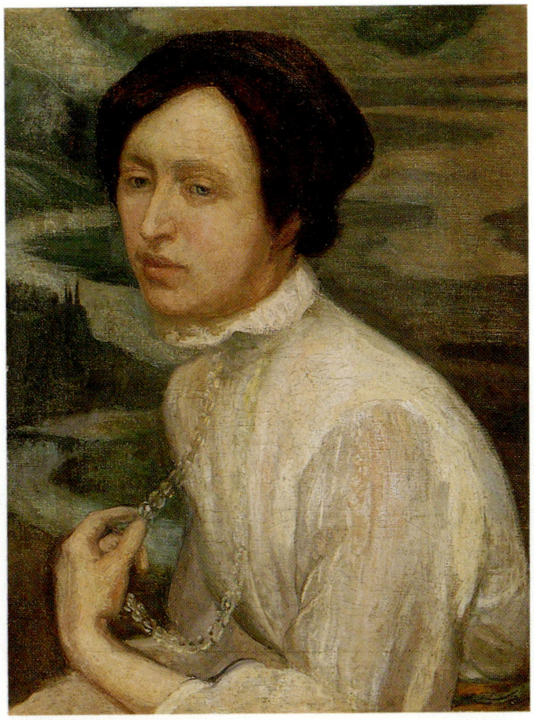

Figure 26
Portrait of Angeline Beloff, 1909, oil on canvas, 58 × 45 cm. Property of the State of Veracruz. Also in the Symbolist tradition, this portrait focuses on the spiritual aspects of Rivera's companion and wife, presenting her in a distant and pensive mood. The city of Bruges appears on the far horizon as a reference to the setting of their first meeting.

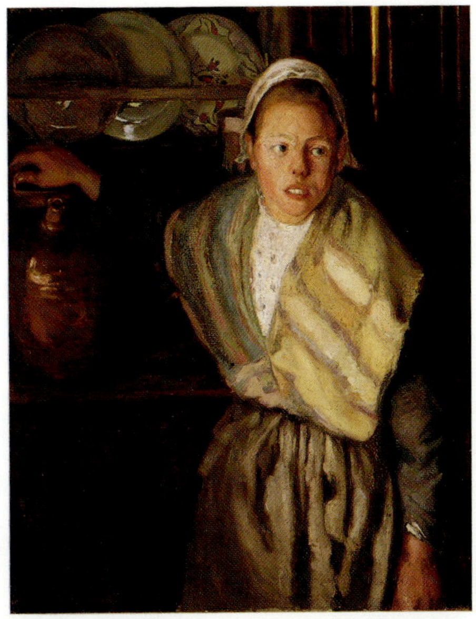

Figure 27
Breton Girl, 1910, oil on canvas, 100 × 80 cm. Mexico City, Museo Nacional de Arte (INBA). This work reveals Rivera's interest in the genre scenes characteristic of Spanish *costumbrista* painting and incorporates the chiaroscuro techniques he had encountered in his study of 17th-century Dutch painting.

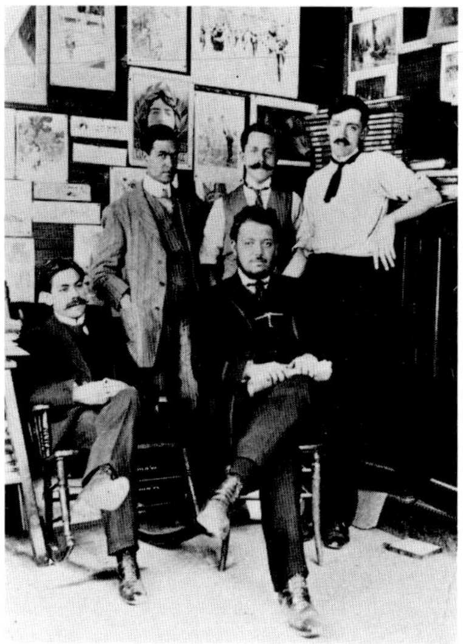

Figure 28
Rivera with members of *Imprenta Garduño*, Mexico, after 1910.

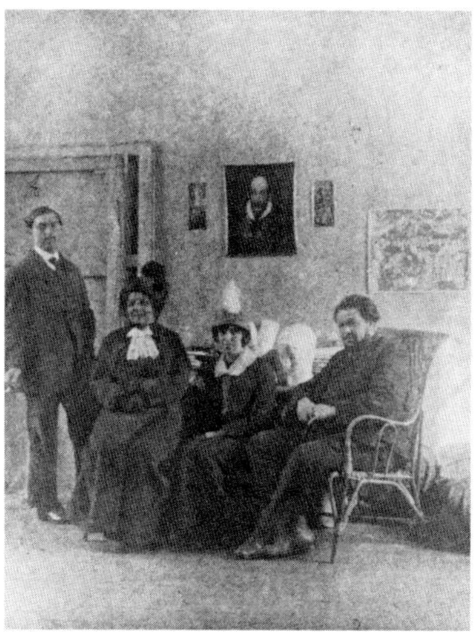

Figure 29
Rivera (far right) with Angeline Beloff, Rivera's mother, and Angel Zárraga in Rivera's Paris studio, ca. 1915.

he exhorts the Mexican people to rise up in armed rebellion on November 20. On that very day, Díaz's wife, Carmen Romero Rubio de Díaz, formally opens Rivera's exhibition, which is a great social and financial success (of the forty works shown, Señora Díaz purchases six and the government seven). Fighting has actually begun two days earlier in the town of Puebla.

1911
Guerrilla actions by Francisco ("Pancho") Villa in northern and Emiliano Zapata in southern Mexico; rebel troops take the border city, Ciudad Juárez, and resistance quickly disintegrates. The Treaty of Ciudad Juárez provides for Díaz's resignation, which he submits on May 25.

June: Rivera returns to Paris, greatly assisted by proceeds from his exhibition. He has missed the first public exhibition of Cubist works in the spring exhibition of the *Société des Artistes Indépendants*.

Rivera and Beloff begin to live together.

Develops a friendship with Amedeo Modigliani; the two artists delight in scandalizing the café crowd of Montparnasse with their bizarre tales and behavior.

Completes two landscapes (both views of the Mexican volcano Iztaccíhuatl) and exhibits them in the Salon d'Automne.

Fall: influenced by the Neo-Impressionist and Divisionist revival in Paris, paints Divisionist landscapes in Catalonia (see fig. 30).

November 6: Madero installed as president of Mexico after a landslide victory in the October elections.

Zapata denounces Madero and, with the assistance of Otilio Montaño, issues his "Plan of Ayala," which calls for immediate land distribution.

Gerardo Murillo returns to Paris and adopts the name Dr. Atl (*atl* is a Náhautl word meaning "water," and Murillo claims to have traveled all the rivers in Mexico).

Justo Sierra, Madero's minister of education, renews Rivera's grant.

1912
Exhibits two Catalonian landscapes in the *Société des Artistes Indépendants* exhibition.

Spring: travels with Beloff to Toledo. Develops a friendship with one of the leading Latin American émigré artists in Paris, Angel Zárraga, and they study the art of El Greco and Ignacio Zuloaga. Rivera adopts and surpasses Zuloaga's style in his most important work of this period, *The Old Ones* (fig. 32).

Fall: returns to Paris and sets up residence at 26, rue de Départ, in a block of artists' studios in Montparnasse.

Reunites with Mexican artists then living in Paris, including Zárraga, Dr. Atl, Roberto Montenegro, and Adolfo Best Maugard.

Influenced by the Cubism of his neighbors, the Dutch painters Piet Mondrian, Conrad Kikkert, and Lodewijk Schelfhout, who derived their approach from studying Cézanne.

Exhibits two paintings in the Salon d'Automne, including the Zuloagesque *Portrait of a Spaniard* (Hermenegildo Alsina).

After a short stay in Paris, returns to Toledo to prepare for a forthcoming January group showing at the Galerie Bernheim-Jeune. The atmosphere of the city of Toledo and its similarity to Rivera's birthplace, Guanajuato, contribute to his attraction to Cubism.

1913
The year 1913 marks Rivera's transition to Cubism, primarily through his study of El Greco and secondarily through his assimilation of the characteristics of the work of Cézanne. During his Cubist period (1913–17), he produces approximately two hundred paintings.

January: exhibits six Toledo paintings in the *Groupe Libre* exhibition (a diverse group of

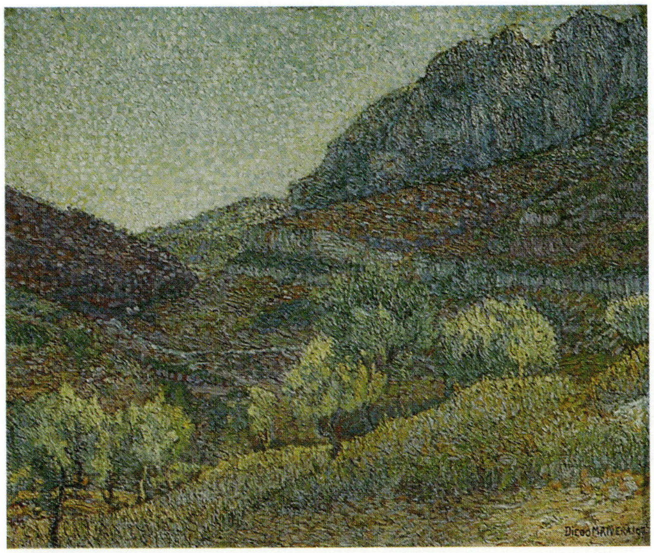

Figure 30
Catalonian Landscape (Montserrat), 1911, oil on canvas, 87 × 107 cm. Property of the State of Veracruz.

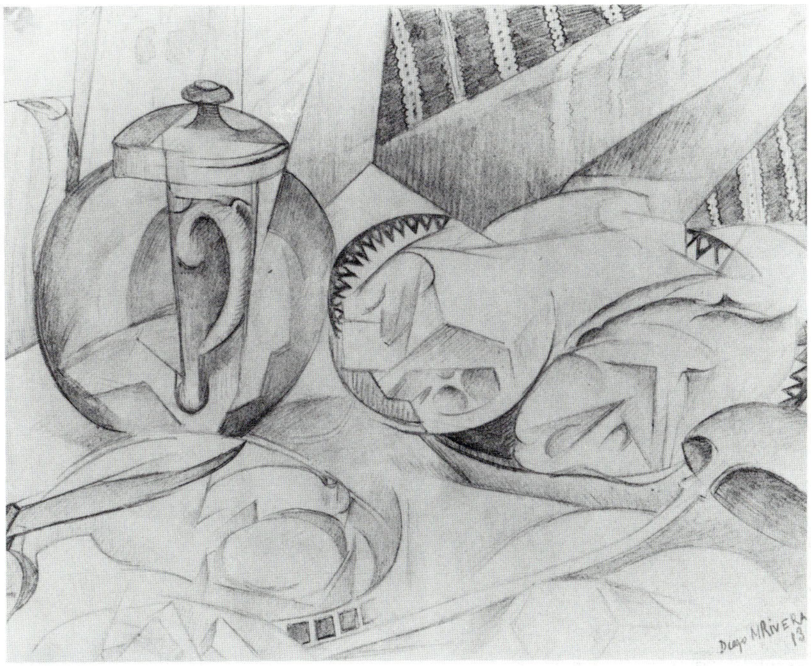

Figure 31
Still Life with Teapot, 1913, pencil, 25.8 × 35 cm. Guanajuato, Museo Diego Rivera (INBA). In this early Cubist drawing, Rivera combined precise rendering in the style of Ingres with the compositional devices of the Cubist idiom.

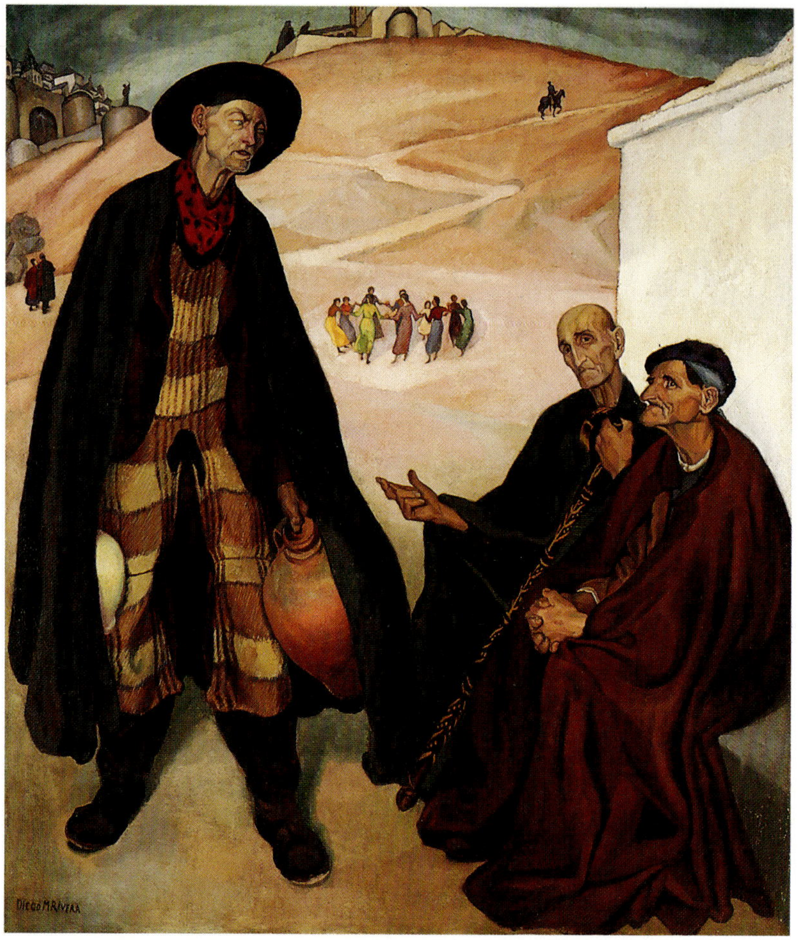

Figure 32
The Old Ones, also known as *En las afueras de Toledo,* 1912, oil on canvas, 210 × 184 cm. Collection of Dolores Olmedo. The influence of El Greco, in particular his elongated figures and characteristic sense of space, as well as that of the Spanish *modernistas,* is evident in Rivera's transformation of a commonplace scene into a monumental image that conveys an aura of spirituality.

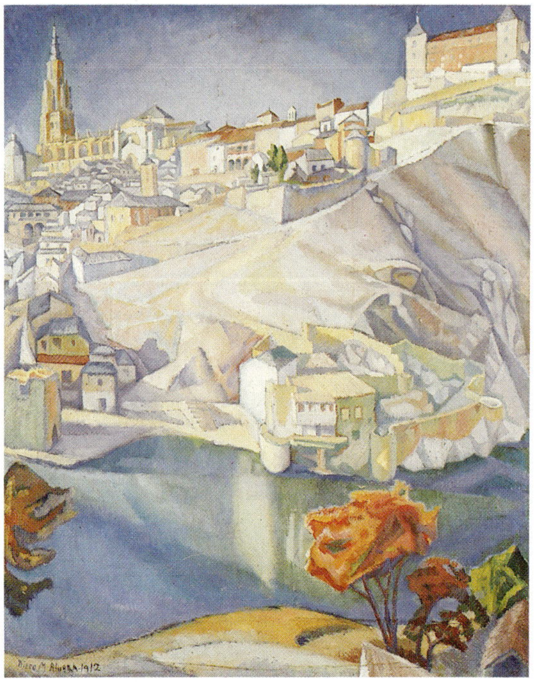

Figure 33
View of Toledo, 1912, oil on canvas, 112 × 91 cm. Fundación Amparo R. de Espinosa Yglesias. This work depicts the same view of Toledo as El Greco's painting of about 1610 (New York, The Metropolitan Museum of Art). It displays the concern for the juxtaposition of forms in space that would ultimately lead Rivera to Cubism.

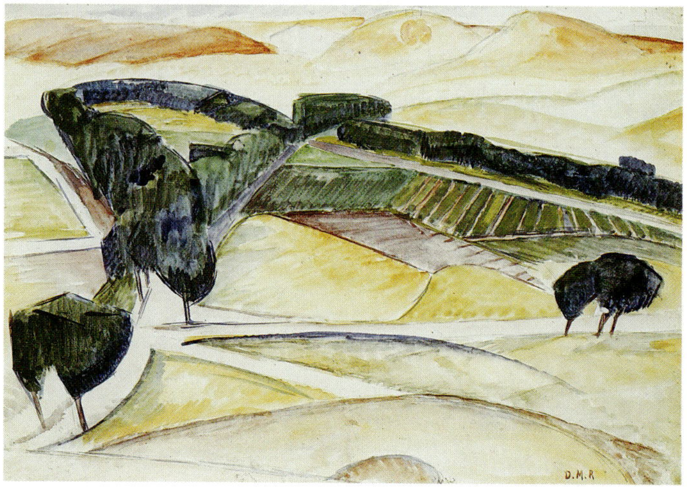

Figure 34
Landscape of Toledo, 1913, pencil and watercolor, 32 × 46 cm. Property of the State of Veracruz.

fourteen artists, all conservative in approach) at the Galerie Bernheim-Jeune. *View of Toledo* (fig. 33) illustrated in catalogue.

Remains in Paris studio preparing for spring exhibition of the *Société des Artistes Indépendants,* in which he exhibits two Toledo landscapes and the large, ambitious salon "machine," *Portrait of Adolfo Best Maugard* (fig. 37). The latter reveals Rivera's interest in the work of Robert Delaunay and his concept of Simultanism. Rivera thought the work his most important to this time and that in "reality [it] marked my entry into the Paris art world,"[2] yet no major critics mention the work in their reviews of the exhibition.

Early in the year returns to Toledo and finally completes his *Adoration of the Virgin and Child*—the first work to successfully incorporate the Cubist elements of El Greco and Cézanne, using one of the most traditional subjects in the history of art.

February 9–18: the *Decena Trágica* (tragic ten days) in Mexico City. Armed conflict spreads among the different factions struggling for power. On February 22, Madero and Vice-President Pino Suárez are murdered, and General Victoriano Huerta takes control of the government. This is the beginning of a civil war that will last over seven years.

Rivera's grant ends with Madero's downfall, and he supports himself and Beloff through the sale of his works.

Late summer: returns to Paris and continues to paint Toledo subject matter.

Exhibits *Girl with Artichokes* (fig. 40) at the Salon d'Automne; this is Rivera's first attempt to portray simultaneously different views of a figure. Also exhibits *Young Woman with a Fan;* the latter is well received and is reproduced in several important journals.

Becomes intimate with the artists (Robert Delaunay, Fernand Léger, Marc Chagall, the Puteaux Cubists) and writers who frequent the offices of the avant-garde review *Montjoie!.*

Late in the year, Rivera's efforts to work in a manner combining Cubism and Futurism culminate in *Woman at the Well* (fig. 42); he develops a brilliantly colored palette unusual for Cubism.

Exhibits his work in group shows in Munich and Vienna.

1914

Achieves a more static portrayal of simultaneity by use of a compositional grid, as in *Sailor at Lunch* (fig. 46) and *Two Women* (fig. 295). Exhibits the latter with the *Société des Artistes Indépendants.*

Begins to include Mexican motifs in his works, probably as a result of viewing the large exhibition of Russian folk art at the 1913 Salon d'Automne.

Meets Juan Gris and adopts some of his artistic language, including golden section compositions, the mixing of sand and other aggregates into his pigments, and a heavy impasto.

Through the efforts of a mutual friend, the Chilean artist Ortíz de Zárate, meets Picasso. Picasso expresses admiration for Rivera's recent paintings, and they talk for several hours about Cubism.

April 21–May 6: Rivera's only one-person exhibition in Paris, twenty-five works, including *Young Man with Stylograph* (fig. 47), from 1913–14 at the gallery of Berthe Weill. A minor scandal ensues as Weill abuses Cubism in her anonymous foreword to the catalogue. In spite of the scandal, the exhibition proves a financial success, greatly alleviating Rivera's penurious situation.

Exhibits in group shows in Prague, Amsterdam, and Brussels.

June 28: assassination of Austrian archduke Francis Ferdinand in Sarajevo; beginning of World War I.

July: Huerta forced to resign, and the struggle between competing factions continues.

Summer: Rivera, Beloff, Jacques Lipchitz, Berthe Kristover, and María Gutiérrez Blanchard undertake a walking and sketching tour of Spain. At the outbreak of the war, they are camped on the island of Majorca, where Rivera paints local landscapes in a less overtly Cubist manner; he uses luminous "tropical" colors and incorporates sand and found objects into his works.

Winter: Rivera's group moves to Madrid, where they join the Spanish Dadaist writer Ramón Gómez de la Serna. A time of abject poverty for Rivera, who talks of enlisting in the French army.

1915

Exhibits his Spanish work in "*Los pintores integros,*" an exhibition organized by Gómez de la Serna, which introduces Cubism to Madrid. The resulting controversy causes the authorities to close the gallery.

Executes Cubist still lifes and "rotative" portraits.

Visits Barcelona with Beloff.

Spring: Rivera and Beloff return to Paris, where he works in a more decorative Synthetic Cubist manner.

April: Villa defeated in a decisive battle at Celaya; Venustiano Carranza consolidates his position as de facto president.

Following his contacts with exiled Mexicans in Madrid and Paris, who inform him of current conditions in his native country, Rivera progresses to a more serious, personal series of paintings reflecting his Mexican heritage. These efforts range from the inclusion of a *sarape* and an *equipal* (a type of chair) in the portrait of his compatriot Martín Luís Guzmán (fig. 51) to overt revolutionary references (rifle, cartridge belt, Zapatista sombrero) and the depiction of the Mexican landscape in the culminating work of this year, *Zapatista Landscape* (fig. 53).

The similarity of the initial stages of Picasso's *Man Leaning on a Table* to the

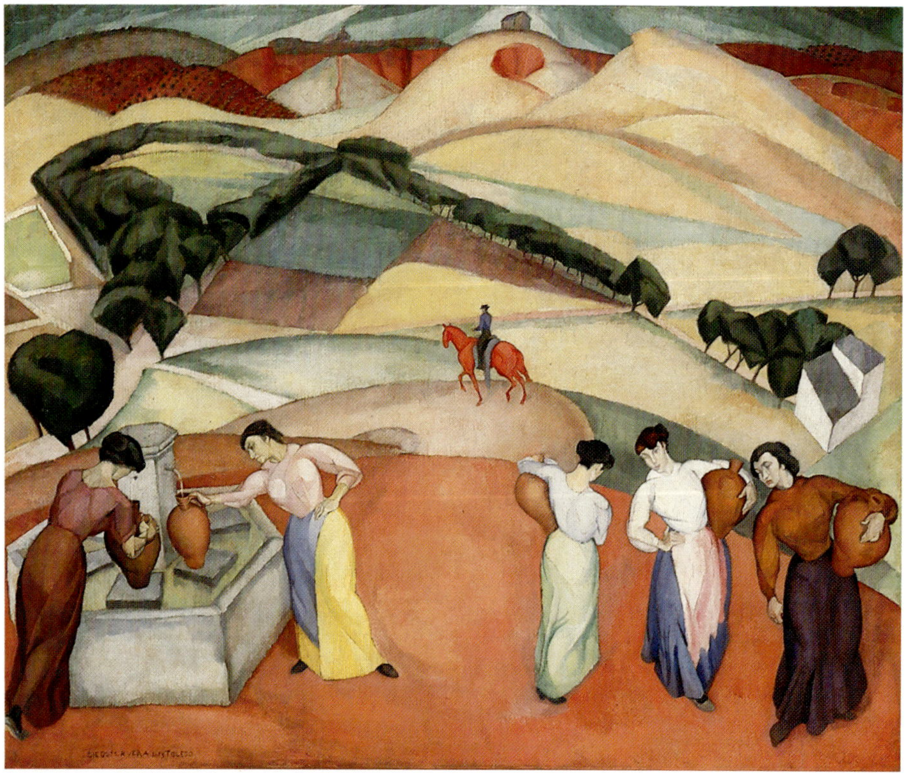

Figure 35
At the Fountain near Toledo, 1913, oil on canvas, 166 × 204 cm. Collection of Dolores Olmedo. This proto-Cubist work demonstrates Rivera's development of abstracted figures and planes and shows his familiarity with the early Cubist work of Piet Mondrian and Lodewijk Schelfhout.

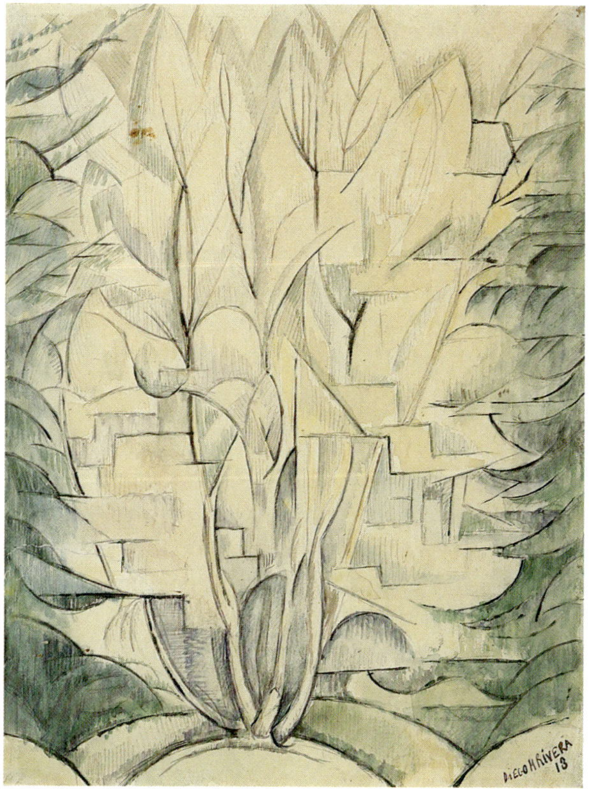

Figure 36
Tree, 1913, watercolor, 33.8 × 26 cm. Guanajuato, Museo Diego Rivera (INBA). This study for a painting entitled *Arbol y muros, Toledo, (Trees and Walls, Toledo),* 1913, exhibits the influence of Mondrian.

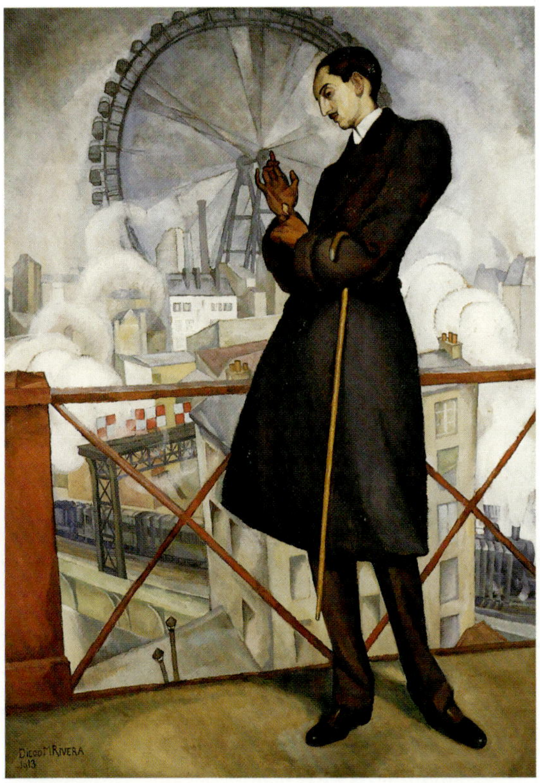

Figure 37
Portrait of Adolfo Best Maugard, 1913, oil on canvas, 226.8 × 161.6 cm. Mexico City, Museo Nacional de Arte (INBA). This portrait of Rivera's friend, the aristocratic Mexican painter Adolfo Best Maugard, combines an El Greco–like elongation of form with the concept of simultaneity as developed by Robert Delaunay.

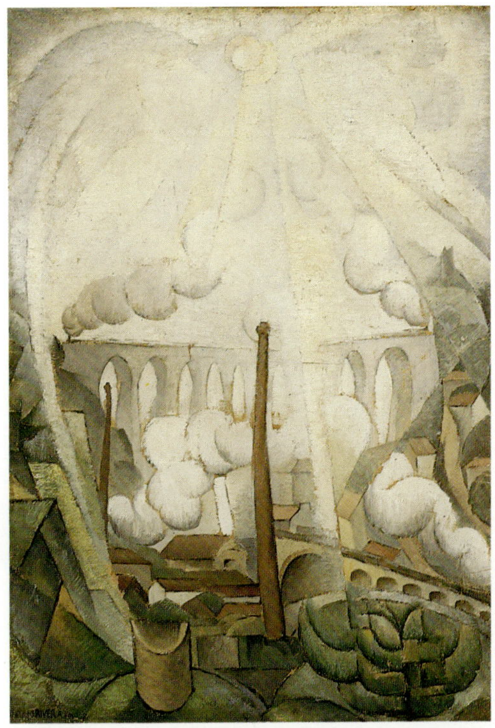

Figure 38
The Viaduct—Sun Breaking through the Fog, 1913, oil on canvas, 83.5 × 59 cm. Collection of Dolores Olmedo.

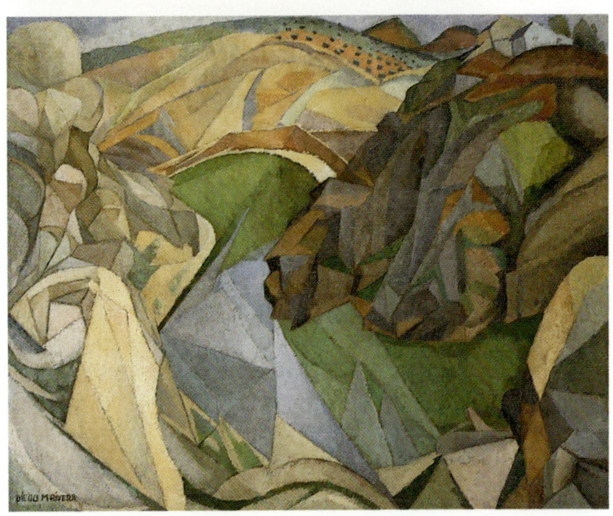

Figure 39
Spanish Landscape, Toledo, 1913, oil on canvas, 89 × 110 cm. Collection of Guadalupe Rivera de Iturbe.

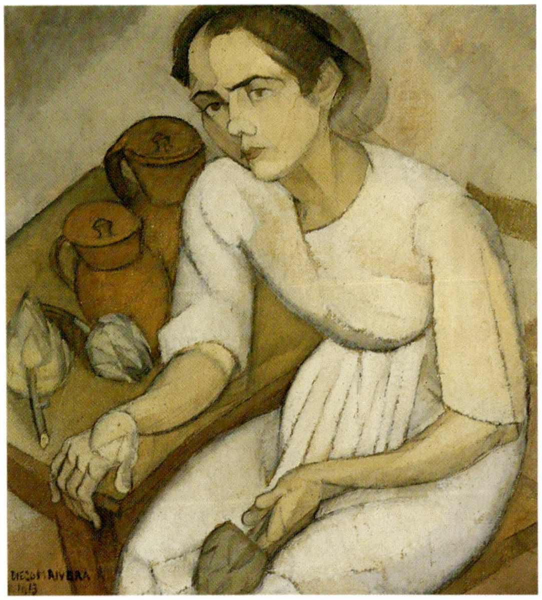

Figure 40
Girl with Artichokes,
1913, oil on canvas,
80.5 × 75 cm. Private
Collection.

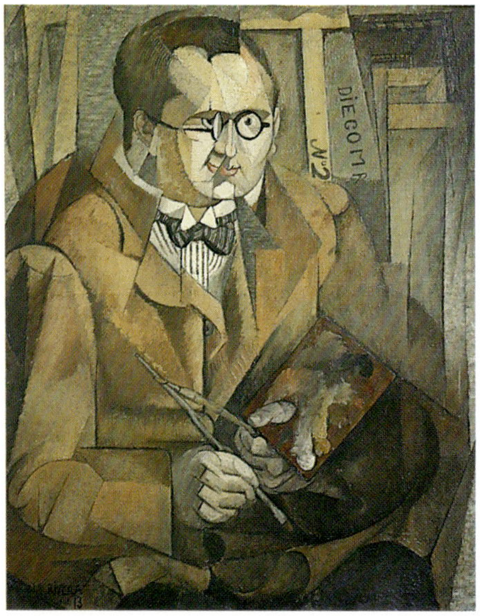

Figure 41
Portrait of the Painter Zinoviev, 1913, oil on canvas, 97.5 × 79 cm. Jalisco, Museo Regional de Guadalajara (Instituto Nacional de Antropología e Historia).

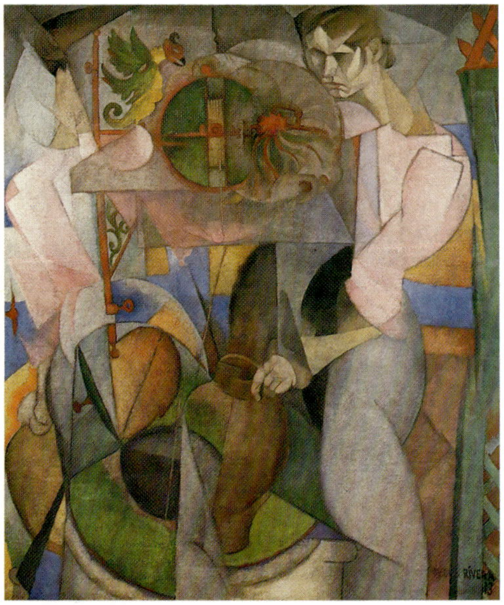

Figure 42
Woman at the Well, 1913, oil on canvas, 144 × 123 cm. (recto of figure 53). Mexico City, Museo Nacional de Arte (INBA). In 1977 this work was discovered under a layer of purple paint on the back of *Zapatista Landscape.*

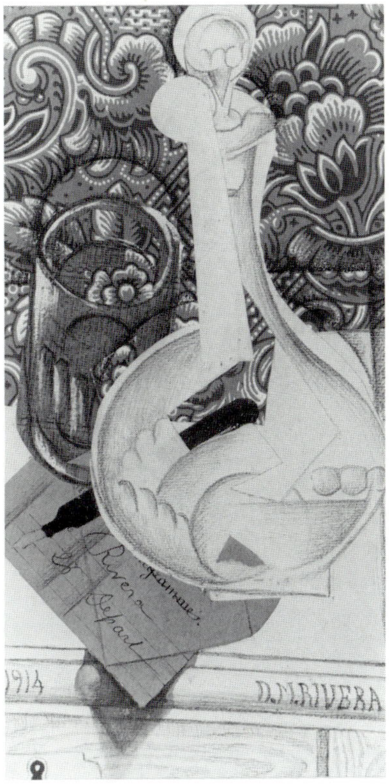

Figure 43
Still Life with Carafe,
1914, collage and gouache, 35.5 × 19 cm. Property of the State of Veracruz. The only known *papier collé* by Rivera, this work is related to the oil painting *Still Life with Stringed Instrument*, 1913, in which the artist used the same flowered pattern, which he derived from a curtain in the Paris studio he shared with Angeline Beloff.

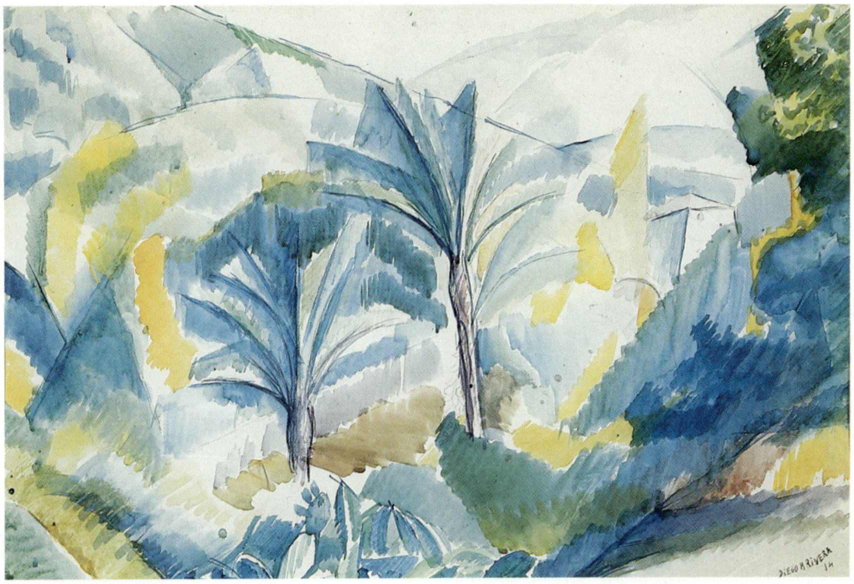

Figure 44
Landscape (Majorca), 1914, watercolor and pencil, 50.8 × 32.5 cm. Guanajuanto, Museo Diego Rivera (INBA).

Figure 45
Sailor's Head (second version), 1914, pencil, 42.8 × 26 cm. Guanajuato, Museo Diego Rivera (INBA). This is a study for the painting *Sailor at Lunch,* 1914.

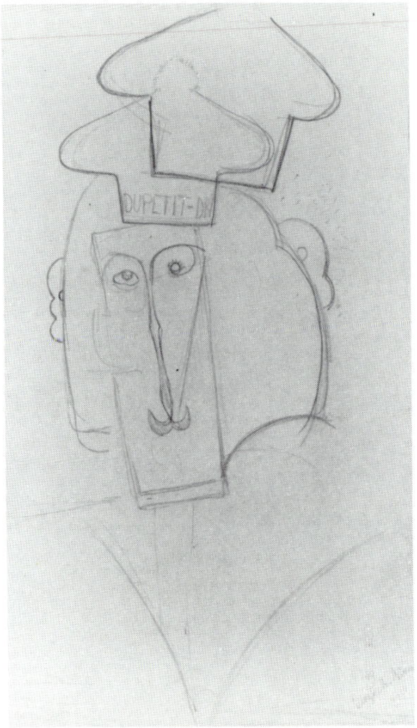

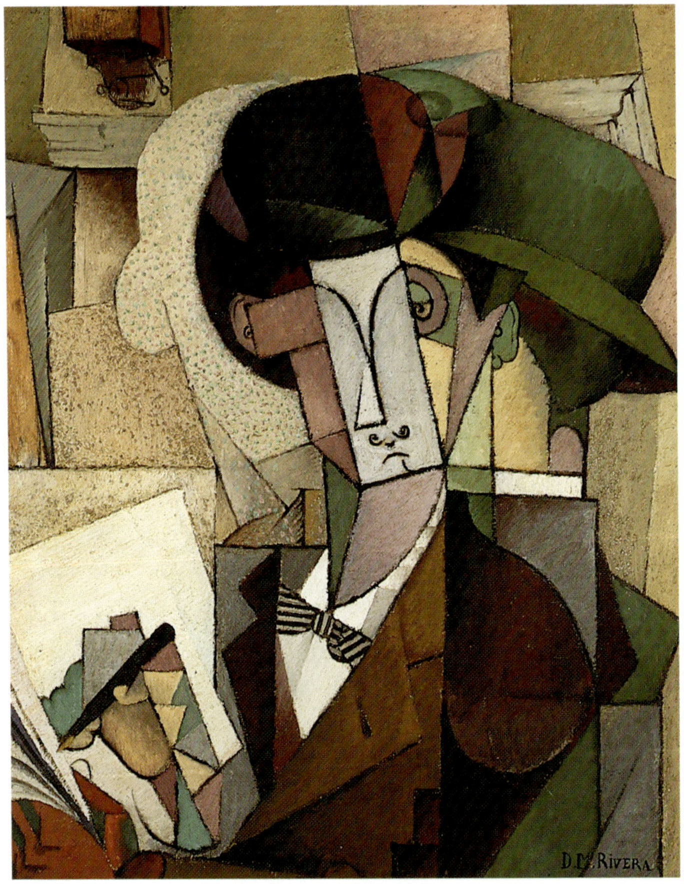

Figure 47
Young Man with Stylograph—Portrait of Best Maugard, 1914, oil on canvas, 79.5 × 63.5 cm. Collection of Dolores Olmedo. A comparison of this work with the portrait of Best Maugard painted the previous year demonstrates Rivera's rapid assimilation of Cubist style, in particular the Synthetic Cubism of Juan Gris with its heavy impasto and rough texture, created by the addition of sand to the paint.

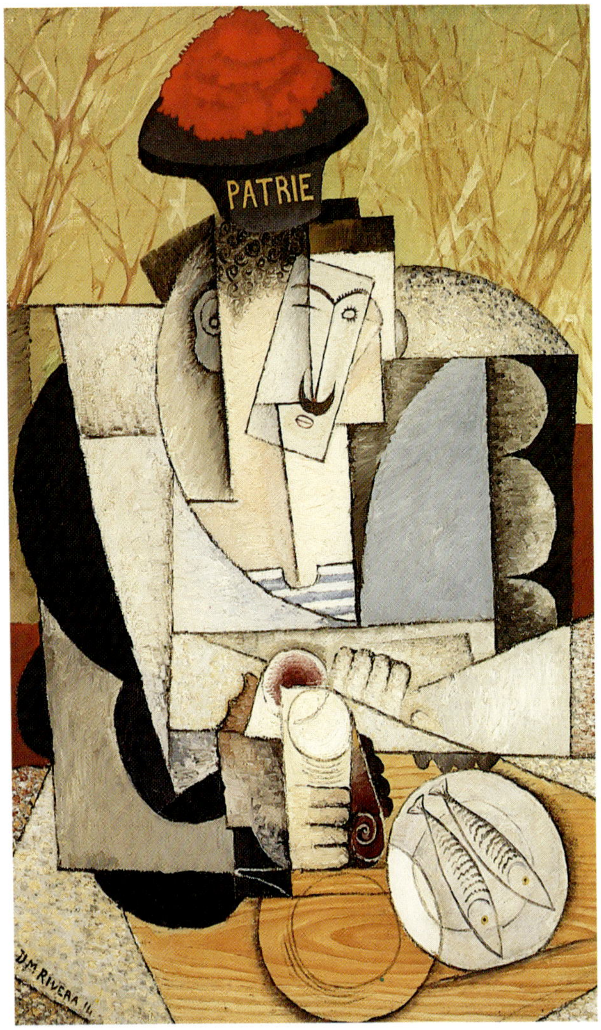

Figure 46
Sailor at Lunch, 1914, oil on canvas, 114 × 70 cm. Guanajuato, Museo Diego Rivera (INBA).

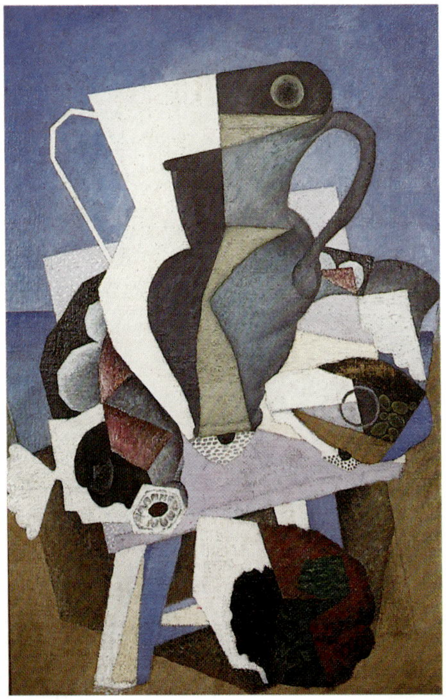

Figure 48
Still Life (Majorca), 1915, oil on canvas, 96.5 × 63.2 cm. Columbus, Ohio, Columbus Museum of Art, Gift of Ferdinand Howald (31.90). Painted in Paris after studies made in Majorca, this work marks the beginning of Rivera's experimentation with pointillist stippling, rich color, and clearly articulated planes.

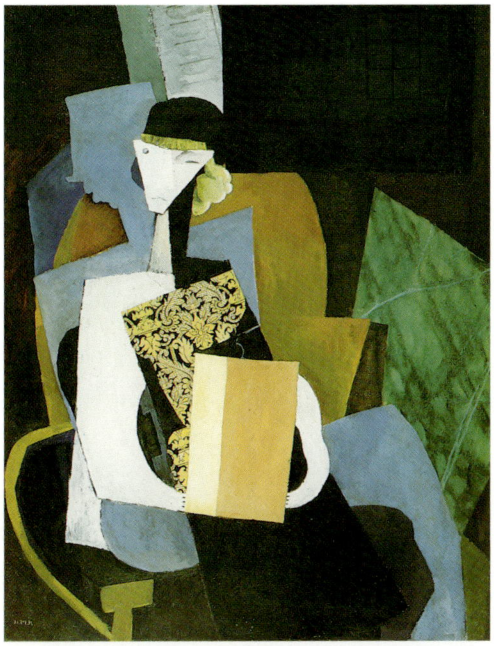

Figure 49
Marevna, also known as *Portrait of Madame Marcoussis,* ca. 1915, oil on canvas, 146.1 × 115.6 cm. The Art Institute of Chicago, Gift of Georgia O'Keeffe (49.579). This portrait, often identified as the wife of the Polish artist Louis Marcoussis, is actually of Marevna Vorobëv-Stebelska, who became Rivera's mistress in 1916.

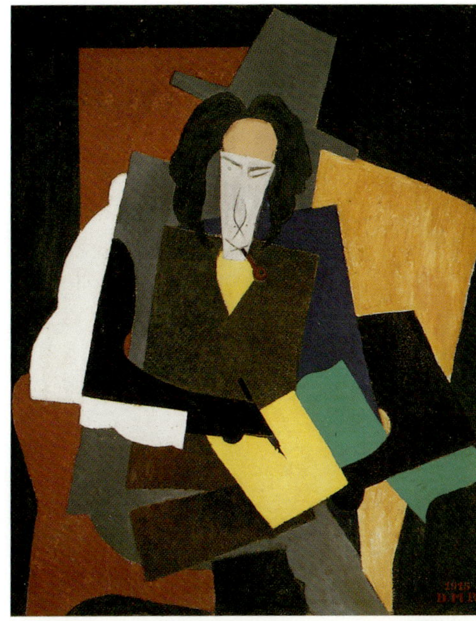

Figure 50
Portrait of Ilya Ehrenberg, 1915, oil on canvas, 110.5 × 89.5 cm. Dallas, Southern Methodist University, The Meadows Museum and Gallery. The Russian writer and poet Ilya Ehrenberg was an intimate friend of Rivera during his years in Paris. This portrait is one of several Rivera painted in which the images are austere and the composition simplified in accord with the artist's growing interest in metaphysical concepts of form.

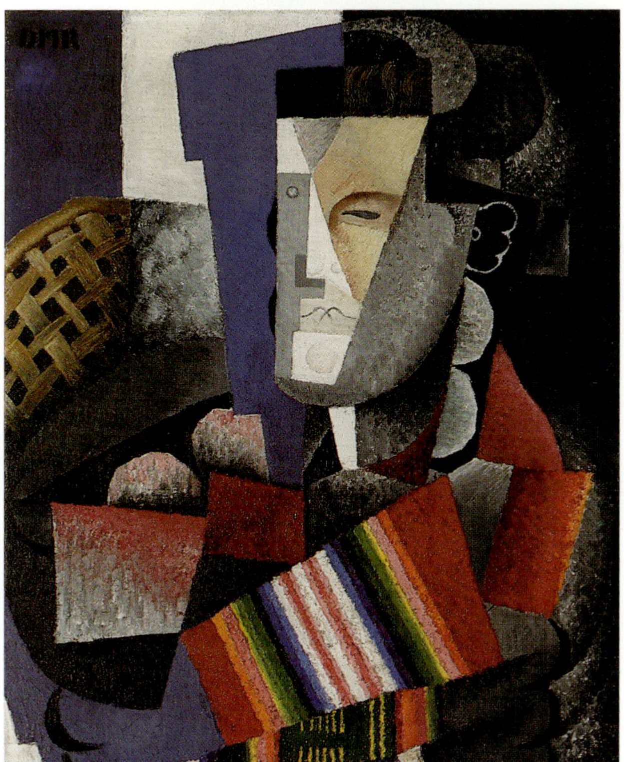

Figure 51
Portrait of Martín Luís Guzmán, 1915, oil on canvas, 72.3 × 59.3 cm. Mexico City, Fundación Cultural Televisa. Among the many Mexican expatriates with whom Rivera associated in both Madrid and Paris was the novelist Martín Luís Guzmán.

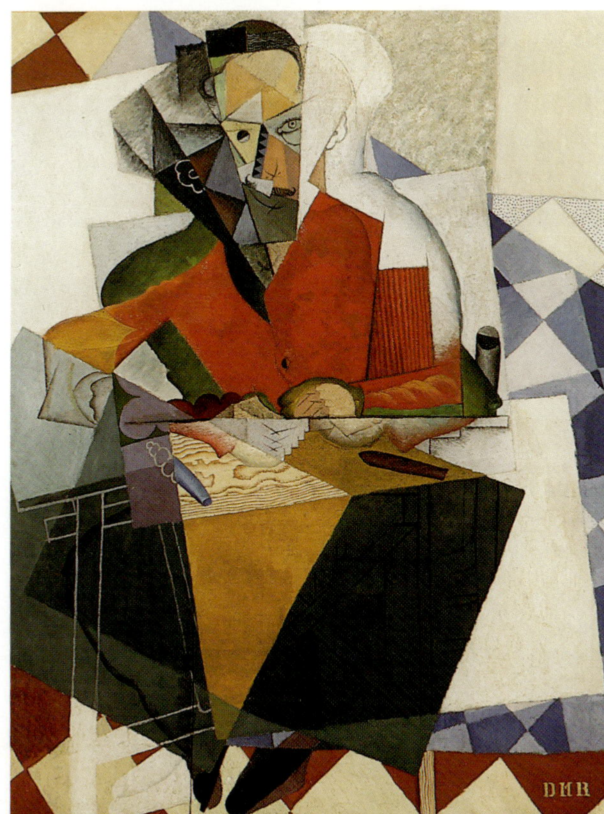

Figure 52
The Architect (Jesús T. Acevedo), 1915, oil on canvas, 144 × 113.5 cm. Mexico City, Museo de Arte Alvar y Carmen T. Carrillo Gil (INBA). Combining abstract and figurative elements, this portrait of Rivera's friend, the Mexican architect Jesús T. Acevedo, was one of the last works Rivera painted in Spain before his return to Paris.

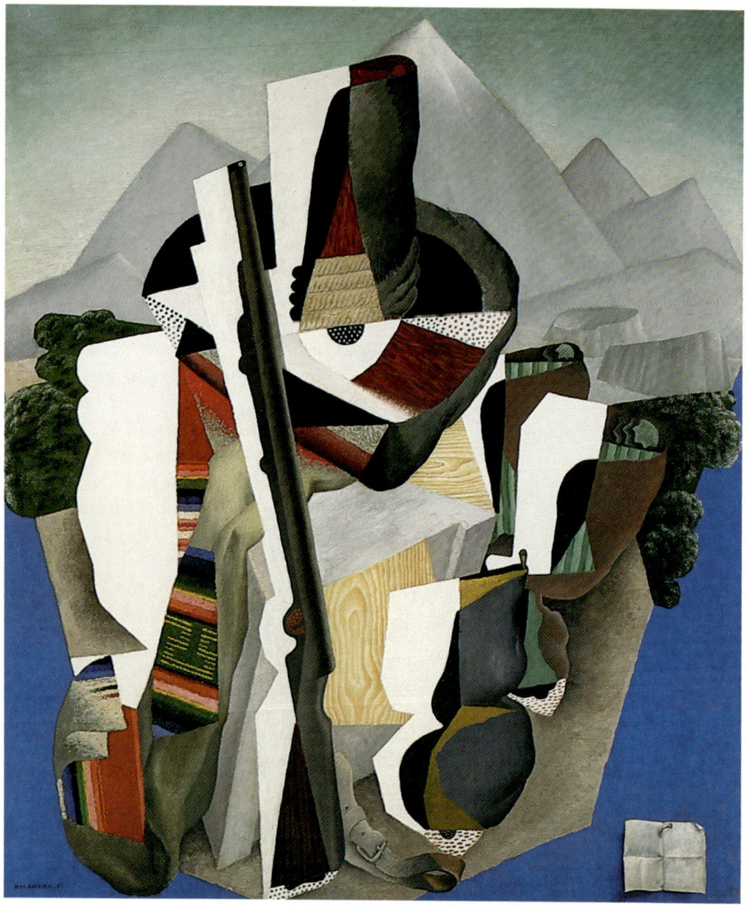

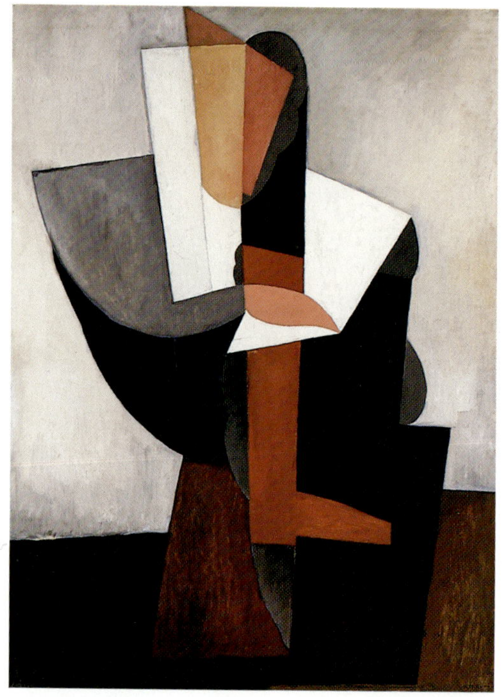

Figure 54
Portrait of a Poet, 1916, oil on canvas, 130 × 97 cm. Mexico City, Museo de Arte Alvar y Carmen T. Carrillo Gil (INBA). The subject of this portrait is Rivera's friend, the Russian theosophist writer Maximilian Voloshin.

Figure 53
Zapatista Landscape—The Guerrilla, 1915, oil on canvas, 144 × 123 cm. (verso of figure 42). Mexico City, Museo Nacional de Arte (INBA). Painted in Paris in the summer of 1915, while the bloodiest battles of the Revolution raged throughout Mexico, this iconic image of Emiliano Zapata suspended in front of a landscape of the Valley of Mexico masterfully expresses, in a Cubist idiom, Rivera's intense feeling for his homeland.

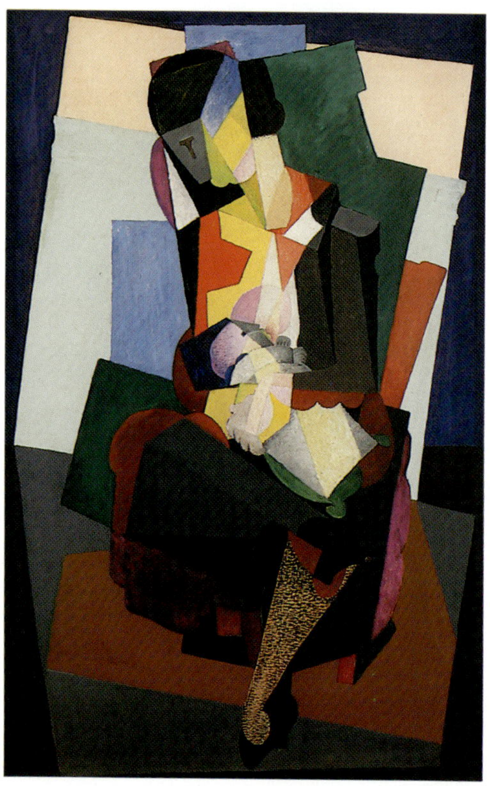

Figure 55
Angeline and Baby Diego—Maternity, 1916, oil on canvas, 132 × 86 cm. Mexico City, Museo de Arte Alvar y Carmen T. Carrillo Gil (INBA).

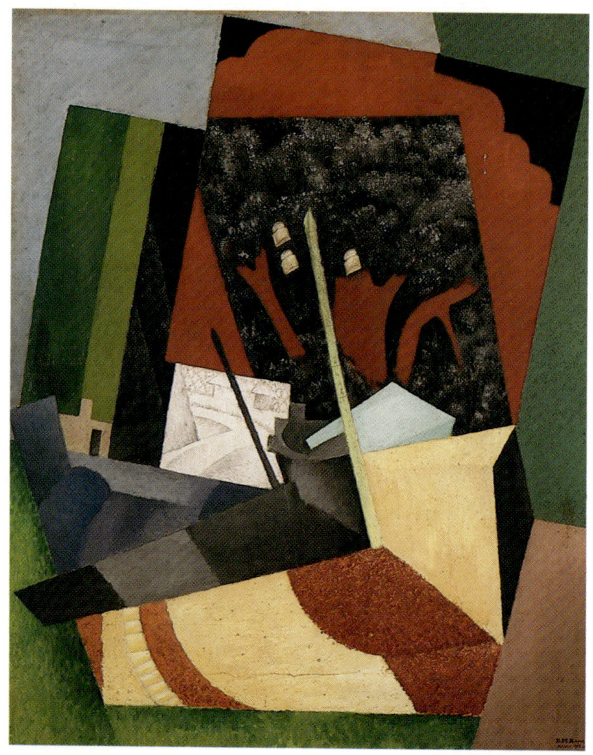

Figure 56
The Telegraph Pole, 1916, oil on canvas with applied sand and other objects, 98 × 79.5 cm. Collection of Dolores Olmedo.

previously completed *Zapatista Landscape* may have contributed to the rupture in relations between the two artists in 1916.[3]

1916

February–March and April–June: included in two group shows of Post–Impressionists and Cubists at Marius de Zayas's Modern Gallery in New York.

August 11: Beloff gives birth to Rivera's son Diego.

October: "Exhibition of Paintings by Diego M. Rivera and Mexican Pre-Conquest Art" at the Modern Gallery.

Díaz dies in exile in Paris.

Mexico lies in ruins: agricultural production has virtually ceased, the transportation and communication networks have broken down, and bandits control much of the countryside. In November the first session of the Constitutional Convention opens in Querétaro.

Son Diego sent to a house of assistance in a suburb of Paris.

Fall: signs a two-year contract with dealer Léonce Rosenberg.

Emerges as a major figure in the "crystal" or "classical" Cubists, a group that includes Gino Severini, André Lhote, Juan Gris, Jean Metzinger, and Jacques Lipchitz, whose works are characterized by an austere classical manner and who advocate a highly metaphysical-scientific approach to artistic production. To this end Rivera studies the scientific writings of Jules-Henri Poincaré and has regular theoretical and metaphysical discussions with a circle of Russian émigrés and with other artists at Henri Matisse's weekly meetings throughout the war years.

Establishes friendships with the Russian writers Maximilian Voloshin and Ilya Ehrenburg (see fig. 50). Ehrenburg's novel *Julio Jurenito* (1921) is based upon Rivera's memories of his childhood, which he related to Ehrenburg on various occasions.

Makes greater use of the technique of mixing sand and other aggregates into his pigments to create relief effects.

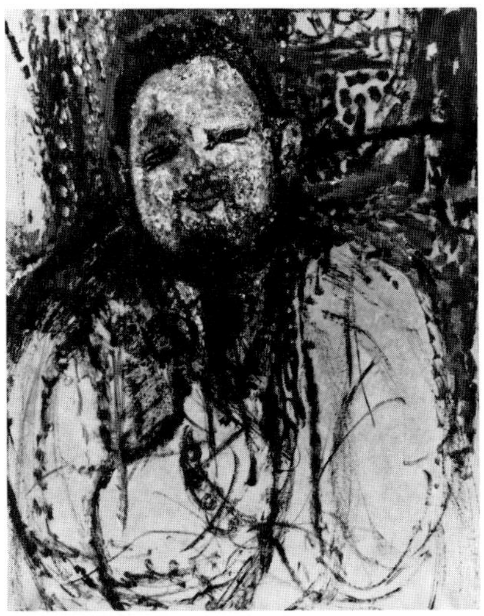

Figure 57
Amedeo Modigliani, *Portrait of Diego Rivera,* 1916, oil on canvas, 100 × 79 cm. Museu de Arte de São Paulo.

1917

Invents an instrument he calls "*la chose*" (the thing)—of which no illustration or drawing exists—possibly to assist him in plotting planar refractions on his canvases.

March: Pierre Reverdy, in Apollinaire's wartime absence the most prominent critic in Paris, denounces Rivera and Lhote by implication in his essay "Sur le Cubisme" in the first issue of his journal *Nord-Sur.* At a subsequent dinner given by Léonce Rosenberg—a collaborator of Reverdy—Rivera and Reverdy engage in an argument that leads to actual physical violence. As a result of what would later be termed "*l'affaire Rivera*" by the critic André Salmon, the artist breaks with Rosenberg. He is ostracized by Braque, Gris, Léger, and others, as well as by his former close friends Lipchitz and Severini.

April: exhibits his work in the first annual exhibition of the Society of Independent Artists in New York.

Leaves Beloff and lives for a six-month period with another Russian émigré artist, Marevna Vorobëv-Stebelska.

Begins executing Ingres-like drawings and continues to study Cézanne—whom he calls "*le père Cézanne*"—as well as the work of Renoir and the 17th-century Dutch masters.

The physician and art historian Elie Faure sponsors a group exhibition, "*Les Constructeurs,*" which includes Rivera; this marks the beginning of his lifelong friendship with Faure, who acts as his mentor in the development of his mature style.

May 1: Carranza formally assumes the presidency of Mexico; the civil war continues.

The October Revolution in Russia. Russian émigrés in Paris plan to return and join the revolution. Rivera and Modigliani apply for visas to Russia, which are denied. Rivera becomes increasingly concerned with the possibilities of art in the service of revolutionary ideals.

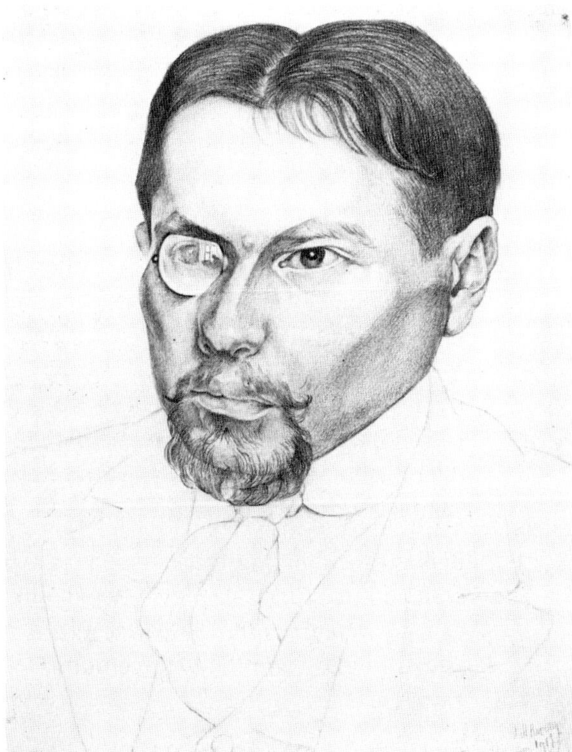

Figure 58
Portrait of Chirokof, 1917, pencil, 30.6 × 23.8 cm. Worcester, Massachusetts, Worcester Art Museum (1928.6). Michael de Chirokof was a Russian painter who established himself in Paris and exhibited in the Salon d'Automne (1910–30). Rivera's self-portrait can be seen in the reflection of the monocle.

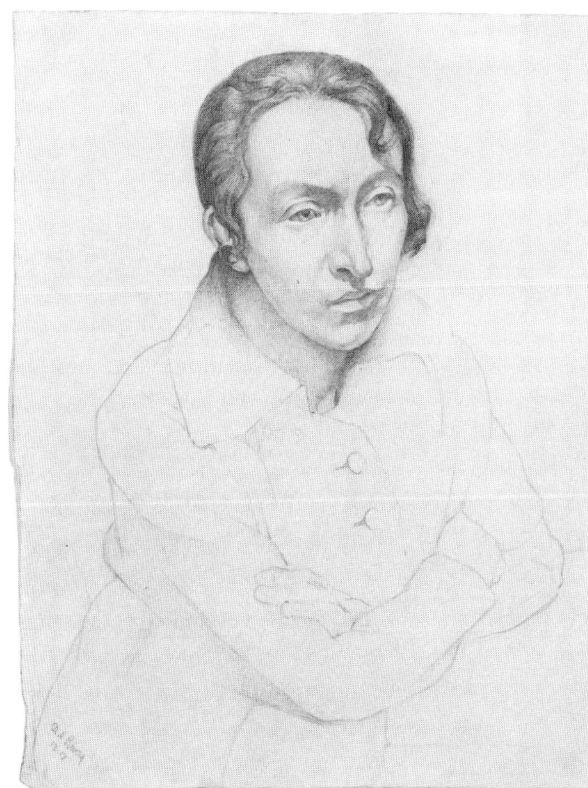

Figure 59
Portrait of Angeline Beloff, December 1917, pencil, 33.7 × 25.7 cm. New York, The Museum of Modern Art, Gift of Mr. and Mrs. Wolfgang Schoenborn in honor of René d'Harnoncourt (36.75). Rendered in the style of Ingres, this sensitive portrait depicts Angeline Beloff, the Russian artist who became Rivera's common-law wife.

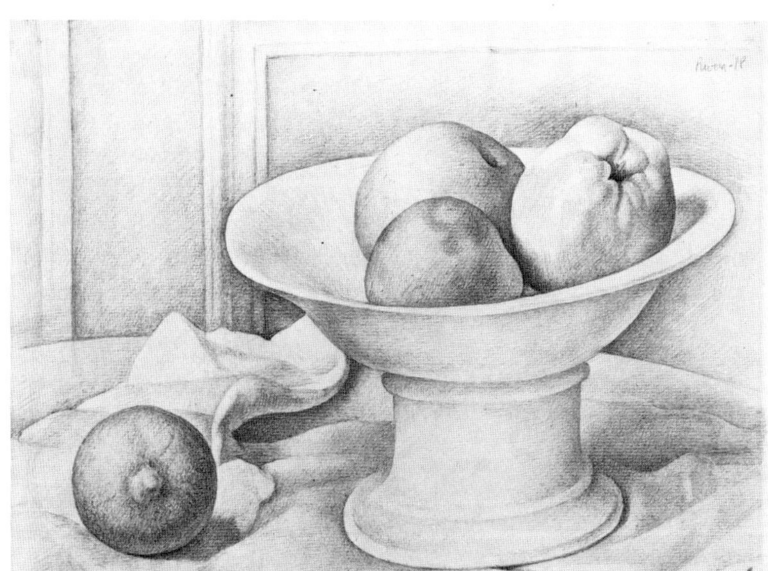

Figure 60
Bowl of Fruit, 1918, pencil, 23.5 × 31.1 cm. Worcester, Massachusetts, Worcester Art Museum (1928.1). Drawn in the style of Cézanne, this work demonstrates Rivera's return to realism after his rejection of Cubism.

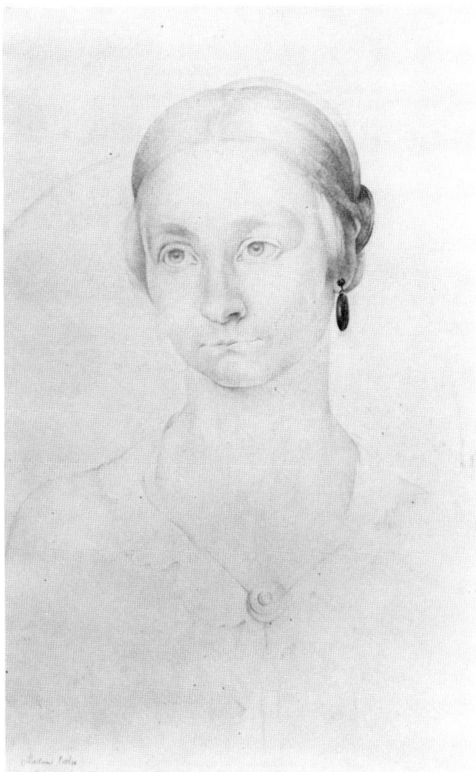

Figure 61
Portrait of Mme. Adam Fischer (Ellen Fischer), 1918, pencil, 47.2 × 30.9 cm. Cambridge, Massachusetts, Harvard University, Fogg Art Museum, Bequest of Meta and Paul J. Sachs (1965.437).

1918
Faure encourages Rivera's "realistic reaction" against Cubism, awakening in him an interest in Italian art, especially the works of Giotto and the Early Renaissance.

May 24: *El universal ilustrado* (Mexico City) publishes photographs of Rivera's Cubist works under the caption "The Outrageous Works of Cubism: Some Paintings in Diego Rivera's 'New Style.' "

Rivera continues his pencil studies and again paints under the influence of Cézanne.

Summer: At the invitation of Jean Cocteau (see fig. 63) and André Lhote, Rivera, Beloff, and the Danish sculptor Adam Fischer and his wife travel to the seaside village of Le Piquey in southwest France.

Fall: Rivera's son becomes ill during a flu epidemic and is brought back to the city; the child dies and is buried at Père Lachaise cemetery. Rivera and Beloff move from Montparnasse to an apartment on the Champs des Mars, rue Desaix, away from the artistic and intellectual circle of Montparnasse.

Alberto J. Pani, the Mexican ambassador to France, urges Rivera to return home to paint for the Carranza government; Rivera declares himself "not ready." He also refuses an opportunity to visit the Soviet Union.

October 28–November 19: participates in a group exhibition at the Galerie Eugène Blot.

1919
Continues to paint in Cézannesque manner; also paints Fauvist landscapes.

David Alfaro Siqueiros (see fig. 77), after a brief stay in Spain, visits Rivera. They discuss the Mexican Revolution and the social role of art.

Carranza consolidates his position as president; Zapata is assassinated on April 10, and in July, Alvaro Obregón announces his candidacy for president.

Summer: Rivera stays with Faure in the Dordogne in southern France.

November 13: birth of Marika, daughter of Marevna and Rivera.

1920
Becomes entranced with the sensuous quality of Renoir.

Continues discussion with Faure on the social necessity of art, especially concerning the possibilities of mural painting. Paints Faure at work, a scene he will later use in his mural program at the Secretaría de Educación Pública (SEP II, 14).

Ambassador Pani commissions portraits of himself (fig. 71) and his wife, purchases *The Mathematician* (fig. 69), and at the suggestion of José Vasconcelos, the rector of the University of Mexico, urges Rivera to go to Italy to study Renaissance art in the hopes of establishing a philosophy of public art that will be adequate for postrevolutionary Mexico.

February: Rivera leaves for Italy. During the next seventeen months, he studies Etruscan, Byzantine, and Renaissance art, especially the works of Giotto, Uccello, Mantegna, Tintoretto, Piero della Francesca, and Michelangelo. Creates over three hundred sketches after various Italian masters, as well as views of Italy and its people.

April: Obregón "pronounces" against Carranza, who flees Mexico City and is assassinated by one of his own followers on May 21.

July: Vasconcelos is named minister of education; he initiates a vast popular education program, including the painting of murals in public buildings.

September: Obregón wins the presidential election by a wide margin.

October–November: Rivera participates in the *"Exposicion d'art français d'avant-garde"* at the Galerie Dalman, Barcelona.

December 15–February 1, 1921: included in an exhibition of the *Société Anonyme* at 19 East Forty-seventh Street, New York (other participants include Matisse, Picasso, Jacques Villon, Georges Braque, André Derain, Albert Gleizes, and Juan Gris).

Figure 62
Portrait of the Engraver Lebedeff, 1918, pencil, 31.1 × 23.8 cm. Collection of Burt B. Holmes. Jean Lebedeff was a Russian engraver, born in 1884, who later lived in Fortenay-aux-Roses, France, and specialized in book illustration. This drawing is a study for a portrait in oil of the same year.

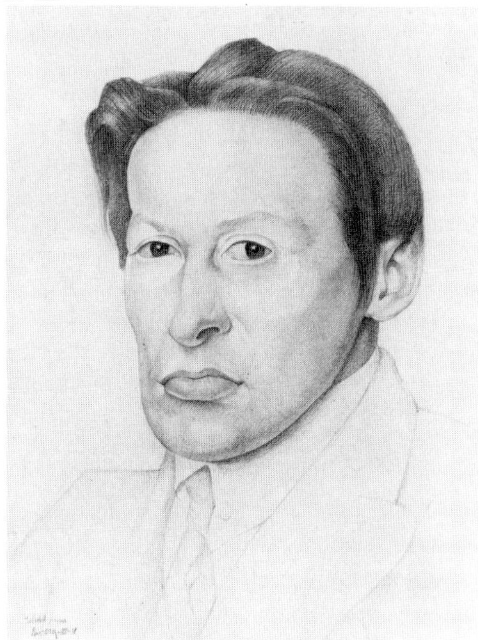

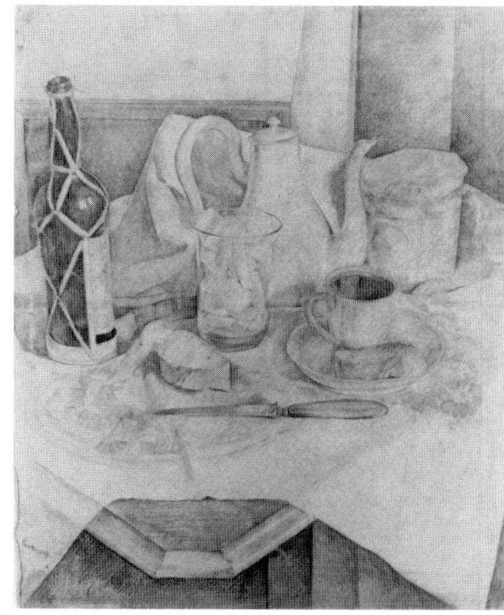

Figure 64
Still Life with Petit Dejeuner and Wine Bottle, 1918, pencil, 48.9 × 40.9 cm. Amherst, Massachusetts, Amherst College, Mead Art Museum, Museum Purchase (1957.37).

Figure 63
Portrait of Jean Cocteau, 1918, pencil, 46 × 30 cm. University of Texas at Austin, Harry Ransom Humanities Research Center, Carlton Lake Collection. The French writer and filmmaker, Jean Cocteau, was one of Rivera's friends during his Paris sojourn. This portrait was made during Rivera's stay with Cocteau at Le Piquey.

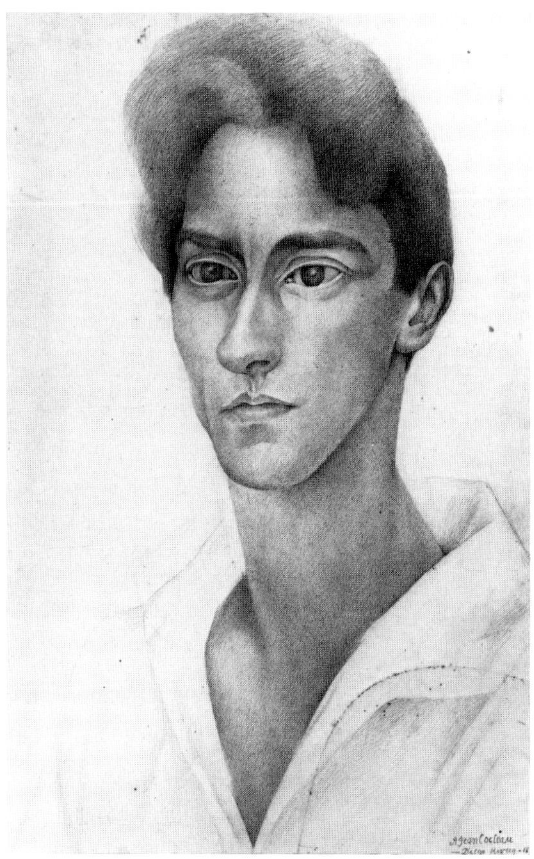

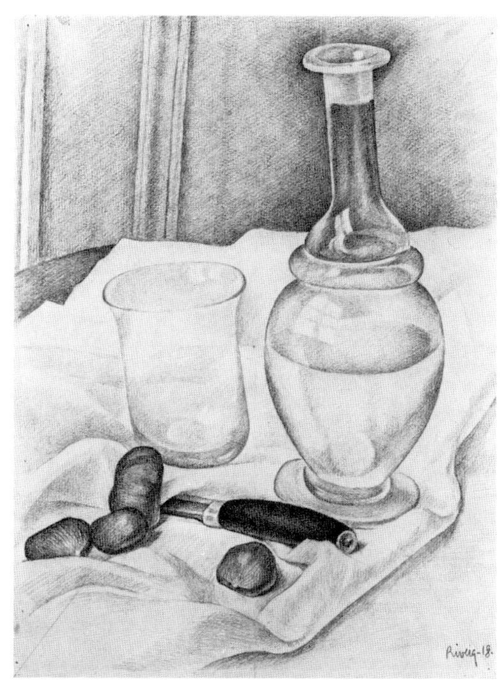

Figure 65
Still Life with Carafe, Knife, and Chestnuts, 1918, pencil, 31.4 × 23.3 cm. The Detroit Institute of Arts, Bequest of Robert H. Tannahill (70.333).

Figure 66
Still Life (unfinished), 1918, oil and pencil on canvas, 45 × 54 cm. Property of the State of Veracruz.

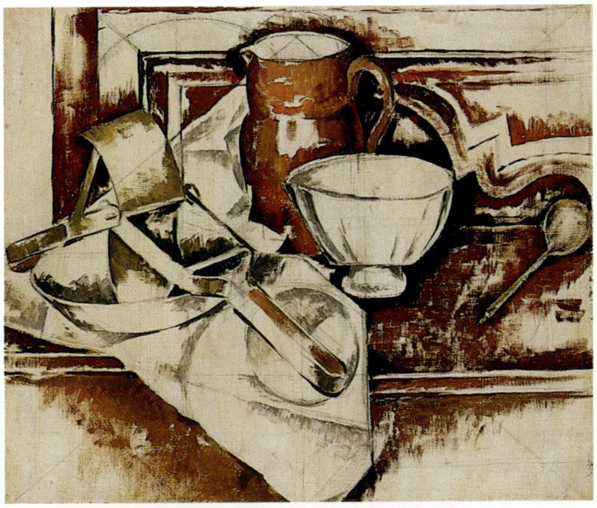

Figure 67
Still Life with Ricer, also known as *Still Life with Garlic Press,* 1918, oil on canvas, 46 × 55 cm. Copenhagen, Statens Museum For Kunst. This painting was once owned by Rivera's friend, the Danish sculptor Adam Fischer, who wrote a lucid and sensitive explanation of Rivera's rejection of Cubism in the Danish art journal *Klingen* in 1919.

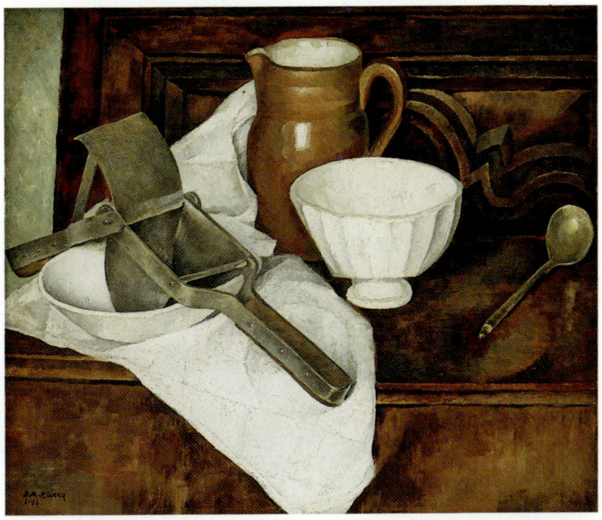

Figure 68
Woman with Geese, 1918, oil on canvas, 62.5 × 81.5 cm. Collection of Dolores Olmedo.

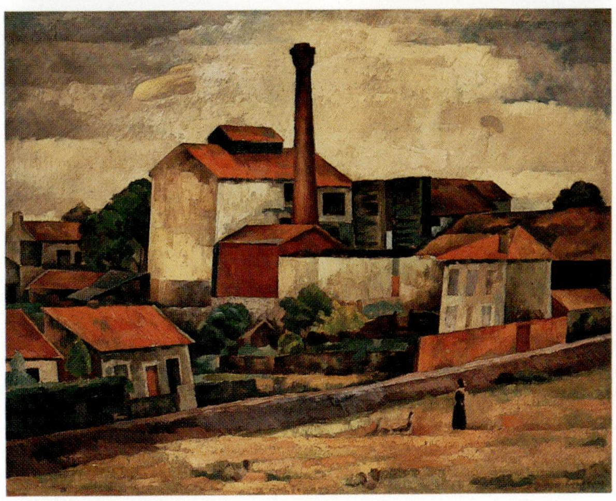

Figure 69
The Mathematician, 1918, oil on canvas, 115.5 × 80.5 cm. Collection of Dolores Olmedo. Carefully composed according to a geometric organization of forms, this work demonstrates Rivera's assimilation of Cézanne's approach to portraiture.

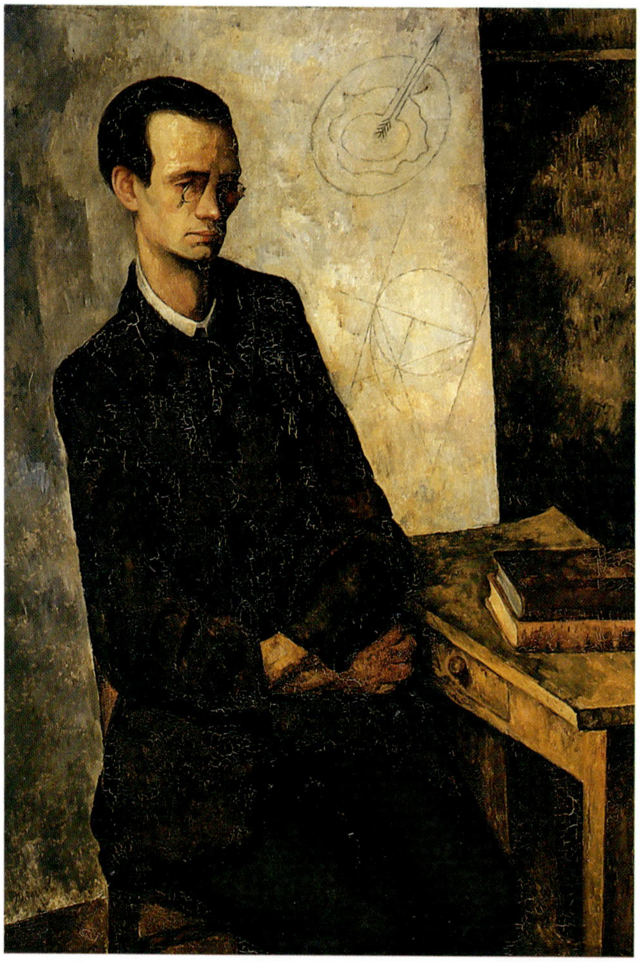

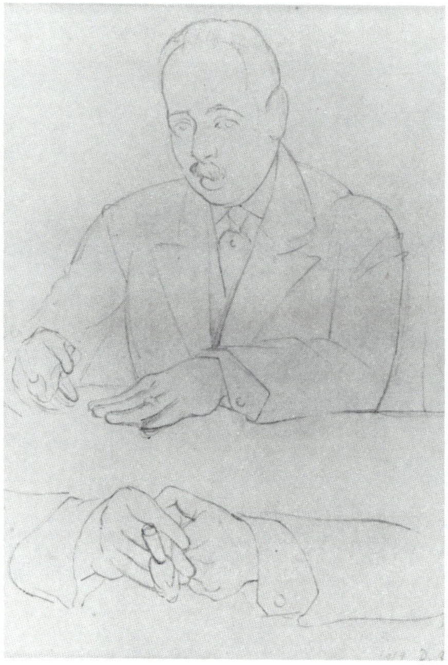

Figure 70
Man with Pipe (Alberto J. Pani), 1919, pencil, 31.4 × 23.5 cm. Guanajuato, Museo Diego Rivera (INBA).

Figure 71
Portrait of Alberto J. Pani, 1920, oil on canvas, 79.5 × 99 cm. Collection of Dolores Olmedo. Alberto Pani, the Mexican ambassador to France, greatly admired Rivera's work and was instrumental in convincing José Vasconcelos, then rector of the University of Mexico, to sponsor Rivera's sojourn in Italy.

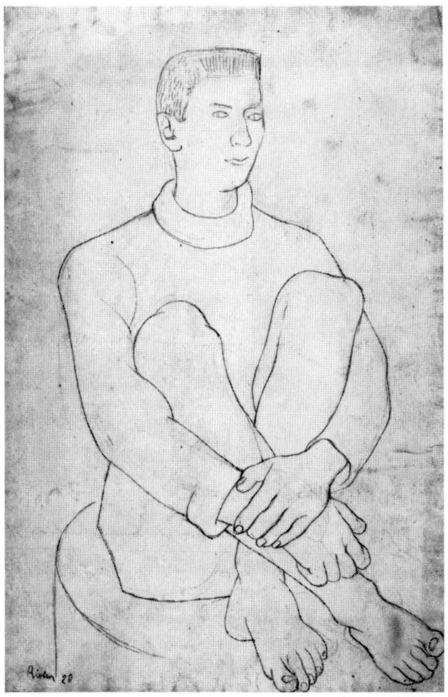

Figure 72
Portrait of Jean Pierre Faure, 1920, pencil, 47.1 × 31.8 cm. The Art Institute of Chicago, Gift of Mr. David Adler (45.21). Jean Pierre Faure was the son of Elie Faure, the French physician, poet, and art historian, who was Rivera's friend and mentor in Paris.

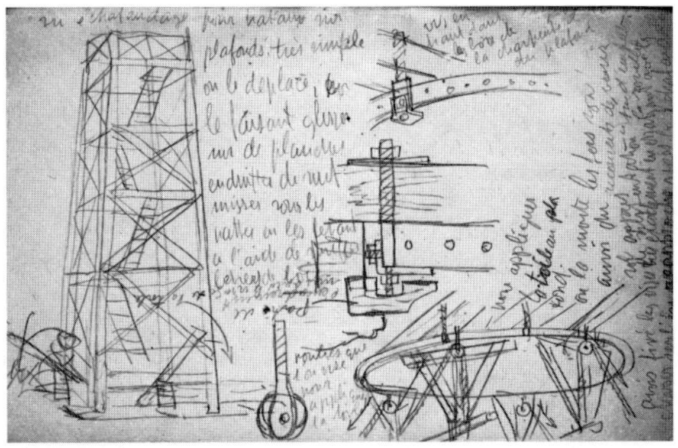

Figure 73
Untitled (from an album of Italian sketches), 1920–21, pencil, 21 × 13.3 cm. Collection of Mrs. Jean Charlot.

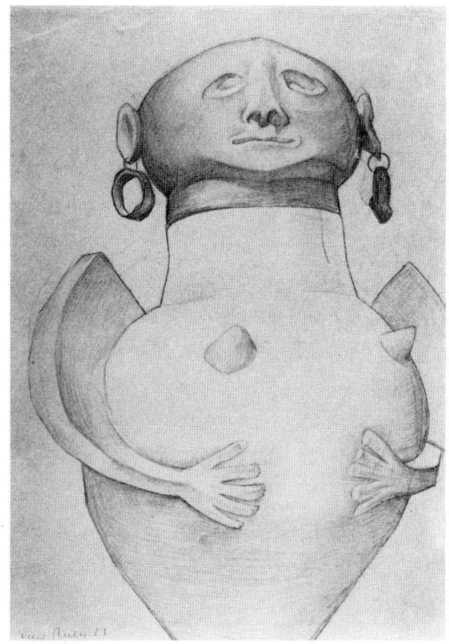

Figure 74
Study of Anthropomorphic Etruscan Vase, 1921, pencil, 32 × 22.2 cm. Philadelphia Museum of Art, Purchase, Lola Downin Peck Fund from the estate of Carl Zigrosser (1976–97–98).

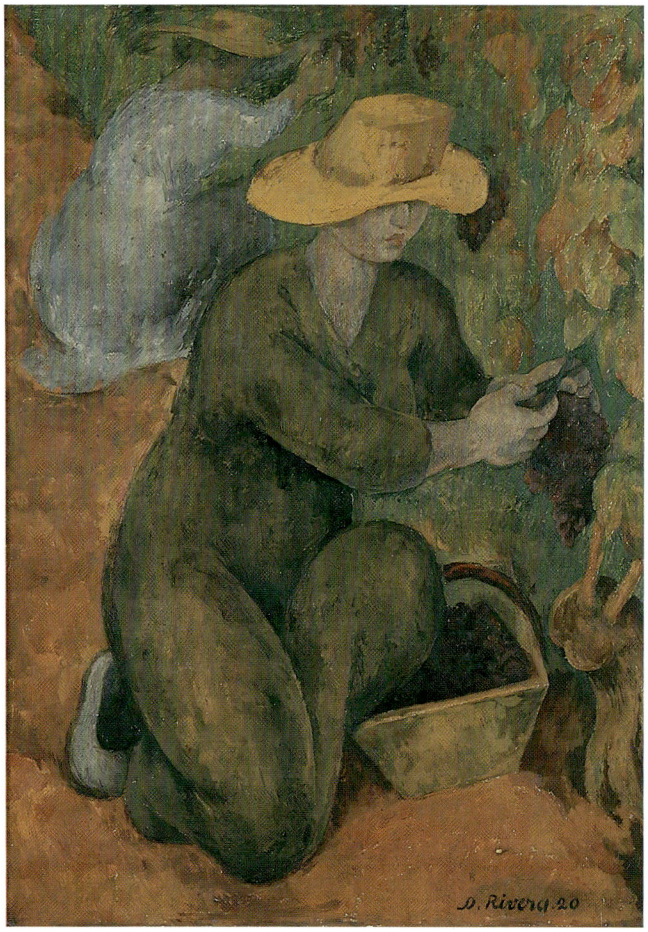

Figure 75
In the Vineyard, also known as *The Grape Picker,* 1920, oil on canvas, 66 × 47.5 cm. Private Collection. In search of a new form of realism, Rivera assimilated the style of Renoir, with its preoccupation with color and its emphasis on sensual full figures and subjects engaged in everyday activity.

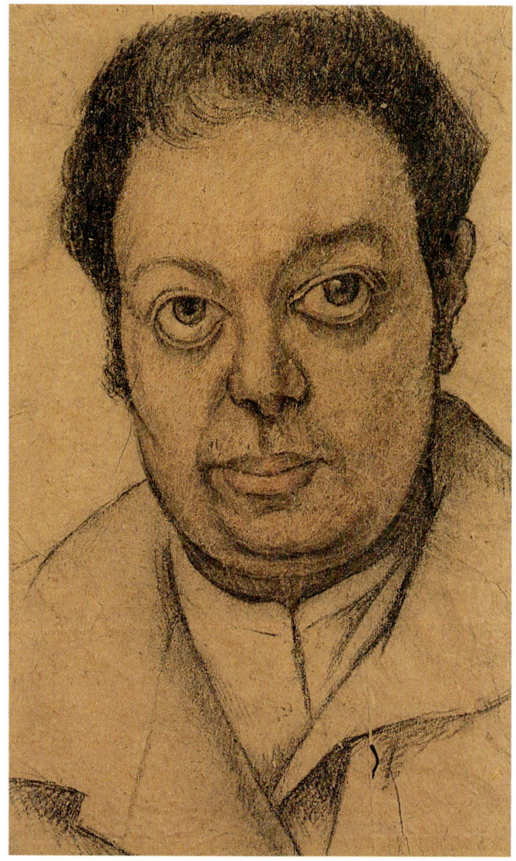

Figure 76
Self-Portrait, 1921, charcoal and red chalk on tan paper, 38 × 24 cm. Collection of Dolores Olmedo. Rivera drew both this self-portrait and his portrait of David Alfaro Siqueiros when Siqueiros visited him in Paris to discuss the role of art in postrevolutionary Mexico. The similarity between the two portraits is intentional, symbolizing the shared ideas of the two artists.

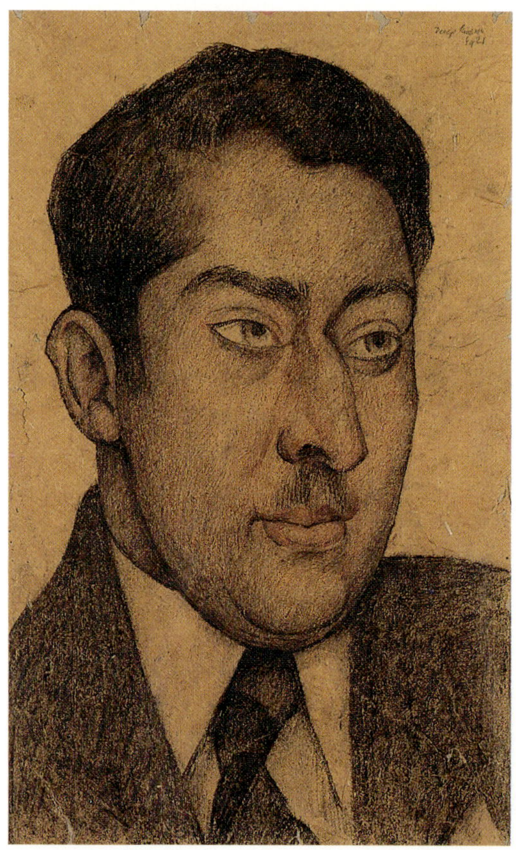

Figure 77
Portrait of David Alfaro Siqueiros, 1921, charcoal and red chalk on tan paper, 38.8 × 24.4 cm. Guanajuato, Museo Diego Rivera (INBA).

III.
The First Mexican Murals

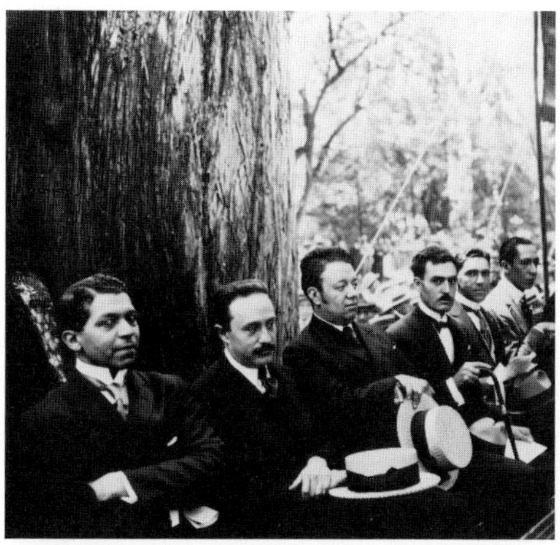

Figure 78
José Vasconcelos and Rivera at a meeting in Chapultepec Park.

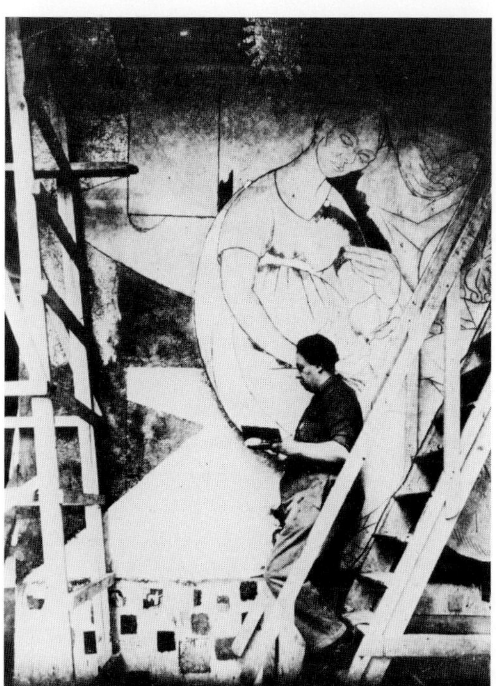

Figure 79
Rivera working on *Creation.*

1921

June: Rivera leaves Paris and Beloff.

July: arrives in Mexico and is "struck by the inexpressible beauty of that rich and severe, wretched and exuberant land."[4] On July 3 he completes a study for a painting of a group of Zapatistas.

Vasconcelos's mural program begins with the decoration of the former Jesuit Church and Convent of Saints Peter and Paul, Mexico City, by Roberto Montenegro, Xavier Guerrero, Gabriel Fernández Ledesma, and Dr. Atl.

Rivera appointed to art-related government positions by Vasconcelos.

Paints Mexican subjects and begins to develop the "classical" figure style that will later appear in his murals.

November: at the invitation of Vasconcelos, travels to Yucatán to view the pre-Conquest sites of Chichén Itzá and Uxmal as part of a group of artists and intellectuals (including Montenegro and Carlos Pellicer) who had recently returned from Europe. Vasconcelos, who accompanies the group, intends to acquaint them with Mexico's heritage.

1922

Early in the year begins the mural *Creation* in the Anfiteatro Bolívar of the Escuela Nacional Preparatoria, for which he draws heavily on his Italian studies. He is assisted by Carlos Mérida, Jean Charlot (who has recently arrived from Paris), Amado de la Cueva, and Guerrero.

June: marries Guadalupe Marín of Guadalajara and moves to a charming old house on the Calle Mixcalco close to the Zócalo (central square of Mexico City).

June 24: Charlot, Ramón Alva de la Canal, Fermín Reveultas, and Emilio García Cahero experiment with fresco on the walls of the open courtyard of the Preparatoria. This is the first use of the fresco technique by 20th-century Mexican muralists.

September 22: Siqueiros returns from Europe.

Tina Modotti's first visit to Mexico; she meets Rivera, Guerrero, and other artists.

Fall: Siqueiros, Rivera, Mérida, de la Cueva, Ramón Alva Guadarrama, Guerrero, Fernando Leal, Revueltas, and Hernán Queto, with the support of José Clemente Orozco, form the Union of Technical Workers, Painters, and Sculptors. Their manifesto proclaims, in part, "We repudiate the so-called easel painting and all the art of ultra-intellectual circles, because it is aristocratic and we glorify the expression of Monumental Art because it is a public possession."[5] Broadsheets printed and distributed by the union develop into a newspaper, *El Machete,* which eventually becomes the journal of the Mexican Communist Party.

December: Vasconcelos funds Rivera's trip to Tehuantepec, whose people and physical beauty greatly impress the artist. On his return he depicts Mexican tropical flora and fauna in the incomplete niche of the Anfiteatro Bolívar. He will continue to draw heavily on his sketches from this trip in his mural work.

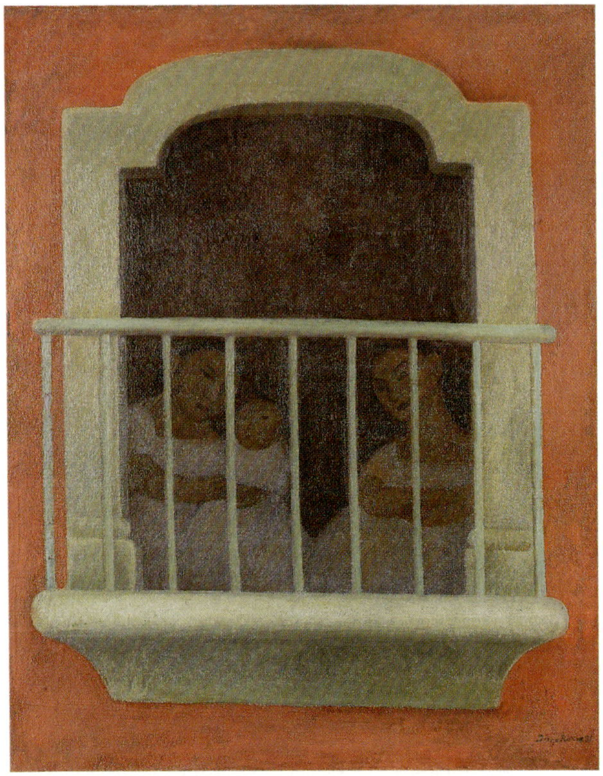

Figure 80
The Balcony, 1921, oil on canvas, 81 × 65.5 cm. Collection of Samuel Goldwyn, Jr. This is one of the first works painted by Rivera upon his return to Mexico after eleven years abroad. Evident here is the joining of an intense interest in Mexican subjects with a classical style derived from Rivera's study of Italian Renaissance murals. The work also demonstrates parallels with the work of his contemporaries in Paris. The balcony motif, so popular with the Cubists and the Fauves, is seen here from the outside in, reminiscent of the work of Goya and Manet.

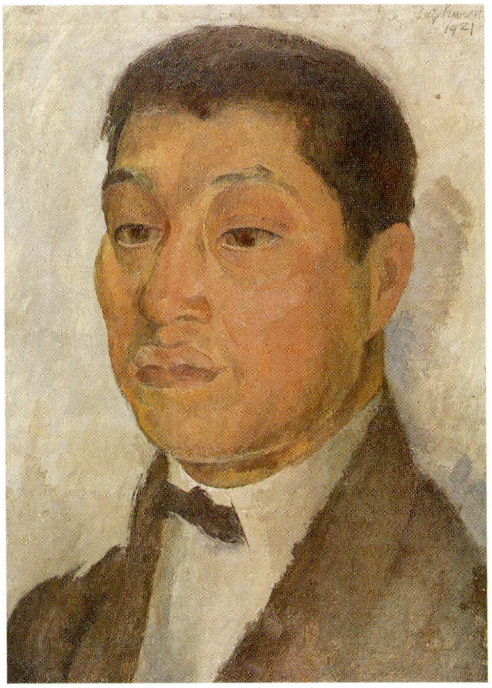

Figure 81
Portrait of Xavier Guerrero, 1921, oil on canvas, 41.7 × 29.9 cm. Collection of Madeleine Blanche Vallier. The painter Xavier Guerrero, a full-blooded Indian originally trained as a house and sign painter, assisted Rivera in his mural work at the Escuela Nacional Preparatoria, the Secretaría de Educación Pública, and at Chapingo. A member of the executive committee of the Mexican Communist Party in the 1920s, he was, along with Siqueiros and Rivera, a founding member of the newspaper *El Machete.*

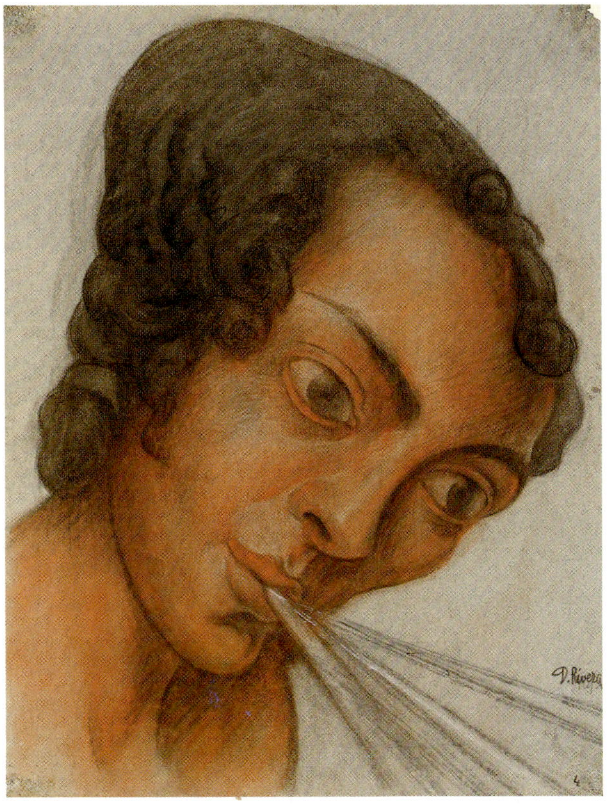

Figure 82
Head, 1921–22, red and black chalk heightened with white on blue-gray paper, 61.6 × 47.5 cm. San Francisco Museum of Modern Art, Albert M. Bender Collection, Gift of Albert M. Bender through the San Francisco Art Institute (64.29). Study for the figure of *Music,* Anfiteatro Bolívar, Escuela Nacional Preparatoria.

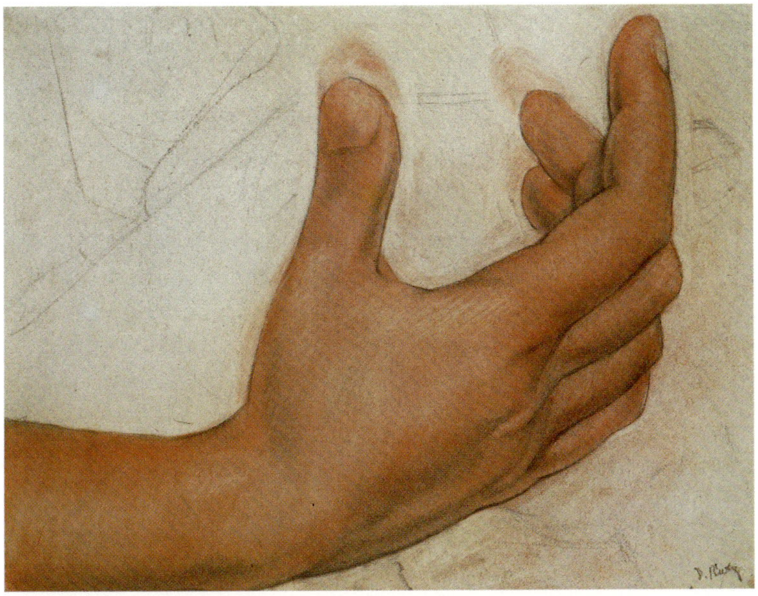

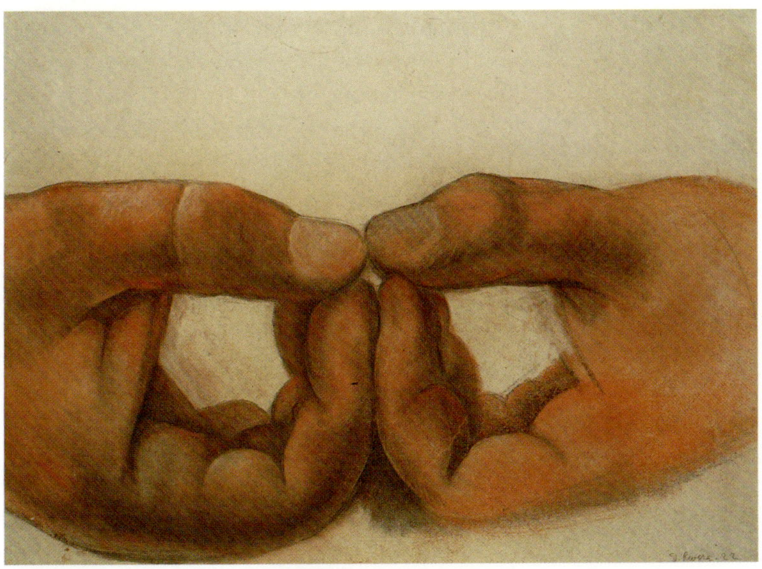

Figure 83
Hand, 1921–22, red and black chalk on light gray paper, 47.3 × 61.3 cm. San Francisco Museum of Modern Art, Albert M. Bender Collection, Gift of Albert M. Bender through the San Francisco Art Institute (64.26). Study for the figure of *Science,* Anfiteatro Bolívar, Escuela Nacional Preparatoria.

Figure 84
Two Hands (palms up), 1922, red and black chalk, 48.9 × 66.1 cm. San Francisco Museum of Modern Art, Albert M. Bender Collection, Gift of Albert M. Bender through the San Francisco Art Institute (64.25). Study for the figure of *Wisdom,* Anfiteatro Bolívar, Escuela Nacional Preparatoria.

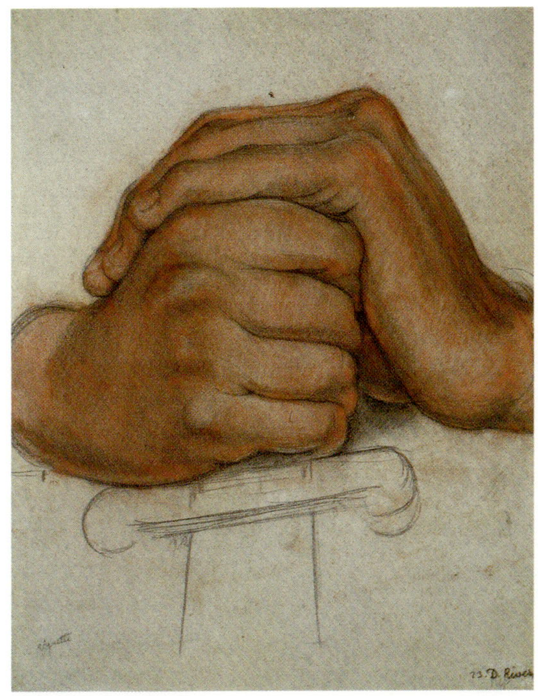

Figure 85
Hands on Sword Hilt, 1923, red and black chalk on light gray paper, 60.4 × 47.3 cm. San Francisco Museum of Modern Art, Albert M. Bender Collection, Gift of Albert M. Bender through the San Francisco Art Institute (64.24). Study for the figure of *Strength,* Anfiteatro Bolívar, Escuela Nacional Preparatoria.

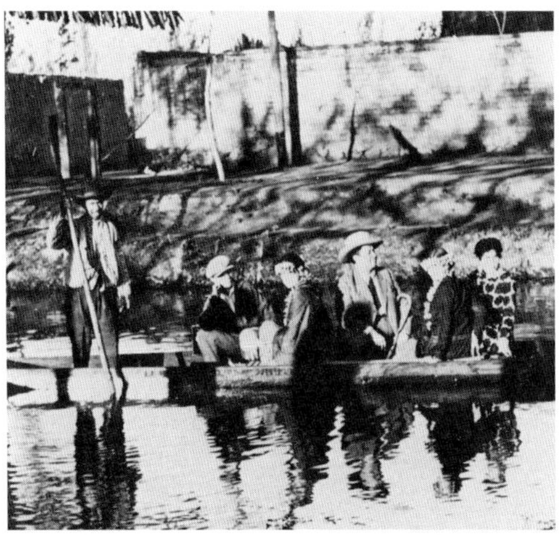

Figure 86
Guadalupe Marín (far right), Tina Modotti, Rivera, María Marín, and Chandler Weston on an outing in Xochimilco, ca. 1924.

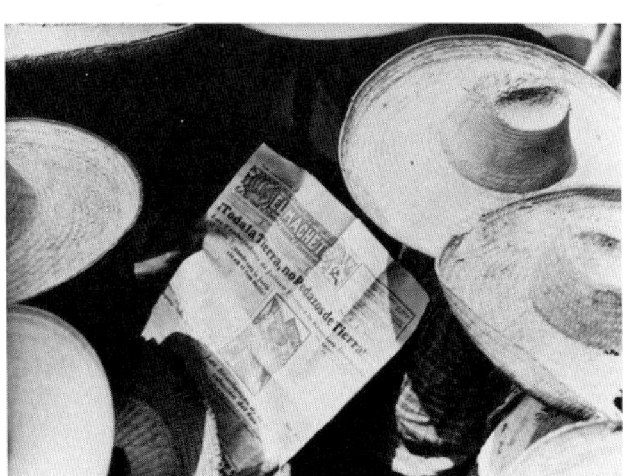

Figure 87
Peasants reading *El Machete,* 1924. Photo by Tina Modotti.

Joins the Mexican Communist Party at the end of the year.

1923

Throughout 1923 Charlot, Revueltas, Orozco, Siqueiros, Alva de la Canal, and García Cahero continue their work at the Preparatoria.

March 9: official inauguration of *Creation;* some reviewers criticize Rivera's use of disparate styles for the various allegorical figures.

March 23: Rivera, Charlot, de la Cueva, and Guerrero, assisted by mason Luís Escobar, begin work on the walls of the east patio of the Secretaría de Educación Pública, which had been dedicated in July 1922. It will take Rivera four years and three months of intensive work, often as much as eighteen hours per day, to complete this enormous program (117 fresco panels covering almost sixteen hundred square meters). Rivera uses nopal cactus juice as a binder in the pigment (to create a polished surface) on several Tehuantepec panels. According to Rivera, this technique reflects the practice of the ancient Mexicans at Teotihuacán. However, technical difficulties cause him to abandon it in favor of traditional European methods tempered by the knowledge of contemporary Mexican masons, which Charlot had employed to advantage in his Preparatoria murals.

The first panels Rivera paints at the Secretaría treat Tehuantepec subjects, as a token of appreciation to Vasconcelos, who is a native of the region.

Throughout the years 1923–27, Rivera, who is earning an average of two U.S. dollars per day for his mural painting, increasingly supports himself through the sale of oils, watercolors, and drawings, often to North American patrons. On occasion he incorporates subjects used in his easel paintings in the Secretaría murals (as in *Bather of Tehuantepec* [fig. 92] and *The Grinder* [fig. 93]).

May 19–August 6: completes six panels in the Court of Labor (SEP I, 7–12), while de la Cueva, Guerrero, and Charlot complete seven panels in the Court of Fiestas, and Mérida and Emilio Amero paint in the public library annex.

June: initial adverse public reaction to Rivera's new style in the Secretaría murals, where he concentrates on the everyday life of the Mexican people, is followed by a series of journalistic attacks, which are diffused by the news of Villa's assassination on July 20 and concern with the upcoming presidential campaign.

July 30: Tina Modotti, Edward Weston, and his son Chandler travel from Los Angeles to Mexico City.

August–September: Rivera assumes control over the entire Secretaría program and forces de la Cueva, Guerrero, and Charlot to stop painting, citing alleged problems of unity, and assigns them menial tasks such as the painting of the heraldic shields of the Mexican states on the second floor. Rivera destroys all their panels, with the exception of Charlot's *Washerwoman* and *Los cargadores* (burden carriers) (SEP I, 35 and 41) and de la Cueva's *The Little Bull* (SEP I, 36) and *Battle Dance* (SEP I, 40).

August 23: Modotti takes Weston to see Rivera's murals at the Secretaría; they later meet Rivera.

October 30: Rivera visits Weston's first exhibition at The Aztec Land, a bookstore and gallery in the center of the city. Weston photographs Rivera, who later incorporates this image in the Secretaría murals.

1924

January 28: Vasconcelos, increasingly dissatisfied with Obregón's policies, offers his resignation.

The press attacks the Preparatoria murals.

June: at the instigation of conservative political groups, students of the school riot in protest against the murals. They present a petition to Vasconcelos demanding that the work be discontinued, and they deface the murals of Orozco and Siqueiros. All

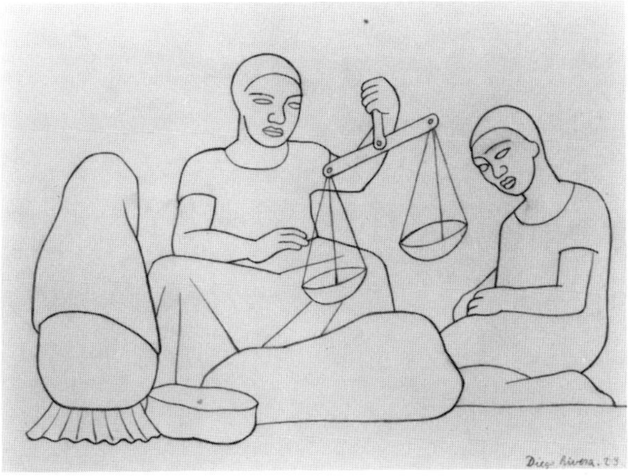

Figure 89
Tobacco Seller, 1923, pencil, 21.2 × 27.2 cm. San Francisco Museum of Modern Art, Albert M. Bender Collection, Gift of Albert M. Bender (35.2695).

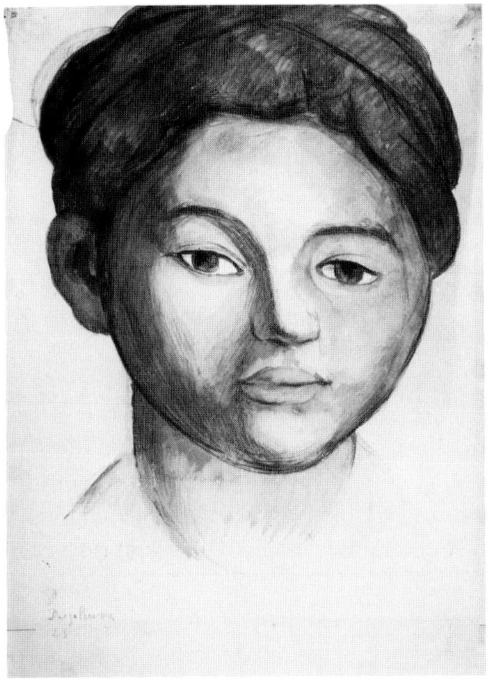

Figure 88
Head of a Tehuantepec Woman, 1923, watercolor over black chalk, 42.8 × 31.7 cm. Philadelphia Museum of Art, Purchase, Lola Downin Peck Fund from the estate of Carl Zigrosser (1976–96–76).

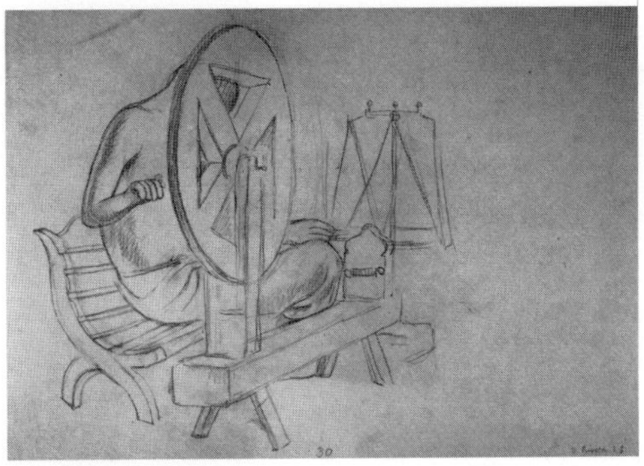

Figure 90
Man at Spinning Wheel, 1923, pencil, 30.2 × 44.5 cm. Philadelphia Museum of Art, Purchase, Lola Downin Peck Fund from the estate of Carl M. Zigrosser (1976–97–81). Study for *Weavers,* Court of Labor (first floor), Secretaría de Educación Pública.

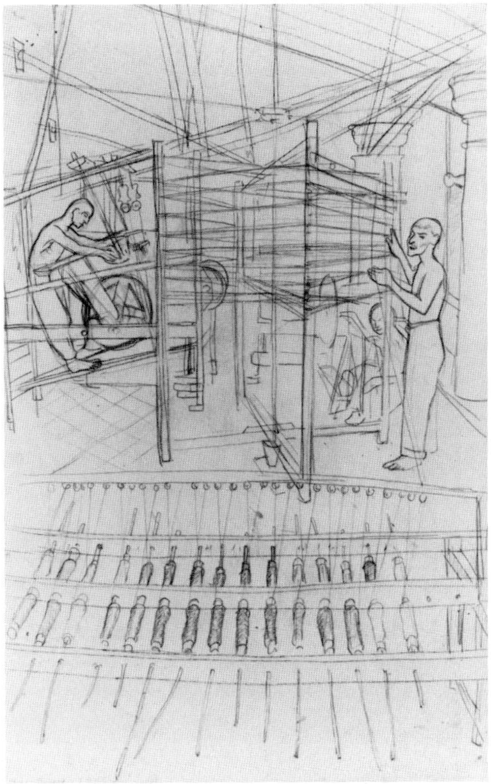

Figure 91
Spinners, 1923, charcoal and pencil, 45.7 × 30.5 cm. Mexico City, Galerías A. Cristóbal. Study for *Weavers,* Court of Labor (first floor), Secretaría de Educación Pública.

Figure 92
Bather of Tehuantepec, 1923, oil on canvas, 63.5 × 53.5 cm. Guanajuato, Museo Diego Rivera, Marte R. Gómez Collection (INBA). Rivera's trips to Yucatán in 1921 and the isthmus of Tehuantepec in 1922 fueled his interest in Indian subjects, providing images for his murals and easel paintings for several years. This painting is related in subject to a panel at the Secretaría de Educación Pública (SEP I, 3b), painted in 1926.

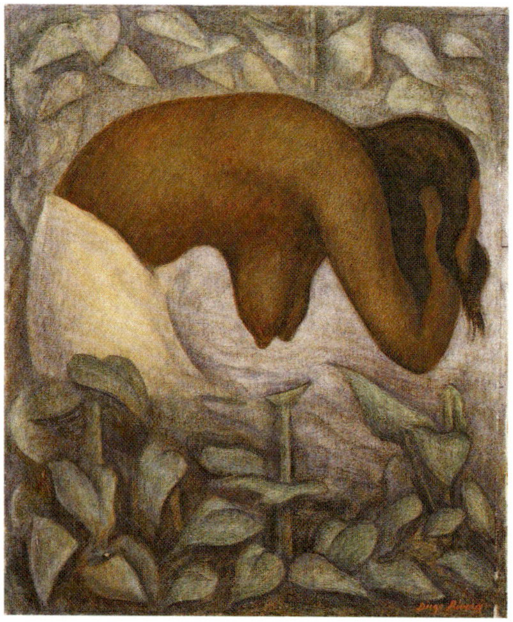

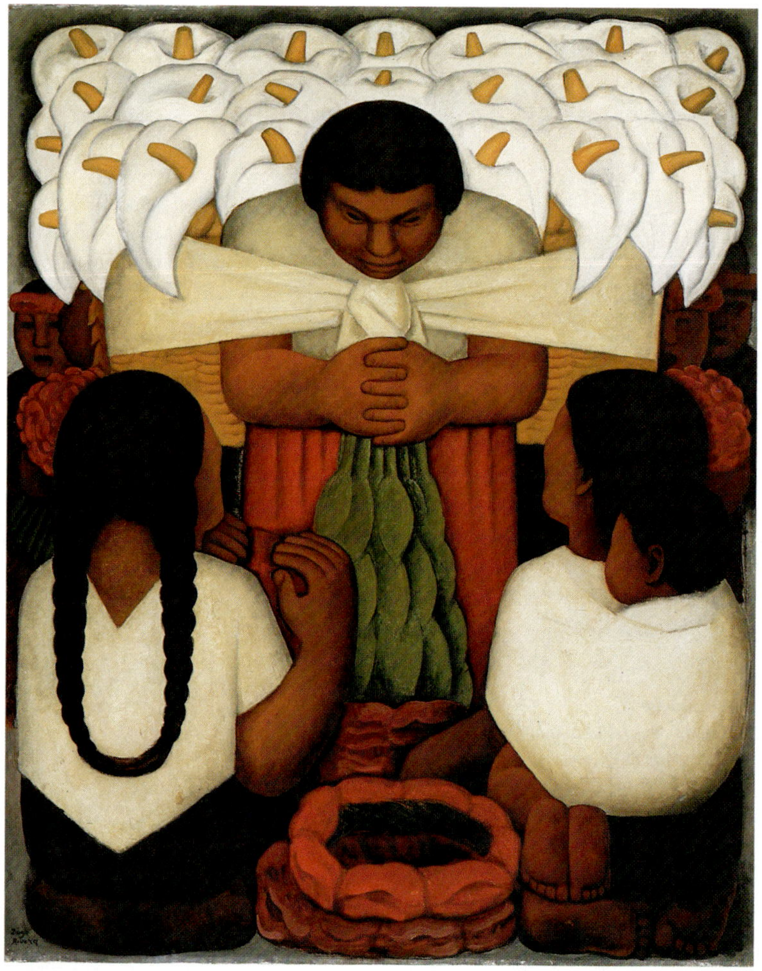

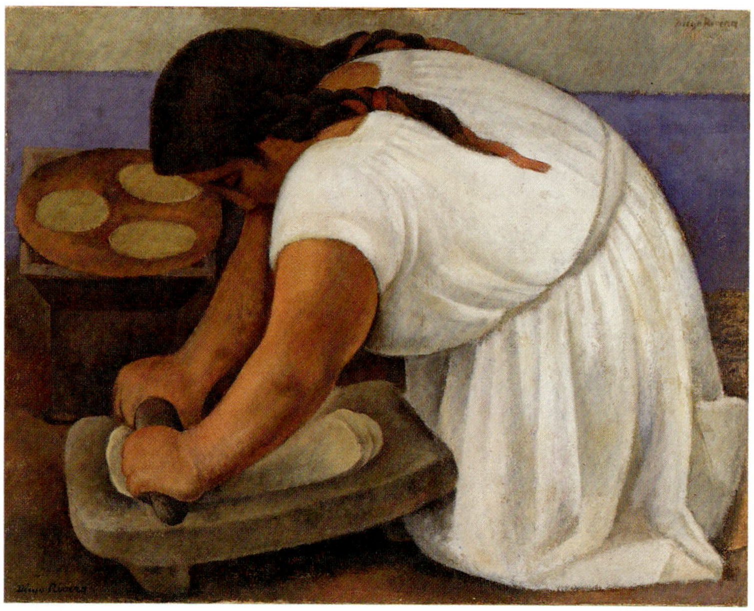

Figure 93
The Grinder, 1924, encaustic on canvas, 90 × 117 cm. Mexico City, Museo de Arte Moderno (INBA). This monumental figure of a woman using a *metate* to make tortillas is one of the best known of Rivera's classical-style paintings of Mexican subjects.

Figure 94
Flower Day, 1925, encaustic on canvas, 147.4 × 120.6 cm. Los Angeles County Museum of Art, L.A. County Funds (25.7.1). This painting is related in subject and style to the panel *Friday of Sorrows on the Canal at Santa Anita,* Court of Fiestas (first floor), Secretaría de Educación Pública.

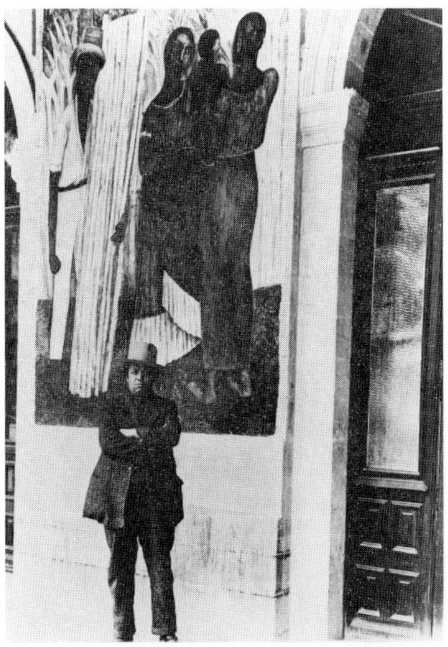

Figure 95
Rivera at the Secretaría de Educación Pública, ca. 1924.

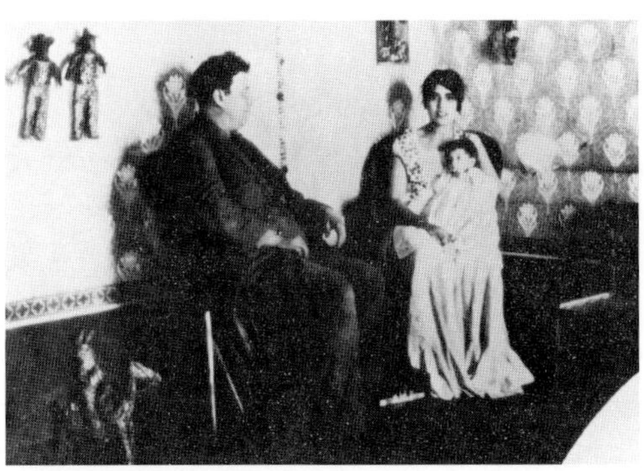

Figure 96
Rivera, Guadalupe, and baby Lupe, ca. 1925.

mural decoration at the school stops. Vasconcelos's resignation is formally accepted on July 3.

July: Rivera, who does not wholly support the counterattack on the students by union artists, resigns from the group.

August: Orozco, Siqueiros, and others are dismissed from their positions as mural painters. Rivera alone successfully weathers the crisis and establishes a congenial relationship with the new minister of education, J. M. Puig Casauranc.

Daughter Lupe born.

While at work on the lower level of the stairway at the Secretaría, Rivera paints the legend "Pearls before Swine" on the prow of a boat as his judgment on the mural controversy (in early 1925, his position vis-à-vis Puig Casauranc assured, he will delete the statement).

November: Modotti photographs the completed stairway paintings.

Rivera begins murals in the administration building at the Escuela Nacional de Agricultura in Chapingo.

December: Plutarco Elías Calles, Obregón's handpicked successor, is inaugurated as president.

Articles on Rivera begin to appear in North American periodicals, and a small but steady stream of artists, intellectuals, and interested lay people from the United States and elsewhere visit Mexico to watch him work on the Secretaría murals.

Paul O'Higgins sees Rivera's work in a magazine and writes to Rivera from California. Rivera invites him to Mexico. O'Higgins (who adopts the name Pablo) becomes one of Rivera's assistants on the Secretaría murals.

1925

January: finishes all the murals in the Court of Fiestas, continues to paint at Chapingo (where he is assisted by Guerrero, Alva Guadarrama, O'Higgins, and Máximo Pacheco), and begins the second- and third-floor murals at the Secretaría.

Siqueiros assists de la Cueva on his murals *The Labor and Agrarian Ideals of the 1910 Revolution* at the Workers Assembly Hall in Guadalajara. With the completion of the mural in March 1926, Siqueiros abandons artistic activity and devotes himself to political activity and union organizing in Jalisco and other western states.

April 26: On the advice of his friend, party colleague, and future biographer Bertram Wolfe, Rivera writes a letter of resignation to Mexican Communist Party officials, stating that he believes himself better able to devote himself to Marxism through his art rather than through militant activities as a party member.

Rivera's painting *Flower Day* (fig. 94) is included in the Pan-American exhibition at the Los Angeles Museum and wins the purchase prize.

June: becomes art editor of Frances Toor's *Mexican Folkways* magazine.

Drawings and mural studies exhibited at the Galerie Beaux-Arts in San Francisco.

Orozco paints the mural *Omniscience* at the Casa de los Azulejos (now Sanborn's Restaurant), Mexico City.

1926

Rivera begins his mural program in the chapel at Chapingo. Tina Modotti and Rivera's pregnant wife are models for the large nudes of the crossing and the end wall (see figs. 100 and 348). Continues to work on Secretaría murals.

Illustrates the first of three albums of drawings devoted to the annual convention of the League of Agrarian Communities and Peasant Syndicates of the State of Tamaulipas Union; some of these drawings are later used to illustrate the book *Mexican Maze*.

Paints *Portrait of Guadalupe* (fig. 110), children's portraits, and other oils, using a colorful palette and graceful forms. Throughout his career, Rivera regularly sketches at the markets, immortalizing the Mexican peasants and flowers.

July: his request for readmission to the Mexican Communist Party is granted.

Separates from Guadalupe Marín.

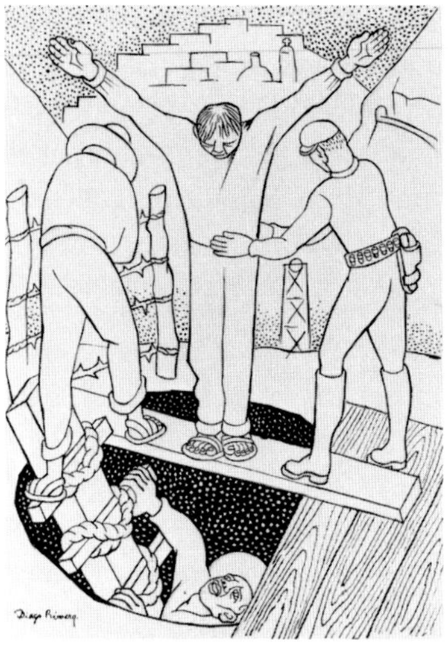

Figure 97
Miner Being Searched, ca. 1925, brush and black ink heightened with white over pencil, 31 × 22.5 cm. Mexico City, Galerías A. Cristóbal. This illustration for the book *Mexiko* (Berlin, 1925) by Alfons Goldschmidt is similar to the panel *Leaving the Mine,* Court of Labor (first floor), Secretaría de Educación Pública.

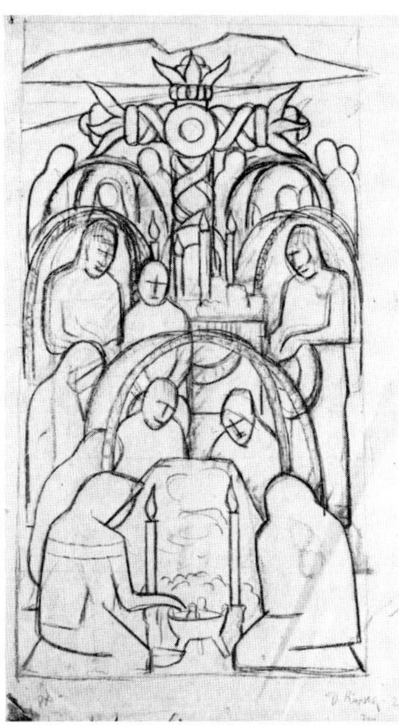

Figure 98
Day of the Dead in the Country, 1925, charcoal, color chalk, and pencil, 46.4 × 30 cm. New York, The Museum of Modern Art, Anonymous Gift (208.40). Study for *The Offering,* Court of Fiestas (first floor), Secretaría de Educación Pública.

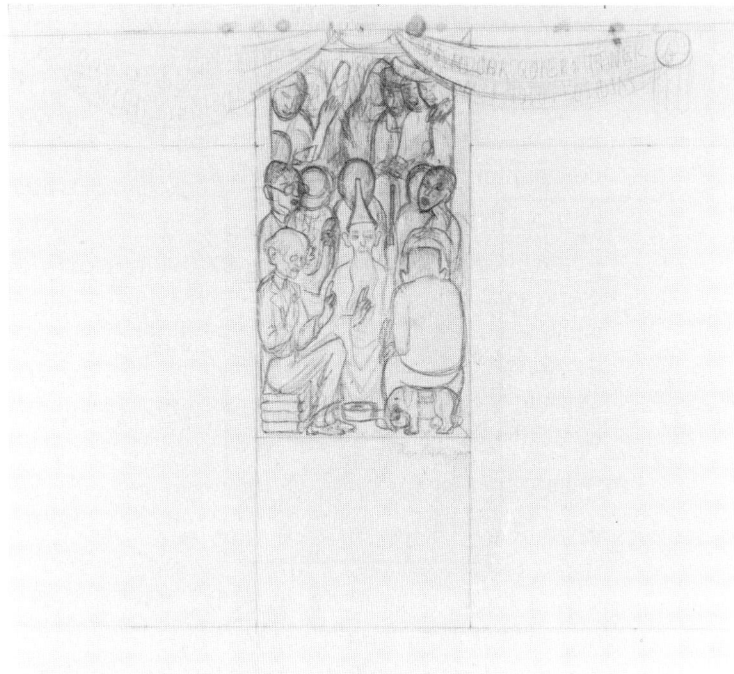

Figure 99
False Learning, 1925, pencil, 48.3 × 53.3 cm. Collection of Rafael Coronel. Study for *The Learned,* Court of Fiestas (third floor), Secretaría de Educación Pública.

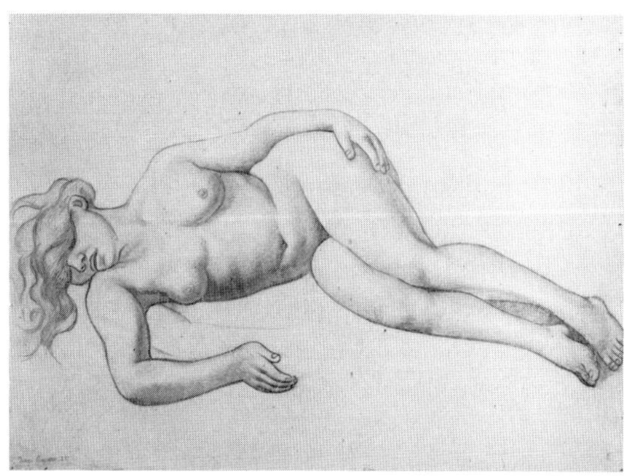

Figure 100
Reclining Nude, 1925, pencil, 45.1 × 63 cm. Philadelphia Museum of Art, Purchase, Lola Downin Peck Fund (1976–97–100). Study for *The Virgin Earth,* Chapel, Universidad Autónoma de Chapingo.

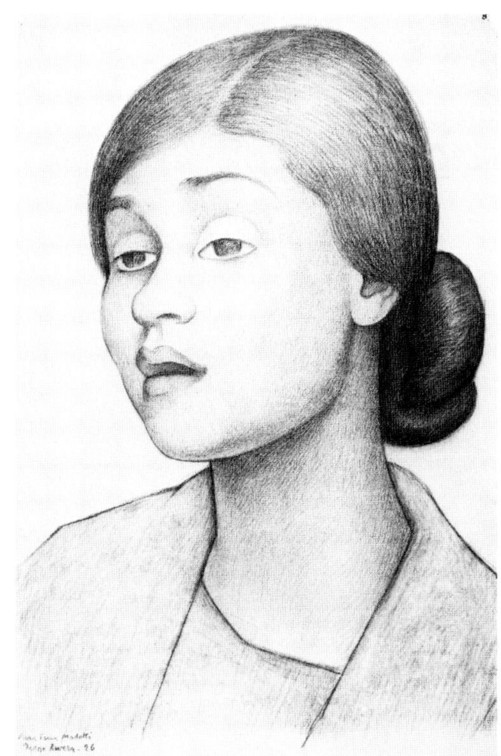

Figure 101
Portrait of Tina Modotti, 1926, black chalk, 48.5 × 31.5 cm. Philadelphia Museum of Art, Purchase, Lola Downin Peck Fund from the estate of Carl Zigrosser (1976–97–89)

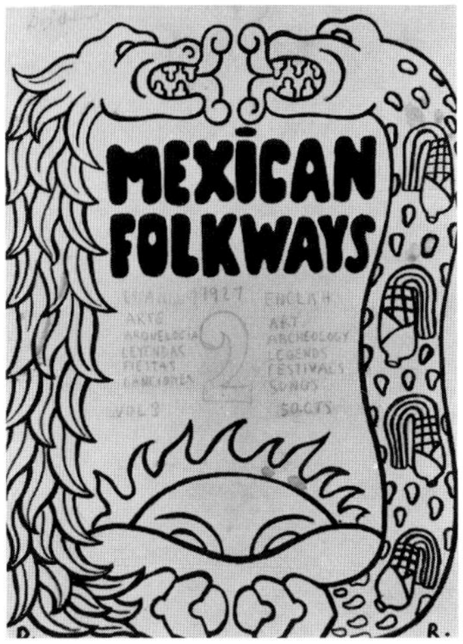

Figure 102
Cover design for *Mexican Folkways,* 1927, black ink, 31.1 × 23.5 cm. Palm Springs, California, B. Lewin Galleries.

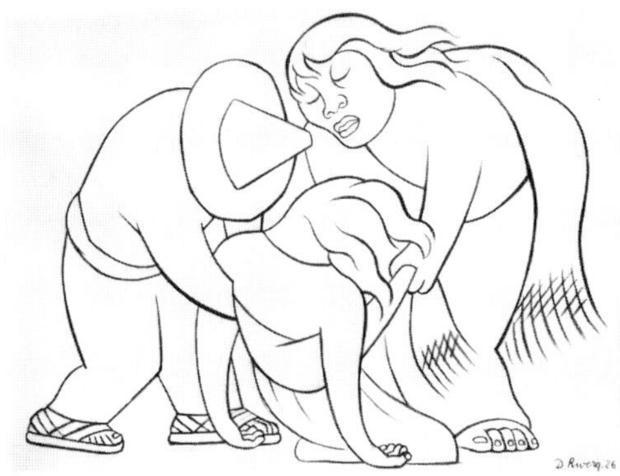

Figure 104
Drunken Woman, 1926, charcoal, 27 × 37.8 cm. San Francisco Museum of Modern Art, Albert M. Bender Collection, Gift of Albert M. Bender (35.2690).

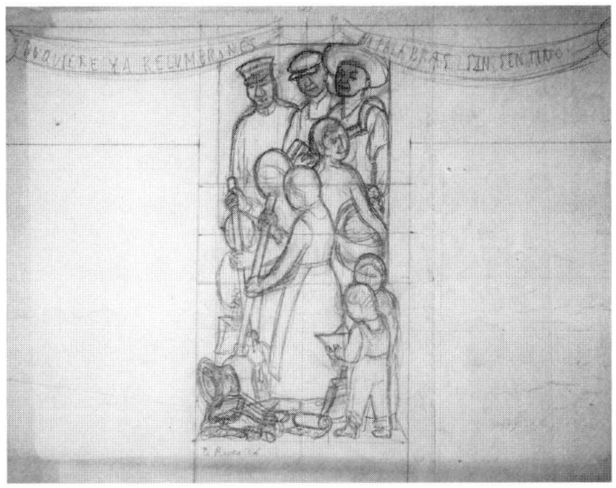

Figure 105
Liquidation of the Feudal Order, 1926, pencil, 33 × 43.3 cm. Philadelphia Museum of Art, Purchase, Lola Downin Peck Fund from the estate of Carl Zigrosser (1976–97–71). Study for *Guarantees—Debris of Capitalism,* Court of Fiestas (third floor), Secretaría de Educación Pública.

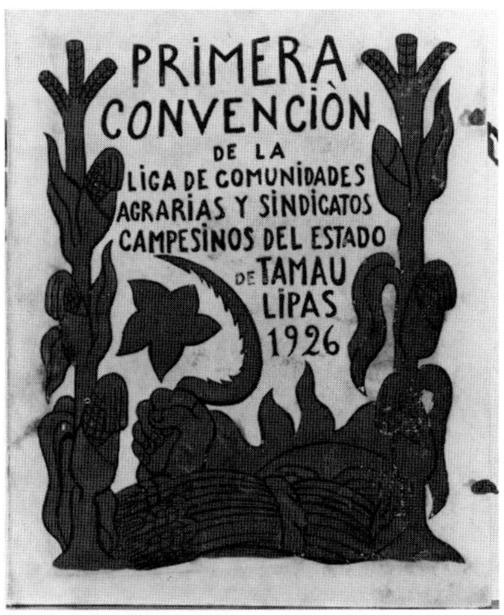

Figure 103
Cover of the album *Convenciones de la Liga de Communidades Agrarias y Sindicatos Campesinos del Estado de Tamaulipas,* 1926, 40.9 × 34 cm. Guanajuato, Museo Diego Rivera, Marte R. Gómez Collection (INBA).

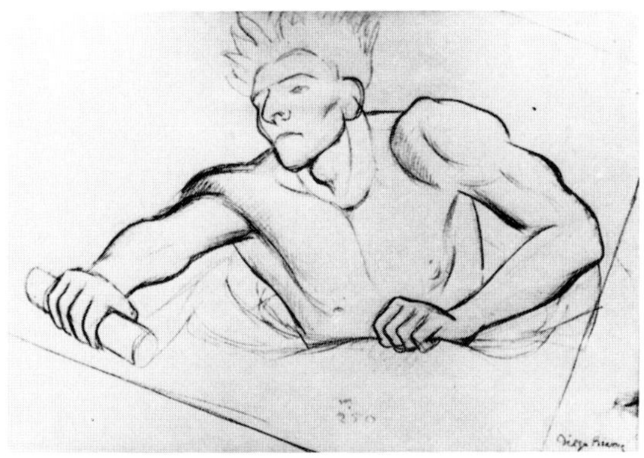

Figure 106
Fire, 1926, charcoal, 30.5 × 45.7 cm. Collection of Dr. and Mrs. David R. Sacks. Study for *The Liberated Earth,* Chapel, Universidad Autónoma de Chapingo.

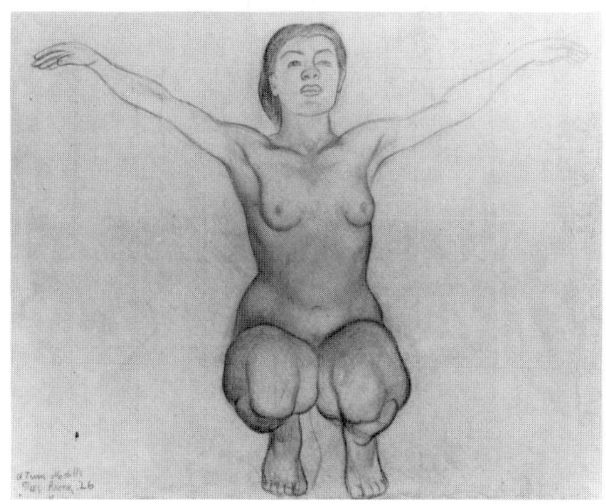

Figure 107
Crouching Nude with Arms Outstretched, 1926, charcoal, 48.2 × 62 cm. The Baltimore Museum of Art, Gift of Blanche Adler (1931.41.2). Study for the central figure in *Subterranean Forces,* Chapel, Universidad Autónoma de Chapingo.

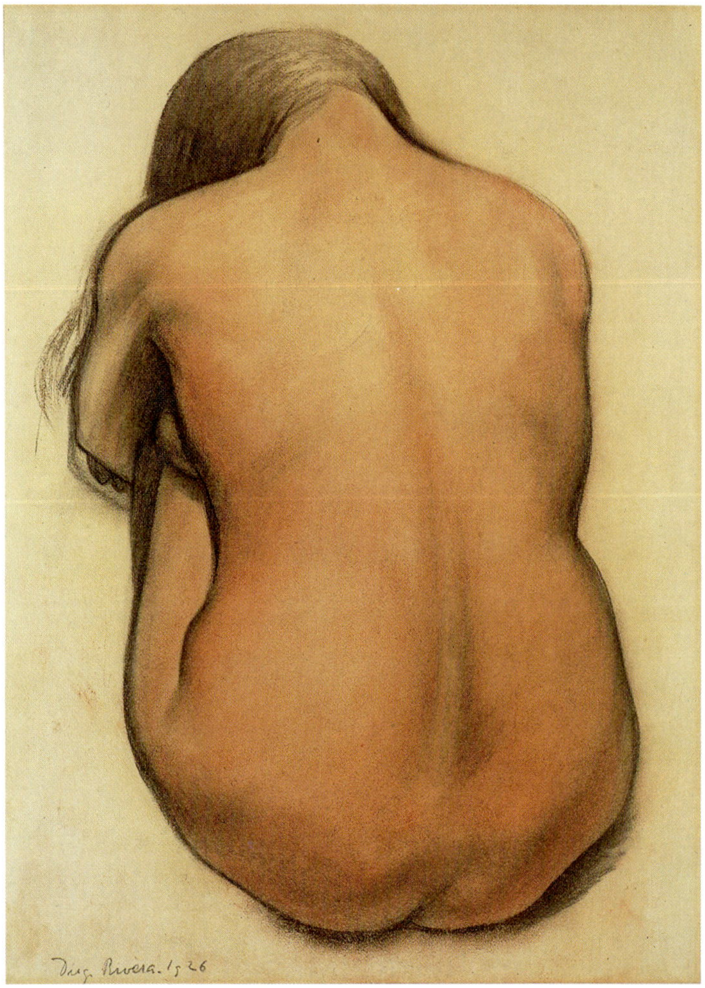

Figure 108
Back of a Seated Nude, 1926, red chalk and charcoal, 63.2 × 48.5 cm. San Francisco Museum of Modern Art, Albert M. Bender Collection, Gift of Albert M. Bender (35.1655). Study for the figure at right in *Germination,* Chapel, Universidad Autónoma de Chapingo.

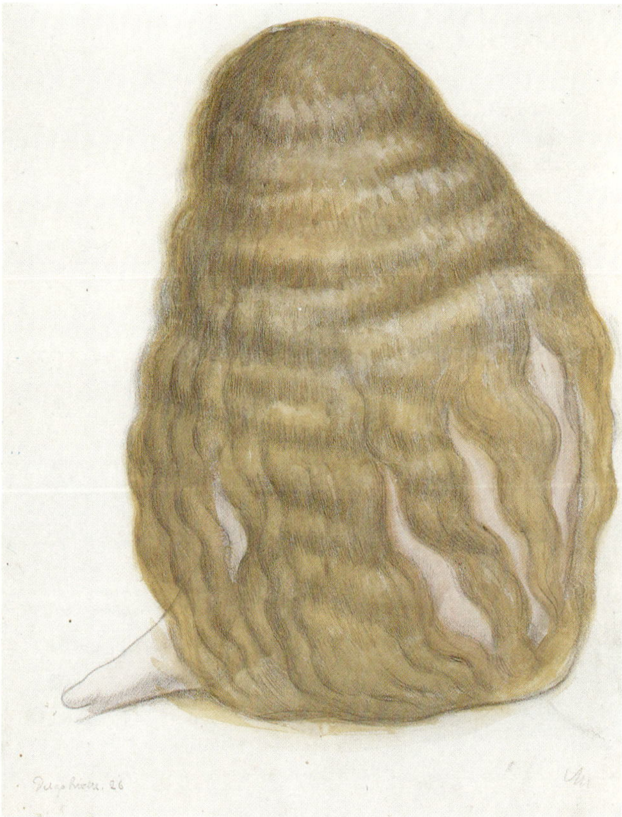

Figure 109
Seated Nude with Long Hair, 1926, black chalk and watercolor, 62.2 × 48.2 cm. The Detroit Institute of Arts, Founders Society Purchase, Matilda R. Wilson and Mr. and Mrs. Walter B. Ford Funds (F1984.27). Study for the figure at lower center in *Subterranean Forces,* Chapel, Universidad Autónoma de Chapingo.

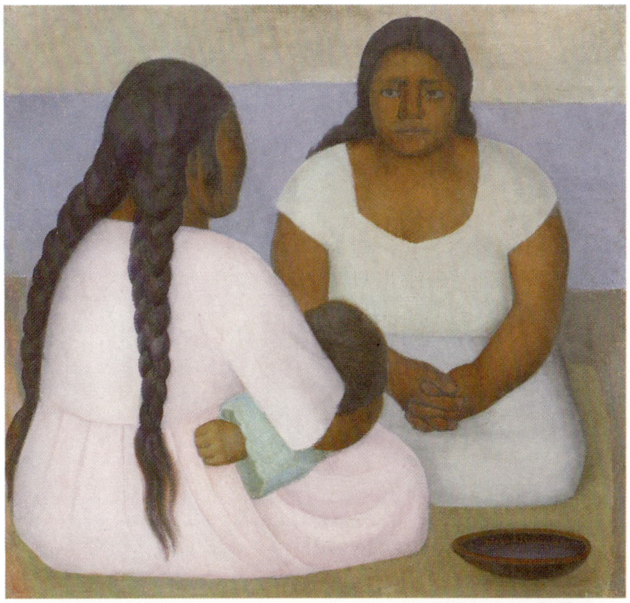

Figure 111
Two Women and a Child, 1926, oil on canvas, 74.3 × 80 cm. The Fine Arts Museums of San Francisco, Gift of Albert M. Bender (1926.22). Women and children were one of Rivera's favorite subjects throughout his career.

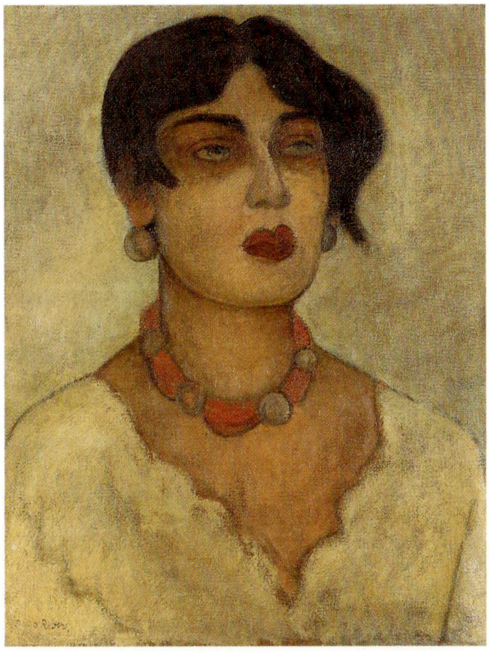

Figure 110
Portrait of Guadalupe, 1926, encaustic on canvas, 67.3 × 56.5 cm. Poughkeepsie, New York, The Vassar College Gallery of Art, Anonymous Loan (L82.1). Rivera's second wife, Guadalupe Marín, was the mother of his two daughters, Guadalupe (Pico) and Ruth (Chapa). Her novel, *La única,* published in 1928, was illustrated by Rivera. This portrait was painted just before their separation in 1926.

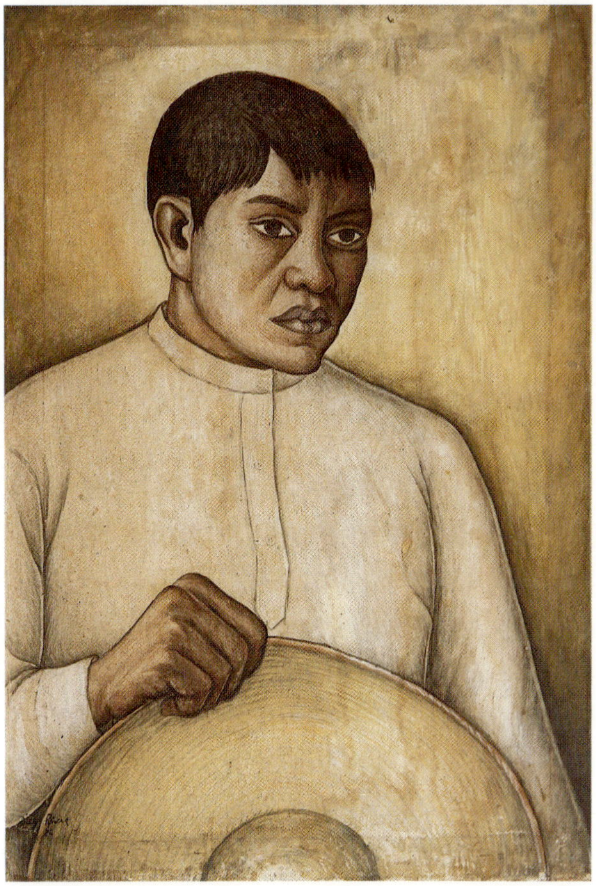

Figure 112
Peasant with Sombrero, 1926, tempera on linen, 69 × 48 cm. Private Collection. Although this specific figure does not appear in the Rivera's murals at Chapingo, it is closely related to the figures mourning the dead peon in the chapel panel *Continuous Renewal of the Revolutionary Struggle.*

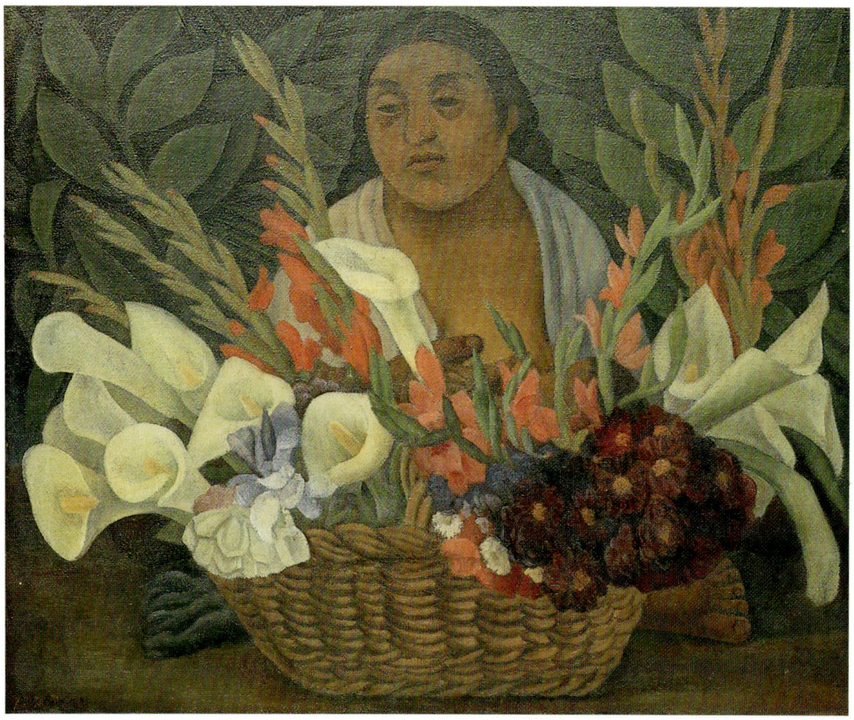

Figure 113
Flower Seller, 1926, oil on canvas, 89.5 × 109.9 cm. Honolulu Academy Arts, Gift of Mrs. Philip E. Spalding, 1932 (49.1).

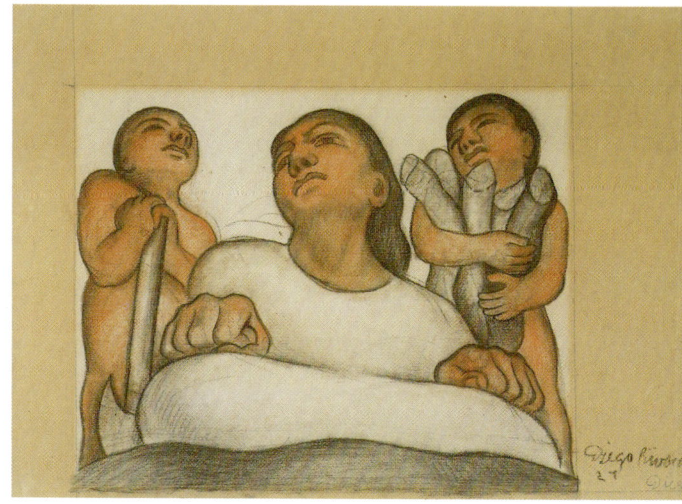

Figure 114
Woman with Two Children, 1927, pastel, 22.1 × 31.3 cm. Philadelphia Museum of Art, Gift of an Anonymous Donor (1956–121–3). Study (not used) for ceiling, Chapel, Universidad Autónoma de Chapingo.

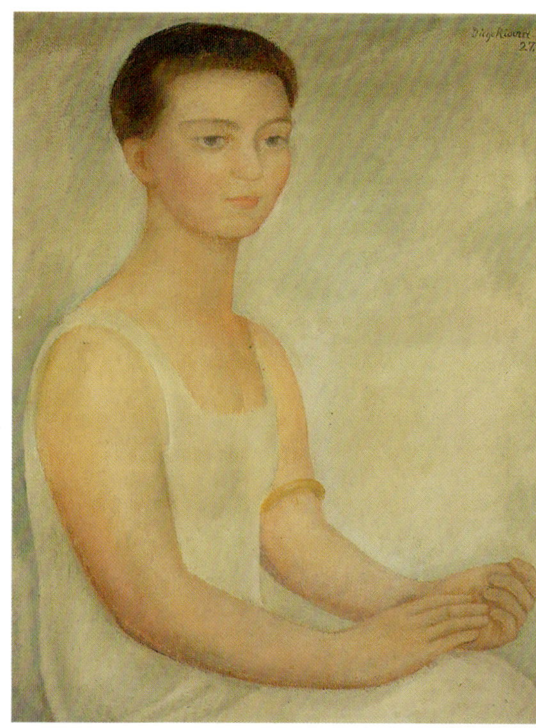

Figure 115
Portrait of Mrs. Dreyfus, 1927, oil on canvas, 82 × 65 cm. Property of the State of Veracruz.

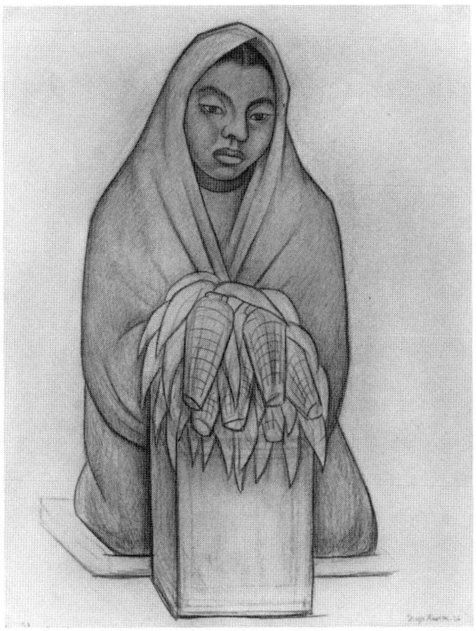

Figure 116
Indian Woman with Corn, 1926, black chalk, 63.2 × 48.3 cm. San Francisco, California Palace of the Legion of Honor, Achenbach Foundation for Graphic Arts, Gift of Albert M. Bender (1927.55).

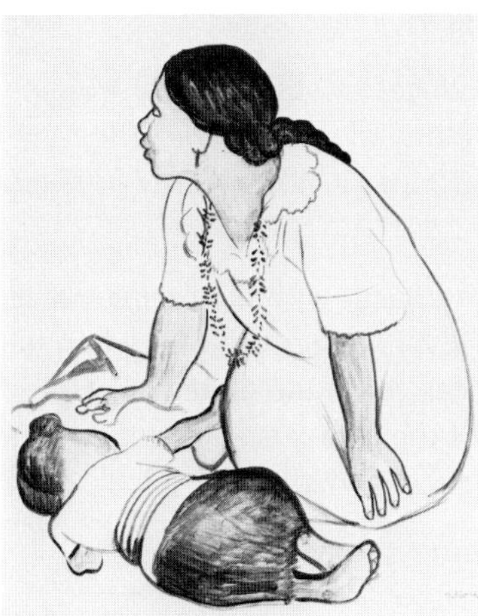

Figure 117
Woman Kneeling over Sleeping Child, 1926, brush and black ink over pencil, 60 × 46.8 cm. Philadelphia Museum of Art, Gift of an Anonymous Donor (1945–66–2).

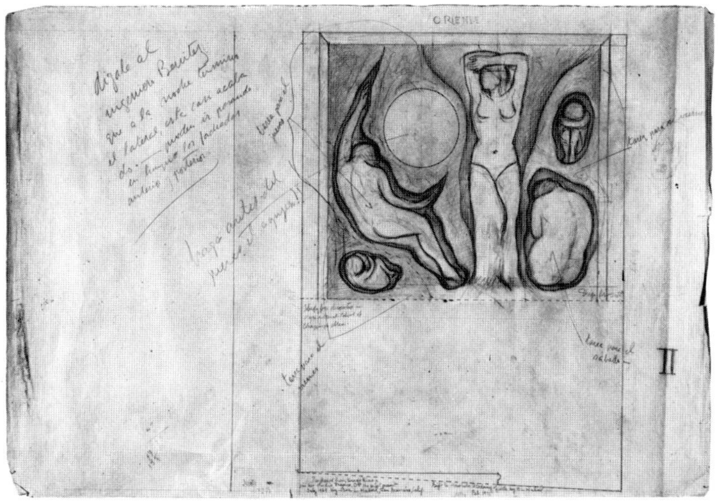

Figure 118
Germination, 1927, pencil, 50.5 × 75.6 cm. Honolulu Academy of Arts, Gift of Miss Bea L. Haberl, 1971 (15.707). Study for panel of the same title, Chapel, Universidad Autónoma de Chapingo.

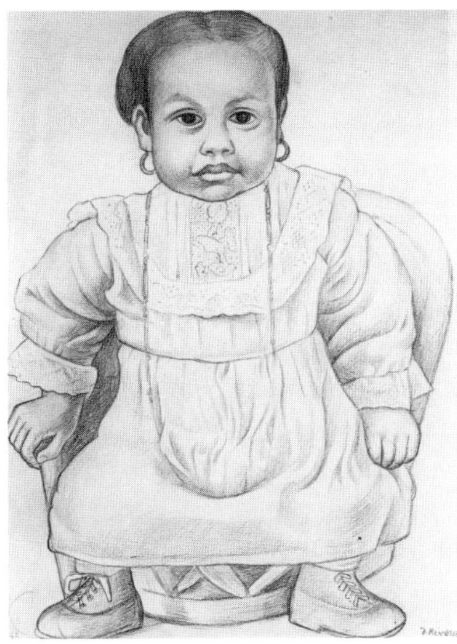

Figure 119
Mexican Child, ca. 1926, pencil, 38.1 × 27.7 cm. San Francisco Museum of Modern Art, Albert M. Bender Collection, Gift of Albert M. Bender (35.2697).

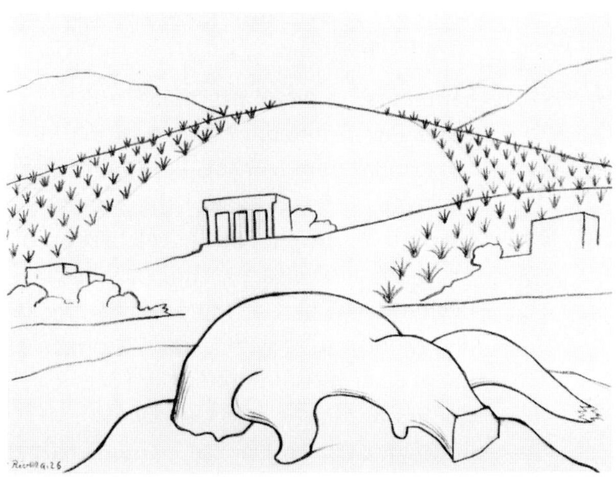

Figure 120
Landscape, Tlalnepantla, formerly known as *Tehuantepec Pass No. 13,* 1926, Conté crayon, 27.3 × 38.8 cm. San Francisco Museum of Modern Art, Albert M. Bender Collection, Gift of Albert M. Bender (35.2707).

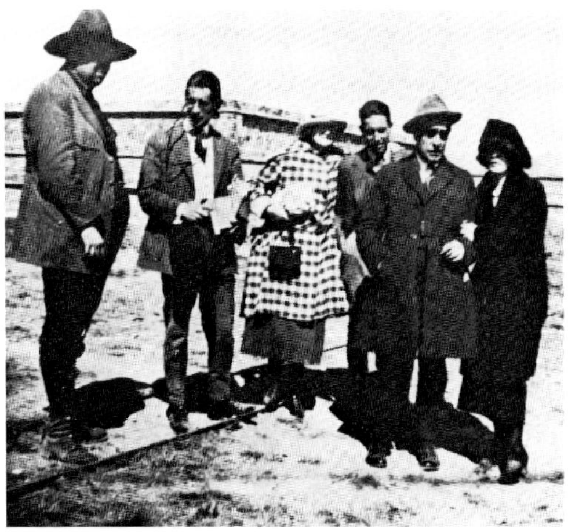

Figure 121
Rivera, Rafael Yela Gunther, Dalila and Carlos Mérida, José Juan Tablada, and his wife at Ciudadela, Teotihuacán, Mexico, ca. 1927.

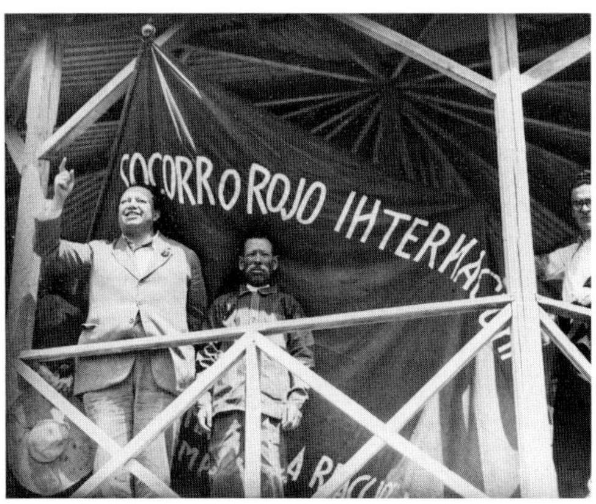

Figure 122
Rivera addressing a meeting of the International Red Aid, ca. 1928. Photo by Tina Modotti.

Orozco resumes work at the Preparatoria and completes several more panels before his painting is again stopped in September.

July: Calles's anticlerical policies result in the cessation of all church services, provoking the *Cristero* revolt in the western states.

Summer and Fall: Rivera active in the Hands-Off Nicaragua Committee.

1927

Falls from the scaffold at Chapingo and is knocked unconscious; head injury results in three months of convalescence during which he is unable to work.

Daughter Ruth born.

The definitive break in Rivera's tumultuous marriage.

Becomes an active member of the Anti-Imperialist League of the Americas as well as director of their publication, *El libertador;* also elected president of the Workers and Farmers Bloc.

Paints the *Wall Street Banquet* panel at the Secretaría (SEP III, 38), with caricatures of Rockefeller, Morgan, and Ford. Designs sets and costumes for Carlos Chávez's ballet, *H.P.* (*Horse Power*) (see fig. 126), the theme of which is the interdependence of the industrial North and the agrarian South.

August: completes the Chapingo murals four days before leaving for a visit to the Soviet Union.

September: a friend from his European years, Edo Fimmen, president of the International Transport Workers Federation, arranges for Rivera to visit the Soviet Union to participate in the celebration of the tenth anniversary of the October Revolution as part of the official Mexican delegation, along with Luís G. Monzón of the executive committee of the Mexican Communist Party, José Guadalupe Rodríguez, director of the National Farmers League, and five worker representatives. Delivers lectures before the Congress of Friends of Russia and is named "Master of Monumental Painting" by the Moscow School of Fine Arts.

November 24: signs a contract with Anatoly Lunacharsky, Soviet Commissar of Education and the Fine Arts, to paint murals for the Red Army Club, but is unable to start work when he is plagued by incompetent assistants, established academic artists who plot against him, and a sinus infection that results in hospitalization.

1928

January 3–21: six of Rivera's paintings and many drawings from the period of 1912–27 are exhibited at the Weyhe Gallery in New York.

February: supports the Union of Former Ikon Painters in their battle against the academic classicists and smaller modernist groups.

Works closely with *Octobre,* a group of Moscow artists who advocate a form of public art based on popular Russian tradition that will promote socialist ideals; they are opposed to both Socialist Realism and the abstract art of the Soviet avant-garde. Rivera's association with *Octobre* will influence his subsequent works of public art.

Sketches Stalin when he addresses the Mexican delegation at the Central Committee Building in Moscow.

May 1: produces a series of forty-five drawings, many of which depict the May Day celebrations in Moscow (see figs. 130, 131).

Rivera's differences with the regime result in the Stalinist government asking him to return to Mexico on the pretext that as president of the Workers and Farmers Bloc he is needed at home.

June 14: returns to Mexico.

June 23: gives an account of his Soviet trip before a Mexican Communist Party gathering.

Mid-July: President-elect Obregón is assassinated by a *Cristero* fanatic and is succeeded by Emilo Portes Gil as interim president.

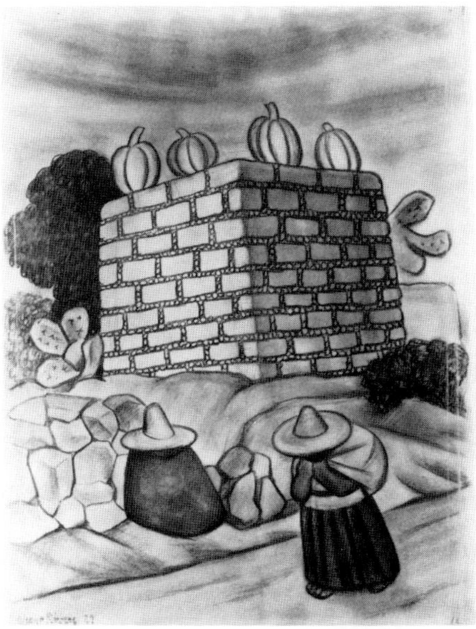

Figure 123
Adobe Hut with Pumpkins on the Roof, 1927, charcoal with red pigment, 63.5 × 48.9 cm. The Detroit Institute of Arts, Museum Purchase (29.338).

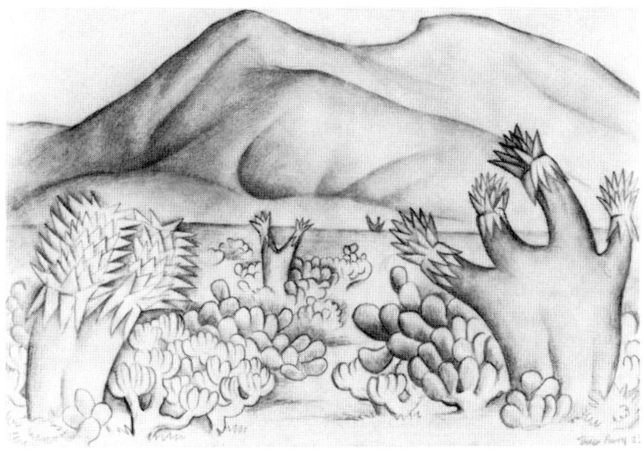

Figure 124
Mexican Landscape, 1927, pencil, 31.1 × 47.2 cm. Cambridge, Massachusetts, Harvard University, Fogg Art Museum, Purchase, Louise E. Bettens Fund (1944.35).

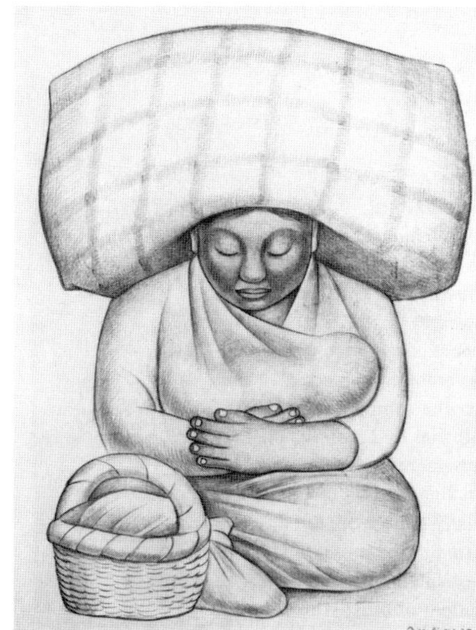

Figure 125
Indian Woman Holding Baby, 1927, pencil, 62.2 × 47 cm. Worcester, Massachusetts, Worcester Art Museum (1928.4)

Figure 126
The Man, 1927, watercolor and pencil, 53 × 74.6 cm. New York, The Museum of Modern Art, Gift of Abby Aldrich Rockefeller (505.41.1). Costume design for the ballet *H.P. (Horse Power)*.

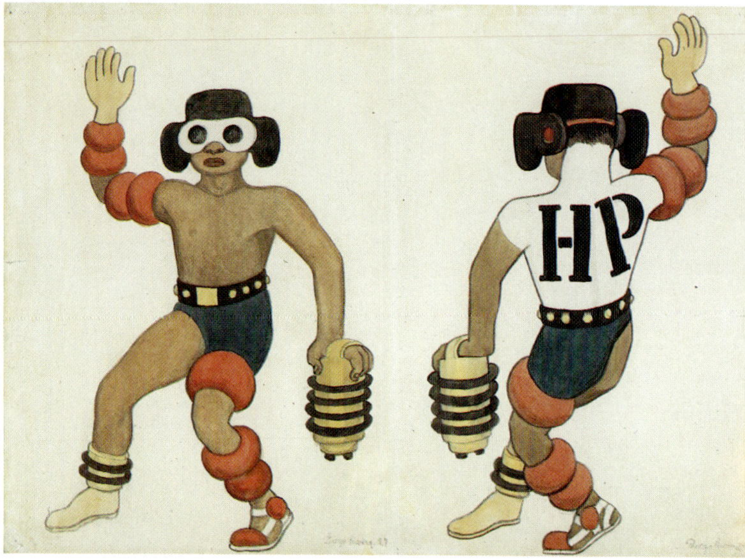

Figure 127
Fiesta Tehuana, also known as *Dance in Tehuantepec*, 1928, oil on canvas 199 × 162 cm. Armonk, New York, IBM Corporation. Painted after the completion of the panel *La Zandunga* in the Secretaría de Educatión Pública, this unusually large work is related to the mural but is executed with greater freedom of brushstroke and movement. La Zandunga is a popular folk dance in the region of Tehuantepec.

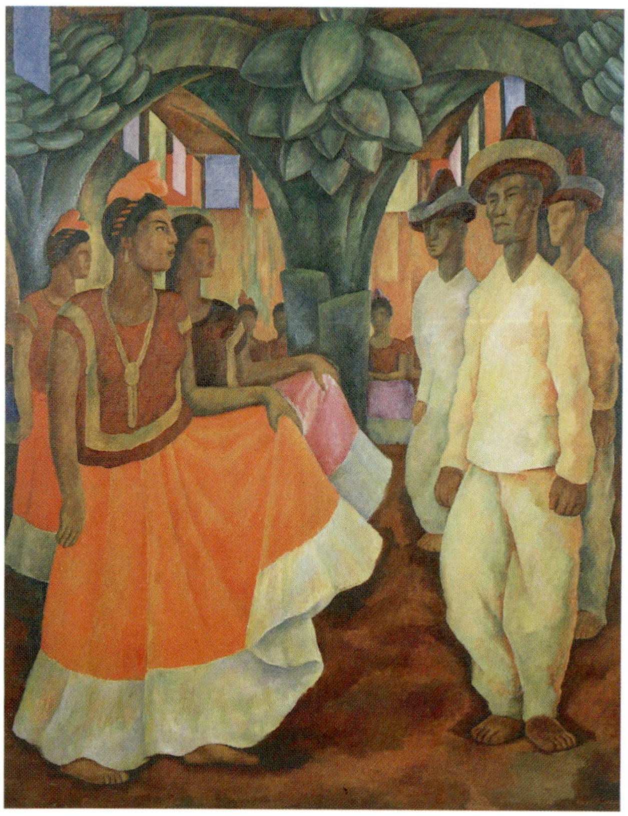

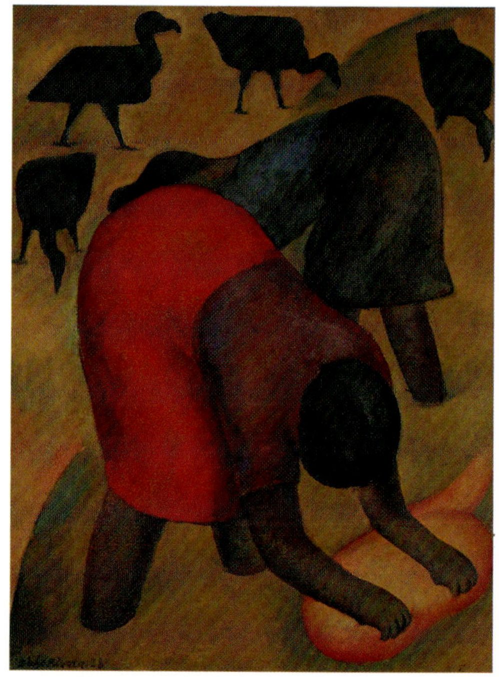

Figure 128
Women Washing Clothes in a River Among Zopilotes, 1928, oil on canvas, 84.8 × 64.8 cm. Collection of Frances de Santos.

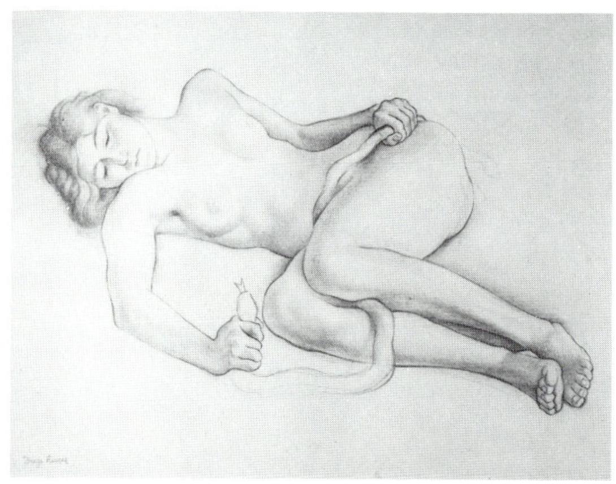

Figure 129
Reclining Nude with Snake, ca. 1929, pencil, 45.5 × 61.2 cm. Philadelphia Museum of Art, Purchase, Lola Downin Peck Fund from the estate of Carl Zigrosser (1976–97–101). Study for the figure of *Continence,* Secretaría de Salubridad y Asistencia.

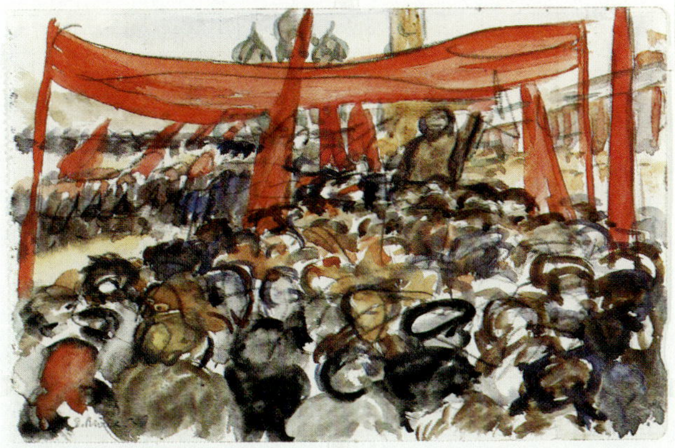

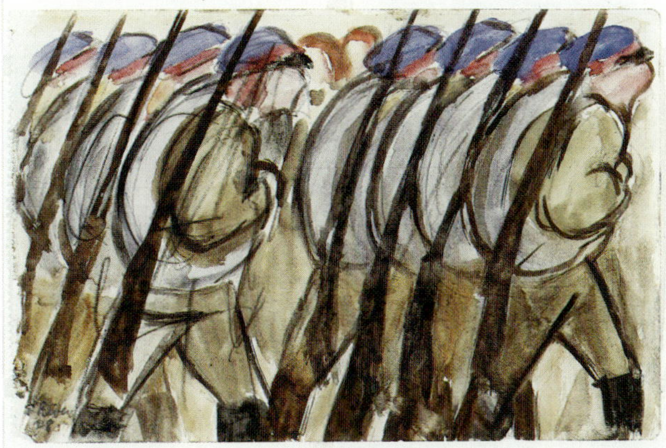

Figures 130–131
May Day, Moscow (two pages from a sketchbook), 1928, watercolor, each 10.3 × 16 cm. New York, The Museum of Modern Art, Gift of Abby Aldrich Rockefeller (137.35.27 and 137.35.30).

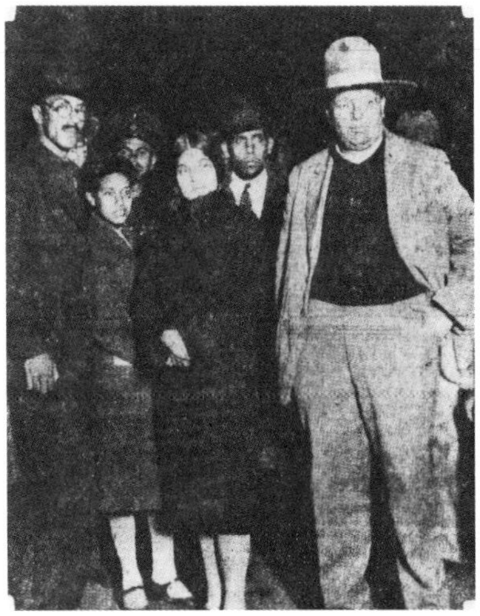

Figure 132
Rivera and Modotti on the way to a court hearing, 1929.

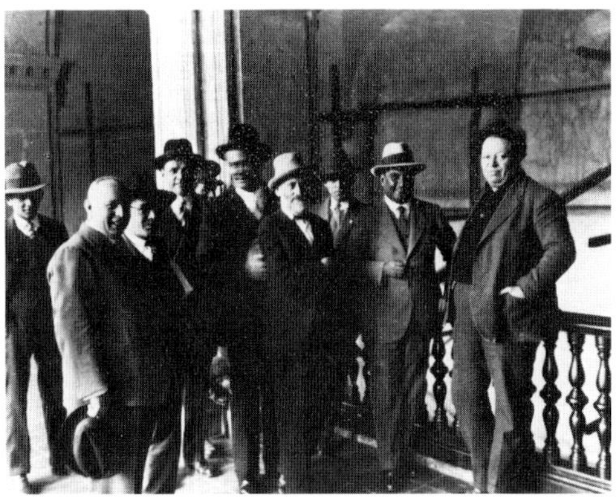

Figure 133
Dr. Atl (with beard) and Rivera at the Palacio Nacional, ca. 1929.

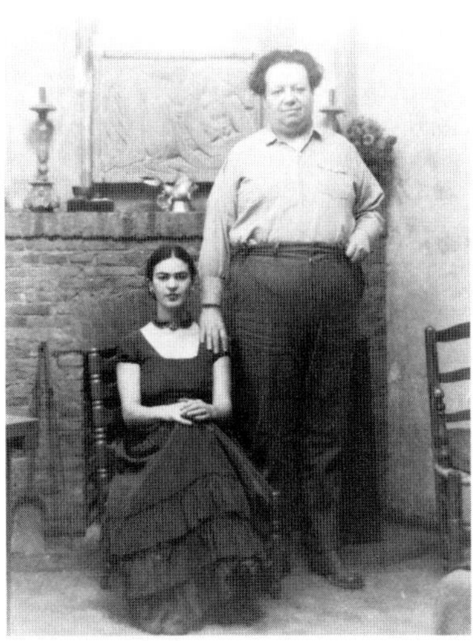

Figure 134
Rivera and Frida at Coyoacán, ca. 1930. Photo by Peter Juley.

Rivera meets Frida Kahlo at one of Tina Modotti's weekly parties. He includes her (along with Siqueiros, Modotti, and the Cuban Communist refugee Julio Antonio Mella) in the *Distributing Arms* panel in the Court of Fiestas at the Secretaría (SEP III, 19).

Paints the large oil *Dance in Tehuantepec* (fig. 127), the first of many paintings he will create throughout his career that are based on successful murals or preparatory sketches for murals.

November: as secretary-general of the Anti-Imperialist League of the Americas, denounces United States president-elect Herbert Hoover's visit to Mexico as an imperialist strategy aimed at undermining the "heroic" army of the Nicaraguan insurgent César Augusto Sandino.

Finishes the Secretaría series.

December: helps organize a protest against the war between Paraguay and Bolivia.

Throughout the winter directs the presidential campaign of the Mexican Communist Party candidate, Pedro Rodríguez Triana.

1929

January 10: Julio Antonio Mella assassinated by agents of the Cuban dictator Gerardo Machado while in the company of Tina Modotti in Mexico City. Modotti is accused of complicity in Mella's murder, and Rivera works to clear her.

January 24: Rivera is elected president of the executive committee of the Workers and Farmers Bloc.

March 4: sends a telegram in the name of the bloc to *El Machete* protesting military uprisings in the states of Sonora and Veracruz. After this Rivera gradually disassociates himself from the openly antigovernment stance of the Mexican Communist Party.

Mexican Communist Party declared illegal; it will remain so until 1935.

April: Rivera appointed director of the Academy of San Carlos. He proposes sweeping changes in the curriculum; students are to combine eight years of daytime factory work with art courses at night, followed by five years of day and night art courses. Rivera's hugely ambitious program draws much criticism, especially from the conservative administration of the adjoining Escuela Nacional de Arquitectura.

May 15: the director of the National Farmers League is murdered in Durango; Rivera and his political colleagues accuse Calles of directing this action.

Rivera paints six large nudes, symbolizing Purity, Strength, Knowledge, Life, Continence, and Health, in the conference room of the Secretaría de Salubridad y Asistencia. He also designs four stained-glass windows on the theme of the elements.

May: the American Institute of Architects awards Rivera its Fine Arts Gold Medal for 1929.

June 7: government attacks on the offices of the Mexican Communist Party and *El Machete*.

July: begins work on his comprehensive history of the Mexican nation on the main stairway of the Palacio Nacional, which houses the office of the president, the Treasury, and other important federal departments.

July and early August: preliminary sketches are traced and transferred to the walls of the stairway.

August 18: begins painting the north wall at the Palacio Nacional. Conservatives criticize the "Communist" tendencies in Rivera's public murals; shortly afterward the government bans known Communists from entering the country.

August 21: marries Frida Kahlo in Coyoacán.

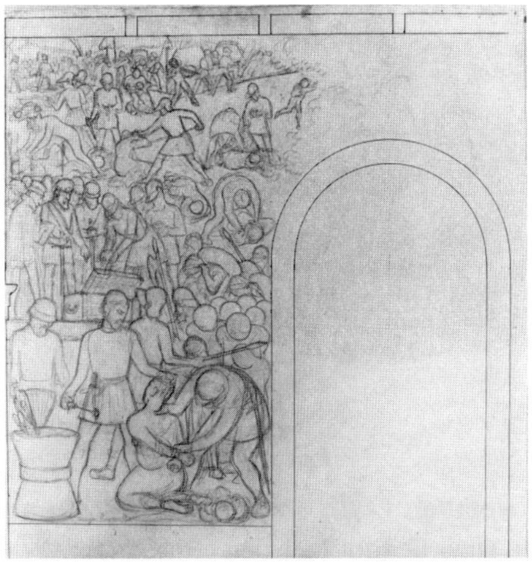

Figure 135
Cortés's Soldiers Torturing and Plundering, 1930, pencil, 41.6 × 43.8 cm. Amherst, Massachusetts, Amherst College, Mead Art Museum, Museum Purchase (1952.16). Study for *The Taking of Cuernavaca,* Palacio de Cortés, Cuernavaca.

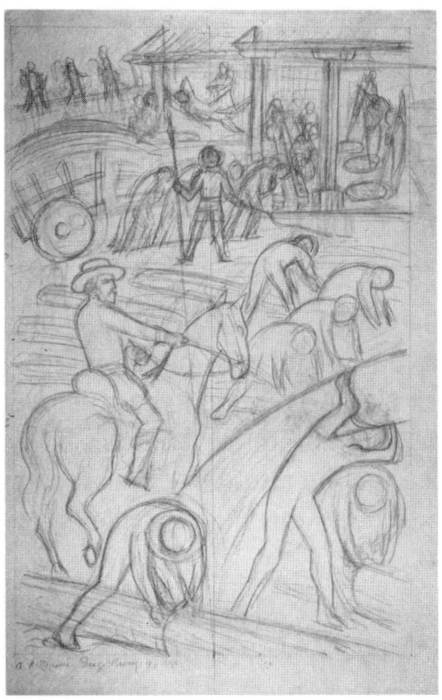

Figure 136
Harvesting Sugar Cane, 1930, pencil, 46.4 × 29.7 cm. Philadelphia Museum of Art, Purchase, Lola Downin Peck Fund from the estate of Carl Zigrosser (1976–97–82). Study for *Sugar Plantation in Morelos,* Palacio de Cortés, Cuernavaca.

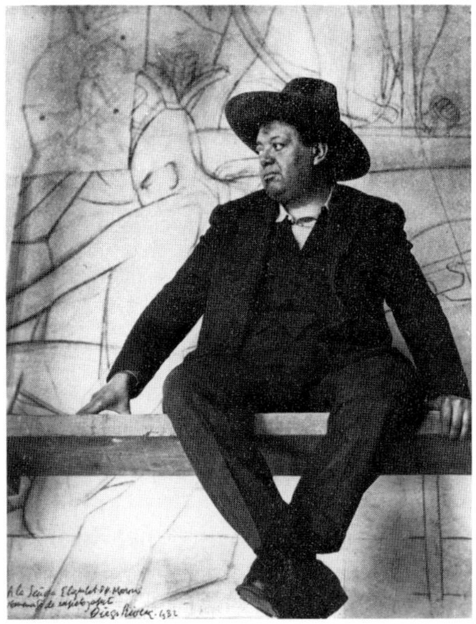

Figure 137
Rivera in front of unfinished mural at Cuernavaca, 1930.

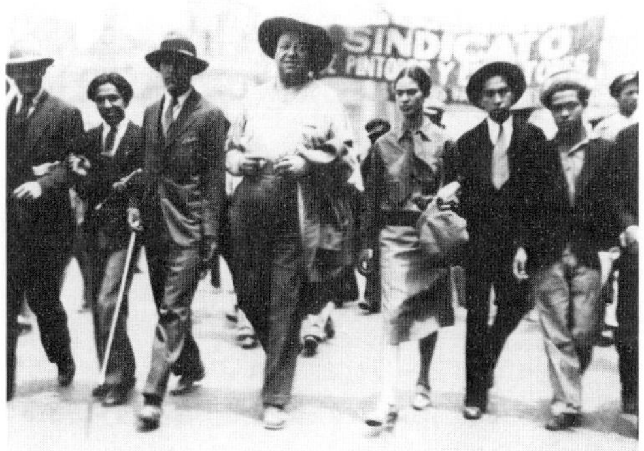

Figure 138
Rivera and Frida Kahlo marching with the *Sindicato de Pintores y Escritores,* ca. 1930.

September 10: expelled from the Mexican Communist Party for disobedience to its policies, including his failure to join in party denouncements of the government and his acceptance of the government-appointed directorship at San Carlos.

September: breaks down from overwork and political pressure and is nursed back to health by Kahlo. Announces his sympathy for political position of Leon Trotsky.

Pascual Ortiz Rubio elected president, but Calles is the power behind the scenes. Labor movements are suppressed and the Mexican Communist Party is the target of unrelenting attacks.

U.S. ambassador Dwight W. Morrow commissions Rivera to paint a mural for the loggia of the Palacio de Cortés in Cuernavaca; the mural is to be a gift to the state of Morelos from the United States as a token of friendship between the two countries.

December: begins to paint at Cuernavaca: nine panels depicting the history of Morelos from before the Conquest to the 20th-century revolution.

Publication of Ernestine Evans' *The Frescoes of Diego Rivera,* a survey of Rivera's murals of 1922–29 and the first book on Rivera in English.

Orozco illustrates *Los de abajo* (The Underdogs) by Mariano Azuelo.

1930
Continues working on the Cuernavaca murals and those in the Palacio Nacional.

April–June: Orozco paints his first North American mural, *Prometheus,* at Pomona College, Claremont, California.

May 10: Rivera forced to resign as director of San Carlos.

Rivera creates a series of paintings and sketches with Tehuantepec themes.

Anti-Communist aggression in Mexico reaches its height with the activities of the fascist Gold Shirts in 1930–31. As a result of tumultuous May Day demonstrations in Mexico City, Siqueiros is placed under confinement (1930–32) in the outlying village of Taxco.

IV.
Rivera's Sojourn in the United States

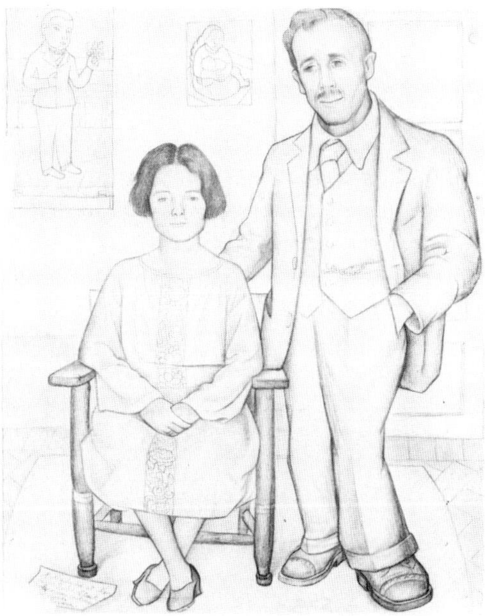

Figure 139
Mr. & Mrs. Ralph Stackpole, ca. 1926, pencil, 64.8 × 54 cm. collection of Mr. and Mrs. Fred H. Altschuler.

1930
September: architect Timothy L. Pflueger announces in San Francisco that Rivera has been commissioned to paint a mural in the Luncheon Club of the new Stock Exchange. Protests appear in the media.

October 13–November 9: Rivera's works are included in an exhibition of twelve hundred objects from various epochs of Mexican art (proposed by Ambassador Morrow and organized by René d'Harnoncourt) at the Metropolitan Museum of Art in New York; the exhibition later tours the United States.

November 7: Rivera finishes murals at Cuernavaca.

Mid-November: arrives in San Francisco.

November 15–December 25: a large Rivera retrospective exhibition (120 works) at the California Palace of the Legion of Honor.

November–December: sketches in the Bay Area in preparation for the Luncheon Club mural and prepares full-scale cartoons, using the borrowed studio of sculptor Ralph Stackpole.

December: begins work on *Allegory of California* for the Stock Exchange, modeling central figure after tennis champion Helen Wills Moody. Moody, an amateur artist, introduces Rivera to William R. Valentiner, the director of the Detroit Institute of Arts. Rivera indicates his wish to visit and study the industrial environment of Detroit.

Sells many of his works to North American collectors.

November: Orozco begins his frescoes at the New School for Social Research in New York (completed January 1931).

1931
February 15: finishes *Allegory of California.*

February 17–March 16: exhibition of Rivera's paintings and drawings at the Detroit Institute of Arts.

March 15: official dedication of the Luncheon Club mural; critical and popular reaction both positive.

April: while vacationing at the Atherton home of Mrs. Sigmund Stern, a prominent San Franciscan, Rivera paints a landscape, including almond trees in bloom and portraits of Mrs. Stern's grandchildren, in the alcove of an outdoor dining area.

April 30–June 2: paints *The Making of a Fresco* in the gallery of the California School of Fine Arts, working day and night since Mexican government officials have requested that he return home as soon as possible to finish the murals at the Palacio Nacional.

May 2: writes to Carl Zigrosser of the Weyhe Gallery in New York that he has been offered seven mural commissions in San Francisco (although these projects do not materialize, the proposals are a measure of Rivera's great contemporary popularity).

May 26: the Arts Commission of the City of Detroit approves Valentiner's proposal that Rivera be commissioned to paint murals for the Garden Court of the Detroit Institute of Arts.

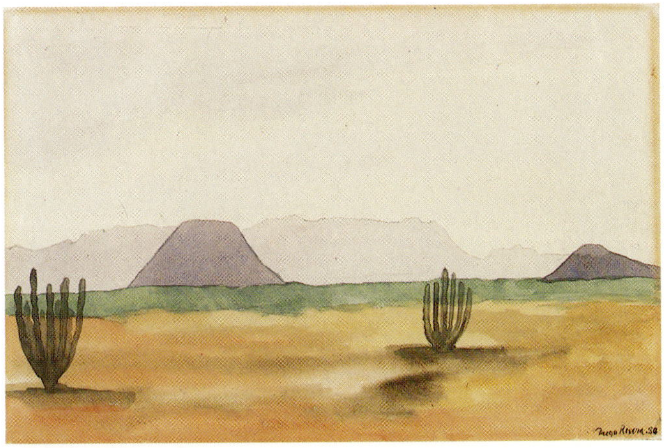

Figure 140
Mesa and Cacti, 1930, watercolor, 31.8 × 48.3 cm. The Detroit Institute of Arts, City Purchase (31.24).

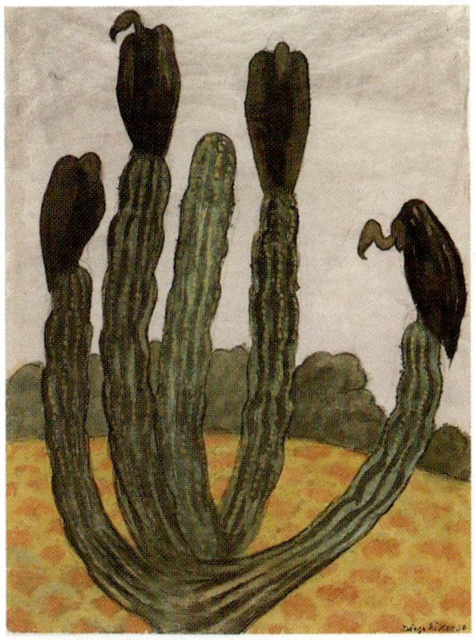

Figure 141
Vultures on Cactus, 1930, watercolor over black chalk, 42.9 × 32.3 cm. The Detroit Institute of Arts, Bequest of Robert H. Tannahill (70.331).

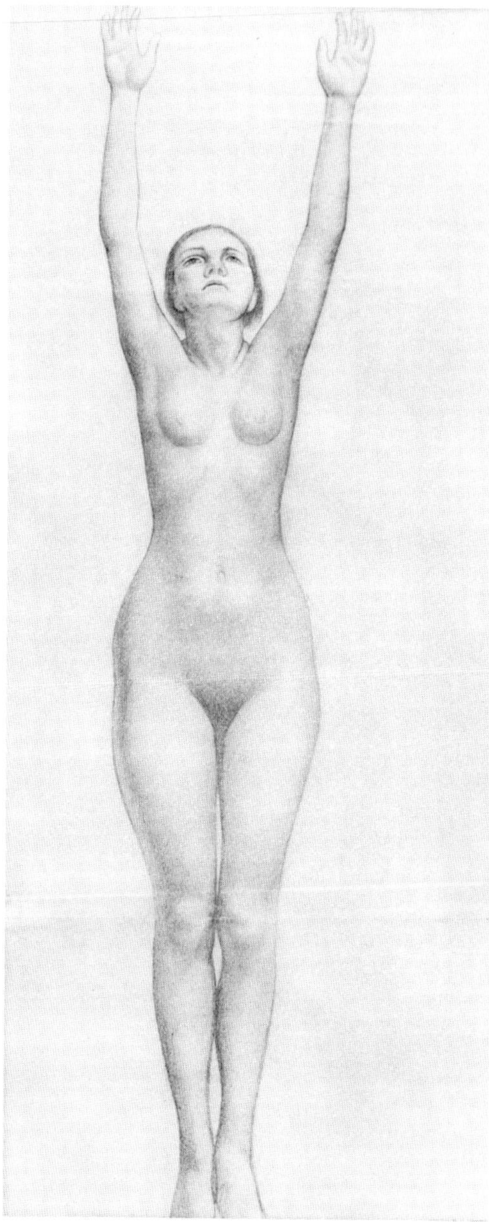

Figure 143
Nude with Arms Outstretched over Head, 1931, pencil, 81.5 × 47.3 cm. San Francisco Museum of Modern Art, William L. Gerstle Collection, Gift of William L. Gerstel through the San Francisco Art Institute (64.16). Study for ceiling, Pacific Stock Exchange, San Francisco.

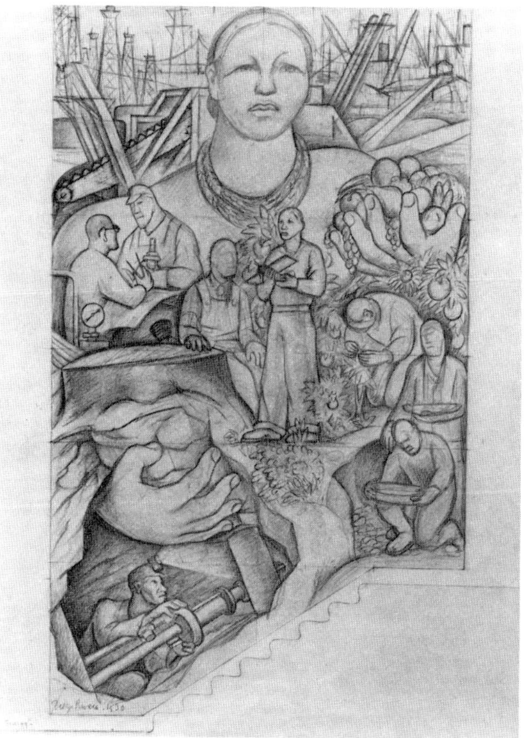

Figure 142
Untitled (Energy), 1930, pencil, 63.5 × 48.3 cm. San Francisco Museum of Modern Art, William L. Gerstle Collection, Gift of William L. Gerstle through the San Francisco Art Institute (64.10). Study for *Allegory of California,* Pacific Stock Exchange, San Francisco.

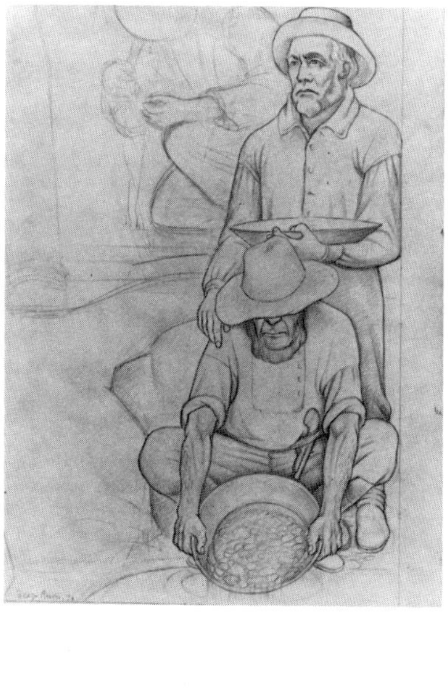

Figure 144
Miners Panning Gold (Marshall's Discovery of Gold in California), 1930, pencil, 61.6 × 47.9 cm. San Francisco Museum of Modern Art, William L. Gerstle Collection, Gift of William L. Gerstle through the San Francisco Art Institute (64.15). Study for *Allegory of California,* Pacific Stock Exchange, San Francisco.

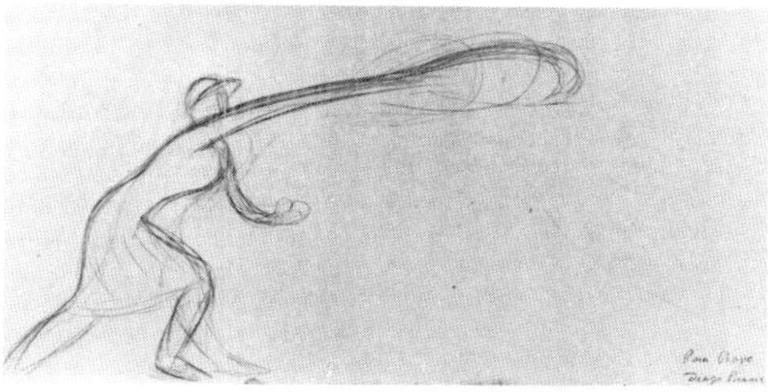

Figure 145
Tenista I (Helen Wills Moody), 1931, pencil, 25.8 × 55 cm. Collection of Rafael Coronel.

Figure 146
Head of a Woman, 1931, red and black chalk, 62.3 × 48 cm. San Francisco Museum of Modern Art, William L. Gerstle Collection, Gift of William L. Gerstle through the San Francisco Art Institute (64.12). Study for ceiling, Pacific Stock Exchange, San Francisco.

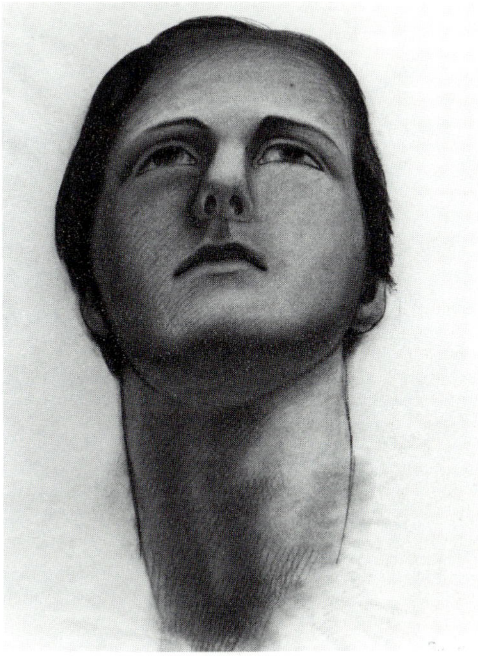

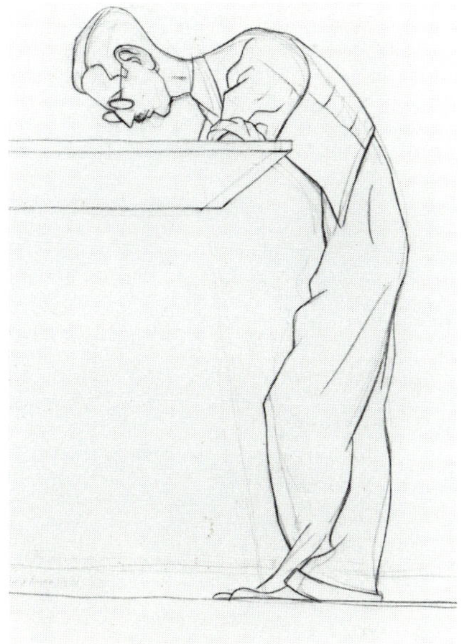

Figure 149
The Draftsman (Albert Barrows), 1931, charcoal and pencil, 55.9 × 43.2 cm. Private collection. Study for *The Making of a Fresco,* San Francisco Art Institute.

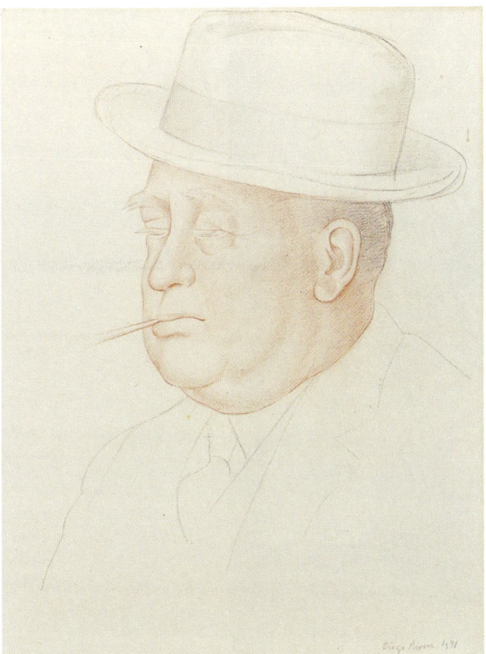

Figure 147
Portrait of Arthur Brown, 1931, red chalk and charcoal, 58.4 × 48.2 cm. San Francisco, California Palace of the Legion of Honor, Achenbach Foundation for Graphic Arts, Gift of Drs. Daniel and Hilary Goldstine and Mr. and Mrs. C. David Robinson through the San Francisco Art Institute (1981.2.26). Study for *The Making of a Fresco,* San Francisco Art Institute.

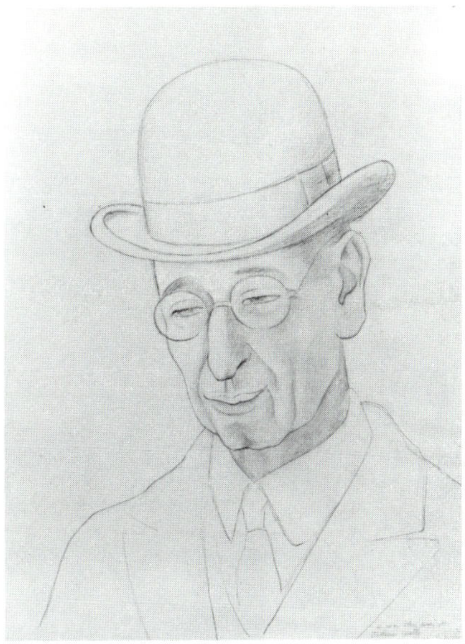

Figure 148
Portrait of William Gerstle, 1931, 60.9 × 45.7 cm. Private collection. Study for *The Making of a Fresco,* San Francisco Art Institute.

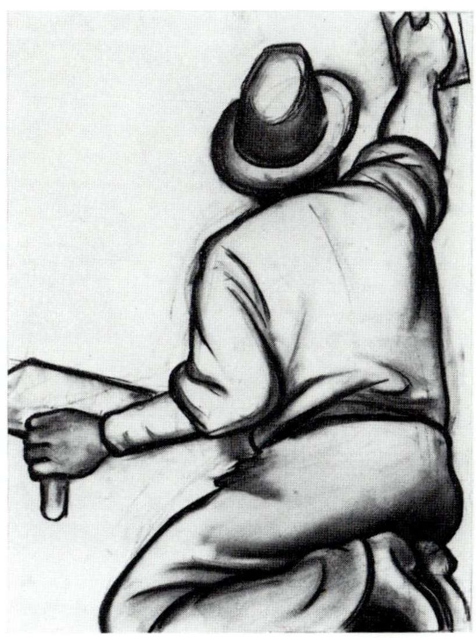

Figure 150
Matthew Barnes Plastering, 1931, charcoal, 60.9 × 45.7 cm. Private Collection. Study for *The Making of a Fresco,* San Francisco Art Institute.

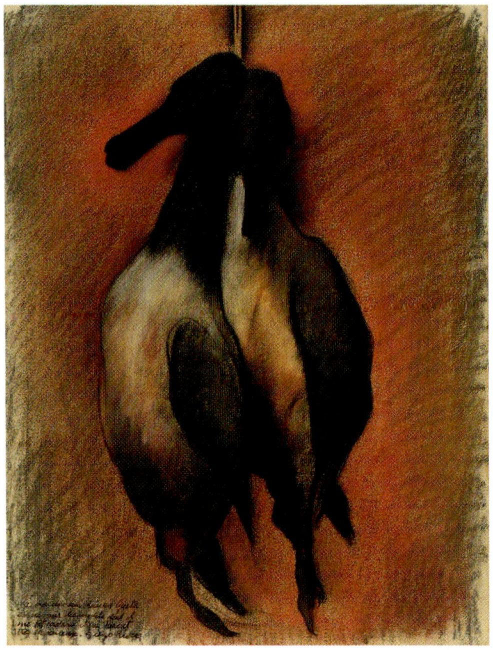

Figure 151
Ducks, 1931, pastel, 61.9 × 48 cm. San Francisco Museum of Modern Art, Collection of William L. Gerstle, Gift of William L. Gerstle (39.179).

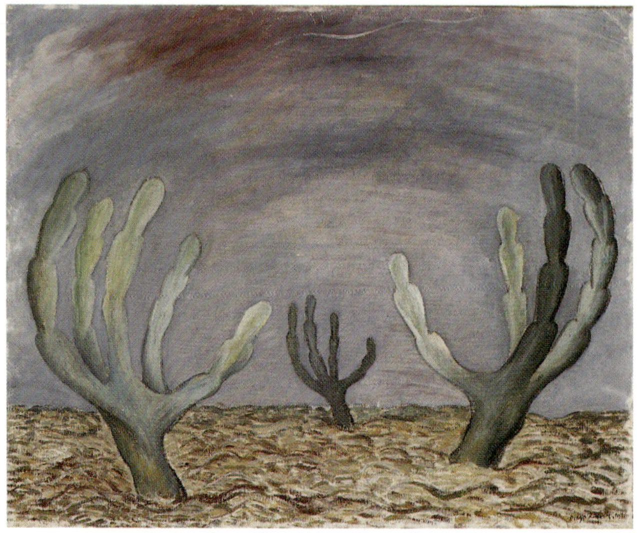

Figure 153
Cactus on the Plains, also known as *Hands,* 1931, oil on canvas, 69.2 × 84.5 cm. Grosse Pointe, Michigan, Edsel and Eleanor Ford House.

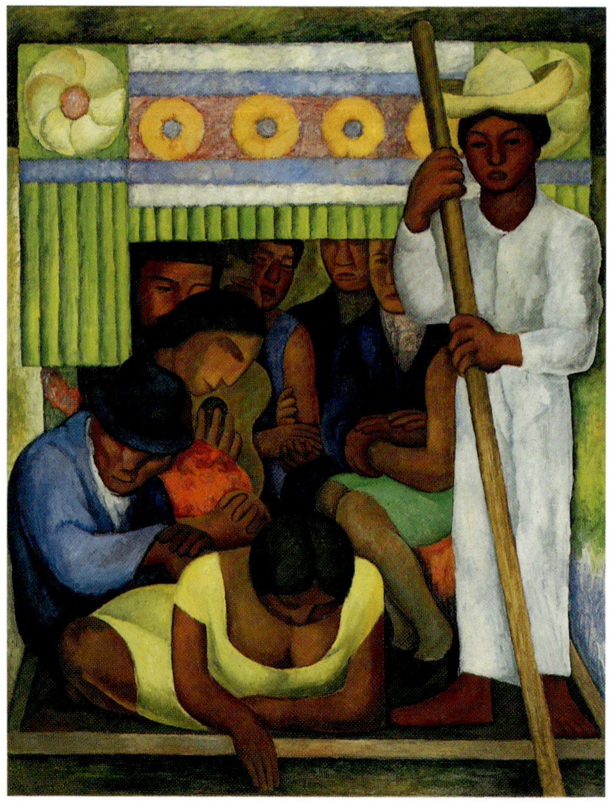

Figure 154
The Flowered Canoe, 1931, oil on canvas, 200 × 160 cm. Collection of Dolores Olmedo.

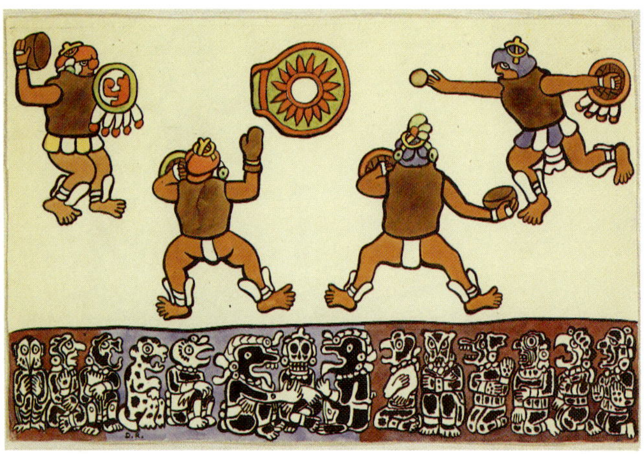

Figure 152
The First Ball Game, 1931, watercolor, 30.5 × 45.7 cm. Private Collection. Illustration for an unpublished translation of the ancient Maya text known as the *Popul Vuh* (Book of the People).

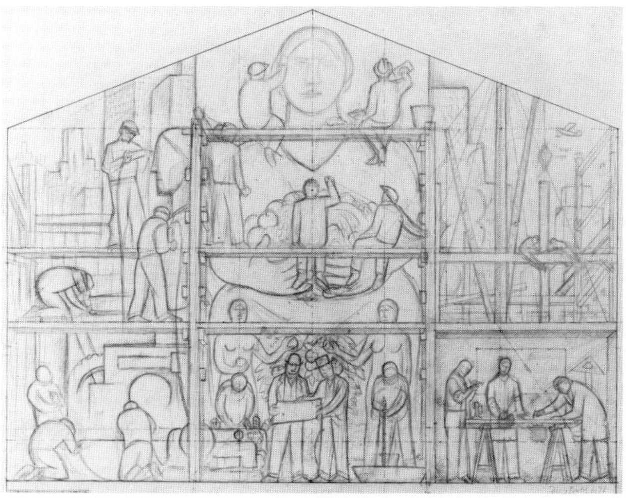

Figure 155
The Making of a Fresco, 1931, pencil, 43.2 × 58.4 cm. Private Collection. Second plan for the mural of the same title, San Francisco Art Institute.

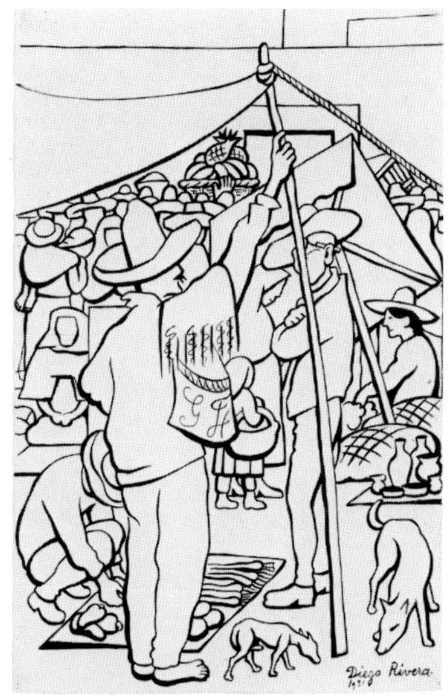

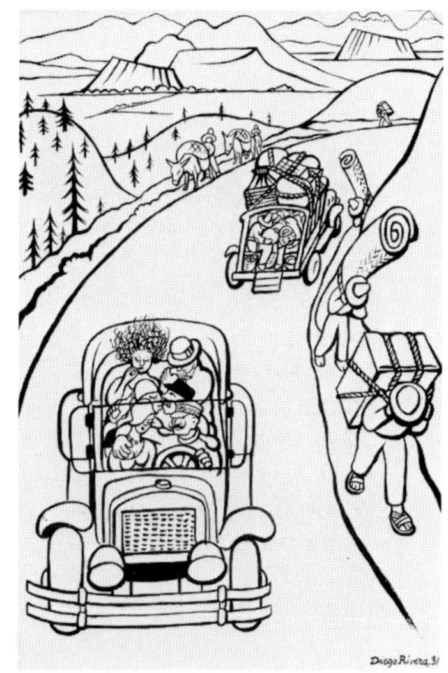

Figures 156–157
Market Scene, 1931, brush and black ink, 48 × 31 cm. Mexico City, Museo Franz Mayer. *Mexican Highway,* 1931 brush and black ink, 48 × 31.6 cm. Philadelphia Museum of Art, Gift of Carl Zigrosser. Both of these works are illustrations for *Mexico: A Study of Two Americas* (New York, 1937) by Stuart Chase.

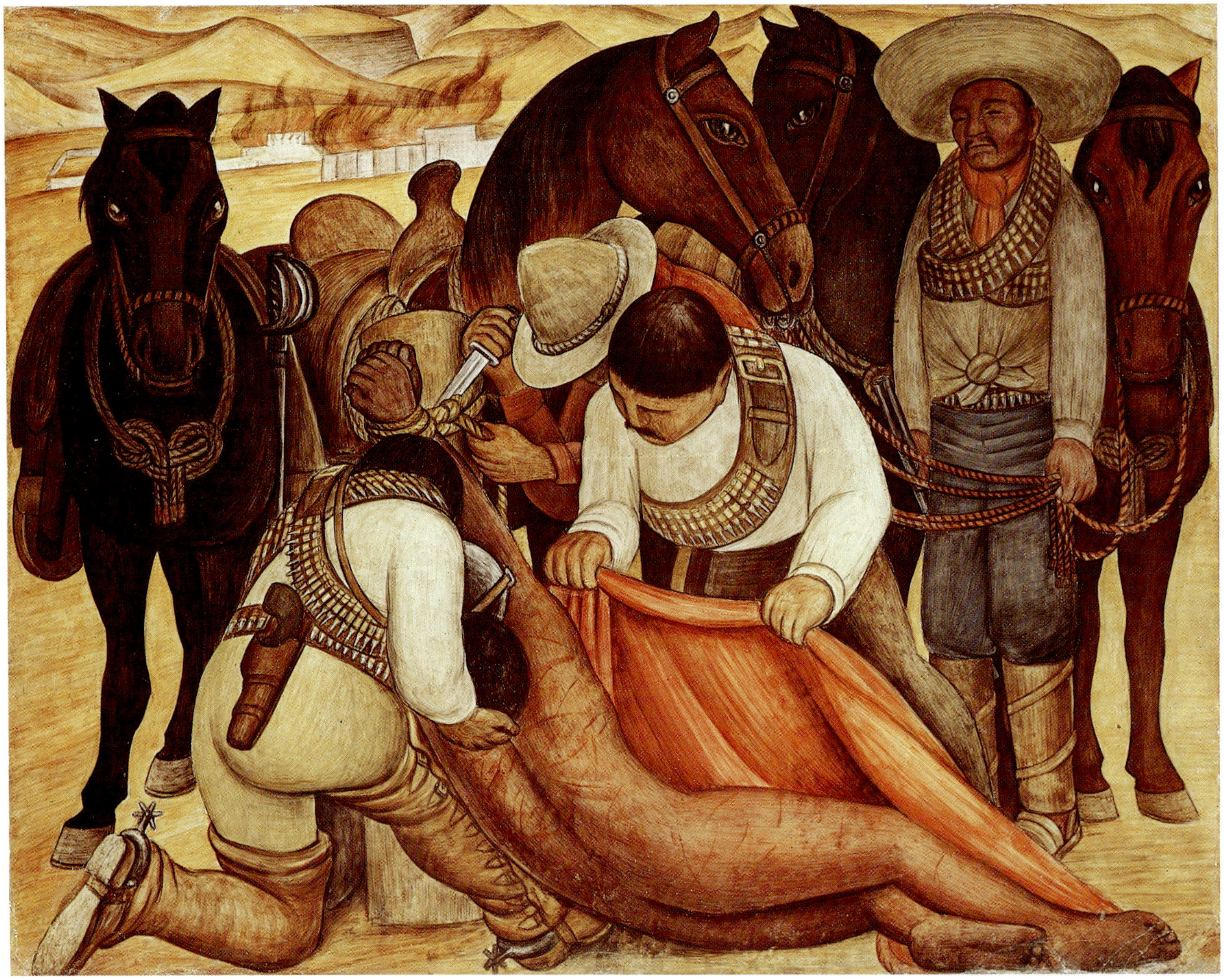

Figure 158
Liberation of the Peon,
1931, fresco, 152.4 × 243.8 cm. Philadelphia Museum of Art, Given by Mr. and Mrs. Herbert Cameron Morris (43–46–1). This movable fresco is based on a panel of the same title, Court of Labor (first floor), Secretaría de Educación Pública.

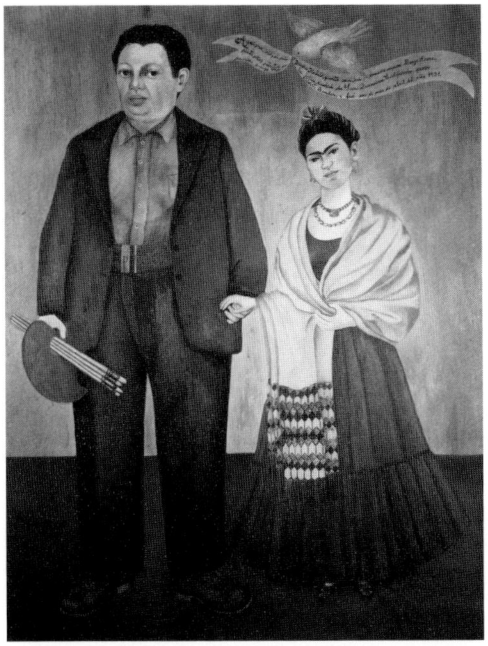

Figure 159
Frida Kahlo, *Frida and Diego Rivera,* 1931, oil on canvas, 100 × 78.7 cm. San Francisco Museum of Modern Art, Albert M. Bender Collection, Gift of Albert M. Bender.

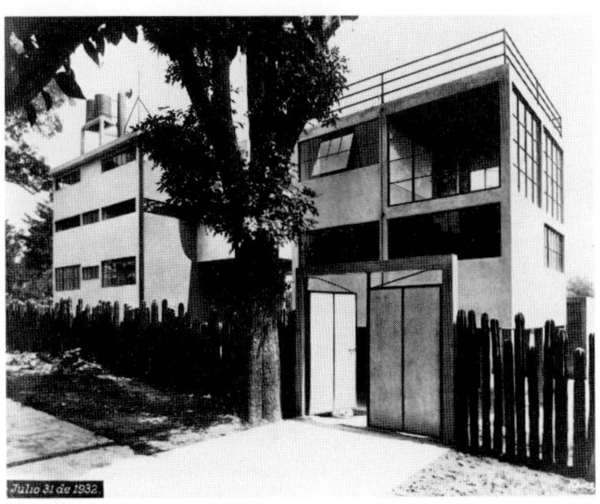

Figure 160
The Rivera residence in San Angel.

June 8: flies to Mexico and by the fourteenth has begun working at the Palacio Nacional. Dissatisfied with work done in his absence by assistants Ione Robinson and Victor Arnautoff, he repaints their work.

Executes a series of drawings and watercolors inspired by the Maya text known as the *Popul Vuh* (see figs. 152 and 358).

With money from his San Francisco projects, Rivera begins to build adjoining house-studios, designed by architect and painter Juan O'Gorman, for himself and Kahlo in the San Angel section of Mexico City.

July: Frances Flynn Paine, art dealer and member of the prestigious Mexican Arts Association, which is financed by the Rockefellers, offers Rivera a one-person exhibition at the Museum of Modern Art in New York.

August: Rivera's Parisian friend and former mentor Elie Faure visits him and views his murals. Their discussions reinforce Rivera's interest in art and technology.

Rivera meets Russian filmmaker Sergei M. Eisenstein, who dedicates a section of his film *Que Viva Mexico!* to the artist.

September: Abby Aldrich Rockefeller purchases Rivera's May Day 1928 sketchbook.

October: finishes the central stairway mural at the Palacio Nacional.

November: collaborates in the organization of the exhibition "*Quatro azules*" (Lyonel Feininger, Alexei Jawlensky, Wassily Kandinsky, and Paul Klee) at the Biblioteca Nacional de México.

November 13: Rivera, Kahlo, Paine, and Ramón Alva de la Canal arrive in New York aboard the SS *Morro Castle*. Rivera paints and sketches on board ship in preparation for his show.

Paints works with Mexican themes, such as *The Flowered Canoe* (fig. 154), *Flower Festival*, and *Cactus on the Plains* (fig. 153).

December 23, 1931–January 27, 1932: Rivera's retrospective at the Museum of Modern Art (143 paintings and works on paper; 8 "portable" fresco panels [5 recreations of themes from the murals at the Secretaría de Educación Pública and Cuernavaca (see figs. 158 and 334), and 3 that treat New York City topics, (see figs. 264 and 265)]) sets attendance records. Almost fifty-seven thousand view the exhibition, the second one-person show held at MOMA, the first being that of Matisse; critical reaction is positive.

1932
The effects of the worldwide depression reach Mexico, and Calles's conservative economic programs come under attack.

January 29: preparation of walls at the Detroit museum begins.

February: Joseph Freeman's article "Painting and Politics: The Case of Diego Rivera," essentially a Communist Party attack on Rivera, appears in *New Masses*. Rivera is denounced as a "renegade" at a John Reed Club meeting in New York.

March 31: world premiere in Philadelphia of the ballet *H.P. (Horse Power)*, conducted by Leopold Stokowski.

March 31: the Ford Motor Company's new V8 model, whose manufacture and production Rivera will paint at Detroit, goes on nationwide display.

April 21: Rivera and Kahlo arrive in Detroit and stay in a hotel across the street from the museum.

May and June: tours and sketches at the Ford Motor Company's Rouge plant and other industrial sites.

Orozco begins his mural at Dartmouth College, Hanover, New Hampshire (completed February 1934).

May 23: the Detroit arts commission approves sketches for the large panels on the north and south walls of the Garden Court; at the end of the month, Rivera requests permission to paint all twenty-seven panels of the court.

June 10: contract signed between the Founders Society of the Detroit Institute of Arts and Rivera for the extended fresco

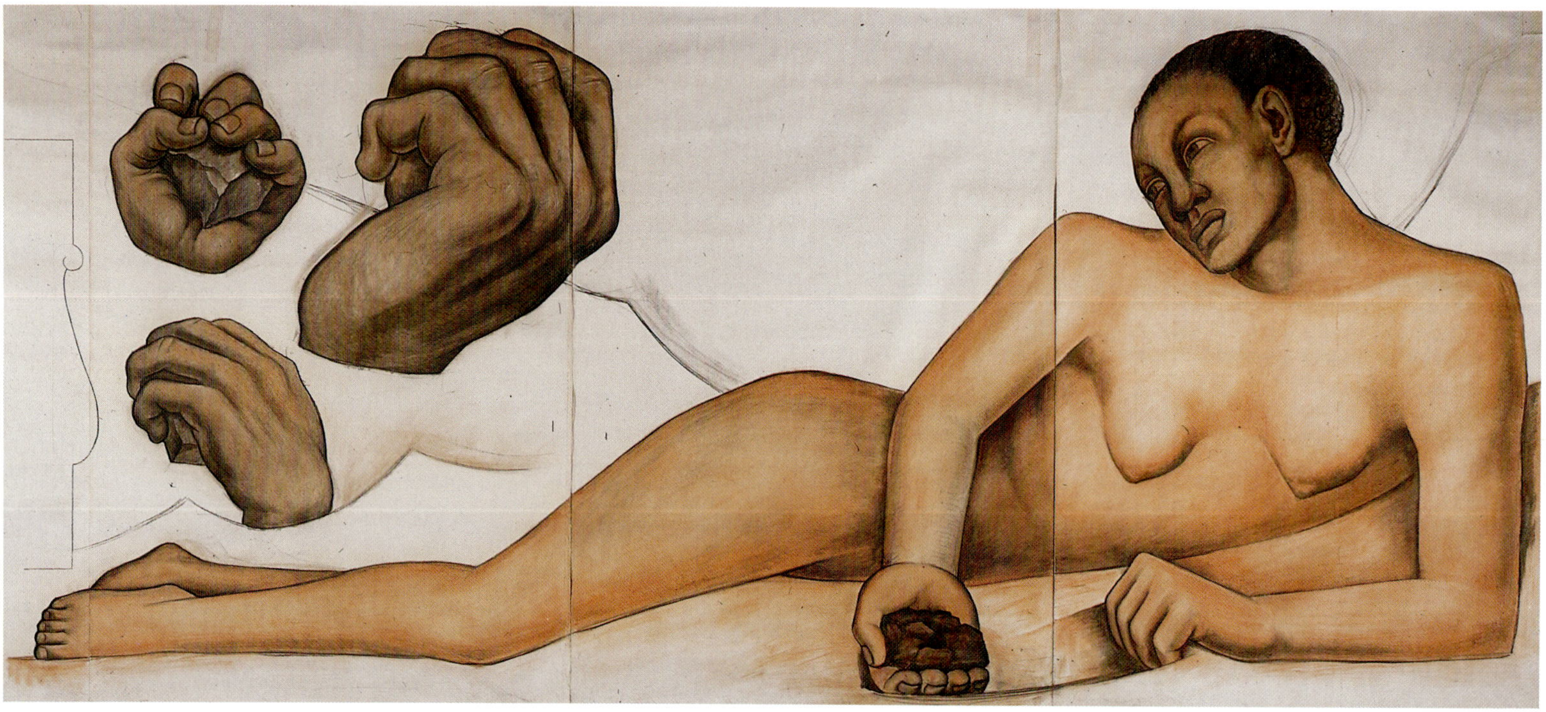

Figure 161
Figure Representing the Black Race, 1932, brown and red pigment with charcoal over light charcoal, 2.64 × 5.82 m. The Detroit Institute of Arts, Gift of the Artist (33.38). Cartoon for the north wall, *Detroit Industry,* Detroit Institute of Arts.

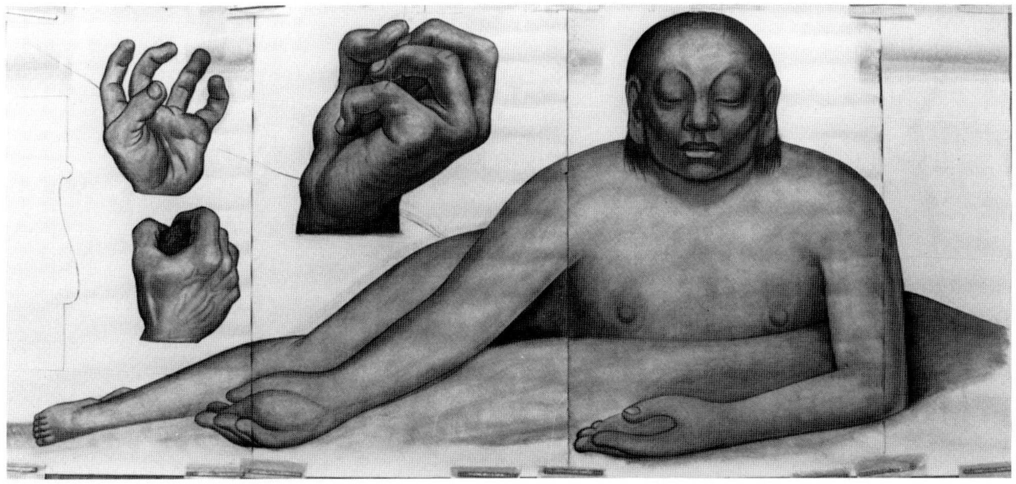

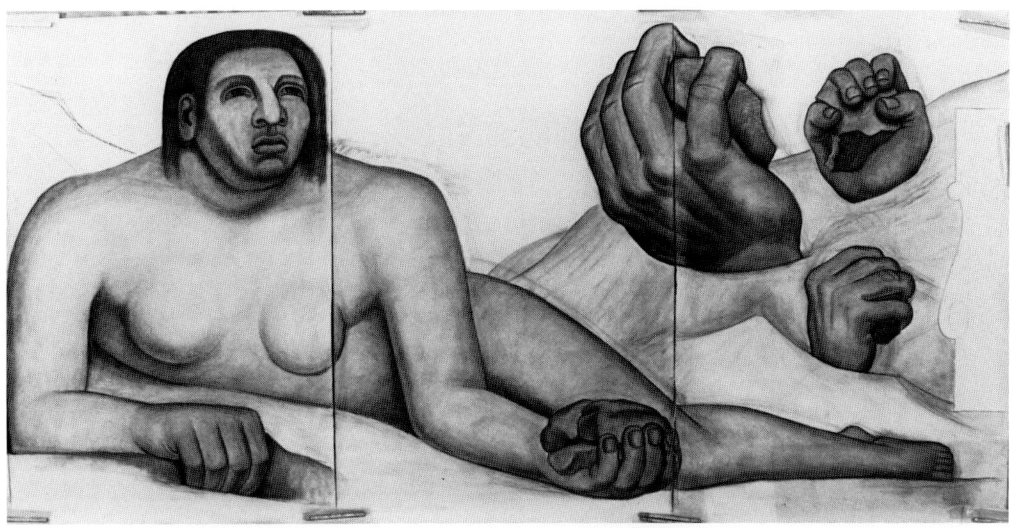

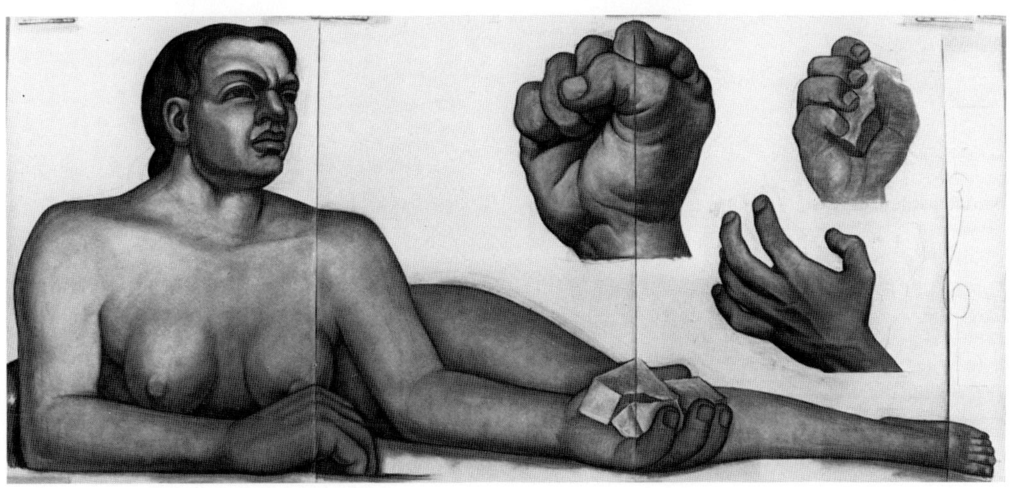

Figures 162, 163, 164
Figure Representing the Yellow Race, Figure Representing the Red Race, and *Figure Representing the White Race,* 1932, brown and red pigment with charcoal over light charcoal, 2.69 × 5.82 m., 2.70 × 5.85 m, 2.71 × 5.84 m. The Detroit Institute of Arts, Gift of the Artist (33.42, 33.45, 33.40). Cartoons for the north and south walls, *Detroit Industry,* Detroit Institute of Arts.

Figures 165, 166
Woman Holding Fruit and *Woman Holding Grain,* 1932, red and brown pigment with charcoal over light charcoal, 2.55 × 2.21 m and 2.55 × 2.20 m. The Detroit Institute of Arts, Gift of the Artist (33.44, 33.43). Cartoons for the east wall, *Detroit Industry,* Detroit Institute of Arts.

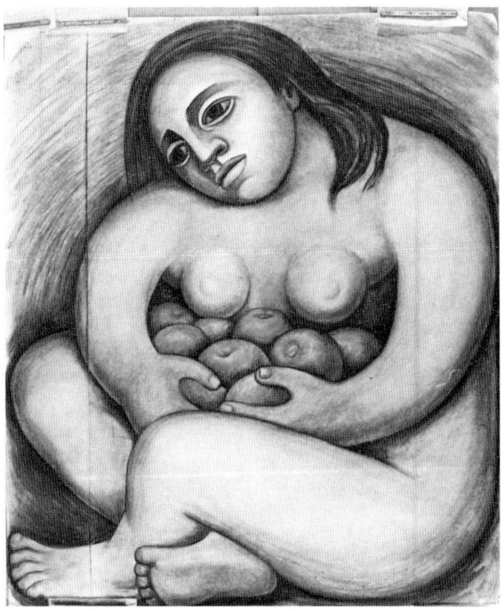

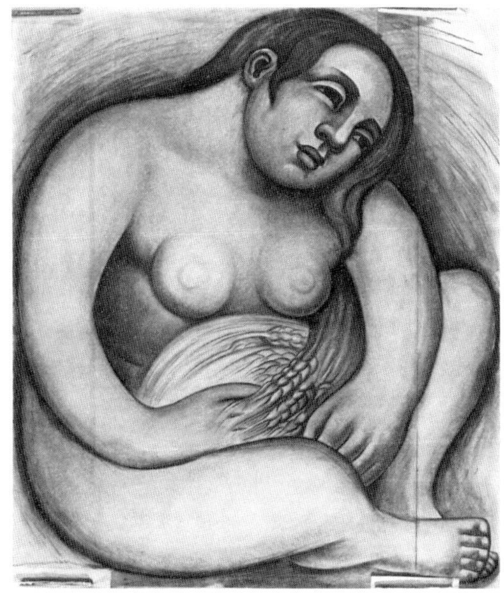

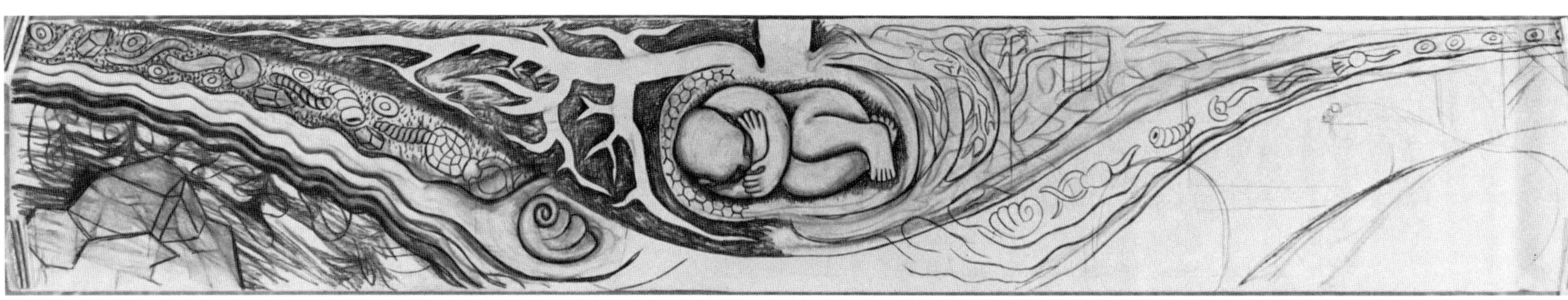

Figures 167
Infant in the Bulb of a Plant, 1932, charcoal with brown pigment over light charcoal, 1.33 × 7.92 m. The Detroit Institute of Arts, Gift of the Artist (33.35). Cartoon for the east wall, *Detroit Industry,* Detroit Institute of Arts.

Figure 168, 169
Commercial Chemical Operations and *Pharmaceutics,* 1932, charcoal, 2.53 × 2.20 m and 2.54 × 2.20 m. The Detroit Institute of Arts, Gift of the Artist (33.46 and 33.37). Cartoons for the south wall, *Detroit Industry,* Detroit Institute of Arts.

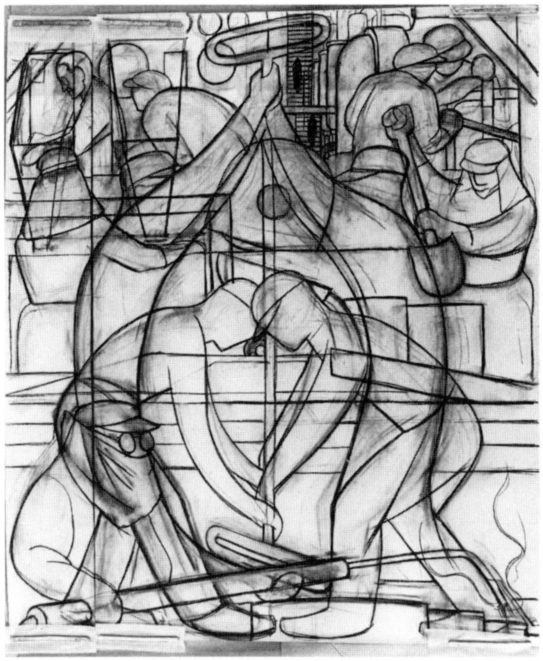

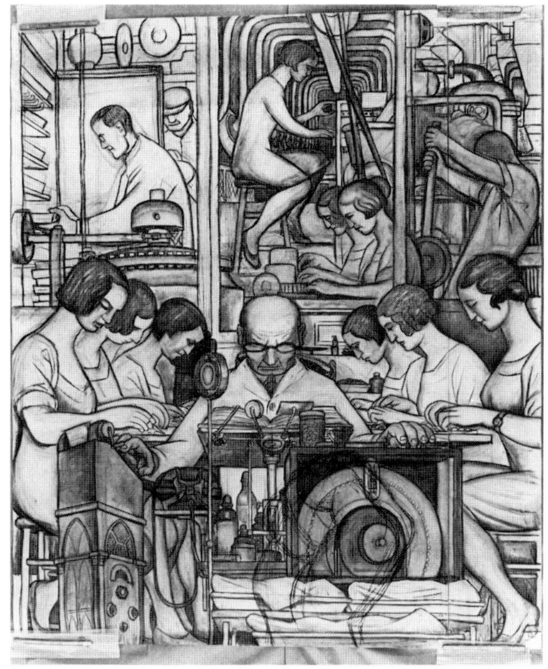

Figures 170, 171
Vaccination, 1932, charcoal with red pigment over light charcoal, 2.55 × 2.20 m, and *Manufacture of Poisonous Gas Bombs,* 1932, charcoal, 2.55 × 2.19 m. The Detroit Institute of Arts, Gift of the Artist (33.41, 33.36). Cartoons for the north wall, *Detroit Industry,* Detroit Institute of Arts.

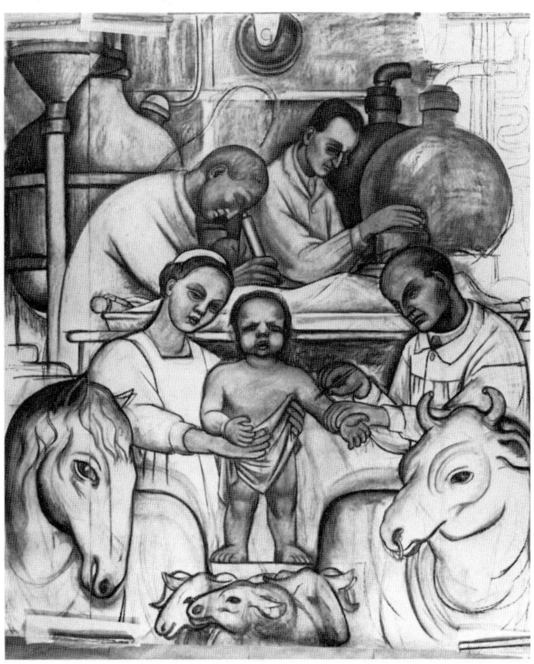

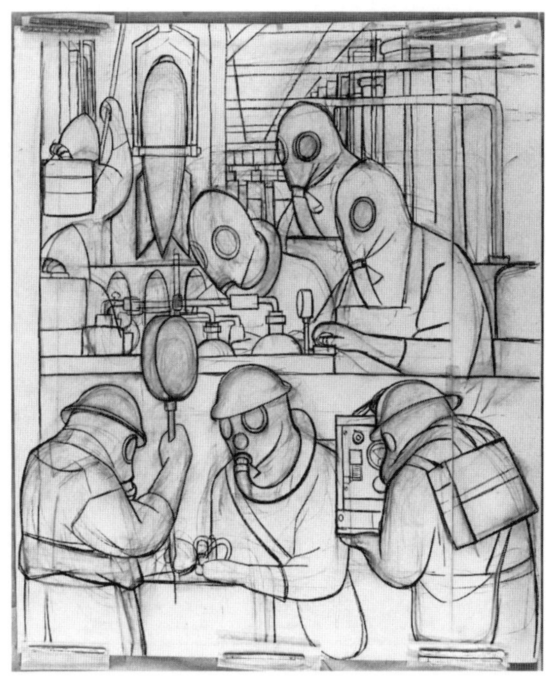

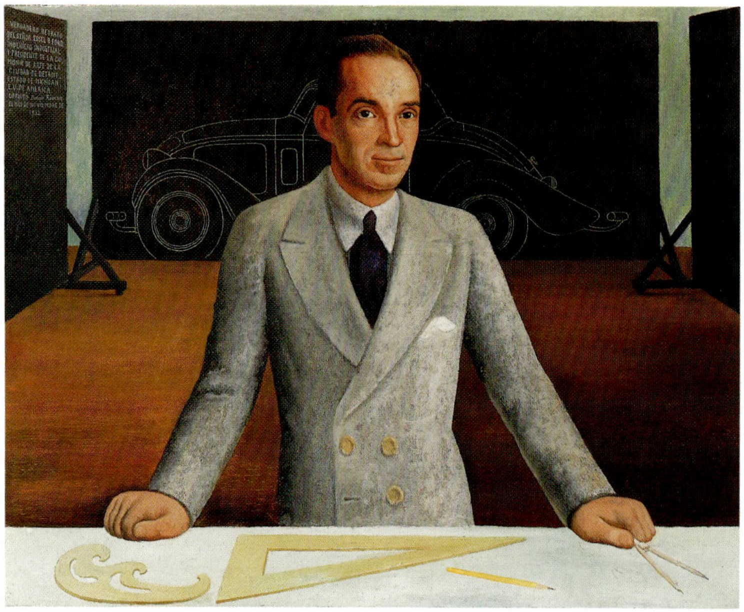

Figure 172
Portrait of Edsel B. Ford, 1932, oil on canvas, 97.8 × 125.1 cm. The Detroit Institute of Arts, Bequest of Eleanor Clay Ford (77.5).

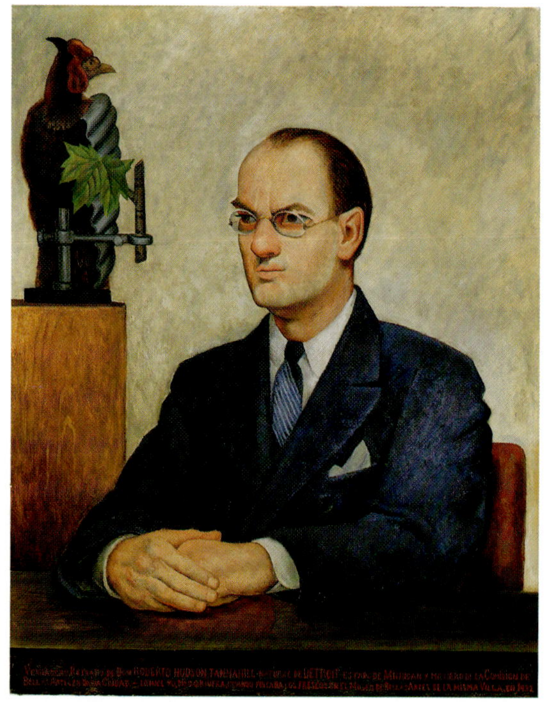

Figure 173
Portrait of Robert H. Tannahill, 1932, oil on canvas, 88.3 × 69.9 cm. The Detroit Institute of Arts, Bequest of Robert H. Tannahill (70.187).

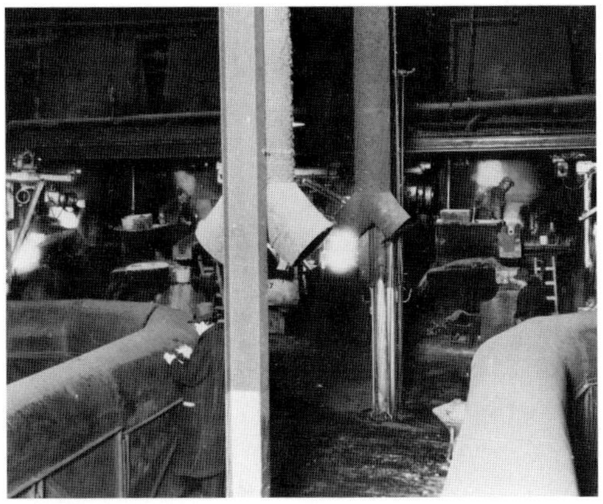

Figure 174
Rivera (left of center in hat) sketching at the Ford Motor Company's Rouge plant.

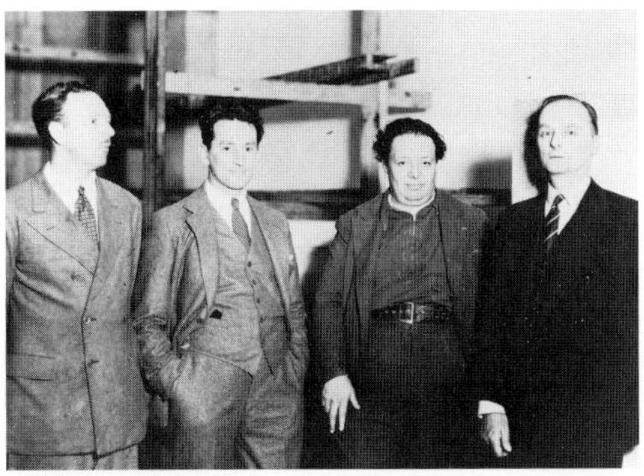

Figure 175
Rivera; Dr. William R. Valentiner, director of the Detroit Institute of Arts; and Rivera's assistants, Clifford Wight and John Viscount Hastings, ca. 1932.

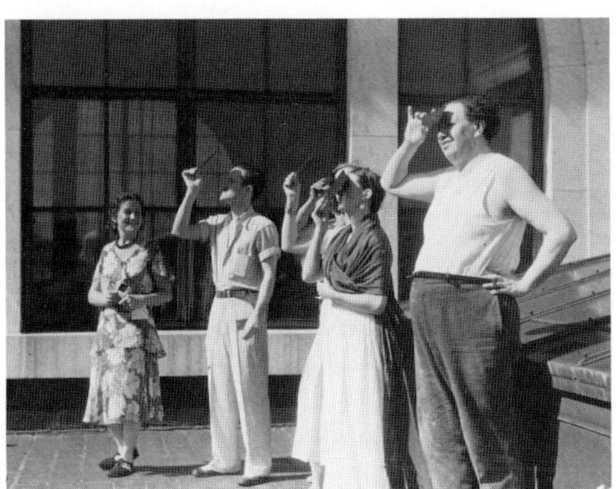

Figure 176
Lucienne Bloch, Arthur Niendorf, Jean Wight, an unidentified woman, Frida Kahlo, and Rivera watching an eclipse on the roof of the Detroit Institute of Arts, August 1932.

project, *Detroit Industry* (funded by Edsel B. Ford, son of Henry Ford and president of both the Ford Motor Company and the arts commission). Rivera begins painting; he is assisted by Clifford Wight, Andrés Sánchez Flores, John Viscount Hastings, Arthur S. Niendorf, Ernst Halberstadt, Stephen Pope Dimitroff, and Lucienne Bloch.

Due to depression-induced budget reductions, the museum's curatorial staff is let go and Valentiner takes a yearlong leave of absence.

During the summer, a vegetarian and acid-fruit diet causes Rivera to lose 100 pounds.

July 4: Kahlo miscarries at Henry Ford Hospital.

July 25: Rivera begins painting the upper registers in the Garden Court.

August 24: at Edsel Ford's request, W. T. Stettler, a Ford Motor Company photographer, documents the mural project with photographs and film.

September 4: after receiving word that her mother is ill, Kahlo, accompanied by Lucienne Bloch, travels to Mexico by train.

October 10: Rivera, Frank Brangwyn, and José María Sert are commissioned to create nine murals in the main corridor of the lobby of the RCA Building in New York, which is then under construction. The paintings are to be done on canvas and delivered by April 1933.

Mid-October: Kahlo returns to Detroit.

November 15: Rivera goes briefly to New York to complete negotiations for the RCA project.

November: Siqueiros is deported from the United States, after painting three murals in Los Angeles in 1932.

Rivera paints portraits of Edsel B. Ford (fig. 172) and Robert H. Tannahill (fig. 173) and creates several lithographs with Mexican themes.

1933

January: Raymond Hood, architect for the RCA project, approves Rivera's mural design (fig. 395) while on a visit to Detroit.

February: Rivera views mural site in the RCA Building for the first time and drastically alters the approved design. The result is a far more explicit commentary on the evils of capitalism and the positive aspects of socialism.

March 13: Detroit murals completed.

March 18: the Detroit murals are officially dedicated and are visited by more than eighty-six thousand visitors in March alone. Conservative clergy, journalists, and politicians raise charges of Communist content, sacrilegious subjects, and the unsuitability of the industrial subject for a museum environment. Protest ends when Edsel Ford publicly supports the murals.

Late March: arrives in New York to begin work on the RCA mural, entitled *Man at the Crossroads Looking with Hope and High Vision to the Choosing of a New and Better Future.* His assistants are Bloch, Dimitroff, Sánchez Flores, and Niendorf; begins to paint at the RCA Building and admits he expects criticism of the mural's political content.

April: Abby Aldrich Rockefeller visits the mural site and praises the section depicting the Soviet May Day demonstrations.

April 24: a *World-Telegraph* article appears with the headline "Rivera Perpetrates Scenes of Communist Activity for RCA Walls—and Rockefeller Jr. Foots the Bill." Other criticisms in the press follow.

May 4: Nelson Rockefeller asks Rivera to replace the face of Lenin with that of an anonymous individual.

May 6: Rivera offers to substitute Abraham Lincoln and other 19th-century North American figures for a group of individuals opposite Lenin, but states that "rather than mutilate the conception I should prefer the physical destruction of the composition in its entirety, but preserving, at least, its integrity."[6]

May 9: the RCA management firm of Todd-Robertson-Todd dismisses Rivera, triggering "the Battle of Rockefeller Center"; the forced cessation of work on the murals incites political protests that receive national and international press coverage. The Communist Party USA continues to denounce Rivera's "opportunism."

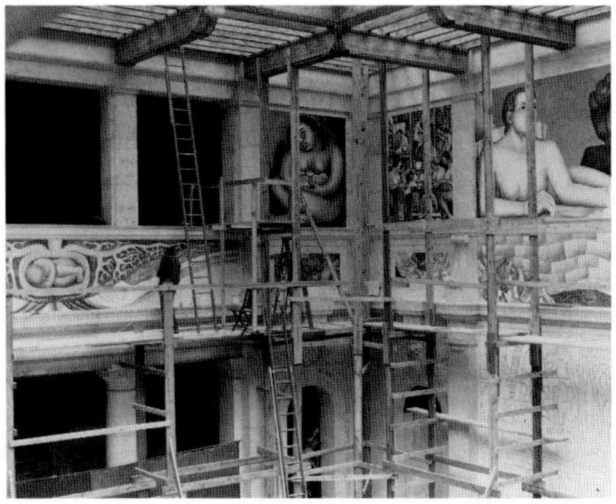

Figure 177
Rivera painting the east wall at the Detroit Institute of Arts, 1932.

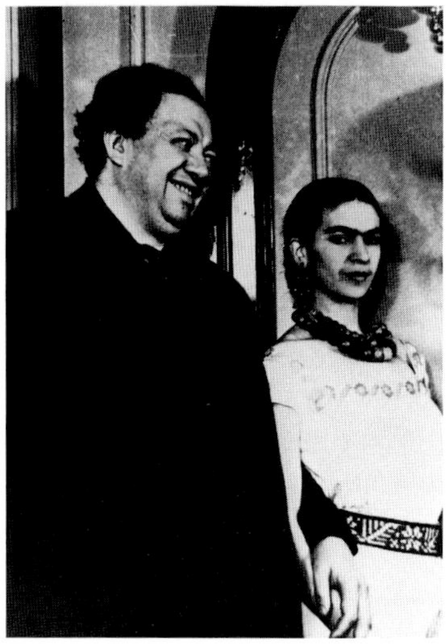

Figure 178
Frida and Diego in New York, 1932. Photo by Carl Van Vechten.

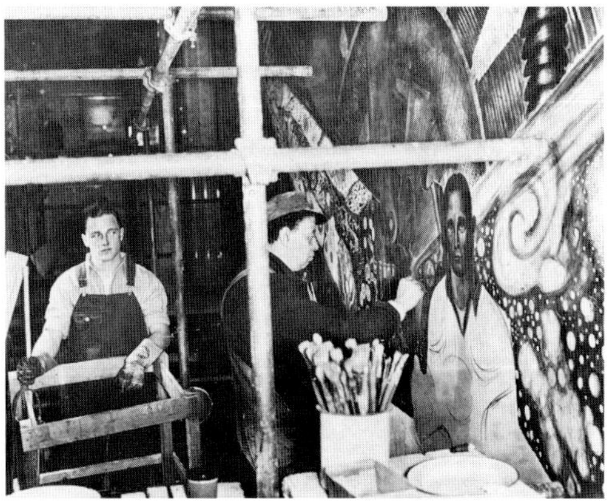

Figure 179
Hugh Curry, Jr., a grand-nephew of Tammany Hall leader John F. Curry and a watchman in the RCA Building, poses for the central figure in the RCA mural, April 1933.

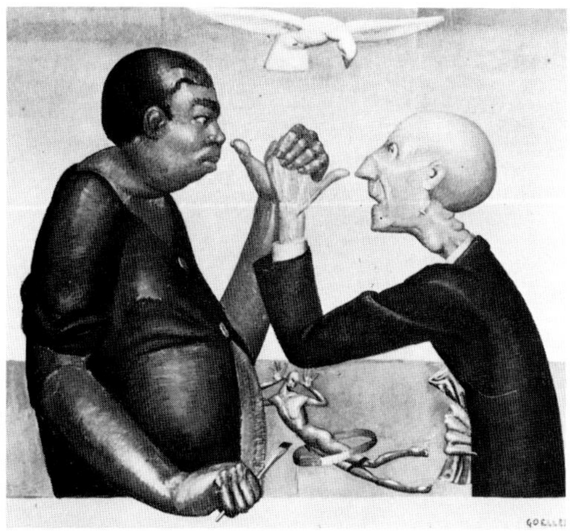

Figure 180
Caricature of Rivera and John D. Rockefeller.

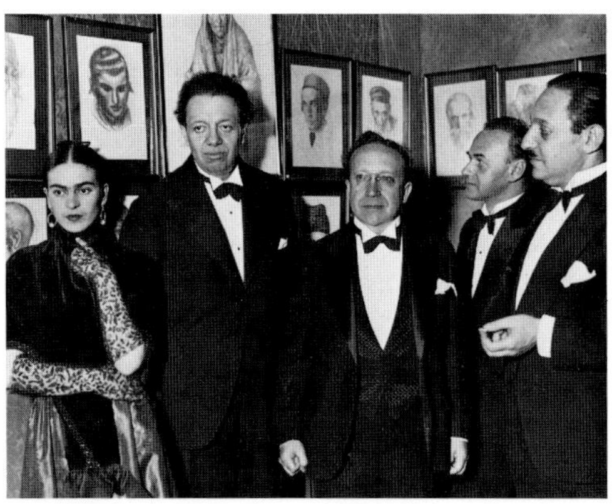

Figure 181
Kahlo; Rivera; Henry Hurwitz, editor of the *Menorah Journal;* Gilbert Seldes, journalist; and Lee Simonson of the Theatre Guild at an exhibition of Jewish portraits by Lionel Reiss, May 1933. The intent of the exhibition was to disprove the Nazis' anti-Semitic theories.

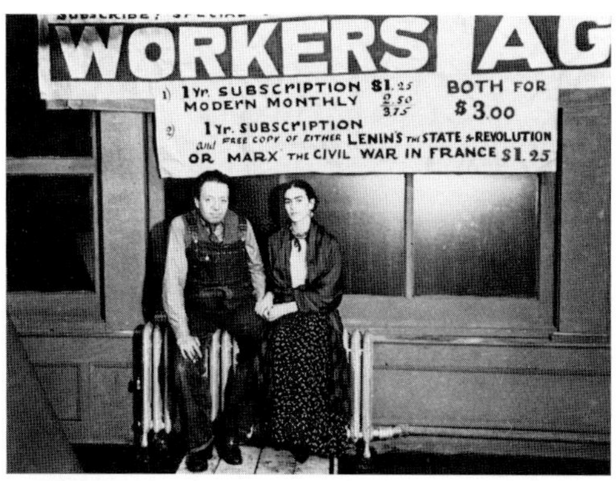

Figure 182
Rivera and Kahlo seated beneath an advertisement for the journal *Worker's Age.* Photo by Lucienne Bloch.

May 11: the RCA mural is covered with canvas painted to match the adjoining blank wall.

May 12: General Motors cancels Rivera's commission for a mural in the corporation's building at the 1933 Chicago World's Fair, bringing to an apparent end his patronage by the capitalist establishment in the United States.

June: agrees to paint a series of twenty-one fresco panels, his *Portrait of America,* for the Communist Party Opposition (anti-Stalinist) at the New Workers School, which is directed by his close friend and future biographer Bertram D. Wolfe.

July 15: Rivera begins painting at the New Workers School. His assistants include Bloch, Dimitroff, Sánchez Flores, as well as Ben Shahn, Lou Block, Hideo Noda, and Arthur Niendorf. This vitriolic series has as its theme contemporary political conditions and the development of revolutionary traditions in the United States.

August 22: receives a commission to execute murals at the new Escuela Nacional de Medicina in Mexico City (this project, however, does not materialize).

December 5: New Workers School farewell reception for Rivera.

December 8–10: public showing of the New Workers School panels and nightly lectures by Rivera.

Completes two small fresco panels for the Communist League of America, a Trotskyite center in New York; his themes are the October Revolution and the IV International (Trotsky's political organization, formed to oppose Stalin).

December 20: Rivera and Kahlo sail for Mexico and on arrival move into their newly finished residence in San Angel.

December 1933–June 1934: the first New Deal art program, in the United States, the Public Works of Art Project (PWAP). The PWAP mural project owed its genesis to the example of the government-supported Mexican mural program, since it was this example that led artist George Biddle to suggest to President Roosevelt that a similar program of direct public patronage be established for United States artists.

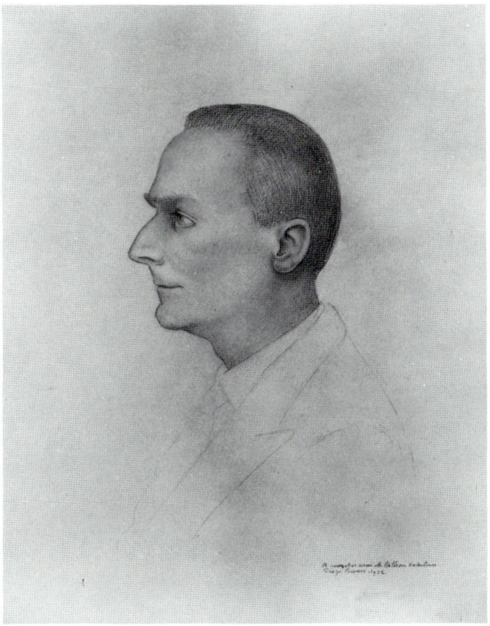

Figure 183
Portrait of William R. Valentiner, 1932, red chalk and pencil, 68.5 × 53.5 cm. North Carolina Museum of Art, Bequest of William R. Valentiner (G.65.10.55).

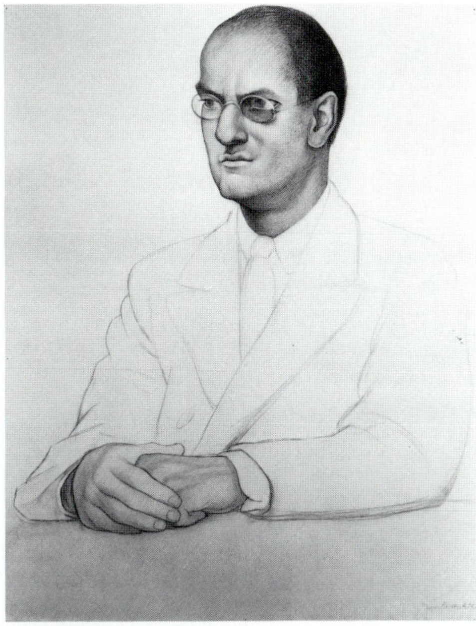

Figure 184
Portrait of Robert H. Tannahill, 1932, red and black chalk, 73 × 57.9 cm. The Detroit Institute of Arts, Bequest of Robert H. Tannahill (70.332).

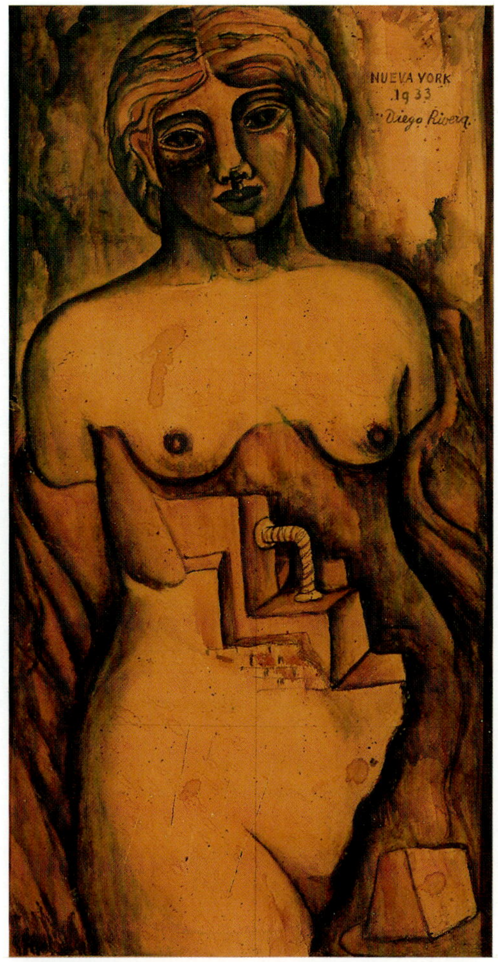

Figure 185
Maternidad mecánica, 1933, watercolor, 47 × 25 cm. Collection of Dolores Olmedo. According to a letter Rivera sent with this drawing to the Mexican Communist poet Carlo Gutierrez Cruz, the drawing "Mechanized Motherhood" was intended as a criticism of the capitalist system's use of machinery as a means for exploiting mankind.

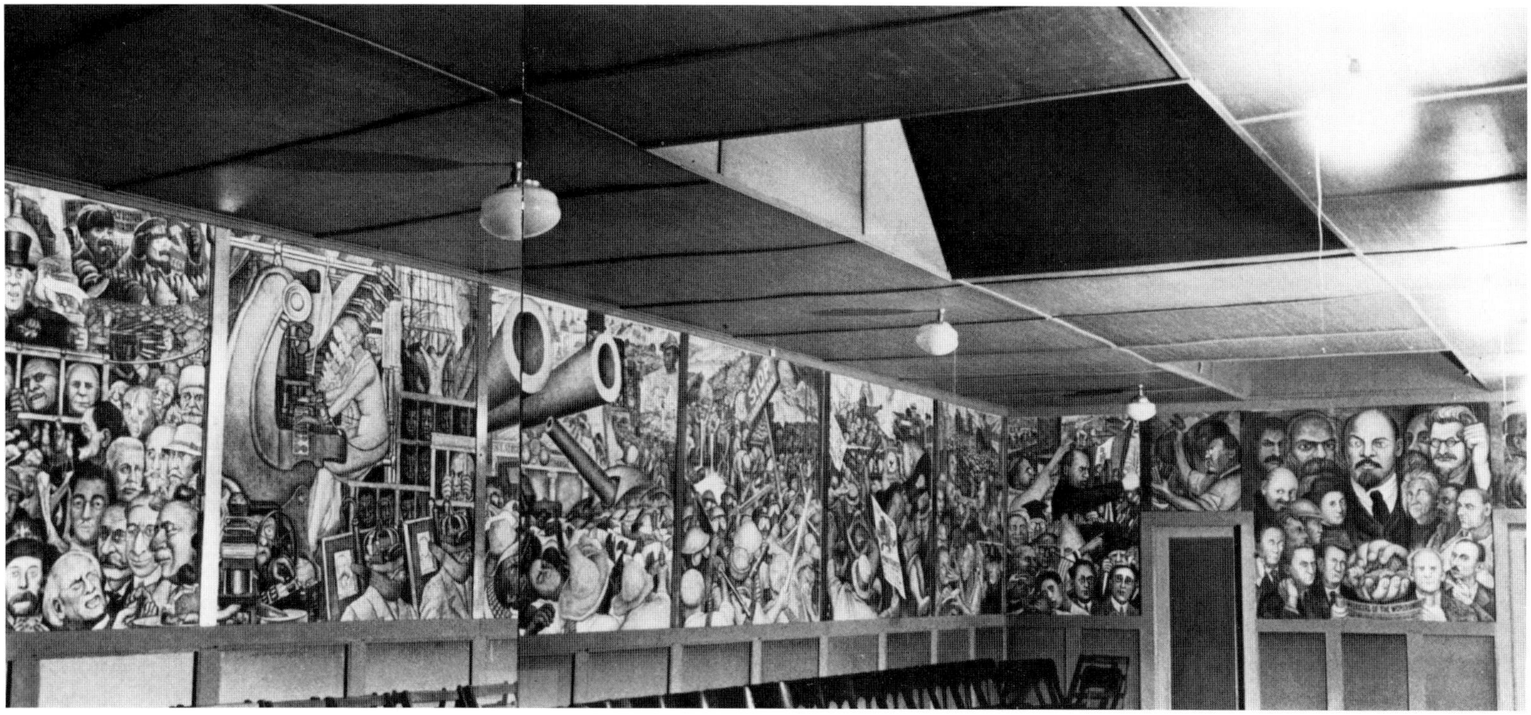

Figure 186
New Workers School
murals, 1933. Photo by
Lucienne Bloch.

V.
Return to Mexico

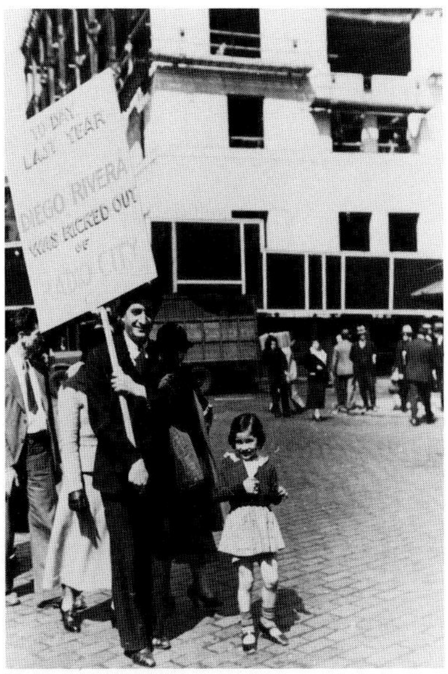

Figure 187
Pickets in New York City on the anniversary of the "Battle of Rockefeller Center," 1934. Photo by Lucienne Bloch.

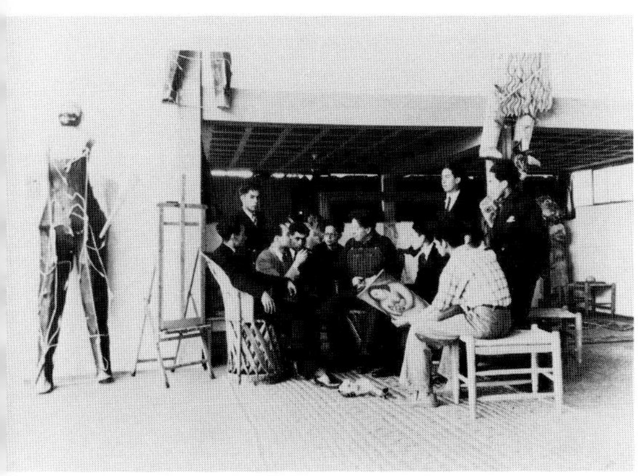

Figure 188
Rivera meeting with the executive committee of the Mexican Communist Party in his studio, ca. 1934/35.

1934

Back in Mexico, Rivera suffers from poor health and depression and does no work for several months.

February 10–11: RCA murals are destroyed. In protest the American Society of Painters, Sculptors, and Engravers and several artists, among them Ben Shahn, Lou Block, and David Margolis, withdraw from the Municipal Art Show at Rockefeller Center, which they then picket.

March: The *Liga de Escritorés y Artistas Revolucionarios* (LEAR, League of Revolutionary Artists and Writers) is founded in Mexico City by Leopoldo Méndez, Juan de la Cabada, and Pablo O'Higgins as a working collective in opposition to fascism and war. They publish a periodical, *Frente a frente* (Face to Face) with the slogan *"ni con Calles ni con Cárdenas"* (neither with Calles nor with Cárdenas). The league attracts both Mexican and U.S. artists. Rivera is an adviser to LEAR.

May 29: Siqueiros's diatribe in *New Masses* denounces Rivera as "saboteur of the collective work."

June 14: Rivera signs a contract to reproduce the RCA murals on a wall at the Palacio de Bellas Artes in Mexico City.

November: begins the final stairway wall, *Mexico Today and Tomorrow*, at the Palacio Nacional. His original sketch (see fig. 189) had shown workers and farmers employing industrial technology to construct a modern Mexico, which he now changes to create a far more politically oriented theme proclaiming the necessity of a Marxist revolution to transform Mexican society.

November 30: Lázaro Cárdenas installed as president of Mexico. Beginning of liberal government reform; by 1940 the Cárdenas administration will have distributed forty-nine million acres of land among one-third of the Mexican population and nationalized the oil industry.

Rivera begins his smaller version of the RCA mural.

Orozco paints the mural *Catharsis* opposite Rivera's mural at the Palacio de Bellas Artes.

Publication of the Wolfe-Rivera collaboration, *Portrait of America*, which becomes a best-seller.

In San Francisco a group of Rivera's assistants and friends paint a series of murals inside the Coit Tower for the PWAP.

1935

Continues working on the stairway at the Palacio Nacional, which he completes on November 20. He also creates a series of watercolors on Tehuantepec themes and the easel paintings *Delfina and Dimas* (fig. 195), *The Flower Carrier* (fig. 193), and *La pepenadora*.

LEAR commissioned by the federal government to decorate the walls of the newly renovated Mercado Abelardo L. Rodríguez in the center of the city. Under the direction of Pablo O'Higgins, several Mexican and U.S. artists (including Ramón Alva Guadarrama, Antonio Pujol, Pedro Rendón, Miguel Tzab Trejo, Angel Bracho, Grace and Marion Greenwood, and Isamu Noguchi) decorate fifteen hundred square meters of wall space in ten months.

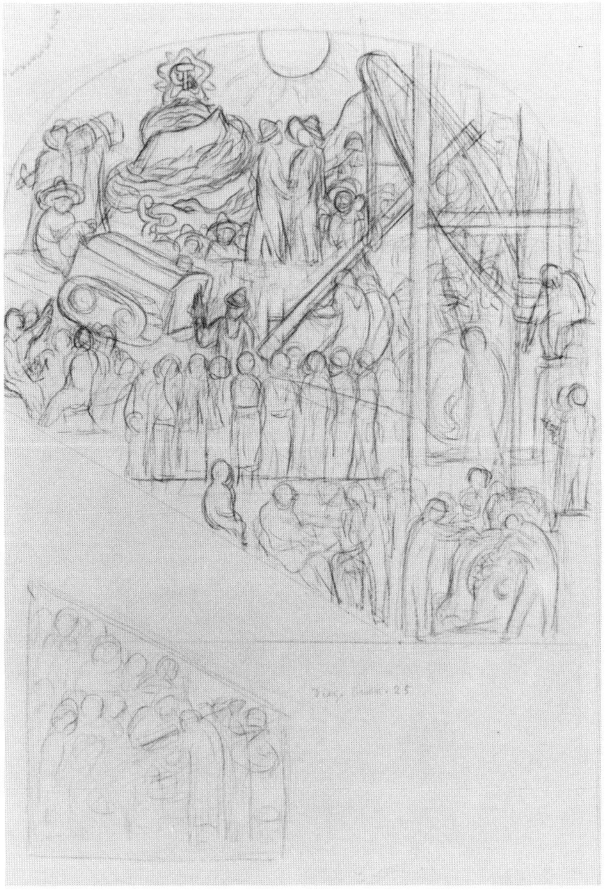

Figure 189
History of Mexico, 1926, pencil. Mexico City, Museo Tecnólogico, Comision Federal de Electricidad. Study for south wall of stairway, Palacio Nacional.

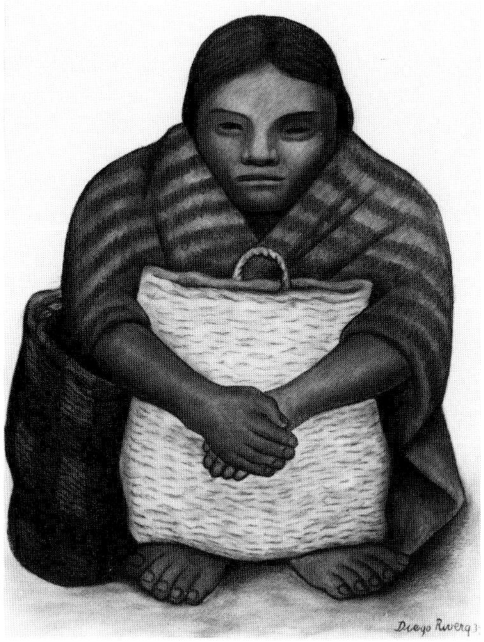

Figure 190
Mexican Woman with Basket, 1935, red and black chalk, 55.4 × 41.9 cm. San Francisco Museum of Modern Art, Albert M. Bender Collection, Gift of Albert M. Bender (35.3400).

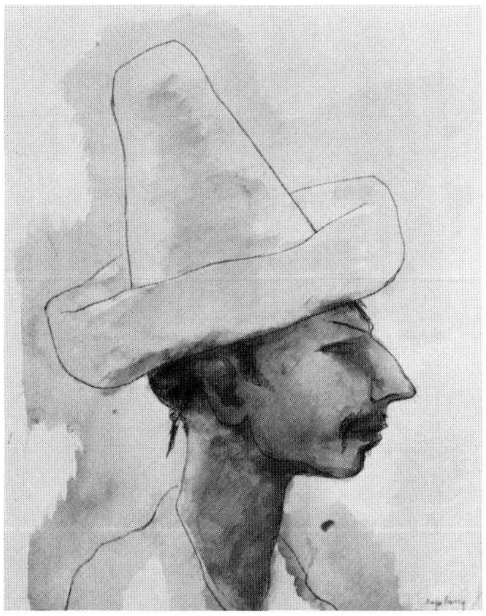

Figure 191
Head of a Man of Tehuantepec, 1935, charcoal and watercolor, 60.9 × 48.3 cm. The St. Louis Art Museum (29.35).

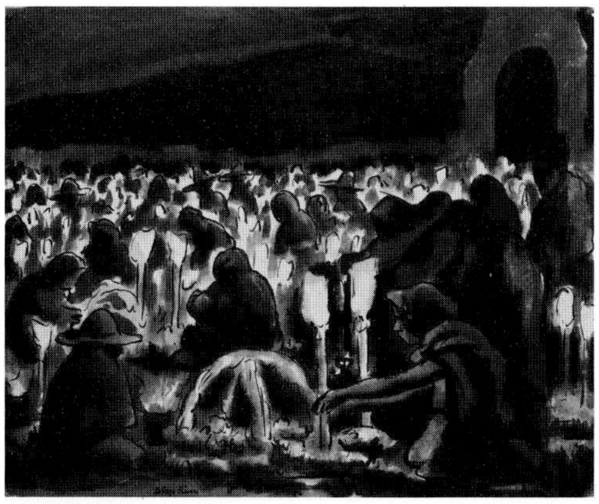

Figure 192
Night of the Dead, 1935, watercolor and black ink, 47.6 × 59 cm. Private Collection.

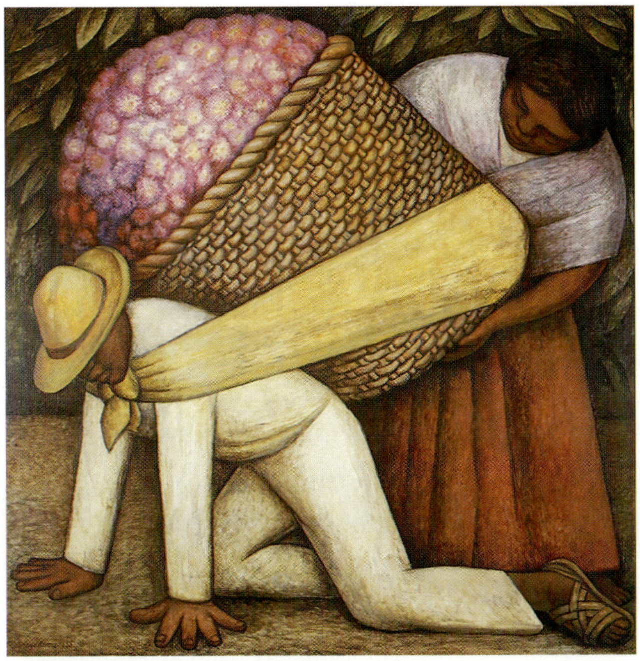

Figure 193
The Flower Carrier, formerly known as *The Flower Vendor,* 1935, oil and tempera on masonite, 121.9 × 121.3 cm. San Francisco Museum of Modern Art, Albert M. Bender Collection. Gift of Albert M. Bender in memory of Caroline Walter (35.4516). Rivera painted this compassionate study of a *cargador* (burden carrier) in response to a letter from his California patron A. M. Bender, announcing a contribution of five hundred dollars to the San Francisco Museum of Art for the purchase of a work by Rivera.

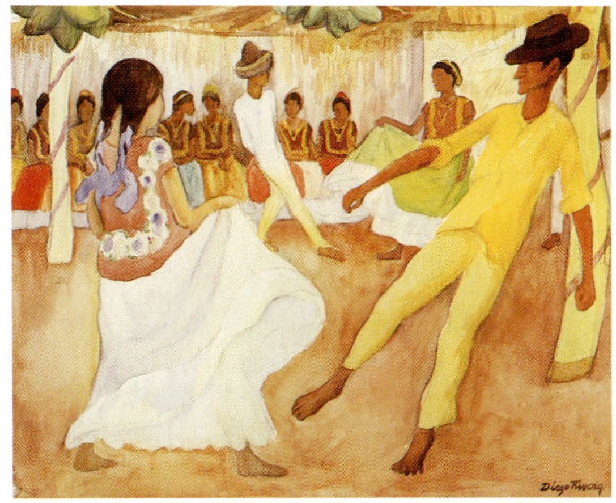

Figure 194
Zandunga, Tehuantepec Dance, ca. 1935, charcoal and watercolor, 48.1 × 60.6 cm. Los Angeles County Museum of Art, Gift of Mr. and Mrs. Milton W. Lipper from the Milton W. Lipper Estate (M.74.22.4).

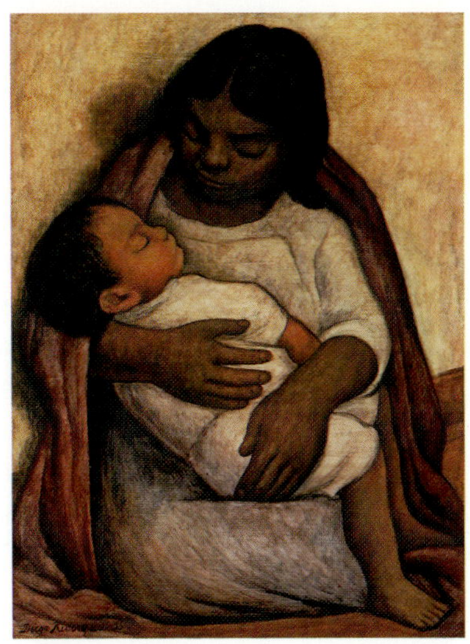

Figure 195
Delfina and Dimas, 1935, tempera on masonite, 80 × 59.4 cm. Private Collection.

Noguchi, who had come to Mexico on a Guggenheim grant, is commissioned to do a relief mural in polychrome cement and carved brick. Rivera is in charge of approving all designs for the murals. He is eventually accused by the artists of being conservative and pro-government.

July: Kahlo and Rivera separate for the first time; she travels to New York to begin a marriage of "mutual independence."

August: during the meetings of the North American Conference of the New Education Fellowship, Siqueiros and Rivera, brandishing pistols, attack each other with inflammatory rhetoric.

October: in answer to Siqueiros's charge that he is a political opportunist, Rivera issues, for the first time in Mexico, a statement outlining his reasons for breaking with the Mexican Communist Party.

Begins a series of sketches of Mexican landscapes and popular customs (by 1940 he will have created hundreds of these in various media).

Alberto Misrachi becomes Rivera's dealer (until 1946). Over the next decade he will also act as mentor, accountant, and banker.

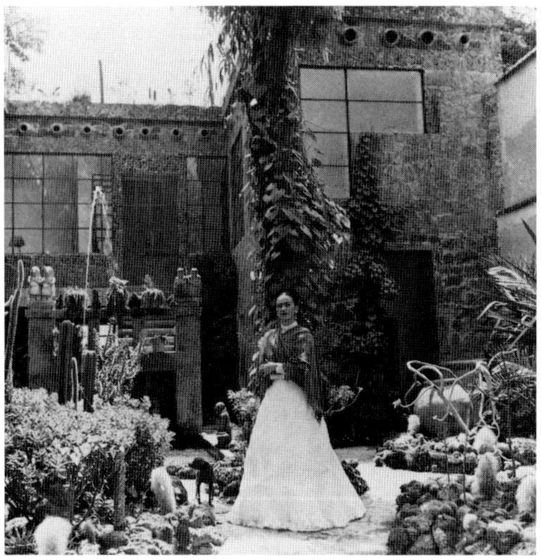

Figure 196
Kahlo in the garden at Coyoacán. Photo by Gisele Freund.

1936

January: LEAR commissioned by the *Sindicato de los Talleres Gráficos de la Nación* (Union of Graphic Workers of the Nation) to decorate the main stairway of the union hall in Mexico City. This is the first mural in Mexico commissioned by a union. The artists who participate are Pablo O'Higgins, Leopoldo Méndez, Alfredo Zalce, and Fernando Gamboa. The theme of the mural is the union struggle and the right to strike.

April: Siqueiros establishes his Experimental Workshop in New York; one of the young artists who works with him is Jackson Pollock.

Late May: Rivera is hospitalized due to a tear duct infection and has operations on both eyes. Later in the year, he will be hospitalized for weeks at a time with eye and kidney infections.

Summer: Alberto Pani, the politician and financier who had previously befriended Rivera in Europe, commissions murals on the theme of Mexican festivals for his new Hotel Reforma in Mexico City. Rivera paints four panels: *Dance of the Huichilobos, Agustín Lorenzo,* the satiric *Touristic and Folkloric Mexico,* and a political caricature of contemporary Mexico, *The Dictatorship*, including recognizable portraits of political, religious, and business leaders. Pani and his associates react by painting out some of the images. Rivera brings suit, wins, and is permitted to restore the works, but they are ultimately placed in storage and later sold to Misrachi.

Orozco begins the first of three murals in Guadalajara, which he will work on until 1939 (at the Universidad de Guadalajara, Palacio de Gobierno, and the Hospicio Cabañas).

September: Rivera joins the Trotskyite International Communist League.

November 21: receives a cable from writer Anita Brenner asking him to ascertain if Mexico would permit Trotsky immediate political asylum. Rivera and his political colleague Octavio Fernández seek out President Cárdenas, who agrees to give Trotsky refuge, but stipulates that he engage in no political activity while in Mexico.

After witnessing a fatal attack on a politician, Rivera paints *The Assassination of Altamirano.*

1937

Between 1937 and 1942, Rivera receives no public walls to paint in Mexico. Aside from his mural for the 1939 Golden Gate International Exposition, his artistic production of these years consists of a huge number of sketches, oils, watercolors, and portraits, including a series of paintings of popular genre scenes, reminiscent of his work in the early 1920s, as an outlet for his passionate interest in Mexican customs and folklore.

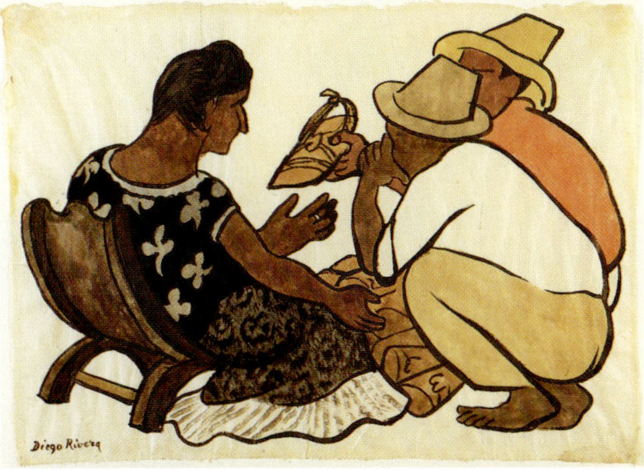

Figure 197
Huarache Sale, 1936, brush in black ink and watercolor, 26 × 37.5 cm. Los Angeles County Museum of Art, Gift of Mrs. Ewing Seligman (M.63.73).

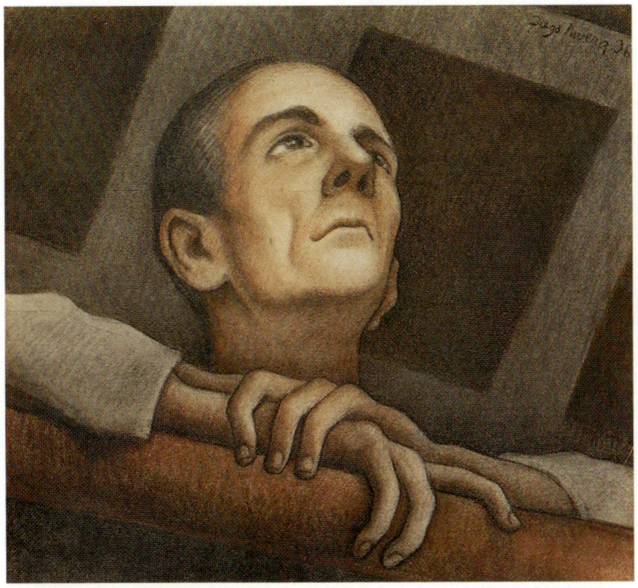

Figure 198
Portrait of a Man (Carlos Pellicer), 1936, pastel, 41 × 45 cm. Property of the State of Veracruz. The poet Carlos Pellicer was a friend of Rivera and secretary to José Vasconcelos during 1922. He later held many government positions related to the arts and was instrumental in organizing the Museo Frida Kahlo (1961) and the Museo Diego Rivera—Anahuacalli (1964). This portrait, with its unusual perspective, is related in tone and pose to the *Portrait of Edsel B. Ford,* 1932 (fig. 172).

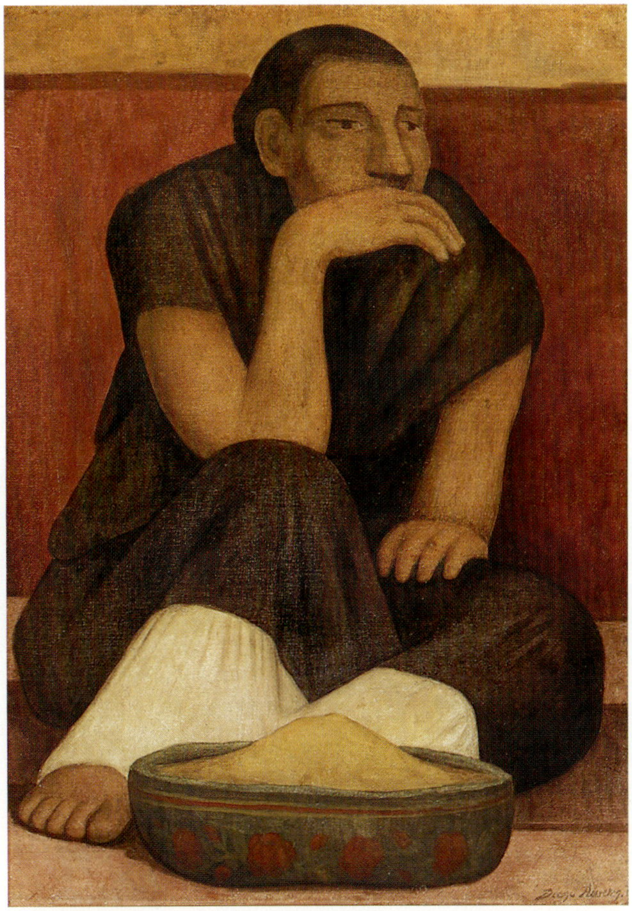

Figure 199
The Pinole Vendor, 1936, watercolor on canvas, 81.4 × 60.7 cm. Mexico City, Museo Nacional de Arte (INBA). In this monumental figure, seated behind a decorative *jicara* (gourd), Rivera has created a Mexican archetype.

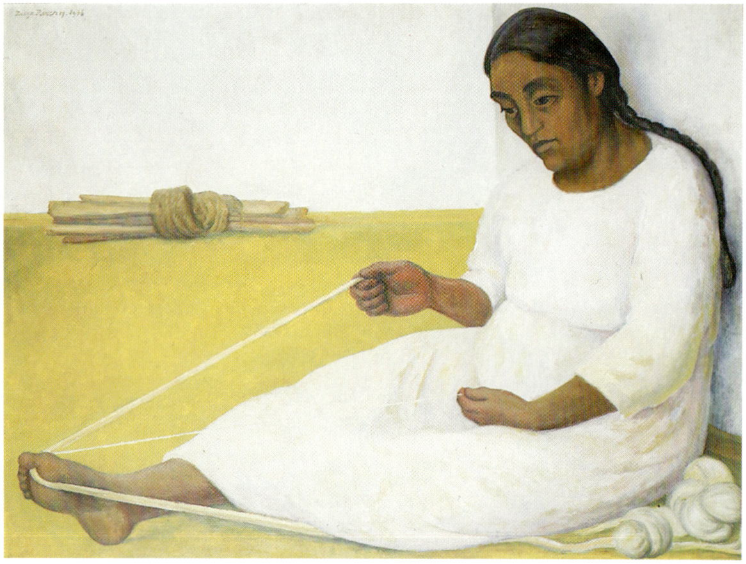

Figure 200
Indian Spinning, also known as *Indian Weaving,* 1936, oil on canvas, 59.7 × 81.3 cm. Phoenix Art Museum, Gift of Mrs. Clare Boothe Luce (68/29).

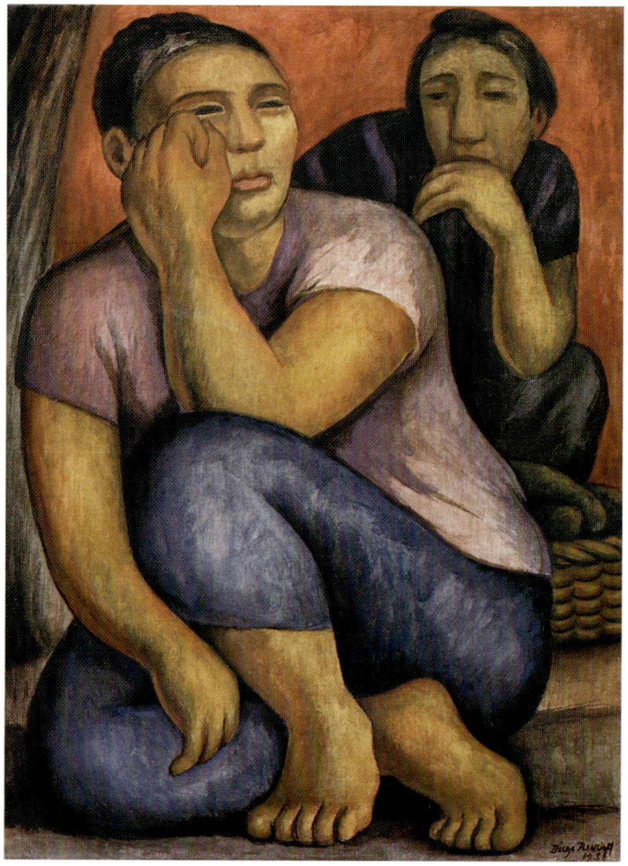

Figure 202
Seated Women, 1936, oil on linen, 80.7 × 60.5 cm. Private Collection. Related to *The Pinole Vendor,* this painting of two crouching women with masklike faces evokes the monumentality and timelessness of pre-Colombian sculpture.

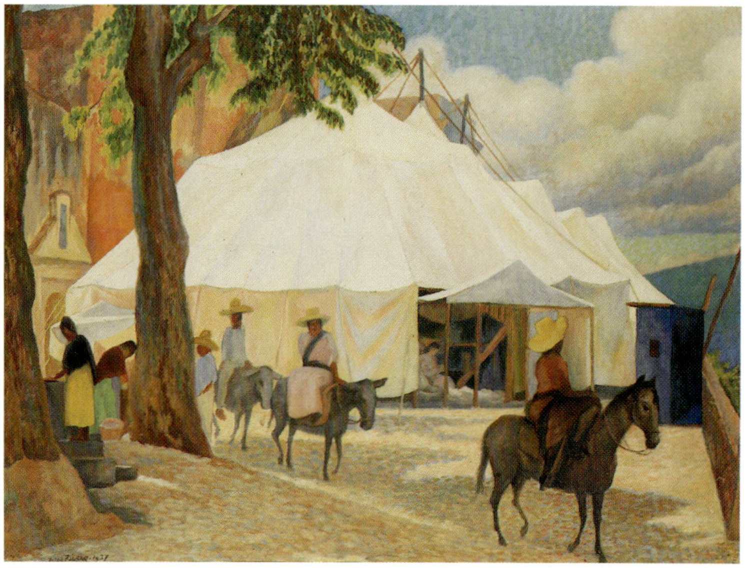

Figure 201
The Tent, 1937, oil on canvas, 54.8 × 80 cm. Collection of the Sollins Family.

Figure 203
Roots, 1937, watercolor on linen, 45.7 × 61.5 cm. Private Collection. Fascinated by the tuberous ferns found near Taxco, Rivera painted six watercolors of this subject on canvas. These works mark the beginning of his concentrated interest in the Mexican tradition of *arte fantástico.*

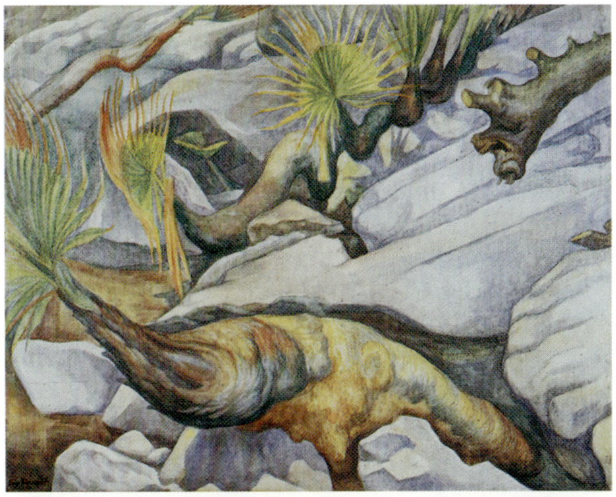

Figure 204
Tecalpexco, 1937, tempera on board, 58.4 × 80 cm. Amherst, Massachusetts, Amherst College, Mead Art Museum, Bequest of Mrs. Phillip Youtz (1975.93).

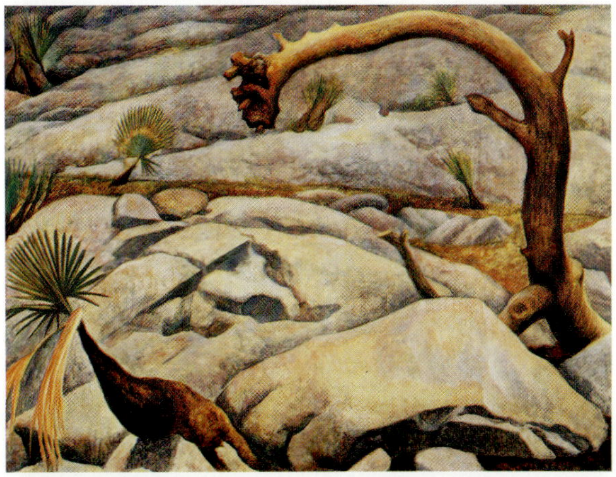

Figure 205
Copalli, 1937, oil on canvas, 91.5 × 114.5 cm. The Brooklyn Museum, Augustus A. Healy Fund (38.36).

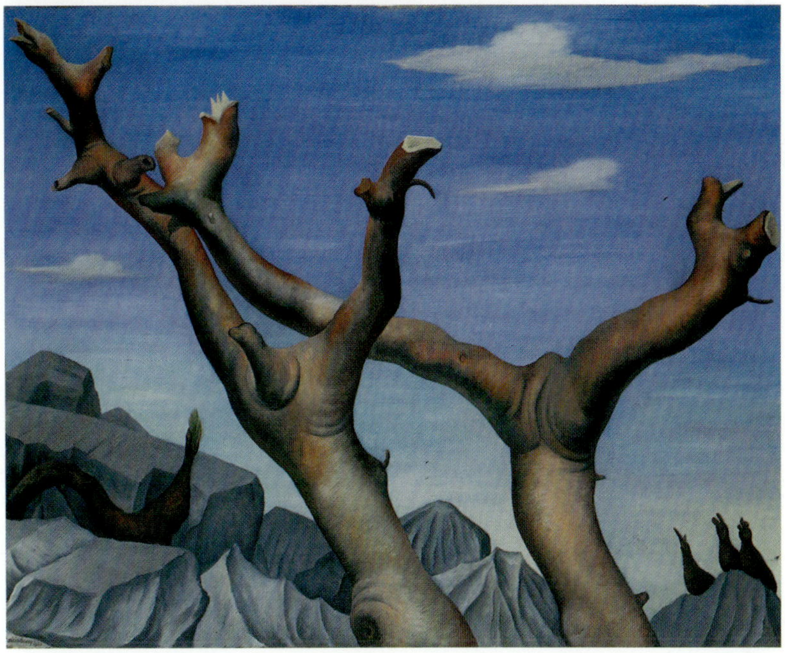

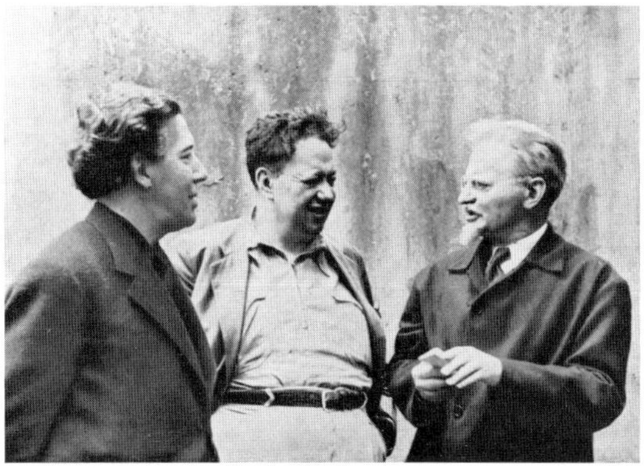

Figure 206
André Breton, Rivera, and Leon Trotsky, ca. 1938. Photo by Fritz Bach. Reproduced from the journal *Minotaure* 12–13 (1939).

January 9: Leon and Natalia Trotsky arrive at Tampico. They will live in the Riveras' Coyoacán home, which is reinforced against attack and guarded by Trotsky supporters, until 1939.

The Mexican Communist Party and *El machete* persist in their attacks on Rivera.

Paints six watercolors on canvas of the strange vegetation near the town of Taxco, including *Roots* (fig. 203) and *Tecalpexco* (fig. 204).

1938

April: André and Jacqueline Breton arrive in Mexico to explore the "surrealistic place *par excellence*."[7] They first stay with Guadalupe Marín, then with the Riveras at San Angel. The Riveras, the Bretons, and the Trotskys socialize and travel together.

June: the Riveras and the Bretons travel to Guadalajara.

July: the Riveras, the Bretons, and the Trotskys travel to Pátzcuaro in Michoacán with the intention of touring local villages by day and discussing art and politics in the evenings, then publishing their talks. Breton becomes enamored of Kahlo's work and offers to organize an exhibition for her in Paris.

In the August–September issue of *Partisan Review*, Trotsky praises Rivera's art.

LEAR dissolves.

Fall: Breton and Rivera sign the *Partisan Review* article "Manifesto: For a Free Revolutionary Art," which was actually written by Trotsky.

Exhibition of Rivera's work at the Galería de Arte Mexicano. Throughout his career, Rivera will maintain a close professional relationship with Inés Amor, the gallery's director and an important figure in the Mexican art world.

Personal and political conflicts develop between Rivera and Trotsky.

October: first issue of the Marxist periodical *Clave-tribuna libre* (Mexico City) appears. Rivera is a member of the editorial board.

November 1: Kahlo's first exhibition, twenty-five paintings at the Julien Levy Gallery, New York; among those attending are Clare Boothe Luce, Isamu Noguchi, and Georgia O'Keeffe.

Rivera delivers a paper at the Congress of the Confederation of General Workers, in which he denounces Stalin's role in the Spanish Civil War.

Eleven years after their separation, Rivera paints a portrait of Guadalupe Marín.

1939

January 7: Rivera resigns his membership on the *Clave* board.

January 11: Trotsky announces he no longer feels "moral solidarity" with Rivera's anarchistic ideas.

Kahlo sails from New York to Paris.

February: Kahlo hospitalized in Paris with a kidney inflammation. When released, she moves in with Mary Reynolds and Marcel Duchamp.

March 10: opening of Kahlo's exhibition at the gallery of Pierre Colle. Her work is well received by Picasso, Wassily Kandinsky, Juan Gris, and Yves Tanguy, among others.

April: Rivera and Trotsky reach a "parting of the ways," and the Trotskys move out of the Rivera/Kahlo home in Coyoacán.

Summer: Rivera and Kahlo separate and are divorced by the end of the year. Rivera continues to live in the San Angel studio, and he and Kahlo continue to see each other often.

August 7: the Mexican section of the IV International denounces Rivera for abandoning the ranks of socialism and supporting the conservative presidential candidate Juan Andreu Almazán.

Rivera begins a series of drawings and paintings of the American dancer Modelle Boss (see fig. 212) that exaggerate the sensuous qualities of her figure.

Siqueiros paints his first mural incorporating the technology of 20th-century industry (such as Duco paint and the airbrush) and revolutionary ideology, *Portrait of Fascism*, at the headquarters of the Mexican Electricians Union in Mexico City.

Figure 207
Mexican Peasant with Sombrero and Sarape, 1938, pastel, 61.6 × 47.6 cm. University of Texas at Austin, Harry Ransom Humanities Research Center, Mr. and Mrs. Dudley Smith Collection (78.24.13).

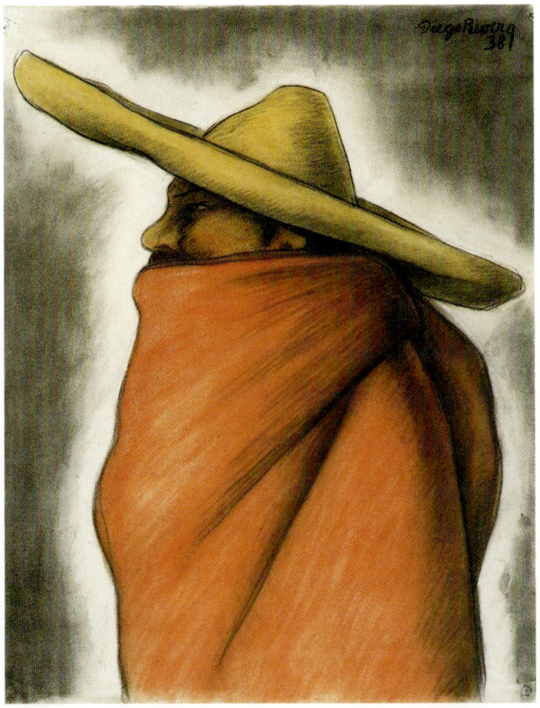

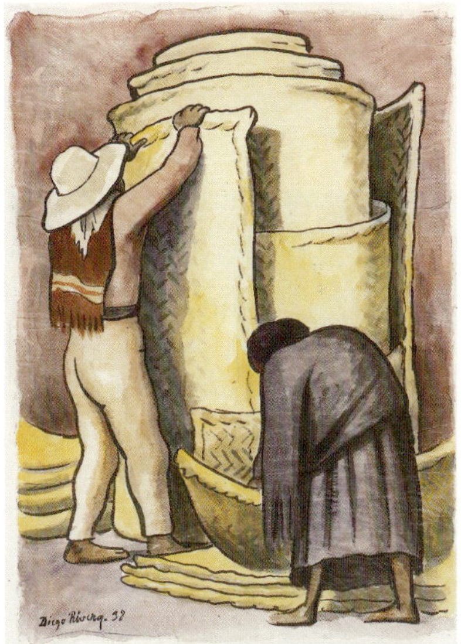

Figure 208
Petate Vendors, 1938, brush in black ink and watercolor, 38.1 × 27.9 cm. University of Texas at Austin, Harry Ransom Humanities Research Center, Mr. and Mrs. Dudley Smith Collection (78.24.6.1). A *petate* is a sleeping mat made of dried palm leaves or grass.

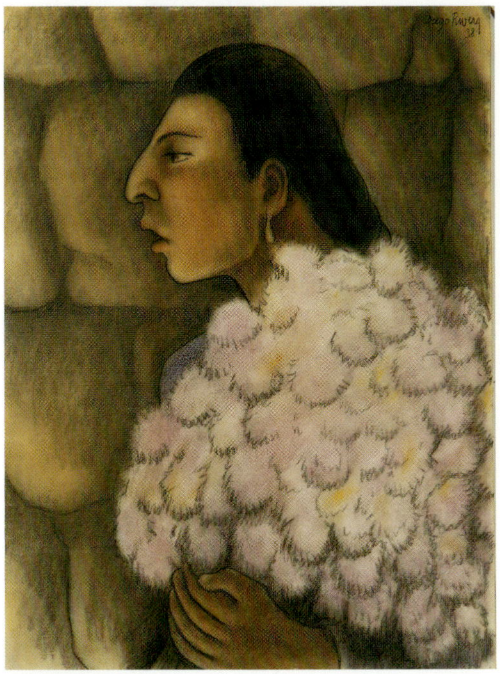

Figure 209
Profile of an Indian Woman with Lilacs, 1938, pastel and charcoal, 63.1 × 47.5 cm. Milwaukee Art Museum, Gift of Mr. and Mrs. Richard E. Vogt.

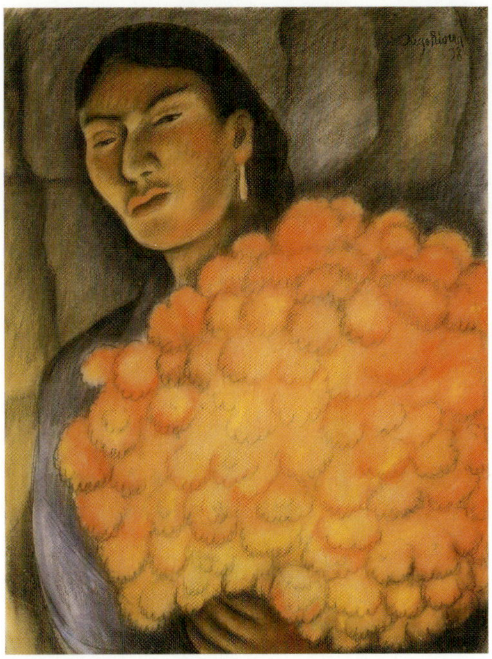

Figure 210
Indian Woman with Marigolds, 1938, pastel and charcoal, 63 × 48.5 cm. Collection of Dolores Olmedo.

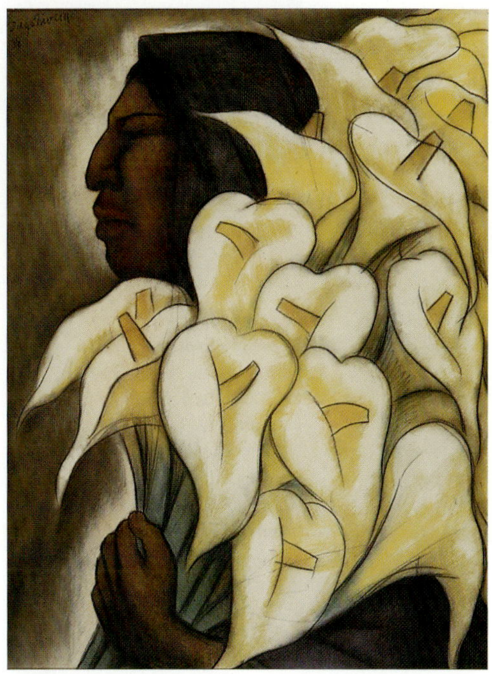

Figure 211
Profile of an Indian Woman with Calla Lilies, 1938, pastel and charcoal, 62.9 × 47.5 cm. Collection of Mr. and Mrs. Kenneth E. Hill.

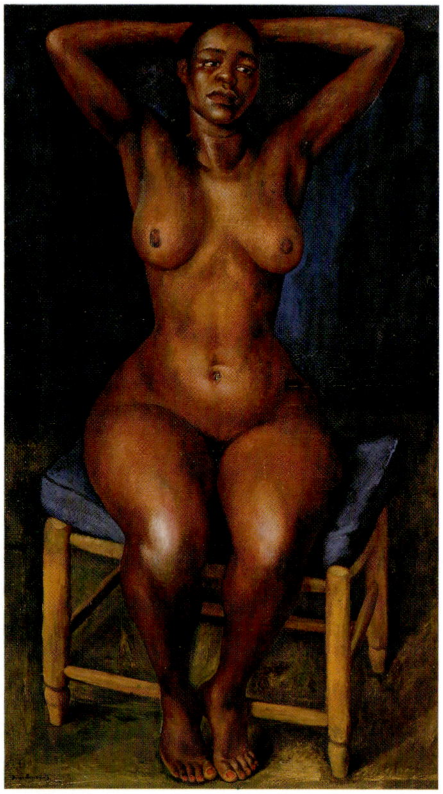

Figure 212
Dancer in Repose, 1939, oil on canvas, 164 × 94 cm. Collection of Dolores Olmedo. This is an early work in a series of increasingly abstracted images of the American dancer Modelle Boss, whom Rivera considered the embodiment of ideal beauty and sensuality.

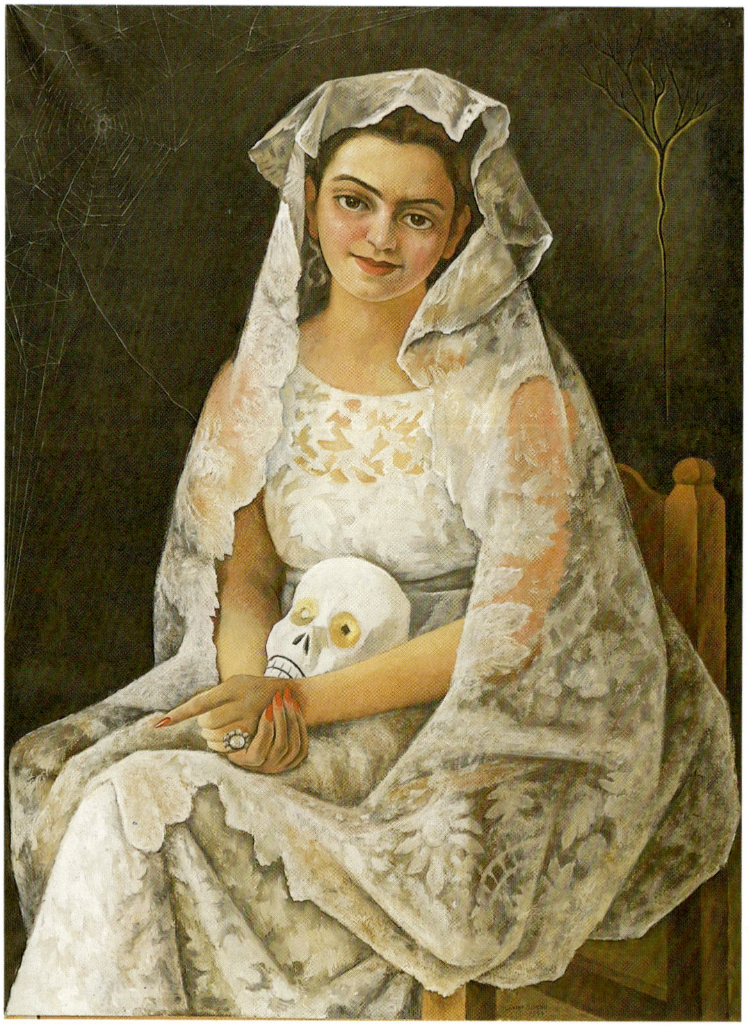

Figure 213
The Lady in White, also known as *Mandragora,* 1939, oil on canvas, 120.6 × 91.4 cm. San Diego Museum of Art, Gift of Mrs. Irving T. Snyder (67.159).

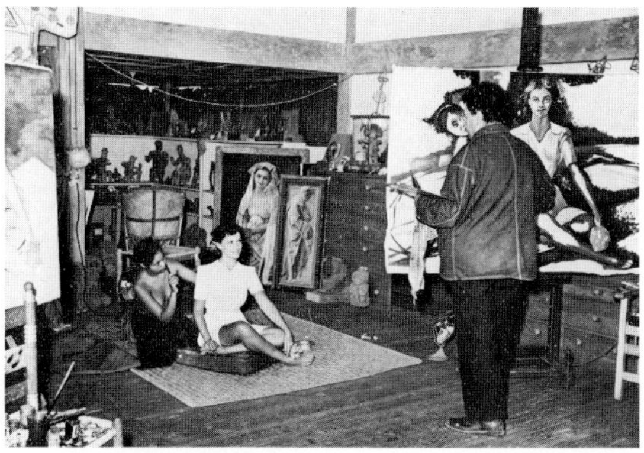

Figure 214
Paulette Goddard sits for her portrait in Rivera's studio, May 1940.

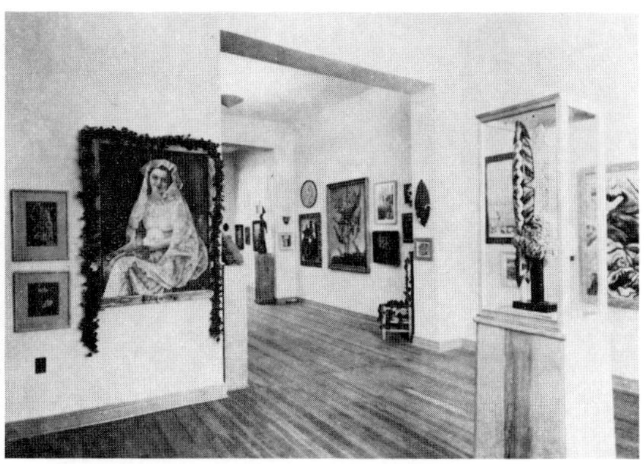

Figure 215
Installation of *"Exposición internacional del surrealismo,"* Galería de Arte Mexicano, Mexico City, 1940.

1940

January 17: *"Exposición internacional del surrealismo"* opens at the Galería de Arte Mexicano, Mexico City. Proposed by André Breton, the show was organized by the surrealist painter Wolfgang van Paalen and the Peruvian poet César Moro. Two of Rivera's works are included (figs. 213 and 217). As a result of this show, European Surrealism briefly attracts the interest of Mexican artists.

Spring: Timothy Pflueger travels to Mexico to invite Rivera to participate in the forthcoming Art in Action program of the 1940 Golden Gate International Exposition.

May 24: Siqueiros, having returned to Mexico following his participation in the Spanish Civil War, leads an assassination attempt on Trotsky in his Coyoacán house. Rivera claims to be under police surveillance.

May: Rivera's article, "Stalin, Undertaker of the Revolution," appears in *Esquire*.

June: Rivera arrives in San Francisco to paint a mural on the theme "Marriage of the Artistic Expression of the North and South on This Continent." He will be assisted by Emmy Lou Packard, Mona Hoffman, and Arthur Niendorf.

Life magazine calls Rivera the "hit" of the Art in Action program, as thousands of spectators watch him paint; the mural (intended for the library of San Francisco City College) presents scenes from Mexican and United States history and shows the fusion of the two cultures in the huge central image.

August 20: Trotsky assassinated by Spanish Stalinist Ramón Mercader. Kahlo, who had become acquainted with Mercader, is questioned by the police. In San Francisco, Rivera, fearing reprisals against himself, stations an armed guard on his scaffold.

September: Kahlo comes to San Francisco and is reconciled with Rivera; they remarry on December 8.

October: with the dissolution of the Communist Party Opposition, the New Workers School frescoes are given to the International Ladies Garment Workers Union; thirteen of the panels go on permanent display at Unity House, the ILGWU's vacation resort in Forest Park, Pennsylvania.

Paints several works depicting his model Modesta in the "classical" style he now reserves for traditional Mexican subjects.

Orozco paints murals in Jiquilpán, Michoacán (birthplace of Cárdenas), and six movable murals for the exhibition "Twenty Centuries of Mexican Art" at the Museum of Modern Art in New York. Several of Rivera's works are also included in this show.

December: General Manuel Ávila Camacho inaugurated as president of Mexico.

December 12–31: exhibition of Rivera's works at the San Francisco Museum of Art.

1941

January: Sigmund Firestone commissions Rivera and Kahlo to paint self-portraits. Rivera paints another almost identical self-portrait at the request of actress Irene Rich (fig. 223).

February: Rivera finishes the Golden Gate Exposition mural as well as private commissions in Santa Barbara and returns to Mexico with his mural assistant Emmy Lou Packard, never again to visit the United States.

Paints traditional Mexican subjects such as *Woman with Necklace, Girl with Sunflower*, and one in a series of calla lily vendors.

His petition for readmission to the Mexican Communist Party is rejected.

Orozco paints a series of murals in the Palacio de Justicia in Mexico City: *The Constitution, Legislation, The Defense of National Wealth*, and *Justice*.

Siqueiros forced into exile in Chile as a result of his role in *"l'affaire Trotsky."* He paints the mural *Death to the Invaders* in Chillán.

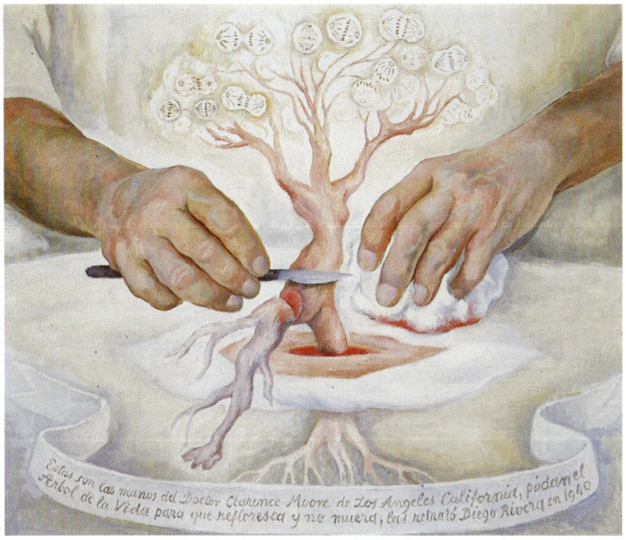

Figure 216
The Hands of Dr. Moore, 1940, oil on canvas, 45.7 × 55.9 cm. San Diego Museum of Art, Bequest from the Estate of Mrs. E. Clarence Moore (70.20).

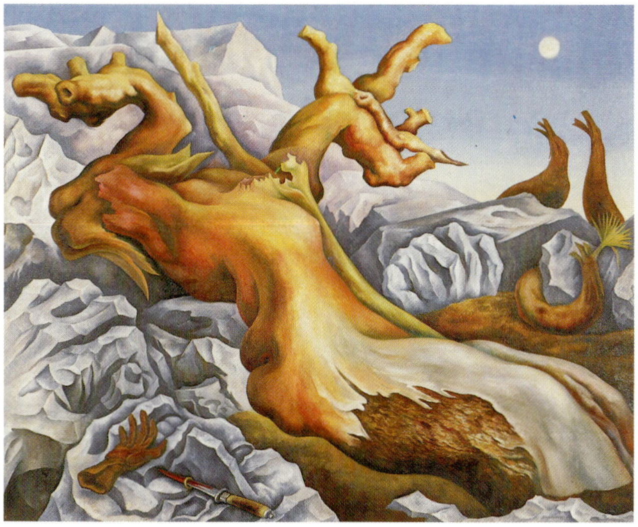

Figure 217
Symbolic Landscape, also known as *Tree with Glove and Knife,* 1940, oil on canvas, 121.6 × 152.7 cm. San Francisco Museum of Modern Art, Gift of Friends of Diego Rivera: Mrs. Sigmund Stern, Mrs. E. S. Heller, Albert M. Bender, William L. Gerstle, W. W. Crocker, Harry Camp, and Timothy Pflueger. This work was exhibited in the 1940 *"Exposición internacional del surrealismo"* under the title *Minervegtanimortvida,* a word invented by Rivera.

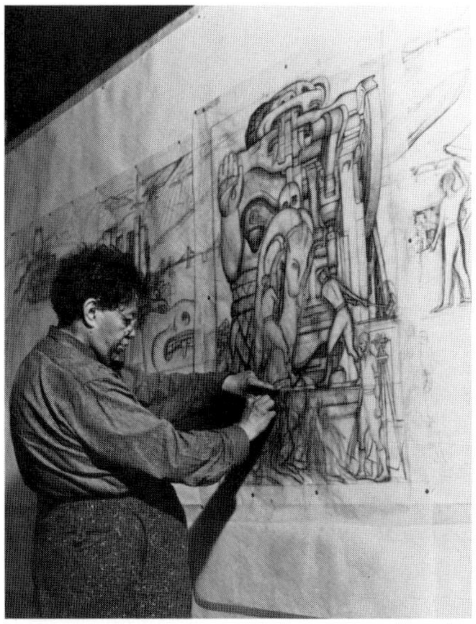

Figure 218
Rivera working on sketches for the Golden Gate mural, 1940.

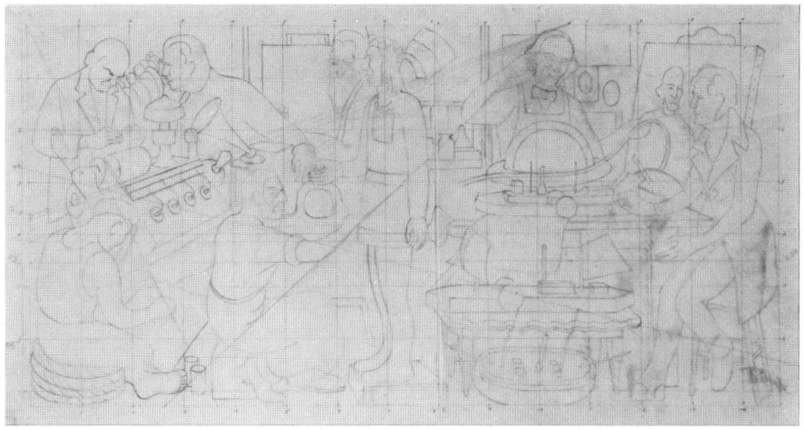

Figure 219
Inventors, 1940, pencil, 45.4 × 80.7 cm. San Francisco Museum of Modern Art, Gift of Emmy Lou Packard (49.140 A-B). Study for *Pan-American Unity,* City College of San Francisco.

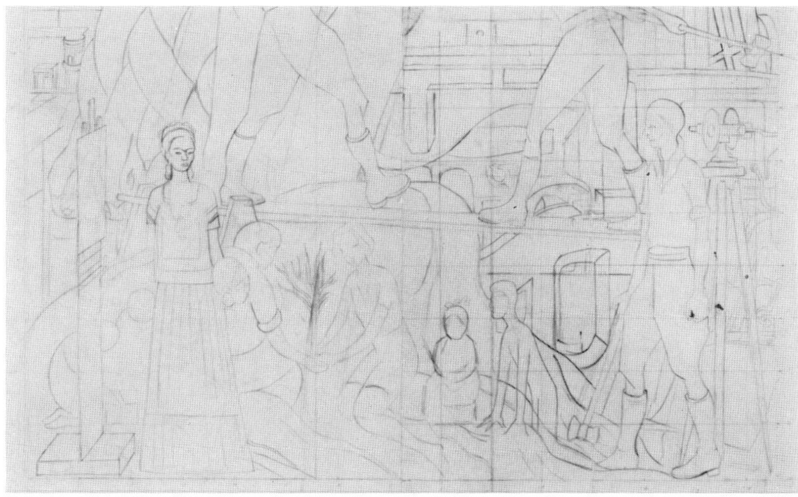

Figure 220
Frida Kahlo, Diego Rivera and Paulette Goddard Holding the Tree of Life and Love, 1940, pencil, 51.2 × 85.4 cm. San Francisco Museum of Modern Art, Gift of Emmy Lou Packard (49.141 A-C). Study for *Pan-American Unity,* City College of San Francisco.

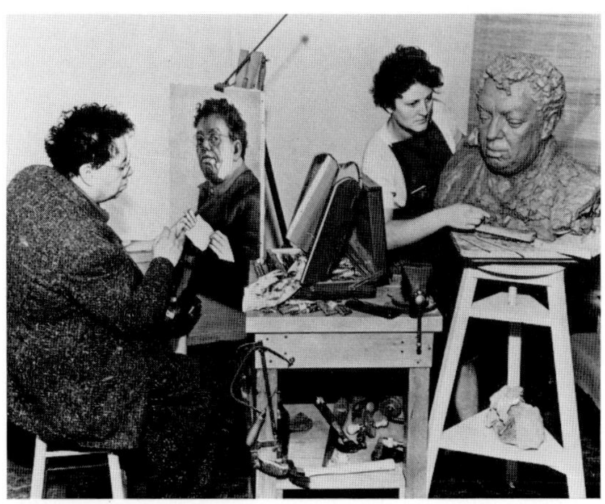

Figure 221
Frances Rich modeling a bust of Rivera, while he paints a self-portrait commissioned by her mother, Irene.

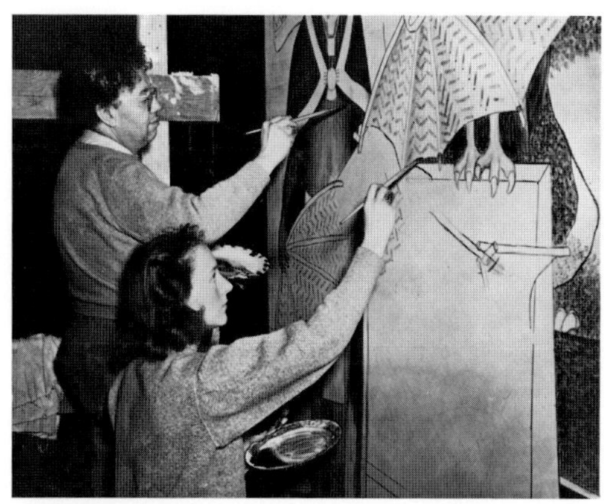

Figure 222
Rivera painting the Golden Gate mural, assisted by Emmy Lou Packard, 1940.

Figure 223
Self-Portrait, 1941, oil on canvas, 61 × 43 cm. Northampton, Massachusetts, Smith College Museum of Art, Gift of Mrs. Irene Rich Clifford, 1977.

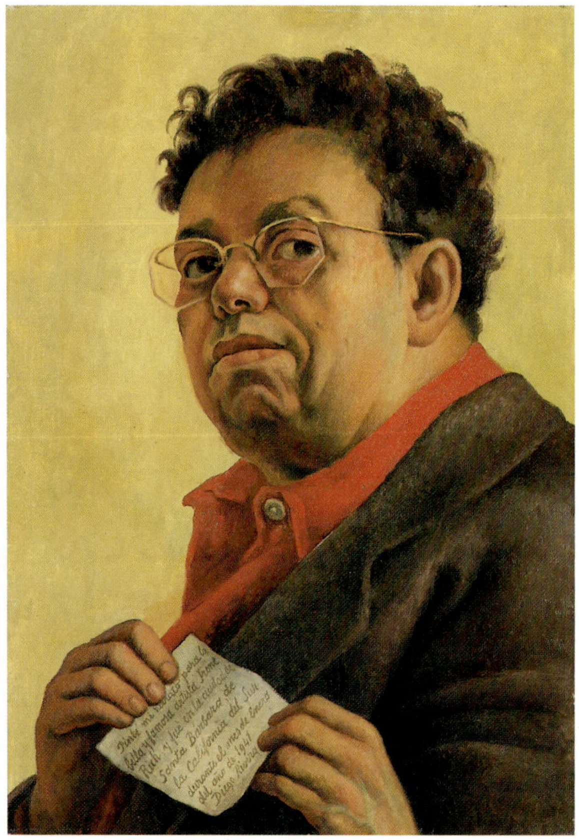

VI.
The Final Years

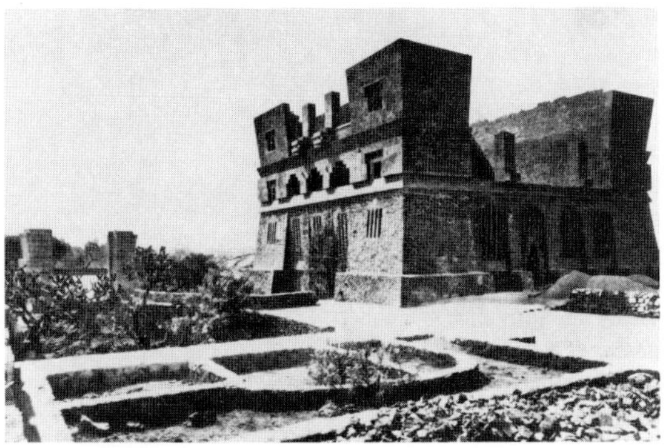

Figure 224
Anahuacalli under construction.

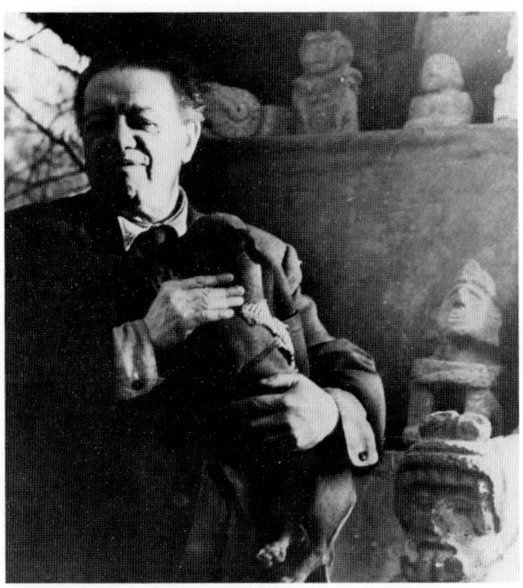

Figure 225
Rivera with one of his dogs. Photo by Gisele Freund.

1942

January: Rivera returns to the Palacio Nacional and begins a series of panels on pre-Conquest cultures for the second-floor courtyard. Completes *The Tarascan Civilization* and *The Zapotec Civilization* and related grisaille panels during the year.

May: after German submarines sink two Mexican tankers, Mexico declares war against Germany.

Paints *Post guerra* and several paintings of flower vendors.

Construction begins on Anahuacalli, a monumental edifice near Coyoacán designed by the artist as a residence-museum-tomb. It will eventually house Rivera's collection of pre-Colombian art (with some sixty thousand pieces, the largest private collection in Mexico). He will work on Anahuacalli intermittently until his death.

Orozco begins a series of murals on the theme of the Apocalypse in the chapel of the Hospital de Jesús Nazareno, Mexico City.

1943

Rivera undertakes two mural projects in Mexico City, one devoted to the history of cardiology at the Instituto Nacional de Cardiología and another in a nightclub, Ciro's, in the Hotel Reforma.

May 15: President Ávila Camacho installs fifteen members in the newly formed Colegio Nacional, including Rivera and Orozco, as representatives of the plastic arts. The members of this prestigious group include the country's most outstanding scientists, writers, artists, musicians, and intellectuals.

Teaches composition and painting at the Escuela Nacional de Pintura y Escultura (*La Esmeralda*); he will serve as a faculty member at the school for several years.

Paints watercolors of the Paricutín volcano (see fig. 227).

Siqueiros paints *New Day of the Democracies* at the Seville-Biltmore Hotel in Havana.

1944

Rivera begins the mosaic decoration of Anahuacalli with pre-Conquest motifs; he uses variously colored native stones as tesserae.

Executes several sketches and an oil painting on the Mexican religious festival known as the Day of the Dead (see fig. 229).

Paints one of the most curious portraits of his career, that of Henri de Chatillon (fig. 345), and the painting *Nude with Calla Lilies* (fig. 230).

Siqueiros returns to Mexico and paints the mural *Cuauhtémoc against the Myth* in a private residence in Mexico City; he founds the Realist Center for Modern Art.

Rivera undertakes research on the history of Mexico by examining pre-Colombian codices and rereading *The True History of the Conquest of New Spain* by Bernal Díaz del Castillo, a member of Cortés's expedition.

1945

Returns to the Palacio Nacional and paints *The Great City of Tenochtitlán*.

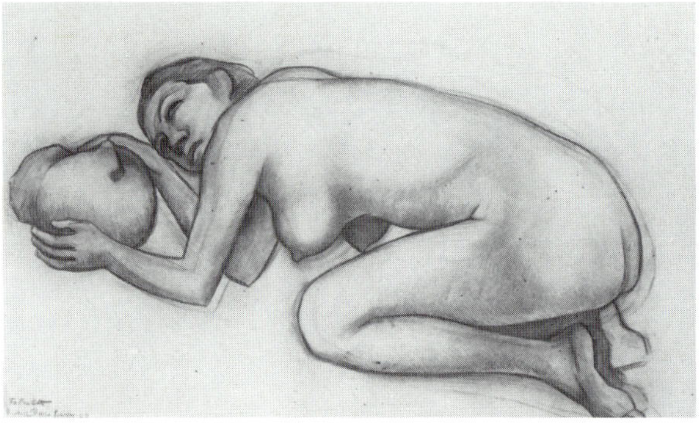

Figure 226
Crouching Nude Holding a Melon, 1943, charcoal on board, 69.9 × 116 cm. Collection of Mr. and Mrs. J. S. Moss

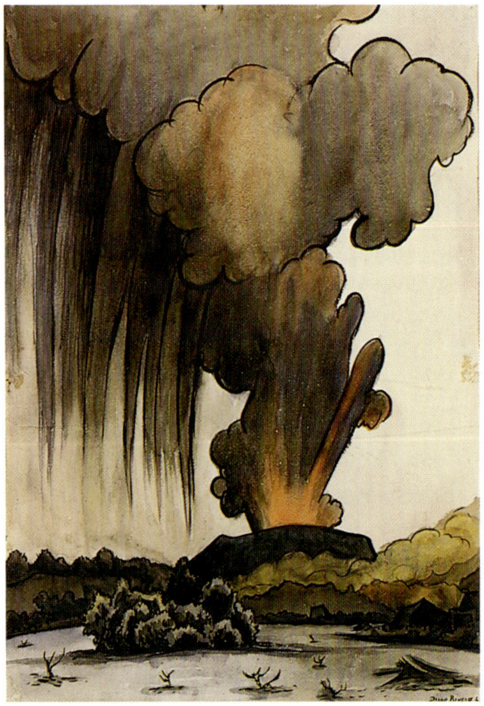

Figure 227
Volcano Erupting (from the album "El Paricutín"), 1943, watercolor, 44 × 31 cm. Guanajuato, Museo Diego Rivera (INBA).

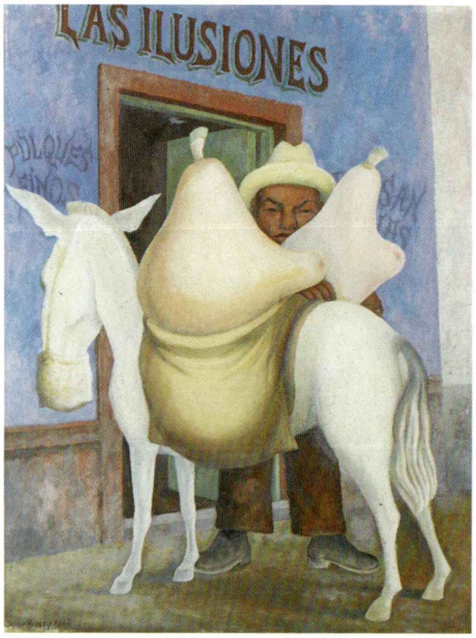

Figure 228
Carregador—Las ilusiones, 1944, oil on canvas, 75 × 59 cm. Museu de Arte de São Paulo. The name of this *pulqueria* (a place where pulque, a liquor made from cactus, is sold) emphasizes the Surrealist character of this work in which Rivera has transformed the sacks carried by the burro into enormous disembodied breasts.

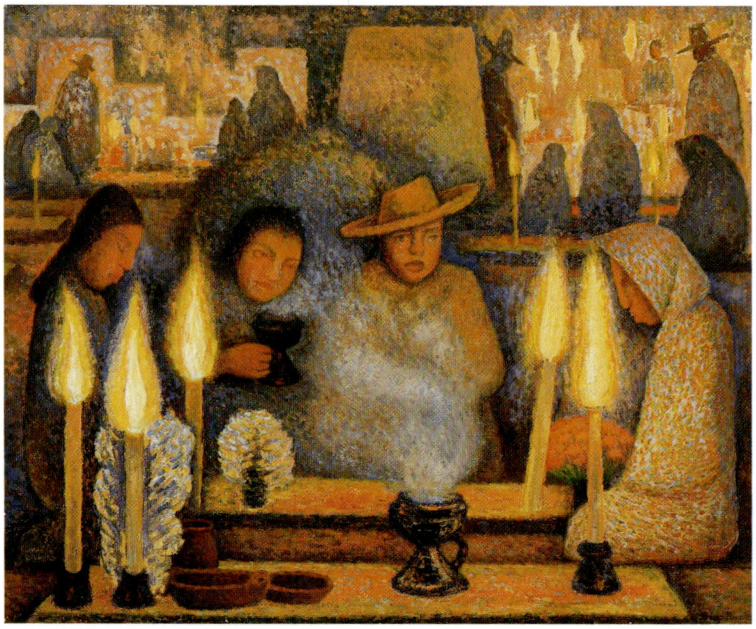

Figure 229
Day of the Dead, also known as *El Velorio,* 1944, oil on masonite, 73.5 × 91 cm. Mexico City, Museo de Arte Moderno (INBA). Here a group of Indians gather around a grave enveloped in the smoke of the incense *(copal)* and the flickering light of candles.

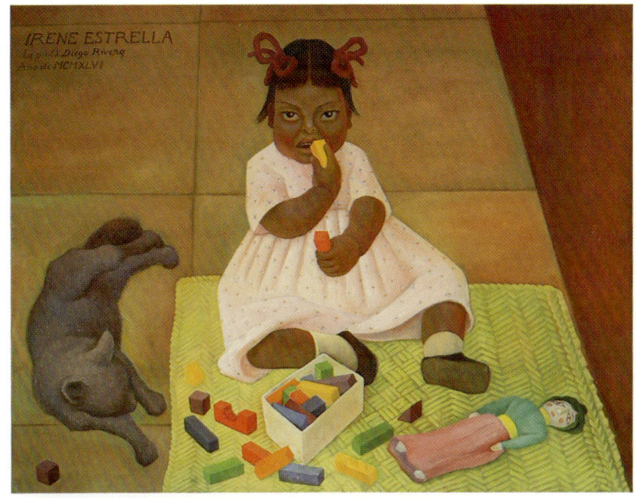

Figure 231
Portrait of Irene Estrella, 1946, oil on canvas, 120.4 × 93 cm. Exeter, New Hampshire, Phillips Exeter Academy, The Lamont Gallery, Gift of Corliss Lamont '20.

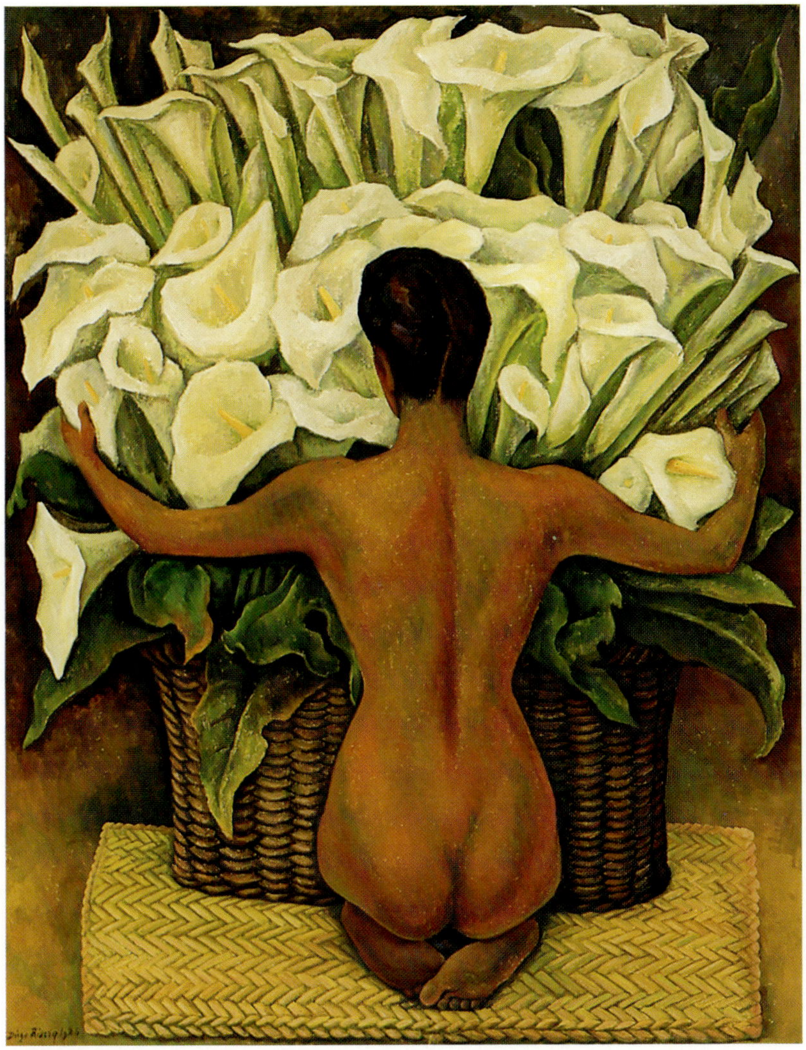

Figure 230
Nude with Calla Lilies, 1944, oil on masonite, 157 × 124 cm. Collection of Emilia Guzzy de Gálvez. In contrast to his highly stylized paintings of calla lily vendors, this portrayal of the artist's model Nieves embracing an immense basket of flowers is a realistic composition in which color, form, and texture combine to create a harmonious unity.

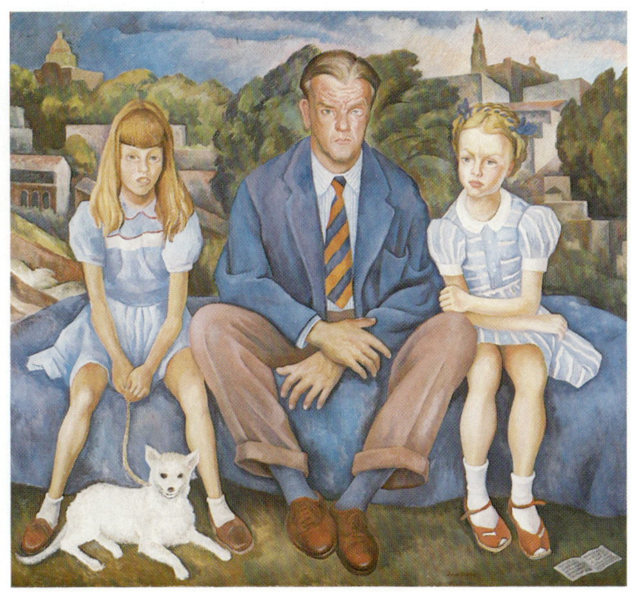

Figure 232
Portrait of the Knight Family, 1946, oil on canvas, 181 × 202 cm. Minneapolis Institute of Arts, Gift of Mrs. Dinah Ellingson in memory of Richard Allen Knight. The Knight family lived in New York but had a home in Cuernavaca, where they became acquainted with Rivera. This compelling work depicts Richard Knight with his two daughters, Nora and Dinah, in front of a view of Cuernavaca.

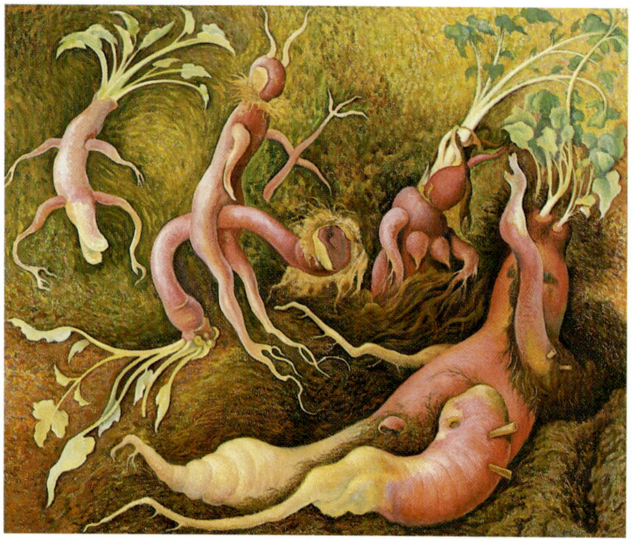

Figure 233
The Temptations of Saint Anthony, 1947, oil on canvas, 90 × 110 cm. Mexico City, Museo de Arte Moderno (INBA). Rivera's use of anthropomorphized radishes to depict a traditional religious theme may be related to the annual radish festival held in Oaxaca City. In the 1930s and 1940s, vendors at the festival competed with each other to create radish sculptures of popular figures such as bullfighters and movie stars.

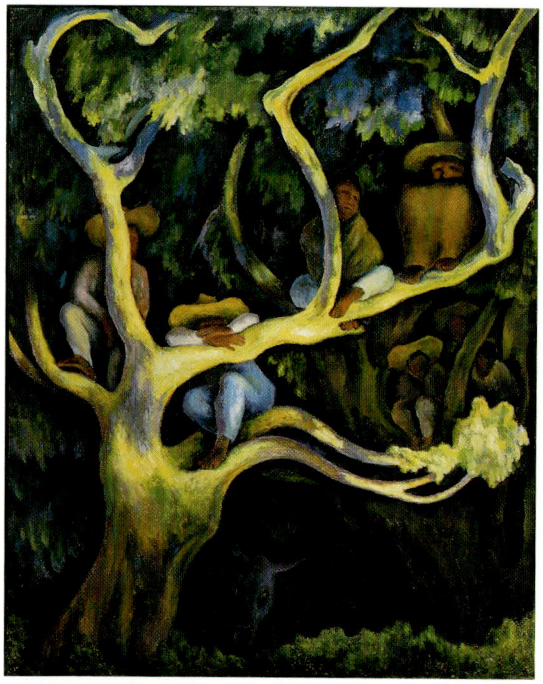

Figure 234
Nocturnal Landscape, 1947, oil on canvas, 111 × 91 cm. Mexico City, Museo de Arte Moderno (INBA).

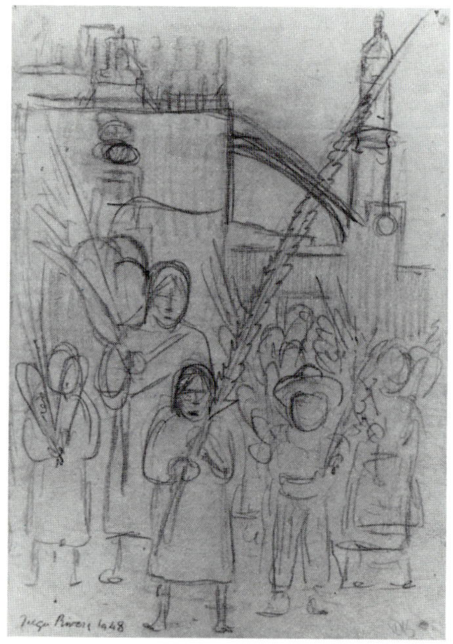

Figure 235
Palm Sunday in Xochimilco, 1948, pencil and charcoal, 38.7 × 28 cm. Collection of Dolores Olmedo.

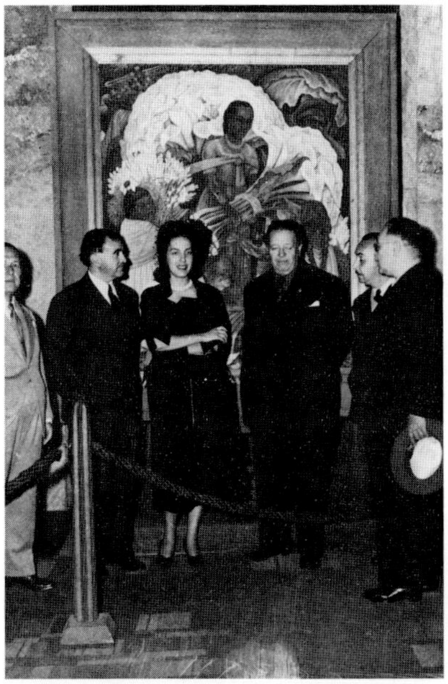

Figure 236
Carlos Chávez, Evangelina Luchica, Rivera, Fernando Gamboa, and Marte R. Gómez at the opening of the *"50 años"* exhibition, August 1949.

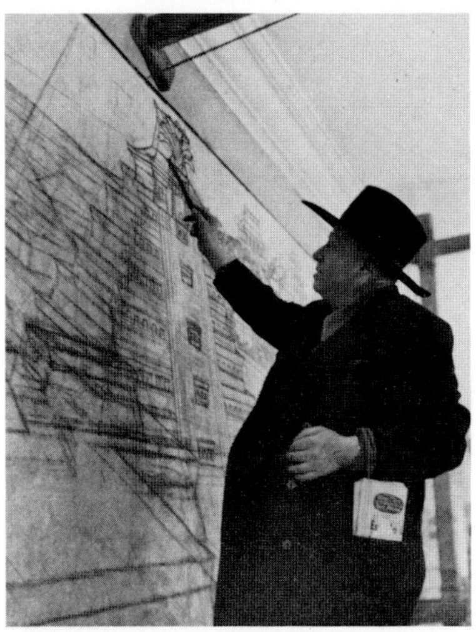

Figure 237
Rivera in front of *The Totonac Civilization* panel at the Palacio Nacional, ca. 1950. Photo by Lola Álvarez Bravo.

February: Mexico hosts the Inter-American Conference on the Problems of War and Peace ("The Chapultepec Conference"), a pivotal event in the restructuring of Pan-American politics after World War II. Rivera is a daily visitor to the conference and announces his plans to paint a mural on this theme.

Paintings include *Tepoztlán*, *The Children of Santiago Reachi*, various watercolors, and portraits.

Siqueiros is allowed his first public wall since 1939, on the third floor of the Palacio de Bellas Artes. Paints *New Democracy* and accompanying panels, *Victims of the War* and *Victims of Fascism*.

1946

Rivera paints a large number of portraits (Cuca Bustamente, Emma Hurtado, Laura Villaseñor, Ramón Beteta, Irene Estrella [fig. 231]).

August: a project that calls for Rivera, Orozco, and Siqueiros to paint murals in Rome for the Italian government, with Mexico donating their fees, is cancelled.

The election of Miguel Alemán as president of Mexico marks the creation of a new political party, the Partido Revolutionario Institucional.

Emma Hurtado becomes Rivera's dealer.

Again petitions for readmission to the Mexican Communist Party, but is rejected.

1947

March: seriously ill with bronchial pneumonia, Rivera is admitted to the American-British Hospital in Mexico City.

Begins a mural commission, *Dream of a Sunday Afternoon in the Alameda*, for the newly constructed Hotel del Prado.

Paints two works with fantastic themes, *The Temptations of Saint Anthony* (fig. 233) and *Nocturnal Landscape* (fig. 234). Also paints several portraits and continues to sketch market scenes and folk customs.

With Orozco and Siqueiros, forms the Commission of Mural Painting, an arm of the Instituto Nacional de Bellas Artes (INBA).

INBA presents a major retrospective exhibition of Orozco's works, followed by another including seventy recent works by Siqueiros, both at the Palacio de Bellas Artes.

1948

Completes the Hotel del Prado mural. His inclusion of the slogan "God does not exist" creates a scandal, with the result that the mural is kept from public view for nine years.

Returns to Chapingo to paint doorway panels with portraits of presidents Manuel Ávila Camacho and Alvaro Obregón.

Paints *The Rural Teacher*, *The Wife of Rebozo Carmesi*, *The Peak of Orizaba*, and *Portrait of Juárez*.

Orozco paints murals at the Escuela Normal Superior, Mexico City, and a portable fresco, *Juárez and Independent Mexico* (Museo Nacional de Historia, Mexico City).

1949

Kahlo readmitted to Mexican Communist Party, but Rivera's petition is again denied.

August–December: first major retrospective of Rivera's work, *"Diego Rivera: 50 años de su labor artistica."* Held at the Palacio de Bellas Artes, it includes over one thousand works and is inaugurated by President Miguel Alemán, who calls Rivera a "national treasure."

September 7: Orozco dies in Mexico City, having earlier in the year completed two murals in Guadalajara.

October 25: Rivera presents his plan for additional murals on the second floor of the Palacio Nacional.

Paints *Flower Stall*, *Flower Market*, and various society portraits.

1950

January: Kahlo admitted to the hospital for operations on her spine. She will remain hospitalized for almost one year; Rivera takes a room next to hers and spends most nights there.

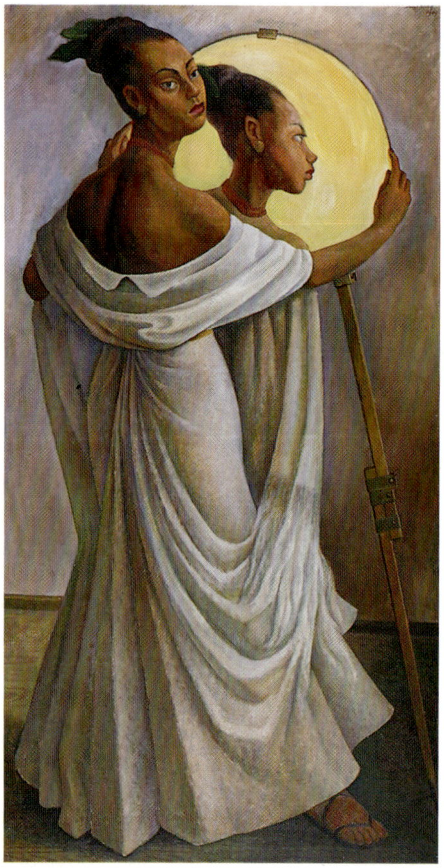

Figure 238
Portrait of Ruth Rivera, 1949, oil on canvas, 199 × 100.5 cm. Collection of Rafael Coronel.

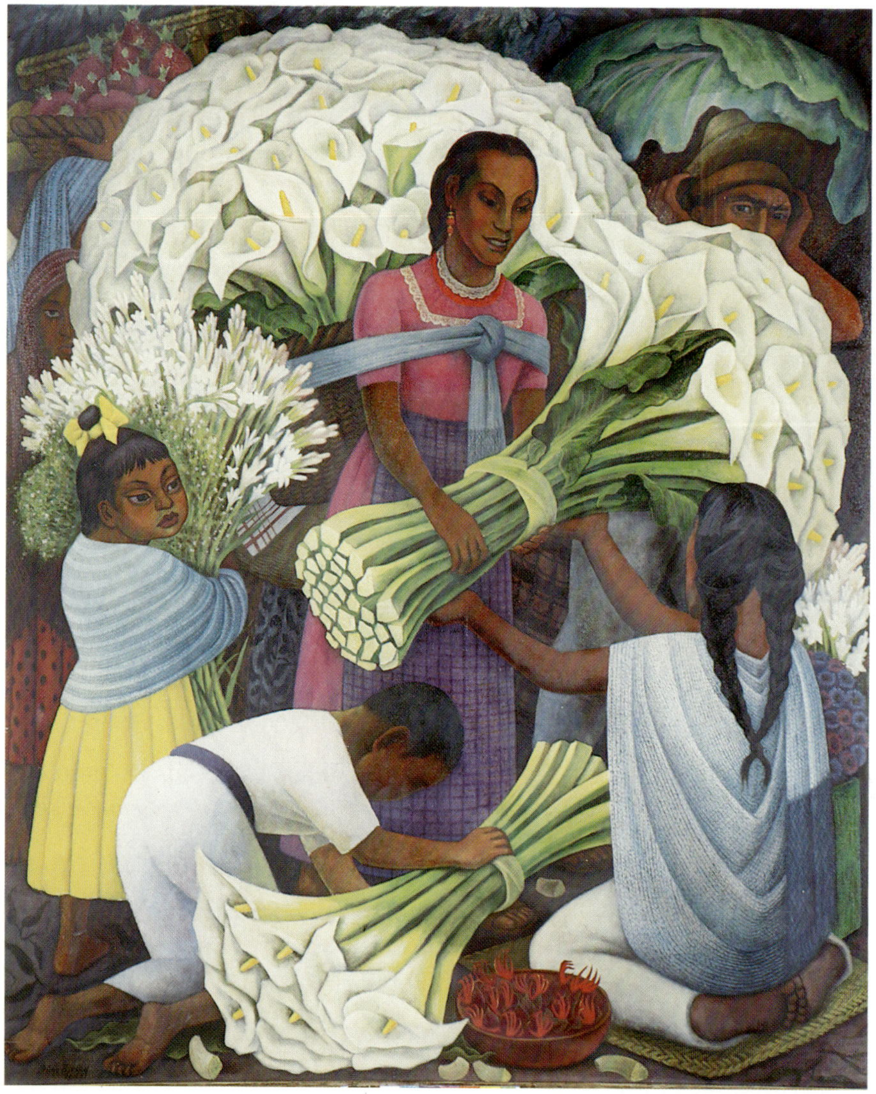

Figure 239
Flower Vendor, 1949, oil on canvas, 180 × 150 cm. Madrid, Museo Español de Arte Contemporáneo. The elongation and angularity of this monumental painting of a flower vendor accompanied by children reflects a change in the classical style Rivera normally used for Mexican subjects.

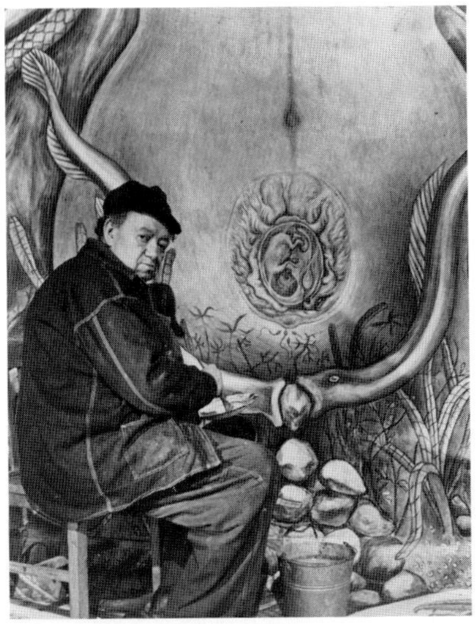

Figure 240
Rivera working on mural at the Lerma Waterworks (Cárcamo del Río Lerma), 1951.

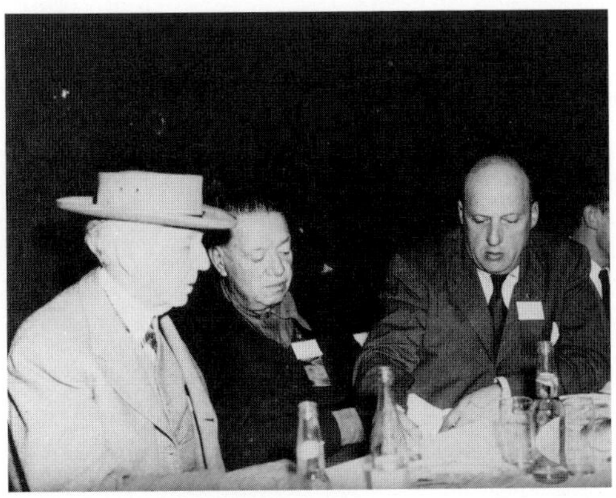

Figure 241
Frank Lloyd Wright, Rivera, and Oscar Stanarov, 1952.

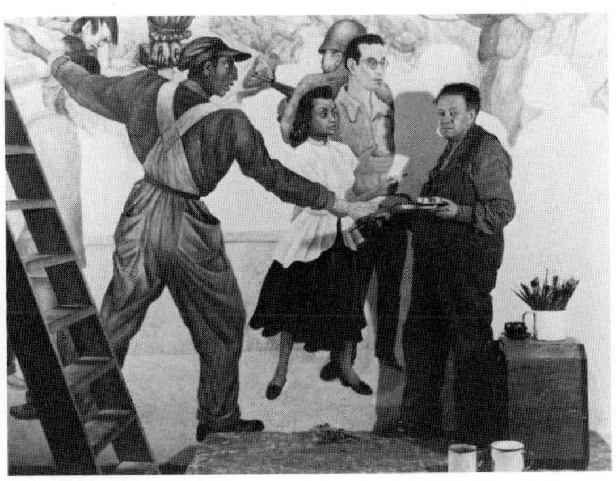

Figure 242
Rivera painting *The Nightmare of War and the Dream of Peace*, 1952.

Completes *The Totonac Civilization* and *The Huastec Civilization* at the Palacio Nacional.

Siqueiros and Rivera illustrate Pablo Neruda's *Canto general*.

Rivera's paintings, along with those of Orozco, Siqueiros, and Rufino Tamayo, exhibited in the Mexican pavilion at the Venice Biennale.

The Mexican government awards Rivera the Premio Nacional de Artes Plasticas (National Art Prize).

Designs the scenery for José Revueltas's play *The Quarter of Solitude*, presented in May at the Arbeu Theater, Mexico City.

Rivera campaigns for the Stockholm Peace Conference, a Communist meeting protesting the atomic bomb.

Siqueiros paints *Torment of Cuauhtémoc* and *Cuauhtémoc Reborn* on the third floor of the Palacio de Bellas Artes.

1951
February: retrospective of Rivera's work at the Houston Museum of Fine Arts.

Completes pre-Conquest series at the Palacio Nacional with the panels *Harvesting Cocoa*, *Maguey Industry*, and *Disembarkation of the Spanish at Veracruz*.

Paints murals (which are intended to be submerged underwater) at the Lerma Waterworks, Mexico City, in an experimental medium combining BKS-92 polystyrene and liquid rubber. Outside the pumping station, Rivera creates a vast mosaic, using plastic resin pigments, which depicts the rain god Tláloc, undulating serpents, fishes, and human figures.

Delivers a series of lectures at the Colegio Nacional on art and politics.

Rivera and Kahlo socialize occasionally with photographer Bernice Kolko, movie star Dolores del Rio, and poets Carlos Pellicer, an old friend, and Salvador Novo, an old enemy.

As her health deteriorates Kahlo becomes more active politically.

Begins research and sketches for exterior mosaic relief decoration of the stadium at the Universidad Nacional de Mexico (UNAM) on the theme of the development of sport in Mexico from pre-Hispanic times to the present.

1952
February: commissioned by INBA to paint a mural-sized painting for an exhibition, "Mexican Art from Pre-Colombian Times to the Present," intended for a European tour. In thirty-five days, paints *The Nightmare of War and the Dream of Peace*, in which Stalin, accompanied by Mao Tse-tung, touches the Stockholm Peace Petition with one hand while with the other (on which rests the dove of peace) he offers the world a pen, while Marianne, Uncle Sam, and John Bull watch. In the background North Koreans are being hung, shot, and whipped by South Korean soldiers, and in the foreground Frida Kahlo (in her wheelchair) and others collect signatures for the petition. The director of INBA, Carlos Chávez, refuses to exhibit the work, pointing out that it makes serious accusations against governments with which Mexico maintains friendly relations.

March 17: at a press conference, Rivera asserts that the Mexican government fears the content of his painting; INBA officials remove the painting from the Palacio de Bellas Artes.

March 19: Rivera returns his advance, and INBA gives him back the painting.

May 1: witnesses accuse Rivera and Siqueiros of inciting violent May Day demonstrations outside the Palacio de Bellas Artes, in which two are killed and fifty injured in clashes between Mexican Communist Party members, fascist Gold Shirts, and the police.

May: with the assistance of the French Communist Party, Rivera arranges for a public showing of his "peace" painting in Paris.

Figure 243
Four Ball Players and Battle Scene with Tiger and Eagle Knights, 1950/57, pencil, 46 × 62 cm. Mexico City, UNAM, Museo Universitario de Ciencias y Arte. Study for mural, Olympic Stadium.

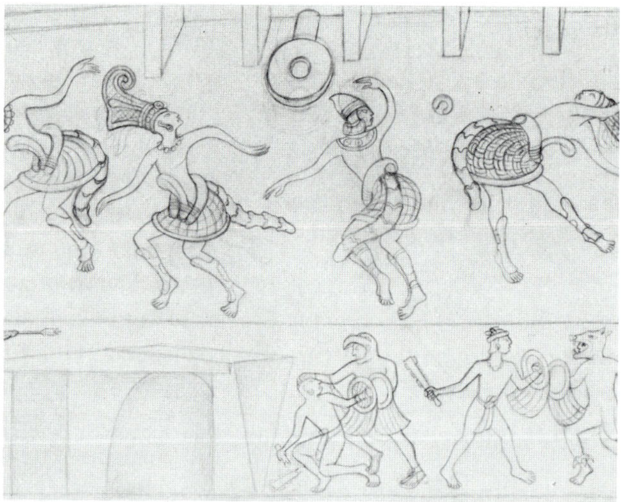

Figure 244
Tiger Knight Offering Heart to Quetzalcóatl, 1950–57, pencil, 46 × 62 cm. Mexico city, UNAM, Museo Universitario de Ciencias y Arte. Study for mural, Olympic Stadium.

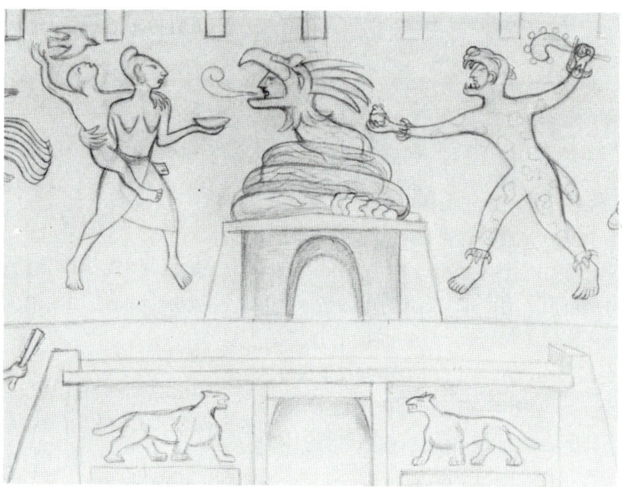

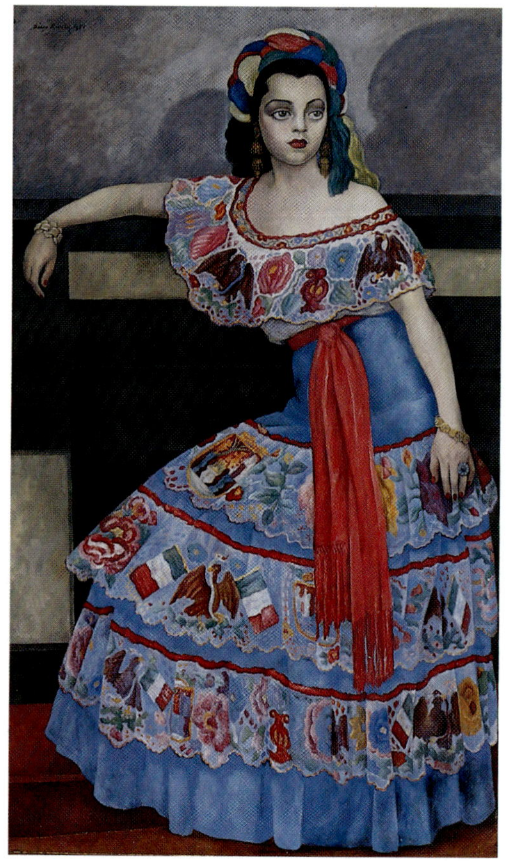

Figure 245
Portrait of Señorita Matilda Palou, 1951, oil on canvas, 200.5 × 123 cm. Collection of the Family of Osceola Heard Davenport.

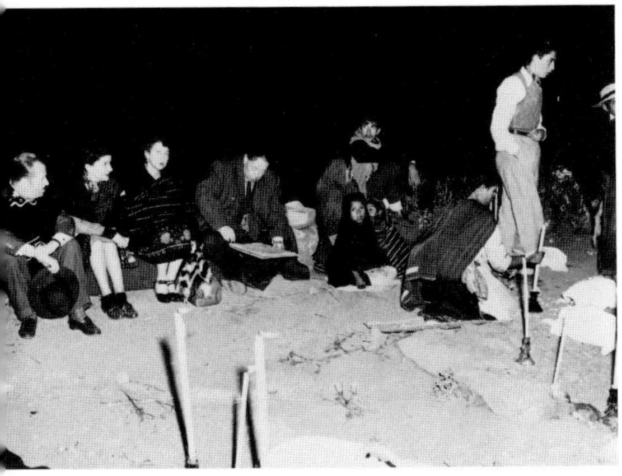

Figure 246
Emma Hurtado and Rivera (center) at a Day of the Dead celebration in Mixquic, ca. 1955.

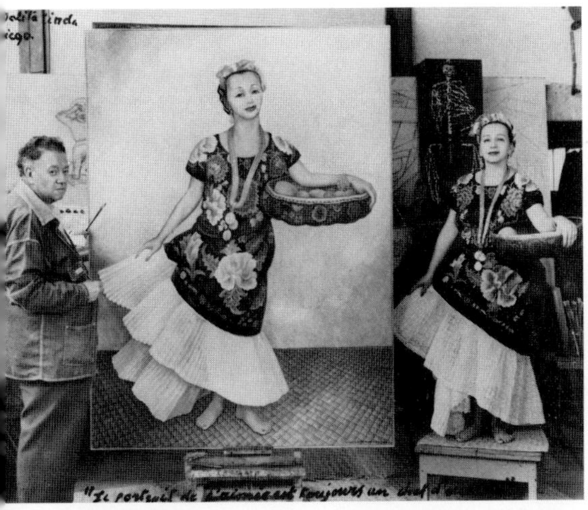

Figure 247
Dolores Olmedo posing for her portrait, 1955.

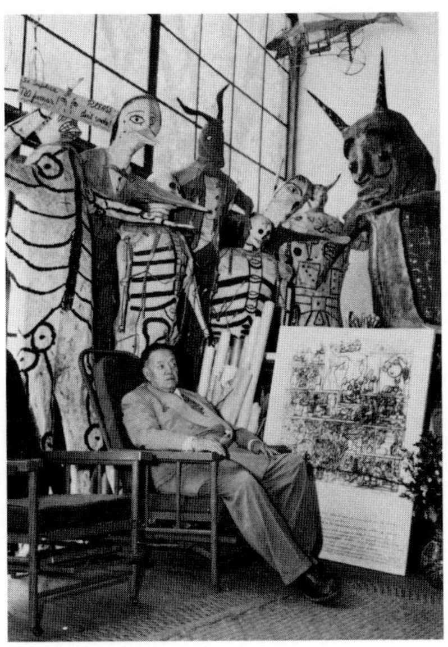

Figure 248
Rivera in his studio, ca. 1956.

Completes only the front section of his mosaic for the stadium of the UNAM when funding is cut off.

Paints *Macuilxochitl (Portrait of Machila Armida)* and *Homage to Ana Mérida*.

Adolfo Ruiz Cortines elected president.

October: Eighth Pan-American Congress of Architects in Mexico City; Rivera meets Frank Lloyd Wright, with whom he shares an interest in pre-Colombian architecture.

December: again applies for readmission to Mexican Communist Party, but his petition is again rejected.

Siqueiros begins his murals at the Hospital de la Raza in Mexico City and at UNAM.

1953

February: José María Dávila commissions Rivera to create a mural for the façade of the new Teatro de los Insurgentes. A scandal erupts over Rivera's image of Cantinflas, the popular Mexican comedian, shown not only stealing from the rich and giving to the poor but also wearing the sacred image of the Virgin of Guadalupe.

March: in the face of a threatened boycott of the theater, Rivera removes the image of the Virgin of Guadalupe from the Insurgentes mural.

April: Kahlo's first one-person exhibition in Mexico, at Lola Álvarez Bravo's Galería de Arte Contemporáneo, Mexico City.

May: Rivera represents Mexico at the Continental Congress of Culture, Santiago, Chile.

August: Kahlo's right leg amputated.

Paints two large oils for the Cuernavaca home of Santiago Reachi, *La piñata* and *La procesion*; these are later installed in the Hospital Infantil de México, Mexico City.

Rivera works with Dr. Gustavo Baz and architect Enrique Yáñez in planning mural decorations for a new medical center in Mexico City.

Fall: Rivera begins the mural *The People's Demand for Better Health* for the Hospital de la Raza. His assistants include Marco Antonio Borregui, Rina Lazo, Teresa Ordialés, Ramón Sanchez, and Melquiades Ejido. This will be Rivera's last fresco commission.

Sends *The Nightmare of War and the Dream of Peace* to the People's Republic of China.

1954

February 10: Andrés Iduarte, INBA director, dedicates the Hospital de la Raza mural.

February 12: Marte R. Gómez, a high-ranking government official and an old friend and patron of Rivera, asks him not to let himself become distracted by other matters but to dedicate himself to finishing the Palacio Nacional murals.

July 2: Kahlo's last public appearance as she and Rivera participate in a demonstration protesting C.I.A. involvement in the ouster of Guatemalan president Jacobo Arbenz Guzmán.

July 13: Frida Kahlo dies.

September 25: the Twelfth National Congress of the Mexican Communist Party readmits Rivera as a party member; his first work after party readmission is the propagandistic oil *Glorious Victory*, a denunciation of the overthrow of Arbenz Guzmán. Rivera sends the painting on tour to the Soviet bloc countries.

Paints a self-portrait and *The Painter's Studio* (fig. 251) as well as beginning a series of four movable murals (finished in 1956), *Río Juchitán*.

1955

Produces easel paintings, primarily portraits.

June: diagnosed as having cancer but continues to work.

July 29: marries Emma Hurtado, his dealer since 1946, at the Galería Diego Rivera in Mexico City.

Paints one of the most successful society portraits of his career, that of his friend and patron Dolores Olmedo (see fig. 344).

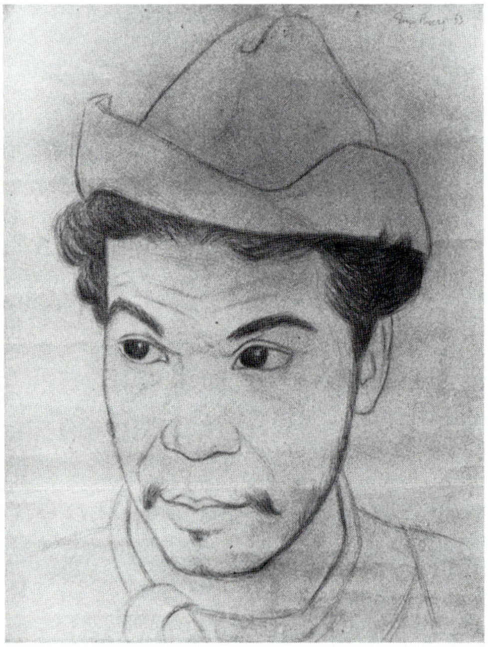

Figure 249
Portrait of Cantinflas,
1953, pencil, 48.3 × 63.5 cm. Collection of Dr. and Mrs. David R. Sacks.

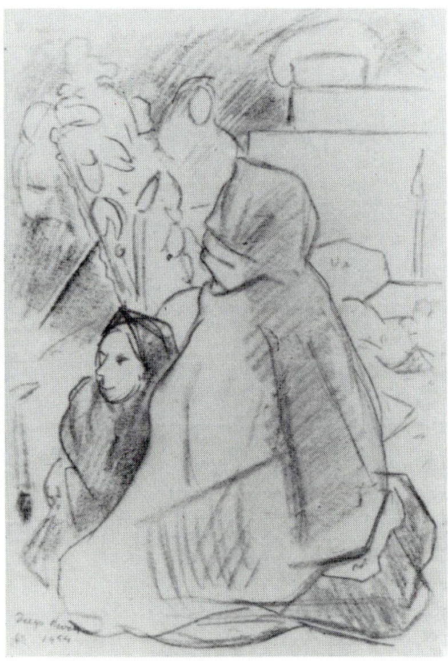

Figure 250
The Offering II, 1954, black chalk or charcoal, 39.4 × 27.7 cm. Collection of Dolores Olmedo.

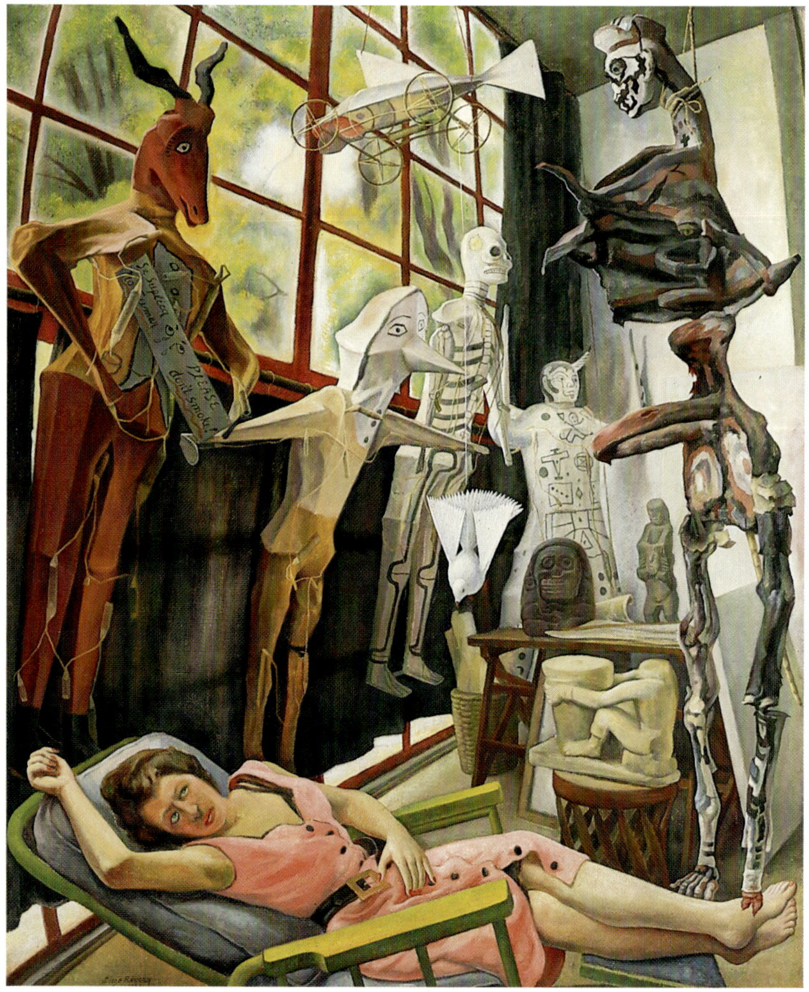

Figure 251
The Painter's Studio,
1954, oil on canvas, 178 × 150 cm. Mexico City, Secretaría de Hacienda y Crédito Público. The subject of this Surrealist work is the artist's San Angel studio. *Papier maché* Judas figures loom like menacing apparitions above the reclining figure of a woman. During the Mexican Easter festivities, these figures are strung with firecrackers and exploded.

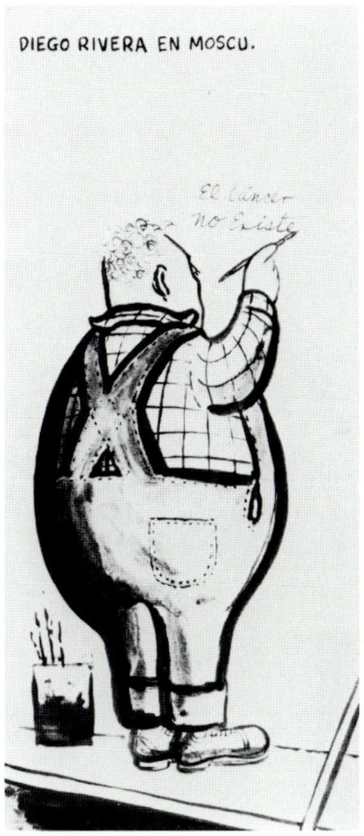

Figure 252
Caricature of Rivera, *"El cáncer no existe."*

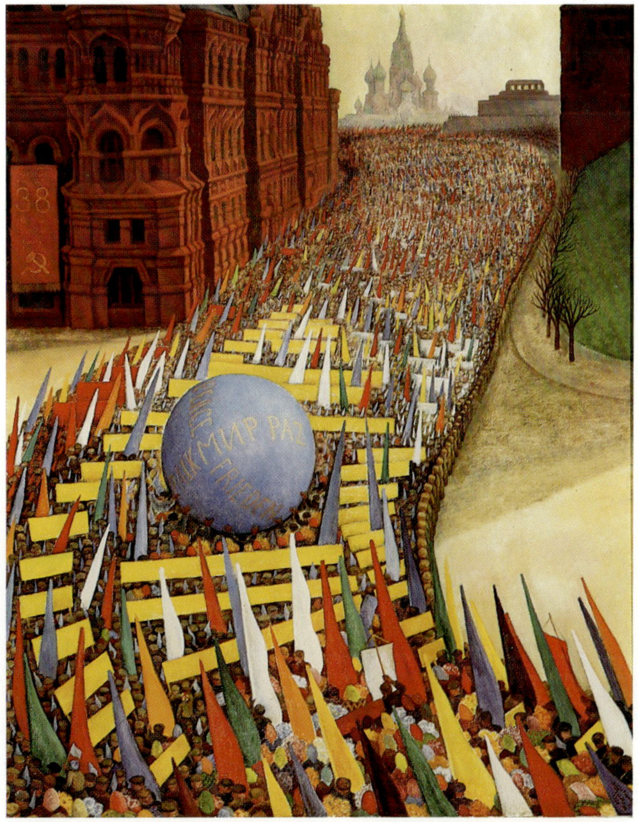

Figure 253
Parade in Moscow, 1956, oil on canvas, 135.2 × 108.3 cm. Mexico City, Banamex. Here Rivera captures the buoyant mood of a parade he saw from his Moscow hotel window. The enormous globe with "Peace" in several languages, the hammer and sickle motif, and the number '38 on the banner allude to the triumph of the October Revolution in this commemorative celebration.

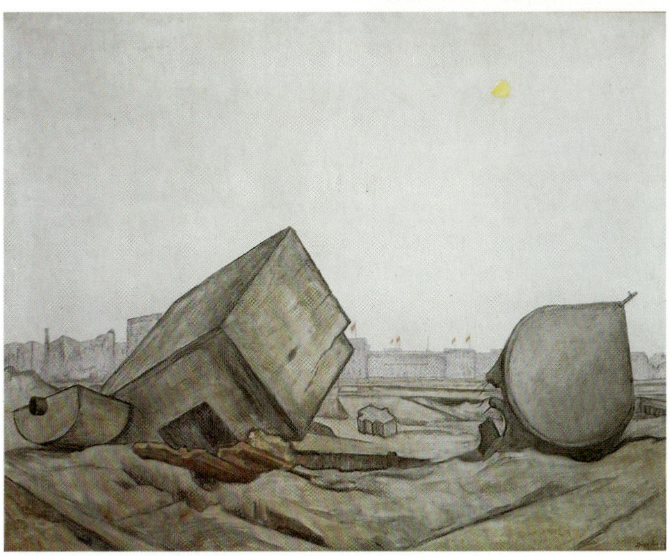

Figure 254
Hitler's Refuge—Ruins of Berlin's Chancellery, 1956, oil and tempera on canvas, 105 × 135 cm. Private Collection. Painted in Mexico from sketches made in Berlin during a stopover on Rivera's trip to the Soviet Union in 1955–56, the work focuses on the ruins surrounding the site of Hitler's suicide in 1945. The severe style and restricted palette befit this dramatic comment on Hitler's regime and the devastation of World War II.

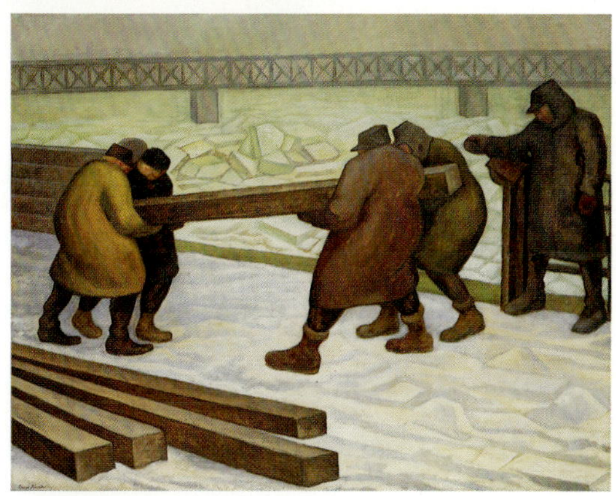

Figure 255
Containing the Ice on the Danube, 1956, oil on canvas, 90 × 116 cm. Mexico City, Secretaría de Hacienda y Crédito Público.

Figure 256
Sunsets (series of twenty), 1956, oil and tempera on canvas, 313.5 × 204 cm. overall (average size 30 × 40 cm.). Collection of Dolores Olmedo. Painted the year before his death from the terrace of the Acapulco home of Dolores Olmedo, this series of sunsets attests to Rivera's deep love of life and his continuous experimentation with color and media.

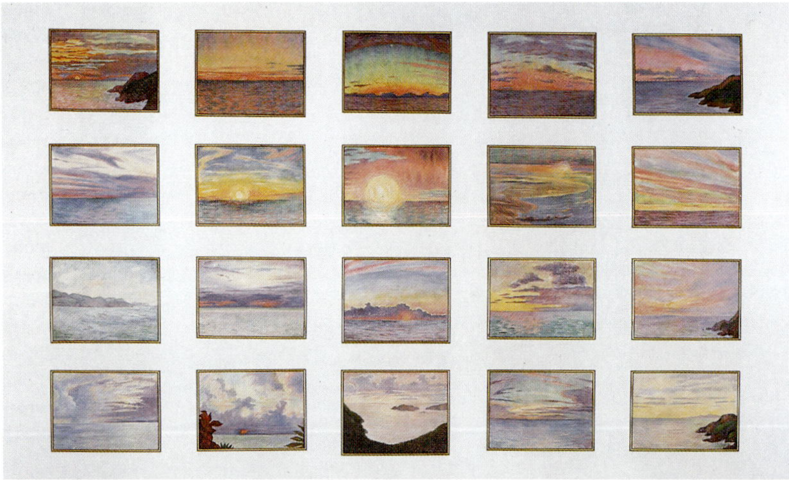

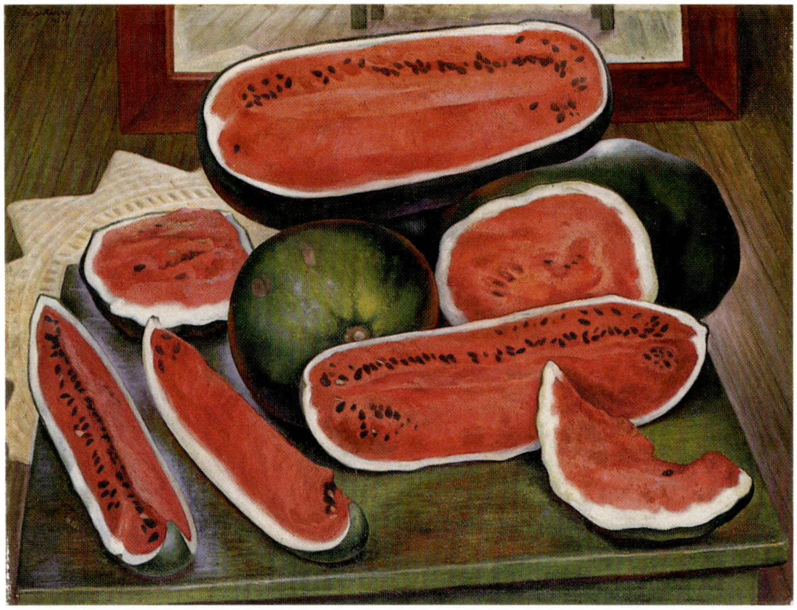

Figure 257
The Watermelons, 1957, oil on canvas, 31 × 26.5 cm. Collection of Dolores Olmedo. This is the last painting Rivera completed before his death.

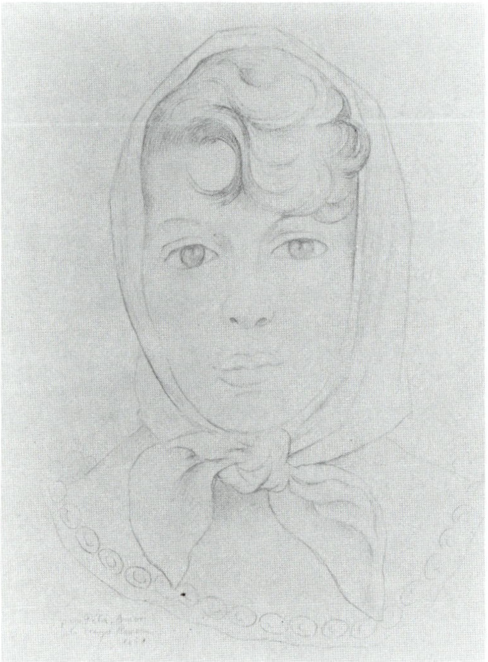

Figure 258
Portrait of Pita Amor, 1957, pencil, 39 × 28 cm. Collection of Dolores Olmedo.

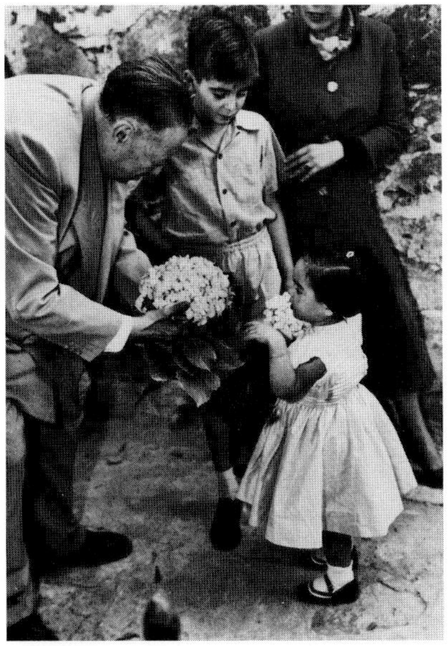

Figure 259
Celebration in honor of Rivera's seventieth birthday.

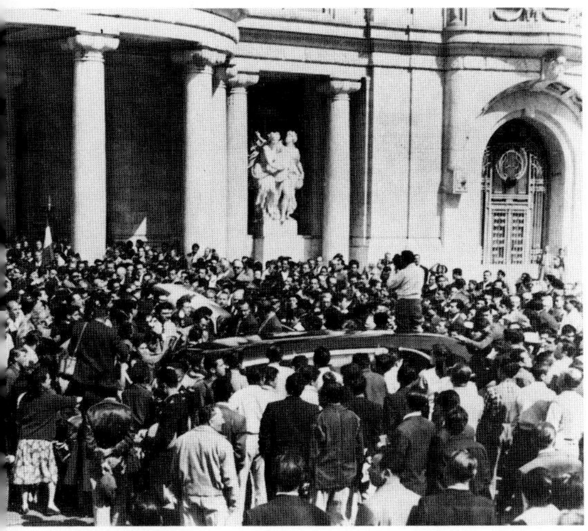

Figure 260
Mourners crowd the entrance to the Palacio de Bellas Artes during Rivera's funeral.

August 16: sets up a trust fund through the Banco de México to administer for the public the structure and collections of Anahuacalli and Kahlo's Coyoacán home as museums.

August 24: at the invitation of the Moscow Fine Arts Academy, leaves for Moscow with Hurtado. His intention is to study contemporary art in the Soviet Union and to seek a cure for his cancer.

October–December: following an operation, undergoes cobalt treatments. Makes numerous drawings and notes during his hospital stay.

1956

January 26: leaves Moscow hospital, saying his cancer has been entirely cured. Recuperates at the National Hotel in Moscow. Paints watercolors directly from life. He and Hurtado meet with friends and colleagues, including Ilya Ehrenburg, who proposes an exhibition of Rivera's work in Moscow.

March: travels to Prague, where he paints *Parade in Moscow* (fig. 253), two Moscow landscapes using his watercolor studies, a painting of a Russian child, and scenes of Prague.

Travels to Poland and East Germany. Makes sketches in East Berlin, including several for the painting *Hitler's Refuge* (fig. 254).

April 4: returns to Mexico, announcing he intends to divide his time between Mexico (in the winter) and the Soviet Union.

April 13: removes the legend "God does not exist" from the Hotel del Prado mural and substitutes "Lecture at the Letrán Academy, 1836," referring to a famous lecture at this mid-19th-century gathering place for poets, novelists, and dramatists.

April 15: at a press conference at the hotel, he announces to an amazed group of journalists, "I am a Catholic."

Recuperates at the Acapulco home of his friend Dolores Olmedo; sketches and paints and does mosaic decorations for her house on the themes of Quetzalcóatl and Tláloc.

Compiles inventories for the Anahuacalli and Kahlo collections.

Exhibition of recent works at the Galería Diego Rivera.

December 8: national homage on the occasion of Rivera's seventieth birthday.

1957

Continues planning for various mural projects as well as frescoes and polychromed sculptural pieces for Anahuacalli, none of which he will be able to begin.[8]

Spring: Rivera's mural at the California School of Fine Arts (now the San Francisco Art Institute), which had been covered by a false wall around 1947, is uncovered, cleaned, and rededicated.

Decorates the Mexico City residence of Dolores Olmedo in mosaic.

September: suffers a blood clot and phlebitis, which paralyzes his right arm.

Continues to paint.

November 24: dies of heart failure in his San Angel studio. Following official honors at the Palacio de Bellas Artes, he is buried in the Rotunda de los Hombres Ilustres at the Pantheon de Dolores, Mexico City. He wills his art to the Mexican nation.

Notes

A major portion of this chronology for the years 1886–1921 has been drawn from *Diego Rivera: The Cubist Years* by Ramón Favela (Phoenix Art Museum, 1984; hereafter cited as Phoenix 1984), the best documented and most accurate description to date of the early years of Rivera's life.

1. Rivera maintained that his paternal grandfather was born in Russia and fought with Juárez after immigrating to Mexico and that his maternal grandmother was half-Indian. While these contentions have not been proved, they are important to any understanding of Rivera's image of himself.
2. Suárez 1962, 115 (I).
3. For an illustration of this work in progress, see *Cahiers d'art* 2 (1950): 284.
4. Wolfe 1963, 145 (I).
5. Brenner 1929, 255 (IV).
6. *New York Herald-Tribune*, 10 May 1933.
7. Rodríguez-Prampolini 1969, 54 (IV).
8. Rivera's plans included further panels in the corridor at the Palacio Nacional and murals for the Museo Nacional de Historia, UNAM, the Teatro Jorge Negrete, and the private residence of actor Emilio Fernández.

Laurance P. Hurlburt

Essays

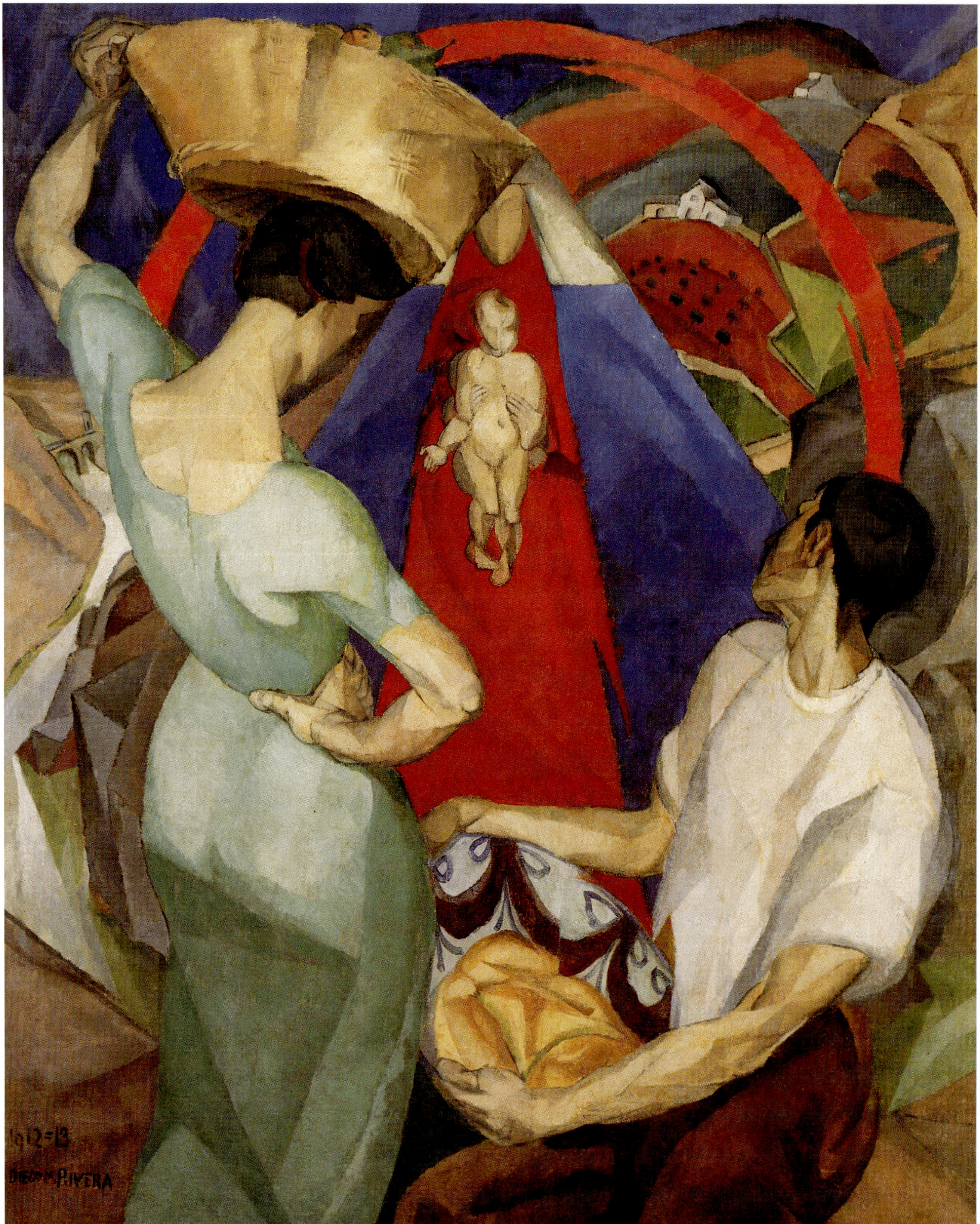
1912=13
DIEGO M. RIVERA

The Influence of the Classical Tradition, Cézanne, and Cubism on Rivera's Artistic Development

Jorge Hernández Campos

Figure 261
Adoration of the Virgin and Child, **1913, encaustic on canvas, 150 × 120 cm. Collection of María Rodríguez de Reyero.**

In his essay on Diego Rivera's Cubist years, Ramón Favela suggests that when the painter formulated his compositions and theories in Paris, he must have been under the influence of José María Velasco's course on perspective at the Academy of San Carlos, which used the text *Compendium of Linear and Aerial Perspective* by Eugenio Landesio. He further observes that the text reflects the original tradition of the Mexican academy, which was based upon Enlightenment ideas and amplified by the 19th century's preoccupation with nature and scientific analysis. According to Favela, it was Rivera's familiarity with Landesio's text and Velasco's teachings that later enabled him to grasp so easily the Cubist concept of a subjective and perceptual pictorial space. He also asserts that for Rivera, who entered the academy at eleven or twelve years of age, the influence of Velasco was extremely important, especially given Rivera's compulsion to rationalize the technical aspects of art based upon scientific and pseudoscientific optical investigations.[1]

Velasco and Landesio's text were not the only influences that had an impact on Rivera's Cubism. In Rivera's memoirs we find discussions about decisive contacts with two other teachers: Santiago Rebull and Félix Parra. Toward the end of his life, Rebull took it upon himself to pass on to Rivera everything that he had learned from the great masters about essential forms and the universal laws to which all possibilities and chance occurrences are subject.[2] Rivera recalls that Rebull stated: "In every great epoch in painting, its masters have elevated forms and colors to their purest state; that is to say, reducing and simplifying them to bring them close to their essence."[3] Rebull also quoted to Rivera passages from Plato's dialogue *Philebus* regarding "the forms that architects draw and construct: the cylinder, the cone, and the sphere."[4]

It was, furthermore, through Rebull the Rivera became acquainted with the theories of the Nazarenes, as Favela points out. As a student in Rome, Rebull frequented the studio of Johann Friedrich Overbeck, which was the gathering place of the Nazarene Brotherhood, and he later became a disciple of Pelegrín Clavé, the Catalan painter who introduced the classicism of the Nazarenes into Mexico.[5] Rivera recalls that Rebull explained to him the secret of the golden section, which was apparently part of the aesthetic ideal of the Brotherhood, and that upon hearing about the golden key to harmonic proportions, which "relates to all organized matter in our universe," he applied it to the anatomic structure of the head. Rivera concluded that

If we construct a Golden Section from the base of the retinal field to the area where the optic nerves spread into the brain, it will be precisely in the center of the crossing of the optic nerve. This same law, then, controls our visual sphere, from the eye outward and from the eye inward. Therefore, when we perceive the division in the Golden Section and its dynamic of harmonious and infinite triangulation of surfaces and voids, we experience visual pleasure, a pleasure as basic and eternal as the atom of Epicurus.[6]

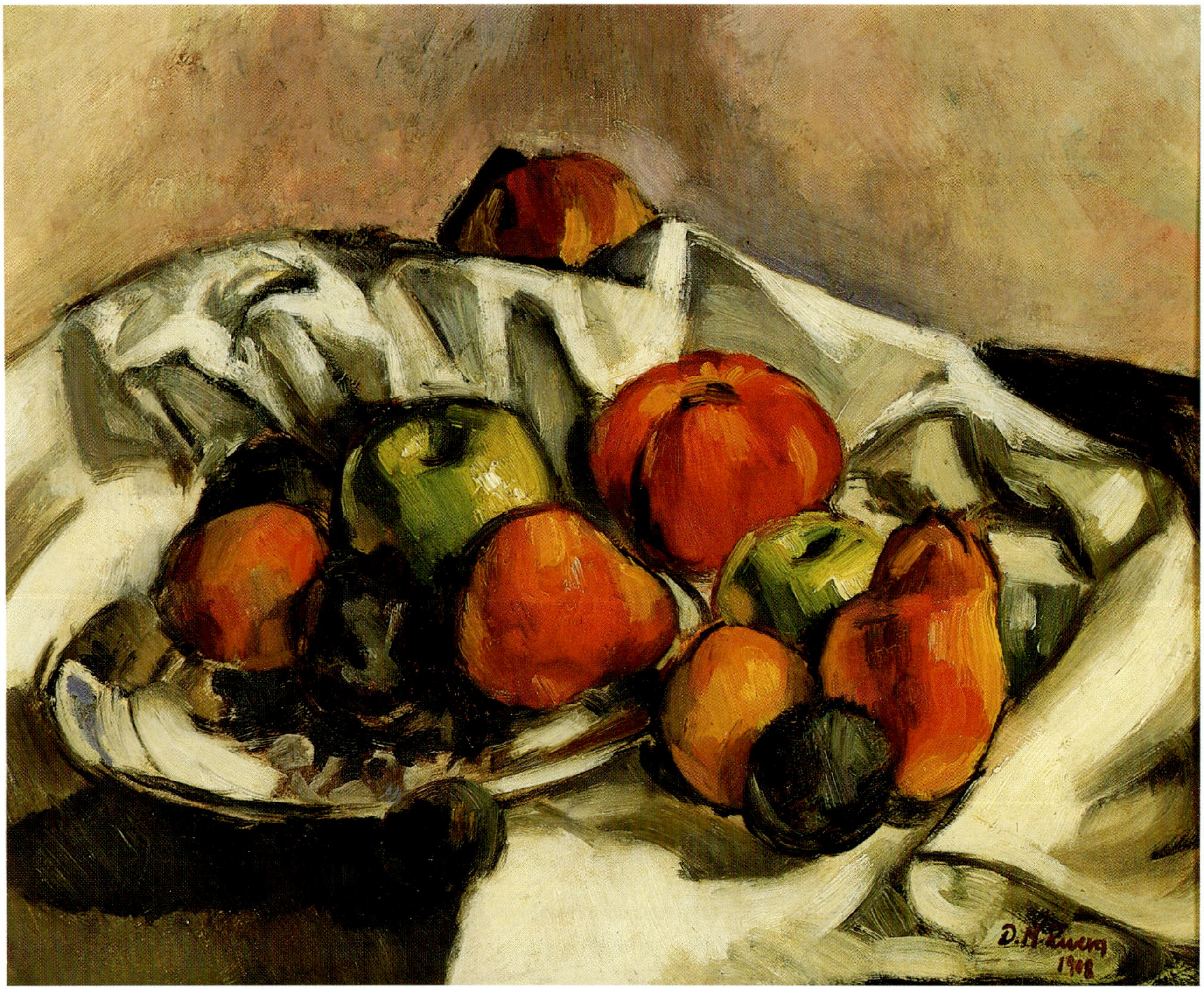

Figure 262
Still Life, **1908, oil on canvas, 38 × 48 cm. Property of the State of Veracruz.**

Félix Parra, who taught chiaroscuro by having his students copy plaster reproductions of famous sculptures, said to Rivera:

Nobody can compose a symphony without knowing the science of harmony, which is the poetic essence of mathematics. Well then, it is the same with our art. . . . In our art, everything is mathematics . . . but in a much more complicated way than in music: mathematics is forms in space; it is . . . construction, be it in stone, metal or paint; mathematics is complete optics with its vibrations of light, partially absorbed, partially reflected, which we call colors . . . the emotions that give life to our works, biology, physics . . . psychology, history . . . yes, even history! . . . and hunger and fear, pleasure, love, life . . . everything![7]

Perhaps Favela is alluding to these ideas when he speaks of the pseudoscientific rationalization to which Rivera was prone. But it is possible that through his teachers the painter had received, in addition to a positivist orientation, the seed of Renaissance scientificism, in which physics and philosophy were a single entity, with philosophy being the dominant factor. In this system, the principle of order is not dependent upon an abstract law, but rather on one based upon a complexity of processes that coexist and interact. It is an order that can be understood by the human intellect through numbers and science, as is true of Platonic metaphysics, in which divine intellect is seen in the infinite nature of mathematical propositions.[8]

Rivera himself provides the key to this connection, or affinity, between his own inclinations, the teaching he received at the Academy of San Carlos, and Cubism. As recorded by Loló de la Torriente:

During the Cubist period, freedom of expression was regained through the construction of new totalities and the use of elements ordered according to their qualitative and quantitative distinctions. Artists were free to use plastic elements based upon what they wanted to express with them within this order of universal, dynamic equilibrium called Cubism. At this time Rivera understood, without a doubt, that the techniques of Rebull, Velasco, and Parra were part of a purely classical tradition already lost in Europe.

Modern artists, driven by the need to reconstruct the basic structure of their craft, were trying to resuscitate that tradition, each in his own way. It was then that Rivera understood how lucky he had been to have gone to the Academy of San Carlos, precisely at the time of the last resplendent rays of its sunset, since around 1903 in Mexico, as twenty years earlier in Europe, this tradition, with its unified curriculum, disappeared. It died with Rebull, Velasco, and Parra![9]

Rivera also maintained that he bore an early admiration for Cézanne. While Rivera was at the academy, there was a considerable clash between factions. On one side were the proponents of tradition: Velasco, Rebull, and Parra. On the other was a group of self-proclaimed modernists, represented by two factions, one led by the German-trained Germán Gedovius, and the other the Franco-Hispanic faction of Antonio Fabrés.[10] Rivera recalls that during that time, Parra brought a very large black man to him at the academy and asked him to paint the man's head in order to demonstrate the efficacy of traditional methods. Afterward, some students from the modernist group compared this work favorably with the painting of Cézanne. Rivera, who had recently found an album of Cézanne reproductions in a French bookstore in Mexico City, was excited by that comparison with "the true master of all who had been able to achieve anything in modern painting, the great Cézanne."[11]

The personal recollections cited above appear in the memoirs that Rivera dictated to Loló de la Torriente between 1944 and 1953 and probably reflect his customary reinterpretation of events. In this case, his student years were probably seen in light of subsequent experience, with a desire to attribute to this formative period a dimension of precociousness and prescience that it did not possess. This is surely the explanation for Rivera's contention that his interest in Cézanne stemmed from such an early period in his career. In contradiction to the artist's romantic memoirs, Favela points out that when Rivera arrived in Spain in 1907, at the age of twenty, it was not in his original plans to go to Paris. Nor could he have had any intention of studying with Cézanne, who had died the previous year. Furthermore, at that time Cézanne's magnificent late work was practically unknown, even in France, where it had influence only upon a limited circle in Paris. It is likewise difficult to believe that in 1903 there could have been the appreciation of Cézanne's work in Mexico that Rivera indicates.[12]

Nevertheless, Rivera's interpretations of his student years must be examined, especially since they were made by the painter toward the end of his life. It is important that Rivera, the major founder of muralism and the Mexican School, cites as influences both the classical tradition, together with the weltanschauung implicit in it, and the Cézannesque-Cubist movement, which has been interpreted not only as a break with tradition but also as the creation of the aesthetic revolution identified with modernity.

Criticism in general has still not taken Rivera's recollections into account. They reflect a break from the pattern of irrational nationalism that has been used by the Mexican School to explain its own development. In the years between 1944 and 1953, when Rivera was dictating his memoirs, the Marxist concept of the spontaneous development of the Mexican School from an historical dynamic became dogma.[13] This theory claims that the Mexican School was rooted in the popularism of the Mexican Revolution and reflected, for the first time, the true indigenous essence of Mexico. This view identified Mexico as a land of workers and peasants, with its own cultural heritage that rejected the colonial past, the culture of the Porfiriato, and the discipline of the academy, along with all foreign influences, especially that of the European avant-garde.

Rivera's memoirs embody a different perspective. They suggest that the genesis of the Mexican School occurred within the broader context of international artistic developments. The Mexican School must be understood as part of an uninterrupted current of realism that, according to art historian Jean Claire, constitutes a separate historical pattern that coexists with the development of the avant-garde (abstractionism, Dadaism, and Surrealism), which has been considered the only history. According to Claire, this additional historical component is a broad return to realism that began in 1919 and continued throughout the period between the two World Wars. This current of realism reflects a reaction against the vanguard and a return to traditional methods of organizing reality.[14] Jean Laude has summarized this parallel history as follows: Around 1919 a discourse occurred in Europe and the United States, which sought to bring an end to, and to warn against, the errors of the past. This discourse refocused on national cultural values and the desire for quality craftsmanship and traditional methods in literature and music. It was based upon works from the immediate past and encouraged the production of new works whose characteristics gave legitimacy to their predecessors. Further, institutional Cubism was rejected, as was Italian Neorealism, not with the intention of avoiding its problematic aspects but rather with the desire to return to a figurative tradition based upon *beau métier* techniques and to reestablish links with pre-Cézannian humanism and perspective.[15]

In order to analyze the impact of realism on the development of the Mexican School, the theses of Claire and Laude must be modified. First, the general return to realism did not begin precisely in 1919, but rather before then. Further, if Cubism was at first rejected, it was later accepted, as both a bridge to and an integral component of realism. In addition, the assertion of a return to a pre-Cézannian perspective is not valid. Rivera maintained that Cézanne was "the father," the bulwark of Mediterranean tradition in the modern European world,[16] and his work demonstrates a Cézannesque influence in 1918. Finally, it was not support and verification that was sought in works of the immediate past, but rather a rejuvenation

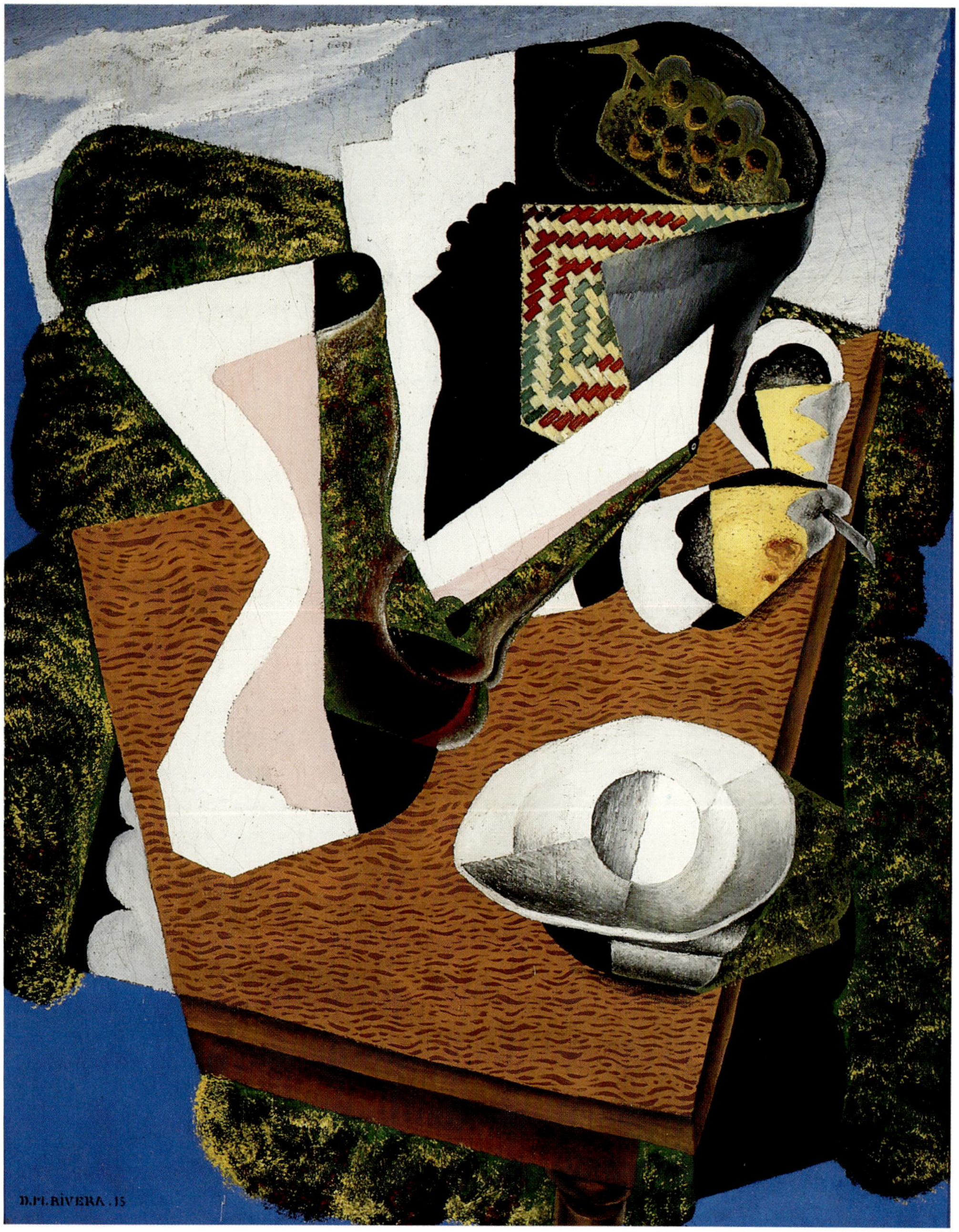

Figure 263
Still Life with Gray Bowl,
1915, oil on canvas, 79.4 × 63.8 cm. Austin, Texas, The Lyndon Baines Johnson Library and Museum.

of the Western tradition of humanism through contemporary revolutionary ideals. The validity of an alternative thesis asserting the importance of a broad tradition of international realism in the development of the Mexican School is reinforced by Rivera's break with Cubism and return to realism in 1918.

It is quite possible that Rivera was unaware of the implications of his reconstructed memoirs. Far from contradicting the theories of Claire and Laude, he places them in what is perhaps a broader and more profound context. Doubtless, this context reflects a vested interest, since it comes from a painter trained in the classical tradition who, in his youth, had a very limited set of models of modernism: first, García Rodríquez, Sorolla, Benlliure y Villegas, Whistler, Liebermann, Carriére, Bastien Lepage (and the skewed opinions of others regarding Sisley and Monet), then Pissarro and Segantini, and finally, the Spanish Academy, which he joined in 1907.[17] In other words, until his second trip to Europe in 1911, Rivera was, measured against artistic developments in Paris, a conservative and marginal artist.

It is apparent from Rivera's own words that he accepted Cubism as the continuation of a search. If, in the development of his aesthetic, Cubism represents a break, it is in the sense that he threw aside the history of modern art, from Mannerism through the turn of the 20th century, and focused on the quattrocento when Brunelleschi, Uccello, Masaccio, and Piero della Francesca ushered in a new epoch with the new scientific tool of linear perspective. Seen in this light, Cubism did more than reopen the problems of classical space, the illusion of an image on a flat plane, and the actual subject of art. It also broadened the problem of space, and human presence in that space, which is implicit in the science of perspective created by Brunelleschi.

This view of Cubism, which is still relatively unexplored, has permeated contemporary criticism perhaps without the complete realization of the critics and has engendered curiously contradictory opinions. In 1954 Jean Leymarie stated that

Cubism resulted in a new lyrical and conceptual pictorial language that put an end to the Renaissance tradition of empirical illusionism.[18] On the other hand, Roberto Longhi, a Piero della Francesca scholar, stated that Piero's work closed an empirical era and opened a scientific one.[19] And Frank Elgar referred to Picasso and Braque, the initiators of Cubism, as the unquestionable heirs to the greatest pictorial revolution that had occurred since Paolo Uccello.[20]

The relationship between the return to realism and the quattrocento needs analysis. The return to realism between the World Wars corresponded to a shift in critical opinion regarding the masters of the quattrocento that became firmly established between 1915 and 1925. Formerly viewed as "primitives," they were now greatly admired. A clear example of this is seen in Longhi's essay in which he gathers and presents 19th-century opinions referring to Piero della Fancesca as "petrified" by the science of perspective and important for the history of technique but not the history of art.[21] Another such opinion was held by Bernard Berenson, who, in 1897 wrote of Piero, "At times you feel him to be clogged by his science.[22] These opinions are quite different from those of thirty years later, such as the statement of the painter and critic André Lhote. In 1930 Lhote declared that one must salute Piero as the first Cubist.[23] And in 1950 Berenson discussed his surprise at the mass admiration for Piero that began around 1925 and at the analogies between Piero and Cézanne that were being made by contemporary painters.[24]

A reevaluation is also necessary regarding the contributions made to Cézannism and Cubism by those artists who represent provincial Western culture (according to the point of view that sees Paris as the epicenter of activity). Guilio Carlo Argan, for example, has stated that up until the time he painted *Les demoiselles d'Avignon,* Picasso was still basically a provincial artist, and although he had obviously known Cézanne's work since 1905, he probably viewed it in relation to El Greco, who was then his ideal. According to Argan, Picasso rejected Matisse's *La joie de vivre* as an offense to the sensibilities, believing that art is not a lyrical effusion, but rather a problem, and that Cézanne was all problem. He further asserts that Picasso's vision in *Les demoiselles* is based on the notion of contradiction as a fundamental principle of history and that for Picasso art is the "decisive intervention in historic reality"[25]—in other words, it is realism. The linking of Cubism with realism is also reflected in the opinion of Pierre Cabanne, who states that Cubism was neither a true nor a false abstraction: it was a pure and new realism, very different from both traditional realism and contemporary abstraction.[26]

When Rivera became a Cubist, he did not break from the Hispanic tradition in which he had been trained in Mexico and Spain, a tradition that was conservative, antireformist, and in dialectic tension with progressive modern culture. Picasso, the genius who created Cubism based on the example of Cézanne, came from that same cultural tradition. Seen from this perspective, Cézanne's work seems even more complex and fertile than has been thought until now. And it should not be surprising, then, that Rivera considered Cubism to be the logical result of the triple influences of Seurat, Cézanne, and El Greco, particularly given his assertion that Cubism is basically classical.[27]

Nor should it be surprising that Rivera abandoned Cubism. In reality he had never felt comfortable with it. It must have seemed too narrow, a small corner of a vast field that had begun to open before him. It seems quite natural that Rivera, encouraged in the postwar period by Elie Faure, a great admirer of Cézanne, should have turned to "father Cézanne" prior to his trip to Italy in 1920. When he took that trip, it was with a nascent awareness of painting as part of an historical continuum. Just as it was possible to move from quattrocento spatial simultaneity through successive juxtaposition to Cubist superimposition of planes and fragmentation of volumes, so was it possible to reverse that movement with Cézanne as a bridge. In so doing, his work gained in human dimension, and he discovered new possibilities within realism.

In his year and a half of travel, Rivera discovered monumental mural painting and began to understand that "what is universal only becomes so when it is profoundly particular."[28] During that period, he created more than three hundred drawings and achieved the integration of intellectual power and artistic vision with which he returned to Mexico.

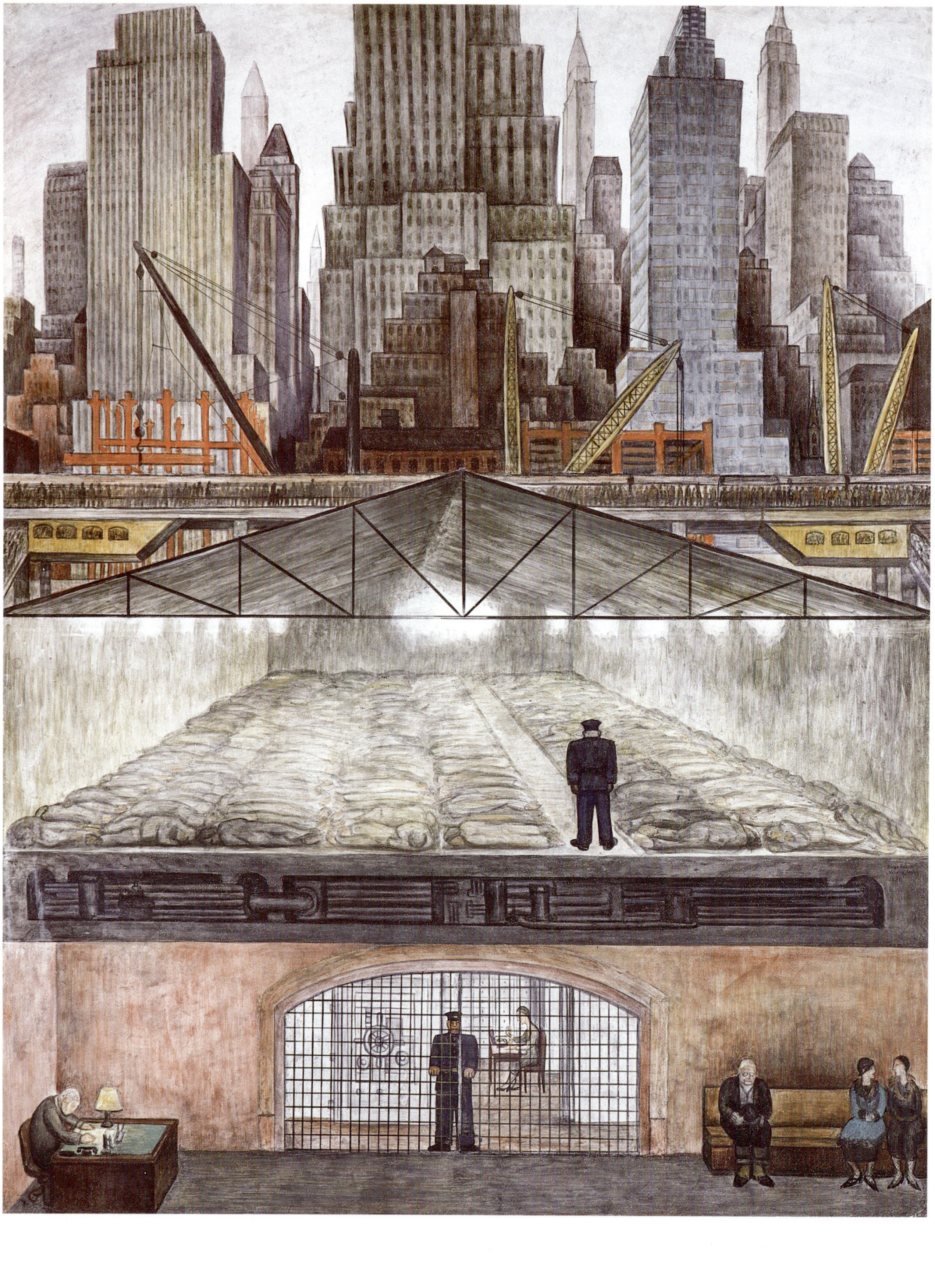

Rivera and the Concept of Proletarian Art

Alicia Azuela

Figure 264
Frozen Assets, 1931, fresco, 239 × 188 cm. Collection of Dolores Olmedo.

The year 1930 was crucial in the career of Diego Rivera for it was then that he began the first of his seven murals in the United States, all but one inspired by that country's industrial society. These mural commissions enabled him to fulfill one of the greatest desires of his life: to create an art that would treat the machine as both an aesthetic object and a generating force in the process of social change.

While this experience was fundamental to Rivera's career from an artistic perspective, it created a conflict between his artistic goals and his political convictions. In the United States, Rivera found himself in a context very different from that in the Soviet Union, where he had first laid the theoretical foundations for his concept of proletarian art. This opportunity to create an art for the proletariat had been made possible by capitalist patrons, and he knew that they would expect him to interpret the realities of an industrial society in a way that would be inconsistent with his own radical views. This situation and its resolution would have far-reaching effects on his work and his theoretical definition of proletarian art.

Rivera's stay in the Soviet Union from late 1927 to early 1928 had decisively influenced his conception of what constituted a truly proletarian art, primarily through his contact with members of the group *Octobre.* (Formed in 1928, *Octobre* exhibited for the first time in 1930 and was dissolved in 1932 by the Stalinist decree "On the Reconstruction of Literary and Artistic Organizations" and the official establishment of Socialist Realism.)

Octobre advocated a public art capable of providing an alternative to both Socialist Realism and the art of the Soviet avant-garde. *Octobre* considered the avant-garde elitist since their art was based on a formal, abstract language that was inaccessible to the masses, and they criticized the Socialist Realists for being on the one hand propagandists and on the other academicists. *Octobre* advocated the creation of an art form that would be at the service of the masses (both workers and peasants) in the international class struggle. This goal would be achieved on several levels: the production of political messages in the various artistic media, the reorganization of communal life through the creation of innovative architecture and industrial design, and the establishment of new forms of public spectacle and new methods of art education. The artist, then, should be a militant, a leader at the head of the revolutionary proletariat, creating the ideological conditions necessary for the construction of a new mode of life.

Although the members of *Octobre* rejected the Soviet avant-garde, they celebrated popular art and respected other forms of art so long as they demonstrated both high artistic quality and acceptable ideological content. *Octobre* saw their own era as a period of transition. They believed that in order for art to fulfill its social function, there must exist a certain level of artistic sensibility, or taste, if communication between artist and worker was to take place. Furthermore, since taste influences selection in the consumption of aesthetic objects, it is thus a factor both in economic change and in determining the form of the art object. Therefore, since the artistic taste of the proletariat had been debased by the "pseudo-art" offered to it by the bourgeoisie, it was of vital importance that the proletariat be educated so that in time they would be able to create their own art. These ideas formed the starting point for Rivera's definition of proletarian art and brought a new dimension to his already long experience in the production of public art.

However, because of a series of artistic and political conflicts with the Stalinist regime, Rivera left the Soviet Union and was not able to put any of these ideas into immediate practice. Paradoxically, his first opportunity to do so would come after the United States ambassador to Mexico, Dwight W. Morrow, who had commissioned Rivera's mural in Cuernavaca, helped make it possible, in the face of an extensive State Department file on the artist's communist activities, for Rivera to enter the United States and undertake his first mural commissions outside Mexico.

Rivera's first three murals in California, those for the Luncheon Club of the San Francisco Stock Exchange, the California School of Fine Arts, and the residence of Mrs. Sigmund Stern, are all fairly conventional in theme—the logical result of the artist's attempt to gain the confidence of a public that disapproved of his political positions. The most interesting of the three for any discussion of Rivera's attempt to create a work of proletarian art in the United States is the mural at the California School of Fine Arts, entitled *The Making of a Fresco* (see fig. 390).

The work is divided thematically into three parts, which are in turn divided into individual scenes by a network of scaffolding. On the left, in ascending order, a sculptor and his assistants cut stone, other workers continue the sculpting process, and factory ventilators, which Rivera saw as "those functional sculptures created by industrial necessity,"[1] complete the sequence. On the right, a group of engineers works on a plan for the skyscrapers being built by the workers above. In the center, architects review blueprints, while a painter and four assistants works on a fresco depicting a monumental worker.

By representing art as a form of work, the composition embodies several crucial points in the Marxist aesthetic: (1) art plays a fundamental role in the creation of the new workers' society; (2) art is thus capable of transforming history; and (3) the artist is a worker in the field of culture who labors in the public service. In line with the theories of *Octobre,* the artist, the architect, the industrial designer, and the engineer are presented as contributing directly to the economy and to the organization of a society's lifestyle through the creation of buildings and everyday objects. A corollary idea is implied: painters and sculptors also contribute to the world of ideas by defining the self-image of the worker.

Although the ideas are essentially Marxist, they are treated in such a way as to make them acceptable to the American public. The actual location is undefined—the workers could be at any site; the urban landscape could belong to any country, any social system. The concepts remain on the level of theory, without reference to how they might actually be applied. Thus, the mural can be read, as it has been up till now, as a sympathetic portrayal of the industrial worker rather than as an attempt to communicate these ideas to the workers of the world. In any case, this approach enabled Rivera to circumvent the compromises that might have been necessary if he had used specific temporal and spatial references and thus to avoid jeopardizing his relations with his patrons by analyzing existing social reality.

Shortly after completing the California murals, Rivera created seven movable panels for the 1931 retrospective of his work at the Museum of Modern Art in New York. In three of these panels, Rivera refers to the terrible conditions in the United States following the economic crisis of 1929, thus embodying for the first time in his United States murals the critical function so important to *Octobre.*

On the lateral panels of the series are scenes set in an electric power plant: on one side a work crew operates electric drills; on the other, welding torches (fig. 265). The central panel, entitled *Frozen Assets* (fig. 264), is a representation of a cross section of New York City. This panel's theme is based on the view, widely held at the time, that the financiers and businessmen had built empires at the expense of thousands of workers and that business had precipitated the economic crisis through bad management and the misuse of capital and public funds. The work is formally uncomplicated and its message is clear. Again, the composition is divided into three parts, the lowest of which depicts a bank vault where wealth is securely kept—that is, imprisoned. In the center the corpses of thousands of workers lie in a sort of warehouse, entombed by the skyscrapers, symbols of economic power, that appear in the upper level.

After *Frozen Assets,* Rivera did not refer directly to any specific historical reality in his work until 1933–34, when he painted his murals for Rockefeller Center and the New Workers School. Whereas the dramatic force of *Frozen Assets* derived from its subtlety, the overtly propagandistic nature of these murals brought them quite close to the style of Socialist Realism that *Octobre* opposed. According to the artist himself, he was first able to crystallize his ideas on proletarian art in his mural at the Detroit Institute of Arts. There, Rivera said: "I was able to analyze the relationship between workers, the means of production, natural resources, and necessary materials, creating a beauty equal to [that of] the proletariat."[2]

Detroit Industry is a synthesis of the observations of machinery and the industrial process that Rivera had made in various Ford factories over a period of three months. During that time he also experienced firsthand the routine of factory work, the growing union agitation, the the plight of the lower and middle classes as a result of the Depression. He avoided any direct references to these problems, however, and chose to treat only the accomplishments of the industrial world of the United States.

Rivera conceived the mural as an epic tribute to the advancements made in Detroit in the fields of pharmaceutics, chemistry, and aeronautics as well as in the automotive industry since these efforts symbolized the best achievements of both intellectual and manual workers. The *Detroit Industry* series consists of various scenes in which workers and engineers carry out their tasks in an idealized setting, presented in the didactic tone often seen in Rivera's works. Also evident is his technique of counterbalancing positive and negative views of a single theme: for example, a scene showing a vaccination is contrasted with the making of poison gas bombs—that is, the benefits of science versus its destructive aspects. Again, however, Rivera did not directly challenge the economic system of the United States, presenting its achievements and problems as simply parts of a whole that, in this instance at least, he accepted as valid.

All of the artist's passion was poured into expressing his fascination with engineering and the aesthetic aspects of the machine. Machines and their function constitute the central theme of the work, and their sheer scale and formal qualities dominate the mural. In spite of himself, Rivera revealed that his artistic interests were above any possible compromise that might be suggested by his political and social ideologies.

In the pamphlet that the Detroit Institute of Arts published after the completion of the murals, Rivera stated that he had intended the work as homage to the workers of Detroit. In his opinion Detroit was a city composed of workers of all races, and it would be there that the cultural values and technological advancements of the American continent would combine to create a new society that would dominate the world. Furthermore, he declared that

on the basis of the unity of prehistoric culture preserved faithfully in Latin America, the industrial power of the United States, the raw materials of the southern continent, and the machines of the north, a new era will arise for humanity in which the worker, now in power, will finally bring peace to the world.[3]

The narrative contained in the mural program begins, according to Rivera, on the east wall, opposite the main entrance to the court, with a description of the geological, economic, and cultural origins of Detroit (see fig. 393). On the west wall the construction of an airplane, the embodiment of the most important technological advances to that time, symbolizes man's achievements in the course of his evolution (see fig. 394).

Also on the west wall are representatives of what Rivera felt to be the two primary and fundamental sources of American technological progress: the exchange of raw materials and technological resources between North and South America and the cooperation between the physical labor of the workers and the intellectual efforts of the engineers. The first premise is presented immediately below the image of aviation in the form of a cargo ship carrying rubber from Brazil, where the workers are shown harvesting the raw material, to Detroit, where industrial laborers receive it for processing. The second premise—the alliance of intellectual and manual labor—is represented by the depiction, beneath the two areas of the American hemisphere, of a worker and an engineer, backed by the mechanisms for producing steam and electricity, forms of energy that together are the driving force of the new industrial civilization.

In the upper registers of the north and south walls, Rivera placed idealized figures representing the four races as a form of homage to the workers of all races who have made progress possible on this continent (see figs. 391 and 392). On both walls, on either side of these figures, Rivera used scenes of industrial activity, specifically in the fields of pharmaceutics and chemistry, to symbolize both the benefits and the destructive potential of technological advancements.

In both relative scale and formal value, the salient scenes in the mural are the central panels on the north and south walls, depicting respectively the various stages in the assembly of a Ford V8 engine and the production of the exterior of the same car. These extraordinary mechanical landscapes capture the concentrated atmosphere of the factories with their continuous movement. Rivera's fascination with machinery resulted in a beautiful, honest, and complete synthesis of the industrial process that masterfully integrates many distinct operations within a single time and space. In line with the ideas of *Octobre,* these two sections of the mural are composed in a totally accessible realistic style, enriched by elements from the classical tradition, Renaissance murals, Cubism, Futurism, and pre-Hispanic art.

The realistic depiction of objects and processes does not, however, detract from the utopian nature of the work. Labor and the industrial process are idealized, with no hint of the negative aspects of the actual environment. Man, machine, and system function in harmony, with no reference to specific problems or adverse working conditions. The workers are immersed in the temporal and spatial realm of production itself, as if that were a separate reality. The worker is but one more piece in the vast machinery that carries out the production cycle with exemplary precision.

In spite of its adherence to many of *Octobre*'s principles, this particular interpretation of social reality and the fact that it was created in the United States, the capitalist country par excellence, separated Rivera somewhat from the fundamental theories about proletarian art that he had espoused as a Marxist and as a member of *Octobre.* Rivera realized this and used the occasion to publish a series of articles presenting his own concept of proletarian art. His aim was to defend himself from attacks by those who questioned the proletarian and revolutionary character of his work.

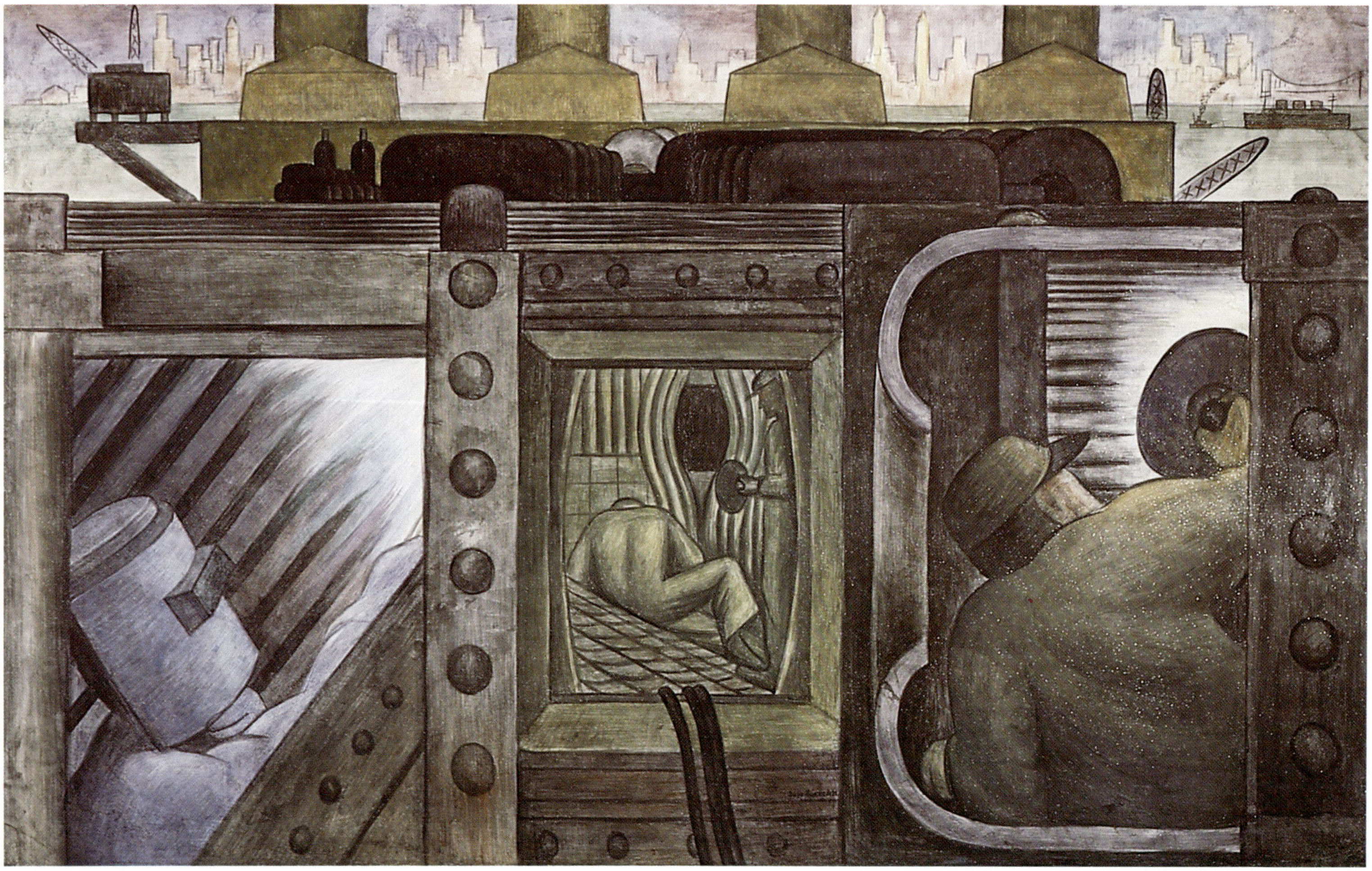

Figure 265
Electric Welding, 1931,
fresco on steel reinforced
concrete, 142.5 x 239 cm.
Collection of Mr. and
Mrs. Marcos Micha Levy.

First of all, he refuted the concept, promulgated by *Octobre,* that the artistic sensibilities of the masses had been seriously crippled by the consumption of the "pseudo-art" of capitalistic societies so that communication between artist and worker was all but impossible. Believing that his work was meaningful to the proletariat as a whole, regardless of the social system in which the workers functioned, Rivera stated that the reception given to his mural by the workers of Detroit proved that

it isn't true that the artistic taste of the North American workers has been created and set by comic strips. . . . If painters insist on creating things that are of no interest to them, then it is only natural that they won't be attracted to them . . . but if they paint things that concern the worker, the response will be immediate.[4]

He added that the worker would always be capable of having an immediate appreciation of beauty on the condition that it was in some way related to his life, expressed his needs, and was thus useful to him.

Rivera's second premise was that the essential characteristic of proletarian art is its usefulness, since it is from this element that the function, meaning, and formal value of any work of art derive. Unlike *Octobre,* however, he did not identify theme as the key to a work's usefulness, nor did he feel that the artist had to expose social injustice. Utility, he declared, could be found "in landscape which, besides depicting man's environment, can reveal new aspects of man himself."[5] In his view, a loaf of bread and an apple, as in a still life by Cézanne, could arouse the sensibilities of the peasant or the worker, since they stem from the same reality.

Usefulness, he concluded, depends upon the artist's formal expertise. If the formal quality of a work is high, then it will be capable of penetrating the viewer's senses, modifying his or her taste, and thereby opening up infinite possibilities in the understanding of reality. Rivera believed that this formal excellence was what gave an art work the ability to communicate:

As long as the work has formal quality and the theme, having sprung from the same environment, is of interest to the proletariat, it will be able to sensitize the worker to his environment and will therefore serve the revolutionary process.[6]

This series of arguments indicate that by the 1930s Rivera had come to believe that the problem of the relationship between the artist and the worker is inherent in the work of art itself and not in socioeconomic influences on the taste and sensibilities of the working class. These statements also make clear how convinced he was of the validity of his contribution to the creation of a revolutionary art for the proletariat. They furthermore reveal the extent to which he was a man of his times, whose attitudes and beliefs had been largely defined by his early training at the end of the 19th century. Thus, although Rivera's contact with *Octobre* enriched both his visual language and his theoretical definition of proletarian art, it left unaltered the way in which he interpreted reality in his art.

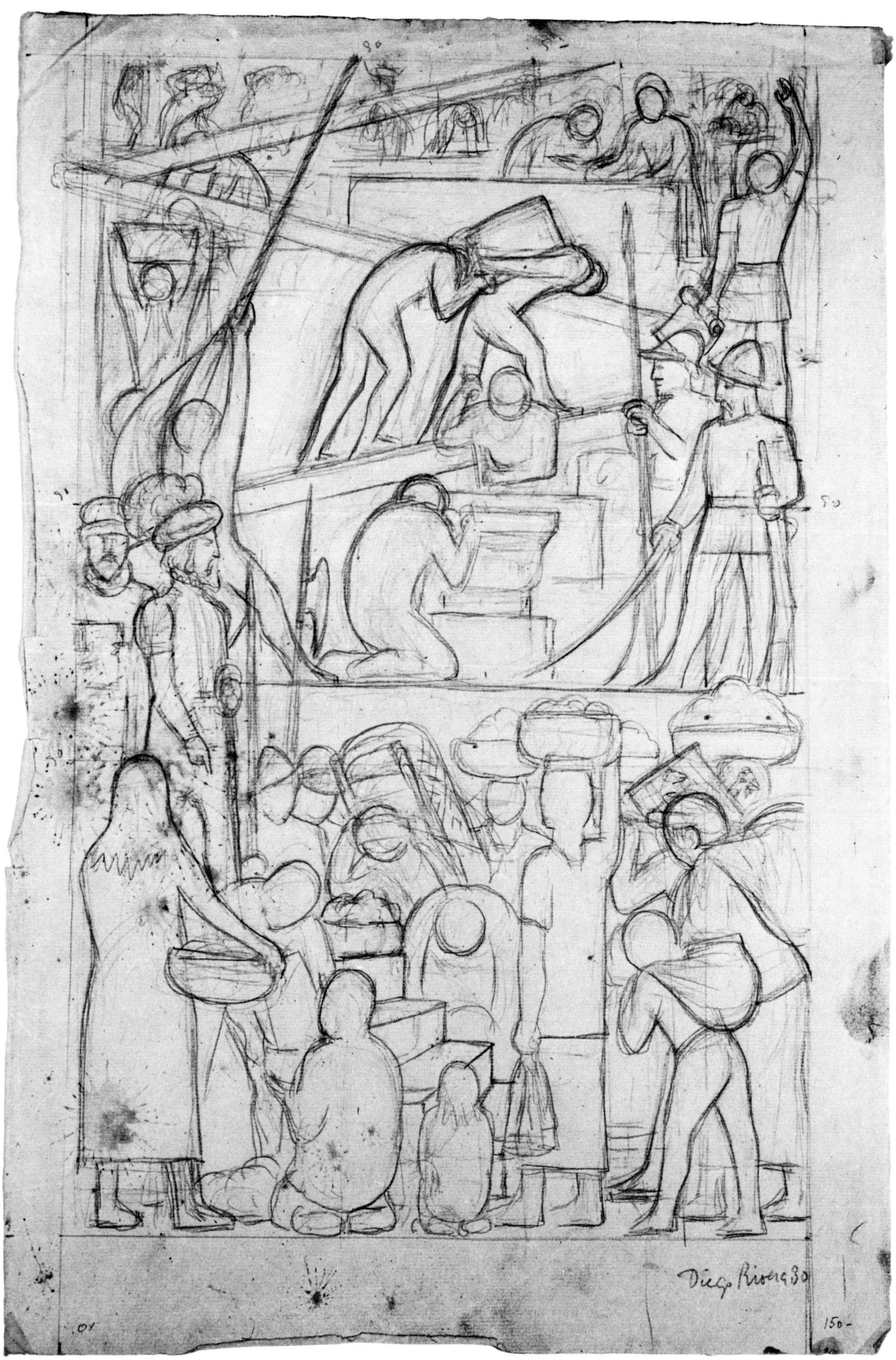
Diego Rivera 30

Rivera's Concept of History

Ida Rodríguez-Prampolini

Figure 266
***Building the Palace of Cortés*, 1930, pencil on brownish paper, 47.9 × 31.8 cm. New York, The Museum of Modern Art. Anonymous Gift (207.40).**

After the triumph of the revolution that began with the overthrow of the regime of Porfirio Díaz in 1910, Mexican artists turned their attention to the problem of how to convey to a largely illiterate population the history of its own political struggles as well as how to introduce them to new revolutionary truths. Artists sought to socialize the language of art by the use of a monumental form of expression—the mural—and thus to help in the creation of a free and cultured society. The three greatest muralists, José Clemente Orozco, David Alfaro Siqueiros, and Diego Rivera, created a body of work that is magnificent in its breadth, power, and mastery. Of the three only Rivera would attempt to create, in clear, legible images, a course on sociopolitical history for his compatriots. The murals of Rivera do not adhere to linear chronology nor do they reflect a didactic objectivity. Rather, they are the product of the artist's interpretation of history from a materialist point of view.

Of all the Mexican muralists, Rivera was the most erudite in the traditional sense of the word. His life experience was broader and richer, as was his imaginative capacity, and, furthermore, as a result of having lived in Europe for many of his formative years as an artist, he had a more profound awareness of the development of Western art. He had also been a participant in the artistic revolution that occurred in Paris in the early years of the century. Like many European artists, Rivera had passed from the lessons of Cézanne to the idealized and conceptual abstraction of Analytic Cubism and then to Synthetic Cubism in the manner of Juan Gris, Jean Metzinger, and Albert Gleizes. It was in several paintings in this latter style that Rivera first introduced references to Mexican history and culture into his work. *Zapatista Landscape* (fig. 53), which reflects a freely interpreted Cubism—its strong, extravagant colors signal Rivera's break with the refinement of French Cubism—contains such allusions to Mexico as volcanoes, a carbine, and a *sarape*. The work is strongly evocative of the country and the revolutionary reality that Rivera was soon to embrace.

Upon his return to Mexico, Rivera abandoned the Cubism that had dominated his work for almost a decade and returned to realism. This abrupt change in his style was the result of his political convictions, which had drawn closer and closer to Marxist ideology as he studied the theory of dialectical materialism.

In the first mural Rivera painted in Mexico, that for the Anfiteatro Bolívar at the Escuela Nacional Preparatoria, his break with Paris is clearly evident, although the true language that he was to develop is not yet apparent and his political convictions are even less so. *Creation* is a transitional work that reflects the influence of the philosopher José Vasconcelos, Mexico's minister of education at the time and one of the driving forces behind the muralist movement. But this first example of Rivera's public art is nevertheless significant. It signals the artist's return to the vocabulary of realism, which he was never again to abandon, and it contains the salient characteristics of Rivera's style: a reliance on the linear language of drawing; two-dimensional composition; sensual forms; and a rich, sumptuous use of color. The theme of this first mural was, in the artist's own words, "the origins of the sciences and the arts, a kind of abbreviated version of the essential history of mankind."[1]

In concert with the aims of the state-sponsored mural projects and their goal of consolidating the revolutionary process, Rivera rejected the classical elements evident in this transitional piece, replacing the classical ideal of beauty with one based on the beauty of the indigenous population and abandoning the traditional subjects of European monumental art in favor of scenes from the history of Mexico. Rivera based his vision of history on a historical-dialectical materialism that was closer to Hegel than to Marx. His inventive presentations of historic events have an almost comic-strip character, which at times borders on a "Hollywoodesque" approach to public communication. No pejorative connotation should be construed from such a description; rather, it is intended to point out the successful modernity of his work.

Rivera's concept of realism presupposes a revolutionary praxis, an analysis of contradictions, and a very real commitment to social struggle. It is necessary, therefore, to ascertain whether or not his work is consistent with his ideological postulations. Such an analysis will also demonstrate the development of his concept of history.

From his return to Mexico onward, the development of Rivera's work is based on a conception of the dominance of theme:

There is no reason to worry about theme being essential. On the contrary, because theme is accepted as a primary need, the artist is completely free to create a perfect plastic form. Theme is to a painter as tracks are to a locomotive. He cannot proceed without it.[2]

Although Rivera conceived of theme with great freedom, his best works, and perhaps his most interesting ones in terms of public murals, are those in which the theme is specifically historical. In Cuernavaca in 1930, Rivera treated the general historical theme of the conquest of Mexico by using the specific example of the region of Cuauhnáhuac. As a symbol of the Spanish triumph, Rivera chose the construction of the very building in which the paintings were done, the palace of the conqueror, Hernán Cortés. The work clearly reflects the submission of the Indians, who, from the moment of their defeat, were reduced to slave labor (see fig. 266). In Rivera's vision, they are dispossessed of their land and customs and reduced to an anonymous mass whose role is that of a Greek chorus, bemoaning a history in which they no longer play a part.

Thesis and antithesis are represented by the benevolence of religious missionaries on one hand and the cruelty of soldiers and government officials on the other, while José María Morelos, one of the major figures in the fight for independence in Cuauhnáhuac, and Emiliano Zapata, the peasant general, provide the synthesis—as symbols of hope and promises of freedom—of the larger struggle between the Spaniards and the Indians.

Rivera treated scientific subjects in frescoes done for two buildings in Mexico City. His willingness to accept suggestions made by his patrons was characteristic of Rivera's complex attitudes toward his work. At the Instituto Nacional de Cardiología, the founder and director, Dr. Ignacio Chávez, not only suggested the theme of the history of cardiology but also provided Rivera with notes on the subject. Like a Renaissance artist who respected the tenets of the church, Rivera took the suggestions of the renowned Mexican cardiologist and with voracious enthusiasm studied the theme exhaustively so that he could faithfully deliver a history lesson on that branch of medicine. Dr. Chávez writes:

But the work of Rivera has yet another value, higher, more subtle and imponderable: its educational value for the younger generations.

It is the evocation of the historic past, with its great lesson of humility: the voice of the masters of yesterday which keeps alive the past's stimulating power; the call of a tradition molded through the centuries which orders us to continue forward.

Youth that passes through the halls cannot but familiarize itself with these great figures of thought, and knowing them all be led to cultivate the holy attitude of veneration.[3]

In the notes he gave to Rivera, Dr. Chávez advanced the notion of an "ascendent progression of knowledge" and underlined the "slow and painstaking" process of overcoming "routine, prejudice, ignorance, and fanaticism." Rivera studied the history of cardiology in minute detail as well as the iconography of the most eminent people in the field. The result was a veritable altarpiece, with the figures of these specific physicians "moving forward, with great determination, in an upward climb."[4] Rivera grouped the figures according to their fields: those who discovered cures, those who made anatomical and physiological discoveries, and those who invented medical apparatuses (see figs. 402a and 402b). These groupings and their order reflect a positivist concept of history rather than the tenets of dialectical materialism.

This positivist view of history appears again in the mural Rivera painted in the Hospital de la Raza, which reverberates with the lessons of his teacher at the Academy of San Carlos, the landscapist José María Velasco, who created a pictorial interpretation of Darwin's *Origin of the Species* at the Instituto de Geología in Mexico City. Using a descriptive and somewhat decorative realism, Rivera created a series of highly detailed scenes depicting the worlds of pre-Hispanic and modern Mexican medicine. With the possible exception of one scene, the mural is free of political denunciations and references to the idea of class struggle. That one scene, appropriate in the larger context of an image created for an institution established to provide health care for the working class, depicts the bourgeoisie being forced to pay part of the cost of treating the workers (see fig. 404). Rivera treated the scene with humor. The director of social security is seen calmly taking the money that will ultimately be used by the very institution in which the murals appear.

In the Hospital de la Raza, Rivera again uses the technique of balancing opposing forces, in this case scenes of illness and cure, arranging them on the wall in ascending order. The pre-Hispanic world is represented in a free, poetic manner, beginning with the act of birth and continuing in a series of groupings that reflect Rivera's encyclopedic investigations of indigenous codices (see Betty Brown's essay in this volume), while the area of the composition devoted to modern medical science is divided into distinct, machinelike compartments.

The murals in the Hospital de la Raza and Instituto de Cardiología are based on a concept of history as the linear, progressive accumulation of knowledge. This approach is very different from the dialectic that Rivera applied in his most ambitious project, the murals for the Palacio Nacional in Mexico City.

Of all of Rivera's works, the stairwell at the Palacio Nacional represents his most clearly defined attempt to develop the materialist concept of history in the context of painting. The most striking feature of the stairwell of the old palace of the viceroys in Mexico City is the dominance of violence in the scenes, the bloody struggles of man against man. However, as one ascends the stairway to the right, the sense of war and cruelty diminishes and one enters a calm and peaceful realm in which Rivera introduces his vision of the pre-Hispanic world (see fig. 384).

The golden age of Mexico as depicted by Rivera is not like those lost paradises, exemplified by Hesiod in *Works and Days*, in which men "lived as gods, with carefree hearts, untroubled by toil and suffering." Nor is it related to the myth of a lost paradise, common to many civilizations, in which there once existed perfect harmony among men and between man and nature. Rivera's pre-Hispanic world is not a problem-free society with no need for legal, military, or governmental structures. Rivera presents instead a political and social structure dominated by a central power, represented here by the figure of Quetzalcóatl, with its own internal and class struggles.

For Rivera, the power of the pre-Hispanic world resided in the strength of the myths and magic used to explain and control the forces of nature. Therefore, this world is surmounted by the central figure of power, Quetzalcóatl, the plumed serpent. Quetzalcóatl also appears in the upper section of the wall, where he is seen departing, illuminated by a setting sun. The latter image represents the end of an age that superficially resembles a golden age. And while this period is depicted without the generalized violence seen in the rest of the mural, there is, again, the underlying tension of opposing forces. At the left is the image of slaves constructing the pyramids, an embodiment of the idea of oppressed and alienated labor. The counterbalance to this repression is expressed through scenes representing the joy of creative work, leisure time, sensual enjoyment, and union with nature. This paradiselike world surmounts a scene of war, or more specifically class struggle. On the opposite wall, the figure of Karl Marx holds a banner in his hand, which reads: "The entire history of human society to the present is the history of class struggle." This quote is given pictorial form in this battle scene that undermines the idyllic society from within.

The wall at the base of the stairway is composed of five large panels, each bounded by an arch. On this enormous surface Rivera presents the actual history of Mexico once the pre-Hispanic mythology had been undermined. In the center of the composition is the Mexican national emblem, an eagle devouring a serpent. This transformation of the plumed serpent, symbol of Quetzalcóatl, is the very antithesis of pre-Hispanic reality, for the plumed serpent was the embodiment of an ideal, a normally earthbound creature capable of soaring to great heights. Around this central symbol of nationality, the history of the conquest of Mexico unfolds and the principal figures in Mexico's history as an independent nation gather. Along the central axis that divides the composition vertically appear the most important figures of Mexican history. Curiously, the first to appear is Hernán Cortés on horseback. Above him is Cuauhtémoc, the fallen eagle. On the same central axis, above the Mexican emblem, is a group of freedom fighters, in the center of which is the priest Hidalgo surrounded by grapevines, symbolizing the introduction of a forbidden element that will break the chains of colonization. Farther above, as the culmination of this core group in national history, is the figure of Emiliano Zapata and the slogan "Land and Liberty." Next to Zapata is a worker who points into the distance to the technological future awaiting the country (see fig. 267). Rivera's intention was to impose a dialectical chronology on a sociopolitical movement filled with contradictions, the synthesis of which provides the basis for further contradictions. The simultaneous presentation of opposites that Rivera used to express a dialectical development of history often led him to sacrifice actual historical chronology, repeating portraits of historical figures or placing them outside their actual time. The mural is nearly illegible because of the visual complexity created by the necessity of presenting in each episode its thesis, antithesis, and synthesis, which in turn provides the thesis for the next episode.

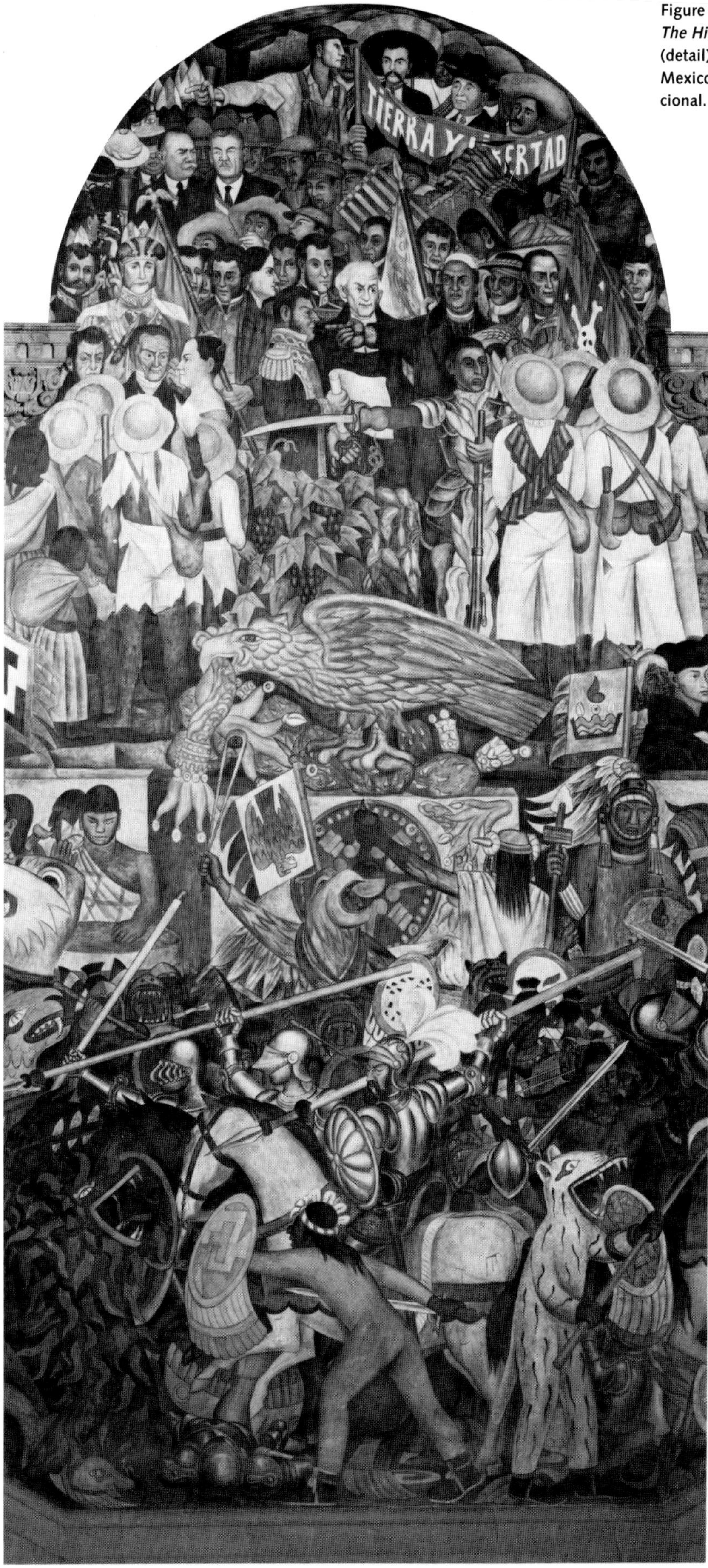

Figure 267
The History of Mexico (detail), 1929–30, fresco. Mexico City, Palacio Nacional.

On the lower part of the wall is a spectacular scene of struggle that borders on the carnivalesque. The combatants are native figures disguised as animals and Spanish conquistadores, representing the two groups from whose confrontation and ultimate fusion was to spring a new race, the mestizo population of Mexico. The genesis of this new protagonist in Mexican history is represented by the rape of an Indian woman by a Spanish soldier at the bottom of the fourth arch.

The series of intermingled yet ultimately discernible scenes always presents contrasting forces. The conquest is followed by colonial rule, which Rivera, with his affinity for completeness, tries to define in all its facets through the use of realistic portraits of actual historical personages. He depicts the royalists and the ecclesiastical orders, civil and religious authorities, viceroys and archbishops, inquisitors and kindly missionaries. Priests, friars, and theologians are presented in both good and bad light, but the underlying theme, the exploitation of the indigenous population, is always evident. The insurgent liberation movement, inspired by the republican model of the United States, is contrasted with the survival of colonialism in the monarchy of Augustín de Iturbide, the concept of empire with that of the Mexican Republic, the first Mexican Republic with the Federal Republic.

The United States ceases to be a model and becomes a threat. The United States eagle appears at the top of the first arch, while the eagle of the French invaders, from whom conservatives had sought support, flees, never to return, through the fifth arch. The empire of Maximilian is destroyed and the Republic, represented by Benito Juárez and a group of liberals, is restored. But immediately there appears a contradiction. The liberal Porfirio Díaz becomes conservative and, with military force and the power of capital, installs the dictatorship that the Revolution of 1910 would seek to overthrow, while above this scene the figure of a worker and the peasant motto of Zapata, "Land and Liberty," preside over the triumph of history.

Throughout this complex dialectic, Rivera never ceases to focus on the contradictions within classes and the class struggle in general. While opposing groups confront each other, those who triumph ultimately turn against their own class. Indians fight among themselves, Spaniards shoot each other, and the people enslave one another. The fratricidal combatants are left faceless. The Indians are masked by their armor. The soldiers fire their modern weapons with their backs turned toward the viewer, as if Rivera wanted to emphasize both the anonymity and the unconscious ignorance of the people, as well as point out the contradictions inherent in the final synthesis.

On the left wall of the stairwell, Rivera developed his theory of universal history, presenting a world locked in a conflict even greater than those previously depicted. The serene figure of Quetzalcóatl on the opposite wall is balanced here by the forces of capitalism, which are protected within a bunkerlike structure. In the modern world, power is no longer in the hands of individuals; rather it resides in social and political systems, which are supported, preserved, and protected by the existence of a mechanized culture such as that in Detroit. This anonymous industrial culture provides the very channel through which money flows from the exploited classes to their capitalistic overlords. All of the forces of industrial capitalism and the ideological structure of the state appear: the military, bankers, the clergy, factory owners, and the intellectuals who serve the bourgeoisie. In a small votive image, Rivera invokes the Virgin of Guadalupe as the cement of the bourgeois structure that feeds off the religious faith of the people, whose offerings pass through the maw of the great machine of capitalist power.

Directly opposite the image on the righthand wall of slaves working on the pyramids is a group of alienated workers constructing a building for the bourgeoisie. In addition, the agricultural environment of the pre-Hispanic world, with its mythology based on the elements, wind, water, air, and fire, is obviously contrasted with the industrial and technological landscape of the modern age.

In this panel, the violence of war is heightened through the use of imagery appropriate to the modern technological and industrial world. The violence is intense near the center of power, yet the figures within the power structure, alienated from reality and cushioned in the limbo of a world where all wants are satisfied, appear completely unaware of what is occurring around them.

Rivera no doubt understood the difficulty of developing in pictorial form a dialectic of history and the forces of liberation, and he often resorted to inscriptions for clarification and amplification. Inscriptions such as "Strike," "Land and Liberty," "Communist," "Agriculturalist," and "Gentlemen of Colon" transmit the ideological message. The smiling figure of a satisfied worker holding *Das Kapital* under his arm is typical of Rivera's incorporation of the written word within his murals

At the very top of the left wall, directly opposite the figure of Quetzalcóatl, appears Karl Marx, while the setting sun that surmounts the mythic pre-Hispanic scene is now a rising sun that illuminates his figure, the prophet of the future, pointing to the world of liberty in the distance. In his hand he holds an inscription that reads: "The entire history of human society to the present is the history of class struggle." This famous quote is the basic argument developed by Rivera in this enormous triptych, in which he attempted both to apply and to test his knowledge and his faith in dialectical materialism and the ideals of the Mexican Revolution.

Like most of the first generation of Mexican muralists, Rivera left a series of writings outlining his political convictions as he undertook the task of producing an art that was completely different from the "pure" art practiced in contemporary Europe.

Rivera conceived of art as an organic, useful human function, as necessary to man as "bread, meat, fruit, water, and air." He attributed a biological importance to art:

Each individual, group, caste, or class that exercises power in human society tries to appropriate, and if successful, take control over the production of art, which is necessary if that power is not to be undermined, challenged, and destroyed by the free exercise of the sensibility, imagination, and the rights of those subjected to the power . . . since art is one of the most efficient subversive agents. As a dialectic counterpart, individuals, groups, castes, or classes in rebellion against those who hold the power to exploit always try to use art and look to it for its inherent subversive power against exploitative power.[5]

Rivera was not the only one aware of the subversive power of art—the rulers were also. In the nationalist program of President Alvaro Obregón, cultural and artistic production in Mexico was strictly monitored, in terms of both internal and foreign policies, since it was seen as both an indicator of the stability of the state and a force in national unification. The birth of Mexican muralism in the 1920s had its roots in the recognition of art's political power. Conscious of the power of art as an agent of change and subversion, Rivera found in his own creativity a form of political praxis that justified his revolutionary beliefs and his collaboration in the nationalistic course taken by the revolution.

In spite of the many conflicts that Rivera had with the Mexican Communist Party, his frequent political vaccilations, and his often public differences of opinion with David Alfaro Siqueiros, he was recognized by many critics and artists, Siquieros included, as the artist who, because of his maturity and talent, established the basic direction of muralism. For example, Siqueiros wrote:

Because of his professional and theoretical maturity, Diego Rivera was, during this period [1922–24], the first to go beyond the aesthetic mysticism of our earliest murals (from the very first period of the Preparatoria) to an art of eloquent ideological purpose as an essential method of developing our general desire for an art bound to the problems of humanity and human society. With his theory and initial works he established the seminal principles, which later permitted more profound formulations. . . . He demonstrated that our movement had pragmatic, universal value.[6]

Rivera's radical shift to realism when he returned to Mexico occurred before the great Stalinist polemic establishing realism as the official language of Soviet art that took place in the Soviet Union between 1934 and 1956. Although this may have affirmed his adoption of realism, through his contact with leftist intellectuals in Paris, Rivera had no doubt already learned that for realism to be truly revolutionary, a proletarian, collectivist spirit was necessary. In 1918, *Proletkult* had already stated:

Proletarian culture should have the mark of revolutionary socialism for the proletariat to assume its new hierarchy, organize its feelings through the new art and shape its vital relations with the new, authentically proletariat spirit, that is, the collectivist spirit.[7]

Rivera's later deviation from this fundamental point is important in understanding the type of realism he adopted for his historical interpretations. To Rivera, individual conscience and personal identification with revolutionary ideas seemed to be sufficient for the creation of a revolutionary art. It is interesting to observe how he resolved his ambivalence regarding the collectivist doctrine and defended his individuality while dressed in worker's overalls. In analyzing his work at the Secretaría de Educación Pública, Rivera described himself as the repository of the sensibilities of the people:

The painter decorated this building with the intention of becoming immersed in himself, eliminating, day by day, anything that was not truly his own, since only a completely personal but totally truthful expression would suffice to achieve his objective. He is an entity identical to the thousands that make up the working class. The artist did not have to adopt a spiritual or philosophical posture or put himself on a political plane. Rather, he simply had to be in touch with his innermost feelings, which were identical to those of all his companions [comrades].[8]

At this point Rivera ceased to be the sophisticated and erudite Paris-educated intellectual and identified himself with the revolutionary proletariat:

. . . if the painter is revolutionary, identified with that part of humanity that represents the positive pole of this great biological phenomenon that we call the Revolution, if he is a worker in the widest class sense, anything that he would do as a good artisan, that is, sincerely, would necessarily be a revolutionary expression, whatever the theme. If an artist in these circumstances paints a portrait and a bouquet of flowers, both paintings will be revolutionary. On the other hand, if a bourgeois artist makes a painting or undertakes a decoration that represents the apotheosis of the social revolution, it will nevertheless be a bourgeois painting.[9]

The subjective aesthetic of these ideas distanced Rivera from party politics and the polemic entanglements of *Proletkult*, which affirmed that only an artist from the proletariat could create the new socialist art and so accomplish the great work of historic interpretation.

Rivera assumed his role as a revolutionary artist by positioning himself on "the positive pole of the great phenomenon that we call revolution" and by defining himself as the equivalent of his comrades—that is, the proletariat. But this conception of the Marxist artist abandoning his bourgeois intellectual background and giving himself over to the revolution is presented by George Lukács as simplistic and romantic. In his analysis of his own particular experience, Lukács states that the "transition from one class [the bourgeoisie] to the class directly opposed to it [the proletariat] is a much more complex business."[10]

Rivera's life and thought reflect a duality, which is revealed in his arguments with the Communist Party on the one hand, and on the other in his dependence on the Mexican political system, becoming its official painter in times that were trying for a militant. But his most important legacy is the hundreds of meters of wall that he painted, and it is to this pictorial text that one must pay attention, since we are reviewing his artistic production and not his ethical position, which, although it surely influenced his work, would require a separate analysis.

According to Marxist theory, the consciousness of the proletariat, understood as a class rather than as a group of individuals, has the power to transform the world and liberate human relations. But that consciousness must be developed. Realism was held to be the artistic idiom capable of heightening the proletariat's awareness since it could reveal and account for the structure of reality.

In attempting a materialist interpretation of history as the story of a succession of class struggles, Rivera played an indispensable role as an intellectual force in both the Mexican Revolution and the universal revolution of the proletariat. His self-imposed task was a nearly impossible one: to use the image as a rationally critical weapon.

In the central panel of the great triptych in the Palacio Nacional, however, the moving forces in society are not clearly determined. Rivera used his enormous capacity for synthesis to create a history of Mexico in which outstanding individuals are the determining forces in the culminating moments of what he viewed as the thesis, antithesis, and synthesis through which that history unfolds.

In another section of this enormous mural, Rivera refers to the *Communist Manifesto* and to Karl Marx as the prophet of the future. He illustrates the triumph of the proletariat through imagery drawn from the technological world, but does not suggest the mechanisms by which that triumph could be achieved. The future becomes a predictable utopia, similar to a promised golden age. Rivera's utopian vision is the product of a mechanistic interpretation of history in which the function of technology will in the future be appropriated by the workers.

This idea is the basis of George Lukács's polemic in the revised preface to the new edition of *History and Class Consciousness:*

The most positive feature of this review is the way my views on economics concretised. This can be seen above all in my polemic against an idea that had a wide currency among both vulgar materialist Communists and bourgeois positivists. This was the notion that technology was the principle that objectively governed progress in the development of the forces of production. This obviously leads to historical fatalism, to the elimination of man and of social activity; it leads to the idea that technology functions like a social "natural force" obedient to "natural laws."[11]

Perhaps Rivera's own extreme individuality prevented him from truly understanding Marxist theory. In this he was not alone, as A. G. Lehman points out: "From 1924 to 1929 it was even possible in France for a number of highly individualistic surrealists to consider themselves Communists in a Marxist sense."[12] Indeed, even today, without a consensus having been reached, discussions continue as to the role of realism within the Marxist aesthetic.

Despite its shortcomings—subjectiveness, ideological lapses that often reflect a simplistic understanding of the dialectic of historical materialism, and illegibility due to a confusion of images and symbols that require a high level of sophistication and historical knowledge to understand—Rivera's mural in the Palacio Nacional is unique and inventive, both practically and theoretically. Apart from its pure aesthetic value, the mural has the merit of being the first attempt ever to present a pictorial interpretation of history conceived of in terms of class struggle, and whether or not Rivera's interpretation of history was correct, his mural stands as both a work of art and a revolutionary document.

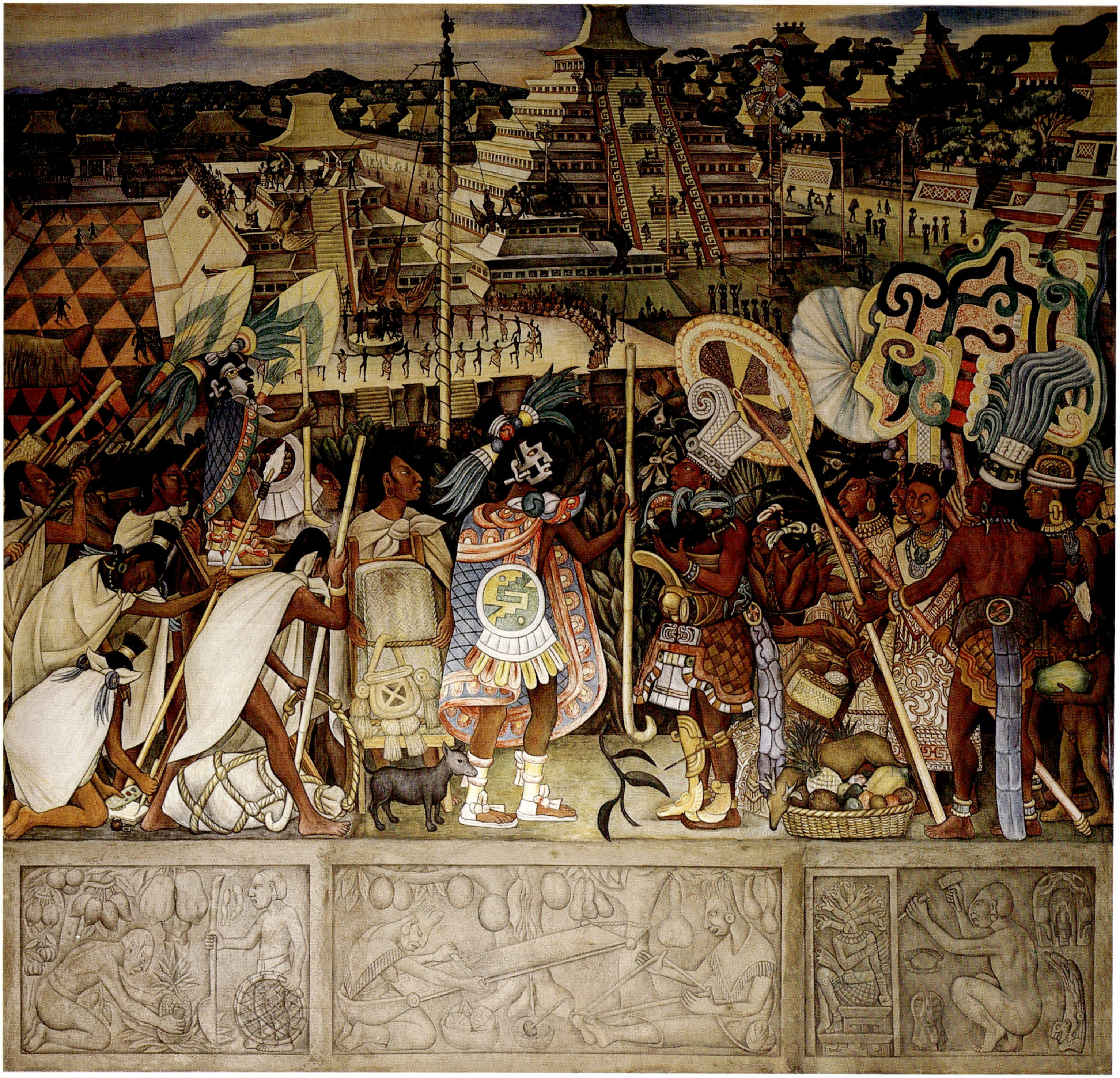

The Past Idealized: Diego Rivera's Use of Pre-Columbian Imagery

Betty Ann Brown

Figure 268
The Totonac Civilization, 1950, fresco, 4.92 × 5.27 m. Mexico City, Palacio Nacional.

At the end of his extended stay in Europe, Diego Rivera traveled to Italy to study the art of the Renaissance. There he was particularly impressed with the mural art of Paolo Uccello, the Lorenzetti, Raphael, and Michelangelo, which he viewed as a kind of "art for the masses." Rivera saw the Renaissance murals as "visual books" for the illiterate, which were intended to function in a fashion similar to that of medieval cathedral façades.[1] When Rivera returned to Mexico, he was determined to create a Mexican Renaissance with his own murals, with the intention that they too would be art for the masses. High on his proselytizing agenda was the revitalization of interest in and respect for the Mexican Indians. While in Italy, Rivera had examined pre-Columbian and Early Colonial Mexican manuscripts in Italian collections, and he continued to study the records and remains of pre-Columbian civilizations that were available to him in Mexico, continually incorporating the fruits of his studies into his murals.

Rivera's interest in pre-Columbian civilizations was personal as well as artistic and political. He was one of the first individuals to develop a sizable collection (sixty thousand objects) of pre-Columbian artifacts, often driving himself to the brink of bankruptcy in order to purchase a prized *"idolo."* In his old age, Rivera designed and built Anahuacalli (the name is a combination of the Aztec words *anahuac* [Valley of Mexico] and *calli* [house]), a four-story "museum-pyramid-tomb" that includes elements of Aztec and Mayan architecture and now houses his collection.

The accidents of history and archaeology have reduced the multitude of pre-Columbian art objects to a fraction of their original number. Virtually no sculptures in wood (which was surely a favored medium) have survived in Mexico; likewise, textile remains are scanty. What we have, for the most part, are monumental sculptures in stone, often basalt; portable works in clay and green stone; the small amount of jewelry that did not fall victim to Spanish smelting; a few murals; and fewer painted books. Rivera was well aware of pre-Columbian sculpture—soon after its discovery he made use of the sculptural image of Xochipilli—and favored the critically acclaimed pieces, such as the masterful Coatlicue, which was found under the Plaza Mayor at the end of the 19th century. Rivera took many ideas from ceramic figurines such as those he collected and housed at Anahuacalli. But his most frequent sources were the painted books that he saw in European collections or studied from such reproductions as those published by Lord Kingsborough in the 19th century.

Many pre-Columbian peoples created pictographic manuscripts, but only a few of these codices survived the Conquest, most finding their way into European collections. None of the indisputably pre-Conquest codices is Aztec in origin. Soon after their arrival, the Spaniards commissioned native painters to make copies of Aztec chronicles

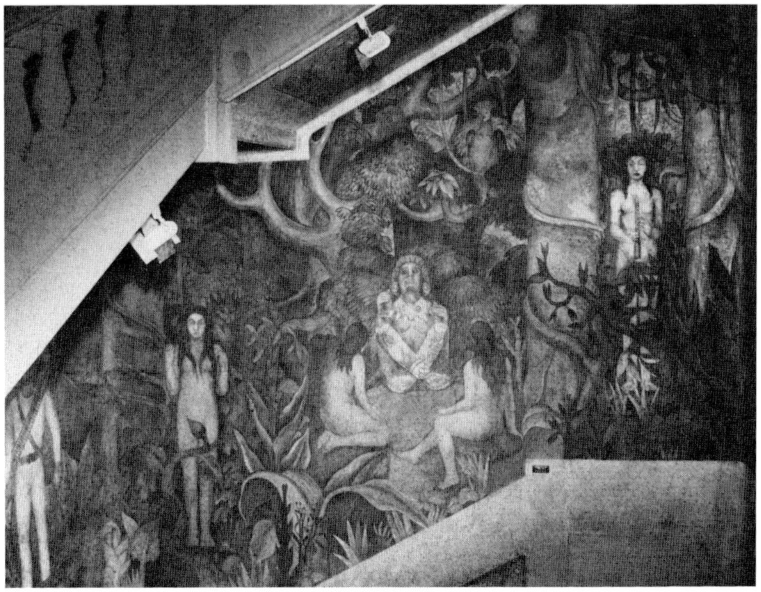

Figure 269
Detail of central section of stairway between first and second floors, 1923/28, fresco. Mexico City, Secretaría de Educación Pública.

as well as to illustrate manuscripts depicting other aspects of the indigenous culture. One of the most ambitious works to use illustrations by native artists is the Codex Florentino, compiled by the Franciscan friar Bernardino de Sahagún in the mid-16th century.

Rivera's favored pictorial sources were not manuscripts of undisputed pre-Columbian date such as the Mixtec Codex Nuttall or the Borgia Group. Nor were they the stiff hieratic images of pre-Columbian murals. Instead, Rivera "seems consistently to have preferred images from after the Conquest and created under European influence."[2] The Colonial-period sources may have been more accessible than the earlier manuscripts or more comprehensible visually (they employ the pictorial conventions of the European tradition, the tradition in which Rivera was trained). Or they may have been more comprehensible conceptually, as most Colonial-period images are accompanied by explanatory texts, generally in Spanish.

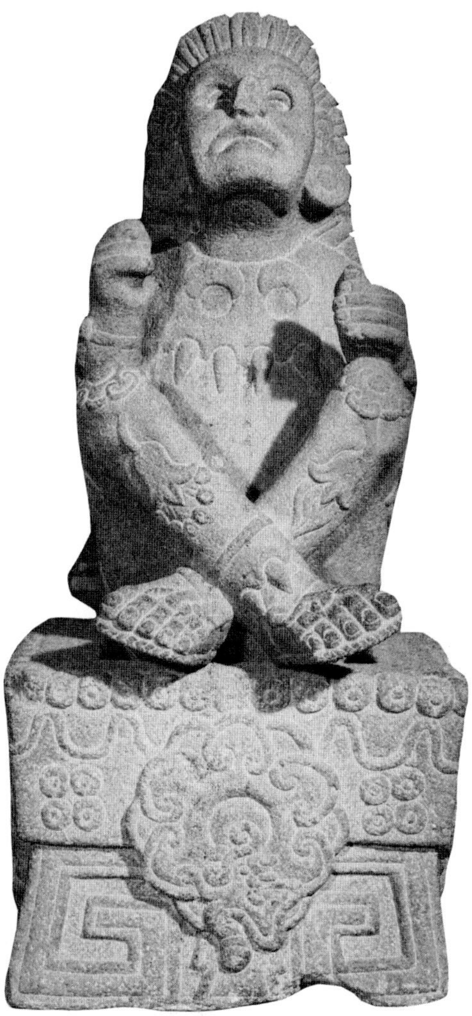

Figure 270
***Xochipilli*, Aztec, ca. 1200–1521, stone, h. 115 cm. Mexico City, Museo Nacional de Antropología.**

The Gods

Rivera was not the first modern painter to champion Indian themes. In 1920, no doubt spurred by the very influential Dr. Atl (Gerardo Murillo), who "proclaimed the value of native craftsmanship and of Mexican culture,"[3] the Guatemalan Carlos Mérida exhibited works in Mexico City that included numerous Mayan images. Rivera himself believed that Mérida was the first "to incorporate American picturesqueness into true painting."[4] And while Rivera was working on his mural *Creation* (1922–23) at the Escuela Nacional Preparatoria, the Frenchman Jean Charlot painted *The Massacre at the Templo Mayor* (the main temple of the Aztec capital, Tenochtitlán) in a stairway of the west patio. In *The Massacre* armored conquistadores attack Indians who are wearing the brilliant feathered costumes of a ceremonial dance. Two years later, Charlot added a portrait of the last Aztec emperor, Cuauhtémoc, to the stairway landing.

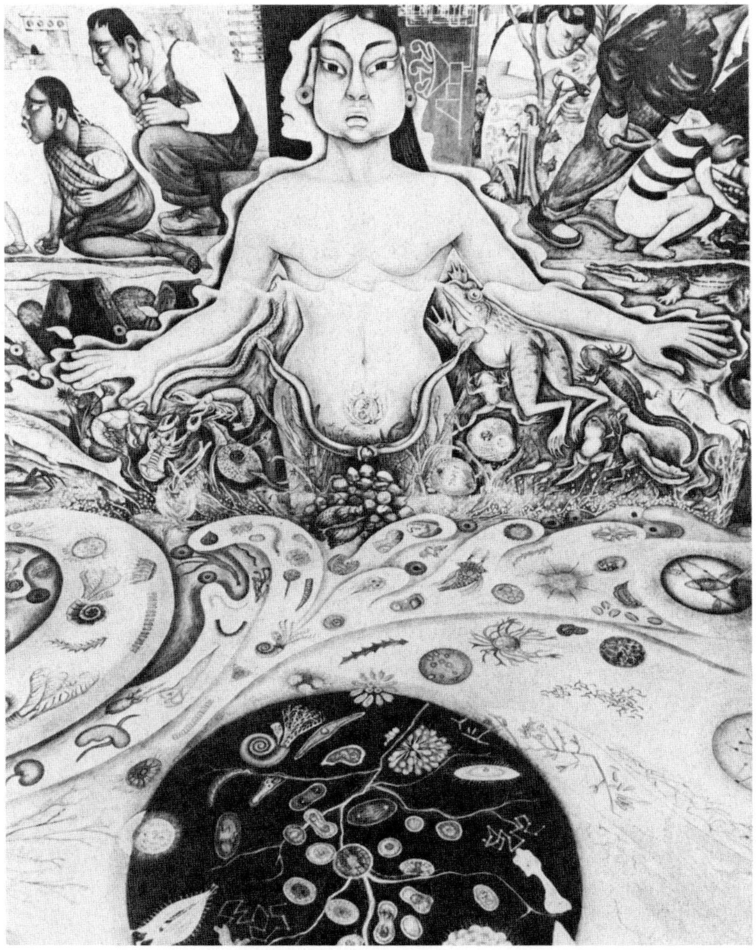

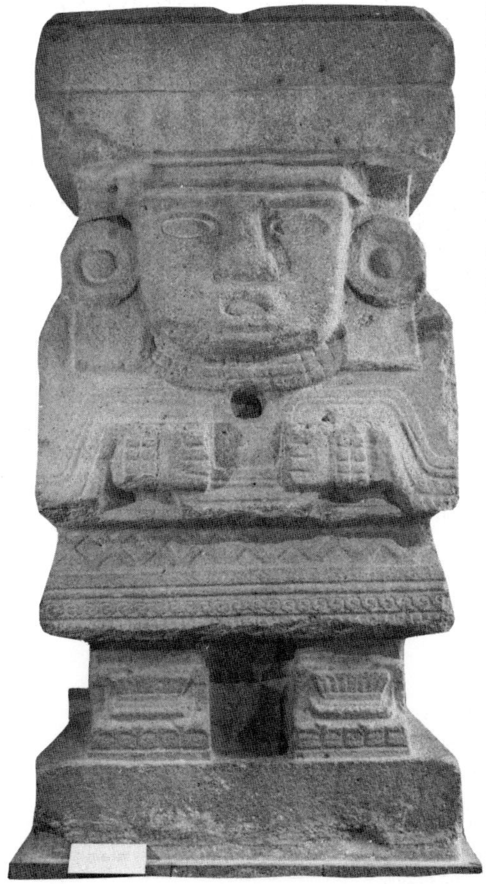

Figure 271
Detail of mural on sides of reservoir, 1951, fresco. Mexico City, Cárcamo del Río Lerma.

Figure 272
Chalchiuhtlicue, Teotihuacán, ca. 300–600, stone, h. 3.2 m. Mexico City, Museo Nacional de Antropología.

Rivera may, however, have been the first to depict an archaeologically accurate image of an Aztec deity. In 1923 he painted Xochipilli, the flower prince, god of dance and springtime, on the stairway of the Secretaría de Educación Pública (fig. 269). The statue of Xochipilli from which Rivera derived his image, one of the most graceful and appealing of Aztec sculptures, depicts an attractive man sitting cross-legged on a small *talud y tablero* platform (fig. 270). The figure's arms are bent, his hands opened in an empty clasp—the statue probably once held paper banners—and his head is angled back as if from the weight of his heavy headdress. He wears a mask, large ear spools, and ornate tied sandals. His entire body is covered with flowers, their beautiful decorative tendrils winding sinuously over his arms and legs. In his mural Rivera eliminated the platform; the god sits on the ground in the clearing of a dense jungle. Otherwise, the depiction of Xochipilli is faithful to its prototype.

Anthropologist Henry B. Nicholson places the god in the same deity complex as Centeotl, the corn god, and says that Xochipilli's principal jurisdictions are "solar warmth, flowers, feasting, and pleasure."[5] Surely Xochipilli is the most beneficent and engaging deity Rivera could have included in his depiction of the Mexican environment.

Years later, when commissioned to decorate the Cárcamo del Río Lerma (Lerma Waterworks), Rivera used single images of other pre-Columbian deities to pictorialize other aspects of the environment. In addition to depictions of plant and animal life, the Lerma murals include a monumental woman whose fertility is indicated by an x-ray view of a child in her womb and by the flow of water around her masklike face. Frogs, snakes, and crustaceans spring from the bountiful hands of this figure, who represents Chalchiuhtlicue, "she of the jade skirts," goddess of water, and sister/wife/consort of the rain god Tláloc (fig. 271).

The best-known depiction of Chalchiuhtlicue is the rigidly architectonic sculpture (fig. 272) from the site of Teotihuacán.[6] Although Rivera's Chalchiuhtlicue has relatively rounded, humanoid proportions, her angular frontality is similar to that of the Teotihuacán sculpture, and the regularized curlicue on the surface of the water around her is similar

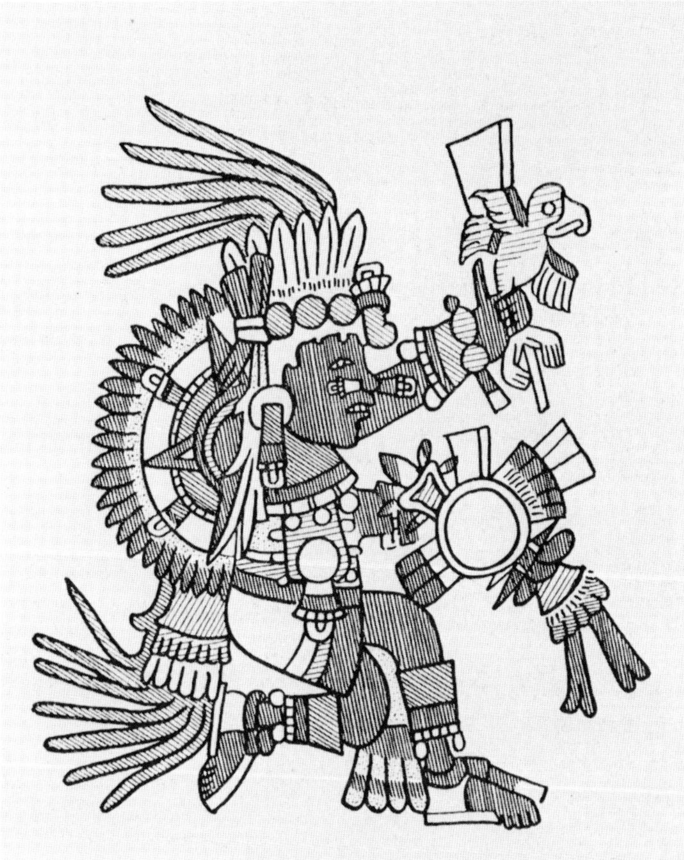

Figure 273
Toniatiuh, Codex Tell-eriano-Remensis, folio 12. Paris, Bibliothèque Nationale.

to the distinctive motif on the sculpture's skirt. Furthermore, the angles of her face, with its snarling, downturned mouth, flanged ears, and prominent ear spools, recall Teotihuacán funerary masks. Above her right shoulder, Rivera has placed a small temple structure, drawn in the same conventional style as those in pre-Columbian manuscripts.[7] The temple's lintel is adorned with the discs that are often read as pictograms for Tláloc, since they are believed to symbolize his characteristic goggle eyes.

Tláloc himself is depicted in the fountain that Rivera designed for the clearing near the reservoir (see fig. 405). The rain god appears as an immense cement figure "sprawled in a shallow pool as if he has plunged from on high."[8] Actually, the god is portrayed in the splayed or "running" position (see fig. 273) typical of pre-Columbian depictions, such as the monumental relief from Texcoco that is generally said to depict the sun god Tonatiuh or the recently discovered moon goddess Coyolxauhqui. Many of the gods in the first section of the Codex Borbonicus, an Aztec manuscript that became one of Rivera's favored sources (see the discussion of the Palacio Nacional murals below), also appear in this pose.[9] Like many archaeological portrayals of the god, Rivera's Tláloc has disc eyes and a twisted nose above a thick, everted lip that is raised to reveal long, tusklike fangs.

Just as Rivera's Xochipilli reveals an optimistic wish for eternal springtime for the Mexican people, so the Tláloc and Chalchiuhtlicue figures must embody a fervent wish for a plentiful water supply for Mexico. The artist's portrayals of the goddess Coatlicue, however, convey more ambiguous messages. At the Detroit Institute of Arts, Rivera portrayed the ominously powerful Coatlicue (fig. 274), earth goddess and mother of Huitzilopochtli (who was the patron war god of the Aztecs) in a radically different environment, with, one would assume, different intentions. Coatlicue's image is covert; only someone quite familiar with the Aztec sculpture of the goddess would recognize her in the mechanized form of the assembly line scene (fig. 275). Coatlicue's presence is more easily discernible in the San Francisco

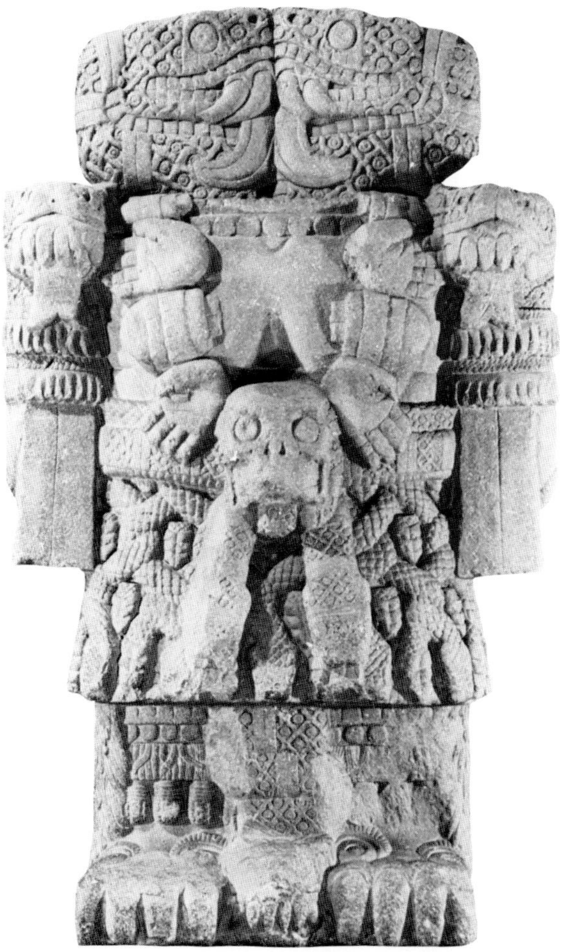

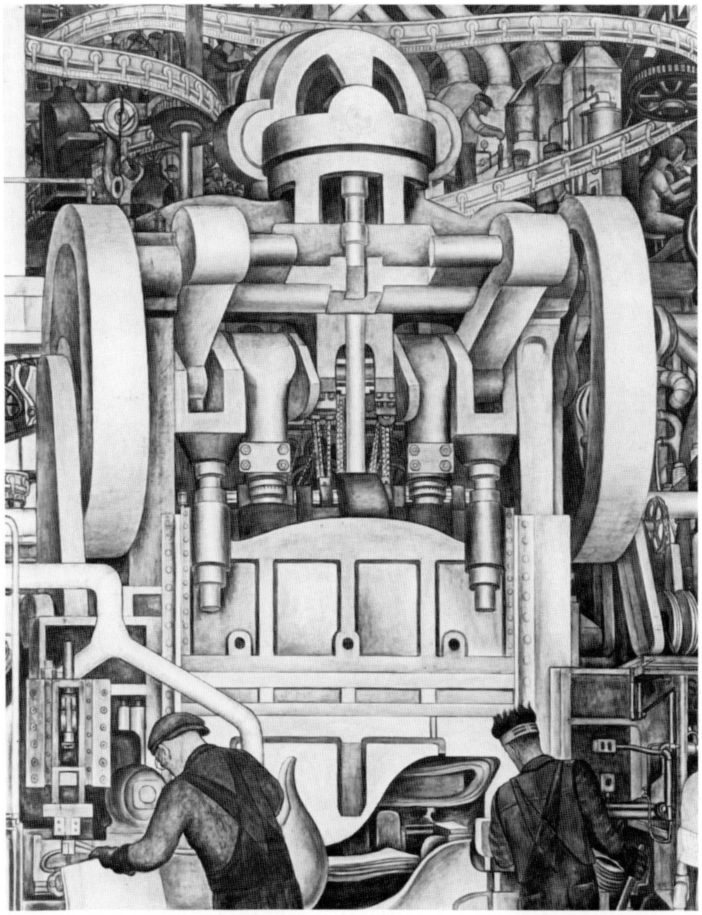

Figure 274
Coatlicue, Aztec, Tenochtitlán, ca. 1487–1521, stone, h. 3.5 m. Mexico City, Museo Nacional de Antropología.

Figure 275
Detroit Industry, (detail of south wall) 1932–33, fresco. Detroit Institute of Arts.

City College mural, where the figure of the goddess is a combination of a similarly mechanical aspect with an anthropomorphic form that includes fangs and a skirt of intertwined serpents (see fig. 401).[10]

The Battles

On the monumental stairway of the Palacio Nacional, Rivera depicted the history of Mexico from the time of the Conquest to the present, as well as "the distant past of Mexico, with allusion to her first mythological history."[11] The compositional focus of the central trapezoid of the stairwell is a large, brilliantly colored eagle (see fig. 384). In choosing the eagle as the fulcrum of his depiction of Mexican history, Rivera was again drawing on ancient sources. The particular guise in which he presents the eagle is taken from the back of an Aztec sculpture known as the *Teocalli de la Guerra Sagrada* (the Temple of Sacred Warfare, figs. 276 and 277). The Teocalli is a small temple model on which relief depictions of the Aztec patron Huitzilopochtli and the Emperor Moctezuma II flank a solar disc on a rectangular block above a pyramidal substructure.[12] Both the god and the ruler have *atl tlachinolli* speech scrolls issuing from their mouths; both speak of sacred war. On the back of the Teocalli is a shallow relief of an eagle perched on top of a nopal cactus. The cactus, in turn, emerges from the reclining body of a skeletal female who represents the surface of the earth. Her body is surrounded by parallel curving lines, the Aztec convention for water, specifically the water that surrounds the islands on which the Aztecs founded their capital city, Tenochtitlán.

The Aztec myths that were recorded by Spanish friars soon after the Conquest include the story of a long migration led by the god Huitzilopochtli, who vowed to bring his followers to a "promised land," which they would know by a sign he would give them, the vision of an eagle upon a cactus with a serpent in its mouth. The eagle-cactus-serpent image symbolizes the foundation of Tenochtitlán and is the emblem on the flag of modern Mexico.

The eagle of the Teocalli, and of Rivera's mural, has no serpent. Instead, like the

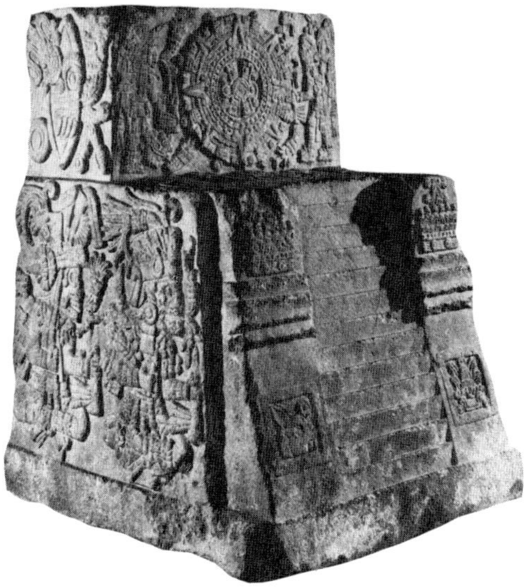

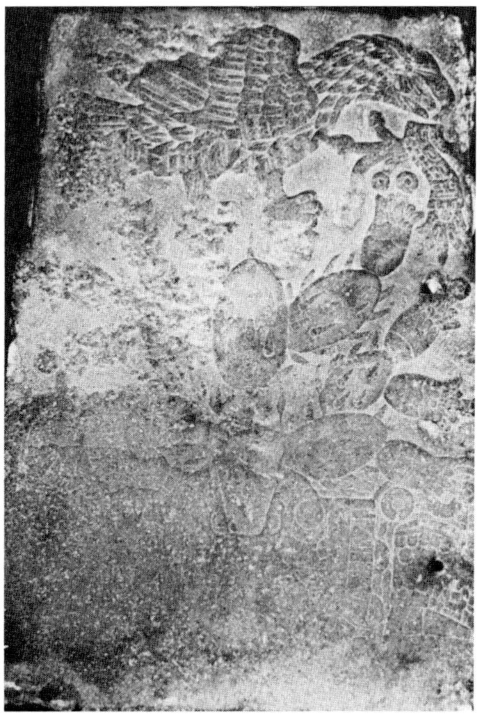

Figures 276, 277
***Teocalli de la Guerra Sacrada* (front and back), Aztec, Tenochtitlán, ca. 1200–1521, stone, 120 × 92 × 99 cm. Mexico City, Museo Nacional de Antropología.**

god and the ruler portrayed on the other side of the monument, it speaks of sacred warfare by means of a speech scroll. The archaeologist Alfonso Caso wrote extensively on the Teocalli and its "sacred-war" symbolism. Caso was one of the experts whom Rivera consulted about the design of his personal museum, Anahuacalli, as well as about the collection to be housed therein, and we can assume Rivera probably knew of Caso's sacred-war thesis.[13] Surely the artist saw the Teocalli eagle as symbolic of the sacred warfare, from the conquest through the Revolution of 1910, that was the crucible in which modern Mexico was annealed.

Beside and below the eagle are scenes of the Spanish Conquest in which Indians battle not only the Spanish conquistadores but other Indians as well. Rivera was well aware that Cortés's victory was made possible by his Indian allies, who joined the Spaniards in battle against the oppressive Aztec empire. The Indian warriors wear the attire of the knightly orders of the eagle, jaguar, and coyote. They carry standards topped with the snarling heads of their mascots and defend themselves with spears, bows and arrows, and obsidian-bladed *macanas,* while guarding their torsos with feather-draped shields strapped over their left arms.

Similar Indian warriors also appear in Rivera's fresco cycle at the Palacio de Cortés in Cuernavaca. The Cuernavaca frescoes portray the Spanish conquest of Mexico from the Indian point of view. Myriad knights, arrayed in splendid attire and accompanied by flamboyantly colorful banners, watch black-painted priests sacrifice a Spaniard atop a pyramid temple. Others battle, in vain, against heavily armed figures in ominous gray armor. An eagle knight is silhouetted against the flames of a burning Aztec city; a jaguar knight stabs a reclining Spaniard with a flint blade. Stanton Catlin has carefully studied these images and finds Rivera's sources to have been both pre-Columbian sculptures—such as the *Head of an Eagle Knight* (fig. 278) and other Aztec warrior figures—and Early Colonial manuscripts,[14] particularly the tribute pages of the Codex Mendoza and illustrations from Fra Bernardino de Sahagún's Codex Florentino, especially from the sections in book II on ritual warfare and gladiatorial combat and those in book XII on the history of the Conquest.[15]

The Civilizations Idealized

Rivera's first panoramic vision of the pre-Columbian world is found on the right wall of the Palacio Nacional staircase, which he generally referred to as a depiction of *"México antiguo"* (see fig. 384). Here we see not only the remarkable range of his research into his country's archaeological past but also the great amount of idealization he imposed upon it. The scene centers on Quetzalcóatl, the feathered serpent. Quetzalcóatl was both a god and a culture hero, the "good" priest who was ousted in shame from the Toltec imperial capital of Tula and who promised to return on an anniversary of his birth, the year Two Reed. (Cortés arrived on the coast in a Two-Reed year, which is one reason Moctezuma II was so afraid of him.)

Quetzalcóatl is seen seated in front of his pyramid-temple, being adored by masses of white-robed Indians who kneel quietly before him. He carries his characteristic curved staff and wears an impressive headdress of green quetzal feathers. On his chest is a pectoral shaped like a cross-sectioned conch shell, which is usually associated with his avatar, the wind god Ehecatl. In the upper section of the composition, Quetzalcóatl appears again, this time astride a huge serpent that flies away from the central solar disc toward the right, or east. (One of Quetzalcóatl's manifestations was Venus, the morning star, which appears in the east.) While the clothing of the serpent-riding image is drawn exactly from the illustration of the god in the Codex Florentino (book I, illus. 5),[16] the headdress of the seated figure

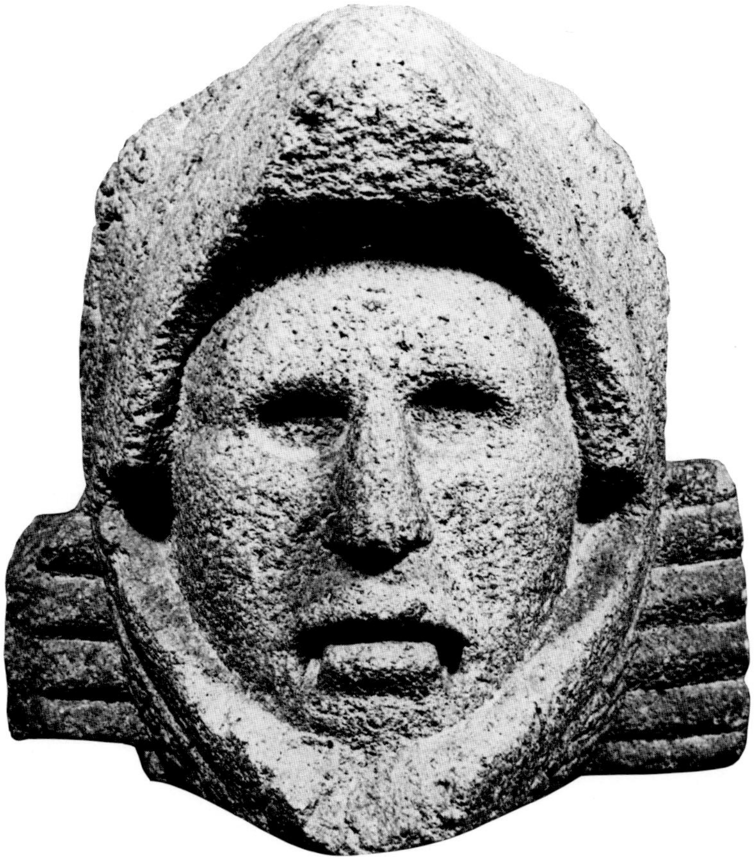

Figure 278
Head of an Eagle Knight,
Aztec, Tenochtitlán, 1300–1521, stone, h. 31 cm. Mexico City, Museo Nacional de Antropología.

seems to be Rivera's invention. The depiction of Quetzalcóatl as having a beard, pale skin, and European features that distinguish him from the surrounding people is of more complex origin. No such pale-skinned figure appears in pre-Columbian art, but tradition had long held that Quetzalcóatl was bearded and fair of skin.

Around Quetzalcóatl are groups of people engaged in all manner of productive activity. Clockwise from center top, they (1) dance with flowered staffs before verdant cornfields, (2) beat the vertical and slit drums that gave pre-Columbian music its percussive vigor, (3) weave on the kind of backstrap looms that many Native Americans still use, (4) create paintings, sculpture, and featherwork, (5) do battle in the jaguar and coyote uniforms discussed above, and (6) carry heavy, basketry-bound burdens as tribute to an impressively clad figure atop a tall pyramidal rise.

People die in the battle scene and backs are bent under the load of the tribute, but all in all this is one of Rivera's most positive historical statements. It includes none of the anger and despair seen in the artist's vision of Colonial Mexico, none of the cynicism and hatred apparent in his numerous critiques of modern life. But if Rivera idealizes the past in his *"México antiguo"* on the staircase, he eulogizes it in the pre-Columbian panels on the second floor of the same building.

The Arts and Industries

The Marketplace

Just six years before his death, Rivera completed a mural series that was the "dream of his old age," the nine panels in the second-floor corridor surrounding the central patio of the Palacio Nacional. The largest of these is a portrayal of the ancient Aztec capital, Tenochtitlán (see fig. 333). A long horizontal rectangle, the mural gives an awesome panorama of the city of Tenochtitlán, perched on its canal-divided "floating island" and surrounded by majestic snowcapped mountains. The sacred ceremonial center with its cluster of glistening white temples stands in the distance. In the foreground, Rivera has depicted the crowded activity of market day in Tlatelolco, Tenochtitlán's twin city. A tall double pyramid looms over the market, just behind the shoulder of the noble who oversees the rich and varied commerce from his basketry litter. He wears the peaked turquoise crown that identifies pre-Columbian nobility and carries an elegant feather fan. Before him nobles and commoners alike examine goods from all corners of the empire. Tropical fruits are bartered for cacao beans. All colors of corn, and corn seeds, are sold. A wrinkled old woman hands tortillas to a shopper,

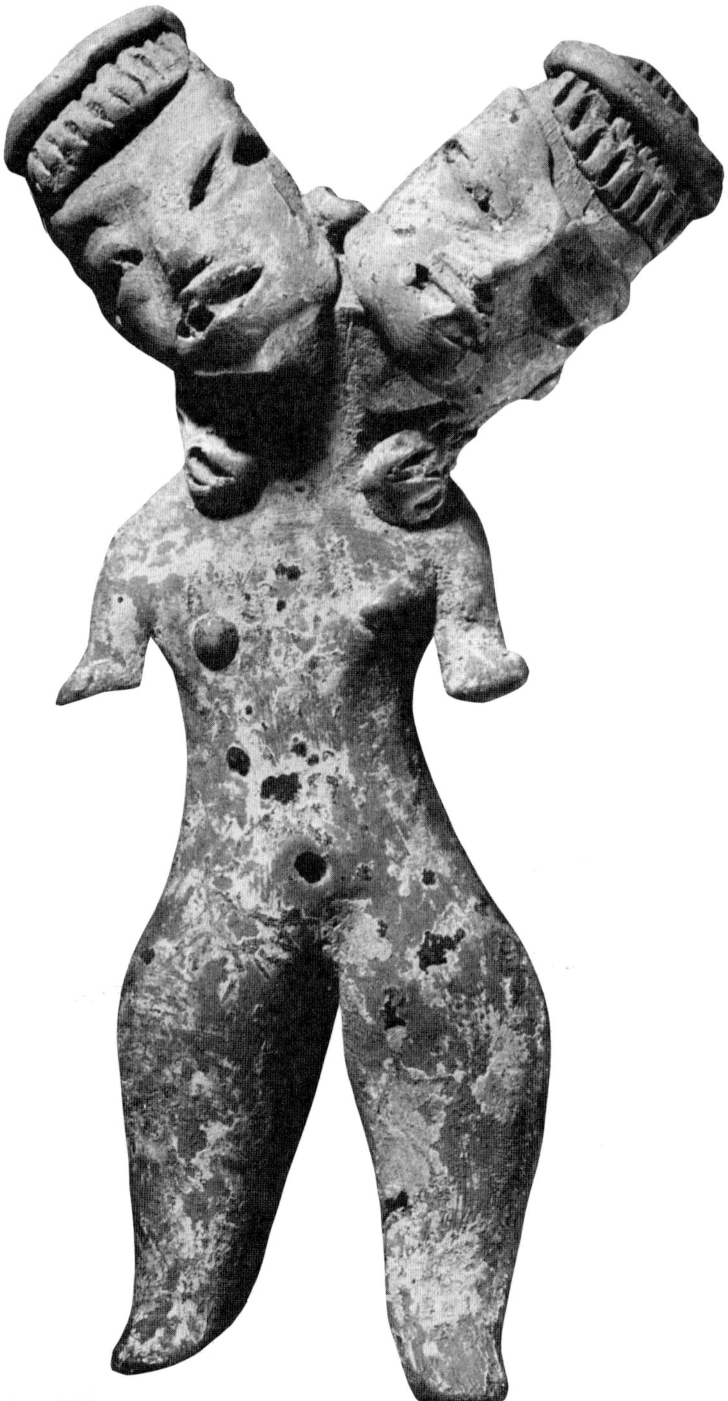

Figure 279
***Figurine,* Tlatilco, ca. 1200–1000, B.C., terra cotta, h. 11 cm. Mexico City, Museo Nacional de Antropología.**

who carries a loaded basket on her back. Herbs and magical concoctions are proffered by a bare-breasted woman who wears a curved nose jewel. A prostitute lifts her skirt to reveal her elaborately tatooed legs. People from the coast exchange fish and fowl. Behind them, numerous ceramics are displayed, from the simple unadorned *comales* (the griddles upon which tortillas are cooked) to urns decorated with the powerful face of Tláloc.

There is exotica certainly: one woman seems, like the tiny clay fertility figures from the early site of Tlatilco (ca. 1000–500 B.C.), to possess two dramatically painted faces (fig. 279). At the opposite end of the mural, a detached human arm is offered for sale. There is much color: costumes vary from simple white loincloths, to striped cottons dyed with Pacific shell purple, to embroidered *mantas* (capes) like those in the Codex Mendoza (fig. 280). And there are moments of touching humanity: a little girl, loaded down with a huge bunch of lilies, has an infant swaddled to her back. Over her shoulder she pulls a wheeled ceramic toy, like the jaguar and monkey toys excavated at Teotihuacán and at Classic Gulf Coast sites (fig. 281).

Below the main mural are five grisaille panels. They depict (1) the planting and cultivating of corn, (2) the harvesting of pumpkins, beans, and fruits, (3) the accounting of tribute for the nobles (this overseen by a jaguar warrior and a priestly figure with the curved staff associated with Quetzalcóatl), (4) the gathering of cotton and weaving of cloth, and finally, (5) the processing of food.

Rivera has portrayed a pre-Columbian world of agricultural abundance. Although there is evidence of class distinction—the noble is elevated above the masses, and visiting traders are clothed according to the Aztecs' strict sumptuary laws—it is neither overwhelming nor oppressive. There is no poverty, no hunger, no suffering. Even the blood flowing down the temple steps seems somehow innocuous. Rivera, a long-term member of the Mexican Communist

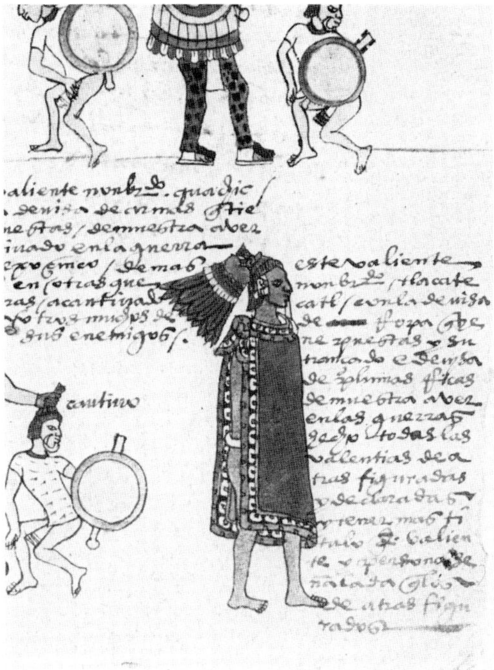

Figure 280
Figure wearing Aztec *manta*. Codex Mendoza, Ms. Arch. A1, folio 64 recto (detail).

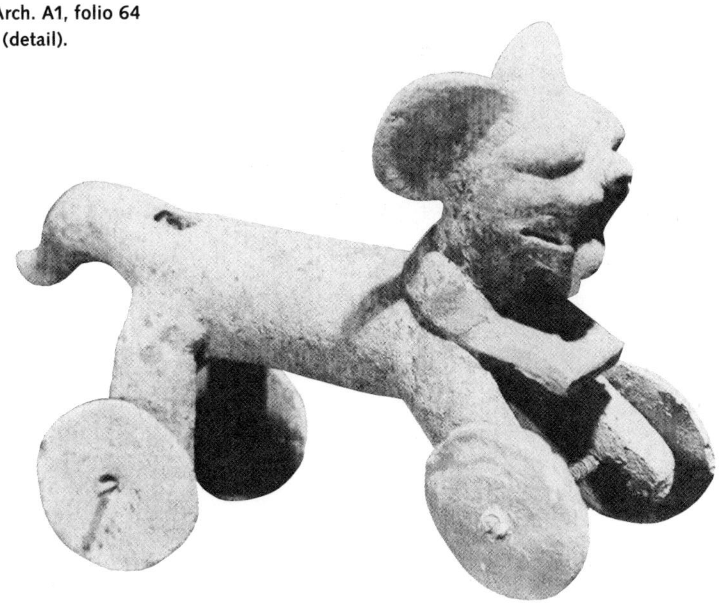

Figure 281
***Jaguar Figurine with Wheels*, Nopiloa, Classic period, terra cotta, l. 18 cm. Jalapa, Universidad Veracruzana, Museo de Antropología.**

Party and an ardent Marxist, seems to have found an economic utopia, a civilization in which the masses are involved with—indeed in control of—the means of production. Rivera paints a pre-Columbian world that is not only romantically attractive in its exotic sophistication but also an historic ideal to which his people should hope to return. According to his biographer Bertram Wolfe, Rivera saw "the return of the feathered serpent as [a symbol] of the recurrence of primitive tribal communism on a higher social level."[17]

Agriculture

In seven smaller panels on the second floor of the Palacio Nacional, Rivera painted equally idealized views of the pre-Columbian arts and industries. These are followed by a final panel that is a harsh indictment of the Colonial period, including a vicious caricature of Cortés. Each of the smaller murals surmounts a row of grisaille panels.

The *Huastec Civilization* panel (fig. 282) shows Indian men and women cultivating and processing maize in the foreground. Immediately behind this scene are two complex symbolic images that Rivera virtually traced from the Codex Borbonicus. Above the women is the corn goddess. Above the men is what appears to be a paper banner lined with red and yellow corncobs, which is suspended on a pole. Although Rivera read this form in the codex as a banner, I would interpret it as a litter or ceremonial platform. In the Codex Borbonicus (fig. 283), a captive dressed as the corn goddess is placed on this construction. In the next view, the impersonator is gone, the implication being that she has been sacrificed to the goddess. Apparently Rivera, who had rationalized even the extensive practice of human sacrifice by the Aztecs, was blinded to the sinister ritual significance of the corn litter.

The grisaille below this scene is also drawn from the Codex Borbonicus. On page twenty-one of this large screenfold book, the primeval creator deities are depicted. On the left, the snaggle-toothed old woman scatters seeds in the archetypal planting ritual. Facing her, and likewise seated on a *talud y tablero* throne, the primordial man acts as a priest, waving a smoking incense ladle and gesturing with the sharply honed bone of self-sacrifice.

Dyeing and Featherwork

The visual arts of the pre-Columbian world are portrayed in two panels. One, *The Tarascan Civilization* (fig. 284), is dominated by huge colored sheets of cloth draped over lines to dry and is sometimes referred to as the "dyeing scene." The other panel, *The Zapotec Civilization*, focuses on the most elite arts—featherwork, jewelry, and other forms of aristocratic personal adornment.

The dyeing scene is compositionally complex. Numerous groups of figures are placed along a zigzagging line that leads to a canoe-filled lake in the rear. In the foreground, men squat over a hide stretched flat by a wooden frame and

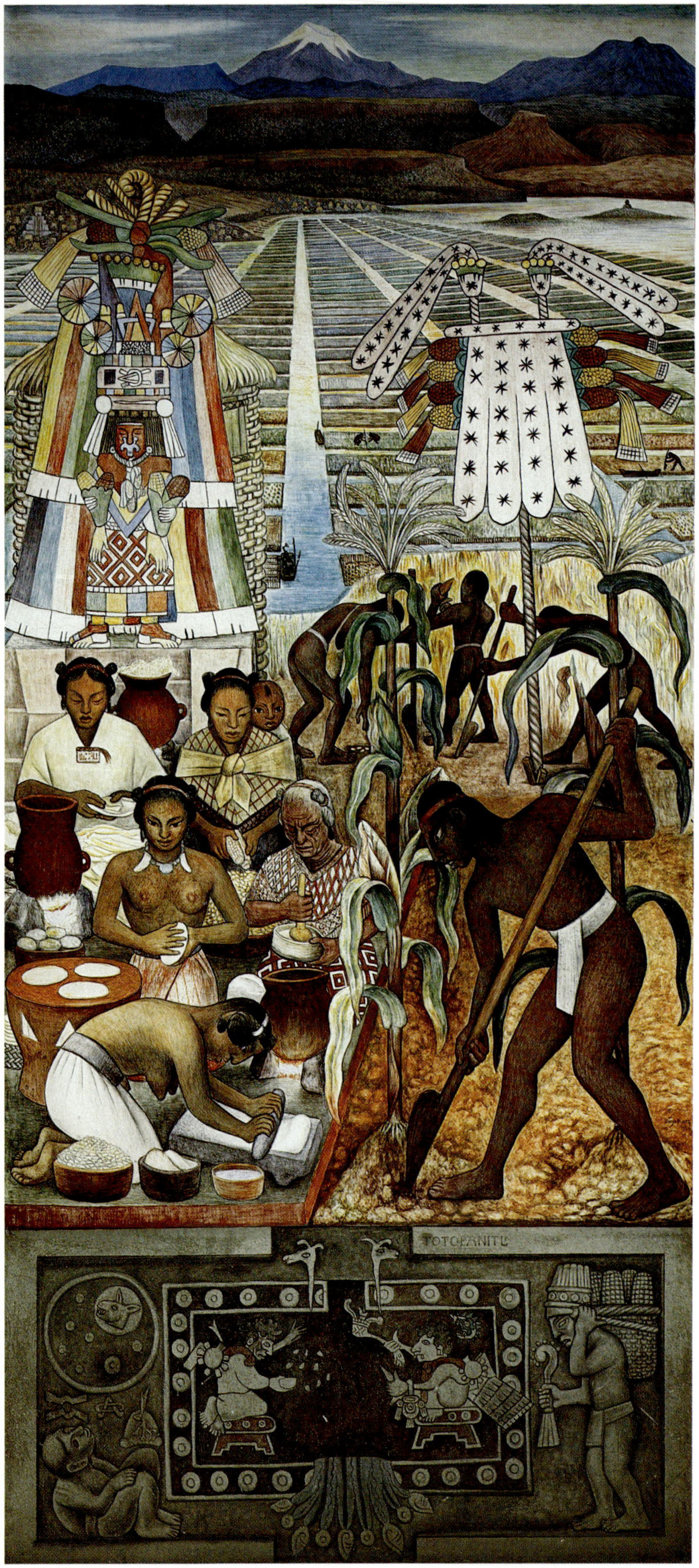

Figure 282
The Huastec Civilization,
1950, fresco, 4.92 × 2.24 m. Mexico City, Palacio Nacional.

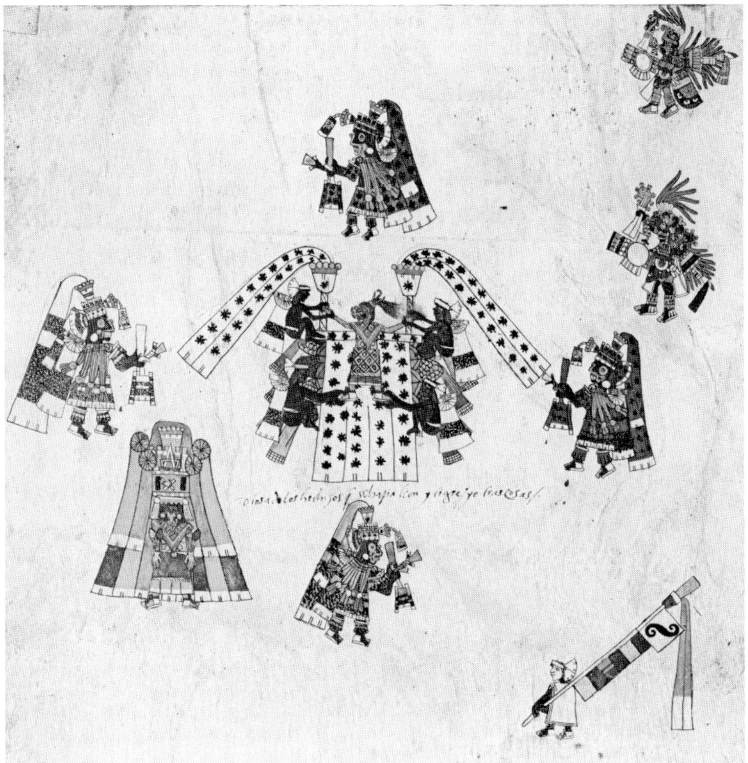

Figure 283
Codex Borbonicus, p. 31. Paris, Bibliothèque de l'Assemblée Nationale.

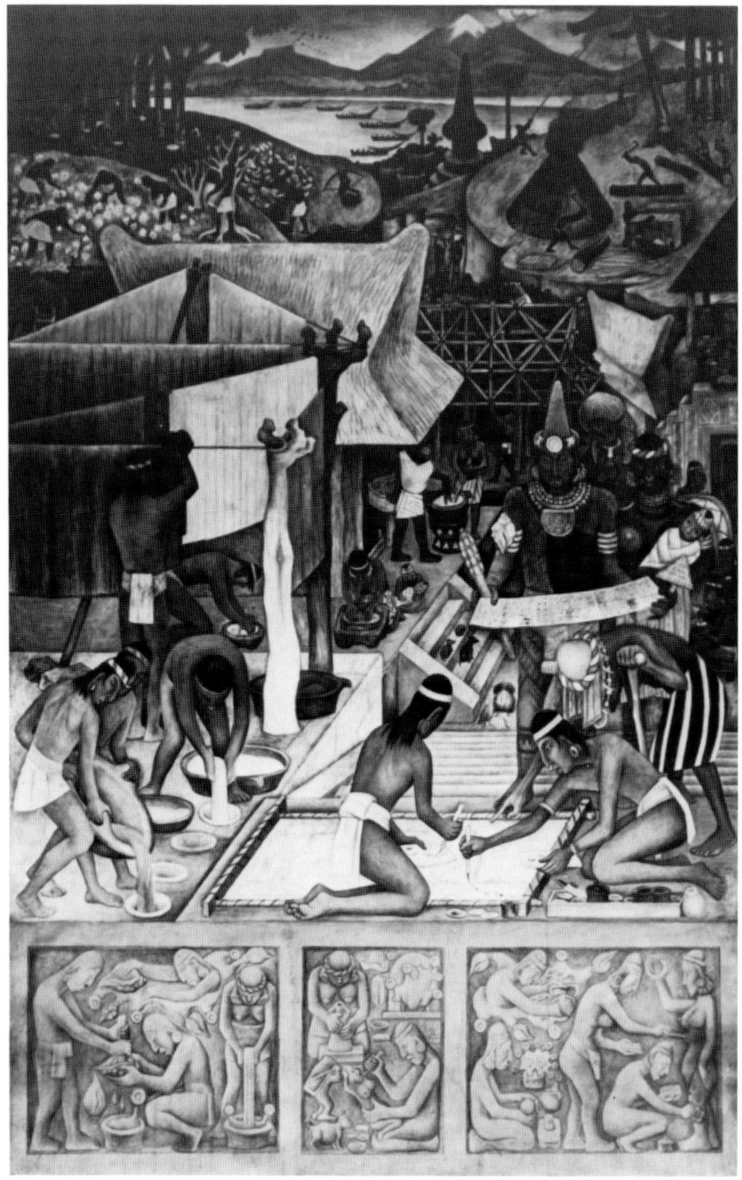

Figure 284
***The Tarascan Civilization,* 1942, fresco, 4.92 × 3.20 m. Mexico City, Palacio Nacional.**

paint upon it as directed by a priest, who wears a tall, pointed hat, abundant jewels (including a conch shell ornament on his upper arm), and grasps a club in his right fist. Before him he has spread open three pages of a *tonalamatl,* a type of pre-Columbian book that records the patron gods and the ceremonies of the 260-day calendar cycle.

With the priest stands a woman, a swaddled child in her arms. Her nose piece and numerous earrings as well as the tatoos on her chest are similar to those found on funerary ceramic figures (fig. 285) from West Mexico, particularly from the modern state of Nayarit. Also typical of that area, and likewise found represented in its claywork, are houses with steep pitched roofs, such as those seen behind the standing couple. But if Rivera intended for this to be a representation of West Mexico, specifically Nayarit, during the time such ceramics were made and placed into the shaft tombs of the honored dead, he erred in two important ways. The Pre-Classic and Classic Nayarit probably did not have painted books like the one the priest holds. Moreover, the lake and snowcapped volcano to the rear are found in Central Mexico, rather than on the Pacific Coast. Rivera has combined images from the earlier cultures of West Mexico with those of the Post-Classic civilizations of Central Mexico, specifically the Aztecs.

To the left of the Nayarit couple, men pour dye into vats, then string the dyed fabric on lines suspended between gnarled tree trunks. Behind these to the right, men fell trees and chop and strip the lumber. To the left, bare-breasted women pick flowers, while other men gather *copal* (resin) from the trees. (Copal was the incense used extensively in religious ceremonies.)

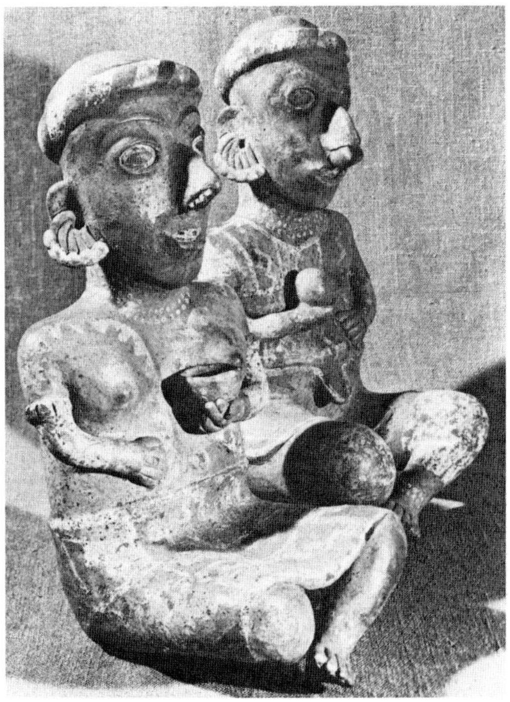

Figure 285
Seated Couple, **Nayarit, 100–500, terra cotta, h. each approx. 33 cm. Mexico City, Museo Nacional de Antropología.**

There are three grisaille panels below the dyeing scene. To the left, men turn conch shells into the trumpets that announce the arrival of political and religious dignitaries. Figures blowing such trumpets have been found in ancient tombs in Colima, as have chubby ceramic dogs such as those being made by the women in the central panel. The grisaille panel at far right depicts the processes of body painting, tatooing, and scarification that are so striking a feature of West Mexican ceramic figurines.

By the time of the Post-Classic Aztecs, the pre-Columbian world had sumptuary laws even more rigorous than those of Tudor England, where only men entitled to be addressed as "Lord" could wear sable. Aztec aristocrats enjoyed the right to wear items that distinguished them from members of the lower classes, but these were not limited to furs. The most valuable items were fashioned from the colored feathers of rare tropical birds. In the Palacio Nacional mural program, *The Zapotec Civilization* (fig. 286) is the second panel that Rivera devoted to pre-Columbian visual arts and is often called the "featherwork scene." It also includes the smelting and shaping of gold and the construction of the headdresses, banners, and shields on which the nobles displayed their totemic crests.

Again, the panel is quite complex in composition. Numerous people are grouped along an angled line that extends into deep space. The surroundings are generally darker and more dense than those of the dyeing scene. The impression is of a forest or jungle environment. In the center foreground, a woman and an old man sew feathers into a round shield according to a design held by the tall, slender man who stands before them. To the left, three kneeling figures work with precious stones—turquoise, obsidian, and others. To the right, no less than thirteen figures execute the various stages of metalworking—grinding, smelting (the fires were stoked by blowing air through long tubes), pouring, hammering, and so forth. It is interesting that Rivera includes women in the feather- and goldwork segments, but there is no evidence that women participated in the production of such elitist artifacts in pre-Columbian tribes.

At the left, two nobles are being arrayed for what must be a ceremonial occasion of great import and drama. The man straightens his turquoise crown in the reflection of an obsidian mirror held up for him by a finely clad woman. He wears large jade ear spools and a pectoral with pendant gold bells. His shoulder cape is patterned with a step-fret motif that reappears on his loincloth. His feather headdress is large and ornate but not figurative like that of his lady, who wears a long fringed skirt and a *quechquemitl* blouse (the poncholike blouse still worn by many Mexican Indian women). Her headdress resembles the "Upper Jaw of the Serpent" configuration found on many Zapotec urns, while the purple striped skirt of the figure dressing the lord is also of Zapotec origin. The woman's jewelry and the headdress and personal adornment of her partner could likewise be Zapotec. Also Zapotec in origin are the twisted hairdos of several of the attendant women.[18] But again Rivera has created a fanciful combination of elements from diverse times and places in the pre-Columbian world. There is no such jungle in Oaxaca, the modern state inhabitated by the Zapotecs.

The grisaille panels present a three-step sequence of lapidary work, a major industry of the ancient Zapotecs, showing the stones being mined and carried away, worked by grinding with bit and drill, and finally being offered to richly attired nobles.

Trade

Another small panel at the Palacio Nacional is generally said to portray the civilization of the Totonacs, the Indians who lived in the Gulf Coast region at the time of European contact (fig. 268). Two groups of people meet in the foreground, one carrying the idol of their patron god, the other baskets of tropical goods. Behind them, in magnificent panorama, is the site of El Tajín, which is located near modern-day Papantla in the state of Veracruz. Rivera

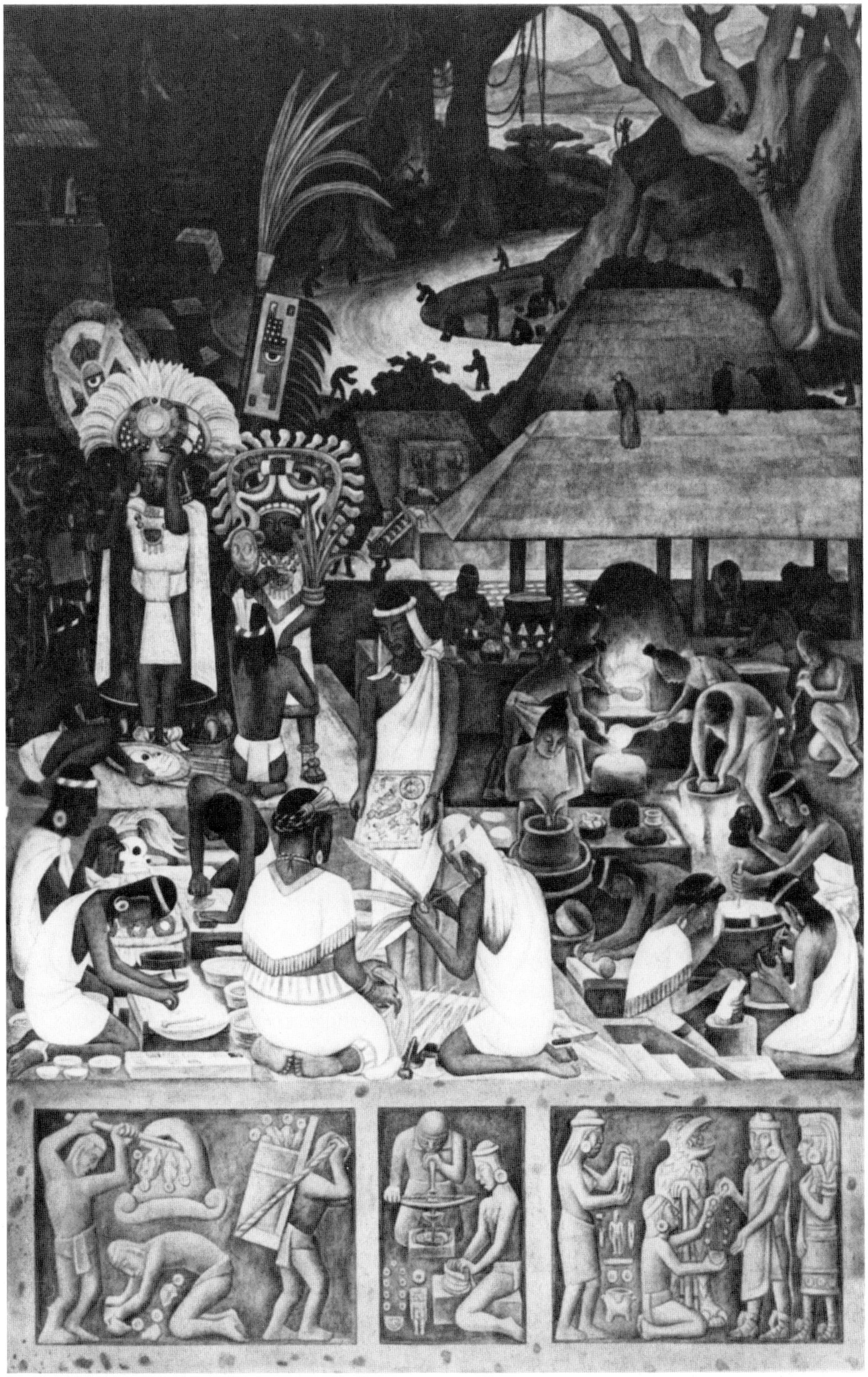

Figure 286
The Zapotec Civilization,
1942, fresco, 4.92 × 3.20 m. Mexico City, Palacio Nacional.

has created a spectacular reconstruction of the archaeological site, with its elegant Pyramid of the Niches and large ball court. The tall pole from which the bird-costumed figures known as *voladores* (flyers) dance was added to the scene by Rivera. Modern voladores certainly perform in the central plaza of El Tajín today, and we know from Colonial sources that some pre-Columbian Indians did a form of the volador dance. But whether the dance was performed when the El Tajín site was an active city (ca. A.D. 100–1000) is a matter of conjecture. Again, Rivera was somewhat eclectic in his treatment of history in the entire panel: the group on the left is surely Aztec and thus late Post-Classic in date; those on the right have faces and outfits derived from Classic-period artifacts.

All but one of the men on the left wear plain white mantas. The exception is one who wears a royal blue cape with an elaborate red and yellow border. He carries a hooked staff and a shield with a yellow and green step-fret design. His face is covered by a compelling black and white mask. The cape and mask are also found on the idol, which is carried shoulder-high on a litter. The idol represents Yiacatecuhtli, lord of the vanguard, the god of the merchants; the man is his priestly impersonator. The image of the man is drawn quite literally from the image of Yiacatecuhtli in the Codex Florentino (book I, illus. 17). Only the masked face and tilt of the head have been changed. In the accompanying text, Sahagún tells us that the merchants

went into the coast lands, looking well for whatsoever goods they could deal in. . . . Greatly were they wearied, much did they suffer to seek out the precious green stones, emerald green jade, fine turquoise, amber, gold; [and] all manner of feathers: the long tail feathers of the resplendent trogon, its red breasted feathers, those of the roseate spoonbill, the lovely cotinga, the yellow headed parrot, the troupial, the eagle, and the skins of fierce animals, rugs of ocelot skins, gourd bowls, incense bowls, tortoise-shell cups, spoons for stirring cacao, stoppers from jars.[19]

Certainly the merchants Rivera portrays are in search of similar luxury goods, because as they approach El Tajín the elegantly attired nobles rush to greet them, their arms laden with the rich produce of the tropical lowlands.

Rivera drew the images of the El Tajín nobles from two sources. The men are derived from a series of relief carvings that line one of the large ball courts at El Tajín (fig. 287). The pre-Columbian ball game pitted two teams against each other on an H-shaped field. The ball was solid rubber and quite heavy, so players protected their bodies with thick padding not unlike contemporary American football uniforms. The game was not just played for sport, however. It was also used to settle disputes, in which case the captain of the losing team could be sacrificed. Like the captain of the ball team in the relief, Rivera's first noble wears a thick protective belt or yoke and a curved chest protector known as a *palma.* His woven headdress repeats that worn by the figure who restrains the sacrificial victim in the relief. The headdress and costume of the man who stands with his back to the viewer are taken from the figure who performs the sacrifice in the relief. The complex interlacing on the huge banner at right echoes the double curves of the relief's border. The woman who smiles and turns toward the viewer is, however, derived from another form of pre-Columbian art. Her peculiar expression and many details of her attire come from the large, hollow ceramic figures of Classic-period Veracruz, commonly called "smiling faces" (fig. 288).

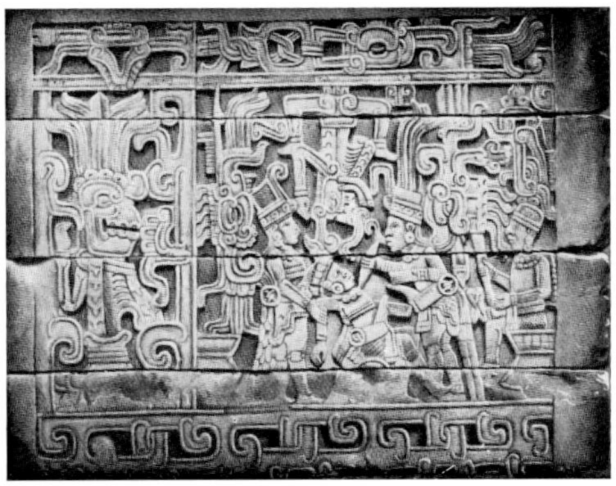

Figure 287
Ball court relief (northeast panel), El Tajín, Post-Classic period, 600–900, stone.

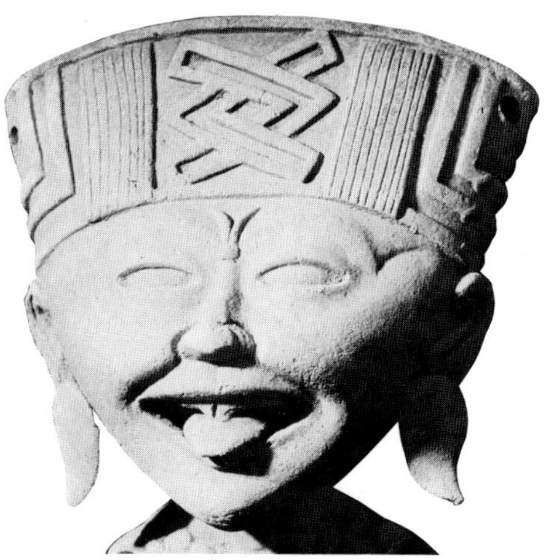

Figure 288
***Laughing Head Figurine,* Veracruz, Classic period, terra cotta, w. 22 cm. Jalapa, Universidad Veracruzana, Museo de Antropología.**

Rivera portrays the El Tajín nobles as happily rushing toward the Aztec merchants, freely offering the bounty of their land in trade. In fact, we know that Aztec trade was often a bellicose enterprise. The merchants frequently incited conflict in foreign lands so that the Aztecs would have reason to conquer the producers of new luxury items and bring the items in as tribute rather than as freely traded goods.

The grisaille panels below show the harvesting of pineapples, weaving on backstrap looms, and, to the far right, a sculptor kneeling with his hammer and chisel before an El Tajín *stela.* Around him are the stone trophies of the ball game—two palmas and a yoke.

A text panel preceding the various panels depicting ancient civilizations makes clear that one of Rivera's primary aims was to illustrate the cultural contributions the pre-Columbian civilizations made to the rest of the world. Translated from Spanish, the panel reads:

The World Owes to Mexico:
Corn, beans, tobacco, chocolate, cotton, hemp, tomatoes, peanuts, the nopal cactus, the maguey, the avocado, the pineapple, chicle . . .

followed by a long list of tropical fruits and vegetables, concluding with "papaya, chile, yucca, jicama." Each Spanish term is followed by its translation in Nahuatl, the language of the Aztecs, demonstrating again the profundity of Rivera's research.

The Final Images of Life And Death

Rivera worked on the façade of the Teatro de los Insurgentes from 1951 to 1953. It was an unusual commission for him. The huge façade, a broad horizontal wall, was an exterior surface and had to be, like the Tláloc fountain, done in mosaic rather than fresco (see fig. 406). The Insurgentes façade is Rivera's only major work with pre-Columbian content on a private commercial structure. Ironically, being outside and facing a major thoroughfare in Mexico City, it is also the most accessible to the public. Like the Chicano murals of Los Angeles, it is seen by whoever drives or buses or walks by. One need not make a deliberate effort to enter the building during certain hours on certain days in order to see it.

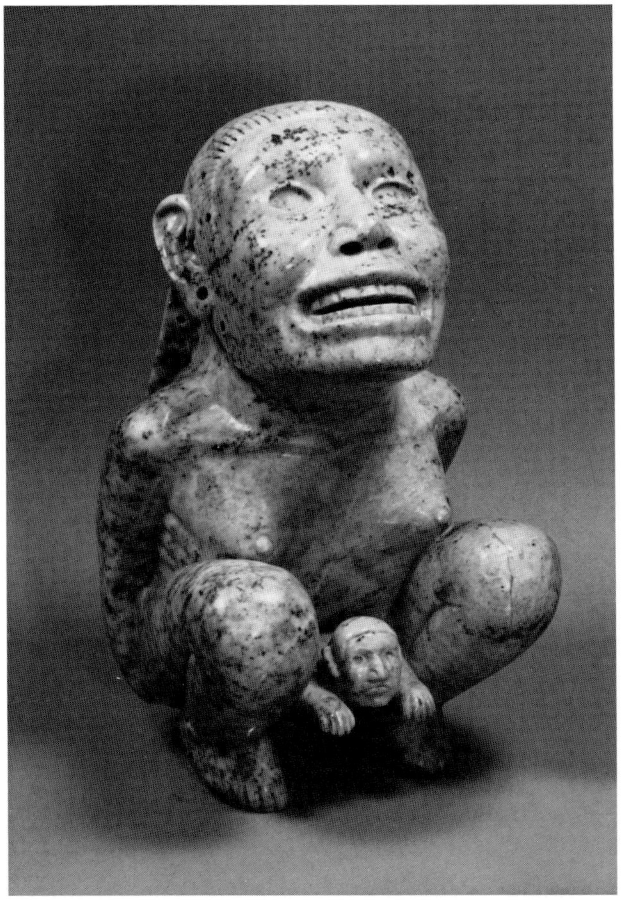

Figure 289
Tlazoteótl, Aztec, ca. 1500, stone, h. 20.6 cm. Washington, D.C., Dumbarton Oaks Research Library and Collections.

Rivera created a variegated cyclorama over the curved façade. Historical figures are merged with contemporary ones—Cantinflas appears as Juan Diego, the Indian who met the Virgin of Guadalupe—in images that unfold behind a huge pink mask and lace-encased hands. To the far right a scene from the pre-Columbian past is presented on three levels. Above, three women dance on a grassy hill. They are the animated embodiments of ceramic fertility figures from the Pre-Classic site of Tlatilco (see fig. 279). Even before the Tlatilco graves were excavated, after being accidentally uncovered by brickmakers in the 1930s, numerous figurines from the site had appeared on the market, the plunder of clandestine digging. Rivera acquired dozens of Tlatilco figurines for his collection, no doubt attracted by the sinuous tatoos on their swollen thighs and the lively vitality of their expressive gestures.

Above the dancers, a red-tongued feathered serpent curls into the sky. Below them, a sacrificial scene takes place on a pyramidal platform. The sacrifice is to be done by a skeletal figure who grasps the long auburn hair of a kneeling Tlatilco woman and raises a flint knife above her head. Grasping the woman's outstretched arms and aiming a spear at the skeleton's chest is a red-skinned man who, with the priestess behind him, may be attempting to stop the sacrifice. This is another example of Rivera's eclectic historical view. The Tlatilco woman resembles ceramic figurines from the Pre-Classic village society; the skeletal figure is taken from the Post-Classic manuscripts known as the Borgia Group, probably specifically from page 7 of the Codex Laud.[20]

An Aztec priest, his skin painted black and his face obscured by a skeletal helmet, dances down the pyramid's staircase, just in front of the stream of blood that flows from the sacrificial platform. To his left are several musicians, one beating a drum and another blowing a conch shell trumpet. To his right is a jaguar dancer, his mask and costume totally disguising the human body underneath. Rivera seems to be saying that a major source of Mexico's theatrical tradition is pre-Columbian ceremony. If so, Mexico would not be alone in having developed the dramatic arts out of religion.

In addition to his study of the more grisly aspects of pre-Columbian culture, Rivera was aware of that culture's battle against death. In both a small grisaille at the Instituto Nacional de Cardiologiá (1943) and his mural at the Hospital de la Raza (1952–53), he glorifies pre-Columbian medical arts. The grisaille shows a manta-clad man dipping leaves into a vaselike container before the reclining body of an aristocratic woman. Above her torso, Rivera has written, "Mexican Medicine. Before the Christian era, the use of the Yoloxochitl [i.e., "Heart Flower" plant] for the cure of heart ailments" (see fig. 402).

The Hospital de la Raza mural (see fig. 404) is bisected by the immense figure of Tlazoltéotl, goddess of dirt, "mistress of lust and debauchery, and she to whom confessions were made,"[21] which Rivera took directly from page thirteen of the Codex Borbonicus. In the Codex, the goddess is shown squatting with a child emerging from her spread legs; she is also the goddess of childbirth. The well-known sculptural depiction of Tlazoltéotl (fig. 289) is represented by the grimacing birth image that swings on a tree limb in the lower righthand corner of the composition. Below the central figure is a series of panels representing all the plants used in pre-Columbian medicine. These are taken from the Codex Badiano. Tlazoltéotl may be considered an aspect or avatar of Toci ("Our Grandmother"), also called Teteoinnan ("Mother of the Gods"). As Sahagún writes, "The physicians, the leeches, those

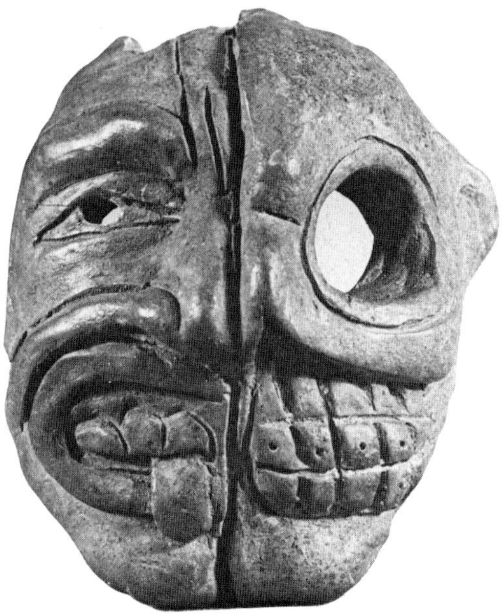

Figure 290
Life/Death Mask, ca. 900–300 B.C., clay. Mexico City, Museo Nacional de Antropología.

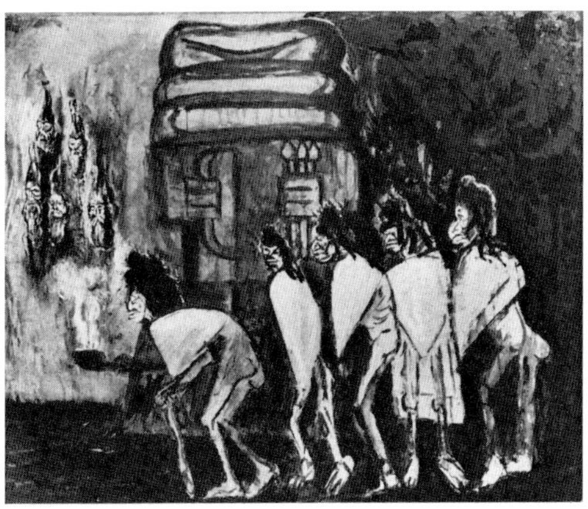

Figure 291
José Clemente Orozco, *Worship of Huitzilpochtli,* ca. 1949, gun cotton and distemper on masonite, 99 × 122 cm. Mexico City, Museo de Arte Moderno (INBA).

who cured hemorrhoids, those who purged people, those who cured eye ailments worshipped her. . . . Also women, those who administered sedatives at childbirth, those who brought about abortion . . ."[22]

To the right of the central figure is a series of layered images depicting pre-Columbian medical practices. Eight of the figures in this section wear the "paper crown with protruding spindles, cotton flowers, and quetzal feathers" found in Sahagún's depiction of Toci (Codex Florentino, book I, illus. 8). The largest of these is a priest who wears the costume of Tlazoltéotl as portrayed on page thirteen of the Codex Borbonicus, and who is proportioned and positioned exactly like the priest who faces a seated Toci figure on page thirty. Clockwise around him cripples approach on crutches, carrying offerings under their bent arms; two men practice dentistry; and others treat an eye infection, perform chest surgery, assist a woman in childbirth, bind a broken arm, treat skin diseases (this image comes from the ceramic tradition of West Mexico, where disease and deformity seem to have fascinated the artists), administer an enema (the giving of hallucinogenic enemas is depicted on numerous Maya funerary urns), and finally use a steam bath. The double Templo Mayor of Tenochtitlán, as well as the round temple of the wind god Ehecatl and the ball court, rises above the horizon line. Below the earth, two mythical serpents face a mask, half skeletal, half fleshed, reminiscent of a particularly striking funerary mask from Pre-Classic Tlatilco (fig. 290).

Rivera as Indianist

The life/death duality represented by the mask and the flanking tree forms of the Hospital de la Raza mural illustrates a basic tenet of pre-Columbian thought: out of death comes life; both are points on an unending cycle of existence.[23] I believe Rivera thought of this concept as parallel to the yin-yang of Oriental thought, which is why he depicted Frida Kahlo holding a yin-yang disc as she stands behind the child Rivera in his mural *Dream of a Sunday Afternoon in the Alameda* at the Hotel del Prado (see fig. 403). Rivera holds the hand of a skeletal woman usually cited as being a *calavera* (skull) figure, a common motif in the art and folk rituals of Mexico. I suggest that the skeletal woman is also an allusion to Coatlicue, the death's-head earth goddess. Her shawl is a feathered serpent, her belt buckle the *ollin* or "earthquake" symbol that is the central icon of the Aztec calendar stone. Mother of the gods and, by implication of placement, metaphorically the mother of Rivera, she is the source of the life and spirit that he loved in Mexico.

Not all of the Mexican muralists glorified the Indian past. In José Clemente Orozco's 1949 easel painting entitled *Worship of Huitzilopochtli* (the central image is actually that of Coatlicue),[24] the idol looms dark and ominous over dessicated Indians who grovel below it in pathetic subservience (fig. 291). The Coatlicue of Orozco's Hospicio Cabañas mural program is similarly intimidating, if not horrific. Again, mistakenly intended as a depiction of the war god, she holds huge weapons in both hands. For this and other reasons, Shifra Goldman calls Orozco a *"hispanista,"* as he was "opposed to Indian glorification, ancient or modern."[25]

Goldman calls Rivera an *"indigenista"* (Indianist). Like many other writers, musicians, filmmakers, and artists of the period, he took an advocacy position and "tended to glorify the Indian heritage and vilify that of the Spaniards as a means of rectifying a historical imbalance."[26]

Rivera's images of the past were definitely influenced by his *indigenista* stance. He portrayed the pre-Columbian civilizations as bright, glorious utopias. This bias led to images so transformed as to be virtually unreal. Goldman says of the Tlatelolco market scene, "The painting gives no hint of Aztec imperialism, which the market symbolizes. Tribute and sacrificial victims were brought to Tenochtitlán from the subject peoples."[27]

Other factors were at work as well. Rivera himself said, "I took grave care to authenticate every detail by exact research because I wanted to leave no opening for anyone to discredit the murals as a whole by the charge that any detail was a fabrication."[28] Numerous scholars have attested to the veracity of Rivera's pre-Columbian images. Jacinto Quirarte, for instance, writes that Rivera "often recorded the motifs so faithfully that they can be read as documents."[29] While this may be true of many individual motifs, Rivera sometimes combined elements and figures in a manner that was both chronologically and spatially eclectic. What might be termed poetic license by a generous reviewer or historical vagary by a critic led him to create scenes involving people separated in time by as much as two millennia or in space by hundreds of miles.

One further point on Rivera's choice of sources. He strongly preferred the elitist images of the most complex pre-Columbian cultures, particularly the Aztecs, to those of the simpler egalitarian societies. Although he employed images from the simple Pre-Classic village society of Tlatilco at the Hospital de la Raza and the Teatro de los Insurgentes and those from the later West Mexico pueblos of Nayarit in the Palacio Nacional, in both cases, he placed figures from these virtually classless agrarian peoples in situations that are clearly Post-Classic in date and Aztec in ambience. I have constantly been puzzled by Rivera's neglect of the agricultural village-dwellers of the pre-Columbian world, especially considering his Marxist politics and his repeated inclusion of modern Mexican peasants in other mural programs. Perhaps he found the pre-Columbian villages insufficient in either exotic visual appeal or cultural sophistication to support his revisionist historical intentions. I am doubly confounded by his neglect of pre-Columbian villagers when I remember that they produced the bulk of the ceramics in Rivera's own collection.

Rivera romantically glorified the pre-Columbian past. He presented a casually eclectic view of pre-Columbian history, often deriving his images from Colonial sources that manifest demonstrable European influence, and his strong preference for the exotically sophisticated culture of the Aztecs gave a skewed view of the Indian populace. But each of these caveats pales when Rivera's total accomplishment in presenting pre-Columbian images is considered. Both the great volume of his mural work and its tremendously positive reception are overwhelming. Rivera achieved his didactic intent. From Indians to tourists to scholars, more people have viewed the pre-Columbian world through Rivera's eyes than in any other fashion. He is the greatest popularizer of pre-Columbian art since Frederick Catherwood illustrated the explorer John Lloyd Stephen's *Incidents of Travel in the Yucatán* in 1843. The only modern artists who have approached Rivera in bringing pre-Columbian imagery to the masses are George Lucas and Steven Spielberg, who employed the Mayan site of Tikal as the rebel camp in the film *Star Wars* and a golden version of the Aztec Tlazoltéotl in *Raiders of the Lost Ark*. If you have seen images of the pre-Columbian world on a streetside mural in East Los Angeles, or on a restaurant menu, or on a souvenir box, odds are they were derived from the work of Diego Rivera, rather than from pre-Columbian originals.

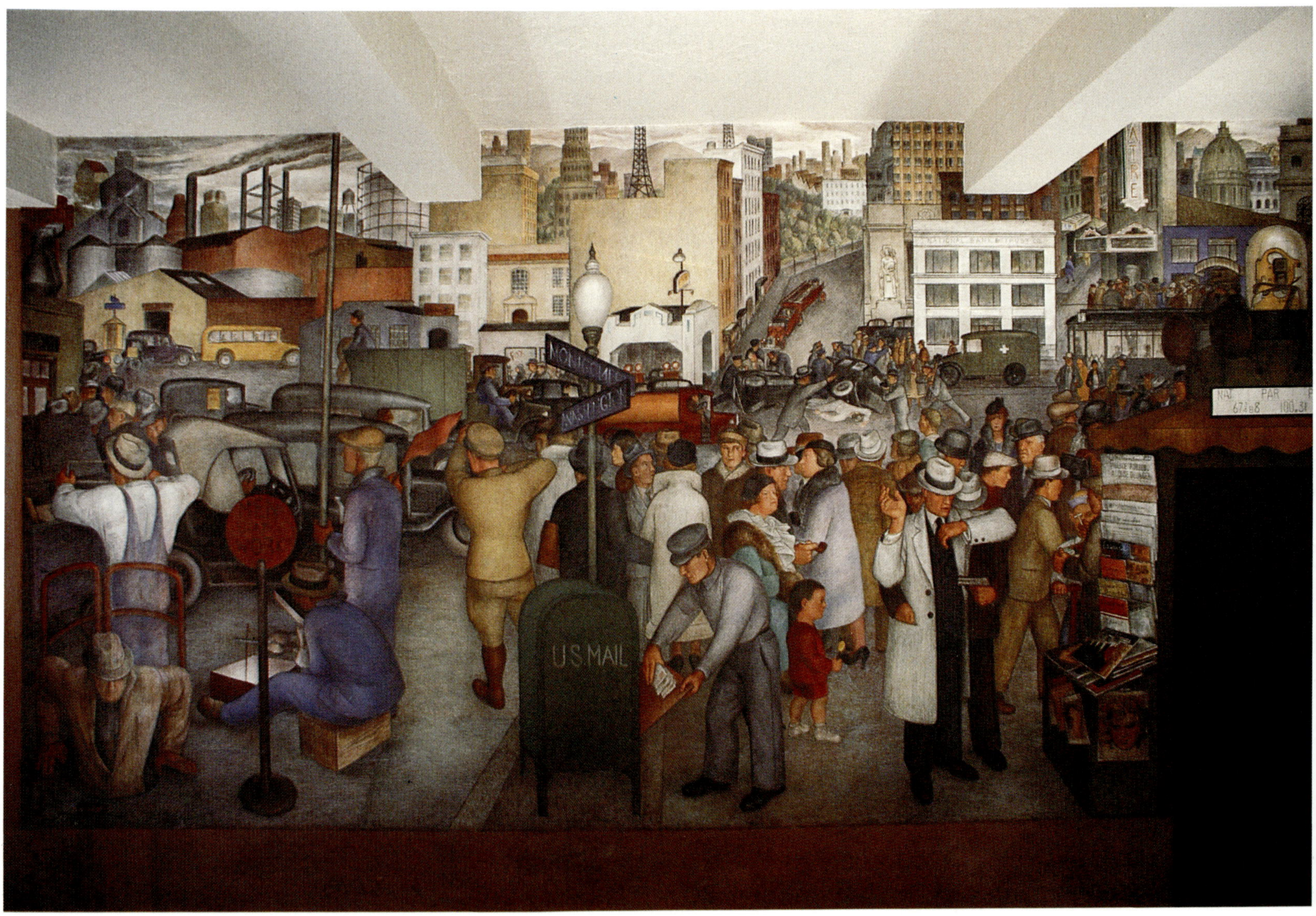
U.S.MAIL

The Influence of Diego Rivera on the Art of the United States during the 1930s and After

Francis V. O'Connor

Figure 292
Victor Arnautoff, *City Life* (left half), PWAP, 1934, fresco. San Francisco, Coit Tower. Photo: © Don Beatty.

The Idea of Influence

[Artists], by the time they have grown strong, do not [see] the [art] of X, for really strong [artists] can [see] only themselves. For them, to be judicious is to be weak, and to compare, exactly and fairly, is to be not elect.[1]

Any discussion of the influence of an artist on an era—especially an artist of Diego Rivera's strength of genius on a decade as turbulent, both creatively and politically, as the 1930s—requires, first of all, a clear idea of what influence means. The idea of "influence" is commonplace in contemporary art writing, but it is usually construed simplistically as involving some sort of larceny of manner and motif based on the seemingly obvious notion that artist A sees artist B's work and does likewise until he develops a "language" of his own, which, in turn, is stolen by artist C—and so on and so on to make the history of art. While there is some modicum of truth in this view, it apprehends only the surface of a profound reality. Life is more various and art a more complex epistemological vehicle than this crude notion of imitation would suggest. We must look deeper.

Let us first consider the various depths of meaning in the word "influence." The word "influence" was understood in the 13th century to refer to the "flowing or streaming from the stars or heavens of an ethereal fluid acting upon the character and destiny of men." It later took on the more general meaning of "the inflowing . . . of any kind of divine, spiritual, moral, immaterial or secret power or principle," and today its only practical definition is the "exertion of action of which the operation is unseen or insensible (or perceptible only in its effects) by one person or thing upon another" (*Oxford English Dictionary*).

So "influence" basically means today an inflowing of some sort from one entity to another—which is not as simple as it may seem if the influx considered is from art into artist. From here the transaction is just as complex a problem of projection and fantasy as was, in other cultures, the comprehension of the zodiac.

The first factor to consider when approaching the problem of artistic influence is basically statistical. The best of any new generation of artists find relatively few strong precursors worthy of reacting against. And the best are themselves few in number. Most artists—I would say close to 95 percent of any generation—follow the line of least resistance. They presume (or worse, are taught) that all problems have been solved and all subjects treated by their predecessors, and they need only follow a received tradition to fulfill themselves as artists and obtain success. The other 5 percent—and here I may be too generous—are capable of more or less overcoming this presumption and reformulating the received tradition of the past in terms of present, and usually very personal, priorities.

The second factor is purely psychological: in order for an artist to be influenced, he or she must be open to a given influence. No artist is influenced by every visual fact encountered. Each personality takes in only what it finds usable—what speaks to it in some way, what it is already predisposed to discern. So a process of unconscious editing and conscious selection is an important factor in being influenced. This psychological predisposition to specific influences has a great deal to do with the biographical reality of the individual artist.

The third factor in the matter of influence in the arts is sociological. In a pragmatic culture such as the United States was during the 1930s—and still is today—the artist is forced to find means with which to handle the very real sense of guilt engendered by his or her compulsion to produce what society at large considers useless things. For most, this requires a cause that justifies the artistic act, the kind of life that act requires, and the resulting product. Such a cause is extrinsic to art but intrinsic to the artist's social environment. During the 1930s, the Depression provided the cause, that of social concern, and therefore an "art for the millions." The Depression also provided a context for Marxist ideology that was not without its own plausibly argued aesthetic dimension. Obviously, all of these factors are operating simultaneously and multidimensionally in time (generations overlap) and space (visual communication is, today, instantaneous).

What does being influenced mean on the level of individual dynamics? The simplest mode of being influenced, as already mentioned, is for an artist to be moved to copy a complex of motifs or stylistic mannerisms from another artist. Young artists do this all the time in order to obtain an initial visual vocabulary with which to express the pressure of imagery within themselves in some approved way. Weak artists, of course, never get beyond this stage. They turn to copying themselves, their tradition, or the latest style—or they drift into teaching. Most, but certainly not all, New Deal and community muralists are in this group.

A more positive way of being influenced is to idealize the precursor in terms of one's own deeply and independently held views of art and its function—or ideological views—or both. The precursor is "copied" not so much on the level of style and motif, though this usually occurs, but on the level of social persona. The influenced artist wants to act as an artist in like manner, but in terms of his own tradition, visual vocabulary, and taste. Thus the precursor's personality, and/or ideological cause, becomes an influence equal to his art. Influence here is moral, not just literal, and the influenced artist finds a comfortable fit in the context of the times. This results in a corpus of art that is easily "dated" as being, for example, typical of the 1930s. Such artists, though fixated chronologically and stylistically, often manage to develop within a self-imposed tradition, since their initial dependency was sociological rather than psychological. Ben Shahn is an example of this group.

The third and most creative mode of being influenced is, however, to be strong enough in personal artistic daemon as to misread the precursor artist in thoroughly individualistic terms. The strength of the strong artist lies in his or her ability, despite overwhelming anxiety, to face down the precursor's apparent omniscience with the one fact the precursor cannot affect, namely the succeeding strong artist's sense of self as an image-maker independent of rivals. Thomas Hart Benton, as we shall see, was such a strong artist.

It ought to be obvious by now that I am stealing the concept of a "strong" artist, as well as the approach here taken, from Harold Bloom's brilliant book *The Anxiety of Influence,* in which he "offers a theory of poetry by way of a description of poetic influence, or the story of intra-poetic relationships."[2] Since I am stealing from Professor Bloom, I shall, from now on, change such words as "poetry" and "poetic" to "art" and "artistic"—the terminology of the visual arts. This does no violence to his meaning and helps to specify mine. Thus, by artistic influence, Bloom does not mean the "transmission of ideas and images from earlier to later artists," which he sees, unlike many traditional art historians, as essentially accidental. Rather he believes that

[artistic] influence—when it involves two strong, authentic [artists]—always proceeds by a misreading of the prior [artist], an act of creative correction that is actually and necessarily a misinterpretation. The history of fruitful [artistic] influence, which is to say the main tradition of Western [art] since the Renaissance, is a history of anxiety and self-serving caricature, of distortion, of perverse, willful revisionism without which modern [art] as such would not exist.[3]

Bloom is only interested in strong artists:

. . . major figures with the persistence to wrestle with their strong precursors, even to the death. Weaker talents idealize figures of capable imagination appropriate for themselves. But nothing is got for nothing, and self-appropriation involves the immense anxieties of indebtedness, for what strong maker desires the realization that he has failed to create himself?[4]

Now, if I misread Bloom with capable imagination, he is saying just this: that a valid hermeneutic must consider the total encounter between the artist and his psychological and sociological environments, which inevitably include the anxiety-inducing reality of other artists, their work, and their motives. Further, this anxious encounter is not linear on the level of causality, but rather dialectic. This implies that an individual work of art is only marginally meaningful in itself unless seen as part of the totality of the artist's creative experience and production. And finally, such an encounter demands that ultimate judgment of an artist's work rests on the strength of this inner dialectic and the extent to which the artist has won out over the anxiety induced both by his involvement with strong precursors and by his resolution of conflict in earlier stages of his own development.

Strong artists are thus capable of selecting out from the welter of potential influences exactly what they require to define their own needs and of discarding the rest. Such predatory artists, indifferent to precise meanings and intentions, systematically misread other artists and their own concerns in former states of development, as their insight accumulates and evolves. This self-Midrash is the salvation of self-creating personalities, and, of course, the despair of scholars. It can eventually be described but never fully explained. The morphology of genius, as the philosophical psychologists from Freud on have been forced to admit, is one of the mysteries of nature. But given such a reality, we can at least try to describe intelligently.[5]

The range of style and image in the work of strong artists tends to be relatively narrow, and they retain their youthful pressure of imagery, renewing its energy within each cycle of their life course.[6] Creative stasis for them is death. They omnivorously assimilate strong artistic precursors and their own experience into even more powerful spiritual expressions. They are the heroic creators weaker artists either copy outright or idealize, wishing they could live such lives though ignorant of their cost. Strong artists are the mirrors of their age. They articulate its myth. They define, in their accomplishments, the history of its art. And they are few.

One of the phenomena of 20th-century art in the Americas is that Mexico produced two such artists at a time when the United States, having lost Albert Ryder in 1917, exiled Arthur Dove to his houseboat in 1920, and not yet aware of the strength of Thomas Hart Benton and Stuart Davis, possessed not one artist of comparable stature. Unlike marginal modernists of the 1920s such as Edward Hopper, John Marin, Alfred Mauer, Charles Sheeler, and Max Weber, who were still trying to figure out what happened at the Armory show so they could imitate it, the Mexicans were busy misreading the School of Paris, the Italian Renaissance, and their own indigenous culture, within the ideological context of Marxism. That the Mexicans were influential in the United States during the 1930s is not surprising; they filled a cultural and ideological vacuum.

Let me say something here about *il tres grandes:* Rivera, Orozco, and Siqueiros. Of the three, I regard Rivera and Orozco as strong artists in the sense just defined. Rivera, of course, is the classicist—the Apollonian, if you will—deriving his style from his profound study of Cubism and Renaissance murals and his capacity to find analogies within the native and Spanish cultures of his homeland. Orozco is the Dionysian, distilling the essential of his style from the satiric tradition of his country and its exuberant Baroque expressiveness. The life's achievement of these two strong artists was both sustained and developmental.

I do not consider Siqueiros a strong artist. Yet the youngest of the three Mexicans is neither a pasticheur nor an idealizer. He belongs to that very small company of artists whose power resides in personally living out an ideological myth. He is the 20th-century epitome of the artist as political propagandist and activist. His art is pure visual rhetoric, intended neither to please nor to inspire, but to persuade.

If Rivera and Orozco epitomize the poles of Apollo and Dionysus, then Siqueiros is Hephaestus, the lame trickster god, flawed but essential to Olympus because of the utility of his craft. The role of Siqueiros in the Mexican mural movement, and more recently in the community mural movement in North America, is thus comparable to that of Marcel Duchamp in the School of Paris and Andy Warhol in the School of New York. Incapable of personal artistic development beyond a certain originality of image, strong enough to ignore if not to misread precursors, and totally subsumed by the motivating ideology of their public stance, such artists synthesize in their lives the myth they cannot readily embody in their art.

The Influence of Diego Rivera on Thomas Hart Benton

I have not joined . . . protesting the indignity put upon Diego Rivera's work in Rockefeller Center because I do not feel, in view of the seriously decadent condition of our own art, that what happens to a Mexican art [sic] is of such importance. . . . I respect Rivera as an artist, as a great one, but I have no time to enter into affairs concerning him, because I am intensely interested in the development of an art which is of, and adequately represents, the United States—my own art. (Thomas Hart Benton in a lecture to the John Reed Club, February 11, 1934).[7]

The statement above was made just hours after the authorities at Rockefeller Center had completed the destruction of Diego Rivera's *Man at the Crossroads* mural during the night of February 10, 1934. It is a classic piece of evidence for the essentially Oedipal origins of Bloom's concept of the "anxiety of influence." Benton, a strong artist if ever there was one, was facing New York's most radical art audience. It was seething with impotent rage over the capitalists' destruction of a comrade's mural. Yet Benton didn't care and said so; his own art, and its ideology, was more important. While Benton and Rivera were almost exact contemporaries—Benton was three years younger—and were quite similar in their capacity as public personalities, the chronology of events, and Benton's own attitudes, clearly indicates that Rivera was Benton's precursor when it came to mural painting. By 1934, however, Benton had worked

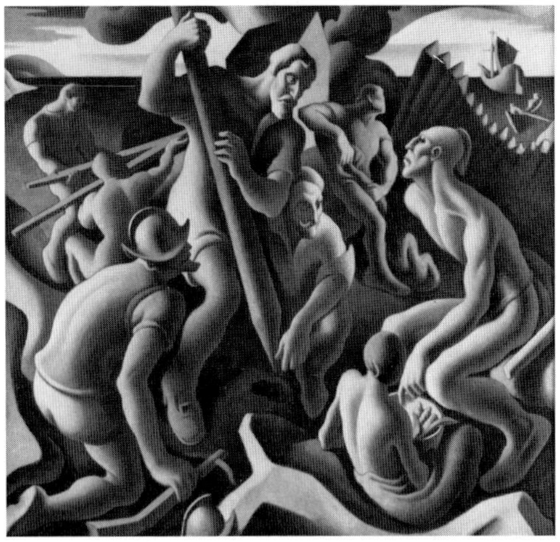

Figure 293
Thomas Hart Benton, *Palisades* (*American Historical Epic* series, 1919–24), oil on canvas, 1.82 × 2.13 m. Kansas City, Missouri, The Nelson Atkins Museum of Art, Bequest of Thomas Hart Benton.

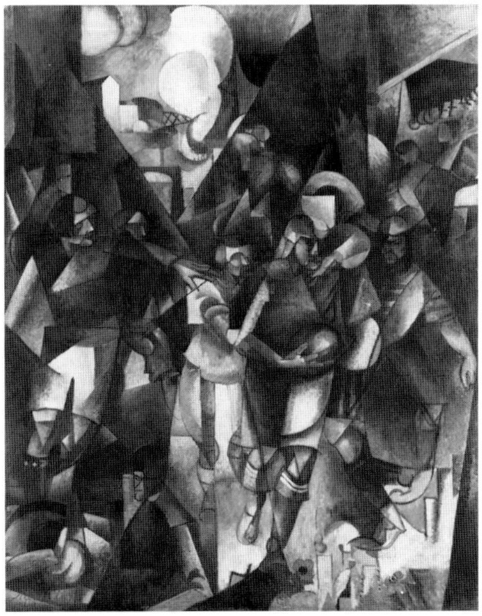

Figure 294
Albert Gleizes, *Football Players*, 1912–13, oil on canvas, 226 × 183 cm. Washington, D.C., National Gallery of Art, Ailsa Mellon Bruce Fund 1970.

through his misreading of Rivera's influence and had created his own mural style. Whatever role as artistic "father" Rivera had played to Benton, the "son" was now his own man.

Benton had promoted himself as a muralist throughout the 1920s, creating groups of large easel paintings, which he called "chapters" in an *American Historical Epic* series (ca. 1920–26). Himself a Marxist during this period, he exhibited these works as potential mural designs,[8] while keeping a canny eye on the Mexicans, as he admits in the following retrospective statement:

I had looked with much interest on the rise of the Mexican school during the mid-twenties. In spite of the Marxist dogmas, to the propagation of which so much of its work was devoted, I saw in the Mexican effort a profound and much-needed re-direction of art towards its ancient humanistic functions. The Mexican concern with publicly significant meanings and with the pageant of Mexican national life corresponded perfectly with what I had in mind for art in the United States. I also looked with envy on the opportunities given Mexican painters for public mural work. After I had completed the second chapter of my history I began to question the practical side of continuing it without similar opportunities.[9]

Benton did not get a wall to paint until Alvin Johnson, the president of the New School for Social Research in New York City, offered him and José Clemente Orozco commissions to paint murals in the schools' new buildings. Benton executed these murals during the winter of 1930–31. In 1932 he did another series of murals for the library of the Whitney Museum of American Art. In 1933 he created a huge mural for the Indiana pavilion at the Chicago World's Fair, and in 1936, after he had left New York City for good, he painted his last wall of the 1930s in the Missouri State Capitol at Jefferson City. These murals are unquestionably the best executed by a citizen of the United States during the first half of the 1930s, and it was not until the last years of the decade that, supported by New Deal art projects, artists such as Ben Shahn were capable of producing a few walls of equal stature.

Although Benton's first three murals were created at virtually the same time as Rivera's murals in this country, Benton does not admit to any dependence on Rivera, making a point of disassociating himself from Rivera's politics, and it is certainly true that Benton's work is free of any direct influence from his Mexican contemporary. Consequently, none of the writers on Benton attributes any aspect of his mural style to Rivera, the consensus being that his walls were created simultaneously, and independently of Rivera's influence. I think such a conclusion is unwarranted, given the stylistic evidence of the murals themselves and the circumstances under which they were painted.

Central to any understanding of Benton's wall painting and its relationship to that of Rivera is the fact that both studied in Paris during the development of Cubism. While Benton later decried the influence of Cubism on the development of an art of "American" values and motifs, Rivera consciously integrated what he had learned in Paris with the Italian Renaissance mural tradition and the indigenous art of his native Mexico. As a result, by the early 1920s, Rivera was going from strength to strength as a revolutionary muralist while Benton was creating the rather desultory "chapters" of his American epic (see fig. 293). These works are highly stylized groupings of heavily modeled figures set in a naturalistic space. They tell simplistic stories derived from popular conceptions of our colonial history. While well designed, and redolent of the formulae of Art Deco academicism that dominated the wall painting of their era,[10] they are, by any standard of judgment, inferior to what Rivera was doing in Mexico and held little promise that their stylistic vocabulary could hold its own against the exigencies of scale and architectural intrusion an actual mural environment would present. Indeed, Benton's artistic development during the early

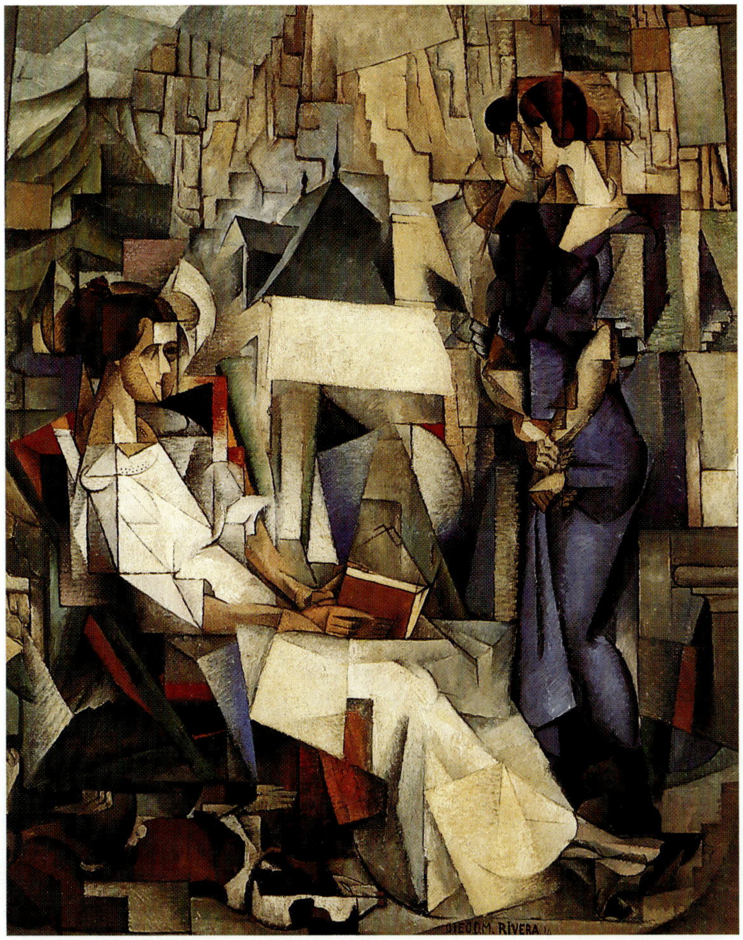

Figure 295
Diego Rivera, *Two Women,* 1914, oil on canvas, 198.1 × 160 cm. Little Rock, The Arkansas Art Center Foundation Collection, Gift of Abby Rockefeller Mauze, 1955 (55.10).

and mid 1920s hardly anticipates the breakthrough evident in his New School murals. Nor is there any possibility that his friendship with Orozco was the key to his sudden creation of ten stylistically powerful and iconographically original murals. Indeed, one glance at Orozco's rigid construct at the New School dispels even the notion of influence from that quarter.

The reason Benton's New School murals are so successful and compelling, is, I contend, that they were created under the influence of Rivera's growing reputation. Further, there is strong evidence that Benton was virtually pushed into emulating Rivera by the very critics who were disposed to promote the flamboyant Missourian as a prototypical American muralist. This was achieved by first promoting him as the prophet of a purely American mural art in opposition to both European modernism and turgid academism—and then with great hopes comparing him to Rivera. Thus Thomas Craven, one of Benton's principal boosters, states flatly (in reviewing four historical panels Benton had designed in the style of his epic series and proposed for the walls of the New York Public Library), "Apart from its aesthetic importance [the show] proclaimed in downright, unequivocal language what I believe to be the beginning of an epoch in American painting—the emancipation of the artist from the French tradition."[11] Another Benton promoter, Lewis Mumford, lamented that no one would give the artist a wall to paint: "Mr. Benton wants space: in a revolutionary moment, such as that Rivera seized in Mexico, he would begin to cover the whole housefront."[12] Even critics who were not totally converted to Benton, took up the theme. Lee Simonson, talking about Benton's skill at imaging heartland America in his easel painting, could say:

If he paints it, and I think that sooner or later, he will, it will be the type of painting I dream about. . . . It will burst out of a two by four frame because it cannot by the nature of its subject be so confined. It will have everything he has learned from the methods of the modern painters, the solidity, the tactile values, the simplification of form, the functional quality of color in expressing form and not merely plastered upon it,—that and everything else which may make it significant for the commentators, just as Rivera's frescoes are.[13]

By 1929 Benton was certainly more than aware of Rivera as a rival. The Mexican's work had been reproduced in the newspapers and art press since 1924. The January 1929 issue of *Creative Art* was devoted completely to Rivera, and the same year a heavily illustrated book about his murals was published by Ernestine Evans.

Indeed, there is evidence that about the same time Benton was becoming acutely aware of Rivera as a superior muralist. As early as 1927 he began to experiment with a style radically at odds with the flat patterns and high horizons of his epic series. A large painting of that year, such as *Bootleggers,* shows a conflation of spatial planes and dissociated pictorial groupings that derives directly from Analytic Cubism.[14] I would argue that Benton's new explorations derive from Rivera's adaptation of the devices of early Cubism in his murals. This is not the Analytical Cubism of Picasso and Braque, but more that of Albert Gleizes's *The Football Players* (fig. 294), in which the figures and their setting possess a greater spatiality and plastic presence. Rivera was well acquainted with such work (he could have seen the Gleizes at the Salon des Indépendents in 1913) and was painting in a similar style in 1914, as his *Two Women* (fig. 295) attests. Benton, who would have known such works only

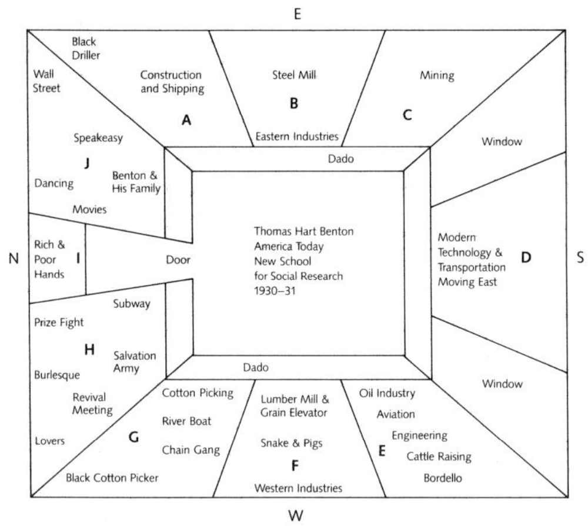

Figure 296
Diagram of Thomas Hart Benton's *America Today,* New School for Social Research. Courtesy of the author.

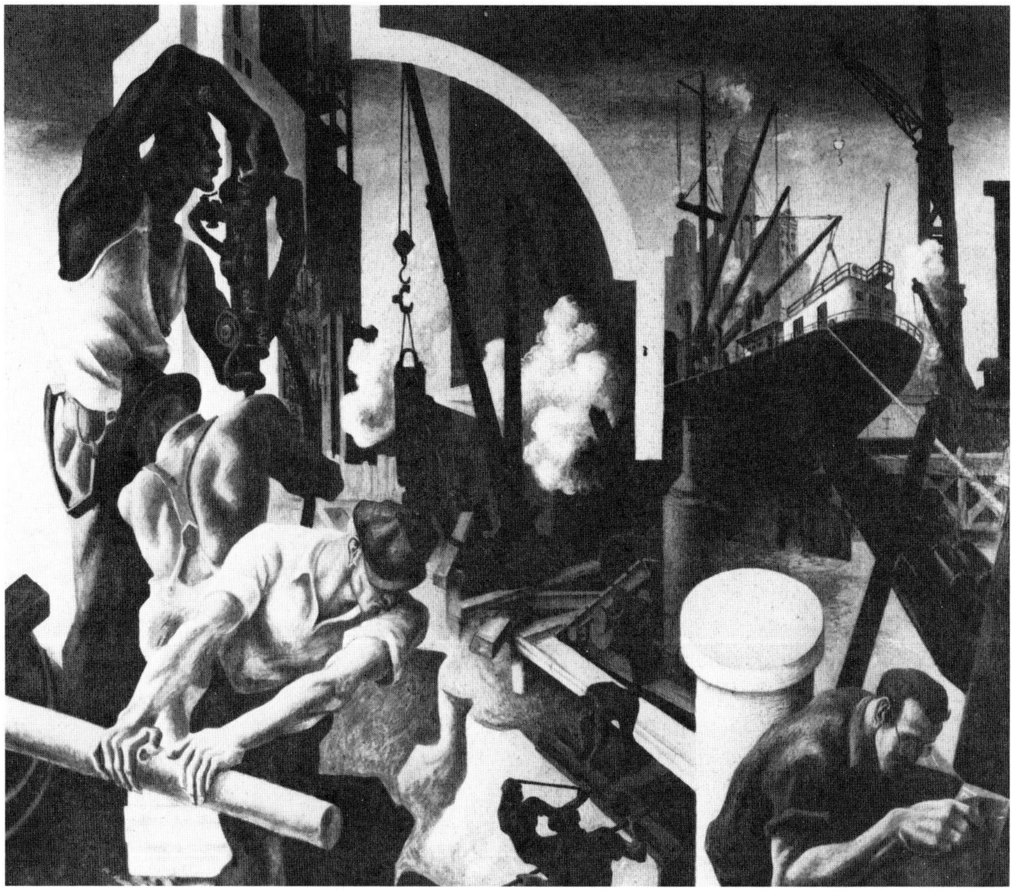

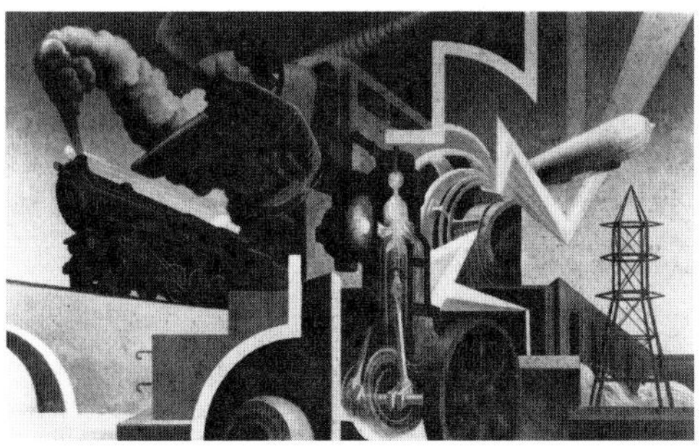

Figure 297
Thomas Hart Benton, *America Today* (see fig. 296 D), 1930, distemper, egg tempera, and oil glaze on linen, 2.33 × 4.06 m. Courtesy of The Equitable.

after leaving Paris in 1911, had come under the influence of the more abstract Cubists such as Delaunay and Stanton MacDonald-Wright. He had also followed a far more desultory and rebellious course of development until the late 1920s, when he was prompted to recognize in reproductions of Rivera's walls far more apt solutions to mural problems than those he had hitherto discovered for himself. This is why paintings such as the two just mentioned can be found to contain in germ all the structural devices Benton employs in his New School panels (see figs. 296–300).

While Benton apparently never went to Mexico and knew Rivera's walls only from photographs, he was nevertheless capable, due to his own early experience in Paris, of immediately perceiving the sophisticated cubistic infrastructure Rivera was using to unify his wall planes while simultaneously violating them with deep recessional spaces. A strong artist, Benton proceeded to misread Rivera's solutions, at first crudely and later with progressive aplomb as he grew in experience and skill. In a series of articles in *The Arts* in 1926 and 1927, Benton offers a thoroughly worked out, if rather mechanistic and literal-minded application of Cubism to the problems of abstract design.[15] Indeed, Benton was the only muralist in the United States who could have even begun to comprehend what Rivera was doing. But Benton was, unlike Rivera, a literal-minded American. He hoped to attain an "American" form that would be free of psychological and intellectual associations and compatible with the essential innocence of the American people. Having thus misread Cubism, modernism, and perhaps the intelligence of his own countrymen, it is not

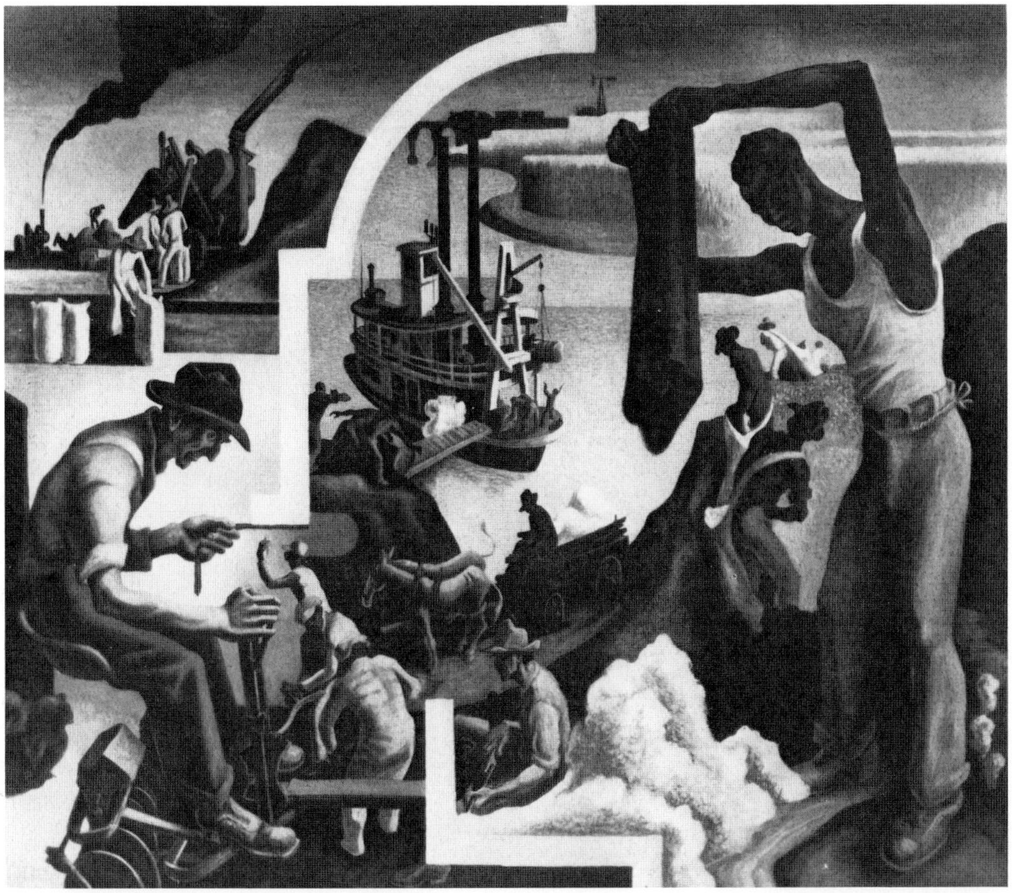

Figures 298, 299
Thomas Hart Benton, *America Today* (see fig. 296 A and G), 1930, distemper, egg tempera, and oil glaze on linen, each 2.33 × 2.69 m. Courtesy of The Equitable.

hard to understand his single-minded misreading of Rivera's murals. But his shallow chauvinism was no match for Rivera's communism (not to mention the Mexican's deeper understanding of modern science and art history), and his natural strength of genius could only seize on what he could recognize: Rivera's ability to energize a wall with cubistic devices.

At the New School, Benton had the opportunity to create his first actual mural, and the result is a surprisingly well-integrated pictorial environment, consisting of ten egg tempera panels arranged around all four walls of a room about thirty feet long by twenty-five feet wide (fig. 296). The panels create an intense visual environment depicting the various industries of the country and a typological anthology of its peoples, derived from Benton's extensive sketching trips during the 1920s (an environment alas destroyed by their recent installation in The Equitable building in New York).

The first image one saw on entering the New School's old boardroom was a lively evocation of modern technology between the windows of the south wall (figs. 296 and 297). This image is highly suggestive of the visual complexity of Rivera's treatment of similar subjects, but it is Benton's in the dynamism of its presentation. Standing at the door and turning directly to either side revealed opposing figures of two huge black workers (figs. 298 and 299) in almost identical poses. These introduce the urban industrial scenes on the east wall and those of rural America on the west—the directional iconography being analogous to the national geography. Thus the program starts with a balance of themes that establishes the visual precedent for similar oppositions of motifs down the long facing walls: cargo ship/riverboat, steel mill/lumber mill, smokestacks/oil rigs, and so on. The eye then returns to the central panel, noting the connection of aviation and energy motifs at its juncture with the west wall and the strong lines of force in the train and airplane hurtling from the rural West to the industrialized East. Only by turning completely around to face north did the viewer turn from images of toil and enterprise to relax amid scenes of their solaces and rewards: family tranquility, religious uplift, sports, the movies, the delights of Wall Street, speakeasies, and the burlesque.

To weave this exuberant iconographic program even more tightly together into an aesthetic whole, Benton used a number of formal devices. Thus, in a manner analogous to his opposition of motifs, he designed the angle of the steelworker's plunger at the right in the central panel on the east wall to continue in the girder at the lower left in the next. At the same position on the west wall, the same angle is reversed in the fence that runs across the division of the panels. Similarly, areas of strong red are used oppositionally at the ends of the east and west walls to "close" the compositions, and the axes of the

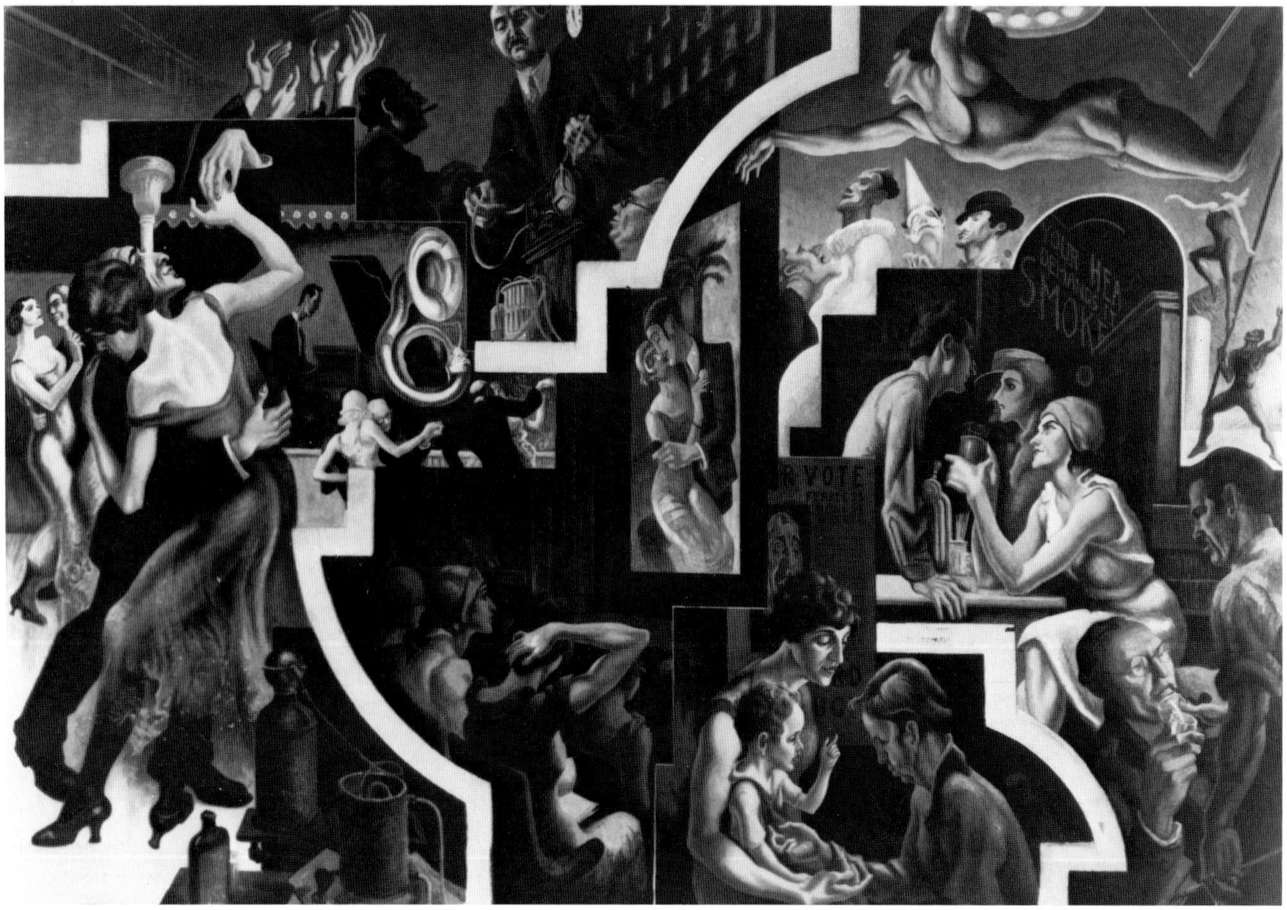

Figure 300
Thomas Hart Benton, *America Today* (see fig. 296 J), 1930, distemper, egg tempera, and oil glaze on linen, 2.33 × 3.40 m. Courtesy of The Equitable.

central panels of each wall act as points of rest for the vigorous lines of force that radiate upward from the center of the east wall and converge downward on the west. All of these devices serve to emphasize the symbolism attached to each of the directions. But most striking and modern, indeed "moderne," of these formal strategies are the angled silver moldings that continue the frame of the panels into the composition and constitute internal partitions for the shifting space planes on which the action of the various scenes takes place. These moldings are also Benton's way of coming to terms with Cubist montage.[16]

Along with these iconographic and formal devices, Benton also employed a system of directional symbolism that goes beyond the merely situational (see my essay later in this volume) and is very much akin to Rivera's early use of such symbolism. Benton's directional symbolism, however, is based on the not unbiased notion of the national geography that might be expected of a Missouri politician's son and only subliminally on a deeper sense of each direction's import. Thus he saw the country as basically divided between the industrialized East and the agrarian West, while the big cities of the North with all their delights and temptations (Benton was thinking of Chicago as well as New York) represented everything the rural imagination felt threatening to the upright values of family and religion: smoking, drinking, dancing, fighting, nightlife, sex—and bankers. Yet the North retains a certain mysterious, morally ambiguous allure about which Benton felt it necessary to remain a bit ambivalent. The south wall is devoted to the brilliance of modern technology: the image is a veritable sunburst of energy centered on the golden disk of a railroad signal. This paean to technology would seem not to square with the social realist theme of the north wall, until placed in the context of the machine-worshipping 1920s.

Furthermore, the three panels on the east wall all present positive, almost idealized images of men at work. There is something of a sense of benign productivity and the grandeur of the rhythms of progress. In sharp contrast, the three panels of the west wall all contain references to the darker, more ominous realities that exist amid the everyday tasks of life. Thus a chain gang works in the cotton panel, a coiled snake lurks to the left of a sow and her litter in the farm scene, and a rather depressed-looking cowboy and Indian consort with a prostitute in the oil-field panel—all in keeping with the West's dichotomous nature.

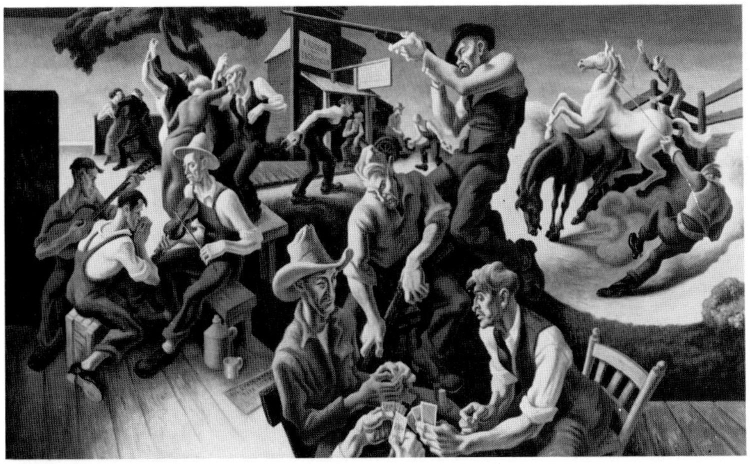

Figure 301
Thomas Hart Benton, *Arts of the West,* 1932, tempera with oil glaze, 2.43 × 3.96 m. New Britain, Connecticut, The New Britain Museum of American Art, Harriet Russell Stanley Fund (1953.21).

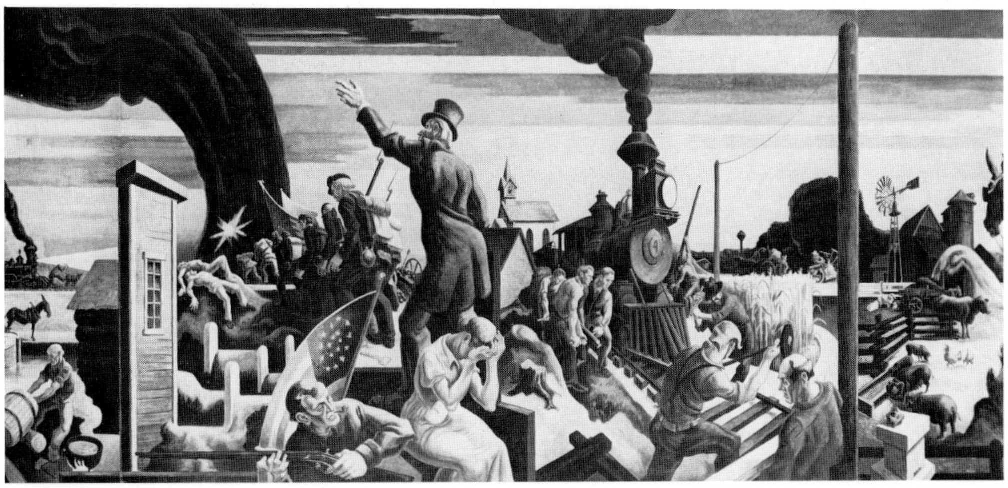

Figure 302
Thomas Hart Benton, *The Social History of the State of Indiana: Civil War and Expansion* (detail), 1933, tempera, h. 3.65 m. Bloomington, Indiana, Indiana University Auditorium.

To sum up then: the east and south walls contain bright, positive images untempered by any negative elements, while the west and north walls present what can in context be interpreted as subjective and value-laden oppositions of good and evil. All this is in keeping with Rivera's similar use of the iconography of the four directions.

I would suggest that the strength of Benton's New School murals lies more in their overall effect than in the details of their energetic but awkwardly crowded design. The reason is to be found in Benton's largely unsuccessful struggle to assimilate Rivera's stylistic influence—to make it his own rather than just copy it. His use of divisional moldings to separate the space planes of his overly complex montages can only be termed crude. This extension, in effect, of the architecture of the room to assist the design is, and looks, arbitrary. But by the time of his next mural environment, created for the Whitney Museum of American Art in 1932, Benton had found his own mural style and had succeeded in creating the semblance, if not the actuality, of an integrated space. The panel *The Arts of the West* (fig. 301) from this group is typical; Benton has eliminated the divisional moldings and created visually logical transitions between most of the figural groupings. Only the broncobusting scene seems left up in the air.

Benton's murals for the Chicago World's Fair of 1933 demonstrate his maturing as a muralist (fig. 302). Here, he has managed to create a fluid panorama of scenes that establishes everything in a single vast space over two hundred feet long. The bumptious rhetoric of *The Social History of the State of Indiana* is devoid of any overt cubistic devices that might challenge the literal, down-to-earth expectations of heartland America.

The Chicago mural set the style for the rest of Benton's career as a wall painter—a style that came to full flower at Jefferson City in 1936 (fig. 303). In *The Social History of the State of Missouri,* the only hint of Rivera is a series of small "predella"

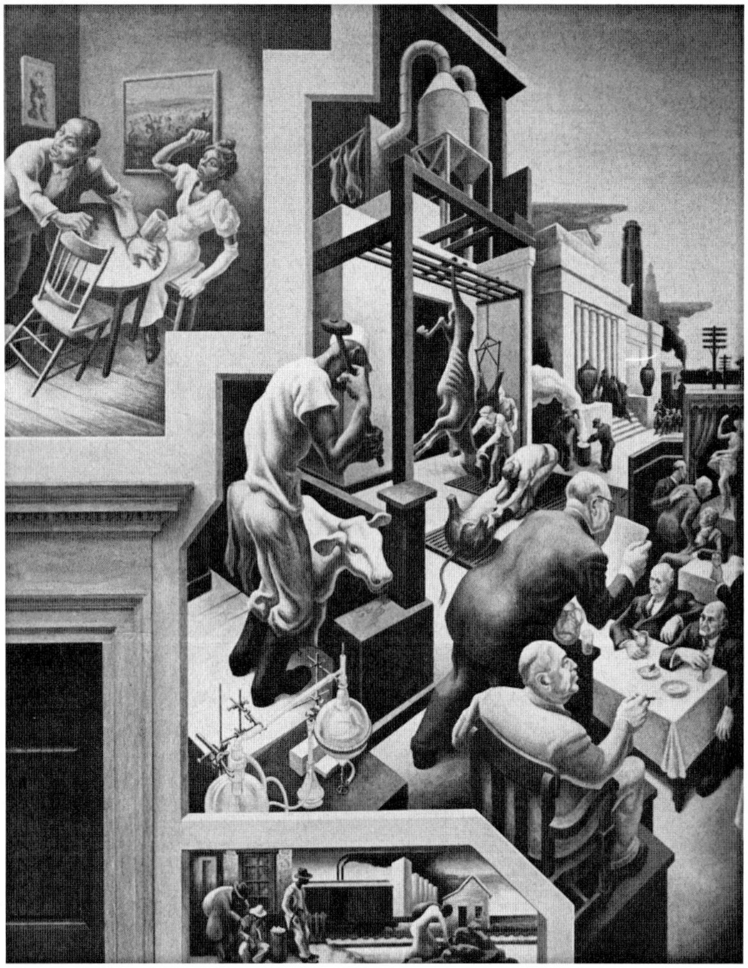

Figure 303
Thomas Hart Benton, *The Social History of the State of Missouri* (detail), 1936, tempera, h. 5.03 m. Jefferson City, Missouri, Missouri State Capitol. Courtesy of the Missouri State Museum.

panels below the major scenes. But this modest appropriation of a device is only vestigial; long before Jefferson City, Benton had cut himself free from his precursor and could, on that riotous evening in February 1934, with the New School, Whitney, and Chicago walls behind him, find the strength to refuse to mourn the loss of a mural by Rivera.

The Influence of Diego Rivera on Ben Shahn

Ben Shahn has humanized the technical methods of the Paris painters. Someone has called the modern French painters "dehumanized." In reality, they are profoundly human, only the humanity they express is a decadent one.

The case of Ben Shahn demonstrates that when contemporary art is revolutionary in content, it becomes stronger and imposes itself by the conjunction of its esthetic quality and its human expression. . . . It demonstrates as well that once art is set in this road, it acquires a progressive rhythm identical with that of its epoch. Hence, Ben Shahn's series on the Mooney case is even stronger and of finer quality than his Sacco-Vanzetti paintings.

The English esthete, John Ruskin, said . . . that lilies and peacocks are beautiful without serving any utilitarian purpose. Sometime later, the great painter Picasso added: "Art is twice beautiful because it is useless." But we painters of the people of the American continent proclaim: "Whatever is not five times useful is not beautiful." (Diego Rivera in a foreword to an exhibition of the work of Ben Shahn)[17]

If Diego Rivera's influence on Thomas Hart Benton was that of a catalyst in the self-definition of a strong muralist, his influence on Ben Shahn—a less robust talent—was that of an active agent. Both Shahn and his second wife have described Rivera's impact as primarily concerned with the technical aspects of fresco painting.[18] The evidence shows, however, that Rivera's influence was also stylistic, and this is best seen by examining the three phases of Shahn's career as a muralist.

Before turning to a discussion of these three phases, something ought to be said about the difference between misreading and misunderstanding Cubism in the development of a mural style. Benton's misreading of Cubism, which was, in effect, a misprision of both the Paris original and Rivera's own misreading, resulted in a well-integrated conceptualization of figures active in a dynamically plastic space—a style that is unmistakably Benton's own. This style can be faulted, perhaps, as rhetorical and overly manneristic, but its formal language is that of a strong and versatile eye, consistently applied and developed over a long and fruitful career.

On the other hand, Shahn's usage of Cubist conventions was essentially a rather unimaginative exploitation of a few visual strategies that permitted the simple juxtaposition of spatially separated events in a decoratively static manner. Both artists were, of course, influenced by the instantaneous scene-shifting of the cinema, the visual multivalence of photomontage, and the various Art Deco devices of the late academic muralists. But these were ancillary to the major impact of an artist like Rivera, to whose walls nearly every progressive muralist looked for inspiration and information.

Certainly the most elemental unifying device utilized by Rivera—and gloriously misread by Benton—was the maintenance of a single foreground and a single sky independent of whatever multidimensional and omnidirectional events took place in the middle and far distance of the composition. Benton tended to expand these areas, especially the sky, to give a spaciousness seldom found in Rivera's densely populated realms. Both artists, of course, were instinctively conscious of the essential centricity of the Cubist matrix. In both Analytic and Synthetic Cubism, the "event" is presented in all its complexity and transparency at the center of a calm background, with an often empty perimeter. This aspect of Cubism allowed these muralists a certain acknowledgment of the vast wall plane involved, while it also permitted a maximum of dynamic action within a modicum of perspectival illusion. One has only to look at the sky in the upper register of the north, west, and south walls of the *Detroit Industry* murals to see how this works—or better, to try to imagine the effect of these walls without it.

In contrast to the expansive viewpoints of Rivera and Benton, Shahn proffers tunnel vision. He consistently breaks the wall plane with abruptly angled recessional spaces that create artificial display areas across the wall, each with its own foreground and many with several different skies. In short, Shahn, like so many early American modernists (one thinks of Charles Demuth or John Marin) misconstrued the Cubists' contextualized pictorial complex as a series of rather arbitrary facetings. But given the larger scale of Shahn's art form, these facets take on a recessional dimensionality within which pictorial events can be shelved seriatim above and below. This leads to a static rather than a dynamic mural design—or at best, as we shall see in his Roosevelt mural, sequential narrative progress across the wall.

Like Rivera and Benton, Shahn was exposed to European Cubism. He had traveled in Europe in 1924–25 and again in 1927–29. But unlike them, his initial contact was with Synthetic, not Analytic, Cubism, and he was further influenced in the 1920s by Cubist-derived styles that were popular in America, ranging from the pioneering early works of Stuart Davis, Charles Sheeler, and Louis Lozowick to the extravagances of Art Deco commercial design. From all this Shahn had already derived the rudiments of the space-frame described above, but it was the influence of Rivera around 1933 that showed Shahn how to use these devices in murals.

It should also be pointed out that Rivera's example confirmed Shahn's own deeply rooted tendency toward a socially engaged, rather than just personal, form of expression. Toward the end of the 1920s, Shahn was becoming more and more uncertain of the modernism he had absorbed in his travels and from his artistic education. Looking back on this time, he recalled, "I had seen all the right pictures and read all the right books . . . but still it didn't add up to anything. 'Here I am,' I said to myself, 'thirty-two-years old, the son of a carpenter, I like stories and people. The French school is not for me.' "[19] And so he turned to the political issues of his day—such as the Sacco and Vanzetti case—to "humanize," as Rivera put it, his modernist methods. This, and his Jewish heritage, would be his ideology.

Shahn's first phase as a muralist centers around his encounter with Rivera. It begins in the spring of 1932 when his career was launched with two virtually simultaneous events. The first was the showing at the Downtown Gallery of a series of twenty-three gouache paintings entitled *The Passion of Sacco and Vanzetti*; the second, the inclusion of a tempera mural study (fig. 304) and full-scale details derived from the series of gouaches in an exhibition at the Museum of Modern Art, "Murals by American Painters and Photographers." This study shows two groups of figures standing before a deep recessional space that is defined by a receding prison wall to the left and an iron fence to the right. The group at the far right, standing near the coffins of Sacco and Vanzetti in front of a courthouse, is a separate configuration unrelated spatially to the rest of the composition. Thus this early and awkward attempt at mural design contains the two basic devices that Shahn would later learn to integrate: the recessional tunnel and the montage. His progress at achieving integration can be seen in his tempera *Apotheosis,* from the *Tom Mooney* series of 1932–33, which was shown at the Downtown Gallery in May 1933. The catalogue for this exhibit was written by Rivera, and it is clear that he has noticed and is encouraging Shahn's stylistic tendencies along with praising his proletarian subject matter: "[Shahn's art] contains all the technical assets of French bourgeois art as well as naiveté of the 'American Folk Art' style, and the broken chiaroscuro and confusion of the world city of New York."[20]

In *Apotheosis* Mooney is shown seated in a narrow central defile of receding walls, while to either side events from his trial take place in the deep recessional space the walls create. This is a far more satisfactory solution than merely standing the figures against the space, as in the Sacco and Vanzetti mural study, but it is still awkward.

By this time Shahn had, of course, met Rivera and had begun to work with him on his mural at Rockefeller Center during March and April. He would also help Rivera at the New Workers School later in 1933. As a result, Shahn learned a great deal, not only about the fresco technique but also about how to organize figures across a wall in a more coherent manner. But it would take time before these lessons could be put into practice: Shahn would not get a wall to paint for another four years. He made studies on the theme of Prohibition for the first of the New Deal art programs, the Public Works of Art Project, early in 1934, but these were rejected and the project ended soon after. During 1934–35, Shahn worked on the New York Emergency Relief Program with the artist Lou Block (who was also associated with Rivera at Rockefeller Center and the New Workers School) on a series of preparatory studies for two one hundred-foot frescoes in the Riker's Island Penitentiary. These proposed murals contrasted the brutal conditions that prevailed in New York City prisons before their reform with the positive effects of new humane policies and rehabilitation programs. Stylistically, they exploited the recessional and montage devices utilized by Rivera and certainly constituted Shahn's best solution of a mural problem to that date. Unfortunately, the sketches were rejected because of their

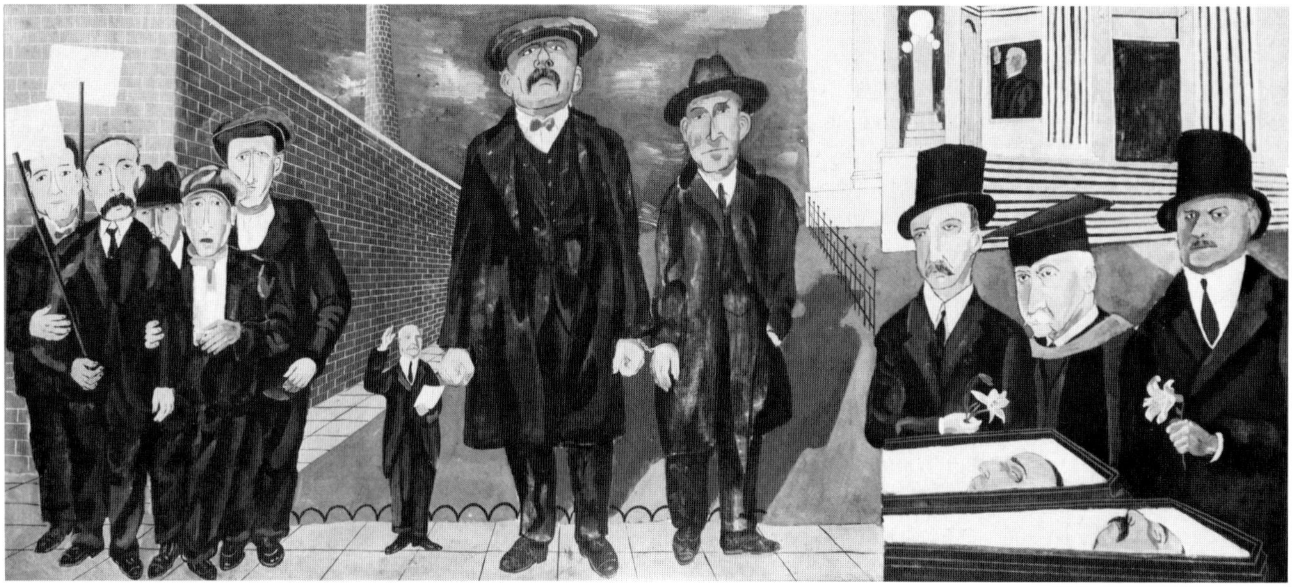

Figure 304
Ben Shahn, *The Passion of Sacco and Vanzetti,* 1932, oil and tempera on canvas sized with gesso and mounted on pressed wood, 53.3 × 121.9 cm. Collection of Mr. & Mrs. H. John Heinz III.

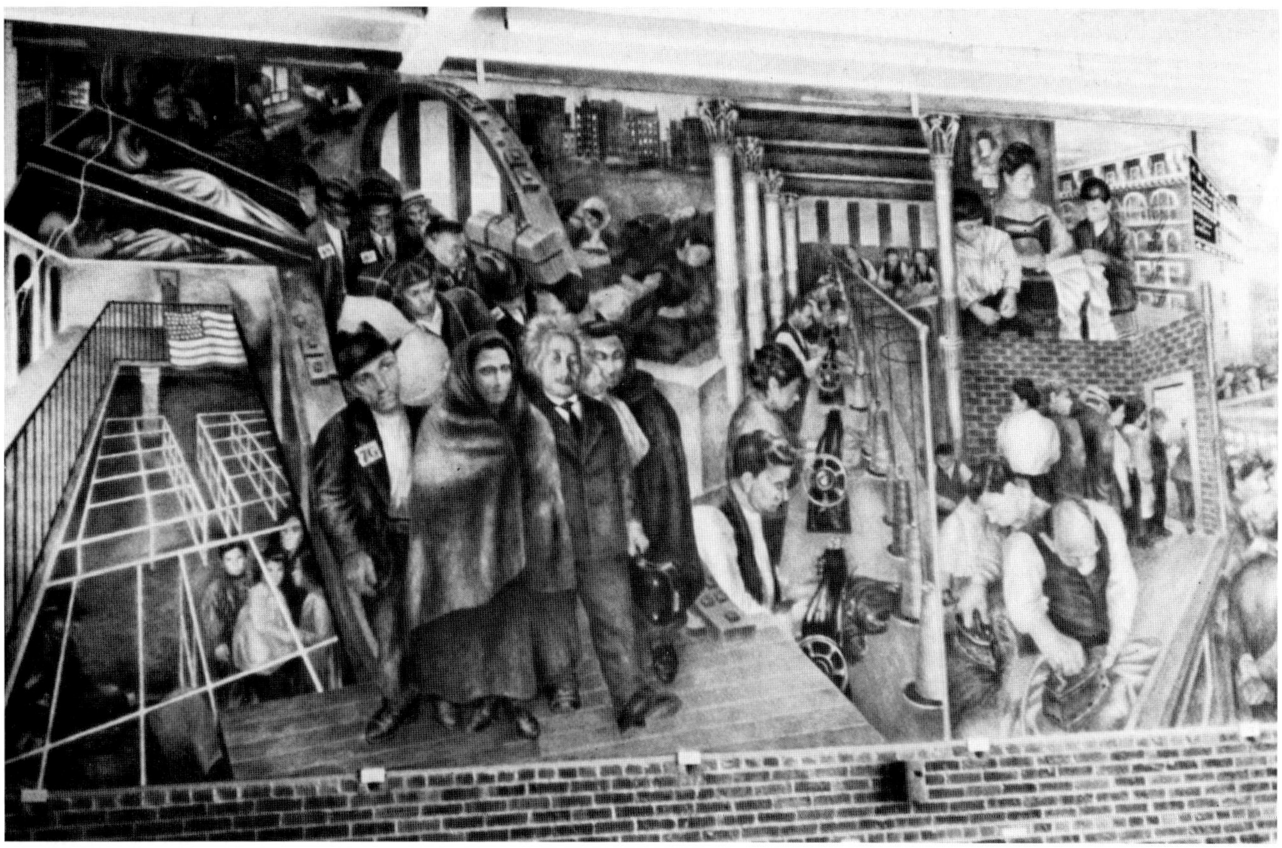

Figure 305
Ben Shahn, *Mural* (left half), Resettlement Administration, 1937–38, fresco, 3.65 × 13.7 m. 45 feet, Community Center and School, Roosevelt, New Jersey.

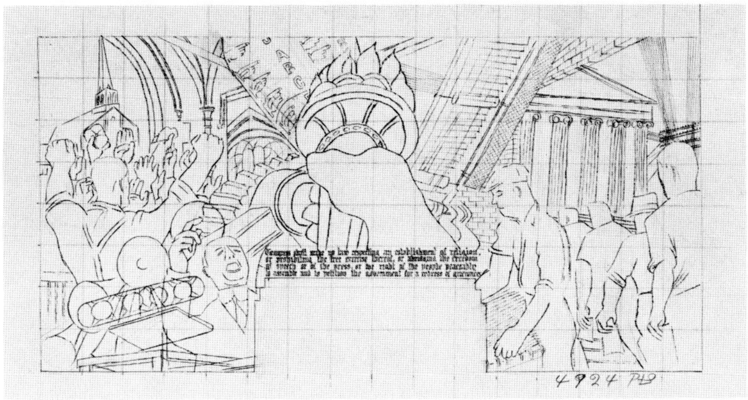

Figure 306
Ben Shahn, *The First Amendment*, sketch for mural in Woodhaven, New York, Post Office, Section, ca. 1939. Present location unknown.

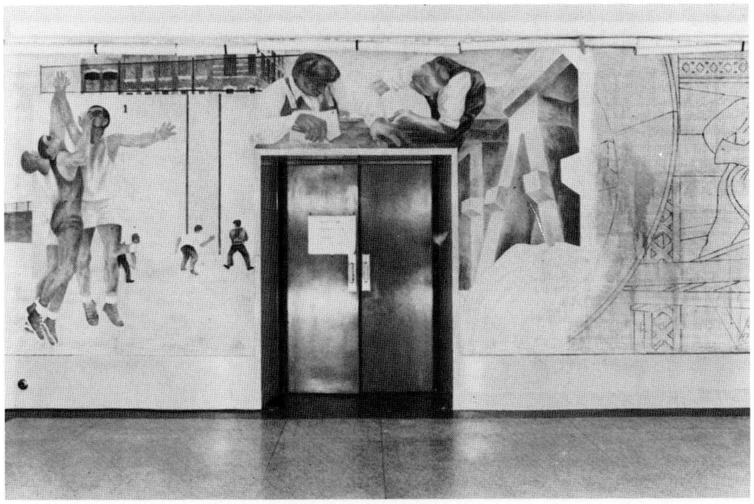

Figure 307
Ben Shahn, *The Meaning and Benefits of Social Security* (detail in progress), Section, 1940–42, egg tempera, h. 2.66 m. Washington, D.C., Health and Human Services Building.

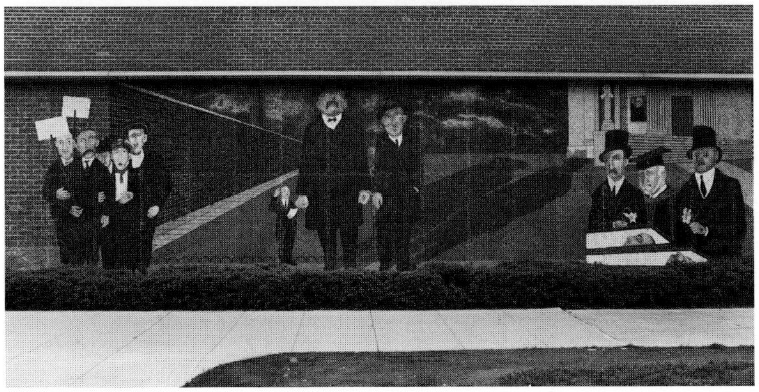

Figure 308
Ben Shahn, *The Passion of Sacco and Vanzetti*, 1967, mosaic, 3.66 × 18.29 m. Syracuse, New York, Syracuse University, Art Collections.

controversial content during the summer of 1935, thus bringing this first phase of Shahn's development as a muralist to a disappointing and frustrating end.

From 1935 to about 1937 Shahn was employed by the Resettlement Administration (later known as the Farm Security Administration or FSA), primarily as a photographer. He was also engaged to paint a mural by this agency. Shahn's second and most successful phase as a muralist began with this commission to paint a mural for a community center at Jersey Homesteads, New Jersey—a greenbelt community settled by Jewish garment workers and later renamed Roosevelt—and continued, through four major mural efforts undertaken for the Treasury Section of Painting and Sculpture, until 1942. (Shahn was never employed on the WPA Federal Art Project, though this is often assumed.)

The Roosevelt mural (fig. 305) is by far the most obviously influenced by Rivera, with its high horizon lines, massively modeled figures, tiers of heads, shifting recessional space planes, and heavy reliance on architectural and industrial elements to serve as transitions. One thinks immediately of Rivera's walls at the New Workers School, though Shahn has created an integrated composition rather than a sequence of discrete panels. The composition "reads" from lower left to upper right, literally from the depths to the heights. It begins in the Ellis Island processing pens, proceeds through the urban sweatshops to the central image of John L. Lewis organizing the garment workers for the CIO, and then onward and upward to scenes of education and fair employment, until, at the upper right, a portrait of President Franklin D. Roosevelt and the members of the community co-op surmount the plan of Jersey Homesteads. The mural thus depicts the saga of Jewish immigration at the turn of the century—the struggle for survival and the achievement of a self-sustaining community. As such it expresses the ideology of the New Deal in its purest form and remains to this day one of the masterpieces of American social realism.

This mural ushered in five years of intense mural activity for Shahn, during which he created murals for the central post office in the Bronx, New York (with his wife, Bernarda Bryson); the post office in Woodhaven, New York; and the main corridor of the new Social Security Building in Washington, D.C. He also prepared designs for a proposed mural for the central post office in St. Louis, Missouri (not executed).

Of these four mural projects, those for the St. Louis and Woodhaven post offices most closely resemble the Roosevelt murals. Each small individual horizontal panel is based upon his now familiar formula in which a central motif in the foreground is flanked by two recessional tunnels going off to right and left (fig. 306).

Shahn's murals for the Bronx post office and the Social Security Building, on the other hand, show the development of a more monumental style. Particularly at the Social Security Building, where he found a more integrated space, Shahn was able to open up many of his compositions and utilize a wider range of images—such as the famous handball court motif—drawn from his FSA photographs, although the device of deep recessionality is retained (fig. 307). These last walls show the final development of his mural style of the 1930s.

Shahn's murals in Roosevelt and for the Treasury Section are among the most eloquent expressions of the social concern of the time and the ideology of the New Deal. They are also, as murals, among the best created as a result of the New Deal art projects, and a very real factor in their quality is Shahn's assimilation of the lessons he learned from Rivera.

Unfortunately, these lessons seem to have been forgotten by the time Shahn returned to the mural about 1956, when he tried to translate his later gouache style and his calligraphy into mosaic murals. These walls of his third phase as a muralist all somehow fail because Shahn cannot find a way to accommodate his loosely composed and delicately colored easel motifs to mural scale and resonance. This is even true in his 1957 attempt to translate his 1932 Sacco and Vanzetti mural study into a mosaic at Syracuse University (fig. 308). Since the wall was longer than the proportions of the study, he simply extended the space between the three groups to no effect but to dilute his composition with a greatly expanded recessional space. If one compares late murals of Benton with the late walls of Shahn, it is very easy to see the distinction between a strong artist, whose style springs from a dynamically expressive personality, and a weak artist, whose walls derive as much from dependence on a cause as on a precursor. Indeed, as Rivera pointed out in his foreword to Shahn's exhibition, "When contemporary art is revolutionary . . . [when] it answers the demands of the collective spirit . . . it acquires a progressive rhythm identical with that of its epoch."[21] And when that progressive rhythm is lost, then an artist who has idealized a cause can only repeat its old motifs.

The Influence of Diego Rivera on New Deal Muralists

There is a matter which I have long considered and which some day might interest your administration. The Mexican artists have produced the greatest national school of mural painting since the Italian Renaissance. Diego Rivera tells me that it was only possible because Obregón allowed Mexican artists to work at plumbers' wages in order to express on the walls of the government buildings the social ideals of the Mexican revolution.

The younger artists of America are conscious as they have never been of the social revolution that our country and civilization are going through; and they would be eager to express these ideals in a permanent art form if they were given the government's co-operation. They would be contributing to and expressing in living monuments the social ideals that you are struggling to achieve. And I am convinced that our mural art with a little impetus can soon result, for the first time in our history, in a vital national expression. (George Biddle to President Franklin D. Roosevelt, May 9, 1933)[22]

The above letter, written by an American artist who had known Rivera and the Mexican mural movement at firsthand since 1928, prompted the chain of events that led, in December 1933, to the creation of the first of the New Deal's cultural support programs: the Public Works of Art Project (PWAP, 1933–34). This "pilot project" revealed a basic tension between the acquisition of quality art by the government and its growing obligation to support jobless artists whatever the level of their skills. As a result, two separate programs were eventually created. The first was the Treasury Department's Section of Painting and Sculpture (Section, 1934–43), which was dedicated to the commissioning, through public competitions, of professional art for new public buildings. The second was organized in 1935 as part of the cultural program of the massive work-relief agency known as the Works Progress Administration (WPA). This program, known as Federal Project No. 1, established separate projects for writers, musicians, and theater people, and its Federal Art Project (WPA/FAP, 1935–43) employed visual artists in all media and provided a weekly wage in return for specified services to tax-supported institutions. These two projects were populated for the most part with young and inexperienced artists. This was especially true of the muralists, few of whom had ever painted a wall before they received their first Section commission or WPA/FAP project. It is not surprising, then, that those who had either worked with or were inspired to emulate Diego Rivera produced some of the more competent early murals created under New Deal patronage.

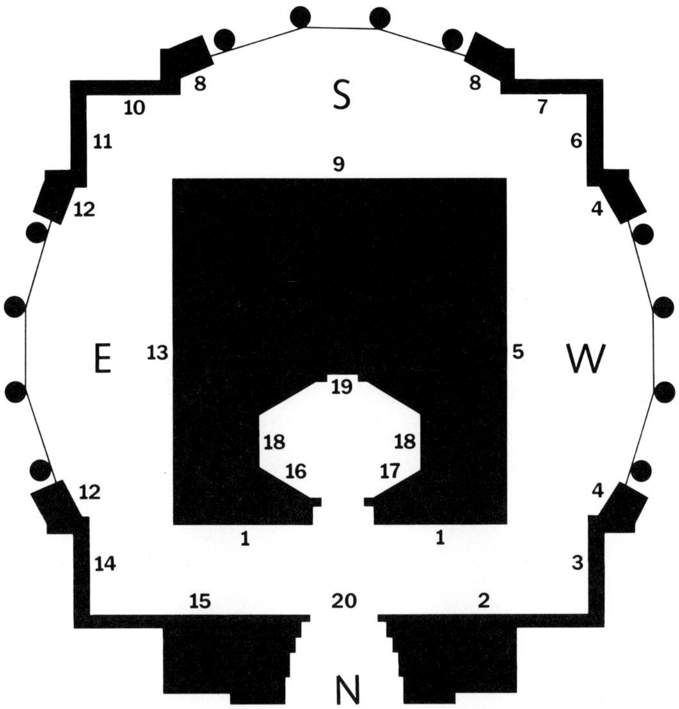

Coit Tower Floor Plan

1. *Animal Force and Machine Force* by Ray Boynton
2. *California Industrial Scenes* by John Langley Howard
3. *Railroad and Shipping* by William Hesthal
4. *Surveyor and Steelworker* by Clifford Wight
5. *Industries of California* by Ralph Stackpole
6. *Newsgathering* by Suzanne Scheuer
7. *Library* by Bernard B. Zakheim
8. *Stockbroker* and *Scientist-Inventor* by Mallette Dean
9. *City Life* by Victor Arnautoff
10. *Banking and Law* by George Harris
11. *Department Store* by Frede Vidar
12. *Farmer* and *Cowboy* by Clifford Wight
13. *California* by Maxine Albro
14. *Meat Industry* by Ray Bertrand
15. *California Agricultural Industry* by Gordon Langdon
16. *San Francisco Bay, East* by Otis Oldfield
17. *San Francisco Bay, North* by Jose Moya del Pino
18. *Bay Area Hills* by Rinaldo Cuneo
19. *Seabirds* and *Bay Area Map* by Otis Oldfield
20. *Power* by Fred Olmsted, Jr.

The following murals are open to the public by special arrangement:

21. *Powell Street* by Lucien Labaudt
22. *Collegiate Sports* by Parker Hall
23. *Sports* by Edward Terada
24. *Children at Play* by Ralph Chesse
25. *Hunting in California* by Edith Hamlin
26. *Outdoor Life* by Ben F. Cunningham
27. *Home Life* by Jane Berlandina

Figure 309
Coit Tower floor plan. Reprinted by permission of the publisher, from Masha Zakheim Jewett, *Coit Tower, San Francisco* (San Francisco: Volcano Press, Inc., 1983), 66.

Nowhere is this more explicitly the case than at Coit Tower in San Francisco, where a group of twenty-six artists employed by the PWAP painted a series of murals early in 1934 (fig. 309).[23] Of the group, two individuals, Victor Arnautoff and Maxine Albro, had worked with Rivera in Mexico, and one, Clifford Wight, had been Rivera's assistant on nearly all of his murals in the United States. With Arnautoff as foreman, these artists created a series of walls almost all of which reflect Rivera's style, facture, and color.

By 1934, Rivera had, virtually single-handedly, forged a strong mural tradition. He was the best, and certainly the most famous, muralist in the Americas, and his walls had become the standard against which those who aspired to be muralists were judged (or judged themselves). Rivera was the role model both sytlistically and ideologically. This is very clear indeed at Coit Tower.

Of all the Rivera-influenced murals in the tower, certainly that by Arnautoff, *City Life* (figs. 310 and 311), is the most successful in assimilating all aspects of the master's manner. Arnautoff had worked with Rivera and had seen his walls in Mexico as well as those in San Francisco, and he well understood the basic principles of a Rivera mural. As a point of reference for this and the next section of this essay, let us summarize these basic principles, using Arnautoff's mural, in terms of the following characteristics:

1. The suspension of the pictorial complex between a clearly defined foreground and a continuous sky, in keeping with the imperatives of Cubist design, not to mention human sightlines, which are almost always just below that foreground. Thus the clearly defined ground plane that leads the eye into the space of the street scene.

2. The maintenance of the wall plane with a relatively high horizon line, here happily justified by the precipitous angles

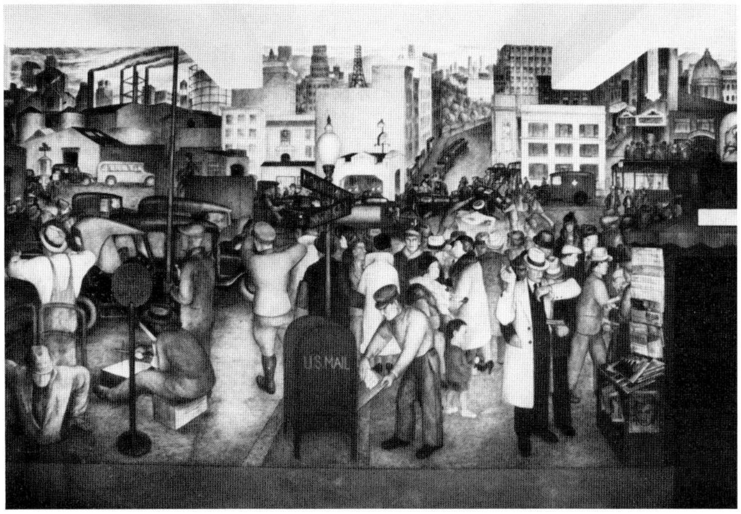

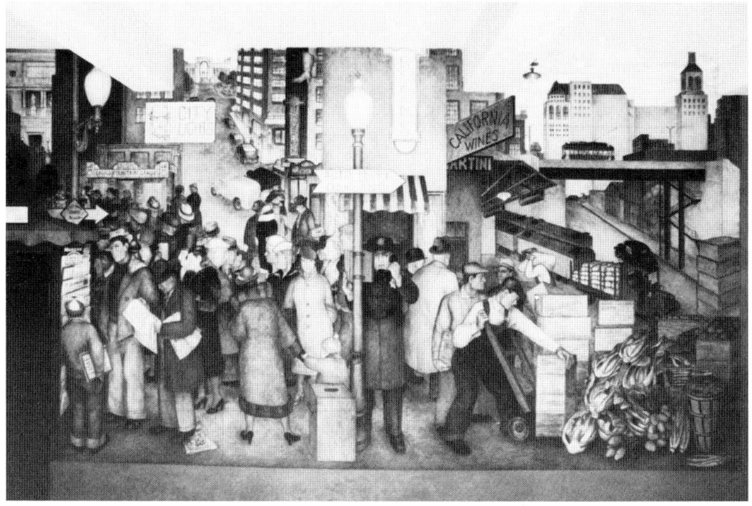

Figures 310, 311
Victor Arnautoff, *City Life*, PWAP, 1934, fresco, 3.04 × 10.36 m. San Francisco, Coit Tower. Photo: © Don Beatty.

of San Francisco's streets, and a visually continuous back plane of depicted walls or skyline.

3. The unification of the wall plane by means of an underlying geometric system based more or less on the principles of dynamic symmetry, as here the ends of the wall are blocked into two squares marked by the two foreground lampposts, with a roughly proportionate rectangle between them. The underlying abstract system always uses pictorial elements, most often in the form of depicted structures, to reveal the informing configuration.

4. The balancing of this geometric system with a true dynamism of occurrence within it, so that each area is filled with implied motion. A worker thus raises himself from a manhole, people walk behind newsstands, cars turn corners, and a series of arrows directs the eye from left to right. Rivera was a genius in maintaining a constant dynamism within the carefully controlled symmetries of his compositions. Unlike Arnautoff, however, few of his followers possessed the power of comprehensive concentration necessary to achieve this occult equilibrium.

5. The simple, bold modeling of figures, derived in part from the precedent of Giotto and his followers, in part from the exigencies of scale, which require legibility at a distance, and in part due to the requirements of the fresco technique, which prompts broad areas of color and form as opposed to meticulous detail.

6. The utilization of a basic palette of earth colors and black to provide a uniform set of tonalities across the wall. This is then skillfully modulated by the symmetrical use of bright colors to achieve a sense of balance and closure, as in the sequence of red manhole, guardrail, blue work suits, and green mailbox in the left panel of *City Life* and the woman in green, policeman in blue, and red handcart in the right.

7. The skillful overlapping of the figures' silhouettes and the massing of their heads in tiers to create a continuous frieze across the length of the wall, beyond and above which discrete vignettes can be depicted in plausible recessional spaces.

8. The use of words and slogans to emphasize the ideological or thematic message of the work. Note the "Men at Work" stanchion to the left, which not only hints of Marxism but also relates to the radical contents of the *Library* mural by Bernard Zakheim on the opposite wall and the *Industries of California* mural by Ralph Stackpole around the corner on the west wall of the rotunda; the copies of *The Masses, Daily Worker,* and *Time*

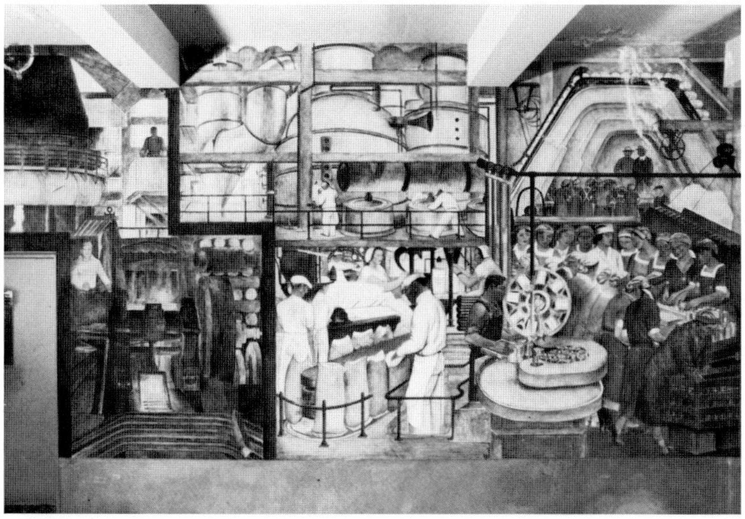

Figure 312
Ralph Stackpole,
Industries of California
(right panel), PWAP,
1934, fresco, 3.04 × 5.18
m. San Francisco, Coit
Tower. Photo: © Don
Beatty.

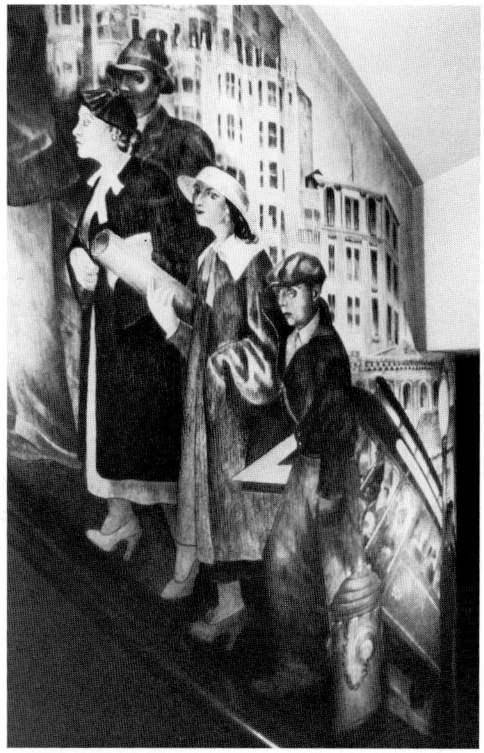

Figure 313
Lucien Labaudt, *Powell*
***Street* (detail), PWAP,**
1934, fresco. San Fran-
cisco, Coit Tower. Photo:
© Don Beatty.

conspicuous at the center; and the signs and labels advertising California wines and oranges, which relate to the agricultural mural by Maxine Albro around the corner on the east wall.

9. And, finally, the attempt to relate the content of the mural to the exterior world by means of some combination of situational or directional symbolism. The Arnautoff mural, on the south inner wall of the rotunda, faces out the window toward the actual intersection, eight blocks to the south, of Washington and Montgomery Streets depicted in the mural. The other murals along the south outer walls of the rotunda, depicting a department store, banks, lawyers, stockbrokers, scientists, a library, and a newspaper office, all relate to the significance of this crossroads of the city's economic life. A similar situational directionality determines the placement of the other major walls and their related panels. Thus Stackpole's mural of local industries on the west wall overlooks the expanse of the city and its waterfront, which lie to the west, and Albro's agricultural mural faces east, the general direction of California's fertile interior.

While Arnautoff's wall displays all these aspects of Rivera's style to best advantage at Coit Tower, his colleagues tended to be less comprehensively successful. Stackpole's industrial mural (fig. 312), while similar in motif to Rivera's Detroit walls, is stylistically dependent on the master's earlier works at the San Francisco Stock Exchange and the California School of Fine Arts, especially the latter's symmetrical, compartmentalized composition and rather stiff deployment of figures. Maxine Albro's agricultural panorama directly quotes the structural device of an orchard's serried perspective from Rivera's 1931 wall at the residence of Mrs. Sigmund Stern, but it also relies on a rigid symmetry to unify the long horizontal wall.

One of the most unusual murals at Coit Tower is that by Lucien Labaudt. Consisting of two walls that face each other across a spiral staircase, the mural depicts San Francisco's Powell Street, which slopes at virtually the same angle as the stairs! Labaudt has successfully managed the almost impossible problems of scale and perspective posed by this peculiar site, though the full effect of this space is beyond the power of photography to capture (see fig. 313). It contains any number of city vignettes and portraits, including those of Mrs. Eleanor Roosevelt and Edward Bruce, the director of the PWAP, who got his test of fire as a government patron at Coit Tower.

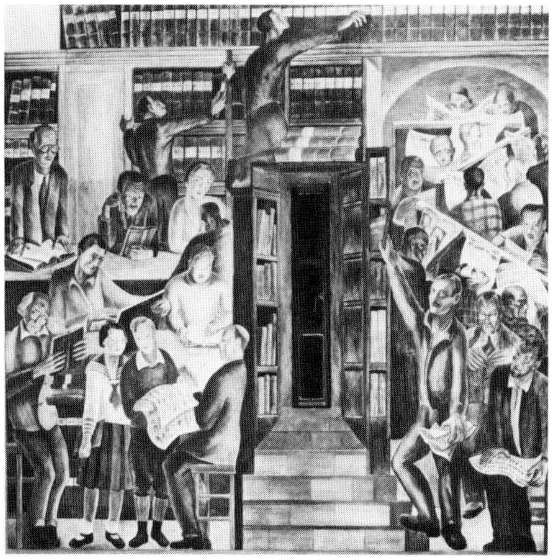

Figure 314
Bernard Zakheim, *Library*, PWAP, 1934, fresco 3.05 × 3.05 m. San Francisco, Coit Tower. Photo: © Don Beatty.

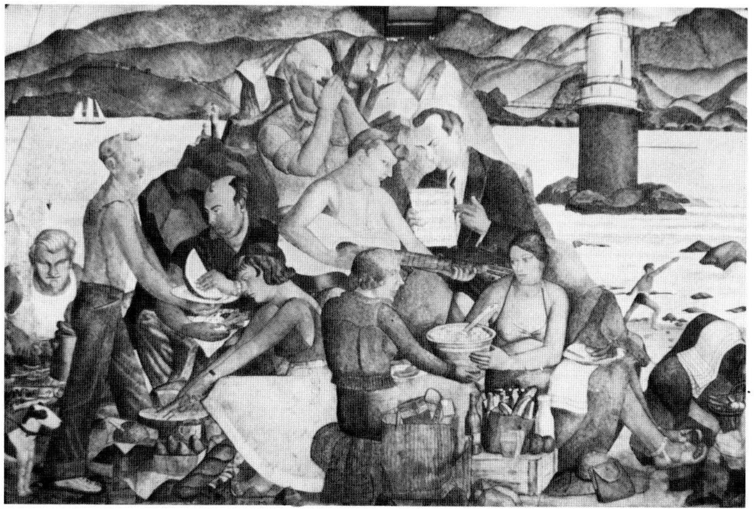

Figure 315
Lucien Labaudt, *Beach Scene* (east wall), WPA/FAP, 1936–37, fresco. San Francisco, Beach Chalet. Photo: © Don Beatty.

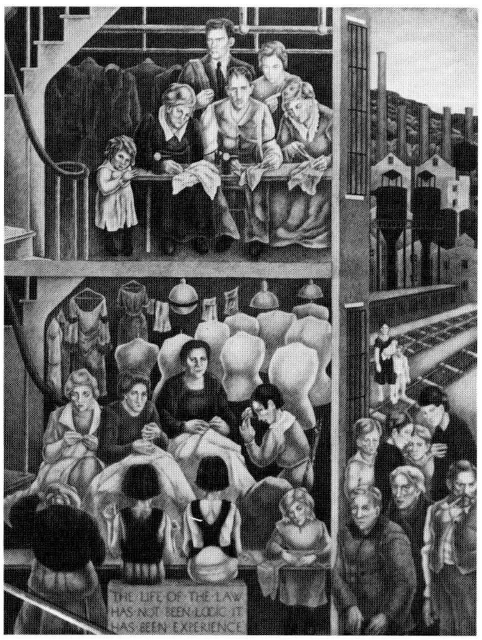

Figure 316
George Biddle, *Sweatshop* panel from *Society Freed through Justice,* Section, 1936, fresco, h.approx. 4.11 m. Washington, D.C., Department of Justice.

For Rivera's style was not the only aspect of his influence operating at Coit Tower. It should be recalled that these walls were painted from January to June 1934, and that early in February Rivera's Rockefeller Center mural was destroyed. This galvanized his epigones at the tower to formal protest and informal vendetta, with the result that equivalents of Lenin's notorious portrait insinuated themselves into the iconography of certain murals. Arnautoff's rather radical newsstand has been mentioned. Bernard Zakheim's *Library* (fig. 314) is replete with provocative headlines in the reading room and revolutionary literature by Marx, Engels, Lenin, and Bukharin on the shelves. And Clifford Wight, no doubt the closest artist to Rivera and the only one who worked with him in New York and who knew personally just what had been lost, included the Blue Eagle of the controversial National Recovery Act along with the hammer and sickle in his design and balanced the legend "In God We Trust" with "Workers of the World Unite!" Although all these provocations had the intended result of a first-class scandal, only Wight's motifs and slogans were finally removed. The rest remain to this day as a record of the political passions of the early 1930s.

Coit Tower is the only mural site in the country that displays so varied a range of walls painted in the style and spirit of Rivera. Although it is true that a number of the Coit artists went on to paint together at San Francisco's George Washington High School under the WPA/FAP, these walls are far less impressive than those done for the PWAP, primarily because the school provided no unified space for a concerted effort. One of the Coit Tower artists, however, found the opportunity to paint an entire building in Rivera's style. Labaudt's Beach Chalet at the western end of Golden Gate Park (see fig. 315), decorated around 1937 with San Francisco scenes, is an overlooked masterpiece of the WPA/FAP and displays a development of style and scope none of the other Coit artists evinced in his or her subsequent work.

Of the nine characteristics of Rivera's style described above, only the broad modeling of figures, the overlapping of silhouettes and massing of heads, and the use of color symmetry and verbal inscriptions tended to be found in most Rivera-influenced New Deal murals. His compositional devices were occasionally copied but seldom understood, and attempts at situational or directional symbolism, while not unknown, were seldom feasible, nor were the artists usually sophisticated enough to employ them. And Rivera's style was hardly the only stumbling block. Hindsight suggests the real problem was just how few artists really understood Rivera's manner or had access to the kind of environmental spaces is which to practice it.

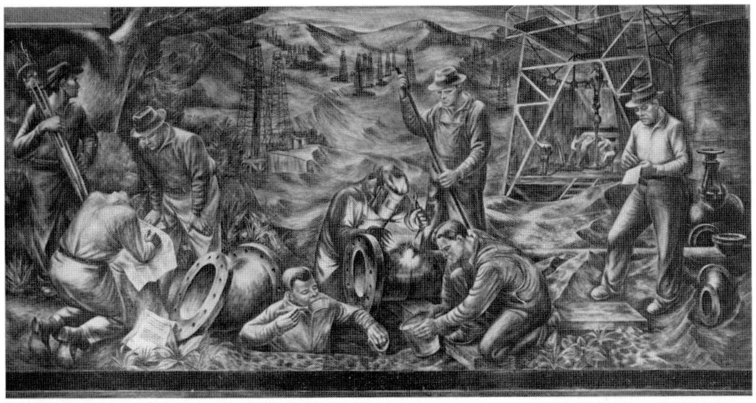

Figure 317
Edgar Britton, *Petroleum: Production and Refining,* Section, 1939, fresco. Washington, D.C., Department of the Interior.

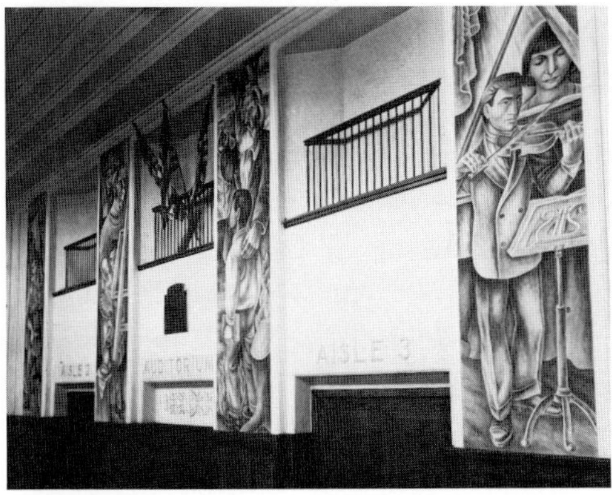

Figure 318
Mitchell Siporin, *Teaching of the Arts,* WPA/FAP, ca. 1938, fresco, 13.10 × 1.06 m. Chicago, Lane Technical High School.

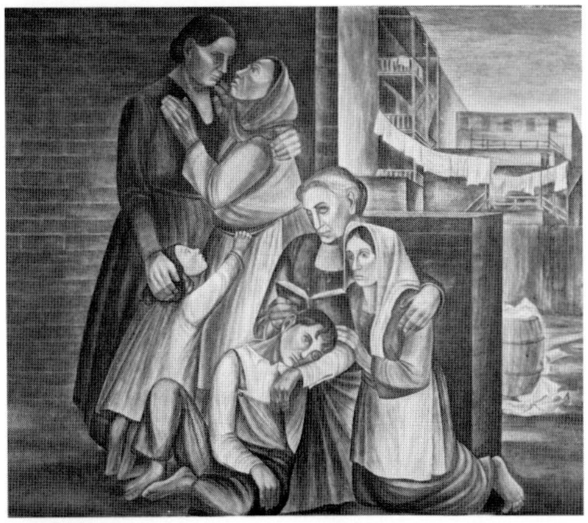

Figure 319
Edward Millman, *Jane Addams* panel, from *Woman's Contribution to America's Progress,* WPA/FAP, 1940, fresco, 2.13 × 2.74 m. Chicago, Lucy Flower Technical High School.

What remains, then, is to touch briefly on a small number of the more interesting Section and WPA/FAP artists who found a visual vocabulary in Rivera's art and politics and, in so doing, to provide an anthology of the stylistic variations his influence prompted.

George Biddle, whose letter to President Roosevelt quoting Rivera provoked the New Deal administration's interest in establishing art programs, was given a prominent wall in the new Justice Department building in Washington, D.C. Biddle had known and worked with Rivera in Mexico in 1928, though his official Section biography discreetly does not mention this.

Biddle's mural, *Society Freed through Justice,* consists of five panels in the Justice Department's fifth floor stairwell. On the left side wall is a depiction of a sweatshop (fig. 316) cut away to reveal two stories as well as a factory-scape outside. This compartmentalized composition, reminiscent of Rivera's similar but more complex solutions in San Francisco and Detroit, faces across the stairwell a similarly organized view of a tenement. Both these side walls flank a central triptych showing an idealized family inside and an idyllic landscape outside. The ethnically specified figures in all the panels are heavily modeled and brightly colored, though one must note their strange lack of cohesion within the space they occupy. Biddle, like so many inexperienced American muralists, could never quite match Rivera's capacity to impose an overall visual logic on a complex composition. Biddle's personal style was characterized by a certain nervous particularity of manner, which, in its urge to accumulate elegant details, seemed consciously to eschew the establishment of any universal canon of human or environmental scale. Thus, only the rigid geometry of his composition combined with the unified sky across the five panels, manages to hold the various subjects together. But despite these difficulties, Biddle's walls constitute one of the most radical social statements sponsored by the Section, and they hold their own with the more pictorially conventional "regionalist" murals by John Steuart Curry nearby.

Typical of the Section's bias toward American scene verisimilitude and regionalism, but nevertheless strongly influenced by Rivera's style, are two murals about the oil industry in the Department of the Interior by Edgar Britton. Titled *Petroleum: Production and Refining* and *Petroleum: Distribution and Use* (fig. 317) and completed in 1939, these panels display all the characteristics of the Mexican's style as adopted by American artists.

Britton was a Chicago artist who, along with Edward Millman and Mitchell Siporin, showed a keen interest in the Mexican mural movement. Siporin, in an essay written for the WPA/FAP, states:

Contemporary artists everywhere have witnessed the amazing spectacle of the modern renaissance of mural painting in Mexico, and they have been deeply moved by its profound artistry and meaning. Through the lessons of our Mexican teachers, we have been made aware of the scope and fullness of the "soul" of our own environment. We have been made aware of the application of modernism toward a socially moving epic art of our time and place. We have discovered for ourselves a richer feeling in the fabric of the history of our place.[24]

Both Siporin's murals (ca. 1938) in the Lane Technical High School (fig. 318) and Millman's *Jane Addams* panel (fig. 319) from a 1940 series, *Woman's Contribution to America's Progress,* at Lucy Flower Technical High School, show their respective adaptations of Rivera's manner.

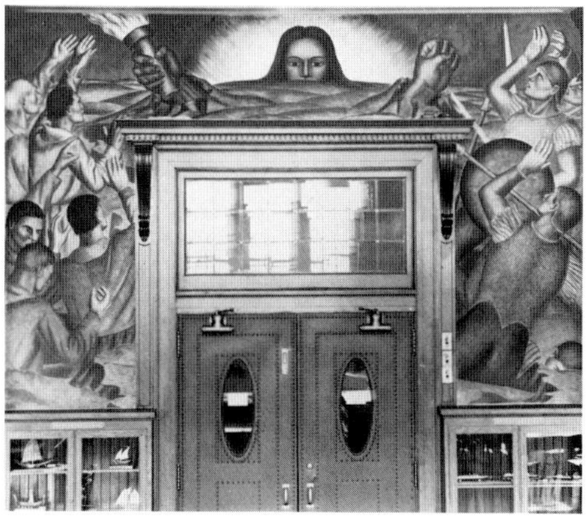

Figure 320
James Michael Newell, *Evolution of Western Civilization* (detail), WPA/FAP, 1938, fresco. The Bronx, New York, Evander Childs High School. Courtesy of the Arts Commission of the City of New York.

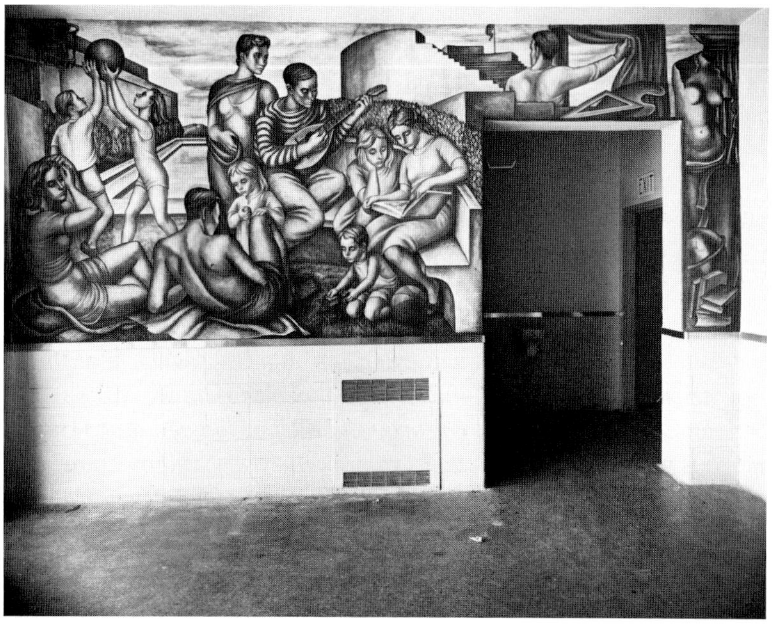

Figure 321
Marion Greenwood, *Blueprint for Living,* WPA/FAP, 1940, one of three fresco panels, area approx. 33.5 sq. m. Brooklyn, New York, Red Hook Housing Project.

The New York City WPA/FAP employed a number of artists familiar with Rivera's mural style. James Michael Newell's *The Evolution of Western Civilization* in the library of Evander Childs High School in the Bronx, completed in 1938, is by far the most ambitious program and the one best suited to its environment (fig. 320). Trained in Paris in fresco, Newell was able to appreciate Rivera's comprehensive eye, and his compositions have a drama and dynamism often lacking in those of other New Deal muralists. He knew Rivera's walls, understood the principles of his style, and was not averse to borrowing motifs as well—such as the hands personifying enlightenment over the door, which burst through the earth as do those on the north wall at Detroit.

As might be expected, those who had "studied" with Rivera understood his techniques and style better than most. It must be understood, however, that Rivera did not take formal students. Rather he permitted talented artists to assist him in the various technical procedures of the fresco process and to watch him paint. In this way artists such as Ben Shahn and Lou Block and the two with whom I shall conclude this section, Lucienne Bloch and Marion Greenwood, learned the rudiments of Rivera's method.

Marion Greenwood's 1940 murals for the Red Hook Housing Project in Brooklyn, New York, are certainly among the most "Riveraesque" of WPA/FAP efforts (fig. 321). Greenwood had been Rivera's "student" in Mexico during the early 1930s and had painted a number of murals there, the most important at the Mercado Abelardo L. Rodríguez in Mexico City in 1935. Greenwood was an artist of great facility and power; she and her sister Grace were acclaimed by Rivera as "the greatest living women mural painters."[25] Greenwood's Red Hook murals emphasize the

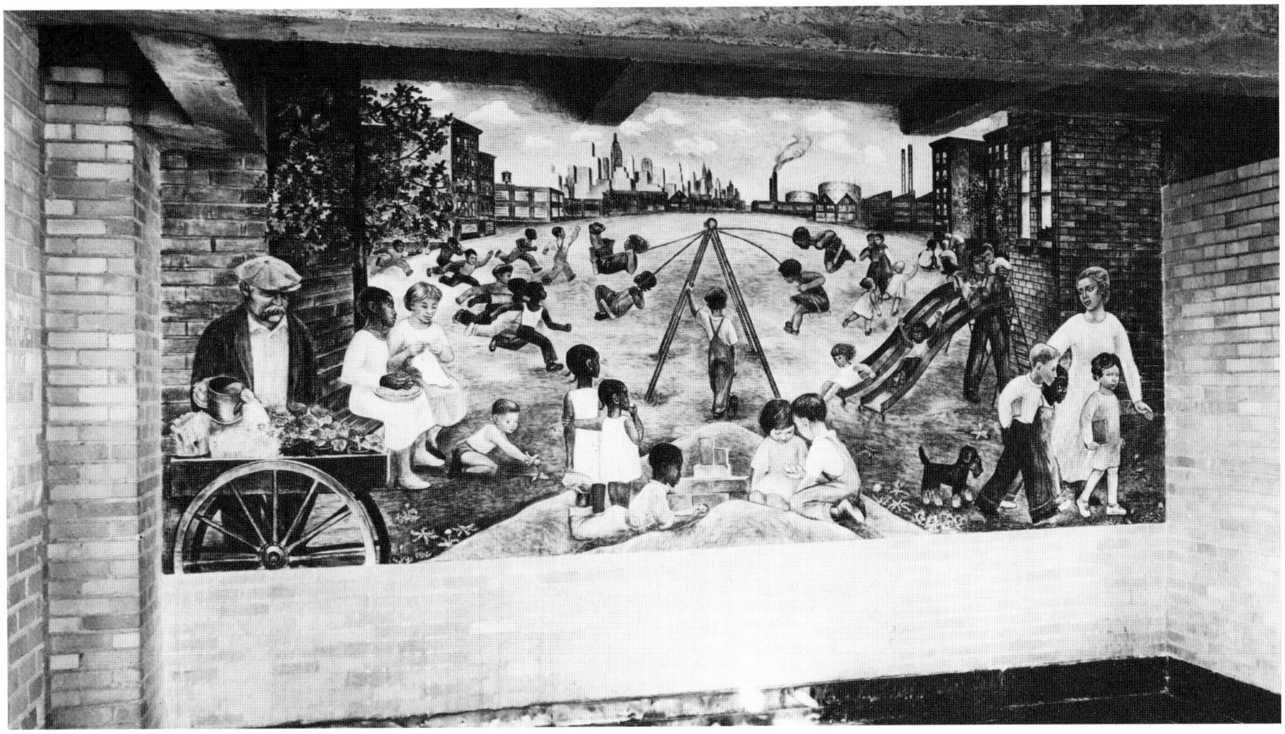

Figure 322
Lucienne Bloch, *Cycle of a Woman's Life: Children,* WPA/FAP, 1936, fresco, area approx. 22.3 sq. m. New York, House of Detention.

decorative more than the dynamic, however, and her skillful balancing and sculptural modeling of the figures make up in visual interest for the static (if not bored) look of these recipients of the New Deal's presumably life-enhancing benefits. The children playing basketball, for instance, might be posing for a lamppost in this *Blueprint for Living,* which was the murals' official title.

Lucienne Bloch's *The Cycle of a Woman's Life: Children,* in the recreation room of the Women's House of Detention in New York City, provides a sharp contrast to Greenwood's stylistic stasis (fig. 322). Bloch first met Rivera in New York in 1931 at the time of his exhibition at the Museum of Modern Art. Later she became his assistant in Detroit and at Rockefeller Center. Thereafter she joined the WPA/FAP in New York City. Her House of Detention mural is a fine example of the application of Rivera's conviction that art's utility is a component of its beauty. Faced with a bleak environment, suspicious administrators, and ignorant inmates, she conquered all with the simplicity and honesty of her craft:

Conversation with the inmates revealed with what sarcasm and suspicion [they] treated the mention of art—as something "highbrow," indicating to what extent art had in the past been severed from the people and placed upon a pedestal for the privilege[d]. . . . To combat this antagonism it seemed essential to bring art to the inmates by relating it closely to their own lives. . . . I chose the only subject which would not be foreign to them—children—framed in a New York landscape of the most ordinary kind. . . . The matrons' . . . conception of an artist was shattered when they saw me work without a smock and without inspired fits. . . . The inmates had a more natural point of view; . . . in [their] make-believe moments, the children in the mural were adopted and named. . . . Such response clearly reveals to what degree a mural can, aside from its artistic value, act as a healthy tonic on the lives of all of us.[26]

The mural is an elegant application of Rivera's methods—especially in its balance of static and dynamic elements within a quite rigid composition. Thus the foreground figures form a varied frieze across the wall plane, with the central group of children and their pile of bricks echoing the skyline. In the middle ground, a riotous playground is stabilized by the triangle of a swing seen from the side, while four swinging children are frozen at the outer limit of their momentum. This image, while actually depicting lateral movement, also gives a marvelous sense of circular motion, as if the children were gathered around a Maypole. It is a classic use of Rivera's device of suspending the central pictorial complex between clearly defined planes of earth and sky, while maintaining a maximum illusion of movement.

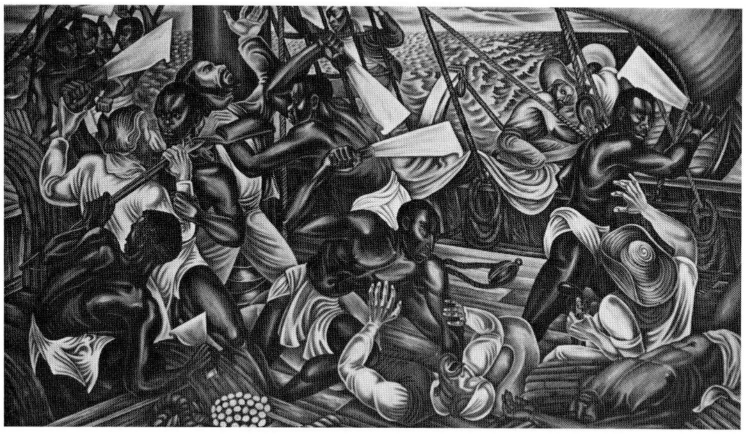

Figure 323
Hale Woodruff, *Meeting on the Amistad, 1839,* 1939, oil on canvas, 1.98 × 3.04 m. Talladega, Alabama, Talladega College, Savery Library.

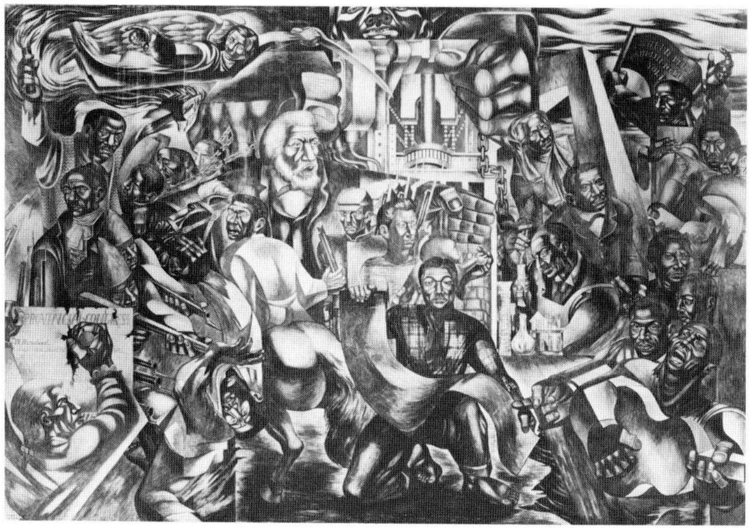

Figure 324
Charles White, *The Contribution of the Negro to American Democracy,* 1943, egg tempera (fresco secco), 3.58 × 5.18 m. Hampton, Virginia, Hampton University, Clarke Hall. Courtesy of Hampton University Museum.

The Influence of Diego Rivera on U.S. Mural Movements after the 1930s

I'm gaining my strength. (A young black man viewing the original *Wall of Respect,* ca. 1967)[27]

Our grasp of values in its first instance is an aesthetic grasp. (Eliseo Vivas)[28]

The onset of World War II brought about the abrupt termination of New Deal mural painting activities, and both the Section and WPA/FAP ended in 1943. After the war, which had erased the last economic vestiges of the Depression, official interest in art support programs ceased. Indeed, public art of any kind was the last thing a reactionary Congress wanted, as the dismal history of federal patronage between 1943 and the mid-1960s makes very clear.[29] Further, many of the younger artists from the WPA/FAP—one thinks of Jackson Pollock, Mark Rothko, Arshile Gorky, Philip Guston, James Brooks—were disillusioned with socially concerned art. These Abstract Expressionists felt that the only valid social statement their art could make was through the authenticity of their personal expression, which others might feel and perhaps act upon in their own lives. Thus they rejected and rationalized Rivera's radical notion that the beautiful had to be "five times useful"—and replaced a social with a subjective humanism.

The only artists in the country to retain the mural as a means of expressing social concern were black Americans. Faced with the realities of de jure segregation and de facto disenfranchisement, and with all the economic and psychological burdens of second-class citizens in a thriving culture, black artists continued to use the mural as the art form traditionally suited to express a people's quest for justice and dignity. And they recognized that the tradition of socially concerned wall painting was best exemplified, not in overcautious New Deal walls, but in the work of the revolutionary Mexicans—especially Diego Rivera.

Rivera's classic style, with its structured forms and its potential for narrative clarity—in contrast to the aggressive visual rhetoric of José Clement Orozco and David Alfaro Siqueiros—appealed to black artists seeking to present a quietly forceful image of their people's history and aspirations.

Early examples of black murals chronologically overlap the New Deal era and obviously took their initial impetus from the resurgence of mural art sponsored by the government. One of the most striking of the early Rivera-influenced walls is a series depicting scenes of the Amistad mutiny created by Hale Woodruff in 1939 at Talladega College in Alabama (fig. 323).

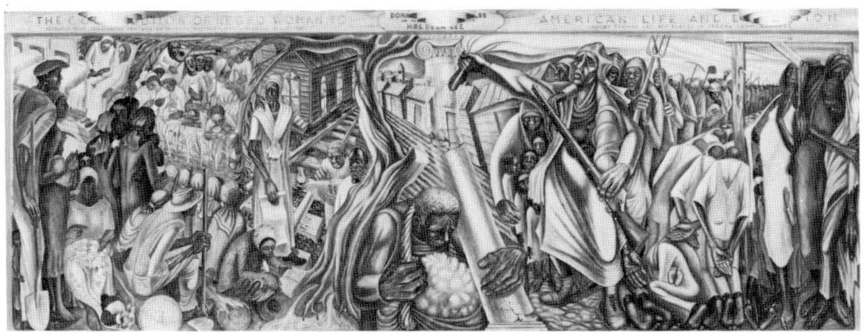

Figure 325
John Biggers, *The Contribution of Negro Women to American Life and Education*, 1953, tempera, 2.44 × 7.32 m. Houston, Texas, YWCA, Gift of the Reverend Fred T. Lee.

Woodruff had studied with Rivera in Mexico and had developed a rather stylized version of his manner. Charles White created a more recognizably "Riveraesque" mural, *The Contribution of the Negro to American Democracy*, in 1943 at the Hampton Institute (fig. 324). And a black artist of the next generation, John Biggers, created a number of impressive murals in Houston, such as his 1953 *The Contribution of Negro Women to American Life and Education* (fig.325) and his 1957 *Local 872 Longshoremen.* But these murals, like so much of the representational art of the Abstract Expressionist years, were ignored by the official world of museums, critics, and art publications. Yet they certainly helped to sustain the hope and ideals of southern blacks until the civil rights movement of the 1960s achieved a consensus for legal—if not, alas, moral—equity for all Americans. And in this sense, these walls were certainly "five times useful"—prefiguring the rallying cry of the 1960s that "Black is Beautiful!"

It was inevitable, given the continuity of tradition in the black community, that the community mural movement—a movement that later became associated more and more with Hispanic concerns—originated in a black ghetto in Chicago. There in 1967 a small group of black artists, led by William Walker, created the original *Wall of Respect* (fig. 326).[30] Walker acknowledges his debt to Rivera,[31] and his murals, perhaps more than those of any other community artist painting during the last twenty years, constitute a clear continuation of Rivera's mural style. This can be seen in his Chicago murals, *Black Love* of 1971 (fig. 327), the dramatically structured *Reinforcement* of 1971–73, and his 1974 *History of the Packinghouse Worker* (fig. 328).

The influence of Rivera on Hispanic muralists has generally been more diffuse, since the Mexicans in general, and Siqueiros in particular, were seen as direct precursors of their social and artistic concerns. Siqueiros was especially influential, since he was still alive and working on his last great mural environment at the Polyforum in Mexico City. From the late 1960s until the artist's death in 1974, a number of community muralists got their basic training working on this vast project.

Also, the expressive rhetorical style of Siqueiros and Orozco was more attractive to Hispanic-Americans, and one finds numerous direct quotations from these Mexicans' murals on community walls and widespread adaptations of their grandiloquent styles. Conversely, there is little concern for Rivera's quieter compositional finesse and subtle iconographic puns.

One important exception to this situation can be found in San Francisco's now famous Bank of America mural of 1974, created by a group of young Hispanic artists in the city's Mission District. San Francisco is the site of three Rivera murals, including his largest and last United States mural, painted in public for the Golden Gate International Exposition in 1940. This work, significantly, was returned to public view in 1961, at San Francisco City College,

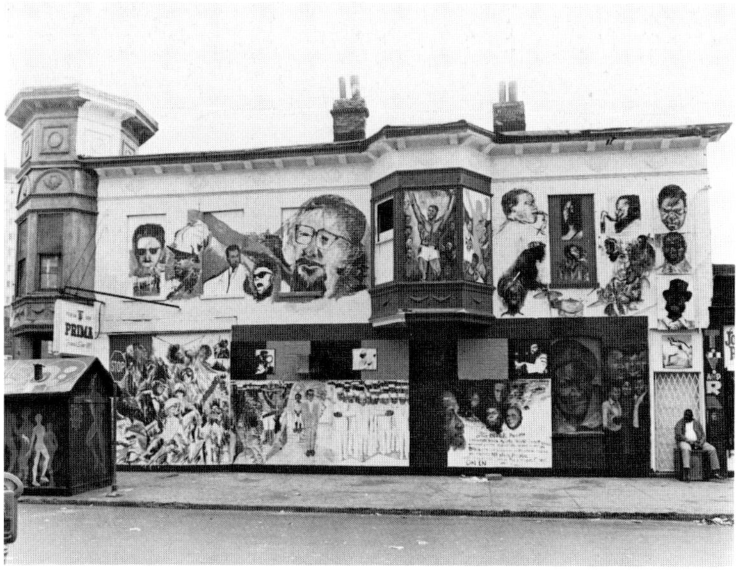

Figure 326
William Walker with Billy Abernathy, Jr., Silvia Abernathy, Edward Christmas, Darryl Colror, Jeff Donaldson, Eugene Eda, Will Hancock, Florence Hawkins, Elliott Hunter, Wadsworth Jarrel, Barbara Jones, Carolyn Lawrence, Roy Lewis, Norman Perris, Wyatt Walker, Mirna Weaver, and others, *Wall of Respect* (detail), begun 1967; this version ca. 1969; destroyed 1971 (see note 30). Chicago, southeast corner of 43rd and Langley Streets. Photo: © Robert Sengstacke.

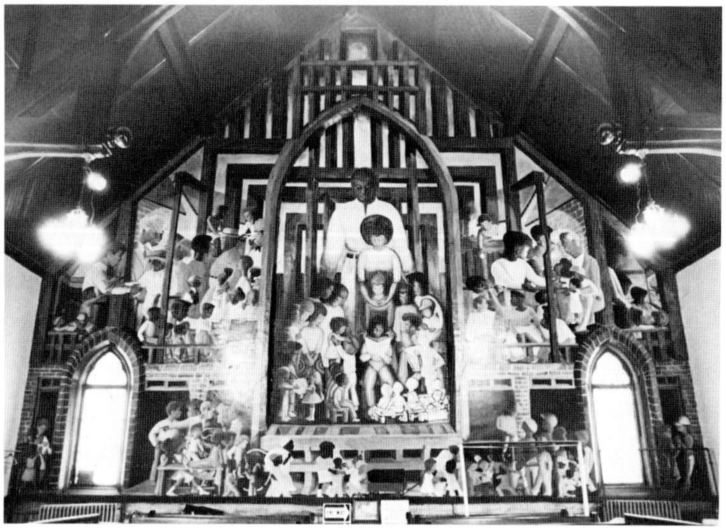

Figure 327
William Walker, *Black Love,* 1971–73. Chicago, Stranger Home, MBC, 617 West Evergreen. Photo: © John Weber.

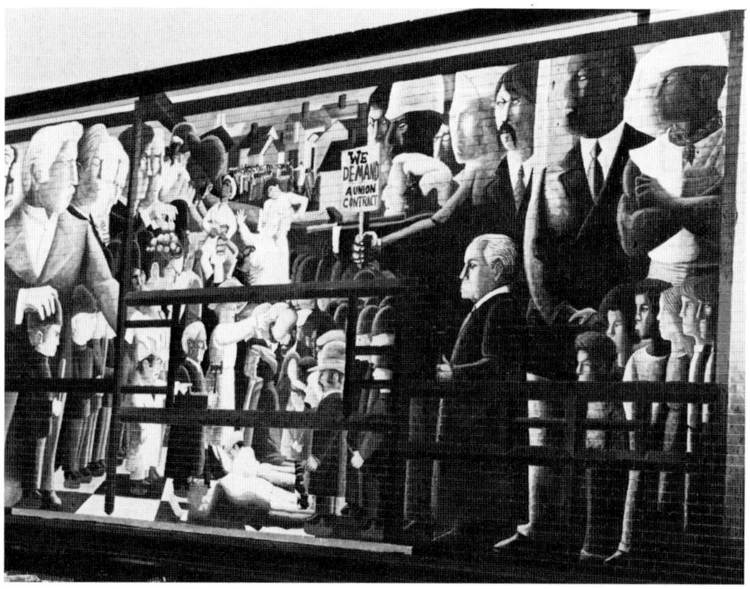

Figure 328
William Walker, *History of the Packinghouse Worker,* 1974. Chicago, Amalgamated Meatcutters Union Hall. Photo: © John Weber.

after twenty years in storage. A vast machine, Rivera's Golden Gate mural contains images of everything from Quetzalcóatl's stomping grounds to Charlie Chaplin's Hollywood, and it is certainly Rivera's worst wall: overcrowded, episodic, repetitious (three portraits each of Chaplin and Paulette Goddard!), and wackily violative of all the classic characteristics of his former manner (see fig. 401). But its sheer size and exuberance, like that of Siqueiros's even more overwhelmingly problematic Polyforum, stood as a model for many youthful community muralists whose aesthetic discrimination was predicated solely on a belief in the social value of art.

The Bank of America mural is formally close to Rivera's style in the Golden Gate mural, and there is certainly also an allusion to it and the California School of Fine Arts mural in the use of monumental figures encased in scaffolding that flank the center of the long wall (figs. 329 and 330) and do much to strengthen its composition. Typically, however, the artist celebrated in this mural is not Rivera, but Siqueiros. One of the central motifs is of a crucified peon pinned to the earth—recollective of Siqueiros's 1932 *Tropical America* mural in Los Angeles. And several portraits of Siqueiros, who died just as the mural was being conceived, can also be found on the wall, the most prominent being to the far left, where his figure, holding aloft an atom, is embraced by a skeleton. Rivera's example was, however, invoked when the young artists had to justify their painting a mural in a branch of a bank alleged to be among the worst exploiters of the poor. They simply pointed to Rivera's mural in the San Francisco Stock Exchange![32]

An examination of two other images can aptly close this discussion of Rivera's influence on community murals. Marcos Raya's *Homage to Diego Rivera* (fig. 331), painted in Chicago in 1972, quotes the entire composition of the Mexican's destroyed Rockefeller Center mural. And at

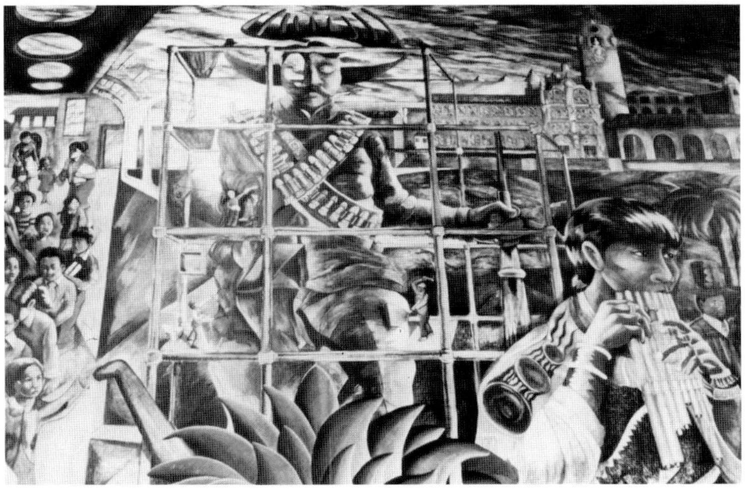

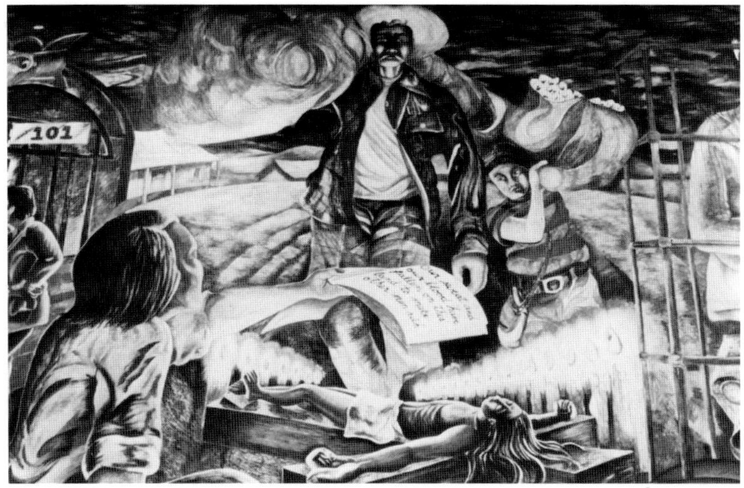

Figures 329, 330
Jesus Campusano, Michael Rios, Luis Cortazar, and others, *Untitled* (details), 1974, oil on fiber board. San Francisco, Bank of America, 23rd and Mission. Photo: © James Prigoff.

Chicano Park in San Diego, California, one of the many painted pylons (1978) supporting the overhead roadway bears portraits of Rivera, Orozco, Siqueiros, and Frida Kahlo (fig. 332), an apt monument to the influence of Rivera, his wife, and his colleagues in the Mexican mural movement on this ongoing chapter in the history of the mural in America.

Concluding Thoughts on Influence and Art as a Weapon

There was not a single tavern, eating house, dairy, wine shop, public bath, hotel, circus, or chapel to any saint whatsoever, which had not been covered with paintings by painters from the people. (Diego Rivera speaking of the folk murals that inspired the Mexican mural movement during the early 1920s)[33]

As a coda to this essay, I want, at least briefly, to acknowledge a vexing problem raised by the obviously value-laden distinctions made in its first part—which the thoughtful reader may discern as being at odds with the philosophy of Rivera and most of the artists discussed. If art is, indeed, a weapon in the struggle for social change, as Rivera and his followers felt it was, does not a hierarchy of values that designates Rivera and his ideological opposite Benton as "strong," Shahn as middling, and the great majority of social artists from the 1930s to today as mere followers contradict art's revolutionary utility?

First, a distinction must be made between the making of art and the uses to which it is put. The psychology of creativity is the same for the revolutionary and the reactionary; it is a human impulse led on by the laws of human environment and life-course development quite independent of ideology. The art historian as psychohistorian must look to the permutations of this human process and the formal power of the image-making involved and not be distracted by ideology. Further, the historian of art, who, as such, is neither a curator nor a critic, must always keep in mind the complex continuity of art objects within personal and social time frames and leave the discrete work of art to be contemplated in isolation by others for other reasons.

Secondly, when the historian does consider the uses of works of art, a distinction must be made between effective image-making and ineffective image-making. If, at a certain point, art is considered a weapon, then the historian must judge whether the art in question shoots true or misses the mark. Thus, while Grace Greenwood and Lucienne Bloch are both competent image-makers, the latter can certainly be said to outshoot the former. Similarly, the well assimilated and deeply felt use William Walker makes of the influence of Rivera is to be valued more than the pastiche of Marcos Raya.

Third, we must consider the reality that art is a weapon for all artists in the furtherance of their particular ideology, but that there are offensive and defensive weapons. The history of art would seem to be the alternation of such weaponry. Sometimes artists use imagery to galvanize

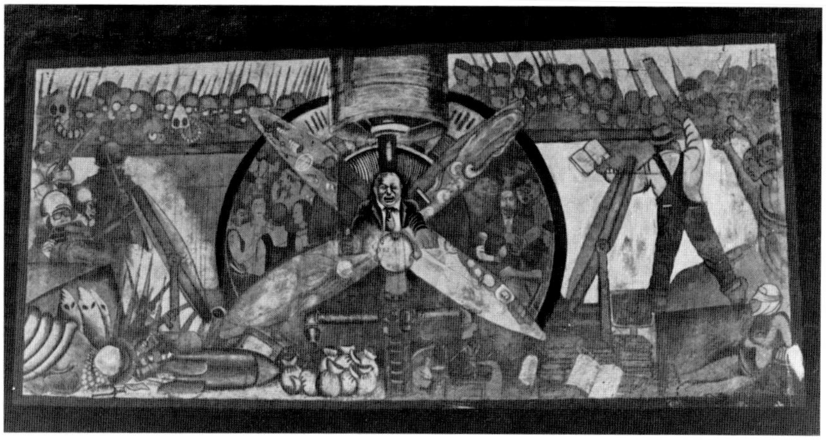

Figure 331
Marcos Raya, *Homage to Diego Rivera,* 1972. Chicago, 1147 W. 18th Street (later destroyed). Photo: © Victor Sorell.

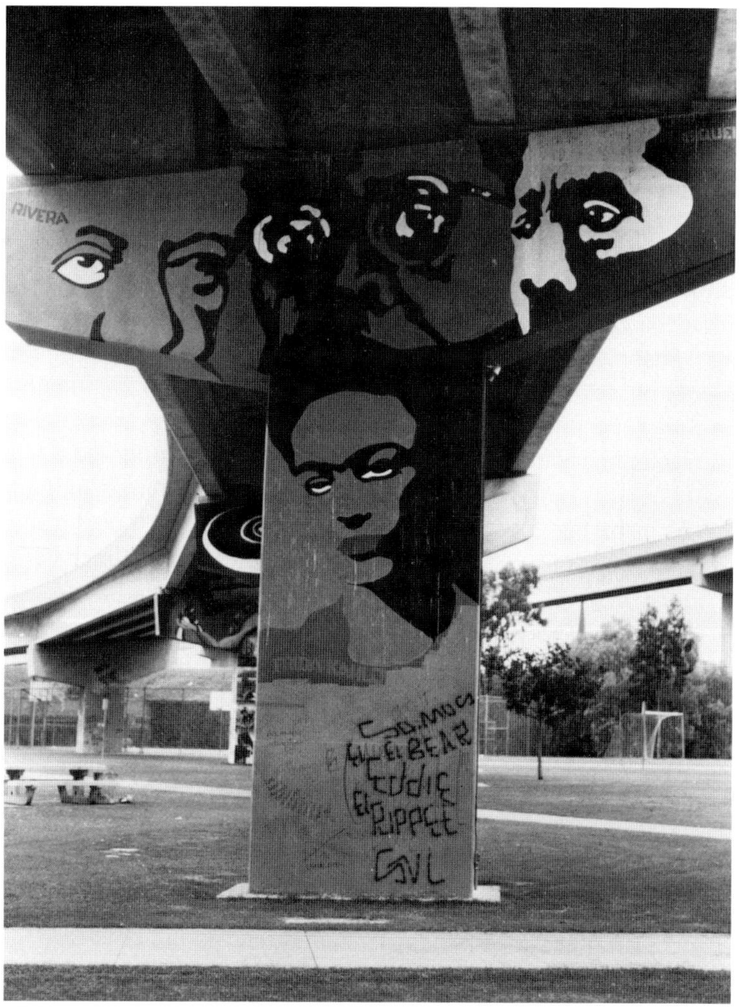

Figure 332
Rupert Garcia (designer), Victor Ochoa and the Barrio Renovation Team (muralists), *Rivera, Orozco, Siquieros, and Kahlo,* 1978. San Diego, California, Chicano Park. Photo: © James Prigoff.

their fellows to political action—as during the 1930s and with black and community muralists. Sometimes artists use art to prompt awareness of inner action—as did the Abstract Expressionists, seeking an authenticity of imagery within the process of painting itself as a way of expressing the human values the political process seemed incapable of conveying. And sometimes artists use art as a defense mechanism against the image-making process itself—as we have seen during the 1960s and 1970s, when color field and conceptual art denied subject and art respectively in order to avoid the realities of social upheaval and ideological aimlessness during the Vietnam war and the turbulence of the counter-culture.

Fourth, and in the same vein, we might pause to meditate on the profound statement of the philosopher Eliseo Vivas, quoted at the start of the previous section, that "our grasp of values in its first instance is an aesthetic grasp." We must constantly distinguish between the aesthetics of the aesthete, for whom art is often a conscious and ongoing substitution for too much gross reality, and the aesthetics of those trapped in that reality, for whom art can project an unexpected glimpse of the possibility of wholeness amid chaos. For Vivas, one of the main characteristics of a value is its "requiredness." Thus he can say: "Values are real and antecedent to our discovery of them; . . . they are a peculiar kind of fact, since they possess 'requiredness' to which we respond, and it is this aspect of value that is the source of the moral imperative."[34] The "moral imperative" can be embodied in an aesthetic response to the self-evident "requiredness," which may, in turn, be embodied in a work of art. Such a work can have an individual or a collective impact—each of which requires its own image of wholeness and its own visual rhetoric. And the historian must make, perforce, judgments as to what is required for the aesthete and what is required for the slum kid who finds his own strength of identity and moral value in the crude images on a wall in Chicago in 1967—or a Rivera who found his on similar walls a half century earlier. The history of art is a matter of ethics as well as aesthetics.

Finally, the distinction we must stop making—or at least historians must stop making—is that between "high" art and artificial subcategories of art such as "folk" art or "primitive" art. For, as we are learning to our surprise, these latter forms of image-making can be of greater power and poetry—indeed of greater strength—than that which our curators and critics promote as the latest aesthetic salvation.[35] Diego Rivera understood this in his respect for assimilation of the folk and primitive art of his native country. But it takes a strong artist to see through the artificial categories into which we segregate art and to realize that it is the image-making process and its results, whatever the provenance or province involved, that convey the essence of human vision. Thus we must value above all the Diego Riveras—who see and act more comprehensively than others—while respecting the best of those who are influenced by such strength of genius.

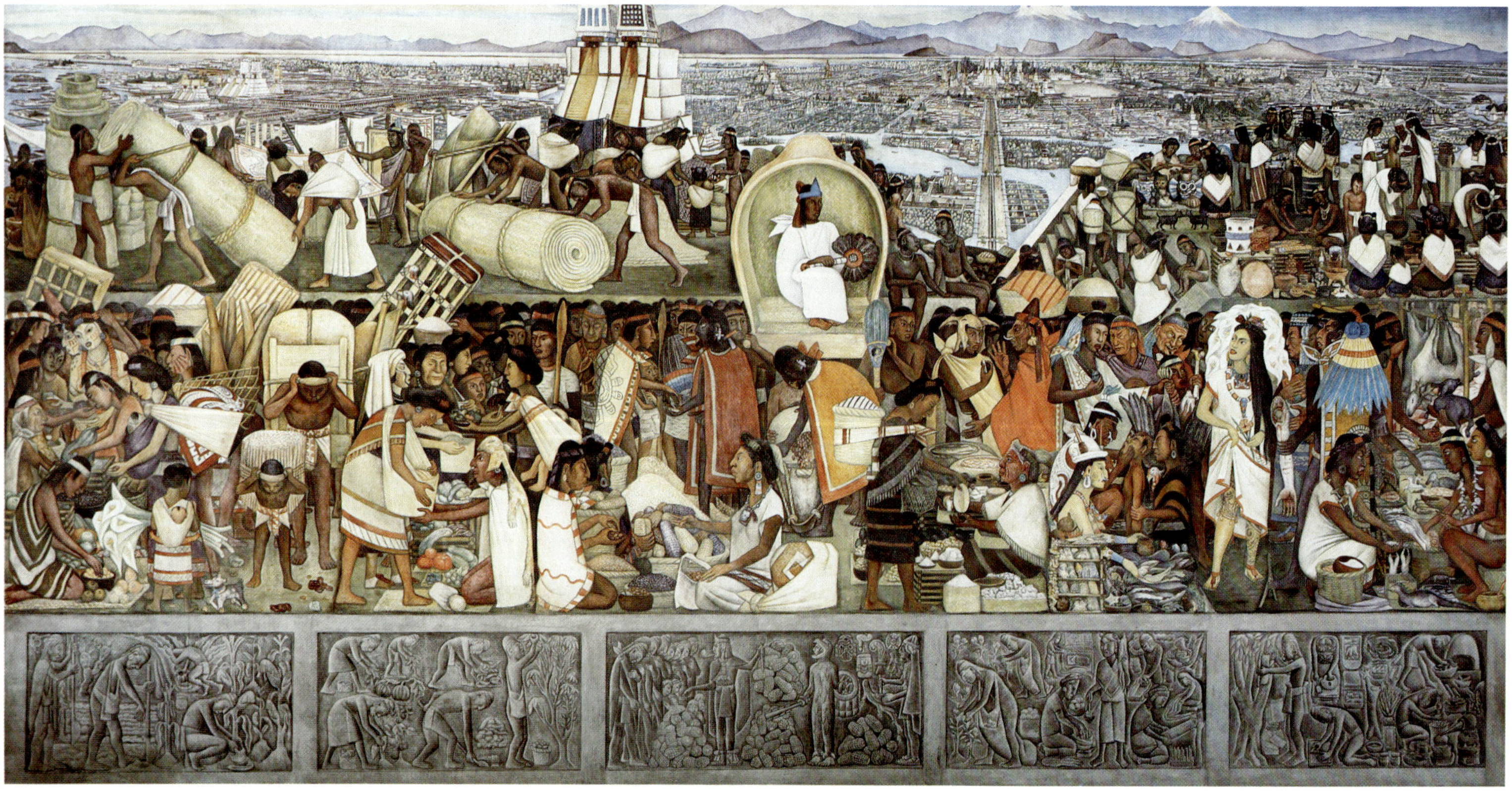

Diego Rivera's Murals in Mexico and the United States

Luis Cardoza y Aragón

Figure 333
The Great City of Tenochtitlán, 1945, fresco, 4.92 × 9.71 m. Mexico City, Palacio Nacional.

Diego Rivera's work as a muralist is the most crucial element of his titanic career. His murals in Mexico and the United States cover more than six thousand square meters—an enormous area in which we often find little of great interest, although Rivera's craftsmanship and technical expertise are always evident. But in this vast expanse, one also finds splendid groupings and details and more than a few inspired figures. The best examples are notable for the dignity of their forms and for the successful integration of their styles and themes with the surrounding architecture.

Herbert Read, in the preface to his *Concise History of Modern Painting,* tells us that he does not discuss Rivera, José Clemente Orozco, or David Alfaro Siqueiros because, "like some of their Russian contemporaries, they have adopted a propagandist programme for their art which seems to me to place it outside the stylistic evolution which is my exclusive concern."[1] Read's observation and his lumping together of the work of these three very diverse artists under the rubric of propaganda constitutes one of the points of departure of this discussion. For the English essayist, the Mexican muralists were not, by reason of their didactic intent, modern painters. But what in Read's mind was a reproach is in fact an essential virtue. Because of its unique character Mexican muralism is perhaps the only completely original contribution by American artists to the development of modern art.

The Mexican muralists did not pay homage to the styles that grew up in Europe after the Impressionists and Cézanne. They forgot about the galleries, the art business, and the prevailing fashions of the day, and almost without pay chose to paint for the people. These actions embodied the ultimate goal of the muralist movement—to create a work unto itself, consciously disconnected from the artistic revolution then occurring in the West. Their works are the most significant creation of Mexico after Cortés, and their "rediscovery" is symptomatic of the profound crisis in contemporary thought as regards the avant-garde art of the early 20th century. As a result of the Eurocentrism of art criticism, the Mexican muralists have been either ignored or, what is worse, misunderstood. Rivera once asked Walter Pach, "Doesn't it seem to you that what is most important is a declaration of American independence in art?"[2] And indeed it is in their departure from European models, in their creation of a truly indigenous art, that the significance of their achievement is to be found.

Who was Diego Rivera when he returned to Mexico from Europe at the age of thirty-five, having lived fifteen years in the midst of the intense artistic revolution that characterized the most innovative period of the School of Paris? He knew intimately the museums and cathedrals of Europe and had participated in the birth of modern painting. He counted among his friends many of the artists who were creating a new vision of reality. Using his skill and his

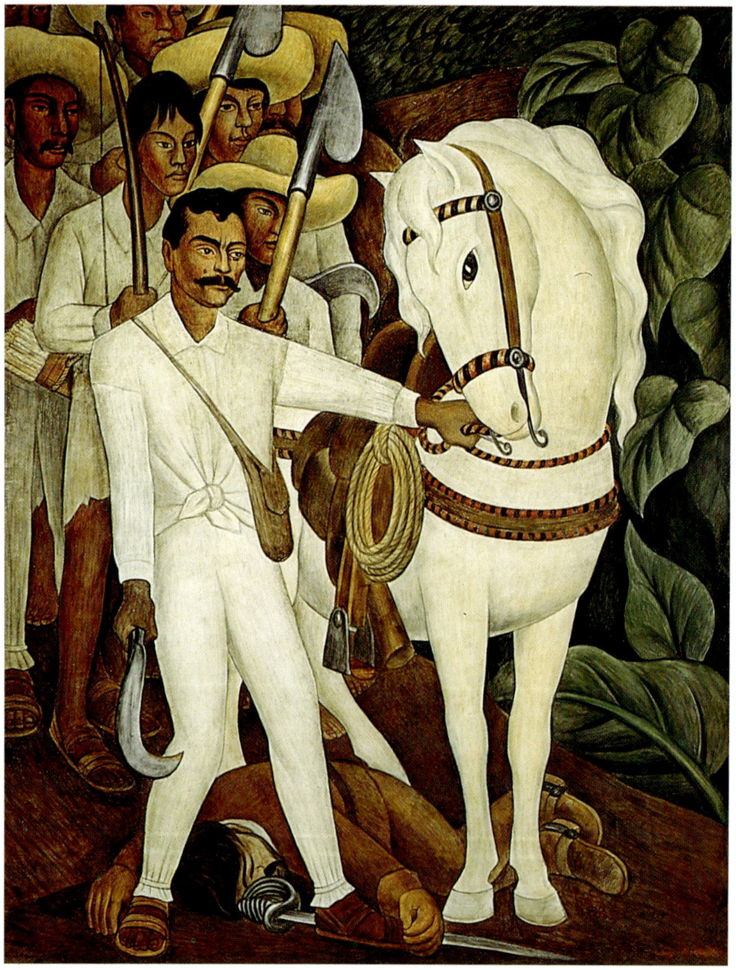

Figure 334
Agrarian Leader Zapata, 1931, fresco, 2.38 × 1.88 m. New York, The Museum of Modern Art, Abby Aldrich Rockefeller Fund (1631.40). This movable panel is based on the *Revolt* panel at the Palacio de Cortés, Cuernavaca.

innate talent, he had immersed himself in that admirable effort. His decision to abandon modernism, then, was not an act of ignorance but of wisdom.

Almost immediately upon his arrival, he began to work. His first mural, for the Anfiteatro Bolívar of the Escuela Nacional Preparatoria, is quite unlike those that were to follow. With his study of the Italian primitives, the art of the Renaissance, and the culture of the Pompeiian Greeks still fresh in his mind, Rivera created an allegorical composition with a Byzantine flavor, which, while it embodies the artist's impetuosity and audaciousness no less than his refinement and the wealth of his artistic experience, is not a great work. Clearly, Rivera had not yet discovered his home ground. In the frescoes for the Secretaría de Educación Pública, his next major work, he found his mature style.

An ardent believer in the Russian revolutionary movement and an acute observer of European disenchantment in the aftermath of World War I, Rivera had returned to a country in the throes of revolution. It was in the face of this turmoil that, in line with his social and political philosophies, he relinquished modernism and dedicated himself to portraying the life of Mexico in murals (and to expounding his ideology in enough pages of prose to make a book). I believe that he was already fed up with the pictorial and literary "isms" of the day, and that on reencountering his own country he experienced a true revelation. And in this rediscovery of his native land, this rescue of what was his own, lies the transcendent genius of Rivera's career. Rivera's role in Mexico's rediscovery of its past and the roots of its culture cannot be overestimated.

Had Rivera, in the face of criticism like Read's, eschewed "propagandistic" art, he would today be only one among many talented modern painters and not the historical artistic eminence he is acknowledged to be. But does his art qualify as socialist realism? The objective of socialist realism is the promulgation of an official vision. Ironically, Rivera, Orozco, and Siqueiros would have been considered formalists in the U.S.S.R. The Mexican government was not socialist much less communist, but in any case these artists painted works whose orientation was manifestly opposed to its ideology and institutions. It is a tribute to José Vasconcelos, Mexico's minister of public education at the outset of the Mexican muralist movement, that he gave the artists total freedom. The same was not true at Rockefeller Center in the supposedly free and open environment of New York. It is ironic that the efforts of the Mexican muralists were never solicited by the socialist countries but rather by the industrial magnates of the United States.

The very vitality of the Mexican muralists has awakened a debate about the relative importance of their work. I believe that their influence goes beyond mere plastic values and their importance beyond the works themselves. These artists created in the Mexican people a consciousness of nationality. This dimension of their work is what makes them "founders" of a truly American art.

Rivera's images are direct, clear, and precise, in accordance with his philosophy that public painting should be both monumental and popular. He is frequently a sensual painter—his work is full of sun, as in his visions of the tropics, his nudes, and his portrayals of fruit and flowers—whose color is opulent and whose compositions betray an incredible versatility. In his murals he concentrated on several persistent themes. Most significantly, his works are saturated with scenes from the history of the battles of Mexico from the mythic pre-Hispanic era up through modern times. His frescoes at the Palacio Nacional, perhaps the most important building decorated by Rivera, are evidence of his concern. Among the panels that refer to Mexico before Cortés, *The Great City of Tenochtitlán* (fig. 333) is outstanding. It is as carefully painted as a miniature, with subtle effects of tone and exquisite color, composition, and design; and it is executed with a softness and spontaneity more characteristic of a watercolor than a mural.

Rivera wanted the simplest man or woman of the people to understand him, and he was an excellent storyteller, although perhaps without a sense of tragedy. When I say that his is not the tragic vein, I am thinking in particular of the murals in the Palacio de Cortés in Cuernavaca, where, although Rivera painted brilliantly the torture the Indians suffered at the hands of the conquistadores, it is the figure of Emiliano Zapata with his white horse (fig. 334) that is unforgettable. The resemblance of this passage to Pintoricchio's murals for the Piccolomini Library in Siena's cathedral is obvious. No one in Mexico was better acquainted with Renaissance painting than Rivera. His re-creation of it here is memorable.

Rivera explained his mural work thus:

Mexican muralism has not brought anything new to the universal plastic arts, nor to architecture, and even less to sculpture. But Mexican muralism—for the first time in the history of monumental painting—ceased to use gods, kings, chiefs of state, heroic generals, etc., as central heroes. . . . For the first time in the history of art, Mexican mural painting made the masses the hero of monumental art. That is to say, the man of the fields, of the factories, of the cities, and towns. When a hero appears among the people, it is clearly as part of the people and as one of them. Also for the first time in history, from the semi-mythic past to the real, scientific, foreseeable future, an attempt was made to portray the trajectory of the people through time in one homogeneous and dialectic composition. This is what has given their work universal value, since this attempt is a real and new contribution to the content of monumental art.[3]

In the frescoes in the United States, Rivera's focus and imagery are similar to those in his Mexican works. He adapted himself completely to his themes: the great factories, the proletariat that works therein, the prodigiousness of the modern age and its industrial genius, the beauty of the machine, and the alienation of mankind. Faced with the dynamic novelty of the culture of the United States, he painted with an astonishment and terror akin to that awakened in the poet Federico García Lorca before a "savage North America."[4] But he never abandoned his Mexican heritage. In Detroit, the artist adapted the form of a classic work of Aztec sculpture, the goddess Coatlicue, a prototypical example of the "huge art" of the ancient Mexicans, which is preserved at the Museo Nacional de Antropología, to represent a monumental group of machines.

What is the relationship of Rivera to Orozco and Siqueiros? While all three artists share the experience of a historic situation in their country and in the world, each interprets these events through a different sensibility and in a distinctive style. But comparisons, as we know, besides being odious, are absurd. Each of the "great ones" (as these three masters are called) had a well-defined personality. Orozco's vehement temperament is evident in his dramatic, biting scenes, which are distinct both from Rivera's serenity and from Siqueiros's obsession with the depiction of movement. Compared to the Baroque character of Siqueiros's works and the frenzy of some of Orozco's compositions, Rivera's works are placid and full of repose. One could call him a classical artist, if such a fluid designation could mean anything precise.

To summarize, there are three criticisms of Mexican muralism: it is anachronistic, it is nationalistic, and it is propagandistic. Such criticisms, however, become less and less relevant as we daily discover the valuable national artistic expressions of countries long ignored by art historians. In the best of Rivera's frescoes, the aesthetic and the political fuse into an artistic unity. He is not simply an ideologue who paints but a great artist. We may forget his ideas, but his images stay with us.

I think it is reasonable to propose, in fact to insist, that Rivera's impact lives on and will not pass away with time. As has happened to religious painting from other civilizations, the element of propaganda in his work grows ever more diffuse, becoming less disturbing to the enjoyment of the works in and of themselves. A master of derivation, which elevated rather than diminished him, Rivera created works that are still vital, that still today embody the universal objectives of truth and beauty.

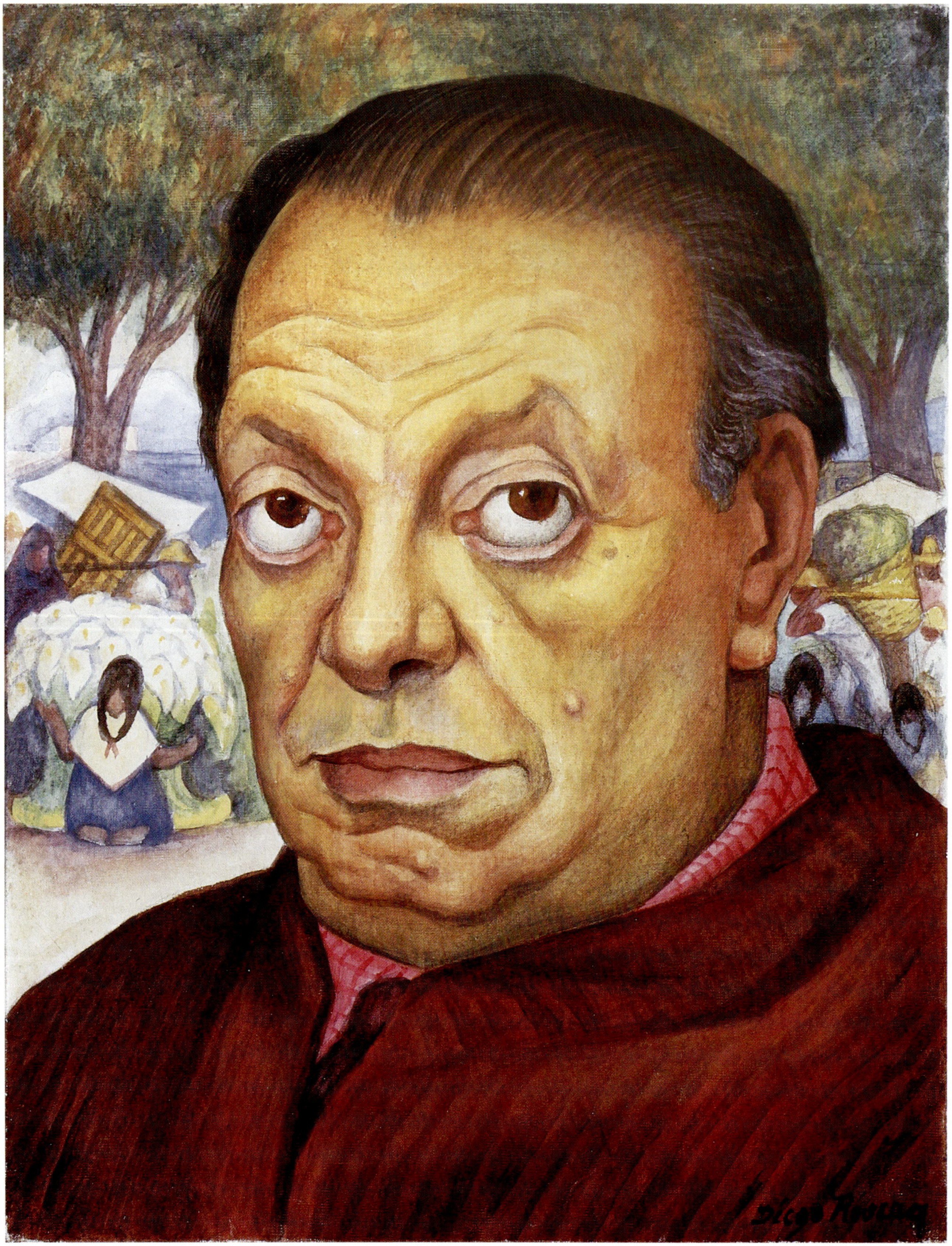
Diego Rivera

The Self-Portraits of Diego Rivera

Xavier Moyssén

Figure 335
***Self-Portrait,* 1949, tempera on linen, 31.1 × 25.1 cm. Collection of Burt B. Holmes.**

Portraiture makes up a significant part of the work of Diego Rivera, especially if one includes the portraits of historic personages that appear in his murals. Naturally, he also did many self-portraits. Between 1906, the date of his first self-portrait, and 1951, when he signed his last, Rivera depicted himself about twenty times, in a variety of formats and media, including drawings, lithographs, easel paintings, and murals. These works form a visual autobiography that reveals all the vicissitudes of human experience.[1]

The primary element in Rivera's self-portraits is the realism with which he always approached his own image. He never idealized his own face, never succumbed to the temptation of seeing himself with uncritical eyes, and he possessed a full consciousness of his true physical appearance. Another outstanding characteristic of Rivera's self-portraits is the treatment of his eyes, those large eyes that observed the world and interpreted it through his art. As in the self-portraits of Pablo Picasso, the expressive power of the eyes immediately draws the attention of the viewer.

While Rivera occasionally depicted himself in full- or half-length, most of his self-portraits are of his face alone. Whether in drawings or paintings, the image is rounded and solidly constructed. Usually there are some background figures that complete the composition, but these never draw attention from the primary aspect of the work, which is the face of the artist.

In 1906, when Rivera was twenty and still a student, he painted his first self-portrait. The composition is weighted toward the left, and the youthful face of the artist with his unruly hair, his large penetrating eyes, and full lips is seen through heavy, contrasting shadows. He created his second self-portrait one year later, while he was living in Spain (fig. 336). Here, there is a flavor of Spanish romanticism in the traces of nostalgia on the artist's face, and a fin-de-siècle bohemianism is hinted at in the presence of the bottle and glass of beer on the table. A comparison with the earlier work makes evident Rivera's professional development as a result of his study with Eduardo Chicharro in Madrid.

Rivera had a natural penchant for drawing, and as a result of the academic training he received from Antonio Fabrés, he developed into a magnificent draftsman. He did several self-portraits in pencil, the first of which dates to 1918 (fig. 337) and was dedicated to Carl Zigrosser, a great connoisseur of graphic art. By that time Rivera had passed through his period of Cubist experimentation and was interested in Cézanne. Very finely drawn, this work is unusual in that it is the only self-portrait to show Rivera with a beard.

In 1921, when Rivera was in Paris, he did two portraits in red and black chalk that are similar in size and technique, one of David Alfaro Siqueiros, the other of himself (see fig. 77). This self-portrait presents the pleasant face of a thirty-five-year-old man, who looks expressively at the viewer with a slight smile. The prominent eyes that were so characteristic a feature of the artist's face are complemented here by strong strokes that make up the rest of the portrait.

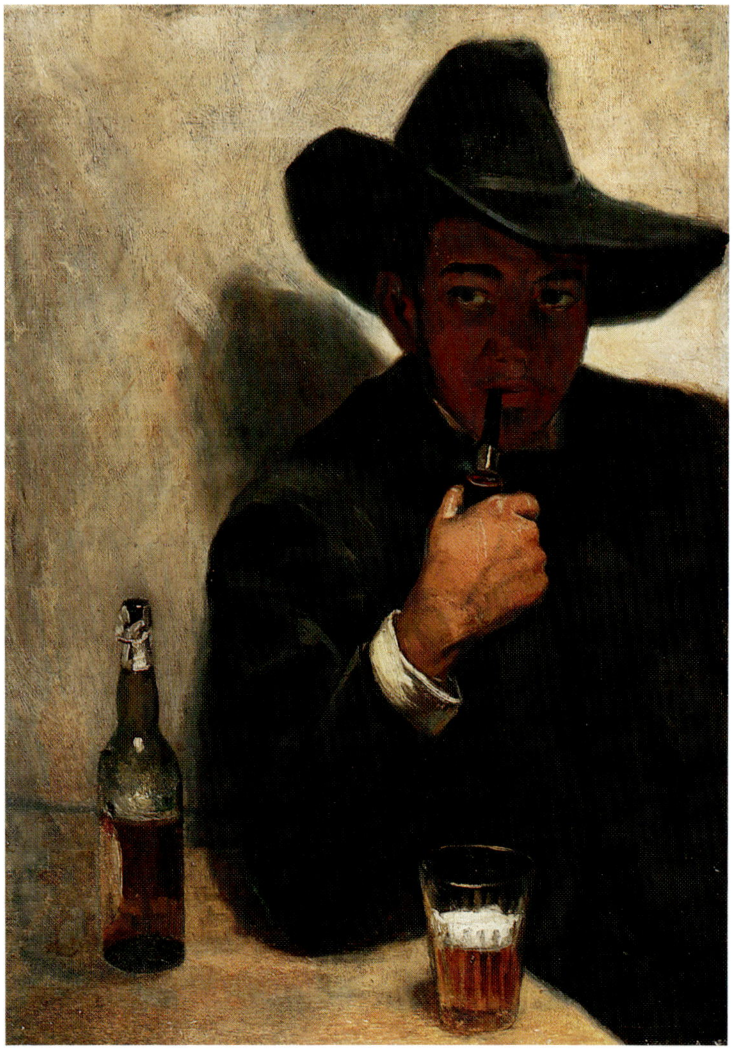

Figure 336
Self-Portrait, 1907, oil on canvas, 84.5 × 61.5 cm. Collection of Dolores Olmedo.

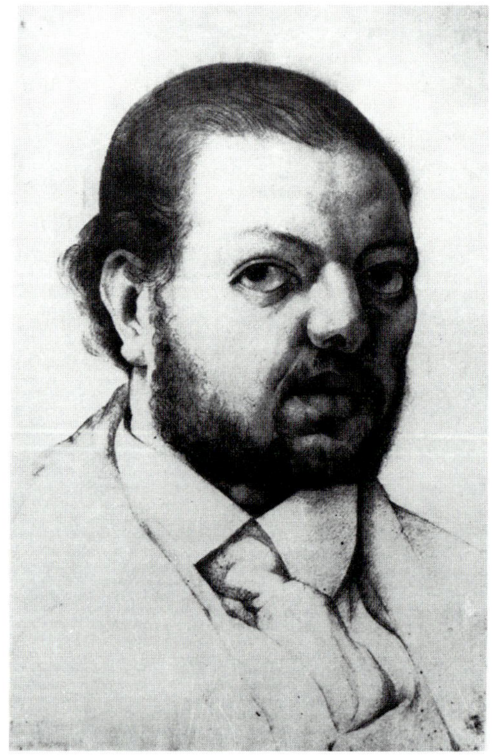

Figure 337
Self-Portrait, 1918, pencil. Present location unknown.

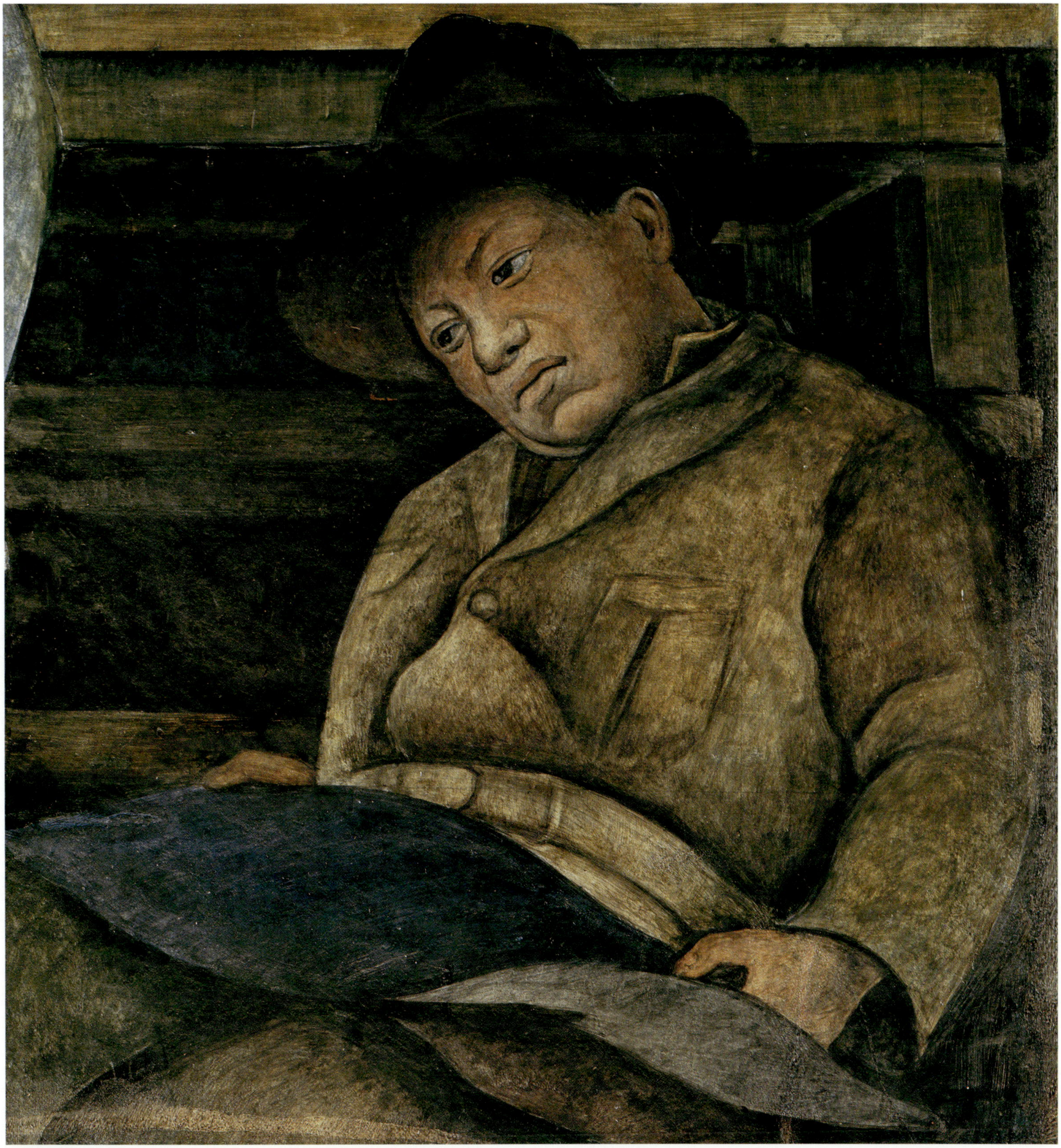

Figure 338
Detail of stairway,
1923/28, fresco. Mexico City, Secretaría de Educación Pública.

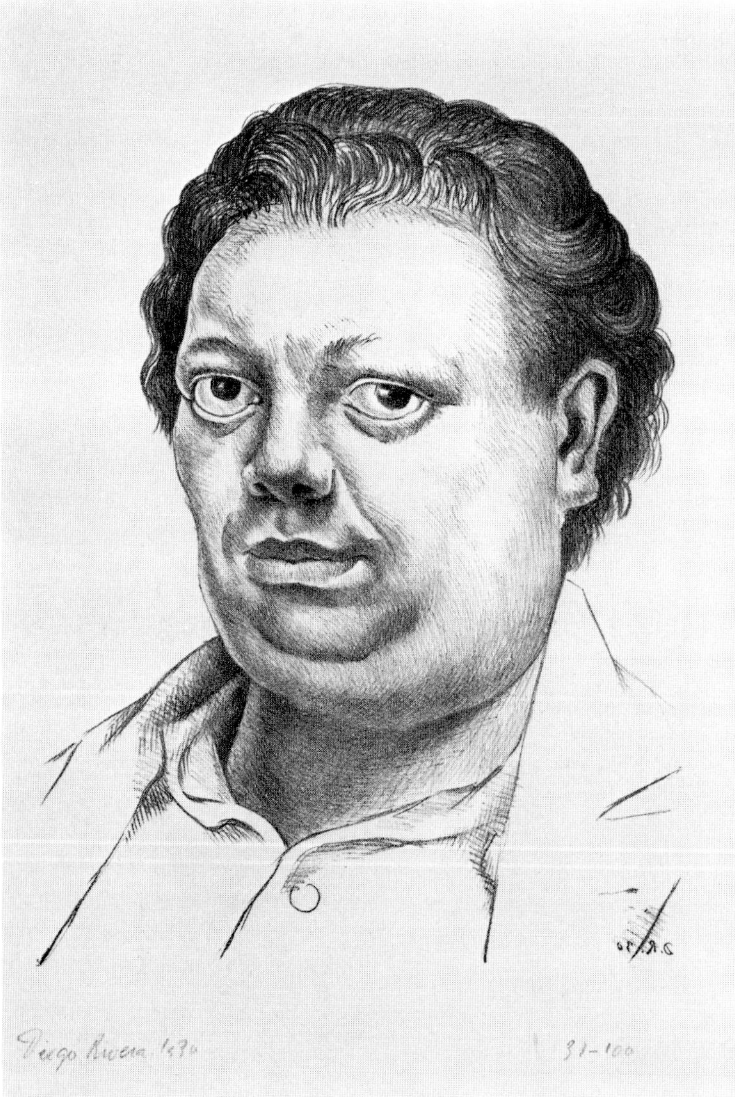

Figure 339
Self-Portrait, **1930, lithograph, 40.2 × 28.3 cm. New York, The Museum of Modern Art, Gift of Abby Aldrich Rockefeller (1557.40).**

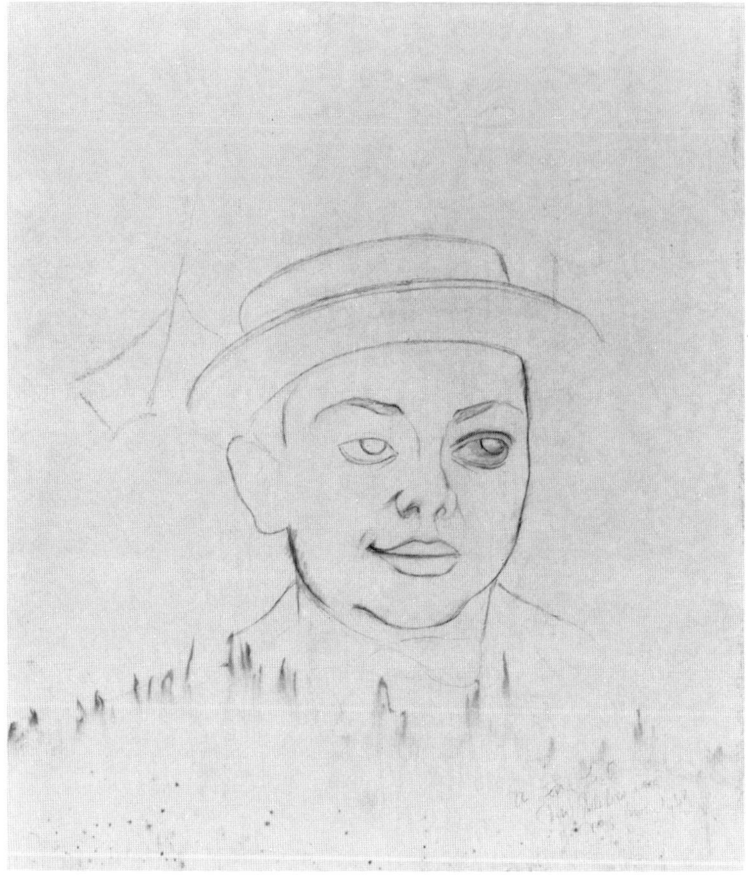

Figure 340
Self-Portrait, **1947, pencil, 61.5 × 52.7 cm. Collection of Rafael Coronel.**

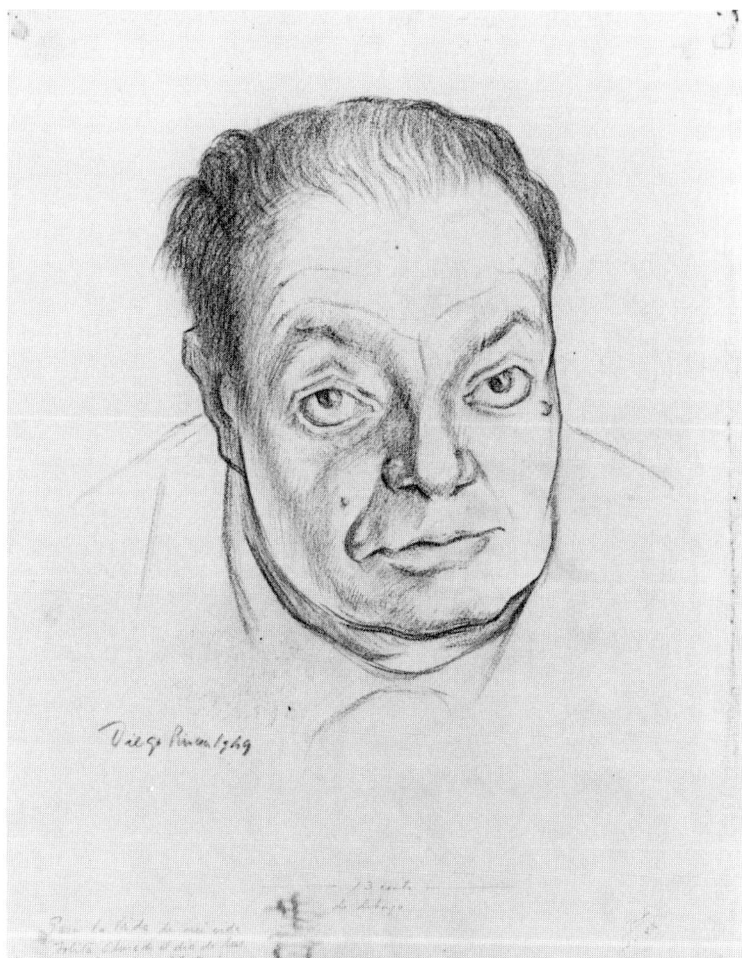

Figure 341
Self-Portrait, **1949, black chalk, 36.2 × 28.6 cm. Collection of Dolores Olmedo.**

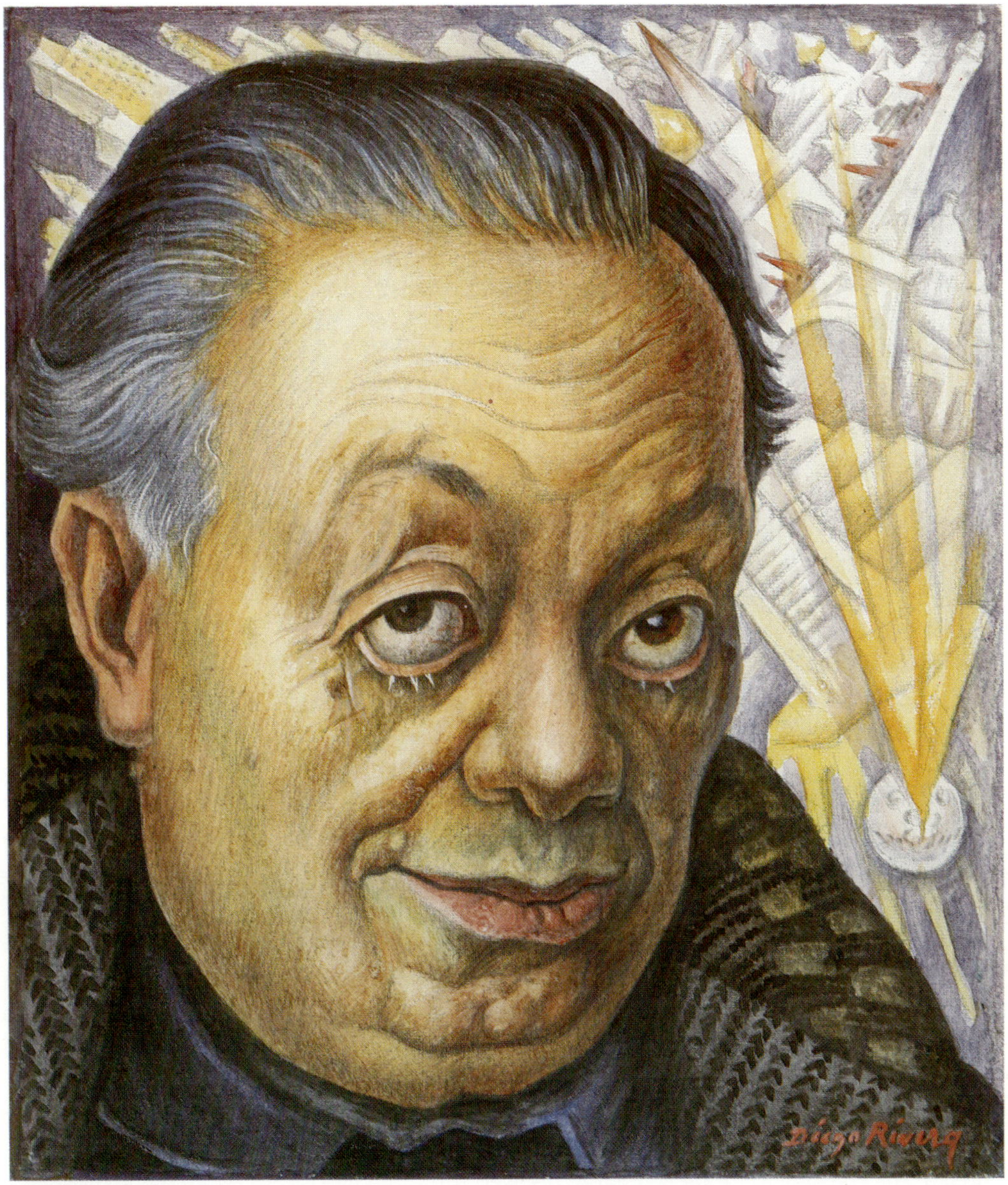

Figure 342
Self-Portrait—The Ravages of Time, 1949, watercolor on canvas, 31 × 26.5 cm. Collection of Marilyn O. Lubetkin.

Between 1923 and 1928, Rivera worked intensely on the murals for the Secretaría de Educación Pública. There, for the first time, he included his own image in two of the panels, imitating the tradition of Italian Renaissance muralists. In the panel *Day of the Dead—City Fiesta,* he appears among a crowd of people that includes humble peasants as well as several celebrated people of the age. It is a *custumbrista* scene, that is, a scene showing the daily life and customs of Mexico. When Rivera returned to his country after many years of residence in Paris, he made numerous sketches of the customs, street life, and festivals of the people during trips throughout Mexico. This work makes evident Rivera's identification with the world whose pictorial interpreter he was to become. He portrayed himself with a straw hat, like one of the masses, and his mischievous gaze and smile betray his happiness in this role.

In 1926, on a wall of the stairwell of the same building, Rivera depicted himself as an architect accompanied by a mural painter and a sculptor (fig. 338). For this self-portrait he used a photograph of himself taken by Edward Weston in which he is seen in half-length, seated and smoking. (Rivera is known to have used photographs as sources for other works as well; for example, he also used a Weston photograph, of Tina Modotti, in creating the panels at Chapingo.) Here the translation from photo to mural is not completely successful; the pose seems forced and unnatural and the placement of the architectural plan over his stomach and legs is awkward. Combined with Rivera's facial expression, the effect is that of an exhausted man alienated by work. Artists frequently refer to photographs in search of formal solutions for their compositions. They also use them as documents, and it is to this purpose that Rivera employed photography in his murals. The fact that he would use the portrait that Edward Weston made of him provokes some questions. Did Rivera have doubts at this time about his ability to know himself? Was he inspired by the image that the photo captured? On the other hand, it is interesting that he did not present himself as a painter but as an architect. If we examine Rivera's egocentrism and the fame he already enjoyed, it is not difficult to imagine that he considered himself the builder of a new Mexican art: mural painting.

In 1929 Rivera had another opportunity to paint himself on a wall, this time in the old palace of Cortés in Cuernavaca. In the rear loggia, he treated the social history of the Valley of Cuernavaca, including the great southern leaders Emiliano Zapata and José María Morelos. Rivera found great similarity between the latter and himself, and to intensify his identification, he altered the physiognomy of Morelos to create a composite portrait of the hero and himself.

Around 1930 Rivera became interested in lithography, creating six works in this medium on themes derived from his murals, as well as one self-portrait, which is so magnificent that were it his only lithograph it would suffice to qualify him as a capable lithographer (fig. 339). Working from a mirror, he captured the robustness of his form. The straightforward expression on his face seems to confirm his self-confidence at this point in his career. One year later, he used the same lithographic stone to print the same self-portrait in a method he called "lithomontage." It is a curious work in which his head appears three times superimposed in different positions.

In 1931 Rivera was invited to work in San Francisco, where he created his first murals outside Mexico. In the California School of Fine Arts he painted an enormous mural treating the theme of the worker controlling the constructive force of a large city. Included in the mural are the artist himself and his students seated on scaffolding (fig. 390). An unusual aspect of this self-portrait is that Rivera presented himself with his back to the viewer and emphasized his buttocks, a detail that was censured by José Clemente Orozco. But Rivera's intention was simply to present himself as just another worker, in defiance of the traditional idea that the artist is a superior being.

Rivera returned to San Francisco in 1940, this time to paint a mural on the occasion of the Golden Gate International Exposition. There he demonstrated his admiration for the world of North American industry as a complement to the world of South American artistry. He felt that if the two worlds could unite they would form a new nation of technicians and artists. He presented his ideas carefully in this work, and he included his own portrait twice. He appears first in a group of Mexican artists working on a painting of American, Latin, and Russian liberators (fig. 401). The second self-portrait appears on the lower section of the wall, where he is seated in front of the actress Paulette Goddard. In this latter portrait, there is a reference to sexual union, symbolic of the new race that would emerge from the union of North and South.

Rivera's talent and his sense of humor allowed him to depict himself in his murals in many guises—architect, hero, painter, scientist. In 1939, in the mural at the Instituto Nacional de Cardiología, he appears among the physicians, again in a composite (see fig. 402). This time his own image is blended with that of the Czech cardiologist Joseph Skoda. But something more surprising happened in 1948 when he painted himself in the Hotel del Prado, poetically altering time by depicting himself as a child in a scene from early in the 20th century (see figs. 403 and 340).

In 1949, when Rivera was sixty-three, he made four self-portraits, one in chalk, two watercolors, and one tempera painting. The compositions of these four works are similar. The head, positioned on an angle, occupies most of the space, and all are done realistically. The chalk drawing reveals the face of a kindly man and represents a synthesis of Rivera's work in this medium (fig. 341). In contrast, the tempera painting is the result of severe self-scrutiny: the artist's face is lined with wrinkles and the heavy-lidded eyes have a sad expression (fig. 335). In spite of this, the work is given a sense of light, color, and gaiety by the background scene of flower vendors, one of his favorite themes. The two watercolors have a lot in common, but the one with the Eiffel Tower and other buildings in the background is the more interesting (fig. 342). In the words of Justino Fernandez, "His gray hair frames his forehead; the ironic look in his large eyes seems to insinuate a warning and the whole of Rivera's life pervades his face, from the wrinkles on his forehead to the sensual and aging mouth. It is Rivera as he knows himself, and he knows himself well."[2]

The last of Rivera's self-portraits with which I am familiar dates to 1951. It is unusual because of the composition's originality. Rivera's smiling face, reflected in a mirror as he draws, is multifaceted, while in a picture in front of him, the double portrait is repeated, inverted as if it were a printed image. Compared with the three images just discussed, Rivera's face is smooth, devoid of the cruel marks of age.

The self-portraits of Diego Rivera reflect his long and fruitful career, from the monumental mural paintings to the most personal drawings. His self-portraits are perhaps the most psychologically profound of all his portraits, reflecting his aesthetic aims and revealing an intimate sense of the man—his desire to identify himself with heroes and intellectuals and to achieve immortality.

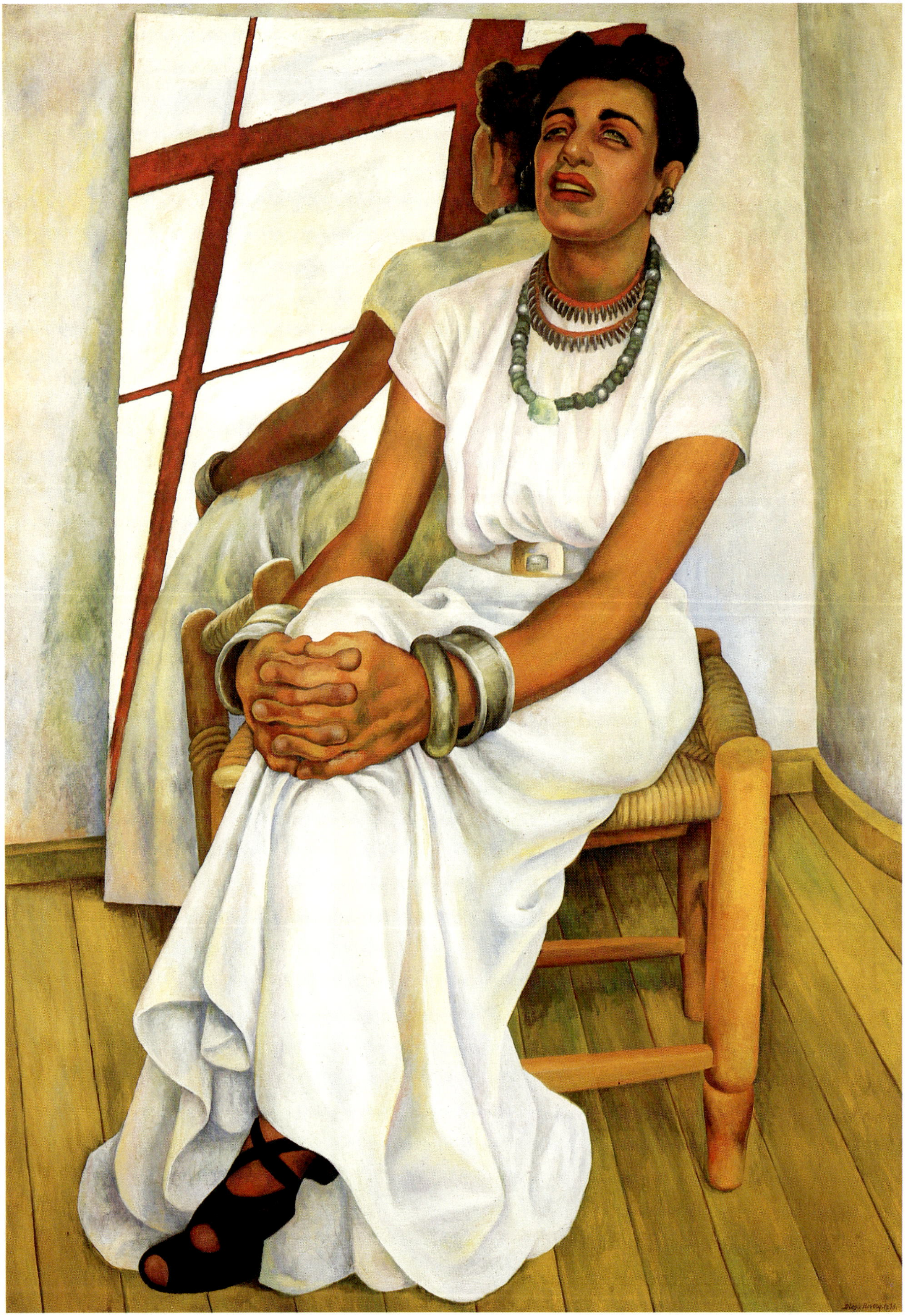

The Portraits of Diego Rivera

Rita Eder

Figure 343
Portrait of Lupe Marín,
1938, oil on canvas, 171.3 × 122.3 cm. Mexico City, Museo de Arte Moderno (INBA).

In 1938, Diego Rivera painted a portrait of Guadalupe Marín (fig. 343). Her actual extraordinary appearance—her height, her large hands, and her strangely transparent eyes—was transformed into a visual image of great impact. She is seated diagonally, and her huge and expressive hands appear in a dominating position, while her green eyes are fixed upon an undetermined spot. Her body almost leans against a mirror that reflects her profile as well as a framed window through which bluish light illuminates the painting and broadens its depth of field.

The portrait of Lupe Marín is puzzling and attractive at the same time in its diversity and richness of elements. Its structure shows a distillation of Rivera's knowledge through the course of his artistic development. His understanding of Velázquez and of Baroque motifs can be appreciated in the strong diagonal that organizes the painting and in the presence of the mirror, signifying visual illusion. Also evident is Rivera's affinity, filtered through a modern sensibility, for the mannerism of El Greco, for whom the human body was essentially emotive form. Finally, the lessons of Cubism are apparent in the delicate balance that the artist has established between the figure and its possible metamorphoses through an intense interrelationship of the diverse elements of the composition. This is made possible by the clever effect of the introduction of a space within space created by the mirror. But Rivera chose to have these motifs undergo a personal synthesis and thus achieved one of his best moments as a portraitist.

His attraction to Lupe Marín, his first Mexican wife—whom he married in church a few years after joining the Mexican Communist Party—had already left its mark upon the walls of the chapel at Chapingo, where, almost a decade before, he had painted her as a pregnant, sumptuous Mother Earth. In this mural, the model, with the impenetrable face of a goddess and an opulent brown body, appears to convey a different meaning: she represents the origin of life and the exaltation of Mexican beauty.

We can see in these portraits two different moments in the work of Rivera. We might say that most of his easel paintings, in particular those that belong to the so-called realistic style, as well as many of his murals, are centered upon portraiture. Our understanding of Rivera's work could be improved by considering this gallery of personages who look at us from his walls, as well as by carefully examining the private portraits, which reveal a more intimate and at times sharper vision of painting as a way of conveying reality and which offer a description of Mexico as Rivera saw it.

These considerations have brought us to divide this reflection on Rivera into two sections: the first one concerns his encyclopedic attitude in mural painting; the second one concerns Rivera with a greater freedom of mind and with more respect for his own fantasies, his exuberance, and his emotions. This division makes it easier to understand his contradictions and his diverse artistic findings.

The Portrait in the Context of Mural Painting

The first aspect of Rivera's muralism, which appears particularly in his monumental work at Mexico's Palacio Nacional, painted in its first phase between 1929 and 1935 and in its second phase between 1941 and 1951, manifests an affirmative, optimistic attitude in which no doubts or fears can be found. All his characters have a precise position in the murals. Risking an overcrowded space within the painting, the artist's main concern was to show each and every one of the participants in the story he was trying to tell of the different moments of Mexican history.

His vision clearly finds its own place among the ideals of the state that made his murals possible:

The groups which came to power during the Revolution, between 1910 and 1917, naturally held, and even continue to claim, that the period born with the Revolution . . . has radically transformed the country and has fully realized the aspirations first manifested by the Mexican people in the War of Independence, then during the Reform, and finally in the Revolution itself; while the Porfiriato is judged to be not only a veritable Middle Ages that denied our history, but also to be the greatest betrayal of its meaning and feeling, its heroes, and its traditions.[1]

Although it is apparent that Rivera's murals offer the possibility, through the analysis of portraits, of an easy ideological exercise conveyed through figures, it is more interesting to apply our skills to the problem of how and why the artist chose certain ways of doing such figures. How can we interpret Rivera's use of carefully and patiently painted individuals to portray this historical moment in a direct and unambiguous fashion?

While his tendency to depict Mexico's history in terms of class struggle illustrates Rivera's debt to Marxist thought, the artist was even more influenced by the ideals of Enlightenment, in particular by the conception of history as an avenue of progress leading to a better future as man exercised his ever-increasing knowledge and by the belief that the best way of obtaining this knowledge was through scientific investigation. Rivera's belief in the latter concept can be seen in the careful order he imposed on his murals. In so doing, he established a taxonomy, which is a concept based in natural history.

Dream of a Sunday Afternoon in the Alameda is perhaps the mural in which portraiture plays the most important part, and through which he introduced new thematic as well as formal conceptions. Realism takes on a new meaning and lets us know more about the artist's mind, going beyond his public attitudes and beyond the ambitious goals he tried to reach in his other murals.

In the central panel, we can see Frida Kahlo and the artist himself. He is in the guise of a strapping ten-year-old boy, although his face is that of a young adult, so he is young and old at the same time. His expression is solemn, especially when compared to the merry figure of death, or *calavera*, whose hand he is holding. Guadalupe Posada, creator of such *calaveras catrinas* (death's-heads of dandies), appears with a serious expression, holding the elegantly dressed skeleton by its other arm.

Beyond the ideological content of the mural, it is worth pointing out the presence of a dreamlike realism. Ambiguity is created in the contrast between the lovely and childish depiction of historical characters and architectural elements, like the gazebo on which the band is playing and the feeling of strangeness that Diego, Frida, Posada, and the *calavera* evoke. This "innocent" realism was intended to show the injustices of the Porfiriato. But it is overwhelmed by the charm of daily life in the open air and tainted with the pleasure the Impressionist painters captured in similar scenes.

The same central panel, in which Rivera pays homage to Posada, appears isolated from the rest of the mural where the motifs are painted with his typical obsessive method. The surrounding commotion contrasts with the silent dreamlike atmosphere of the central panel. And the portrait of Diego as a child deprived of innocence is there to perpetuate his own myth as Posada's apprentice and heir, as a rescuer of Mexican beauty, and as a spokesman for his own history. In opposition to Posada's extraordinary engravings, Diego introduced a concept of death as a decorative reference, and did not let the terrible side and the deep humor of Posada mix into his own harmonious organic vision of social and individual values.

Rivera interprets the history of Mexico as a continuous struggle to organize a social and political identity and creates from his own imagination the elements that could bring the country into the realm of modernity. In this process, he intertwines the bourgeois democratic aspect of the Mexican Revolution with vague notions on how to build a proletarian culture. The result would not be a democratization of art, but rather a didactic, sometimes doctrinaire painting in which portraiture occurs on three different levels: as part of a system that organizes nature in the manner of 18th-century humanism; as an ideological vehicle; and as the testimony to his intimate world as an individual and as an artist.

Easel Portraits

In the writing of Rivera, as well as that of critics, there seems to be a need to avoid analysis of portraiture even though it is an important and complex part of his total work. Along with the changes in Rivera's style, particularly those that took place at the end of the 1940s, he seems to have abandoned his reverence for good drawing as well as his coloristic sense, previously well balanced by his regard for classical harmony. In these late works, especially in the murals, there appears a strident, extremely decorative phase, with a more highly narrative quality clearly resembling cartoons. A few examples of this period are the murals in the Teatro de los Insurgentes of Mexico City, the landscapes of Acapulco bay, and the portrait of Linda Christian. All these works show a Rivera who, notwithstanding his reverence for history, is full of contradictions between his visual language and his political attitudes, between his Marxist ideas and his interpretation of national values.

The easel portraits of this period have been considered both frivolous and uneven. Most of them are of society women, some dressed in regional costumes and seated on an *equipal* (a type of Mexican chair that is a common motif in the artist's work from the Cubist period on), others wearing fashionable contemporary clothes. In the latter, Rivera often included pre-Hispanic artifacts set on shelves in the background. He also painted many portraits of Mexican movie stars, including that of Maria Félix, which does not present her at all as the beauty that appeared on the Mexican screens of the time, but rather as an unexpressive doll. The same can be said of his portrait of Dolores del Rio, painted a few years before, in 1938, in which, although she was an exemplar of the refined and sophisticated Mexican beauty, the actress appears with the huge eyes that are a characteristic feature of his paintings of sweet-faced children.

Taken together, these late portraits constitute a kind of painted x-ray of Mexico's emerging upper classes, linked to the growing industrialization: these politicians' wives, society matrons, and actresses were the only ones who then wore Mexican costumes and collected Mexican artifacts, merely as touches of color, as proof of their *"mexicanidad"*, in the same way that they decorated their houses with Rivera's paintings of smiling Indian women and children.

The counterparts of these paintings—which probably ended up as an essential part of the decoration of their subjects' houses—are the portraits of Indian children with big, smiling eyes and Indian women seen from behind or from the sides, with huge, beautiful calla lilies in the background or foreground that make them recognizable all over the world.

Something like a spell has been cast upon these portraits made for the bourgeoisie. In them, Rivera stands in violent contradiction to the painter of epics intended for the working class that he pretended to be. Little has been said, though, in defense of the psychological depth of these works; and even less has been undertaken in terms of their formal analysis or of an ordered chronology. His great number of easel paintings reveal a different Rivera, more openly sensual, with the special taste for and great skill at abstract drawing of *petates* (straw mats), *rebozos* (shawls), and embroidered dresses, as well as plants and flowers. His background of deep, saturated colors of indigo blue and mustard yellow are abstracted, as if he painted a wall or a backdrop for his model. He decorated the scenery with domestic items such as fruits and flowers and with the many extraordinary lilies.

Rivera was not a mimetic portraitist. He focused instead on the essential characteristics of each individual's personality, sometimes with malice, at other times with respect, or with an accent on eminence of character in the classical manner. He used some motifs of Expressionism when he exaggerated specific body parts for expressive effect, as in the previously mentioned portrait of Lupe Marín.

He made a very special use of the subject's hands as a means of defining their characters, painting them as small and stiff to suggest a limited interior life or, more often, particularly in the case of female sitters, as disproportionately large in relation to the rest of their body. Another curious feature of these portraits, which probably consisted of an adopted mannerism, that the artist employed in a large number of them is the inexactness of figural proportions. For example, one arm is often slightly longer than the other. The formal origin of this stylistic feature is probably found in Ingres, the great defender of 19th-century classicism.

In this phase of Rivera's work there is a veneration for woman that is apparent in the treatment of skin, which has a delicate, transparent quality in the manner of Renoir. One of the best examples of this is the portrait of Mrs. Beteta, whose rosy-skinned blond beauty and green eyes are framed by an indigo background and by thick vegetation. Here, one can appreciate Rivera's gourmet appraisal both of pictorial craftsmanship and of a use of color that links him with the Impressionist painters.

This personal interpretation of the Impressionist style is also evident in his love for Mexican exuberance, which is portrayed in complicated and varied foliage and sumptuous dresses. In the most skillful of his richly embroidered and highly ornamented paintings, he treats the Mexican costumes with the virtuosity of the draperies of classical sculpture. Two good examples of this are the *Portrait of Mrs. Carrillo Flores* (1948), in which the subject is wearing a beautiful dress from Tehuantepec and a turquoise blue shawl, her face displaying great serenity and dignity and the *Portrait of Dolores Olmedo* (fig. 344). There is an intense luminosity at this time in Rivera's pallette that is hardly seen in Impressionist paintings, for it was inspired by the light of the Mexican landscape and by colorful Mexican costumes.

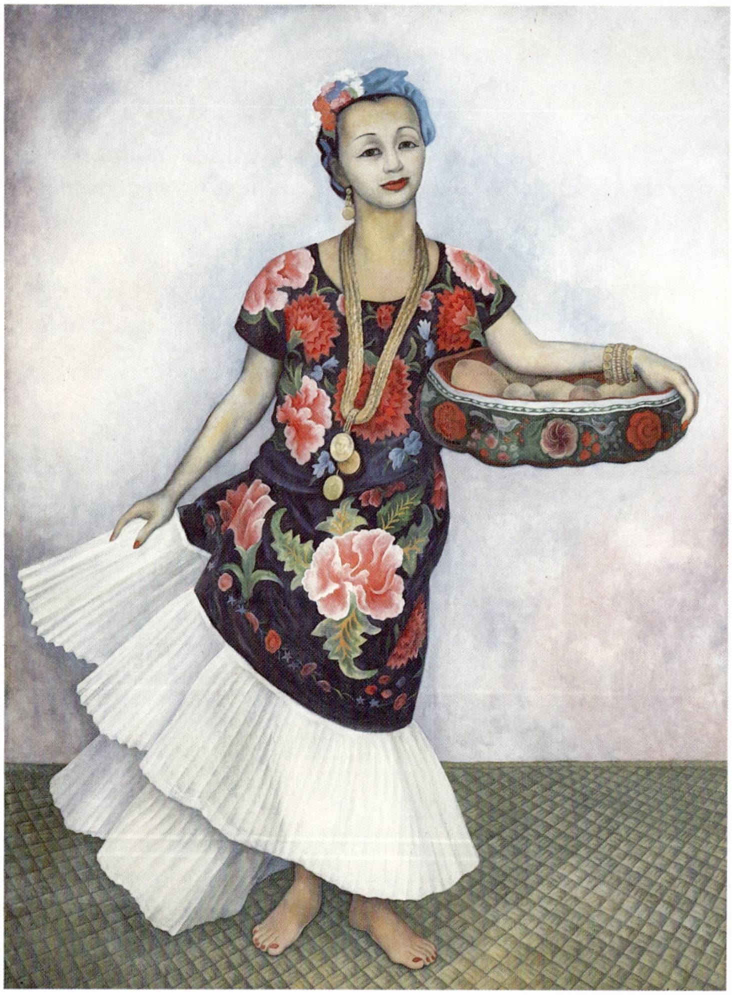

Figure 344
***Portrait of Dolores Olmedo*, 1955, oil on canvas, 200 × 152 cm. Collection of Dolores Olmedo.**

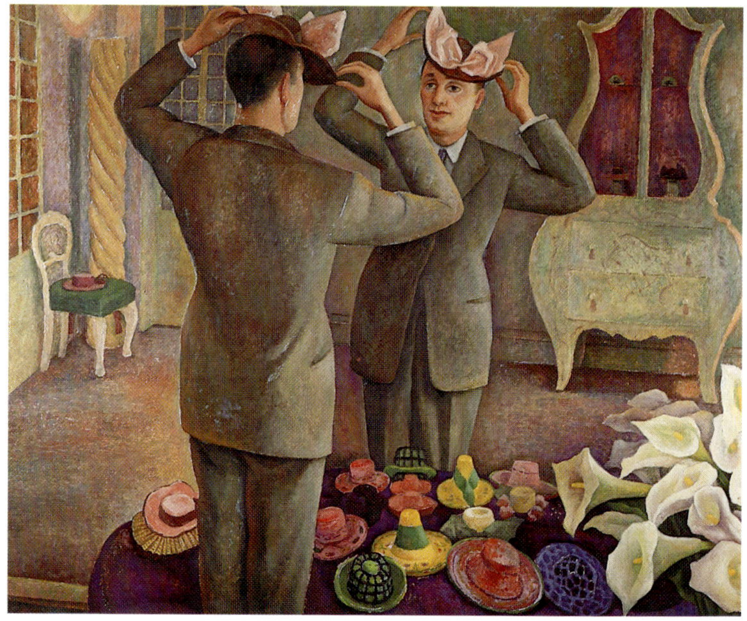

Figure 345
***The Milliner* (Henri de Chatillon), 1944, oil on masonite, 121 × 152 cm. Collection of Mr. and Mrs. Marcos Micha Levy.**

Other portraits from the same period remind us of his skill of observation. The *Portrait of Adalgisa Nery* (fig. 346) captures the sitter's elegance through a concentration on line: the spreading lines of her suit lapels, the ascendant lines of her feathered hat, and the ironic lift of her eyebrows.

Perhaps the most charming and psychologically penetrating portrait of the 1940s and 1950s is that of Henri de Chatillon, *The Milliner* (*El modista*) (fig. 345). Again, Rivera used a mirror to create a spatially complex painting, according to a pattern that fascinated him, yet one that appears effortless. The milliner pokes gentle fun at himself as he tries on a lady's hat, while the hats themselves look like so many colorful Mexican candies. In these portraits where he used the artifice of the mirror, Rivera undertook a series of experiments that are rarely found in his mural painting.

In the Guise of a Conclusion

When Rivera arrived in Spain in 1907, he was mainly preoccupied with the possibility of a different treatment of the human body. The first symptoms of change appear in works such as *El Picador* (1909), in which he exaggerates certain parts of the body in order to attain a higher expressiveness. During his Cubist phase around 1913, he painted the portrait of Jacques Lipchitz (1914) following the principles of Analytic Cubism, which was almost at its hermetic point. His intelligent and long-mediated transition from Cubism back into realism, through the lessons of Cézanne, is exemplified in his magnificent *The Mathematician* (1918). This portrait is built according to an intuitive geometry based in planes and axes; in it we find a Diego Rivera who can lay aside color and discourse and present us with the most essential part of his sensibility.

It is worth mentioning that, even during this so-called realistic period of his career, Rivera often experimented with other stylistic solutions to the problems of portraiture. In *Homage to Ana Mérida* (1952), for instance, he employed the Futurists' concept of the simultaneous presentation

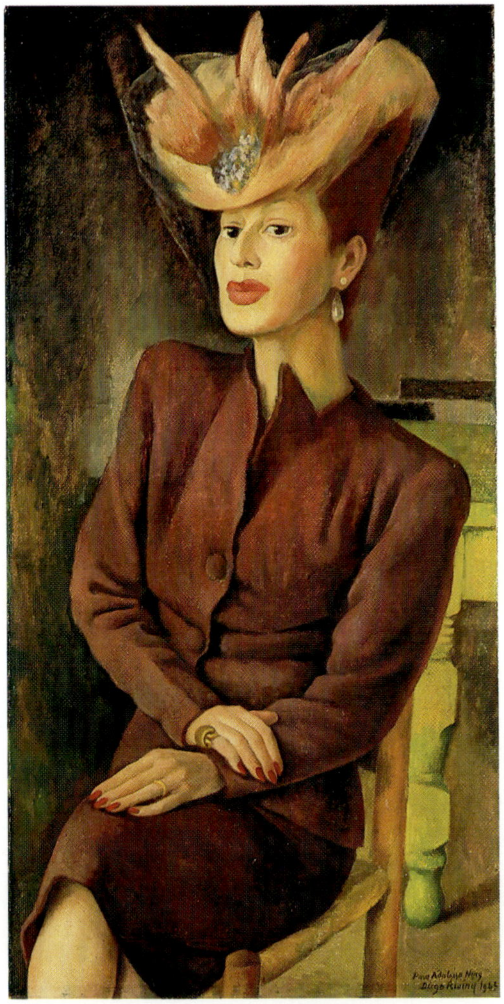

Figure 346
Portrait of Adalgisa Nery, 1945, oil on canvas, 123 × 62.4 cm. Collection of Rafael and Dora Mareyna.

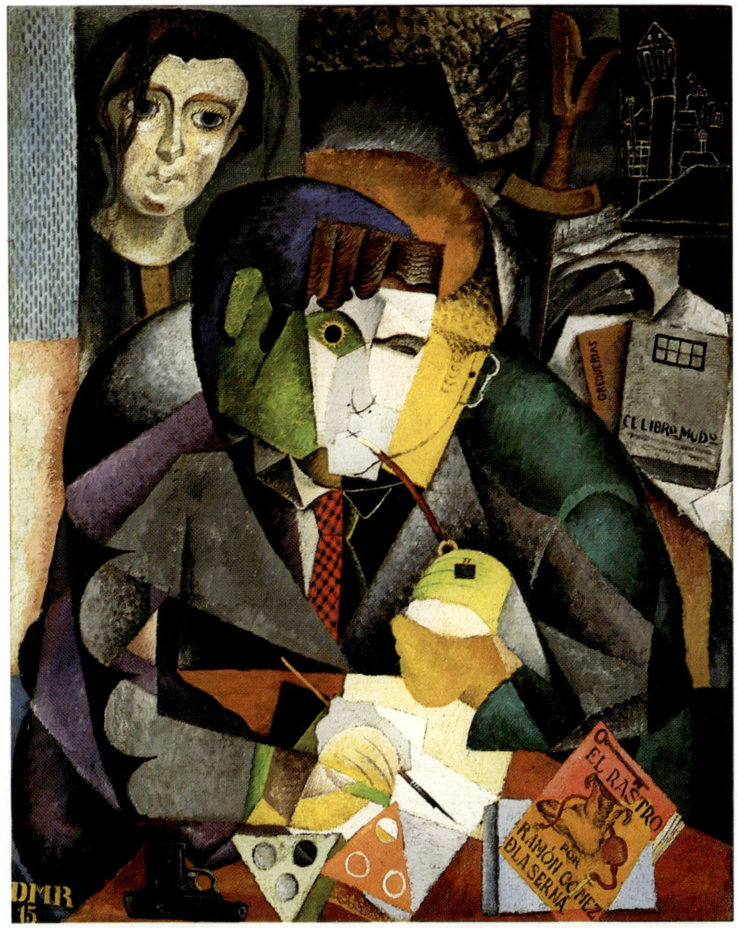

Figure 347
Portrait of Ramón Gómez de la Serna, 1915, oil on canvas, 109 × 90 cm. Collection of Placido Arango.

of multiple viewpoints to suggest movement, inspired in this case by the use of chronophotography in Marcel Duchamp's *Nude Descending a Staircase* (1911–13).

The portrait of Ana Mérida suggests a Rivera who needs a change of style and new aesthetic answers. His early years at the Academy of San Carlos and his life in Europe between 1907 and 1921, when so many changes occurred in the world of painting, were experiences that could not be laid aside. It is very evident that they did play an important part in Rivera's capacity for surprising changes, in which we can recognize his mastery of many diverse styles.

This brief analysis of some of Rivera's portraits is an attempt to illustrate the fact that it is in his quest for a new interpretation of the human figure and a new conceptualization of space that Rivera's credentials as a truly modern artist are to be found.

The portraits in his murals, however, reveal an opposite attitude. Here, Rivera seems uninterested in breaking new ground. He is instead a meticulous pilgrim who stops at the borders of similitude and who sees his mission as affirming on these walls his own understanding of the ideological concepts of the Mexican Revolution and demonstrating, through his figures, that that heroic feat is achieved. In this manner, the two missions to be accomplished in his murals—to convey the existing social order with the loving meticulousness of a botanist, and to have faith in the concept of art as an instrument of social change—place Rivera in the philosophical and visual framework of the past.

This essay intends to open a debate on Diego Rivera's work and warn of the danger that lies in defending his modernity as an easel portraitist. Rivera was, as an artist and as a man, an essentially contradictory person, with an odd and excessive personality. Perhaps this fact serves as the best guide for future analysis of various aspects of his work and explains the diversity of style and intent in his murals and his easel portraits.

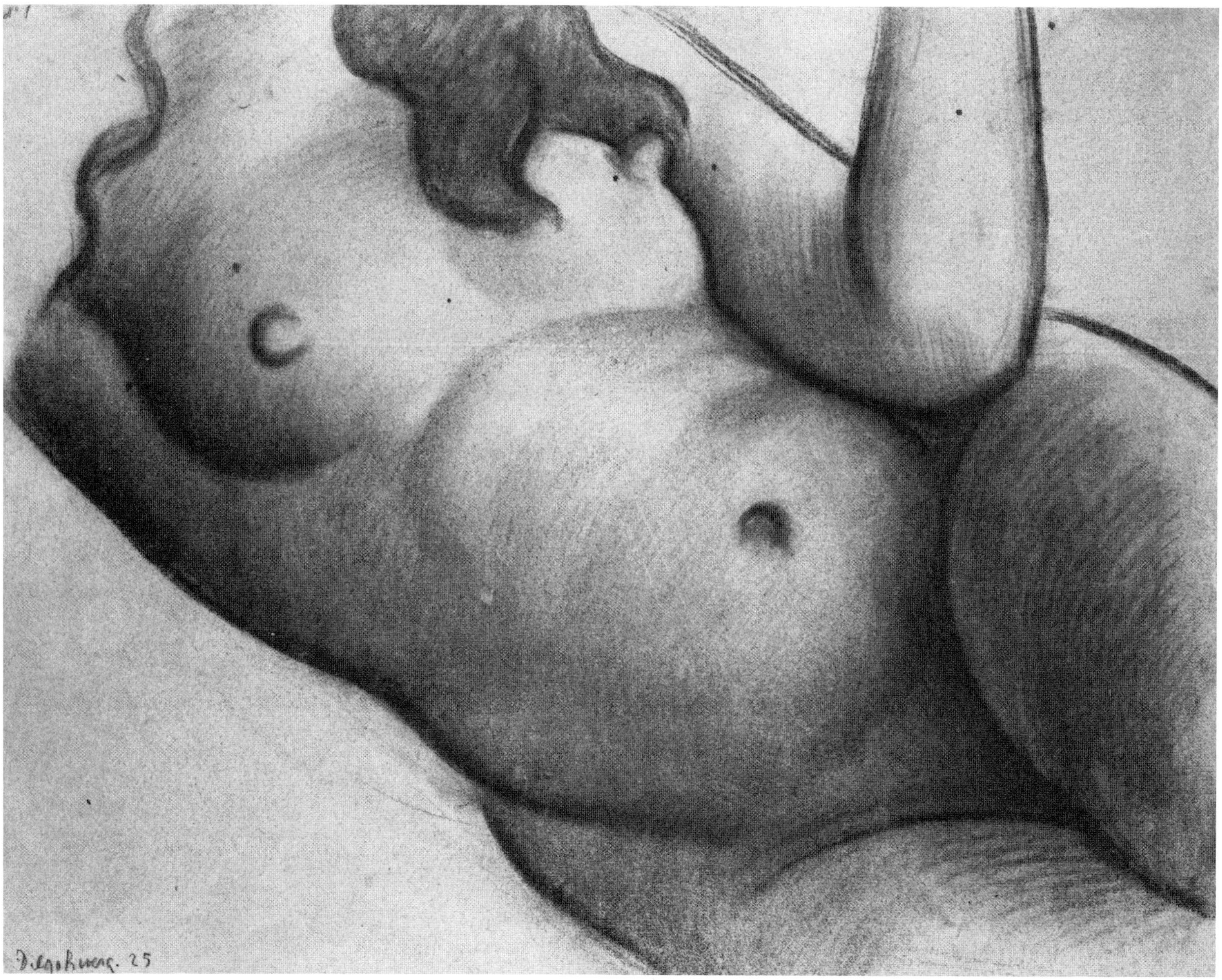

Rivera as a Draftsman

Ellen Sharp

Figure 348
***Torso of a Woman*, 1925, charcoal on tan paper, 47.9 × 63 cm. Philadelphia Museum of Art, Purchase, Lola Downin Peck Fund from the estate of Carl Zigrosser (1976–97–96).**

In July of 1921 Diego Rivera, at the age of thirty-five, after working in Europe for fourteen years, returned to Mexico. His art was to take an entirely new direction in his homeland. As he himself later related:

My homecoming produced an aesthetic exhilaration which it is impossible to describe. . . . I was in the very center of the plastic world, where forms and colors existed in absolute purity. . . . The very first sketch I completed amazed me. It was actually good! From then on, I worked confidently and contentedly. Gone was the doubt and inner conflict which had tormented me in Europe. I painted as naturally as I breathed, spoke, or perspired. My style was born as children are born, in a moment, except the birth had come after a torturous pregnancy of thirty-five years.[1]

Rivera had been persuaded to return to Mexico by an invitation from those in power in the government to join a cultural revolution—that is, more specifically, to participate in a project that has come to be known as the Mexican Mural Renaissance. It was typical of Rivera that he would immediately set down his impressions of his return to his native land in a sketch—that he should express his exuberance and delight through a graphic medium. From infancy he had had a passion for drawing, displaying the natural talent that was reinforced and refined by rigorous training at the Academy of San Carlos. The great mural projects that he was to undertake were built on the solid foundation of his genius and skill as a draftsman. In planning his murals he used drawing in much the same way as an architect does in designing a building. The drawings he created in preparation for murals in Mexico and the United States from 1922 to 1933, in all their clarity, beauty, and originality, will be the focus of this essay. However, to understand how he arrived at his more mature drawing style, it is necessary to review his formative years as an artist—the long period of gestation that Rivera referred to, with characteristic colorful hyperbole, as "torturous."

A drawing of a train with locomotive, car, and caboose (fig. 349) made by Rivera at the age of three is the earliest drawing that has survived as an indication of his precocious talent. It is most interesting for its subject matter, the first evidence of Rivera's lifelong interest in machines and technology. Several of Rivera's biographers relate that his father, recognizing his young son's talent and wishing to encourage it, set aside a room in their home in Guanajuato as a studio. Everything was removed from the room and blackboards were arranged around the walls, none of them higher than the point the child could reach standing on a chair. Rivera, rather than playing with other children, spent many hours there, drawing on the walls or lying on the floor producing countless sketches drawn from his imagination.[2]

Two later pencil drawings, now in the collection of Rafael Coronel, *Wounded Rider on Horseback* (1895) and *Devils Tossing a Devil in a Blanket* (1895; figs. 350 and 351), have a lively, calligraphic line. They recall the early drawings of such master draftsmen as Henri de Toulouse-Lautrec or Pablo Picasso, both of whom can be compared to Rivera as artists who

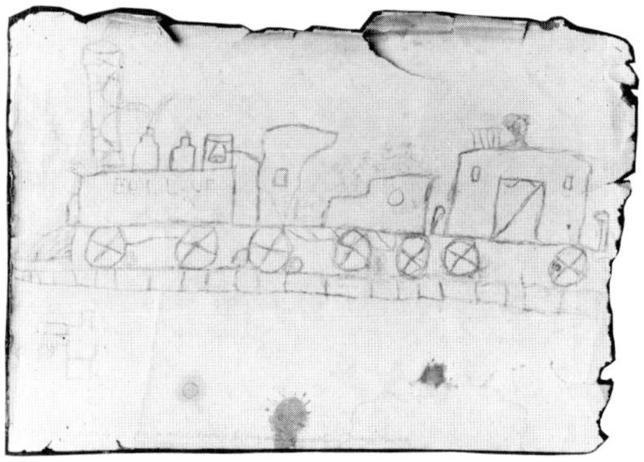

Figure 349
The Locomotive, 1889, pencil, 34 × 44.2 cm. Museo Diego Rivera-Anahuacalli.

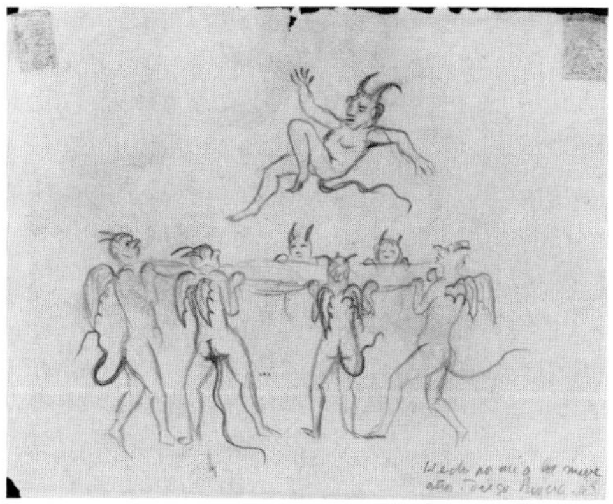

Figure 351
Devils Tossing a Devil in a Blanket, 1895, pencil, 12 × 18 cm. Collection of Rafael Coronel.

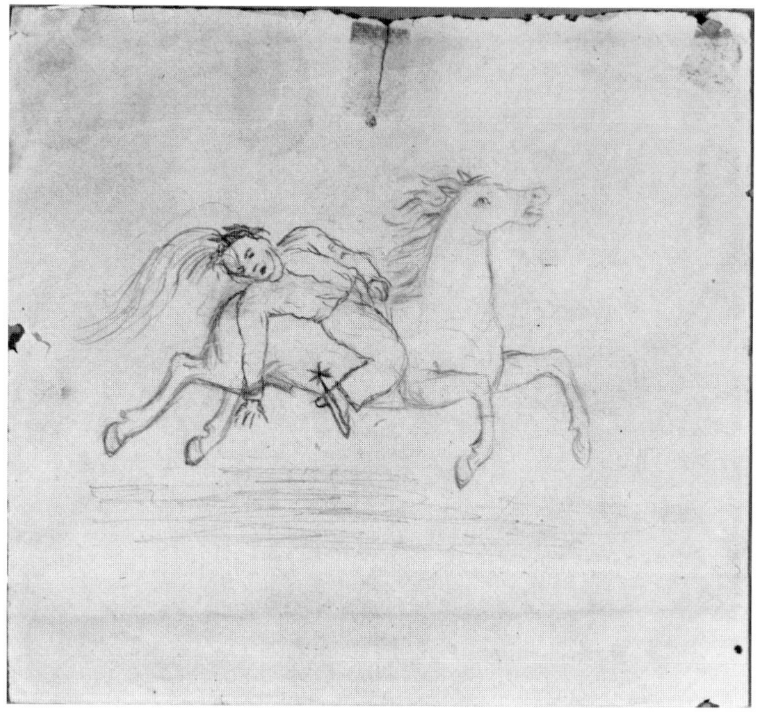

Figure 350
Wounded Rider on Horseback, 1895, pencil, 12.4 × 13.7 cm. Collection of Rafael Coronel.

as young children evidenced an exceptional talent for drawing, which they developed into a highly expressive tool as a basis for their oeuvre. Rivera's action-filled *Wounded Rider on Horseback* reminds us of Picasso's pencil drawing *Bullfight, Malaga* (1890) (Barcelona, Museo Picasso), executed when the Spanish artist was the same age as Rivera.

In 1892 Rivera's family moved to Mexico City and, four years later, he enrolled in night classes at the Academy of San Carlos, which at that time included the National School of Fine Arts as well as the School of Architecture. He was a regular student at the academy from 1898 to 1905.

Before enrolling in painting courses, all students at the academy were required to complete the course in life drawing, and courses in life drawing were only open to students who had completed the tedious copying of lithographic charts of the human anatomy, models of geometric solids, ornaments in low and high relief, and figures from bas reliefs and plaster casts (see figs. 7 and 11). That Rivera accomplished these steps with amazing success for one so young is demonstrated by drawings still preserved in the archives of the academy. Especially handsome is *Head of a Woman* (fig. 9), a copy after a lithograph by Charles Gleyre. This drawing is a reminder of the influence of one of Rivera's teachers, Santiago Rebull, who continued the classical tradition of the Nazarenes that had been established by Pelegrín Clavé, director of the academy from 1847 to 1868 and an ardent admirer of Johann Friedrich Overbeck and Peter Cornelius, members of this German expatriate group who lived and painted in Italy in the first decades of the 19th century. Rebull was also a disciple of the great French 19th-century draftsman Jean-Auguste-Dominique Ingres. Rebull early recognized Rivera's ability as a draftsman and encouraged him. Other teachers at the academy to whom Rivera acknowledged a debt were Félix Parra and the landscapist José María Velasco, who, in his drawing classes, taught perspective and optical theory, based on geometry and the trigonometry of space. What significance the Catalonian artist Antonio Fabrés Costa, Rivera's painting instructor from 1903 to 1905, held for the artist is a matter of conjecture, since he is not mentioned in Rivera's memoirs. In contrast to Parra, who gave his students prints after the masters to copy, Fabrés relied on photographs, and his position as subdirector of the academy no doubt gave his views considerable weight, as he himself stated: "You know very well that, in my system of drawing, approved by the Government so that today IT IS THE LAW, there is no such thing as drawing from prints. If we keep it for the first years it is only with the understanding that, eventually, we shall be able to replace the prints with photographs."[3] Perhaps we can assume that Rivera's later use of photographs for reference in constructing elements of the composition of his complex fresco cycles was a practice introduced to him by Fabrés. Fabrés seems to have prepared Rivera well for his encounter with Spanish realism as practiced by the then-renowned Spanish master Eduardo Chicharro y Agüera, with whom Rivera worked after obtaining a pension to study in Spain from 1907 to 1909.

Only a few drawings have been located from the period in Mexico after Rivera left the academy in 1906 or from his first trip to Europe (1907–10). Those that we have had an opportunity to view confirm what his paintings from those years convey. Rivera was not yet cognizant of the revolutionary Cubist avant-garde. His drawings reflect the art movements dominant in Mexico at the turn of the century and his association with the Mexican neo-Symbolist group *Savia Moderna.* This is especially evident in a charcoal, gouache, and ink drawing of 1906, *Dead Horse* (fig. 16), a macabre, mysterious image in which the undulating trail of carnivorous insects, which have picked clean the skeleton of a horse in the foreground of the drawing, is interwoven with the sinuous ribbon of a stream that bisects the composition and whose curves are repeated in the swaying forms of the trees at the right. Two drawings of 1906, *Confluence of the Rivers* (fig. 15), a pastel, and *Cerro de las campanas, Querétaro* (fig. 18), a gouache, are Whistlerian in mood and style, with their vaporous atmosphere and delicate hues. Rivera's 1909 trip to Bruges, a city beloved by the Symbolists, is recorded in a charcoal drawing of a night scene, *Béguinage à Bruges* (fig. 25). This drawing, in which the shadowy forms emerging out of the darkness are created by striations of black charcoal, is reminiscent of the drawings of Eugène Carrière and Henri Fantin-Latour. It is also a significant document since it is dedicated to Angeline Beloff, the Russian painter and printmaker who, after their first meeting in Bruges, was to become Rivera's companion and common-law wife until his return to Mexico in 1921.

No drawings by Rivera have been located for the years 1910–12; and for the period 1913–17, the years when Rivera was working in the Cubist mode, only about fifteen drawings are today available for study—five are included in this exhibition. None of these works has the dense shaping of form, achieved with short, feathery, angular strokes of the pencil or pen laid closely together, or the architectonic structure seen in the Analytic Cubist drawings of Picasso and Georges Braque. Rivera's Cubist drawings, such as *Still Life with Teapot* (1913; fig. 31) or *Paris Cityscape—"Foll"* ca. 1913; (fig. 352), have a clarity of outline and a linear delicacy that are more in the manner of the drawings of Juan Gris of 1912–13 and Picasso's pasted paper and charcoal drawings of the same period. In addition, Rivera's drawings have a more precise geometric composition. Rivera's *Still Life with Carafe* (1914; fig. 43), is his only known paper collage. It is an accomplished Synthetic Cubist work with collage and gouache combined with charcoal. The graceful curve of the carafe and the skillful simulation of the wood grain of the table, both executed in charcoal, contrast effectively with the more ornate floral background in gouache.

After the war, many of the artists involved with Cubism turned away for a while from their experiments and returned to traditional modes of expression. It has been suggested that this Neoclassical period was a reaction to the chaos and brutality of the war years, that it evidenced a need for order and simplicity. Like Picasso and Gris, Rivera created at this time a number of realistic portrait drawings in a style that has been termed Ingresque. In contrast to Picasso's portrait drawings of these years (1917–20), which are usually executed in pure outline with minimal shading and the subject shown three-quarters length, seated, Rivera's portraits are bust-length and more sculptural. The focus is concentrated on the facial expression, with the shoulders and chest lightly sketched. In these portraits Rivera demonstrates his versatility as a draftsman in masterly fashion as he varies the type of modeling of the face to suit the character of his subject. For example, his sensitive, tender portrait of Angeline Beloff of 1917 (fig. 59) uses a delicate pencil stippling technique, which is intensified around the eyes, nose, and mouth. Rivera's mistress at that time, Marevna Vorobëv, described Angeline: "To me, she always looked like a kind of bird, a little parakeet . . . this intelligent woman who looked so frail but was endowed with uncommon strength of mind. . . .[4] Bertram Wolfe has also provided a verbal portrait of Angeline that parallels Rivera's interpretation: "Birdlike in her movements and lightness, in the poise of her head slightly tilted to one side when she was lost in contemplation, in the delicately aquiline profile, in the lips always pursed into the shadow of a meditative smile. . . ."[5]

In the *Portrait of the Engraver Lebedeff* (1918; fig. 62), Rivera models the fleshy planes of the face more broadly, and the contrasts of the light and dark areas are greater. Lebedeff confronts us with a direct, quizzical gaze. Although Rivera's portrait drawings of this period are often compared with those of the 19th-century master Ingres, there is really more of an affinity with the portraits of the Nazarenes, to whose work, as has been noted above, Rivera was introduced during his student years. The penetrating yet introspective scrutiny of Lebedeff reminds us of similar attitudes seen in such portraits as Overbeck's *Self-Portrait* of 1844 (Florence, Uffizi).

During the same years that Rivera was creating these realistic portraits employing classical drawing techniques, he also drew still lifes, no longer Cubist, but reflecting his admiration for Cézanne and the influence of Juan Gris. In these still lifes, he utilizes the same objects again and again but in different arrangements, most often against the same background, a wall with wood paneling. Like the portraits, the still

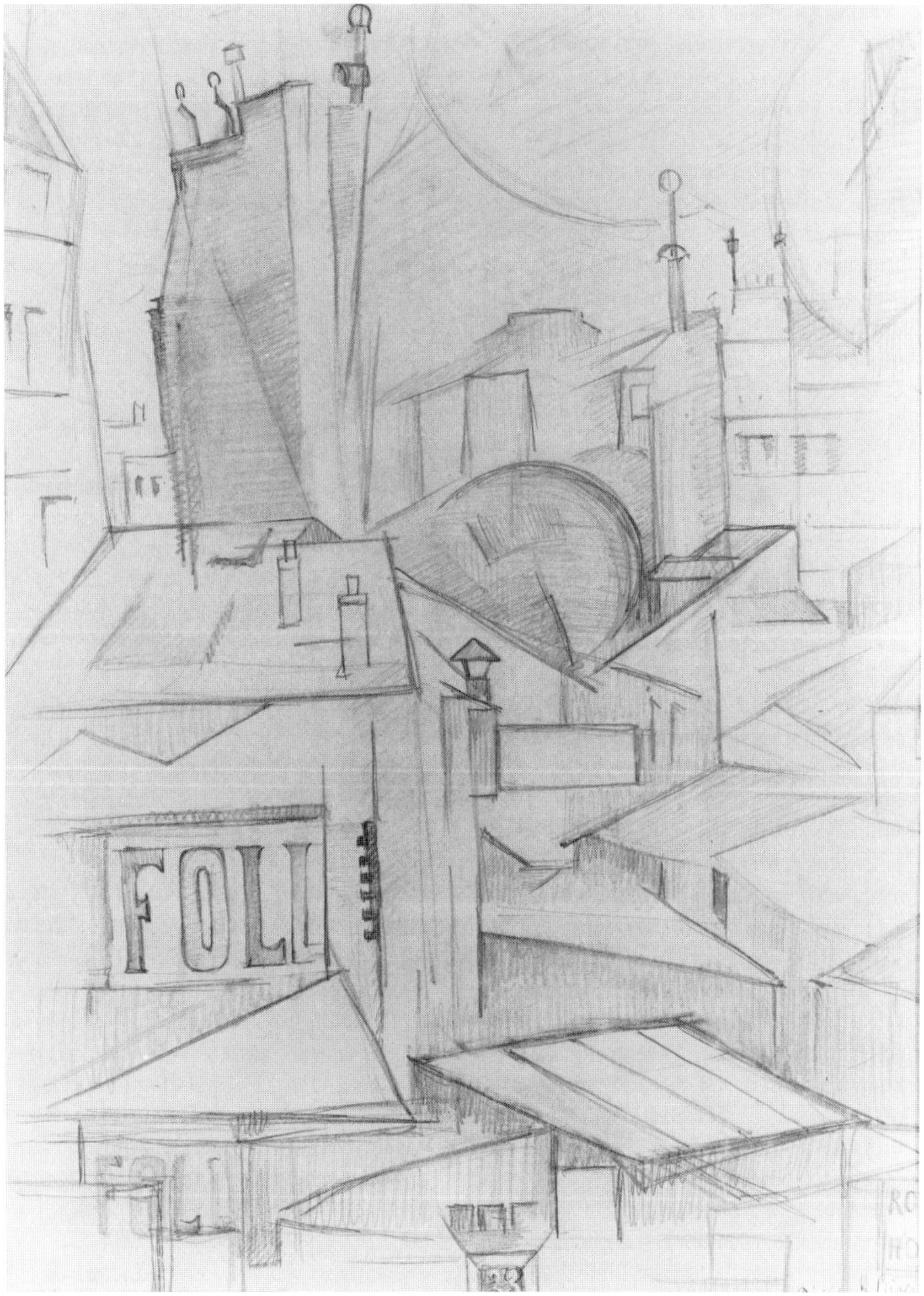

Figure 352
Paris Cityscape—"Foll,"
ca. 1913, pencil, 33.4 × 25.8 cm. Guanajuato, Museo Diego Rivera.

lifes are executed on fine laid papers with French watermarks and, as in the *Portrait of the Engraver Lebedeff,* by rubbing his pencil with varying degrees of pressure over the surface of the sheet, Rivera picked up the tooth of the paper, thus creating textured shading. This technique is evident in the handsome still life *Bowl of Fruit* (1918; fig. 60), in which the globular forms of the fruit are juxtaposed with the rhythmical ovals of the bowl. This still life emphasizes Rivera's penchant for volumetric, round forms. His *Nude Woman,* a pencil drawing of 1919 (fig. 353), is further evidence of this inclination. The apple-shaped breasts and the exaggerated, eccentric curves of the body of this nude recall the woman in Picasso's *Sleeping Peasants* (New York, The Museum of Modern Art), a tempera, watercolor, and pencil drawing of the same year. This predilection for monumental nudes represents yet another aspect of the Neoclassicism of this period.

Rivera's *Portrait of Jean-Pierre Faure* (1920; fig. 72) is yet another example of Rivera's proficiency as a draftsman. This pure contour drawing with its minimal shading again has parallels with Picasso's Neoclassical drawings of these years, as well as with those of Gris. The informality of the pose of the young man and the angularity of the line suggest that this is a rapid sketch rather than a more finished portrait or still life such as those previously cited. Throughout his career Rivera sketched constantly. So inveterate a habit was this that those who knew him recall that he always had sketchbooks of different sizes at the ready, tucked in several pockets about his person. The earliest substantial body of sketches that we have available for study are those that he made on his trip to Italy in 1920–21, a trip financed by Alberto Pani (see figs. 70 and 71), then the Mexican ambassador to France, so that Rivera might study the art

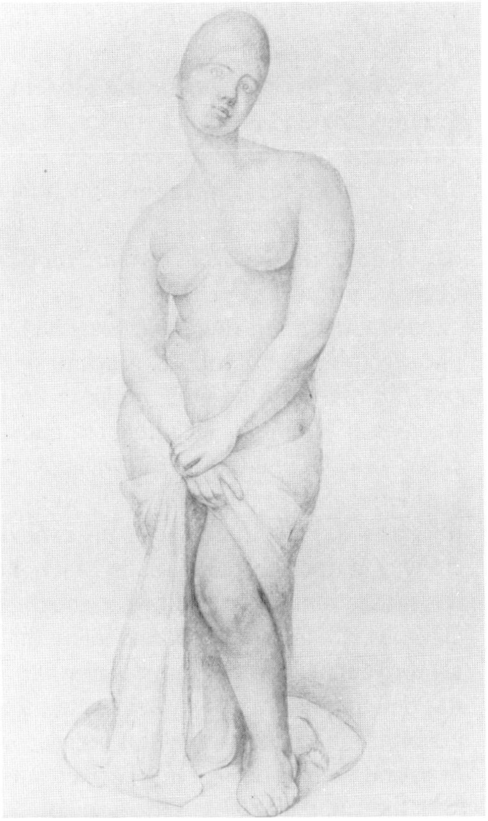

Figure 353
***Nude Woman,* 1919, pencil, 47.8 × 31.3 cm. Guanajuato, Museo Diego Rivera.**

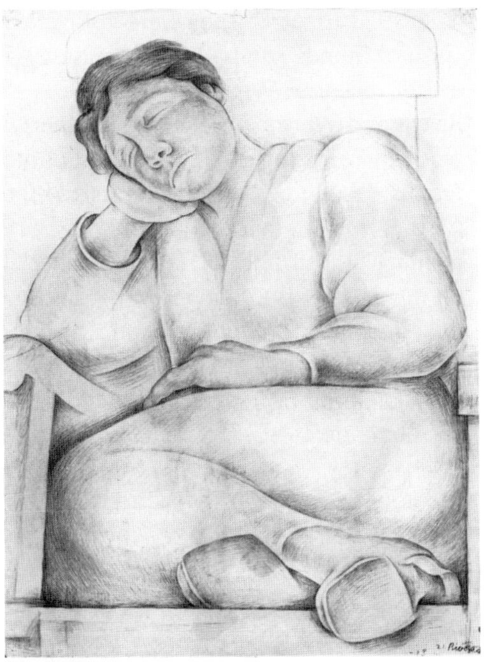

Figure 354
***Sleeping Woman,* 1921, pencil, 58.4 × 45.7 cm. Harvard University, Fogg Art Museum, Bequest of Meta and Paul J. Sachs (1965.436).**

of Italy, especially the mural work of the great artists of the quattrocento and the cinquecento. Rivera recalled: "My Italian travels took me from Milan southward to Florence, Rome, Naples, and Pompeii, and then northward, along the Adriatic coast, through Venice. . . . During my seventeen months in Italy, I completed more than 300 sketches from the frescoes of the masters and from life."[6]

Many of these sketches have disappeared, or are scattered widely throughout public and private collections in Mexico, the United States, and Europe, often unidentified as being from his Italian journey. Fortunately, Angeline Beloff entrusted a significant group of these drawings to Jean Charlot, who kept them bound together. Of the thirty-one sketches in the Charlot collection, twelve are studies of paintings or frescoes with color notes, analyses of the geometric construction of the compositions, or indications of the scale of the works in relation to their architectural setting; eleven are sketches of heads of men and women, quite obviously done from life. There is one study of Etruscan sculpture and one genre figure, a female drug addict giving herself an injection. One sheet is especially interesting (fig. 73) for we can see that Rivera is already concerned with the practical problems of the muralist. He noted on the sketch of a scaffold: "A scaffold for working on ceilings, very simple to move by sliding it over planks greased with lard, slipped under the front legs raised by means of wooden screw levers."[7]

While in Italy Rivera visited museums containing Etruscan antiquities. The relationship between Etruscan art and pre-Hispanic art seems to have fascinated him. The inventory of drawings from his estate, now housed in the Museo Frida Kahlo, lists "Notes and sketches of little Etruscan bronzes in the museum at Arezzo similar to Prehispanic art." There were several sketches of Etruscan vases in the collections of Angeline Beloff and of Alberto Misrachi, which have been dispersed and cannot be presently located. A finished drawing in the collection of the Philadelphia Museum of Art (fig. 74) is a copy of a well-known Etruscan terra-cotta canopic urn (from Castiglione del Lago, second half of the seventh century B.C., Florence, Museo Archeologico), which itself recalls a clay vessel in the Museo Diego Rivera–Anahuacalli (Teotihuacán II, first–third centuries A.D.). This later vessel is in the form of a seated hunchback, who wears similar large, round pendant earrings and whose arms likewise emerge from the body of the vase. The wit and humor in Etruscan art would have attracted Rivera. A lively humor pervades much of his work throughout his career, from the previously mentioned rambunctious sketch of devils done at the age of nine to the studies for the murals at the University of Mexico's stadium, executed when he was in his sixties, with their insouciant dancers and ball players patterned after figures in pre-Hispanic codices (see fig. 243). The humanizing of the funerary urn to suggest the figure of the departed would also have drawn Rivera to this particular work. In his drawing he makes the eyes, nose, and mouth more humanoid than in the original urn. His pencil delighted in delineating the full, round form of the body of the urn, its curve accentuated by the angular, winglike arms that emerge from it. The vase is depicted from a low viewpoint as if it were on a shelf slightly above the artist's head. The focal point of the drawing is the head of the vase, which is more densely shaded than the rest of the composition.

Another finished drawing from his Italian trip is *Sleeping Woman* (fig. 354). The massive figure of a woman asleep in a chair is seen from a similar low vantage point. These two drawings are prophetic of the direction that Rivera's draftsmanship was to take in Mexico—simplified, monumental, humanistic, often with parallels in pre-Hispanic art. A smaller version of the sleeping woman, a quick sketch, has recently come to light on the art market. Rivera, if he was attracted to a face or a figure, would often lightly sketch it, repeat the image more fully delineated, and then

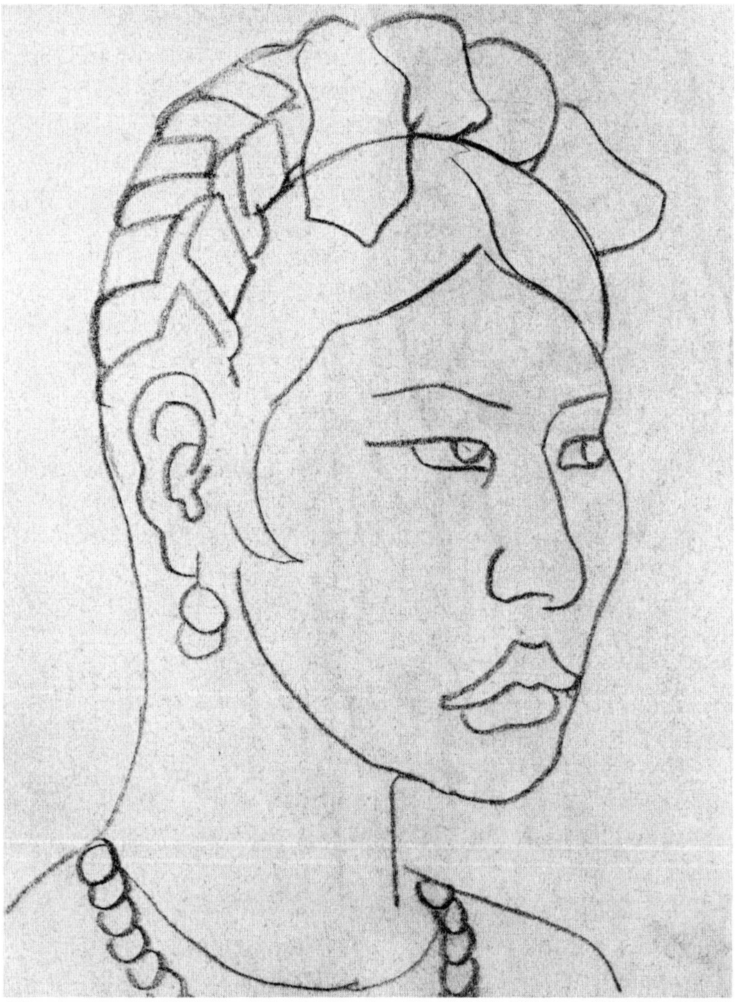

Figure 355
Woman of Tehuantepec,
from a sketchbook of Tehuantepec scenes, 1923, pencil, 22.2 × 16.5 cm. Private Collection.

finally develop it into a larger, finished drawing, or incorporate it into a painting or fresco.

By the time Rivera returned to Mexico, he had already demonstrated his skill in a variety of media—pencil, charcoal, ink, gouache, and watercolor—but in his very first Mexican drawings, created for the mural *Creation* in the Anfiteatro Bolívar, we see his power as a draftsman expanding. There followed a decade (1921–32) of astonishing achievement.

An emphasis on monumentality of form, a trend that had begun to emerge in his portraits and still lifes of 1917–19 and in some of the drawings he created on his trip to Italy, is full-blown in the series of drawings of heads and hands for the allegorical figures in *Creation,* executed in charcoal and red chalk, often on a gray-blue paper (see fig. 82). In the studies for Wisdom and Science (figs. 83 and 84), the hands seem to grow out of the sheet, filling it almost completely with their graceful gestures. We are reminded of the frescoes in the Vatican by Raphael and Michelangelo, in which the gesturing hands play a major role in the unifying rhythm of the composition.

In the studies for the chapel of the Escuela Nacional de Agricultura at Chapingo, such as *Torso of a Woman* (1925; fig. 348) and *Back of a Seated Nude* (1926; fig. 108), the figures' breadth of form and their scale in relation to the size of the sheet are similar to the studies of hands. However, the contours of these later drawings are more sharply defined with bolder strokes of charcoal. The model for *Torso of a Woman,* which is a study for the fresco panel entitled *The Liberated Earth* on the altar wall of the chapel, was Rivera's wife Guadalupe Marín. Rivera recalled that in 1921 he created his first portrait of Guadalupe, then a second and a third. Then he made four or five sketches of her hands: "Held at her breast, her extraordinary hands had the beauty of tree roots or eagle talons."[8]

The model for *Seated Nude* was the photographer Tina Modotti. Modotti posed for most of the other nudes in the frescoes at Chapingo, including the panel called *The Virgin Earth* on the wall opposite the altar of the chapel. The study for this panel is not as dramatic as the charcoal study of the torso of Guadalupe Marín, but it is just as sensual. In contrast to the vigorous strokes and broad modeling that capture Guadalupe's voluptuousness, in this drawing Rivera conveys with the shading of his pencil the softness of female flesh and with gently curving strokes outlines the languid curves of the body of Modotti (see fig. 100).

It is tempting to speculate on the possibility of artistic interaction between Rivera and the photographer Edward Weston, who was with Modotti in Mexico from 1923 to 1926. They were in Rivera's circle of friends and part of the stimulating artistic milieu of Mexico at that time. Rivera and Weston admired each other's work and exchanged drawings and photographs.[9] We know that Rivera utilized the portrait Weston made of him in 1924 when painting his self-portrait "as an architect" on the walls of the stairwell of the Secretaría de Educación Pública. Jean Charlot, who was one of Rivera's assistants for *Creation,* and for the first frescoes at the Secretaría, relates:

While Rivera was painting "The Day of the Dead in the City" in the second court of the Ministry we talked about Weston. I said that his work was precious for us in that it delineated the limitations of our craft and staked out optical plots forbidden to the brush. Diego, rendering meanwhile a wood texture with the precise skill and speed of a sign painter, countered that in his opinion Weston did blaze a path for

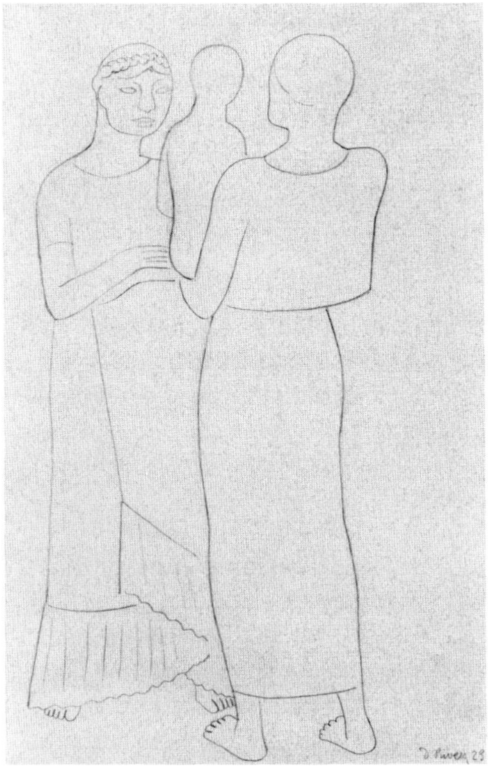

Figure 356
***Two Standing Women Conversing, Tehuantepec,* 1923, pencil, 33 × 21.6 cm. San Francisco Museum of Modern Art, Albert M. Bender Collection, Gift of Albert M. Bender (35.2705).**

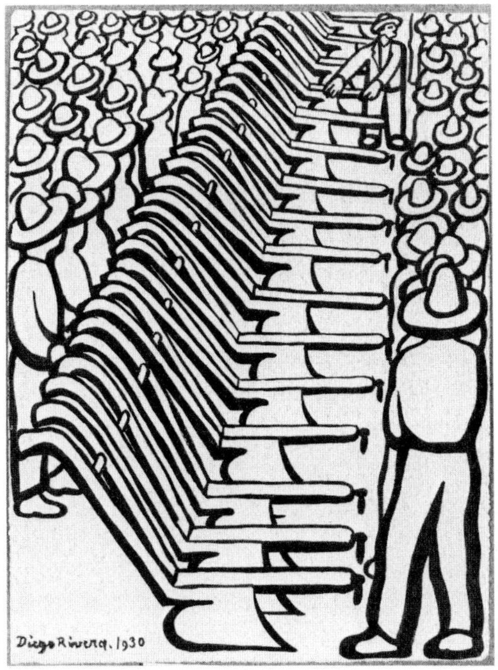

Figure 357
From an album illustrating the *Convenciones de la Liga de Communidades Agrarias y Sindicatos Campesinos del Estado de Tamaulipas,* 1930, brush in black ink, 31.1 × 23.5 cm. Guanajuato, Museo Rivera, Marte R. Gómez Collection (INBA).

a better way of seeing, and, as a corollary, of painting. It is with such humility at heart that Rivera had painted with a brush in one hand and a Weston photograph in the other his self-portrait in the staircase of the Ministry.[10]

Weston, like Rivera, had experienced a regeneration of his art when he came to Mexico. Realizing that Mexico had sharpened his vision and shaped the future direction of his art, Weston later observed: "Go to Mexico, and there one finds an even greater drama, values more intense—black and white, cutting contrasts, am I theatrical because I see important forms importantly?"[11] In Mexico Weston abandoned completely his previous pictorial approach with soft focus and painterly effects. His work gained in purity and strength as did Rivera's draftsmanship.

After his return to Mexico not only did Rivera produce remarkable drawings in a sculptural mode, but he also created pure outline drawings with greater virtuosity. At the end of 1922 Rivera traveled south to Tehuantepec, one of Mexico's most picturesque regions. The trip was financed by José Vasconcelos, the minister of education, who initiated and was in charge of the government's mural program. After viewing *Creation,* which is European in inspiration and style, Vasconcelos wanted Rivera to learn more about Mexican art and culture. The trip was an unforgettable experience for Rivera, and the sketches that he made were to serve as inspiration for future works for many years. Rivera was particularly impressed by the majestic women of Tehuantepec, who, with their long dresses falling in stiff folds and their braided coiffures, seemed like figures from antique Greek or Roman art. In a sketchbook he depicted a series of heads in profile and full face, the contours outlined with strong, sure strokes of a soft pencil, endowing the female physiognomy with great dignity (see fig. 355). In *Two Standing Women Conversing, Tehuantepec* (1923; fig. 356), one of three similar drawings in the San Francisco Museum of Modern Art, Rivera with economy of line and clarity of outline suggests a casual encounter in village life. The Tehuantepec outline drawings have a casual serenity which is not present in the charcoal drawings of 1926, such as *Drunken Woman* (fig. 104) and *The Eating Place.* In these later drawings, the outlines are bolder and seem to be deliberately employed to convey the tougher, more miserable aspects of Indian life. In *Drunken Woman,* Rivera suggests with curvilinear strokes the weight of the inert body that an Indian woman and man are trying to lift and carry away.

During the years 1929–31 Rivera made numerous drawings as illustrations for various publications. Executed in brush and black ink, they are yet another type of pure outline drawing in his repertoire. At the Museo Diego Rivera, in his birthplace in Guanajuato, there are three albums containing 133 drawings in this technique, which were commissioned by Marte R. Gómez to illustrate the meetings of the League of Agrarian Communities and Peasant Syndicates of the State of Tamaulipas in 1926, 1927, and 1928. These drawings utilize a broad brushstroke to outline form, and areas of solid black ink highlight many of the compositions. In a single drawing repetition of certain motifs, such as hands, or the heads of peasants wearing sombreros, is a powerful compositional device for conveying a mass reaction (fig. 357). There are many effective vignettes in these albums utilizing hands holding sickles, ears of corn, the sun, the moon, or the stars. Rivera designed a beautiful cover for these albums using those motifs in red and black on parchment (fig. 103).

Rivera also designed covers for *Mexican Folkways,* a magazine published by Frances Toor in English and Spanish to promote interest in the study of Mexican culture and art. Rivera served as art editor and wrote numerous articles for this periodical. His cover with the sun rising behind two feathered serpents was used for several issues and was printed in different color combinations. On the drawing in this exhibition (fig. 102), Rivera's penciled note indicates that two colors are to be used. Rivera created two other cover designs for *Mexican Folkways,* which were equally as effective as this one.

For illustrations in Stuart Chase's book *Mexico: A Study of Two Americas* (New York: MacMillan, 1931), Rivera utilized the same brush in black ink technique. The drawings for this book do not have the strength and power of those in the Tamaulipas albums. Their outlines are not as broad, their forms not so angular. The general mood is less somber, gently satirical rather than militant (see figs. 156 and 157). Rivera's brush displays a more energetic, pliant line in the drawings he made in 1931 as illustrations for an English translation by John Weatherwax of *Popol Vuh,* the sacred book of the ancient Quiché Maya (see fig. 152). This translation and the drawings by Rivera were never published. Especially effective in this group of illustrations is the one depicting the hero-brothers, Sun Tiger and Moon Tiger, extracting the emerald teeth from the Giant Macaw, Seven-Times-the-Color-of-Fire, and replacing them with kernels of corn (fig. 358). The excruciating pain of the miserable giant is graphically expressed in the jagged, nervous rhythm of Rivera's line.

All of Rivera's talent as a draftsman and the skill and versatility that he had acquired in his years as an apprentice and as an independent artist in Europe were drawn upon when he created his great frescoes. Like the great Renaissance and Baroque masters, in developing his compositions he used drawing in the classic manner. First thoughts, sketches, compositional studies, studies of individual figures, full-scale cartoons, all are represented in his oeuvre. Unfortunately, a complete series of drawings of each type for one mural project is not available for exhibition. The drawings have been scattered across several continents in public and private collections and many have disappeared. A large group of over fourteen hundred drawings, now housed in the Museo Frida Kahlo in Coyoacán as part of the Rivera trust, cannot be lent. However, we do have some fine examples of each type.

The Tehuantepec sketchbook contains rapid sketches of women and children bathing (fig. 359), which were later more fully developed and incorporated into the first panels executed for the frescoes in the Secretaría de Educación Pública. We have cited above some of his most beautiful studies for individual figures in the frescoes for the chapel at Chapingo. There are several compositional studies, including one for the panel entitled *Day of the Dead in the Country* in the second court of the Secretaría (fig. 98) and those for the loggia of the Palacio de Cortés in Cuernavaca (figs. 135, 136, and 266). Other drawings show the entire composition for a large wall surface, such as the *History of Mexico* for the stairway of the Palacio Nacional (fig. 360), *Production and Manufacture of Automobile Motors,* and *Manufacture of Automobile Bodies and Final Assembly* for the north and south walls of the Garden Court at the Detroit Institute of Arts, and *Man at the Crossroads* for Rockefeller Center (fig. 395). Although these particular drawings are not final versions, they nevertheless have all the basic elements of the final composition. Rivera had a remarkable ability to conceptualize swiftly a complex, immensely detailed subject, fitting it skillfully into the architectural elements of the space.

With regard to his mural for the stairway of the Palacio Nacional, he recalled that, on his way home from Moscow in 1928, he embarked for Mexico from Hamburg and that on deck during the voyage he watched a brilliant sunset: "At that moment, the conception of the National Palace stairway mural which I had begun to plan in 1922, flashed to completion in my mind—so clearly that immediately upon my arrival in Mexico, I sketched it as easily as if I were copying paintings I had already done."[12]

Rivera's detailed compositional studies with their multitudes of small figures provide a striking contrast to the full-scale cartoons that have survived. The Detroit Institute of Arts is fortunate to have in its collection thirteen of the cartoons for the *Detroit Industry* frescoes.

The first definition of *cartoon* in *Webster's Unabridged Dictionary* is "a design for or study drawn of the full size, to serve as a model for transferring or copying—used in making fresco paintings, mosaics, tapestries, and the like, as Raphael's cartoons." The word *cartoon* derives from the Italian word *cartone,* meaning heavy paper, and was first used in the mid-fifteenth century in Italy to refer to the full-scale drawings used for models for fresco painting. As the compositions of frecoes became increasingly complex, it was no longer possible for the artist, who had to work quickly on the wet plaster, to transfer the design from memory from the sinopia or from a small-scale drawing of the composition. Cartoons were needed to maintain the coherence of the whole scheme.

The nature of the fresco medium requires that the artist work in a way different from the manner in which he would work on a painting. Since it is necessary to paint on the plaster while it is still wet, the wall has to be completed in sections. While working in Detroit, depending on the humidity and temperature in the Garden Court, Rivera had from eight to sixteen hours to complete a section. It is customary in mural work to start at the top

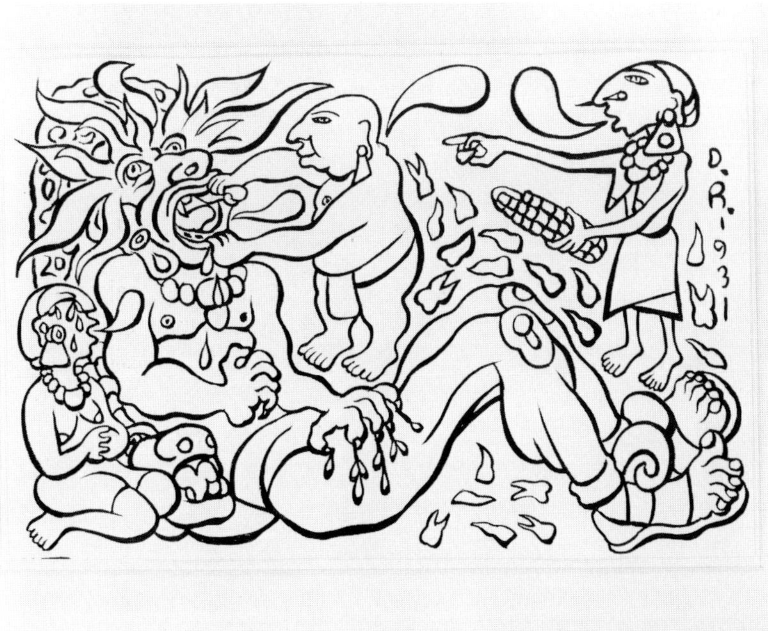

Figure 358
Seven-Times-the-Color-of-Fire, **1931, brush in black ink, 30.5 × 45.7 cm. Private Collection.**

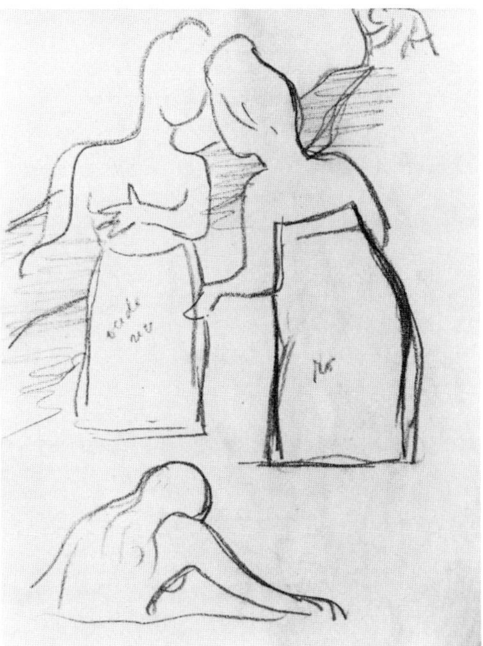

Figure 359
Women Bathing, **from a sketchbook of Tehuantepec scenes, 1923, pencil, 22.2 × 16.5 cm. Private Collection.**

of the wall and work downward. This succession avoids the spilling of paint on an already executed section and also permits the regular lowering of the scaffold as the work progresses. Usually the patches of wet plaster are laid from left to right. Thus the artist is not free to proceed from the center of the composition outward as he would in a painting. As the artist moves down the wall, his forms normally come forward. All of these elements, technical problems as well as optical phenomena, require the painter to envision the entire fresco. Changes are very difficult to make. Once the wet plaster dries, the carbonation that occurs binds the pigment into a solid crystalline mass.

The difficulties of working in fresco provided a challenge that Rivera obviously enjoyed. His was a methodical, cerebral approach to painting, so he did not find laborious the careful planning demanded by fresco work. From sketches and from drawings of individual figures, he developed compositional drawings of increasing detail and finish. He then enlarged the final small-scale drawing into a cartoon. (For the *Detroit Industry* cartoons, he was able to obtain a German-made, wove, all-rag paper of fine quality that came in large, seventy-two-inch-wide rolls.) The cartoon was then attached to the wall for viewing in relation to the setting.

The cartoons for the panels depicting the four races of man and for the two panels *Woman Holding Fruit* and *Woman Holding Grain* are executed in black, brown, and red over preliminary drawing in fine charcoal (see figs. 161–166). The outlines of the figures are reinforced with charcoal. For the color Rivera appears to have used dry pigment, the same as he would have used for painting the fresco. Tests made with pastel sticks and with Conté crayon indicate that he could not have obtained the same soft areas of color with these sticks as he achieved by brushing the dry pigment into the paper to shade his drawings. He varied the color of

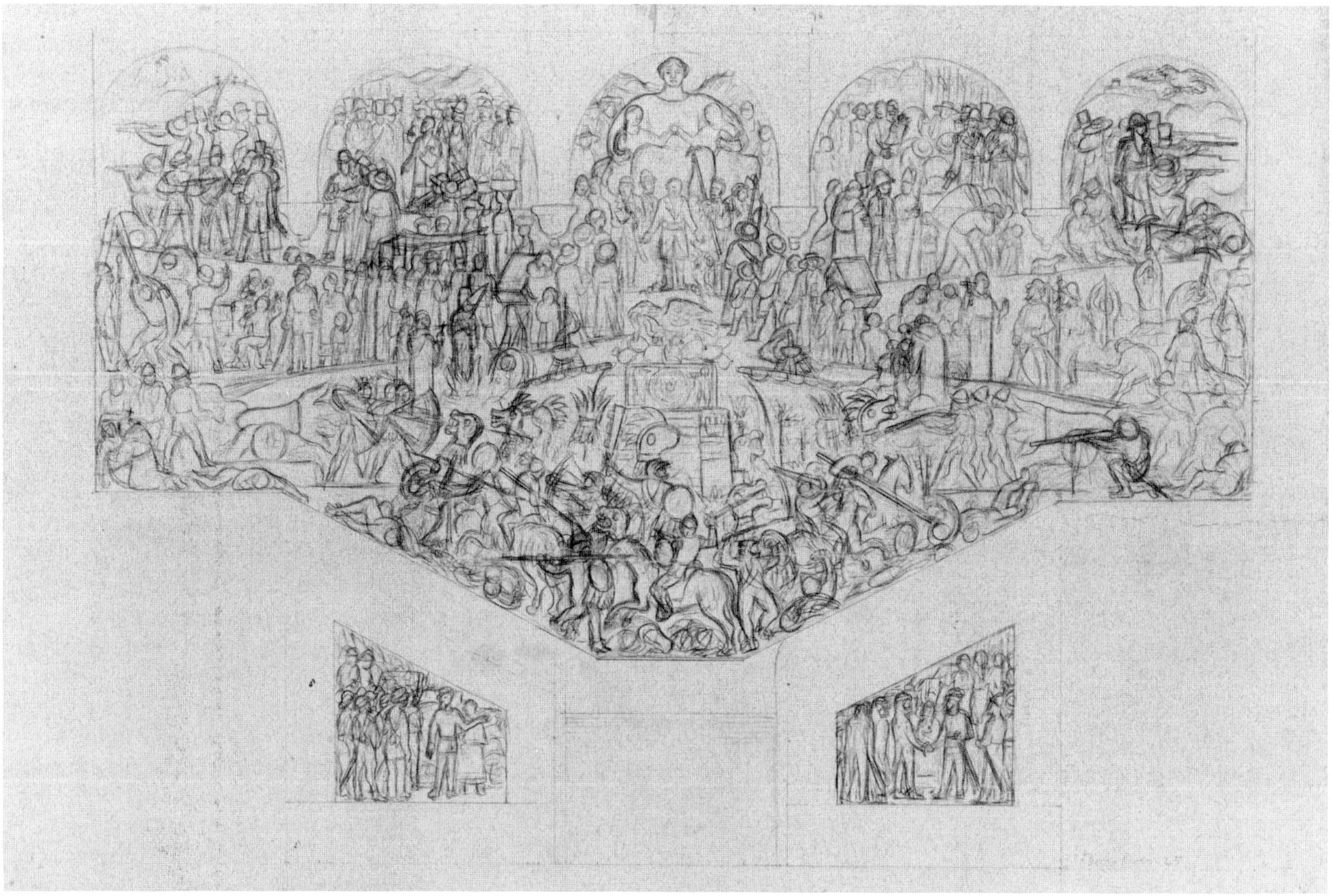

Figure 360
Study for *The History of Mexico,* central wall, Palacio Nacional, 1925, pencil. Mexico City, Museo Tecnologico, Comision Federal de Electricidad.

his drawings subtly for the different races—the Asian race is more ocher in tone than the other races; the American Indian race, more red; and the black race, more brown. There are two cartoons depicting the black race, one more finished than the other. The two versions indicate that Rivera took great pains to work out the size of the figures in relationship to the great hands that emerge out of the ground beside them. Rivera must have realized that he had created works of grandeur and beauty. There are no traces of pricking, slicing, or tracing for transfer on the cartoons. Evidently Rivera used them only for reference while he was working on the panels.

The drawings that Rivera created in 1932 for the Detroit frescoes represent a high-point in his career. But after them, as before, he remained a compulsively prolific draftsman. In the late 1930s, a period when he received no mural commissions, he produced a series of drawings and watercolors depicting the Mexican people and the Mexican landscape, for both of which he had a deep abiding affection. He made countless, rather ordinary, studies of peasants, especially children, which were aimed at the tourist trade and, as Rivera readily admitted, provided him with grocery money and the means to acquire pre-Columbian art for the museum he was planning. However, there are also many drawings from this period that are handsome, unusual works—glowing pastels of Indian women carrying flowers (see figs. 209, 210, 211), watercolors of the Mexican landscape in all its vast, mysterious beauty, and accomplished genre studies of peasants at market (see figs. 197 and 208) in brush and black ink with watercolor.

In 1957, the last year of his life, before he suffered a blood clot and an attack of phlebitis and lost the power to move his right arm, he executed a pencil drawing of the poet Pita Amor (fig. 258), which is exquisite in the simple clarity of its line. Like the great Japanese artist Hokusai, also a passionate draftsman, Rivera could have signed himself as Hokusai did in his seventy-fifth year—"The Old Man Mad about Drawing." An undated drawing in the collection of Rafael Coronel of a little Mexican dog is small and unpretentious (fig. 361). It recalls some of the animal studies in the pages of Hokusai's well-known sketchbooks, the *Mangwa.* With none of the sumptuous beauty of the drawings for the chapel at Chapingo or the magnificence of the monumental Detroit cartoons, it, nevertheless, with its humor and its simplicity, its acuteness of observation and its humanity, epitomizes Rivera—the man, the artist, and the superb draftsman.

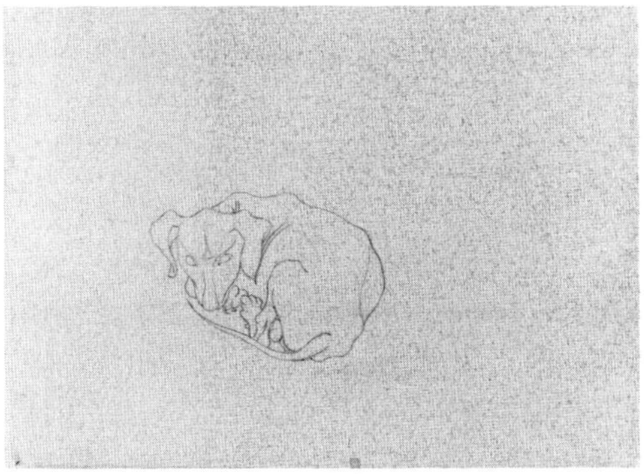

Figure 361
Dog Lying Down,
undated, pencil, 44 × 60 cm. Collection of Rafael Coronel.

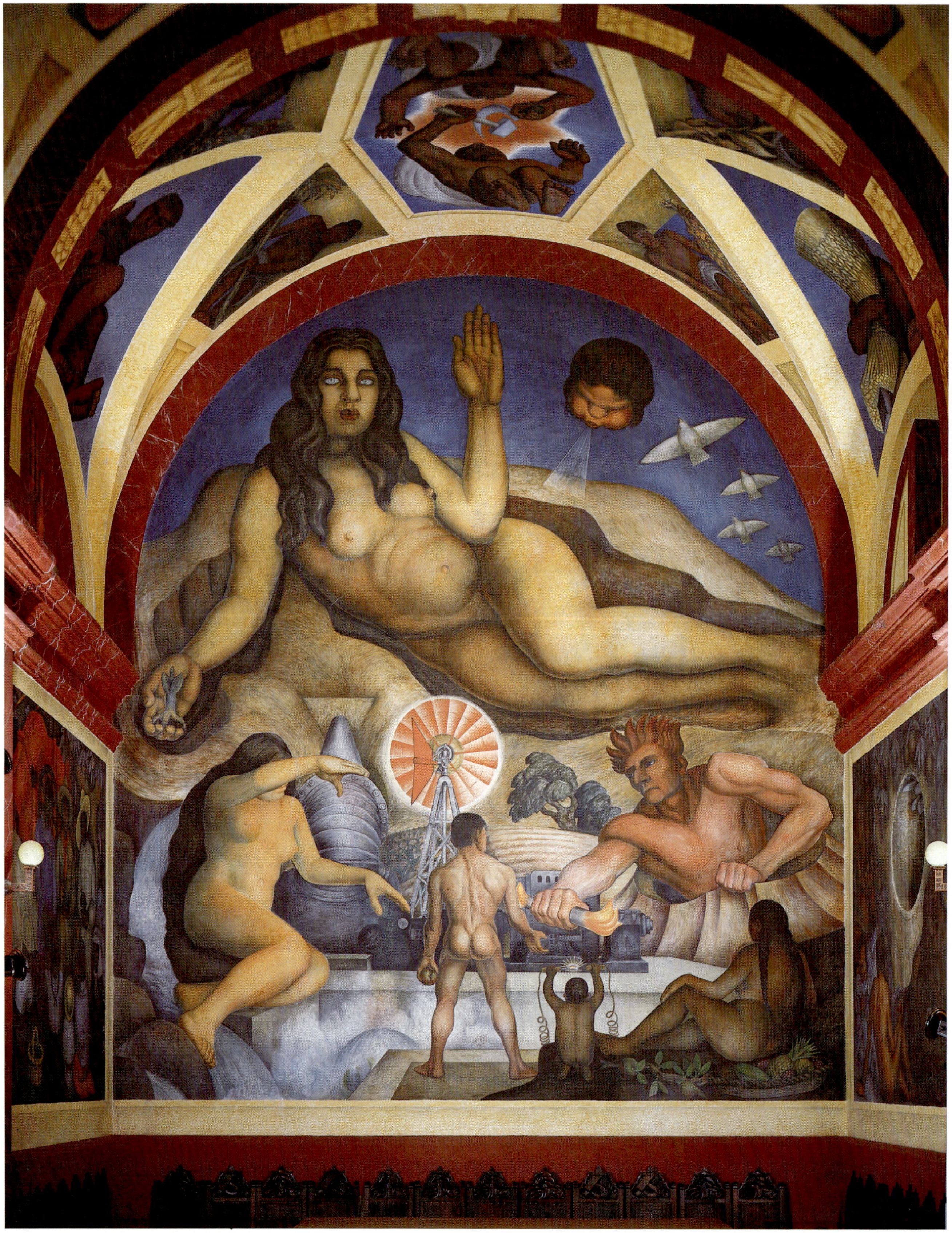

An Iconographic Interpretation of Diego Rivera's *Detroit Industry* Murals in Terms of Their Orientation to the Cardinal Points of the Compass

Francis V. O'Connor

Figure 362
***The Liberated Earth with Natural Forces Controlled by Man*, 1926–27, fresco. Chapel, Universidad Autonoma de Chapingo.**

When Diego Rivera had finished painting his murals on the walls of the Detroit Institute of Arts' Garden Court in March 1933, both he and various commentators were forced to explain their contents to a generally hostile public. These explanations consisted of neutral descriptions of the literal subject matter of the twenty-seven panels and generalized statements concerning the more obvious relationships between them (see, for instance, Rivera 1933 [V] and Pierrot and Richardson 1933 [I]) Since these descriptions were composed under pressure of controversy, they were meant to calm the angry rather than to enlighten the curious. Neither Rivera nor his patrons were in a position to provide a more elaborate interpretation of the mural program's philosophical, scientific, or political implications when its most innocent details were arousing popular wrath and the threat of destruction was a possibility. Today, unencumbered by old passions and with a deeper understanding not only of the genesis of these murals and their content but also of Rivera's career as a whole, it is possible to deduce from their parts the essence of their unity as one of the most brilliantly and comprehensively conceived and executed mural cycles in North America.

It is in the nature of wall painting to create pictorial environments. It is clear from internal iconographic evidence that Rivera conceived the Detroit images as an integrated system and that his principle of unity was the orientation of the Garden Court's four walls to the cardinal points of the compass. As we shall see, there is ample precedent for the utilization of such an iconography both in the history of wall painting and in Rivera's own experience and practice.

The Iconography of the Cardinal Points

Any discussion of the iconography of wall painting must take into consideration the symbolism of the cardinal points of the compass. Walls exclude the cosmos; murals create an interior cosmos. Great muralists—like great architects—are sensitive to the relationship of inside to outside and conform the interior symbolic environment they create to the phenomena of the exterior world.

Diego Rivera, more than his artist colleagues in Mexico and the United States, had been exposed to the simple yet profound tradition of the directions through his study of Italian Renaissance and indigenous Mexican iconography. One finds, therefore, that the informing principle of unity in his two great environmental mural programs—at Chapingo and at Detroit—is their directional orientation.

The simplest thing to be said about the orientation of a mural environment is to show how it is related to the sun, which rises in the East, shines from the South into the lightless North, and sets in the West.[1] This quotidian reality is seldom thought about, and its profound poetry is lost to the modernist mind. Yet almost all earlier cultures utilized the directions to locate themselves and their beliefs in the natural cosmos.

If we put aside our old-fashioned penchant for consigning the "primitive" to the "childhood" of our race and culture, we can come to appreciate how early man watched the skies as avidly as we scrutinize the media, and with richer mythogenic results. But we must also realize that each early society developed its own particular cosmic myth, and the complexity and the infinite variations of interpretation each society imposed upon the import of the heavenly bodies, their movements, conjunctions, and schedules tend to obscure the more universal aspects of directional symbolism. The universal symbolism of each direction is derived from humankind's perception of the phenomena apparent in that direction. For example, for all peoples the warm, light-giving, crop-helping sun lies to the South. However, there is a myth-specific symbolism that is determined by actual knowledge and experience of what lies in or comes from a particular direction. Thus, the South can be perceived as evil because it is the site of an untraversable desert or a shaman's bad dream. All of humankind experience the universal phenomena, but the specific associations depend on circumstances. We shall see, for instance, how Christianity reversed the East-to-West orientation of the temple for myth-specific reasons. One must concentrate then on the meaning humankind as a whole has always given to the various directions, independent of specific mythic constructs. What is needed is a certain essentialism of viewpoint—a certain common sense of things. In this, I am following the method of the historian of mythology, Joseph Campbell, whose incisive cross-cultural studies of mythic imagery provide a model for understanding mythic structures, independent of the eccentricities of specific societies or scientific knowledge.[2]

Needless to say, the universal symbolism of the cardinal points is quite innocent of modern astronomy. It is descriptive, however, of something deeply embedded in our common sense of the cosmos as it appears and is felt. Artists in the past, and often today, perceived this common sense of the directions more urgently than most, and no art form displays such awareness more frequently than the mural. What follows, then, is a compendium of humankind's ingrained attitudes toward its orientation in nature, drawn from a wide range of sources, but dependent on none in particular.

East

For almost all humans, the East is the focus of greatest importance simply because it is the direction from which the light of the sun first comes each day. It is now becoming increasingly apparent that prehistoric and ancient shrines and temples in both the old and new worlds have entrances oriented to the East—most often to the point at which the sun rises at the summer solstice. Whether it be the great cliff temple of Ramses, the onetime astronomical observatory at Stonehenge, a Celtic passage tomb, a pre-Columbian temple, or a Kiowa-Apache tepee, the door faces East to catch the rising sun and thus renew life after the deadly darkness of night. If the precinct is special enough, its axis is aligned to the solstice, which marks the longest day and shortest night, from which the greatest agricultural cycles can be measured and the harvests and hunts calculated. Thus the East has taken on a highly positive symbolism: it is a spiritual focus, a source of illumination and regeneration that overcomes the darkness that the West induces and night terrifyingly prolongs.

West

The West swallows the sun. It is a place of opposites: light and darkness, and by extension life and death and all natural dichotomies. Artistic manifestations oriented toward the West are amazingly consistent in the duality of their iconography (the Christian Last Judgment on a West wall being a typical example).

In its path from East to West, the sun moves on its relentless annual schedule, arching from North to South, from solstice to equinox to solstice. What humankind has perceived here—the apparent rebirth of the sun each dawn and its death at dusk—has been more important for symbol-formation than what we know about a round earth revolving around the sun. For these phenomena were felt before they were understood, and artists such as Rivera can still imagine them symbolically despite scientific knowledge.

While the East and West are clearly defined in terms of this drama of solar motion, the North and South find their universal import in contrast to each other.

South

The sun shines from the South, creating warmth and inducing growth. The South is associated with fertility and a wide range of positive values. It is the place from which the exterior of things is revealed; it is the direction of everyday reality. Iconographically, it is most often symbolized by some sort of opening toward it: a row of windows or a door leading into a courtyard or cathedral close. It is the direction of daylight, noon, bright blue skies, and reflecting surfaces—opening nature's infinite splendors to our consciousness.

North

Of all the four directions, the North is the only one that is not a source of light, except at night, when the polestar becomes the hub of the heavens and the exact determinant of the other three directions. It is associated most frequently with the nocturnal powers and their impenetrable mysteries. It is a place of darkness, bleakness, loneliness, and emptiness. If the South is the place of external tangibilities, then the North is the place of the inner mysteries of things. If the South is consciousness, the North is unconsciousness.

Both South and North are also, in a sense, infinite in their extension, despite their solstitial limitations, and thus symbolize a capacity for spiritual ambition and growth. These poles of endless potential are opposed to the limited path from birth to death, symbolized each day by the sun's journey across the zenith from East to West.

Rivera's Knowledge of Mural Tradition and the Development of his Sense of Directionality in his Murals through 1930

The most important artistic influence on Rivera's murals was the Italian Renaissance. During 1920 and 1921 he traveled in Italy for seventeen months, and it is known that he visited all the major mural sites including Padua, where he would have seen Giotto's Arena Chapel.[3] That he knew the Arena Chapel murals is clear from the quotations of motifs from them that appear in his later murals. Thus the *Embrace* from his Secretaría de Educación Pública cycle and *The Continuous Renewal of Revolutionary Struggle* panel from Chapingo are derived from Giotto's *Joachim and Anna* and *Lamentation* panels respectively. Since the Arena Chapel is typical of the Renaissance tradition's treatment of directional symbolism in a complete mural environment, and since its orientation is similar to both Chapingo and Detroit, it deserves a brief analysis here.[4]

Giotto's murals at Padua were created about 1305. His program was designed to serve three purposes. First, he wished to accommodate his patron, Enrico Scrovegni, in his reason for building the chapel: to expiate his father's sin of usury (a transgression so notorious that the elder Scrovegni is to be found in Dante's *Inferno*). Second, he wanted to acknowledge the festival of the Annunciation of the Virgin, which had been celebrated by the people of Padua at the old Roman arena that once occupied the site of the chapel. Third, he desired to portray, in his own way, the life of Christ, and the Last Judgment—the two most important themes an artist could engage at the time.

To accomplish this, he divided his walls into four registers or levels containing fifty-five major pictorial panels separated by decorative bands and trompe l'oeil architectural elements, some of which contain vignettes related to the major panels (see fig. 363). This traditional pedagogical format was often found in murals and altarpieces. As Gombrich points out, it would be two hundred years before Leonardo da Vinci would question this basically medieval convention.[5]

There are three ways to "read" Giotto's program. The first and simplest is to follow the biblical narratives of the lives of the Virgin and of Christ, which begin in the upper left corner of the South wall and wind across the walls (skipping across the Last Judgment on the West wall), with scenes such as the Annunciation on the eastern arch acting as a fulcrum.

The second way to read the program is in terms of correspondences of event and meaning between the upper and lower tiers of the christological panels. Thus, to take two obvious examples: the *Massacre of the Innocents* surmounts the *Flagellation* on the South wall and the *Raising of Lazarus* is above the *Resurrection* on the North.

A third, and far more comprehensive approach, is to see the various events depicted in terms of the traditional orientation of the chapel to the cardinal points: altar to the East, door to the West, South to the right, North to the left. In keeping with the distinction made earlier between culture-specific interpretations of the directions and their more universal import, it must be noted that Christian churches, unlike almost all "pagan" temples, place their altars and not their doors to the East. The reasons for this are complex, but can best be summarized by pointing to early Christianity's distaste for emulating pagan forms, especially any animistic interpretations of nature, and its theological identification of Christ as the "light of the world." For the Christian, true light was within the church, not exterior to it, and the newly baptised were turned at the door away from the West and its unsettling dualities toward the East and its focus of certainty.

It is clear that Giotto was sensitive to the meaning of the directions both in terms of the iconographic tradition he inherited and his own rather radical, humanistic sensibility. Thus around the eastern altar he placed an image of God the Father and the engendering of Christ at the Annunciation. To the West, the direction of opposites, the great *Last Judgment* shows Christ summoning the elect from the South and banishing the damned to the North. The apocryphal legend of Joachim and Anna, parents of the Virgin Mary, and all the public, but nonmiraculous, events of Christ's life appear on the South wall, while on the North one sees in contrast the life of the Virgin, the marvels surrounding her betrothal to Joseph, and the miraculous and/or mystical events of Christ's life. Also, along the bottom register of the walls, Giotto placed grisaille depictions of the Virtues on the South and the Vices on the North, thus corresponding to the southerly orientation of the elect in the Last Judgment as well as the position of the Virgin of the Annunciation on the right side of the eastern arch and the northerly placement of the damned, with Judas occupying a position correlative to Mary's but on the left. Thus the South is the place of virtue and everyday public activity, whereas the North witnesses spiritual mysteries—such as miracles and sin. Giotto's Arena Chapel is, then, a mural environment of enormous power and complexity that is best understood as a unity when seen in terms of its directional orientation.

When Rivera returned to Mexico he began a study of native Mexican art (see Brown essay in this volume). One of the things he would have noticed was the striking correspondences between Aztec

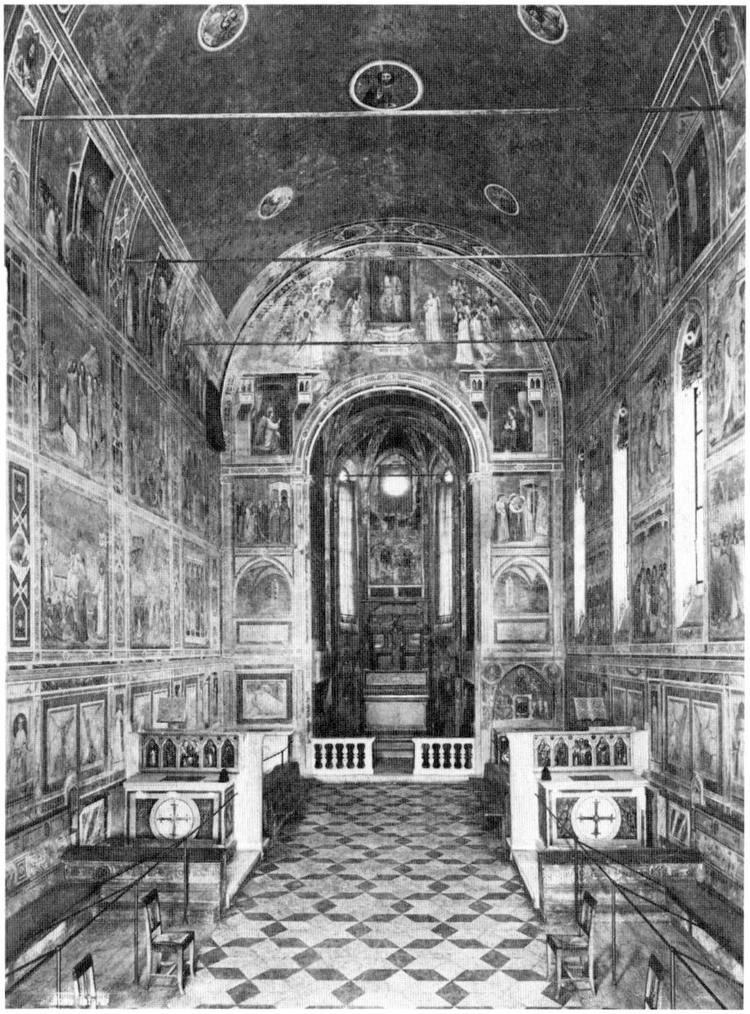

Figure 363
Giotto, *Arena Chapel*, Padua, Italy, ca. 1305, interior looking east.

and Christian directional symbolism that existed despite enormous cultural differences. A page from the Codex Féjerváry-Mayer (fig. 364), which shows the areas of the world with their corresponding gods, can serve here to illustrate the Aztec directional system. Rivera could have learned this from many similar sources, but this particular codex was published in Paris in 1901, and Catlin includes it among the sources Rivera would have been able to consult in researching his murals at Cuernavaca.[6]

The famous page depicts the god of the heart of the mountain and earthquakes at the center (which, for the Aztec, was the fifth direction) surrounded by four trees representing the cardinal points, each of which is flanked by two deities.

Just as with the Arena Chapel, where it was necessary to differentiate between the cultural factors that determined that the altar be at the East and the universal import of the East as the source of renewed light, so too it is necessary here to distinguish between the symbolism of the trees—which display the directions' universal import—and the contrasted gods and goddesses, who relate to Aztec mythology's tendency to balance positive and negative forces within its pantheon. Following Nicholson, this complex image can be interpreted as follows.[7]

To the East (at the top), a budding tree surmounts the eight-pointed disk of the rising sun, which symbolizes the universal sense of light and regeneration associated with this direction. Appropriately, the beneficent sun god presides here, accompanied, however, by the god of the sharp-cutting knife, who reminds us that human sacrifice was a major means of propitiating the Aztec gods.

To the West, a tree with a leafy trunk and bare branches displays the symbolism of opposites always associated with this direction. It is flanked by the goddesses of flowers and drunkenness who represent the opposition of beauty and decay, ecstasy and violence.

To the North (to the right here, since the entire image is conceived of as if viewed from below, which reverses the lateral directions), the tree bears human hearts, or

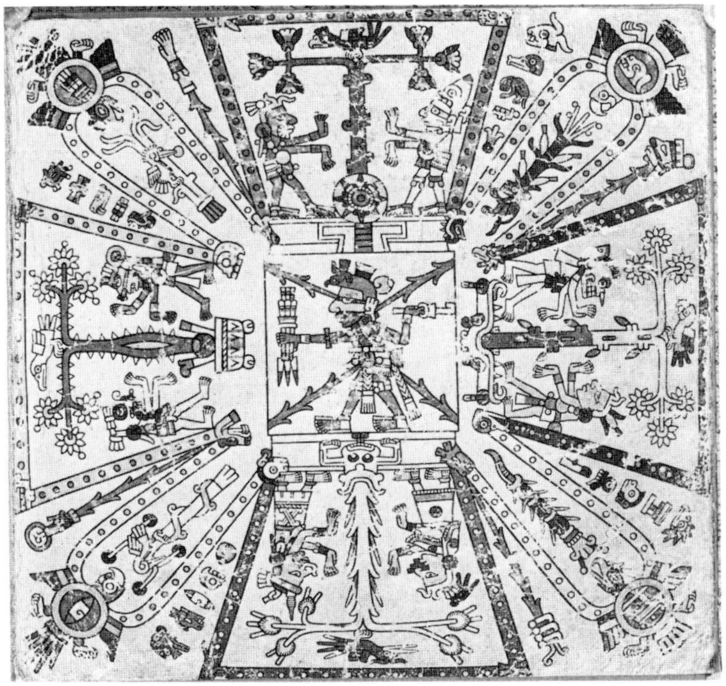

Figure 364
Page one, *Codex Féjerváry-Mayer,* Mixtec. Liverpool, England, Merseyside County Museums.

bloody knives, in keeping with the dark forces implicit in this lightless direction. Here the god of corn presides with the god of the dead, as if to emphasize the life-death-rebirth cycle of the earth's fertility and the violence with which maize is ground into food.

Finally, to the South is a tree in full leaf with an oval opening in its trunk, emblematic of the generative forces associated with the sun's daylong path. Here the god of rain and possibly the god of the underworld are found, who from above and below the earth assist the sun in the all-important agricultural cycle.

Rivera's developing awareness of the universal aspects of directional symbolism, and how they are always couched in a myth-specific context, can be traced in the programs he devised for his murals at the Secretaría de Educación Pública in Mexico City, the Escuela Nacional de Agricultura at Chapingo, and the Palacio de Cortés in Cuernavaca, between 1923 and 1930—an iconographic evolution that anticipates his definitive employment of directional symbolism at Detroit.

Rivera's first opportunity to create a major mural program came in 1923 when he was given the walls of the two great courts at the Secretaría. The long axis of this vast, three-story building runs East to West from the entrance. The murals are arranged between doors, which open into the interior, along the walls of the loggias that run around each story. The two courts are open to the sky and are separated by a crossover at the second and third levels. Thus the smaller, square court, which Rivera called the Court of Labor, has three courses of murals to the North, East, and South, and the larger, rectangular Court of Fiestas is similarly decorated to the South, West, and North (see SEP diagrams, p. 248).

As Wolfe points out, Rivera faced the enormous task of establishing a revolutionary iconography for Mexico from scratch,[8] and so we must look upon these walls—initially intended to be painted by a team of artists under Rivera's supervision—as tentative and experimental. Yet it is plain that Rivera was, from the beginning, conscious of directionality, and the walls of the Court of Labor bear his first exploration of its possibilities.

Wolfe says that the Court of Labor "is divided according to the location of its walls to correspond with the main divisions of the country: north, central, and south."[9] Yet the first glance at the program does not seem to bear this out, in terms either of a situational interpretation (the industries of northern Mexico are on the South wall, for instance) or of a more universal common sense of the directions (the East wall is filled with opposites).

The key to understanding Rivera's first approach to directionality is to realize that he understood the Secretaría's walls *as exterior walls* open to the sky and not as an interior environment. Thus the walls of the Secretaría were conceived not as transparent to the direction they occupy, but rather as mirroring the direction they faced (or perhaps the direction occupied by the viewer).[10] Thus, on the first level of the Court of Labor, the depictions of southern industries and cultures such as weaving, dyeing, sugar growing and processing, Tehuanas, and so forth are all found on the North wall, while northern mining scenes are found on the South wall. The East wall, facing the West, takes on its burden of opposites, with scenes to its left (northern) side, of oppressed miners—one of whom takes the pose of the crucified worker—and a more benign scene of pottery making to the right (southern) side, with the powerful image of the embrace at the center, balanced by placid farmers awaiting the harvest of revolutionary hope. And across the length of the building from this West-facing East wall, at the far end of the Court of Fiestas, the East-facing West wall bears a central depiction of the celebration of the First of May flanked by scenes of Mexican Easter festivities and Aztec pleasure gardens. Thus is the direction of light and regeneration symbolized in terms of Rivera's revolutionary concerns and the traditional rejoicings of the people.

This directional conceptualization of the walls as exterior surfaces facing the subject is perhaps most clearly demonstrated on the second level of the Court of Fiestas. Here the walls bear depictions of the coats of arms of most of the thirty-one Mexican states—and bear out literally Wolfe's statement that Rivera conceived the walls to correspond to the three areas of the country: the North, the central region, and the South. These areas must be comprehended as they would be felt from Mexico City, since Mexico runs from the Northwest to the Southeast, with its central states mostly to the West and Southwest of the capital. This is clearly to be seen in the arrangement of these heraldic devices, which were painted by Jean Charlot and Amado de la Cueva in 1924 under Rivera's supervision. The South-facing North wall of the second level of the Court of Fiestas bears the escutcheons (from right to left as one faces the wall) of the states of Yucatán and Campeche through Tlaxcala, a number of which are to the East of Mexico City, but considered to be in the "south" of the country. On the West wall are the arms of the central states from Guerrero and Michoacán on the right to Morelos and Querétaro on the left. And on the North-facing South wall, are the emblems of the northern states from San Luis Potosí to Sonora.[11]

Rivera's sense of the directionality of exterior walls is perhaps more succinctly and elegantly demonstrated by his murals in the Palacio de Cortés at Cuernavaca, which he painted in 1929–30. There a similar architectural situation prevailed, with the murals painted on the East-facing wall of a loggia overlooking the valley (see fig. 386). The entire program is conceived of directionally in terms of historical events that took place in front of the painted wall. It traces Mexican history from the Spanish conquest to the agrarian revolution and does so beginning on the North wall and ending on the South Cortés having invaded the area from the North in 1521 and Zapata having invaded the capital in 1911 from the South.[12] The resulting program was no doubt doubly agreeable to Rivera the Marxist, since it forced the chronology of these events to proceed from "right" to "left" as one faces the exterior wall of the palace, and it followed the historical sequence from invasion to revolution.

Although the Secretaría and the Palacio de Cortés demonstrate Rivera's sense of the directionality of exterior walls, his conception of the interior walls of the chapel at Chapingo—which he painted from about 1926 on, while still working on the Secretaría—shows his more traditional awareness of the directional symbolism of closed environments.

Before the 1910 Revolution, the assembly hall at Chapingo was the Catholic chapel of a vast, privately owned hacienda. It is oriented thirty-six degrees to the Northeast in the general direction of the summer solstice, which is at sixty-five degrees to the Northeast.[13] This is more than appropriate for the assembly hall of an agricultural school and not atypical for a Christian church in a rural setting. It is evident from the program that Rivera treated the space as if it were oriented in the traditional manner on a true West to East axis—and the walls will be so designated here for convenience. It should be noted, however, that the actual orientation is close to Northeast-Southwest, and as we shall see, this tends to endow the windowed "South" wall and its agricultural personifications with the combined light/growth symbolism of the East and South, while the scenes of social exploitation and revolution on the "North" wall are associated with the dichotomous/mysterious import of the West and North.

This secularized chapel provided Rivera with the opportunity to emphasize two philosophical ideals of overwhelming pertinence to the agricultural students who would gather within it. The first, of course, was the grim imperative of revolution with its commitment to violent land reform; the second was the manifest beauty, fertility, and awesomeness of the mothering earth. Rivera thus takes his themes from his Marxist/humanist ideology rather than from Christian or Aztec mythology and articulates them in terms of the universal common sense of the four directions that an agrarian peasantry would understand as easily as Rivera's agitprop imagery.

His program begins in the western vestibule of the chapel, where he appropriately sets up an opposition of everyday life and subterranean death in terms of his two great themes: revolution and agriculture (see diagrams, p. 259).

Thus, the northern wall of the vestibule depicts a Communist agitator rousing the people by pointing to the hammer and sickle with one hand and to oppressed miners slaving in a pit with the other (fig. 365). Here the point is first made that the revolution can only germinate when the people are stirred to their depths, flower when they are made aware of their exploited condition, and ripen when they achieve a program of social betterment. On the southern wall the red-shrouded corpses of the revolutionaries Zapata and Montaña are shown buried beneath a fruitful cornfield—the seeds of a revolution symbolized by the great red sunburst that surrounds the first of the six circular windows in the southern wall (fig. 366). Here the point is that the revolution is a matter of growth—slow and cyclic—and demands the sacrifice of the fruitful blood of martyrs.

This dramatic contrast between the poles of revolutionary agitation and fertile martyrdom presages the four bays of symbolically complementary wall panels on the long walls of the chapel's nave. Thus as one enters beneath an oppositional image—the sleeping virgin earth grasping a phallic shoot—on the western inner arch, to the right is an allegory of the subterranean forces of the earth in the form of female personifications, while to the left appear social realist depictions of the "earth enchained by capital, army, and

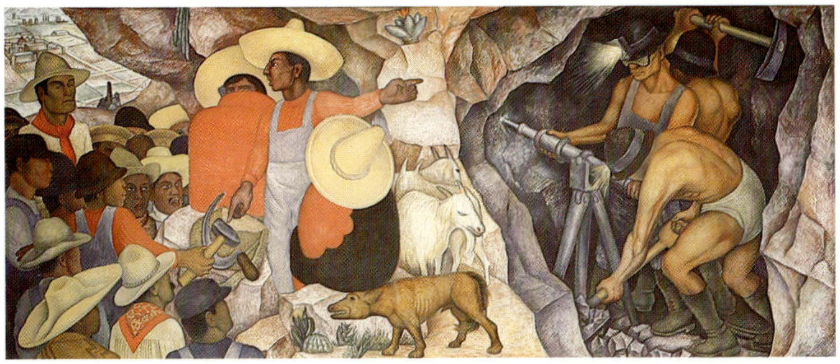

Figure 365
***Birth of Class Consciousness,* 1926–27, fresco. Chapel, Universidad Autonoma de Chapingo.**

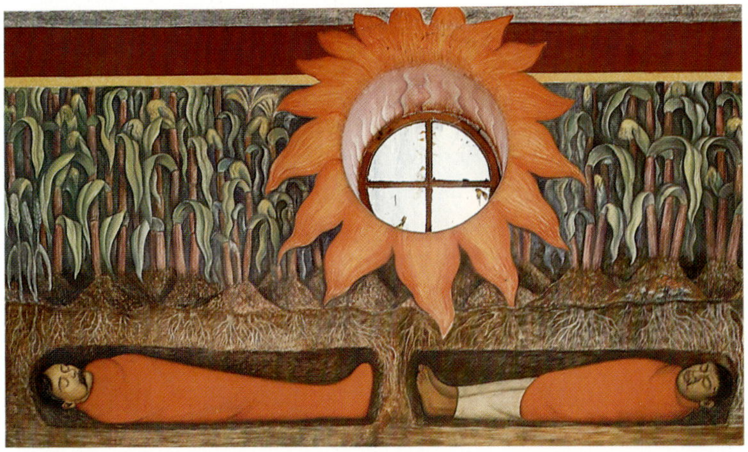

Figure 366
***Blood of the Revolutionary Martyrs Fertilizing the Earth,* 1926–27, fresco. Chapel, Universidad Autonoma de Chapingo.**

church" and "the oppression of the many by the few." Similar female personifications of "germination," "flowering," and "fruitfulness" on the southern wall (all beautifully grouped around the circular window openings) are opposed to images of the instigating, fighting, and winning of the revolution. These contrasted themes are joined on the great eastern wall in the allegorical personification of the fertilized earth (modeled after Rivera's pregnant wife) surrounded by the four elements and depictions of humankind in control of the land and its abundance (fig. 362). And in keeping with the solar iconography of the summer solstice, all these figures are set around the bright disk of a windmill's vanes, which suggests both the spoked circle of the Aztec sun glyph and the aureole of a Catholic monstrance.

At Chapingo, Rivera thus devised a purely secular program in terms of the broad symbolism of the directions and the traditional orientation of the architectural environment of a Christian church. By the time he reached Detroit, he was ready to elaborate an even more ambitious program and to make it explicitly manifest in terms of the cardinal points of the compass.

The Detroit Murals

I have had here a very heavy job of preparation especially a job of observation. The frescoes will be twenty-seven, making together a single thematic and plastic unity. I expect it to be the most complete of my works; for the industrial material of this place I feel the enthusiasm I felt ten years ago at the time of my return to Mexico with the peasant material. (Diego Rivera on the Detroit murals)[14]

While Rivera was at first offered only the two main walls, North and South, of the Garden Court of the Detroit Institute of Arts, he soon arranged to paint the entire room, since, in fact, the vast space offered him an opportunity he had had only once before—at Chapingo—that of painting a directionally integrated mural environment. Indeed, only at Chapingo and Detroit did Rivera have the chance to formulate a program comparable to Italian Renaissance environments such as the Arena or Sistine chapels. As discussed previously, Rivera's earlier murals in Mexico from about 1922 to 1930 and in California during 1930 and 1931 were all on single walls or else grouped around patios or stairwells. But it was only in a complete,

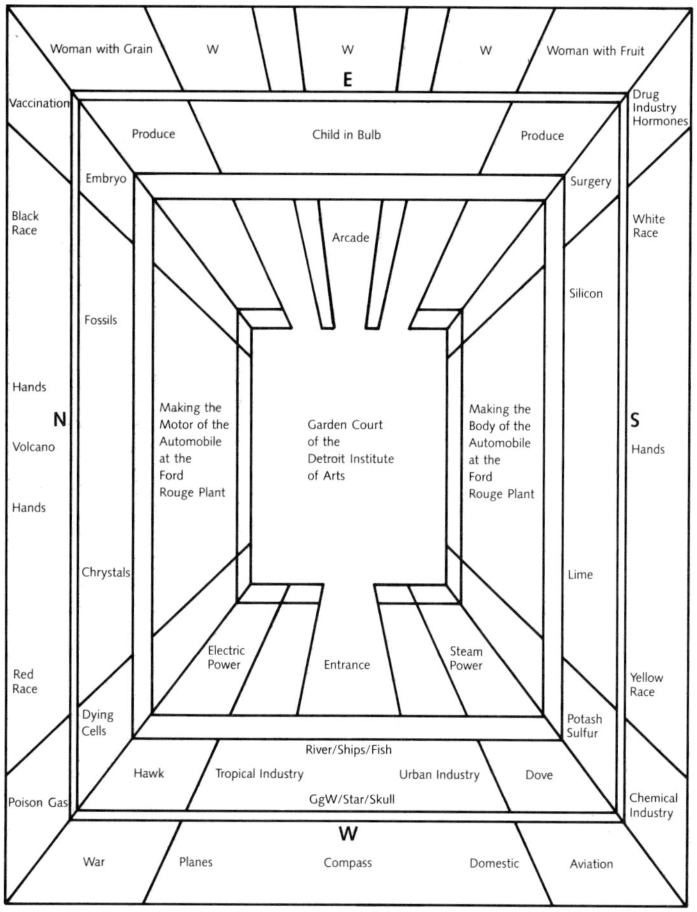

Figure 367
Diagram of the Garden Court. Courtesy of the author.

closed environment that he could go beyond such situational directionality and visual punning to reinforce and unify his iconography by engaging our common sense of the cosmos.

At Detroit Rivera made his awareness of the directions explicit (see fig. 367). Over the door of the West wall he placed a mariner's compass painted in grisaille within a blank rectangle that can be read as a plan of the Garden Court with its North wall at the top (see fig. 368). Thus the court itself becomes the measure of its own universe of imagery. Since the court's North wall is orientated about thirty-five degrees to the Northwest, the compass needle points, as it must, slightly to the right toward due North. What must be deduced from the compass face is that the West to East axis of the Garden Court points almost exactly to the summer solstice, which in Detroit is roughly fifty-five degrees to the Northeast.[15] This motif, overlooked in earlier interpretations of the mural program, thus emphatically declares Rivera's awareness of the directions and their central importance in the development of his iconographic environment. The placement of the compass on the West wall is entirely appropriate given the oppositional nature of the instrument, with its four equal but opposite points. The motif directly below the compass—a star set on a square that bisects a human head into a skull on its North side and a face on the South, the whole surmounting two cargo boats sailing in these directions—further emphasizes this oppositional theme. In this one image Rivera states the theme of three directions: the oppositional nature of the West, the dark essentialism and interiority of the North, and the open explicitness of the South.[16]

On the East wall directly opposite this thematic epicenter of his mural program, and visible, through the West door of the Garden Court, from the central door of the museum, is the bright image of a child sleeping in a pod—an image of life and rebirth that, as we shall see, was as simultaneously personal and universal for Rivera as was the allegorical portrait of his pregnant wife on the East wall at Chapingo. But just as this revivifying image of the child on the East wall provides the symbolic and optical focus of the iconographic program, the details on the West wall, as they did at Chapingo, introduced a set of ideas elaborated throughout the entire mural sequence. To the North, Rivera groups an overwhelming array of motifs that emphasize the deep internal nature and working of things and people, their chthonic essence and cultural potential, and their capacity for evil as well as good. To the South, his equally complex imagery speaks to external factors and forces, brightness, growth, and the ironies of civilization.

This overall directional dichotomy is first made explicit on the West wall, where the North side of the grisaille panel beyond the skull shows laborers in the depth of a jungle rubber plantation extracting the essence of a raw material from nature while fish leap from the deep (see fig. 368). The upper area of the North side depicts war planes. An aviator with a stricken face and shaven head, his hands seemingly rending his garments, stands as if prepared for some rite of sacrifice or mourning. Other figures wear zoomorphic oxygen masks and echo the contiguous panel on the North wall that depicts the manufacture of poison gas (see fig. 391). Below all this, the implicit violence is made explicit by the image of a hawk killing a bird—a creature, as Rivera noted, of its own species.[17] Below this side of the West wall, flanking the entrance, is an electrical generator, which consumes matter to make raw energy. This is presided over by a stern conflation of Henry Ford and Thomas Edison, who served capitalism by creating profit out of the resources and robotlike labor of others—as the small panel above the dynamo suggests.

To the South of the West wall, on the side of the fleshed face, the grisaille panel depicts a prosperous city, employed workers, and sail- and motorboats skimming the water's surface. Above, a passenger plane is shown being assembled at the Ford aircraft division. Its peaceful utility is emphasized in the panel below, which shows a dove eating an insect, a species lower than itself. Flanking the door to the South is a steam engine, which recycles water to create energy, and the strong, impassive image of the archetypal worker (who resembles Rivera)—the creator of value as opposed to profit (fig. 394).

Over the door in the West wall is carved the famous saying of Hippocrates, *Vita brevis, longa ars.* This inscription came with the room, yet it falls naturally into Rivera's directional schema, with the idea of life's brevity to the South and the extended mystery of art to the North. The art referred to, of course, is healing, and the rest of the saying reads: "The opportunity [is] fleeting, the experiment perilous, the judgment difficult." For if life's shortness is nothing new under the sun, skill at diagnosing its ills requires an experienced knowledge and intuition that goes to the heart of the matter.[18]

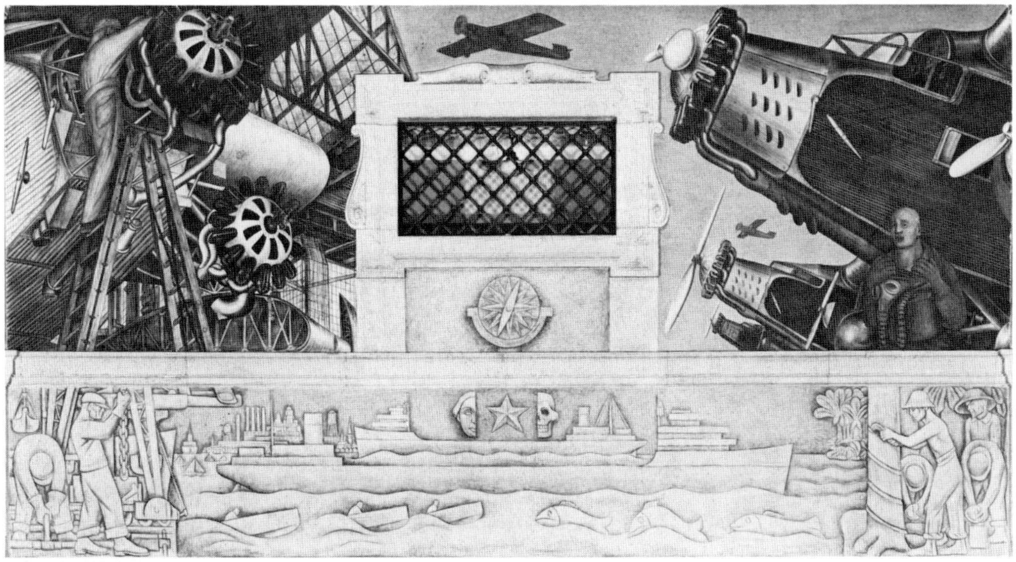

Figure 368
***Detroit Industry,* West wall (detail), 1932–33, fresco. The Detroit Institute of Arts, Founders Society Purchase, The Edsel B. Ford Fund and Gift of Edsel B. Ford.**

If the dominant themes of the North wall speak to the heart of matters, those of the South wall proclaim the commonality of matters. This contrast between the interior and exterior of things and processes, between their dark, mysterious, metaphysical, chthonic, and unconscious dimension and their explicit, self-evident, political, telluric, and conscious aspects is, as discussed earlier in several contexts, the difference between our common sense of North and South. That Rivera's program for the walls in these directions reflects these ideas will become clear in the analysis that follows. But one need merely glance at the walls to note that he has placed the dark tonalities to the lightless North and the brighter to the sunlit South (as if the walls themselves were translucent to their directions) or read the simplest description of the main panels to learn that the motor, the interior force of the automobile, is manufactured to the North and the car's exterior body to the South (see figs. 391 and 392).

Certainly there is no more powerful image of interior forces than the volcano, which leads to the molten core of the planet itself. The upper two central registers of the North wall depict the cone of a volcano and its vent through a strata of minerals and fossils that recall the depths in time and space of the earth's geologic and organic evolution. The natural resources derived from these subterranean regions and used in manufacturing automobiles are seized and brandished by human hands that thrust through the slopes of the volcano, thus associating the worker with profound chthonic forces. To either side of this panel recline androgynous personifications of the red and black races holding iron ore and coal respectively. These figures represent the "uncivilized" Native American and African cultures, whose depth and potential was not yet fathomed by Western humankind. The appearance of these exploited peoples on the North wall indicates that Rivera, who was partly descended from native Mexican stock, wished to emphasize their chthonic dignity and vitality as well as to prompt the guilt their presence would stir in the darker psyche of "civilized" humankind.

On the South wall, the upper two panels echo the configuration of those to the North. But here, instead of a natural volcano, one finds a stepped pre-Columbian structure. The hands here seem to express distress and defiance. The personifications represent the "civilized" white and yellow races, with the drum of a fluted Greek column appearing behind the classical visage of the Caucasian and the ruins of the Great Wall behind the Oriental. They hold, respectively, limestone and sand, and the panel directly below represents limestone strata, the fossils that form the basis of sandstone, and crystals of silica.

If we consider for a moment the industrial transformations of the four materials held by the four personifications, we find that the coal and iron ore of the northern entities must be completely consumed to release their interior product, whereas the changes of form that limestone and silica undergo to make building blocks or glass, for instance, are extrinsic to their nature. Similarly, the proletarian hands to the North grasp at things from the interior of the earth to survive, while to the South they react to exterior forces, either pleading for or demanding survival.

Flanking the two upper panels on the North and South walls are four smaller ones that depict or refer to aspects of Detroit's chemical and pharmaceutical industries. They are best understood in terms of their relation to each other, to their opposites across the court, and to the directions they occupy and abut.

That Rivera had some profound misgivings concerning the chemical industry's potential for evil over good is suggested by his placing an ominous depiction of masked figures making a poison gas bomb (and below it a graphic demonstration of the bomb's devastating effect on human cells) at the Northwest end of the North wall. Directly opposite, at the Southwest end of the South wall, is a more benign portrayal of a commercial chemical plant, though the protective headgear of some of the workers still points to the dangerous nature of even the most useful chemicals. This ambivalence is emphasized in the small panel below, which depicts crystals of sulfur and potash along with organic sacs. McMeekin interprets this panel as referring to both life and death, first, because it depicts living organic forms being generated spontaneously from the primordial chemical "soup," and secondly, because the two chemicals shown can be combined to make either poison gas or soap.[19]

This dichotomous nature of the chemical industry, emphasized by its westward placement, is further underlined by the treatment of the figures in the two panels. On the North wall the nefarious bomb is contrived by six persons so swathed in protective gear as to appear subhuman. Their humanity is utterly submerged in the amorality of their war work. In contrast, of the eleven figures in the correlative panel on the South wall, only one appears to engage in a dangerous task, and the two at the center are working a plunger so energetically that they are shown simultaneously both bent and erect in a flash of Cubist conceptualization unique to the entire program but quite appropriate to the quotidian dynamics of the South.[20]

The pharmaceutical industry's more beneficent nature prompted Rivera to place it to the East of the long walls, with a sense of immunological research and vaccination at the Northeast end and a drug laboratory to the Southeast. Beneath the former is a depiction of a human embryo amid cells and crystals; the latter surmounts the image of a surgical operation.

While it is apparent from these panels that Rivera is spoofing the "religion of science" so prevalent in the 1920s and 1930s, with allusions to the nativity of Christ in the vaccination panel and a gothic "radio pulpit" reminiscent of the demagogic Father Coughlin in the lab scene (not to mention "eggheads" twenty years before baldness and white coats became associated with scientific dogmatism)—the import of these walls and their dependent panels is open to a more complex interpretation, independent of both Rivera's skeptical humor and old controversies.

It is certainly appropriate that the vaccination panel appears on the North wall, given the essential interiority of innoculation against disease. This reinforcement of the body's immunological system against invading microbes is a positive pendant to the biological havoc wrought by poison gas at the other end of the wall. It is interesting, however, to note that Rivera at first planned to paint the pharmaceutical lab in this space on the North wall. He had even begun the sinopia on the walls.[21]

Why he changed his mind is not known precisely, but since the lab scene shows the preparation of hormones from the endocrine glands of animals, it is reasonable to speculate that he thought the scene more appropriate as a pendant to the more benign chemical plant panel. McMeekin finds abstract symbols of androgyny in the lab panel;[22] but one can go further and suggest that the mannish heads on the curvaceous female workers emphasize the fact that certain hormones can induce an androgynous appearance, and that this external effect was more appropriate to the South wall. (That it was also appropriate for girls arranged like monks in a choir can be left to speculation.)

It can also be suggested that the two smaller panels refer to the internal and external styles of medical practice embodied in homeopathy and allopathy. Rivera, whose vegetarian diet at this time was probably dictated by the principles of the former,[23] would certainly have known that vaccination was the closest allopathic medicine came to the doctrine of similars inherent in much folk medicine and at the heart of homeopathy. He seems to have attempted to illustrate this doctrine in the small panel beneath the vaccination scene. Here a human embryo encounters an egg-shaped cell with a skull for a nucleus. This motif surmounts a grouping of crystals, and all is surrounded by an organic mass of chromosomes and cells. McMeekin notes that an interpretation of this panel akin to that for the similar panel beneath the commercial chemical scene—that of organic life emerging from the primordial "soup"—is farfetched since human embryos are too complex for such direct genesis.[24] Rather, what Rivera seems to be trying to illustrate here is the esoteric homeopathic principle of *simul similibus curentur* (like cures like). The skull at the center of the cell symbolizes the regenerative potential of a mineral or organic substance that induces pathogenic symptoms in the healthy that are akin to those it can cure when used as a medicine in someone diagnosed as suffering from similar symptoms. This reliance on the latent congruence of matter's energies, parallel with an essentially psychosomatic theory of illness, is at the heart of most folk medicine and those therapies that take a holistic view of disease.[25]

Directly opposite the embryo panel, the small panel beneath the hormone lab depicts the primary recourse of allopathy: surgery—here showing the removal of a brain tumor surrounded by the dissected organs of the alimentary and reproductive systems. Surgery, unlike homeopathic remedies and their like, which are internally preventive, opens the body to external intervention and is thus appropriate to the symbolism of the South.

Before turning to the two large industrial panoramas on the North and South walls, it would be appropriate to say something about the four side panels of the East wall that abut the "medical" scenes just discussed. Rivera's early drawings indicate that he intended to celebrate the agricultural industries on this wall (see fig. 369), and the large panels in its upper register depict two buxom female personifications, one holding cereals, the other fruit. Again Rivera has followed the logic of directional symbolism, placing grains, which must be milled to obtain their intrinsic product, toward the North, and fruits, whose good parts are as externally available as are the benefits of limestone, silica, or surgery, to the South. Below these panels are still lifes of vegetables, no doubt memorializing the gargantuan vegetarian meals from which he daily derived the renewing energy to paint these frescoes (see fig. 393).

It has already been noted that the manufacture of the internal combustion engine is shown on the North wall and the making of the external body of the Ford V8 on the South. The industrial specifics of these operations, so ingeniously conflated and presented by the artist, do not concern this essay except where they play a roll in its directional symbolism. Rather the overall formal qualities of these two walls will be shown to intensify this symbolism by means of three strategies: the compositional matrix in which the complex of details is unified, the way the workers are portrayed, and the analogies to be drawn from the shapes of the machines that dominate the walls. But as this discussion will make clear, Rivera has gone beyond directional symbolism alone to make a philosophical statement concerning the political condition of the worker.

As with the Christian and pre-Colombian models discussed earlier, where a distinction must always be made between the universal import of the four directions and their myth-specific contexts, so also with the murals of the Garden Court. For while it is plain that Rivera recognized that the court's orientation was identical to that of a Christian precinct like the Arena Chapel and arranged the major motifs accordingly, the Aztec in him and/or the communist materialist could not help but note that the gods/social forces came in both positive and negative guises. Thus, in a manner similar to that of the pre-Colombian codex mentioned earlier, he places oppositions of good and evil not only on the West wall, where they are overt, but also covertly within the imagery dedicated to the other directions. This is most explicit in the eight "scientific" panels on the North and South walls, which have just been discussed. But it is more pervasive and subtle in the allusions to "mechanomorphic" forces presiding over the assembly line and its inhabitants in the two large panels.

The first thing that can be said about the compositions of the two industrial scenes is that they contrast closed and open systems. There is no visible exit from the interior depicted on the North wall except through the blazing furnaces at the center top, which are directly beneath the vent of the volcano above. The recessional space at the center between the rows of oversize spindle machines ends in a wall. There are no windows letting in light. This sealed-in

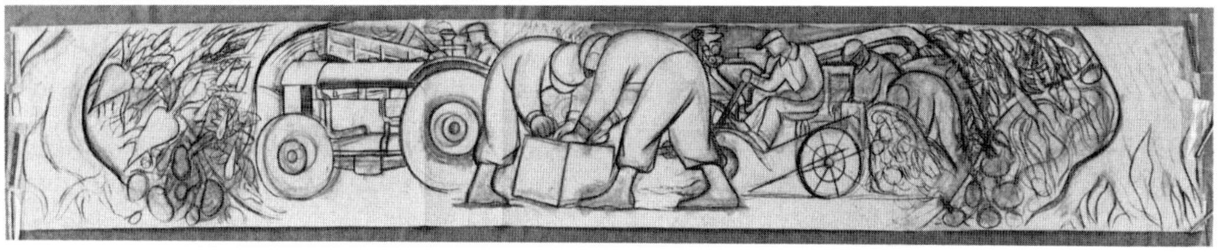

Figure 369
Agricultural Scene,
1932/33, preliminary sketch (not used) for East wall, *Detroit Industry,* black chalk over graphite, 133.4 × 791.8 cm. The Detroit Institute of Arts, Gift of the artist (33.39).

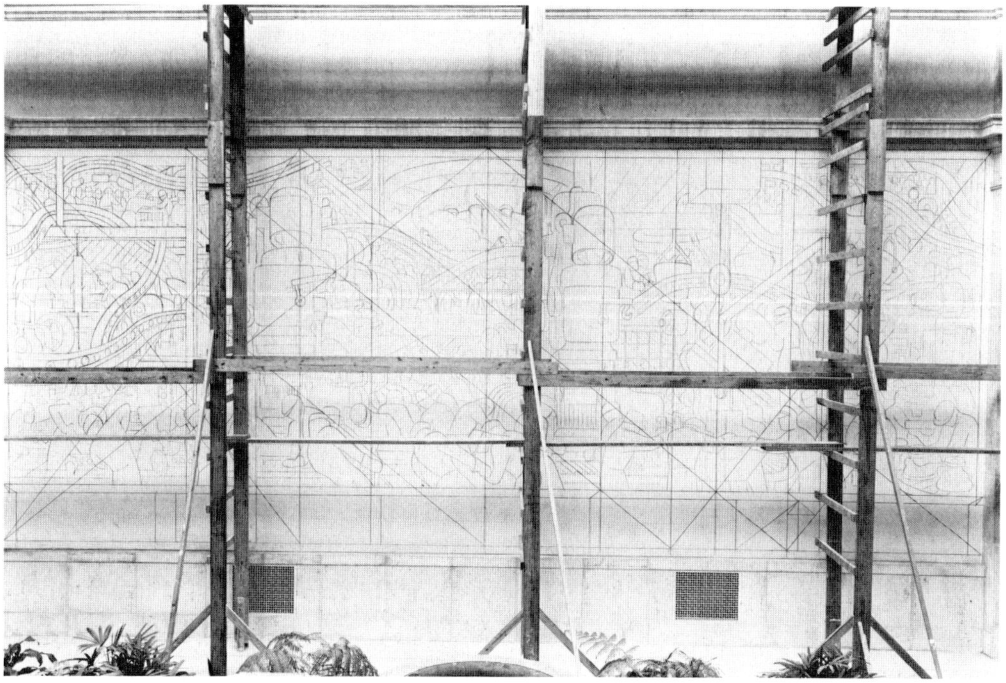

Figure 370
Sinopia for North wall, *Detroit Industry,* 1932.

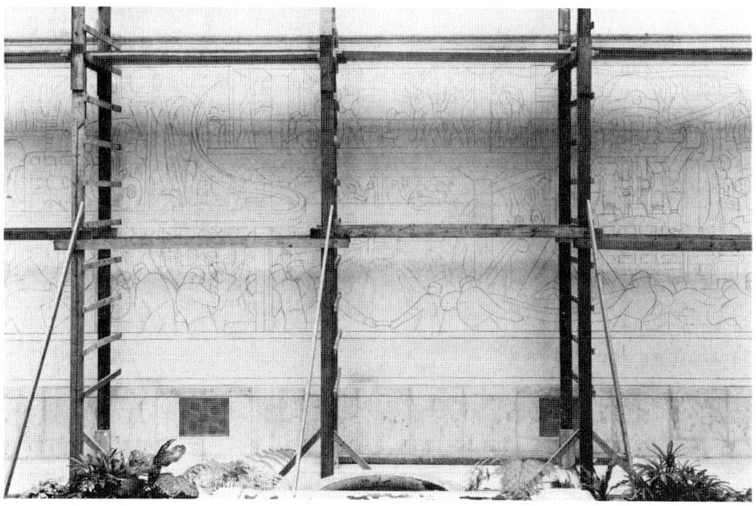

Figure 371
Sinopia for South wall, *Detroit Industry,* 1932.

space, lit as it is by flame and phosphorescence, resembles a vast subterranean inferno. In contrast, the South wall, painted in cooler tonalities, gives access to the exterior world. Windows and skylights can be seen across the top of the factory, and the central recessional space, viewed head-on from a point on the final assembly line, opens in the far distance to allow a red car to drive out into the sunlit parking lot beyond. This central opening is also entered from the outside by a group of tourists who gawk at the cars being put together. In terms of directional symbolism, this space is analogous to the opening in the trunk of the southern tree depicted in the codex, and to the general tendency of all South-facing walls to be open to the sun either figuratively, as here, or literally by means of windows, as at Padua and Chapingo.

Similarly, the overall structure of the two large panels emphasizes their directional import. On the North wall, Rivera worked out an elaborate compositional system loosely based on the theory of dynamic symmetry.[26] Photographs of the sinopia for both walls (figs. 370 and 371) show this clearly. The North wall is divided into two overlapping square and rectangular patterns. The two great squares at the end of the wall are easily recognized in the maze of other lines if one simply drops the height of each end along the bottom edge of the panel. The space between the squares creates a proportionate vertical golden rectangle between the squares at the top of which are the furnaces. The wall appears to be composed asymmetrically because the dead-ended recessional space at the center is viewed at an angle from the right (an angle, by the way, that is approximately the same as that by which the actual wall diverges from true North). Thus the edge of the left square aligns with the back row of tall spindles, i.e., large drills, while edges of the right square align with the center of the spindle at the right front. This ingenious solution permits the entire composition to avoid the appearance of symmetry, even though it is organized into five vertical rectangles all roughly proportionate to each other. Sweeping across these underlying rectangles are diagonals that create dynamic lines of force along which most of the workers' actions are aligned in rhythm to the harmonic proportions these diagonals define. In this use of dynamic symmetry, we have the most interiorized aspect of the North wall, since the underlying compositional matrix, visible in the sinopia, is invisible in the finished mural. But this matrix controls the figures of the workers with a regimentation akin to that enforced on the Ford assembly line itself,[27] while seducing the eye with a proportional elegance that belies the human situation depicted.

The South wall, while similarly composed in terms of dynamic symmetry, is perfectly symmetrical in appearance, with the two great squares at either end clearly defined along the inner edge of the round columns of the welding buck at the top center and the edges of the opening in the grisaille "fence" at the bottom (see fig. 392). The composition here is thus far more open and frontal, and the workers are in less obvious thrall to controlling diagonals, which are barely visible in the sinopia.

Yet both walls emphasize the integration of the worker into the industrial process—but not in any "social realist" sense of protesting his condition. Rather, Rivera chose simply to describe, in devastating detail, his dichotomous situation: serving machines that serve him. The modern man in Rivera loved modern technology, and the former Cubist in him could revel in its aesthetic elegance of structure. The Marxist Rivera, however, was well aware of the workers' condition in Detroit and had only to read the newspaper to learn of worker unrest and Ford strikebreaking techniques. And the Native American in him, perhaps more than the Christian capitalists he served, understood that nothing good came without its evil counterpart, and that life in nature was a balancing of these forces rather than an absolute denial of evil and a futile quest for absolute good. This attitude is certainly part of the elaborate iconography he created with the materials out of which Ford made cars, Dow chemicals, and Parke-Davis drugs. And it is also evident in the manner in which Rivera depicted the most conspicuous workers.

On the North wall, the figures that make up the frieze of workers across the foreground of the industrial scene are strikingly individualized. Many are portraits of Rivera's assistants and Ford employees (see fig. 391). The faces reflect a wide range of ages and ethnic origins. In this way Rivera emphasizes their interior personalities and distinguishes their essential humanity from the vast mechanical and artistic design into which they are locked. This contrast between the workers and their infernal surroundings is even more starkly achieved in the vaccination and poison gas scenes on the North wall. In the former, all the figures are individualized—each of the three scientists at the top bears distinct ethnic characteristics, while the central group consists of portraits of Jean Harlow, the recently kidnapped Lindbergh baby, and Dr. William Valentiner, the director of the museum. This scene of human scientific progress is sharply contrasted to the retrogressive processes of the war industry shown at the other end of the wall, where those engaged in them are unable to show their faces lest they succumb to the very weapon they contrive.

On the South wall, appropriately, only the faces of outsiders are specifically individualized: the factory boss at the left, the row of tourists in the center, and the donor portraits of Edsel Ford and Valentiner at the right corner. The workers are either seen from the rear or what is visible of their faces is generalized. This is true even in the chemical and pharmaceutical panels, where the four visible male faces in the former appear the same, while the presiding doctor in the latter is shown radically foreshortened and the ten girls around him have the heads of androgynous classical statues.

Rivera thus portrays the workers on the North wall, enclosed in their natural habitat creating value for themselves and their community, as human beings with ethnic histories, specific personalities, and individual dignity. Only those who compromise with outright evil are faceless. The workers on the South wall, on the other hand, are seen from the outside. They appear not as individuals but as factors in exterior processes controlled by bosses, owners, and consumers. They become interchangeable ciphers with inarticulate wants—as the hatband one wears suggests by reading "We want . . ." Beer, of course, was what was wanted, since the prospect of Franklin D. Roosevelt's inauguration, which would occur soon after this panel was painted, promised the end of Prohibition. But much more was obviously needed by these workers, and Rivera chose not to trivialize those issues, while perhaps suggesting that what the workers needed was an organizing voice.

The portrayal of the workers is also a function of the symbolism of light as it pertains to the directions. It is significant that Rivera has omitted electric lights in his factory scenes, even though photographs of the Rouge lines[28] show numerous shaded bulbs suspended over the work areas. On the North wall the major light source is fire and the luminescence of molten metal. This reddish light is reflected off the sides of the spindles and infuses the entire subterranean scene with a warm illumination that, under any circumstances, would favor the human face by etching its features and dramatizing its character. On the South wall, where daylight floods in from outside, the workers' faces lose their specificity and become tonal masks (as if painted by Fairfield Porter). For the South deals with externals of vision, whether it be the car's body or the worker's persona, and the North reveals the driving inner force, whether it be that of the car, of transformed matter, or of the worker's personality.

Presiding over this subsidiary world of opposites are the dichotomous gods of Rivera's Aztec homeland in the guise of machines. Indeed, the most conspicuous

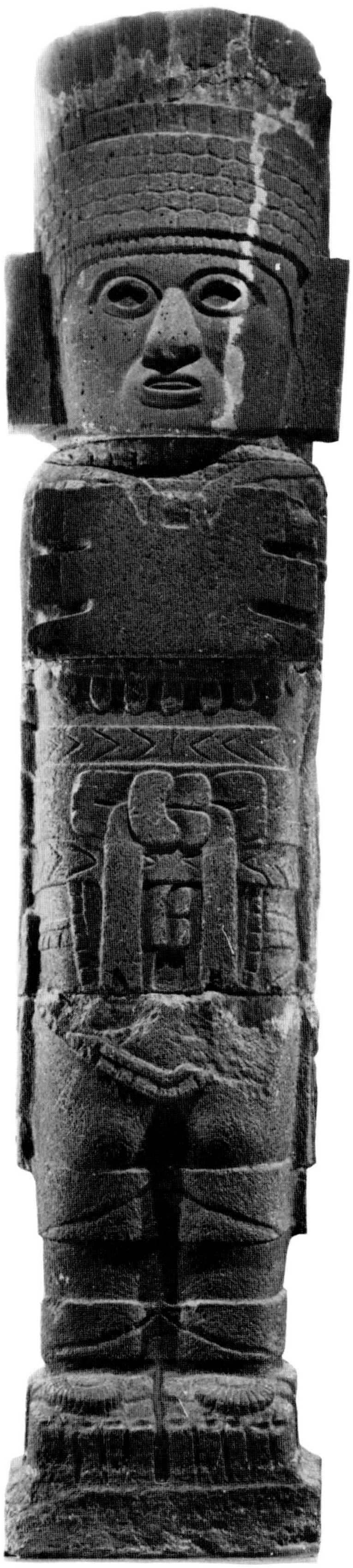

Figure 372
***Atlante of Tula,* stone, h. 4.6 m. Mexico City, Museo Nacional de Antropología.**

motifs in these complex panoramas are the tall alleys of deliberately overscaled spindles on the North and the huge stamping presses on the South. In keeping with the directional symbolism, the spindles drill to size the valve ports in the engine block and are thus engaged with the very interior structure of the motor itself. The stamping presses, in contrast, apply external forces to shape the doors, fenders, and cab that constitute the outside of the car.

More significant, however, is the way these machines allude to the pre-Columbian sculpture of Mexico. Rivera, who collected such sculpture, was well aware of this[29] and consciously enlarged the spindle machines to resemble what Kozloff has plausibly identified as the *Atlantes,* or warriors, from the Aztec pyramid at Tula (fig. 372),[30] whose forms—with their round heads, flat chests, and striated aprons—are uncannily similar to the Ford spindles. These ancient guardians, originally the internal columns of a temple sanctuary surmounting a five-stepped pyramid, thus preside over the internal world of the worker. His external world to the South, however, is dominated by presses that Rivera intended to resemble the Aztec goddess Coatlicue.[31] This deity, whose most impressive manifestation is a statue, eight feet tall, now in the Museo Nacional de Antropología in Mexico City (see fig. 274), represents the struggle of the opposites in nature and human society. Burland characterizes Coatlicue as "the Serpent Lady: Mother Earth from whom all gifts of food grow. She is also the Cipactli monster which presents her as the devouring mother who is at once the womb and the grave."[32] The iconography of this goddess can thus be related to almost all aspects of life and death, to androgyny, war and peace, human sacrifice, the various heavenly bodies, and the four directions.[33] Coatlicue's ominous "mechanomorphic" transformation into a stamping press appears on the West side of the South wall, presiding over the exterior world of the factory workers—not to mention the donor portraits. Rivera originally planned a motif from the Coatlicue statue—the skull at its center and its raised hands open to the directions—in the place on the West wall now occupied by the more explicit compass.[34]

Rivera's subtle references to these Aztec entities underly the political commentary he is covertly making in these murals. On the North wall, where he has depicted the individualized workers as totally immersed in the interior world of industrial and artistic rhythms—willing adjuncts to high technology—he places guardian spirits to protect their dignity. On the South wall, where the workers are vulnerable to exterior forces, he represents the dichotomous spirit of those pressures as totally dominating and all-powerful.

It remains to say a word about the grisaille reliefs that fence in the industrial scenes just analyzed. These depict a day in the life of the workers, beginning in the Northwest corner where they punch in at the time clock and enter the infernal world of their labor, symbolized here by the fiery transformative processes of the steel mill. In the Northeast corner, they pause for lunch close by Rivera's image of his own vegetarian meals. At the Southeast corner, appropriately, fertilizer is made, followed by scenes of spare parts being made, Henry Ford teaching, glass being manufactured, and finally, the day's work over, the workers leaving the plant at dusk to enter the outside world at the Southwest corner. These panels thus sum up the thematic material of the murals and again emphasize the symbolism of the four directions.

Let us conclude by turning to the main panel of the East wall. As stated earlier, the East is the place of light, altars, sacraments, and regenerative symbolism. Rivera's sketches show that he first thought of an agricultural motif of farmers and tractors, perhaps with Chapingo in the back of his mind, for this wall. But something happened to Rivera between these early ideas and the wall's actual execution that sheds light not only on the meaning of this wall of light but also on Rivera's ideas about social realism and political radicalism at this time, as well as on the overall philosophical orientation of this mural environment.

Rivera was accompanied in Detroit by his wife, the artist Frida Kahlo, who was pregnant. She was a brilliant, beautiful woman and a talented painter in her own right. But her life had been blighted as a child when she was severely injured in a bus accident that crushed her pelvis and resulted over the years in the slow deterioration of her spine. Her paintings are graphic in their depiction of her tormented self-image and the agony of endless operations and orthopedic procedures. Her great wish was to have a child by her husband, but despite several attempts, she always miscarried. She did so again in July 1932, while Rivera was working on his murals. Her pain was shared by her husband, who immortalized his lost child as a symbol of rebirth on the East wall—thus bringing his iconographic program, so obsessed with conflict and irony, to a hopeful and dramatic focus. He described this motif as follows:

This germ—a child, not an embryo—is enveloped within the bulb of a plant which sends its roots down into fertile soil deposited in the hollow bed of an ancient lake, above strata of sand, layers of water and salt, and deposits of iron, coal and limestone—which constitute the actual geological composition of the soil of Michigan and the primordial reason for the existence of the city of Detroit.[35]

But granting this autobiographical dimension to the work, we must ultimately ask what is the overall meaning of this mural environment, especially since it was created by a Communist artist painting in Depression-riven Detroit while Ford guards were actually shooting striking workers at the Rouge plants. Where, then, is the radicalism one expects of a social realist artist?

To be radicalized indicates a psychological state more than a political stance. I am referring to those complex, primary motivations that determine patterns of behavior that society perceives as extremes when compared with its conventional modes of procedure. Inherent in the process of radicalization is some violation of human expectation so extreme, so crushing, so devastating to the individual's sense of entitlement or exemption within the norms of his ethos, that he must either succumb to the utter negation of his integrity or rebel. Injustice, therefore, is the basic motivating force behind the radicalized personality; the dream of perfect justice, the goal.

Why is it, then, that Diego Rivera's greatest mural is so lacking in a politically radical vision. As a world-renowned Communist, he was certainly not inclined to coddle his capitalist patrons. But as a great artist, he understood instinctively the inutility of depicting the immediate turmoil. Rather he chose a more understated yet no less devastating image of the Ford workers: integrated into a vast, mechanized, aesthetically elegant system of industrial production to the point where they become anonymous organic connectors within the relentless rhythms and needs of a geometric whole. Rivera loved the machine; he also understood what the machine could do to people. But the machine had never done anything to him—and it thus could not radicalize him.

In contrast, I would suggest that Rivera's wife Frida was the true radical—radicalized by profound physical misfortune. Her art cries out against the injustice of a pain-racked fate. Rivera lived with no such fate and had the genius's incapacity for a permanent commitment to the failed lives of others, either in society or in his wives, as Hayden Herrera makes so clear in her biography of Kahlo. Rivera, never touched by violence, could never be a radical. He was a humanist, not a revolutionary, totally engaged by a personal, not a political, vision.

And perhaps he understood more than most who read it, that the inscription he found already carved on the West wall of opposites, with the words *Vita brevis* to the South, where life is born, flourishes, and dies in broad daylight, and the words *longa ars* to the North, where life's eternal, internal mysteries prevail, was a saying of Hippocrates that refers to the art of healing, not image-making. And perhaps he knew that the stark depiction of an open wound is a less effective political statement than the creation of a healing interior cosmos where the tragedies of being alive can be raised to inspiring symbols of wholeness, hope, and renewal—as his miscarried child proclaims from the East of his masterpiece—poised between those natural opposites that neither personal nor political outrage, whether in society or art, can ever hope to unite.

Notes

Jorge Hernández Campos, pages 119-123

1. Phoenix 1984, 12–15 (III).

2. Torriente 1959, I: 206 (I).

3. Ibid., 211.

4. Ibid., 212.

5. Phoenix 1984, 19 (III).

6. Torriente 1959, I: 218 (I).

7. Ibid., 237–38.

8. For a discussion of this subject, see Giorgio di Santillana, *Processo a Galileo, studio storico-critico* (Milan: Arnoldo Mondadori Editore, 1960), 146–165. In this study di Santillana discusses the conflict resulting from the breakdown of the system in which physics and philosophy were one. He also describes the Aristotelian-Platonic universe that anti-Galilean orthodoxy sought to defend. The 16th-century humanist Pope Urban II, writes di Santillana, "lived in a variable and infinite world of significant forms and perceptible substances, where names and attributes were manifold and subject to discourse. . . . He considered that any new natural conclusion should enrich the world, not reduce it to geometric space." This conflict instilled the need to reconcile opposites, especially in Counter-Reformation Spain. Perhaps it is the echoes of this conflict, so characteristic of the culture of Latin countries in general, that are heard centuries later in the process from Impressionism to Cubism, in which Spaniards such as Picasso and Juan Gris, and the Mexican Rivera, participated.

9. Torriente 1959, I: 239 (I).

10. Germán Gedovius was born in 1867 in Mexico, the son of a German father and a Mexican mother. Deaf and mute, he was sent for treatment to Hamburg, where he lived with his paternal grandmother. Around 1883 he entered the Royal Academy of Munich, where he studied painting, absorbing the influence of Wilhelm Leibl, Arnold Böcklin, Hans von Marées, and others. See Fausto Ramírez, "La obra de Germán Gedovius, una reconsideración," in *Germán Gedovius: Una generación entre dos siglos: el porfiriato y la pos-revolución,* exh. cat., Museo Nacional de Arte, Secretaría de Educación Pública (INBA), 1984.

11. Torriente 1959, I: 242 (I).

12. Phoenix 1984, 21 (III).

13. The establishment of this dogma was stimulated by the program of *"mexicanidad"* instituted by President Miguel Alemán (term 1946–52). His program for national development focused on industrialization and the opening of Mexico to foreign capital.

14. Jean Claire, "Données d'un probleme," in *Les realismes,* exh. cat. (Paris: Centre Georges Pompidou, 1981), 8.

15. Cited by Claire (note 14), 9.

16. Torriente 1959, II: 19 (I).

17. Torriente 1959, I: 227 (I).

18. Jean Leymarie in *Nouveau dictionnaire de la peinture moderne* (Paris; Fernand Hazan, 1963), 76–79.

19. Roberto Longhi, *Piero della Francesca (1927), con aggiunte fino al 1962,* (Florence: Sansoni, 1975), 202.

20. Frank Elgar in *Nouveau dictionnaire* (note 18), 42.

21. Longhi (note 19), 185.

22. Cited by Longhi (note 19), 182.

23. Cited by Longhi (note 19), 210.

24. Cited by Longhi (note 19), 221. Further, Roberto Longhi provides an early personal corroboration of Claire's theory of an *"histoire autre"* when he states that his own theory of "modern culture," adopted around 1910, was not based "in Cubism, nor in the 'metaphysical' movement, which had not yet occurred, but rather in the reconstructive Post-Impressionism of Cézanne and Seurat. These artists, with their capacity for synthesis of form and color through perspective (*'le tout mis en perspective,'* in words attributed to Cézanne, which may be taken as authentic), did not engender the aesthetic confusion of the past fifty years. Rather, they initiated a critical search, one which could recapture the history of a great poetic ideal that surfaced in the first half of the Quattrocento. In short, Piero was rediscovered critically by Cézanne and Seurat . . . and not by the genial rhapsodist Picasso."

25. Giulio Carlo Argan, *L'arte moderna, 1770/1970* (Florence:Sansoni, 1977), 510.

26. Pierre Cabanne and Pierre Restany, *L'avant garde au xxe siecle* (Paris: Edicion André Ballard, 1969), 182.

27. Torriente 1959, II: 25 (I).

28. Ibid., 85.

Alicia Azuela, pages 125-129

1. Rivera 1934d, 17 (V).

2. Rivera 1933d (V).

3. Diego Rivera, unpublished pamphlet, Detroit Institute of Arts Research Library Files.

4. Rivera 1933c (V).

5. Rivera 1933e, 275 (V).

6. Rivera 1933c (V).

Ida Rodríguez-Prampolini, pages 131-137

1. Rivera 1925 (V).

2. Rivera 1929 (V).

3. Chávez 1946 (I).

4. Ibid.

5. Rivera in the introduction to Mexico City 1947, 56 (III).

6. David Alfaro Siqueiros, *No hay más ruta que la nuestra.* (Mexico: 1945).

7. Quoted in Elga Gallas, *Teoría marxista de la literatura* (Mexico City: Siglo, 1973), 19: 62.

8. Rivera 1925, 17 (V).

9. Ibid.

10. George Lukács, *History and Class Consciousness,* Rodney Livingstone, trans. (London: Merlin Press, 1971), 33.

11. Ibid., 33.

12. A. G. Lehman, "The Marxist as a Literary Critic," in *George Lukács, The Man, His Works and His Ideas,* G.H.R. Parkinson, ed. (London: Vintage Books, 1970), 173.

Betty Ann Brown, pages 139-155

1. Although Rivera clearly thought of the Italian frescoes as "popular art capable of nourishing the masses" (Wolfe 1963, 115 [I]), and even so politically enlightened an art historian as Shifra Goldman (1982, 111 [II]) writes that the Mexican muralists hoped their works "would serve, as in the Renaissance, like a 'painted book,' " I would argue that the Italian murals were neither accessible to nor intended for the masses during the Renaissance. Certainly this is true of the main religious commissions, from Giotto's Arena Chapel to Michelangelo's Sistine Ceiling, which were created for private chapels available only to the wealthy elite.

2. Catlin 1964, 448 (II).

3. Edwards 1966, 169 (IV).

4. Charlot 1962a, 72 (IV)

5. Henry B. Nicholson, "Religion in Pre-Hispanic Central Mexico," in *Handbook of Middle American Indians,* vol. 10 (Austin: University of Texas Press, 1971), chart opposite page 408.

6. The ruins of Teotihuacán, centered around two large temples known as the Pyramid of the Sun and the Pyramid of the Moon, are found in a small valley contiguous with the Valley of Mexico and thus quite close to modern Mexico City. Teotihuacán culture flourished during the Early Classic period, i.e., A.D. 300–600.

7. See Donald Robertson, *Mexican Manuscript Painting of the Early Colonial Period: The Metropolitan Schools* (New Haven: Yale University Press, 1959), 19.

8. Edwards 1966, 262 (IV).

9. The Codex Borbonicus is housed in the Bibliothèque de l'Assemblée Nationale in Paris, where Rivera could have viewed it during his years of residence in that city. He could have continued his study of this book by consulting the facsimile edition published by Ernest Theodore Hamy in 1899 (Paris: Ernest Leroux). Rivera, like most scholars of his time (including the eminent Alfonso Caso), no doubt considered the Codex Borbonicus an authentically pre-Columbian document. Today, many scholars hold that it is Early Colonial in date.

10. Jacinto Quirarte, "The Coatlicue in Modern Mexican Painting," *Research Center for the Arts Review* 5, 2 (April 1982): 5.

11. Edwards 1966, 205 (IV).

12. Emily Umberger, "Montezuma's Throne," paper delivered at the Symposium on the History of Art at the Frick Collection, New York, 1976. Umberger, through analysis of the glyphic and pictorial elements on the Teocalli, confirms not only that Montezuma II commissioned the monument, but also that he used it as an imperial throne.

13. March 1960, 195 (I).

14. Stanton Catlin (1964 and 1978 [II]) has thoroughly documented the sources of the Cuernavaca images. My discussion here relies heavily on his.

15. Catlin (1964, 448 [II]) asserts that when Rivera depicted pre-Columbian images, he did so in the flat, stylized manner of pre-Columbian art and that a "more naturalistic treatment was reserved for themes identified with foreign and private interests." If this were the case, one could argue for a simple and direct equation between Rivera's mural style(s) and his political opinions. I read his images as more complex and would assert that both the often reproduced jaguar warrior of the Palacio de Cortés battle scene and the crouching coyote figure of the *Crossing the Ravine* segment are as perceptually rendered as any conquistador. Both animal-costumed figures have naturalistic anatomical proportions; both their positions are realistic, involving foreshortening and overlap; and both are depicted with light-dark shading to give the impression of three-dimensionality. None of these pictorial conventions was part of the pre-Columbian Aztec repertory.

16. See Arthur J. O. Anderson and Charles E. Dibble, trans. and ed., *Florentine Codex: General History of the Things of New Spain* (Sante Fe: The School of American Research and the University of New Mexico, 1970).

17. Wolfe 1963, 264 (I).

18. See Frank Boos, *The Ceramic Sculptures of Ancient Oaxaca* (New York: A. S. Barnes and Co., 1966), 92–119

19. Anderson and Dibble (note 16), 41–42.

20. See *Codex Laud. (Bodleian Library). True Color facsimile of the old Mexican manuscript* (Graz: Akademische Druck-und Verlagsanstalt, 1966).

21. Anderson and Dibble (note 16), 23.

22. Anderson and Dibble (note 16), 16.

23. Perhaps the most concise illustration of the life-out-of-death concept in pre-Columbian thought is the Aztec glyph for grass *(malinalli),* which has the plant growing out of the skeletal jaws of the earth. Of course the earth goddess Coatlicue, with her death/fertility iconography combines the two as well.

24. Quirarte (note 10), 1–8.

25. Goldman 1982, 114 (II).

26. Ibid.

27. Ibid.

28. March 1960, 168 (I).

29. Quirarte (note 10), 1.

Francis V. O'Connor, pages 157-183

This essay is a development of a lecture, "The Mexican Muralists and New Deal Artists: Thoughts on the Dynamics of Influence in Art," which I gave at the Detroit Institute of Arts as part of its "Mexico Today" symposium on Saturday, November 4, 1978. I want to thank Linda Downs, Curator of Education, the Detroit Institute of Arts, for her continuing support of this research.

1. Harold Bloom, *The Anxiety of Influence: A Theory of Poetry* (New York: Oxford University Press, 1973), 19. The words "poets," "read," etc., have been changed to apply to the visual arts.

2. Bloom (note 1), 5.

3. Bloom (note 1), 30.

4. Bloom (note 1), 5.

5. For a recent study of the psychology of the creative genius, see John Gedo, *Portrait of the Artist* (New York: Guilford Press, 1983), especially chapter 6.

6. For my ideas concerning the developmental psychology of the artist's life course, see "The Psychodynamics of the Frontal Self-Portrait," in *Psychoanalytic Perspectives on Art*, (Hillsdale, NJ: The Analytic Press, 1985), 169–221.

7. Excerpt from an unpublished lecture given by Thomas Hart Benton to the John Reed Club at the Irving Plaza Auditorium, New York, February 11, 1934, Jackson Pollock Papers, the Archives of American Art, Smithsonian Institution.

8. For a discussion of this period in Benton's career, see Matthew Baigell, *Thomas Hart Benton* (New York: Harry N. Abrams, 1973), 68–74.

9. Thomas Hart Benton, *An American in Art: A Professional and Technical Autobiography* (Lawrence: The University Press of Kansas, 1969), 61–62.

10. The Art Deco mural, as created by artists such as Eugene Savage and Hildreth Meière during the 1920s and 1930s, was an outgrowth of the so-called "American Renaissance" mural movement that flourished ca. 1900. These younger academic artists tried, with some success, to bring the traditional allegorical conventions for wall painting up to date with "moderne" devices such as simplified classical motifs, streamlining, and industrial materials such as glass and chromium. Benton was well aware of this style—as the newly restored silver moldings of the New School murals attest. But he was not about to copy these newer conventions wholesale. For a discussion of these matters, as well as the restoration of the New School murals, see Emily Braun and Thomas Branchick, *Thomas Hart Benton: The American Today Murals* (New York: The Equitable and Williams College, 1985) ext. cat.

11. Thomas Craven, "American Month in the Galleries," *The Arts* 11 (March 1927): 151.

12. Lewis Mumford, "Thomas Hart Benton," *Creative Art* 3 (December 1928): xxxvii.

13. Lee Simonson, "The Palette Knife," *Creative Art* 3 (October 1928): xxxii.

14. See Baigell (note 8), 129, pl. 92.

15. Thomas Hart Benton, "Mechanics of Form Organization in Painting," *The Arts* 10 (1926): 285–89 and 340–42; *The Arts* 11 (1927): 43–44, 95–96, and 145–48.

16. Since there is no evidence that Benton ever saw a completed mural environment by Rivera, I hesitate to attribute every device found in the New School murals exclusively to the Mexican's influence. Benton was also well aware of the American academic mural tradition going back to Constantino Brumidi. As the son of a congressman in the period 1897 to 1905, he would have seen more of the U.S. capital's best murals than any tourist. (Many of Brumidi's best environments are off limits and virtually unknown, even to art historians—a situation I hope to correct in my forthcoming history of the American mural.) Benton himself admitted seeing the academic murals that were being painted by the masters of the American Renaissance in the Library of Congress while he was in Washington. Further, he certainly saw the major murals of Paris and New York and knew a number of muralists and architects. He would have discovered the oppositional and directional logic of mural environments from many sources. Rivera's impact was more stylistic than formal in this respect.

17. Excerpt from Diego Rivera's foreword to the catalogue of an exhibition of the *Tom Mooney* series of gouaches by Ben Shahn presented at the Downtown Gallery, New York, May 2–20, 1933. Reprinted courtesy of the Kennedy Galleries, New York.

18. See John D. Morse, ed., *Ben Shahn* (New York: Praeger, 1972), 20, and Bernarda Bryson Shahn, *Ben Shahn* (New York: Harry N. Abrams, 1972), 133, 135, 287–88.

19. James Thrall Soby, *Ben Shahn: Paintings* (New York: George Braziller, 1963), 10.

20. See note 17. For a color illustration of *Apotheosis,* see New York, Kennedy Galleries, *Ben Shahn* (exh. cat.), 1968, no. 4.

21. See note 17.

22. George Biddle, *An American Artist's Story* (Boston: Little, Brown, 1939), 268.

23. I am indebted to Masha Zakheim Jewett, *Coit Tower, San Francisco: Its History and Art* (San Francisco: Volcano Press, 1983), for much of the historical information concerning these murals and their creators.

24. Francis V. O'Connor, ed., *Art for the Millions: Essays from the 1930s by Artists and Administrators of the WPA Federal Art Project* (Greenwich, CT: New York Graphic Society Ltd., 1973), 69.

25. *Washington Post,* April 12, 1936.

26. O'Connor (note 24), 76–77.

27. Quoted by the muralist William Walker on p. 5 of Cockcroft/Weber/Cockcroft (see below). I wish to acknowledge my indebtedness to Cedric Dover, *American Negro Art* (Greenwich, CT: New York Graphic Society Ltd., 1960); Eva Cockcroft, John Weber, and John Cockcroft, *Toward a People's Art: The Contemporary Mural Movement* (New York: E. P. Dutton, 1977); and Alan Barnett, *Community Murals: The People's Art* (Philadelphia: The Art Alliance Press, 1984) in the writing of this section and to thank John Weber and Victor Sorell for their help in obtaining photographs.

28. Quoted in Hugh Curtler, *A Theory of Art, Tragedy and Culture: The Philosophy of Eliseo Vivas* (New York: Haven Publications, 1981), 51.

29. For this history, see Gary O. Larson, *The Reluctant Patron: The United States Government and the Arts, 1943–1965* (Philadelphia: University of Pennsylvania Press, 1983).

30. It should be noted that the *Wall of Respect,* as with so many community murals, was very much an ongoing project. As with Native American wall paintings, its communal purpose took precedence over its status as a work of "art" and the wall's montage of panels was changed in keeping with the community's interest. The first version was completed in 1967, many minor changes were apparently made thereafter, and major changes and additions occurred in 1969. The version of the wall reproduced here appears to date from about 1969. For accounts and pictures of earlier versions of the wall, see Cockcroft/Weber/Cockcroft and Barnett (note 27). A full history of the wall's pictorial evolution until its destruction in 1971 has yet to be reconstructed.

31. See Barnett (note 27), 396.

32. See Cockcroft/Weber/Cockcroft (note 27), 233–34.

33. Quoted in Rodríguez 1969, 133 (IV).

34. Quoted in Curtler (note 28), 11.

35. The recent sobering spectacle of the Museum of Modern Art's exhibition " 'Primitivism' in 20th-Century Art: Affinity of the Tribal and the Modern," in which the numinous power of the native creations eclipsed the "aesthetic" presence of the modern and contemporary works, serves fair warning that many of the pretensions of "modernism" no longer can be sustained in the face of authentic human image-making (a.k.a. art). See the two-volume catalogue edited by William Rubin (New York: The Museum of Modern Art, 1984) for a number of brilliant restatements of modernism's shaky case.

Luis Cardoza y Aragon, pages 185-187

1. Herbert Read, *A Concise History of Modern Painting* (New York: Praeger, 1968), 8.

2. Walter Pach, "The Relationship between North American Culture and the Work of Diego Rivera," in Mexico City 1949, 207 (III).

3. Quoted in Tibol 1979, 27 (I).

4. Federico García Lorca, *Antología poética* (Mexico City: Costa Amir, 1944).

Xavier Moyssén, pages 189-195

1. In all of Rivera's numerous writings, there is no reference to his ideas on self-portraits. His brief introduction to the catalogue of the 1947 exhibition "Forty-Five Self-Portraits of Mexican Painters" does not discuss the theme of the show but rather the function of art in politics.

2. Fernández 1950, 81 (II).

Rita Eder, pages 197-201

1. Arnaldo Córdova, *La ideología de la revolución mexicana* (Mexico City: Ediciones Era, 1979), 15.

Ellen Sharp, pages 203-213

1. March 1960, 124 (I). The sketch Rivera refers to is *Zapatistas,* Puebla, July 3, 1921, which is reproduced in Mexico City 1949, pl. on p. 113 (III). This loosely drawn pencil sketch of seated peasants wearing sombreros has color notations in French and betrays the artist's obvious pleasure in depicting the large, round shapes of the hats.

2. New York 1931, 10 (III) and Wolfe 1963, 18–19 (I).

3. Charlot 1962, 144–46 (IV).

4. Vorobëv 1962, 199 (IV).

5. Wolfe 1963, 68 (I).

6. March 1960, 122–23 (I).

7. Jean Charlot, "Diego Rivera in Italy," *Magazine of Art* 46,1 (January 1953): 10.

8. March 1960, 126 (I).

9. Edward Weston, *The Daybooks of Edward Weston* (Rochester NY: Eastman House, 1961), I: 31.

10. Jean Charlot, unpub. ms. (chapter omitted from Charlot 1962a [IV]), Jean Charlot Collection, University of Hawaii at Manoa.

11. Weston (note 9), II: 250.

12. March 1960, 157 (I).

Francis V. O'Connor, pages 215-229

I am grateful to Linda Downs, Curator of Education, the Detroit Institute of Arts, for inviting me to give, on March 20, 1977, the first lecture on Rivera's *Detroit Industry* murals since they were eclipsed by controversy in 1933. This essay constitutes a thorough revision and development of my extemporaneous remarks at that time. I also wish to acknowledge her subsequent generosity in sharing the fruits of her own research into these murals and in creating several opportunities for me to participate in conferences concerning them. I am also indebted to Dr. Laurance P. Hurlburt, whose unpublished history of Mexican muralists in the United States has been a valuable source of information.

1. In the strictest sense of the word, to "orient" something is to turn it toward the Orient—the East—the direction of the rising sun. Similarly, the architectural term "orientation" derives from the fact that the axes of most early temples and other major buildings ran from East to West, with the entrance at the East, but it has come to refer to the overall directional symbolism of a building or environment.

2. See Joseph Campbell, *The Hero with a Thousand Faces*, The Bollingen Series XVII (Princeton, NJ: Princeton University Press, 1949); *The Masks of Gods: Creative Mythology* (New York: The Viking Press, 1968; and *The Mythic Image*, The Bollingen Series C (Princeton, NJ: Princeton University Press, 1974).

3. Jean Charlot to Linda Downs, private correspondence, April 12, 1978. Rivera mentions Giotto in Rivera 1929 (V).

4. I have relied here on the essays in James Shibblebine, ed., *Giotto: The Arena Chapel Frescoes* (New York: W. W. Norton & Company, 1969).

5. E. H. Gombrich, *Means and Ends: Reflections on the History of Fresco Painting* (London: Thames & Hudson, 1976), 10–11.

6. See Catlin 1978 (II).

7. Irene Nicholson, *Mexican and Central American Mythology* (London: The Hamlyn Publishing Group, 1967), 94–96.

8. Wolfe 1963, 173 (I).

9. Ibid., 172.

10. I am grateful to the muralist John Weber for pointing out (private conversation, August 24, 1984) the different sense a wall painter has of an exterior wall as opposed to an interior wall. Inside, enclosed by four walls and a ceiling, the outer direction is the most important and the mural becomes, in a sense, a window to it. Outside, on the other hand, facing a wall open to the sky, the situation immediately in front of the wall takes on an added force.

11. I want to thank Professor Stanton Catlin for his generous help in identifying and locating these coats of arms and giving me a sense of how Mexicans think about the directions of their country. A complete listing of the coats of arms on each wall can be found in Suárez 1972, 275 (IV). While it is clear from the evidence that Rivera was fully conscious of both the universal and the situational directionality of walls, it is unclear whether all the sequences of mural panels at the Secretaría were conceived in such terms. Why, for instance, are the arts on the North-facing South wall of the Court of Labor, or why are images of the proletarian revolution in the *corrido* series on the same wall of the Court of Fiestas? Obviously a more detailed directional analysis of this vast and complex program is called for; here we must be content to establish a beginning to Rivera's evolving awareness of this matter and proceed with the subject of this essay.

12. Laurance P. Hurlburt, "Diego Rivera in New York, 1933: Contrasts to the *Detroit Industry* Murals," unpublished lecture given at the Detroit Institute of Arts, March 5, 1983.

13. I am indebted to Professor Dorothy McMeekin for her assistance in establishing the precise orientation of Chapingo and Detroit. At Chapingo, to put the matter more accurately, the axis of the chapel is at azimuth thirty-six degrees and the summer solstice is at azimuth sixty-five degrees (private communication, December 27, 1984).

14. Quoted in Wolfe 1963, 306 (I).

15. According to McMeekin, the North wall is thirty-five to thirty-six degrees to the West of due North and the East wall points to azimuth fifty-four to fifty-five degrees, while the summer solstice is at azimuth fifty-six to fifty-eight degrees at the latitude of Detroit.

16. It should be noted that this motif is at the center of a long panel that is painted, like the compass, in grisaille. This gives the trompe l'oeil effect of its being carved in stone—an effect often utilized in Italian Renaissance murals, as seen earlier in Giotto's Virtues and Vices. Rivera also uses this technique in the small panels that "fence in" the vast industrial scenes on the North and South walls. While these dozen panels, emulating metal relief, are perfectly plausible in this context, one wonders why Rivera chose grisaille for the horizontal panel over the West door. While he might well have thought of echoing the relief carving of the caryatids above the arched windows around the court, one suspects this artistic reason was supplemented by a political joke. The central motif of this panel is a star, which, if the panel were polychrome like the rest of the wall—and given Rivera's communist ideology—would have had to be colored red (as is the almost hidden star on the worker's glove in one of the lower panels). This, as he could well have imagined, would have caused his patrons and everyone else to see red. So he painted it the color of the 250 million-year-old limestone of which the Garden Court is constructed and no one ever noticed. Also, as I suggested in my original lecture, it is likely that the star is actually red underneath its tan paint and stands there as an echo of Rivera's sardonic humor, serious ideology, and profound sense of life's oppositions.

17. Rivera 1933a, 291 (V).

18. See the last page of this essay for further reference to the inscription from Hippocrates.

19. Dorothy McMeekin, "Science and Its Broad Cultural Context in the Detroit Murals," unpublished lecture given at the Detroit Institute of Arts, March 5, 1983.

20. Linda Downs, "The Detroit Murals: New Insights and Changing Views," unpublished lecture given at the Detroit Institute of Arts, March 5, 1983.

21. See Stettler negative #2773 (8-24-32), Detroit Institute of Arts photographic files.

22. McMeekin (note 19).

23. See Wolfe 1963, 308 (I), and Dolores Olmedo to Linda Downs, private correspondence, September 1984, concerning, respectively, Rivera's diet and his interest in both homeopathy and allopathy.

24. McMeekin (note 19).

25. McMeekin (note 19) makes a brilliant analogy between the formal composition of the embryo panel and that of the industrial scene on the South wall, yet this small panel is on the North wall. It is possible that Rivera originally designed it for the South wall and that it was transferred to the North when he decided to place the hormone lab to the South. Unfortunately, there does not seem to be any photographic evidence indicating the vaccination scene was ever considered for the South wall.

26. Detroit 1978, 70 (III), and Hurlburt (note 12).

27. Hurlburt (note 12).

28. See Detroit 1978, figs. 93 and 114 (III).

29. Rivera 1933a, 291 (V).

30. Kozloff 1978, 224 (II).

31. Walter Pach, as quoted in Hurlburt (note 12).

32. C. A. Burland, *The Gods of Mexico* (New York: G. P. Putnam's Sons, 1967), ix.

33. Justino Fernández, as cited in Hurlburt (note 12).

34. Campbell 1974 (note 2), 157, and Detroit 1978, fig. 53 (III).

35. Rivera 1933a, 289–91 (IV).

Mural Census

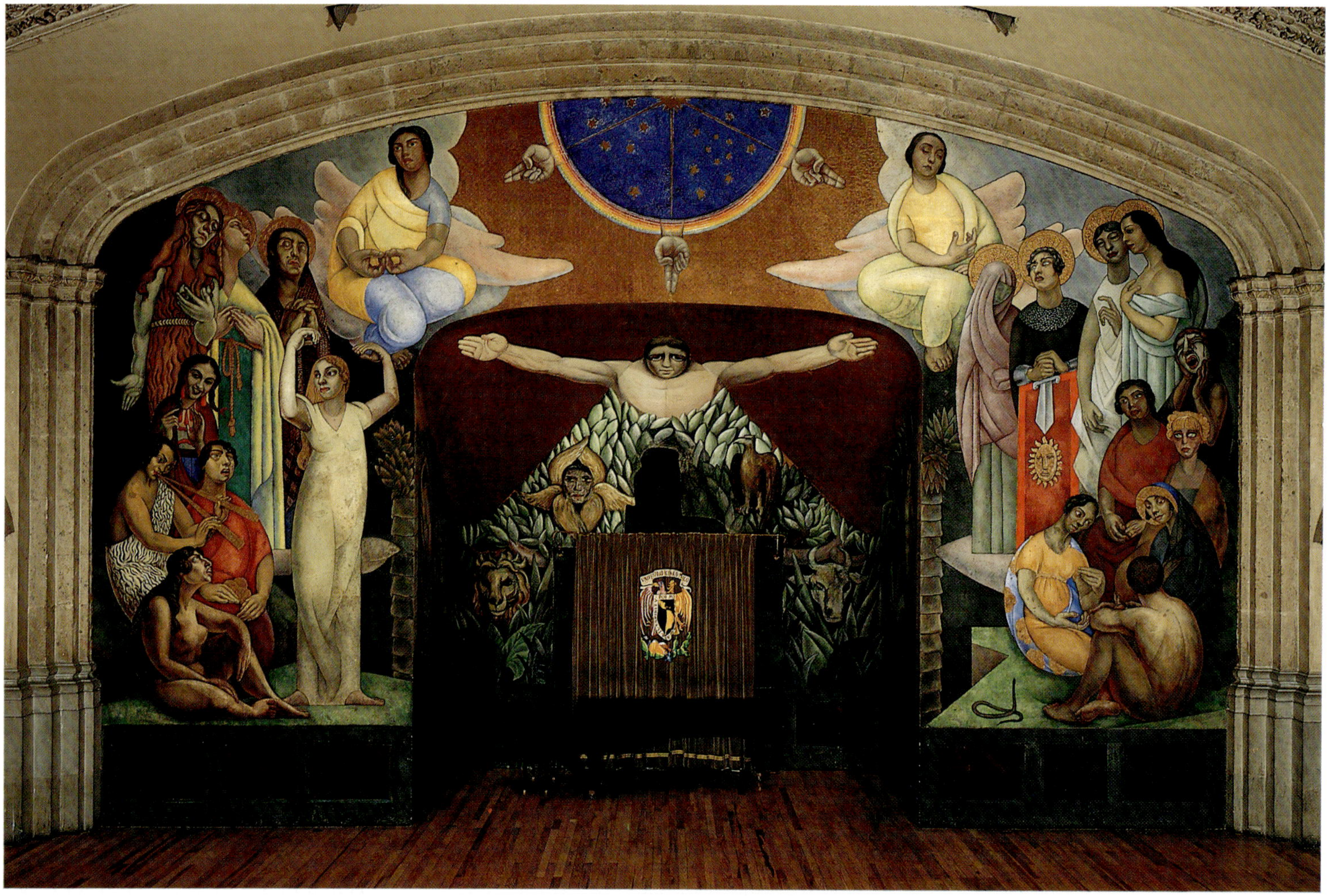

Anfiteatro Bolívar

Mexico City

Figure 373.
Creation, 1922–23, encaustic and gold leaf, 7.08 × 12.19 m. Mexico City, Escuela Nacional Preparatoria, Anfiteatro Bolívar.

Diego Rivera's first mural in Mexico was commissioned early in 1922 by José Vasconcelos—the recently appointed minister of education under the revolutionary government of President Alvaro Obregón—within six months of the artist's return from his long stay in Europe. In the eyes of his Mexican contemporaries, Rivera's assignment was at once the most formidable and sought after (although not actually competed for) of the initial commissions that launched the minister's plan for a publicly visible art program as a complement to his new centralized national education policy.

The Escuela Nacional Preparatoria was an upper-class institution of special importance to Licenciado Vasconcelos, a dissident alumnus from the last years of the Díaz dictatorship. Its handsome, recently finished auditorium, the Anfiteatro Bolívar, offered the most auspicious formal assembly area in which to begin to realize his grand ambition to eliminate illiteracy and to elevate and consolidate the cultural condition of the nation as a whole.

The classical design, symbolic imagery, magnified figure scale, and vivid color of the resulting work seem to have satisfied the minister as shown by his renewal of rather open-ended patronage to Rivera soon afterward. Although Wolfe called it a "false start," the problems Rivera faced in working out a mural program that would bridge the differences between his own Cubist perspectives and the minister's complex philosophy can be considered both ingeniously and solidly thought through and resolved.[1]

The problem was to devise a composition that would symbolize the potential fusion of native indigenous tradition with the moral imperatives of the Judeo-Christian religion and the intellectual standards of Hellenic civilization; in the latter case including in particular the premise of the astronomer-philosopher Pythagoras, with whose thought Vasconcelos was deeply imbued, that a mathematical and mystical harmony of numbers underlies universal reality.

Vasconcelos's commission had a further purpose: to replace the stigma of another mural, remembered from his own student days at the Preparatoria, that once occupied the principal stairway of the main school building, Juan Cordero's 19th-century *Triumph of Science and Labor over Ignorance and Sloth,* an emblem of positivism, the utilitarian philosophy of the Díaz era, which his egalitarian and more broadly visionary policies were designed to supersede.[2] There can be little doubt that he felt Rivera's appointment had been vindicated, despite outside attacks and ridicule. In art historical perspective, the mural must be considered a major painting in the international tradition of rationalized Art Nouveau, or "Art Deco," as it has come to be called.

Although the sequence of events has not been precisely determined, Jean Charlot's account confirms that Rivera's work in the enclosed area of the Anfiteatro had to overlap in time with the first mural assignments being carried out by members of the Union of Technical Workers, Painters, and Sculptors in the nearby open courtyard of the school. There, the erection of scaffolds in the stairways and along three floors of patio corridors, together with the uninhibited, untidy working habits of experimenting mural painters, and, above all, the unconventional forms that began to appear on the walls as the artists strove to create a native Mexican style, provoked the students into slanderous, rock-throwing attacks against the painters and school administrators. Some of the murals were damaged, and arming themselves with pistols, the artist fought back. The confrontation lasted well over a year and eventually escalated to implicate the official authorities in the newly reformed Ministry of Education, including the minister himself. Through it all Rivera seems to have continued to work more or less unmolested in the auditorium. After more than a year of tumult, a full-blown student riot prompted a presidential decree in August 1924 that caused all mural work at the Preparatoria to be suspended.[3]

By this time the scene of artistic opportunity had shifted to the new Secretaría de Educación Pública. On completion of his Anfiteatro mural, Rivera had received an appointment as "Head of the Department of Plastic Crafts" in the Ministry of Education and was already working on designs for the first court at the time the building was dedicated in July 1924. But he did not completely escape the effects of the controversy at the Preparatoria. In the end it was Rivera who was fixed upon, through spoken and written criticism and general public outcry, as the leader of the whole offensive movement in mural art. He succeeded in deflecting this accusation by making public statements that, to the dismay of his colleagues, minimized the importance of the uprising and the resultant damage to the aims and self-respect of the artists' group.

The theme of the mural, creation, is presented as a composition of human and animal figures with conventional symbolic attributes shown in unconventional associations. The two principal figure groups are arranged vertically to the left and right of the auditorium's proscenium wall and are positioned on either side of a deeply recessed central niche.

The overall composition is an exposition of individual tenets of Vasconcelos's Pythagoreanism, adapted to Mexico's interracial and postrevolutionary social circumstances, as interpreted and grouped together allegorically by the artist.[4] The program's motif-by-motif sequence begins at the top of the proscenium arch with a symbol (diag. 1) representing *Primal Energy* (or "light one" in Rivera's own description),[5] a sky disk with stars and sun rays framed by a rainbow arc.[6] From the edge of the disk extend three half-closed hands that point downward to the figure in the niche and to the figures assembled on the right and left walls. The index and middle fingers of each hand point outward toward the world; the others are folded in, signifying father and mother as "origin," or perhaps suggesting the Pythagorean concept of duality. Within the curve of the rainbow are two constellations: a hexagon of stars to the left, standing for the feminine principle, and a pentagon of stars to the right, for the masculine.

In the niche, *Emergent Man* (2), outstretched arms and hands suggesting both sacrifice and offering, emerges from a mass of heavy foliage. Azuela suggests that this depersonalized image is the Pantocrator (the godhead or lord of the universe, commonly associated with the authority figure of Christ in Byzantine iconography), here symbolizing the universal logos.[7] The religious implications of the scene are balanced by the placement of the figure, the New Testament symbols of the ox, lion, and eagle, and the wing-capped head of a man in a tropical jungle, where the inclusion of other natural creatures heightens the allusion to biological evolution. *Emergent Man* prefigures the commanding human figures of Rivera's later mural work, such as "Man the Controller of the Universe" in the RCA Building and the feminine symbol of California at the San Francisco Stock Exchange.

On either side of the proscenium, above the seated figures of Adam and Eve, conceived as a mestizo couple, ascend personifications of the virtues and creative forces that sustain the human race. Arranged according to a Christian-Classical hierarchy, these opposite, symmetrical figure groups represent the respective emanations of the masculine and feminine spirits.

On the left, Eve, or *Woman* (3), an indigenous nude with heavy features and a dull expression, looks upward. *Dance* (4) is a white-clad blond woman from Michoácan, whose pose and folded tunic conjure the rhythmic movements of a creole dancer. *Music* (5), a faunlike figure clad in a goatskin, plays a double flute, accompanied by *Song* (6), a dark, clear-eyed Jaliscan creole, who holds three Hesperidean apples in her lap. *Comedy* (7), a sophisticated creole from the central plateau with braided hair, a pendant necklace, and earrings, smiles mischievously.

Above this pyramidal group, three standing figures with halos represent the three theological virtues. *Charity* (8), covered by her long reddish hair, offers her breast in the attitude of nursing. *Hope* (9), a Castilian type, looks upward to the central motif. *Faith* (10), a pure Indian from the sierras of the Valley of Mexico, stands in prayer. Nearest the symbol of light, *Wisdom* (11) rests on a cloud meditating; with her hands she makes a sign that signifies both infinity and the macrocosm and microcosm.

On the right, Adam, or *Man* (12), his back to the viewer, looks at *Fable* (13), a figure wearing a diadem and cowl, who gazes at him bemused. To his left, *Knowledge* (14), with darker face and serious expression, appears to be explaining something to him. Behind her sits *Erotic Poetry* (15), a figure with green eyes, white skin, golden hair, and a bleary-eyed stare. *Tradition* (16), an indigenous working woman wearing an earth red rebozo, rests her hands in her lap, feigning detachment. *Tragedy* (17) holds a grief mask before her face. *Prudence* (18), a creole dressed in a green tunic, converses with *Justice* (19), a pure Indian type. Looking into the distance, *Strength* (20) leans on the edge of a shield bearing an image of the sun, symbol of divinity, her dagger and armour signifying defense against temptation. The head and hands of *Continence*

(21) are veiled with a violet cloak. (In view of their positions in the composition and their depiction with halos, it is obvious that *Prudence, Justice, Strength,* and *Continence* were conceived as parallel in rank to the figures representing the theological virtues of faith, hope and charity. In Vasconcelos's perspective these virtues were equally important as aids to spiritual purification.) Finally, *Science* (22), like the corresponding winged figure of *Wisdom,* rests on a cloud contemplating the scene below while compositionally uniting it to the central symbol of the cosmos.

The overtones of Rivera's naturalist, rather than metaphysical, outlook on life notwithstanding, the mural *Creation* seems fairly and fully to present Vasconcelos's belief that the "fusion of racial strains [represented by the mestizo couple] . . . education through art . . . the practice of virtues taught by the Judeo-Christian religion, and the wise use of science to control nature can lead Man to absolute truth."[8]

The change in feeling from shiny luminosity on the face of the proscenium to tropical earthiness in the niche (completed last, after Rivera had traveled to the simple, natural world of Tehuantepec in late 1922) anticipates the artist's turn away from a classical-universal experience toward a universal-indigenous outlook, wherein virtues derive from native experience and surrounding local phenomena, that would soon become central to his work at the Secretaría de Educación Pública.

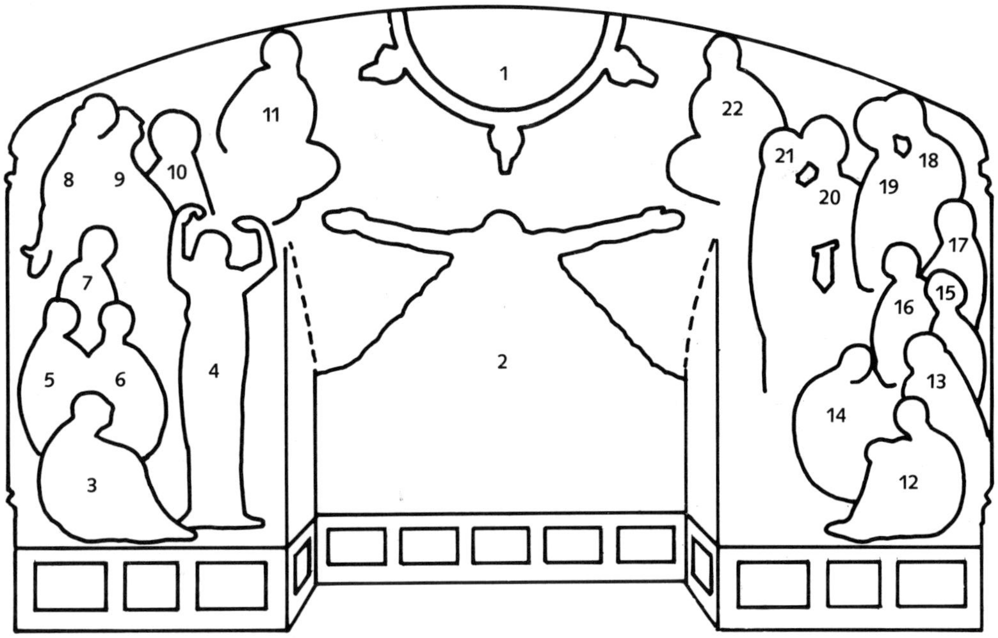

1 Primal Energy

11 Wisdom
10 Faith
9 Hope
8 Charity
"Theological Virtues"
7 Comedy
6 Song
5 Music
4 Dance
Emanations of the Spirit of Woman
3 Woman

22 Science
21 Continence
20 Strength
19 Justice
18 Prudence
17 Tragedy
16 Tradition
15 Erotic Poetry
14 Knowledge
13 Fable
Emanations of the Spirit of Man
12 Man

2 Emergent Man

Summary

Location: Mexico City, Justo Sierra 16

Site: Auditorium of the former Escuela Nacional Preparatoria. Built between 1902 and 1910 as part of an addition to accommodate growing enrollment at the school, the auditorium was designed in keeping with the late Baroque architecture of the original building (the Colegio de San Ildefonso, built 1739–49).

Theme/Subject: *Creation*

Format: The principal wall is in the shape of an inverted U and surrounds a square niche under a slightly protruding diminished arch. The niche was intended to house an organ, a shape Rivera took into account when the mural was planned. The two elements form a proscenium that faces an audience area of some nine-hundred seats.

Date: 1922–23 (inaugurated March 9, 1923). Niche probably completed in early 1923.

Medium: *Main wall:* Encaustic and gold leaf
Niche: Primarily encaustic (combined with experimental fresco?)

Dimensions: *Main wall (above dado):* Approx. 7.08 × 12.19 m
Niche (above dado): Approx. 4.36 × 5.85 × 2.75 m

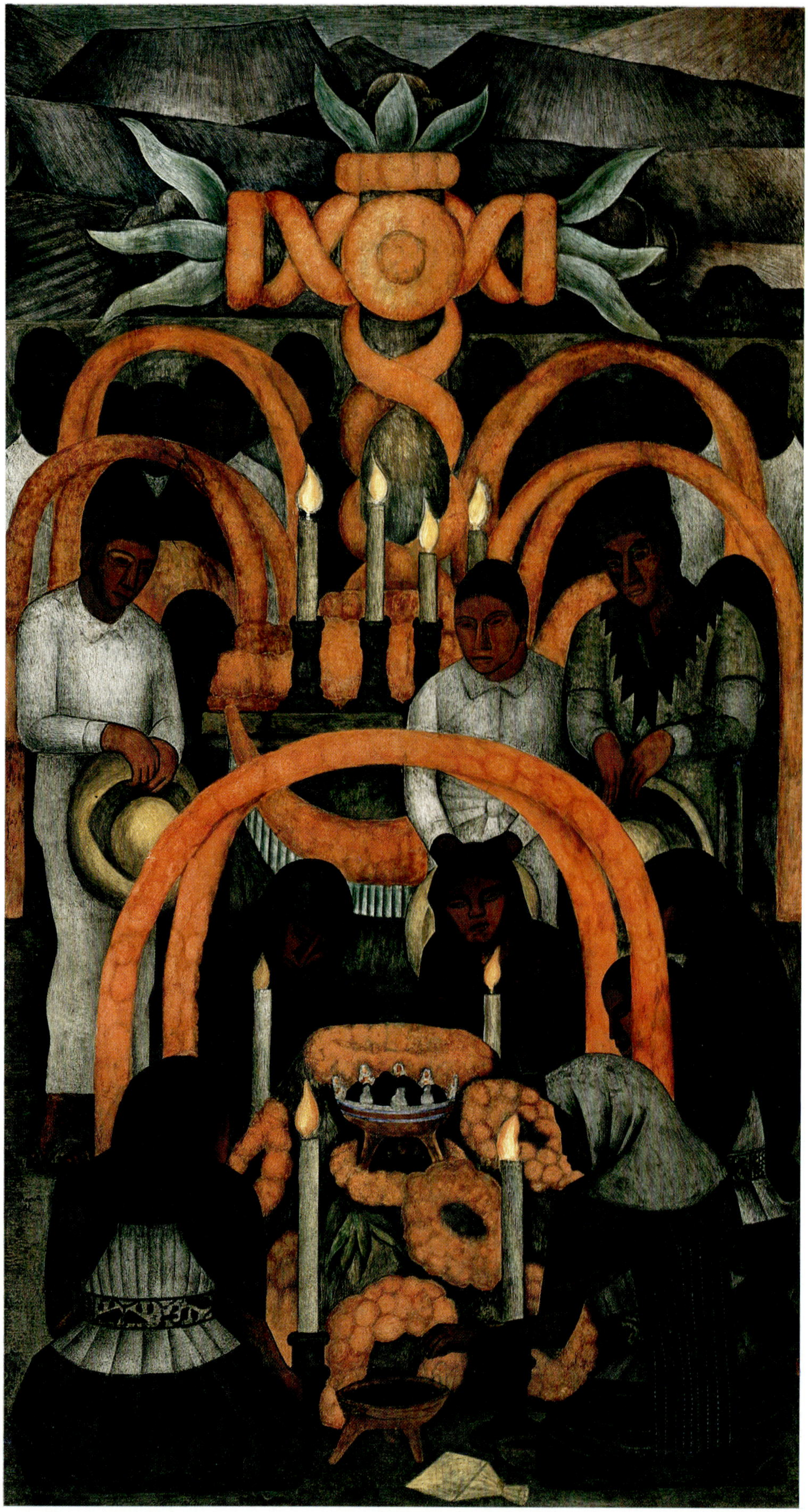

Secretaría de Educación Pública

Mexico City

Figure 374.
Day of the Dead—The Offering, August 1923–24, fresco, 4.15 × 2.37 m. Mexico City, Secretaría de Educación Pública, Court of Fiestas (first level).

If the murals on the patio walls and stairways of the Escuela Nacional Preparatoria were the crucible of the Mexican Mural Renaissance, the immediately following fresco decorations in the new Secretaría de Educación Pública (Ministry of Education building), a block and a half away, were soon to become the most extensive, systematically planned, and widely known achievements of the movement's embattled, contentious yet comradely, and, to other pioneer artists, frustrating first decade. At the center of the controversy over this undertaking and the discord that soon arose among his fellow members in the painters union was Diego Rivera. On the basis of a vague title given him by the minister of education, José Vasconcelos, he maneuvered himself into overall command of the building's decorative program at the expense of his colleagues. Confirmed in his authority by the succeeding minister, he proceeded unopposed. What he went on to accomplish overshadowed all other mural activity, much of which was diverted away from Mexico City as a result, during most of his following four years of work in the immense headquarters of the new national education program.

Whatever the ultimate effect on the development of the early mural movement of his personal takeover of the whole building's decorative plan—which soon led to the withdrawal of the other painters working there—his 116 principal fresco compositions, together with related motifs that tie them together into a synoptic view of the Mexican nation *redivivus populi* and that integrate them with the architecture, have come to occupy the same position with relation to the Mexican Mural Renaissance as Masaccio's Brancacci Chapel frescoes to the Florentine quattrocento. More significantly for the art of their time, they quickly became the pivotal work in opening an altogether new highway for the future of art over the next two decades in and beyond Mexico. In reviving and perfecting the art of fresco painting, they provided the chief model for a widely followed return to mural painting and an equally influential, form-setting example in their emphasis on indigenous American cultural values and socially conscious themes, projected in large scale in public places for broad popular exposure and interaction. They awakened and gave shape to an era in modern art and in widespread popular feeling on both American continents.

The Secretaría de Educación Pública, designed by Federico Méndez Rivas and constructed in thirteen months (June 1921–July 1922), was in effect an immediate consequence of the Mexican Revolution. It was conceived and carefully laid out to accommodate the functions of the reformed Ministry of Education, which, in place of the previous system of independent state control, was now the center of a new federal system of education that

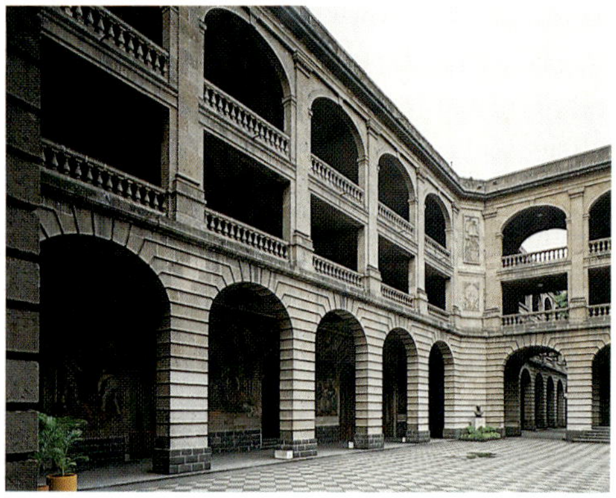

Figure 375.
Courtyard, Secretaría de Educación Pública.

would coordinate and implement all teaching activities throughout the country, from elementary through university levels. Under José Vasconcelos's direction, the ministry was not only to produce "the didactic materials, publish practical manuals and basic literary texts" for distribution throughout the country, but was also to "enrich the leisure time of the people through cultural festivals, choirs [*sic*], and popular events as well as to bring about a new sense of participation in the realm of ideas."[1] Vasconcelos wanted the Secretaría to be "a work in stone . . . a moral organization, vast and complex with big rooms in which one may hold free discussions under high ceilings and where ideas may expand without any sense of obstruction," and that is indeed what it became.[2]

The Secretaría is a three-story building divided into two parts, each of which is built around a courtyard surrounded on three sides by open corridors (on all levels) that serve as a continuous promenade connecting the various offices, workrooms, and meeting places (see fig. 375). On one side of the smaller courtyard is a handsome interior stairway, and on the opposite side is an elevator entrance. All of the corridor walls facing the two courts as well as the walls of the stairwell and the elevator shaft were made available for decoration by Vasconcelos.

From among the many artists working at the Escuela Nacional Preparatoria, four—Jean Charlot, Amado de la Cueva, Xavier Guerrero, and Rivera—were given ministerial assignments for corridor murals in the Ministry of Education's new headquarters. Rivera, however, soon took control of the project and his colleagues' plans were upstaged. By July 1924, as his phenomenal inventiveness and productivity gathered momentum and authority, Rivera had gained possession of all but a very small portion of the available wall space with the full approval of the new minister, Puig Casauranc. Even before he had finished his final series of panels at the Secretaría, he had come to be seen in international eyes, if not unanimously in Mexican eyes, as the central and in effect the superior figure in a national art phenomenon of formidable proportions. Whatever his strategy and tactics had been in opening his way to such an achievement, Rivera's work at the Secretaría, only the second site in his career as a muralist, must be seen for what it is—a tour de force as an architectural and pedagogical decorative program and the primary element of a three-part artistic source from which the Mexican Mural Renaissance derived much of its formal character and its humanistic-nationalistic direction. The other indispensable elements are, of course, to be found in the contemporary work of Rivera's fellow patriarchs and rivals-to-be, José Clemente Orozco and David Alfaro Siqueiros.

Rivera's mural program at the Secretaría represents a cosmography of modern Mexico, presenting the life of the Mexican people in several allegorical series based on their work, their struggles for social improvement, their achievements, and their popular festivals.[3] Over the span of its execution, Rivera evolved a new visual dialect—an artistic vernacular based on Mexican reality and the popular consciousness—that moved beyond the precepts of the program's original patron, Vasconcelos (whose philosophy advocated the combination of classical traditions and indigenous virtues), toward a Marxist-socialist interpretation of national life wholly concerned with that which is native to Mexico.

The Court of Labor

The mural decorations on the walls surrounding the smaller of the two courtyards, the Court of Labor, are unified by a progressive treatment of the theme of labor. The eighteen main panels on the ground floor (including those in the elevator alcove) were painted by the artist with substantial assistance from Xavier Guerrero, in a sequence of execution, rather than thematic order, that begins at the north end of the crossing and moves around the courtyard in a clockwise direction. Representing various aspects of physical labor, the subjects of these panels are

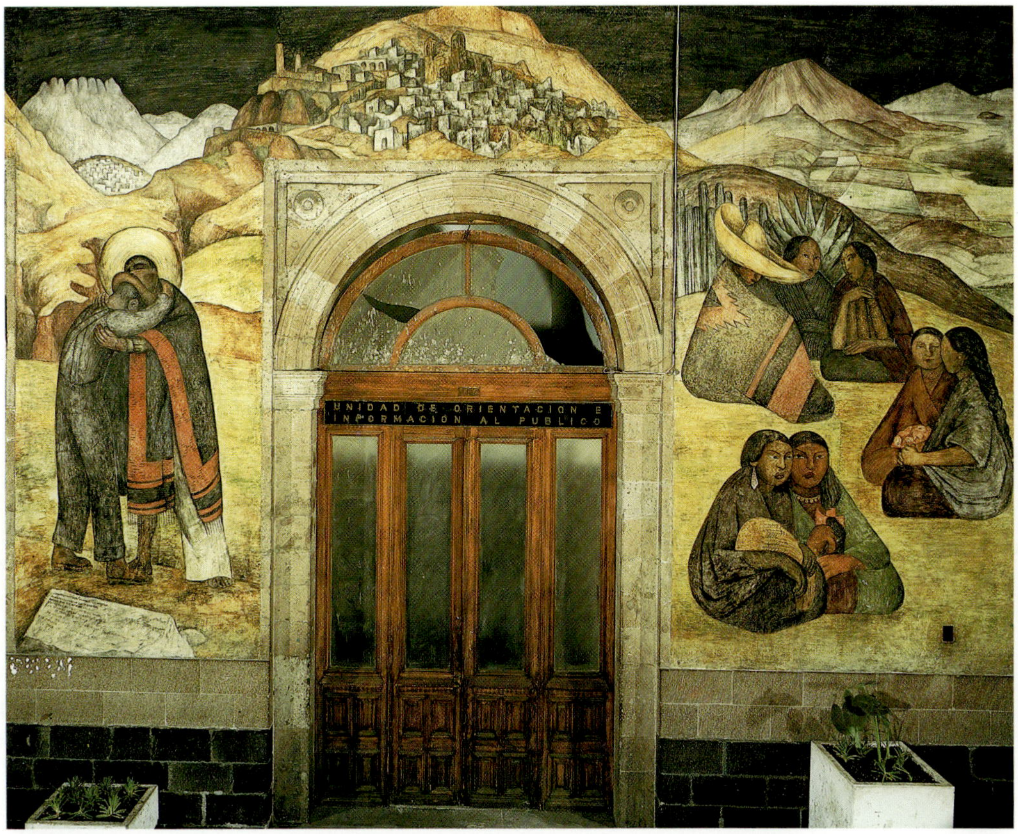

Figure 376.
Embrace and *Peasants*, March–July 1923, fresco mixed with nopal juice, 4.78 × 1.83 m and 4.78 × 2.47 m. Mexico City, Secretaría de Educación Pública, Court of Labor (first level).

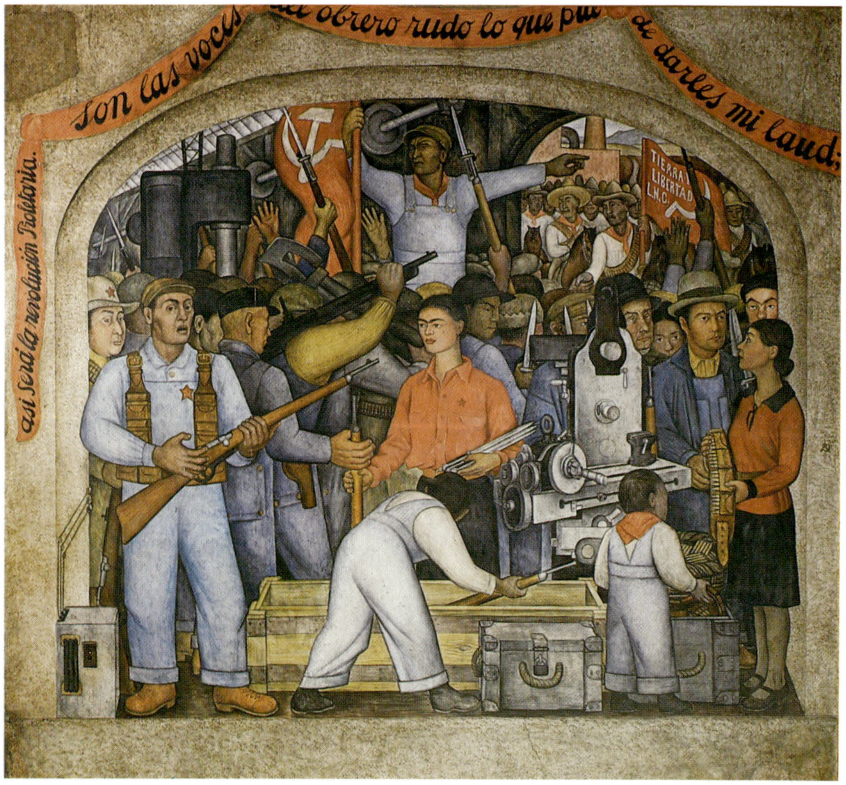

Figure 377.
***Distributing Arms*, ca. November 1928, fresco, 2.56 × 3.58 m. Mexico City, Secretaría de Educación Pública, Court of Fiestas (third level).**

based on the agricultural, industrial, and handicraft economies characteristic of Mexico's various regions. The emphasis throughout the series is on native folkways and on the life of the working-class and peasant sectors of Mexican society.

The first six panels (I, 1–6), which face south, portray the people and productive activities of the tropical areas of Mexico—the Isthmus of Tehuantepec in the state of Oaxaca—with prominence given to the depiction of the Tehuanas, the regal women of a matriarchal Indian society near the southern Pacific coast.[4] Rivera's glorification of this indigenous community makes clear his belief in the necessity of revising traditional (i.e., white) social standards.

The west-facing panels depict the occupations and industries of Mexico's western highlands—mining, farming, and the making of pottery. This is the first point in the series at which revolutionary political implications arise. The first two panels in the group, *Entering the Mine* and *Leaving the Mine* (I, 7 and 8), pointedly allude to the subjugation of the workers by outside interests (the mines were generally foreign-owned or controlled) by invoking the familiar imagery of the Way of the Cross and the Crucifixion, while the third (I, 9; see fig. 376), depicting an embrace between a farmer and a worker, is an allegorical presentation of the theory of the mutual interest of these two sectors of the proletariat and the potential power of their alliance.

The final six panels, which face north, present scenes from the vast highland regions of northern and north central Mexico—its human occupations, social conditions, and "redemptive actions."[5] The Mexican Revolution developed in the country's northern heartland, and these panels convincingly portray the region's austere landscape, insurrectionary mood, and aspirations toward regeneration. Although composed more as large pictures than as murals,[6] *Liberation of the Peon* (I, 15; see fig. 158) and *Rural Schoolteacher* (I, 16) are among the most impressive compositions in the artist's work as a muralist.

The twenty motifs on the second level of the Court of Labor symbolize the intellectual, scientific, and professional aspects of work. Designed to simulate an architectural frieze of individually framed sculptural reliefs, these motifs were executed in frescoed grisaille. The series consists of freely conceived symbolic arrangements of everyday items of professional interest and use, combined with human figures in classical attitudes. Scenes and symbols of contemporary science and the professions are balanced by scenes showing scientific study and experiment by ancient Mexicans. Newer technologies are presented by descriptive logos of X-rays and electrical devices; medicine, by realistic images of growing plants, a serpent, a laboratory experiment, and an operating room. Scenes symbolizing chemistry, surveying, astronomy, and war are also included. In several of the more recondite compositions, Rivera seems to be attempting to develop a new socialist symbolism.

The series can be seen as a scientific-industrial-socialist "zodiac" with masonic as well as Christian overtones. In its modernizing, technological outlook it is also a foil to the real sculptural reliefs representing Plato, Buddha, Bartolomé de las Casas,[7] and Quetzalcóatl, which face the courtyard on the third level and which embody the Hellenic-universalist philosophy of Vasconcelos.

The twenty-one fresco panels on the third level of the Court of Labor are the thematic culmination of Rivera's symbolic program, although not the last painted in his six-year period of activity at the Secretaría. These figural compositions apotheosize the proletarian partisans of the Mexican Revolution, celebrate the fraternity of peasant and worker, and symbolize the arts and sciences, native husbandry, native dances, and horsemanship. As a group they may be seen as allegorical testimonials to man's highest achievements, a view that is denoted by their placement at the topmost level of the Court of Labor.

The central position in the series is occupied by a repetition of the theme of the meeting of peasant and worker (III, 11), which first appeared at almost the same point in the ground-floor sequence (I, 9). Here, however, this meeting is more explicitly a political union and produces the new "Revolutionary Man," who rises with arms outstretched in the background, a figure that bears a distinct resemblance to the *Emergent Man* at Chapingo, created just one year earlier, and the earlier figure of the same title at the Anfiteatro Bolívar.

The Court of Fiestas

Rivera's decorations for the Court of Fiestas cover the first- and third-level walls. The ground-floor sequence begins on the south wall next to the crossing and proceeds around the courtyard, ending where the north wall meets the other end of the crossing. Of the twenty-four main panels in this series, four are by artists other than Rivera (I, 35–36 and 40–41). The series theme is the popular festivals of the Mexican people, both religious and secular. Rivera saw these communal celebrations, in which votive and festive aspects are to a greater or lesser degree combined, as carrying on the spirit of the ritualized social existence of the ancient Mexicans. His aim was to integrate these rituals into a redefined, specifically Mexican, proletarian society that would embrace the full gamut of the nation's colorful popular life and supersede the Spanish colonial tradition.

In this series, as in the Court of Labor, the walls facing north and south reflect the festivals of those regions. The nine panels on the south wall focus on the festivals of the peasant farmers of the north central area of Mexico—the festivals surrounding the corn harvest and the celebration known as the Day of the Dead—as well as the parallel celebration of the latter in the city (see fig.374). The three-panel sequence at the center of the series commemorates the restoration of the Indian communal lands (the *ejidos*) by the Constitution of 1917.

At the beginning and end of the west wall are two panels that carry the theme of festivals into the city on a more exuberant, carnivalesque note. These panels, *Burning Judases* (I, 28) and *Friday of Sorrows on the Canal at Santa Anita* (converted by popular custom into a joyous flower festival) (I, 33), bracket a solemn four-part frieze depicting the celebration of May Day in the city by both farmers and workers. This sequence constitutes the largest wall space devoted to a single theme in the Secretaría complex and was no doubt meant to impress upon the viewer that echoes that of *Embrace* (I, 9), the smaller, earlier panel exactly opposite this group in the Court of Labor.

Murals by Rivera occupy only five of the nine interdoorway areas on the north wall; of the four remaining, two were painted by Jean Charlot and two by Amado de la Cueva, artist assistants to Rivera until late in 1924. In keeping with the mirroring compass directional emphasis of the program, Rivera's panels depict two southern dances and a southern market scene. The sequence begins with Rivera's *Ribbon Dance* (I, 34), which replaced a panel on the same subject by Charlot,[8] one Rivera had destroyed, and ends with *La Zandunga* (I, 42). The continuity of the festival leifmotif is interrupted, however, by Charlot's two surviving panels on work themes, *Washerwomen* (I, 35) and *Burden Carriers* (I, 41), which were executed before Rivera took full control of the building's decoration and which follow the original decorative plan of alternating work and festival themes, at least on the ground floor. De la Cueva's panels, *The Little Bull* and *Battle Dance,* were done at the same time, but since they fell into the new overall festival grouping of the Court of Fiestas they survived.

The central position in the north-wall sequence is again occupied by the scene of a large gathering, this time a three-part market scene (I, 37–39), which clearly shows Rivera's growing command of medium, composition, and detail. It is typical of his portrayals of the crowded places of Mexican daily life—loaded with particulars of character, dress, incident, momentary expression, and uncomplimentary characterizations of "enemies of the people."

The second floor of the Court of Fiestas is decorated with the escutcheons of the states of Mexico (all but Baja California), painted under Rivera's supervision by Charlot, de la Cueva, and other members of the Union of Technical Workers, Painters, and Sculptors.

The third-floor walls contain the two major series in the Secretaría program, the "Corrido of the Agrarian Revolution" and the "Corrido of the Proletarian Revolution" (*corrido*—song, popular ballad). The "Corrido of the Proletarian Revolution" begins on the south wall with the distribution of arms as Mexican peasants and urban workers join together to attack the established order under the guidance of white soldiers with Slavic features who wear overalls bearing red stars (III, 19).[9] This panel contains portraits of Frida Kahlo (whom Rivera had recently remarried and who is shown distributing arms), David Alfaro Siqueiros, and Tina Modotti (see fig. 377). The following panels depict scenes from the revolutionary struggle, the establishment of workers' cooperatives, and the triumph over capitalism (a Slavic-featured man in a Russian cap and red-starred overalls appears as a leader in several panels). The series ends with the figure of the peasant leader Zapata, who figuratively introduces the agrarian *corrido* that begins on the adjacent west wall. The "Corrido of the Proletarian Revolution" was painted after Rivera returned from his stay in the Soviet Union in 1927–28, and its revolutionary mise-en-scène, wherein Russians play a prominent role, reflects the idealistic regard in which the Soviet revolution was held by members of the international intelligentsia, including that of Mexico, during the second half of the 1920s.

The "Corrido of the Agrarian Revolution," executed nearly two years before the "Corrido of the Proletarian Revolution," begins at the lefthand end of the west wall, where a woman, modeled on the well-known *cancionista* Concha Michel, sings the *corrido* surrounded by a group of dark-skinned workers of the soil.[10] In the panels that follow, a group of peasants plans a revolution while women and children eat supper; the rich are shown greedily increasing their wealth through the stock market (this scene [III, 38] includes caricatures of John D. Rockefeller and J. P. Morgan) and dining on gold (III, 36). Other panels depict the simple existence of the *campesinos*, who, although they may be poor, lead healthier lives because of their proximity to the land—the source of all true wealth. The panels contain several demeaning portrayals of Rivera's former patrons and friends, such as José Vasconcelos, who appears seated on a marble elephant in the panel entitled *The Learned*, which mocks the conventional intelligentsia.

Rivera's visual emulation of the *corrido*, a popular musical form familiar to all Mexicans, as a means of engaging the attention of a mass audience long accustomed to receiving news of events in song and verse, was a radical artistic innovation. In the "Corrido of the Agrarian Revolution," Rivera aimed at translating the feeling of the *corrido*, a sentiment-laden and satirical art form, into visual terms, as witnessed by the soft outlines of his figures, the warm, earthy feeling of color and light, and the caricatures of the property owners who hold the day-to-day fate of peasants in their absentee hands.

In the "Corrido of the Proletarian Revolution," the application of the same device is less successful because it has been pushed into a more remote, Northern European cultural and political context. Here the themes are more abstract and beyond the horizons of local reality, borrowed as they have been from an outside revolutionary experience that can only be made relevant by an intellectual exercise that is essentially foreign to the sensuous and nostalgic form of the *corrido*. The difference that this transference made in Rivera's style is striking: the proletarian scenes are more linear; their shapes, more sharply focused; the realistic representation of details—clothing, rifles, bayonets—more careful; the color, brighter and less organic; and there is an almost photographic delineation of the features of the personalities. The overall tendency is toward a new, ideologically oriented realism, in which the political element is never immune to modification but in which scientific and technological phenomena, as well as the panorama of history, come to play increasingly important roles.

Stairway

The walls of the main stairway, which connects all three levels of both patios on the south side of the Court of Labor, are rectangular in elevation. Except for the double doorway openings on the second and third levels, they are uninterrupted as they fold at right angles around the balustraded staircase. Rivera treated the surfaces of this box-shaped area as a single continuous composition that shows the Mexican landscape and its native inhabitants in an ascending sequence that follows an imaginary route from the tropical regions at sea level to the high central plateau. This connected series of scenes provides a vertical counterpoint to the main horizontal corridor series that are linked by the stairway, thus unifying the whole scheme according to the country's topography and corresponding ecology as well as (along the corridors) its main geographical directions.

The first scene encountered on entering the stairway is that on the south wall.[11] It represents the undersea world, as symbolized by an allegorical figure plenishing the waters. On the adjoining wall to the right is another marine vista, bounded on the left by a rocky shore and capering fishes. Draped classical figures, representing tropical islands, float on the sea's surface. The next wall shows a deep-sea diver being unsuited, while other crew members of a steam launch examine his finds. Above them a wind symbol wafts inland three allegorical figures representing clouds. At the far right edge of the scene, a cane field and a corner palm tree announce the ascent to the tropical interior. Adjoining these motifs, on the east wall, the guardian figure of a Tehuantepec woman is poised against a background of the cane fields, oil derricks, and fruit trees that signifies the mineral and agricultural resources of Mexico's tropical regions. The ascent to the second level begins on the east wall with a scene showing the tropical paradise of the littoral: bathing nudes, a woman daydreaming in a hammock, and a jungle of plants of varied color, size, and shape. In the background are the foothills of the mountains, dotted with the straw huts of a peasant settlement. To the right a Zapatista sentinel from the hills of Morelos marks the transition to higher subtropical lands. Behind him the upland gorges show the positive effects of industrial progress: a railroad tunnel and trestle and terraced hillsides.

The south wall depicts a deep jungle landscape in which Xochipilli, the Aztec god of flowers, feasting, and frivolity, appears in a trance, surrounded by nude female votaries. Undulant and upright tree forms, embraced by winding vines and surrounded by opulent plant forms, glorify the prodigality of untamed nature and thus echo the primitive impulses and code of native libido. The scene on the next wall shows a colonial hacienda, where an estate manager oversees the planting and harvesting of sugarcane while lying in a hammock. The final scene on the second level shows a peon sharpening his machete in the shadows of a cave, an allusion to the Indians' revolt against their callous oppressors.

The ascent to the third level begins with the burial of a dead worker in the highlands. The red standards held by onlookers are a reminder of the proletarian cause for which he gave his life. In the background, above the volcanic cones and austere plains of the Valley of Mexico, allegorical nudes in contorted postures glorify his sacrifice, while mourning his passing. On the south wall, a triple flash of lightning strikes down figures representing the three enemies of the people, militarism, clericalism, and capitalism, as if in immediate retribution for the victim in the previous scene. Centered on this wall is an Indian woman seated in the manner of Xilonen, the Aztec goddess of corn and the "spirit of young growth."[12] She holds two ears of corn, while in her lap are stems of wheat. Behind her a tractor plow, power lines, railroad freight cars, and a storage silo represent modern agricultural progress. At the right, a soldier, an armed peasant, and an armed worker, the latter two holding hands, present the political triad of brotherly alliance that protects the new social order.

In the center of the main wall on the third level, against a background construction scene, symbolizing the building of a new world, a teacher and a class of children represent education in the workplace. To the left a farmer and a worker confer with an engineer, and to the right a surveyor and a chemist stand behind a doctor as he attends an Indian mother and her infant. In the final scene, next to the doorway, Rivera portrays himself. His seated figure is accompanied by that of the sculptor Martinez Pintao and a figure with his back to the viewer, who is allegedly the painter Jean Charlot.[13]

Although there are allegorical elements at the beginning and the end of the composition and a single historical reference (to the Zapatistas) near its midpoint, the greater part of this considerable space is an empirically treated representation of Mexico's exotic natural and human surroundings. It is almost as if the artist were a latterday Baron von Humboldt, or a scientific geographer with a romantic point of view. However, Rivera's free interpretations of physical phenomena move beyond simple description to a new formulation of artistic vision, which employs smooth, rhythmic, curvilinear means to reshape the observed forms with a firm sense of artistic three-dimensionality. From this point on, this new sense of "form" becomes the hallmark of Rivera's mature style, a style that will soon be recognized as one of the basic styles, if not the primary style, of the Mexican Mural Renaissance as a whole.

In the stairway sequence, finished according to Charlot in January 1925,[14] he describes the changes in landscape and native life as the land rises from the tropics to the high plateau with the thoroughness and attention to detail one would expect from a natural scientist. Also evident is his pride in the variety and richness of Mexico's natural and human heritage, the depiction of which drew him ever deeper into the magical aspects of the living phenomena of his theme. The result is one of the Rivera's most masterful panoramas, both in its organization and its unfolding exposition, which takes artful advantage of one of the most confining and complex of his mural sites. It seems likely that it was in this stairway mural that Rivera found himself and his master style as a Mexican artist. It is also where he set his highest standard for establishing the relationship between art and ideology. Here the experience of his real world is cause; and ideology, which emerges in the top register, is consequence. At Chapingo, where rational and logical analysis set the framework, the reverse is true. In the artist's humanistic vision, and in his method, the balance of art and ideology depends on the theme and circumstances at hand, always within the larger perspective of loyalty to human needs in the face of historical forces, exploitation, and oppression.

The correlation between the changing effect of altitude on climate, ecology, and culture and the fulfillment of the destiny of the working class as the ruling authority in human affairs, implied in the scenes on the upper level of the stairway, anticipates Rivera's systematic treatment of the idea of parallelism between nature and evolution in human society in the chapel at Chapingo.

Except for the two "Corrido" series, the complex of mural decorations at the Secretaría follows no strict sequence on which appreciation of its form or comprehension of its content depends. For clarity in description, the above discussion has treated each courtyard in turn, going from first to third levels, always moving in a clockwise sequence, and ending with the

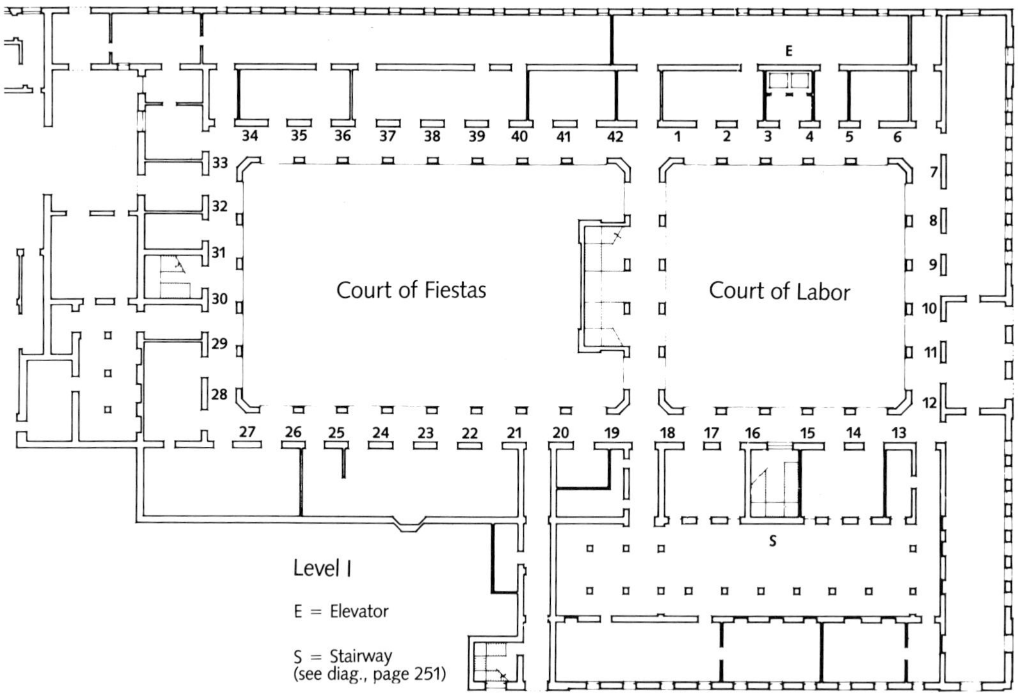

three levels of the stairway as an independent but interconnecting unit. In light of Rivera's general preference for hierarchical arrangements, another sequence could be followed. This would begin on the ground floor and proceed all the way around both courts, move to the second level to repeat this procedure, and then finish on the third level, where, jumping ahead, it would begin with the "Corrido of the Agrarian Revolution," followed by the "Corrido of the Proletarian Revolution," and finally end at the central (rather than the last) composition on the east wall of the Court of Labor, with the emergence of the new "Revolutionary Man." In both sequences the stairway functions as a sort of obligato, a dialectical metaphor for the upward trend of revolutionary progress.

Ideologically and symbolically, the "Corridos of the Agrarian and Proletarian Revolutions" represent the penultimate phase in Rivera's pictorial conception (at least in his work of the 1920s) of the process of social change in Mexico and its role in the international revolution against the overall established order. These two series set the stage for his apotheosis of a classless Mexican society, centered in native traditions and cultural values, on the top level of the adjoining Court of Labor, and, together with that final series anticipate and lay the groundwork for Rivera's summary dictum on the logics of social revolution in the chapel at Chapingo.

Summary

Location Mexico City, Calle de Argentina 22, between Justo Sierra and Venezuela

Site: Secretaría de Educación Pública, built between 1921 and 1922 (Federico Méndez Rivas, architect)

Theme/Subject: *A Cosmography of Modern Mexico*

Format: All walls of a three-story cloister surrounding a double patio, as well as the walls of a stairway connecting the three levels, and those of a ground-floor elevator alcove. The smaller patio, which is the first entered from the street, is called the Court of Labor, the larger patio, the Court of Fiestas.

Date: 1923–28

Medium: Experimental and true fresco made part of the wall structure. (A conservation program in the 1960s and 1970s remounted several compositions onto movable frames. To repair paint losses from earlier defacements, the entire series was extensively in-painted, especially on the ground-floor level.)

Dimensions: Painted areas cover linear wall distances approximating one-half the length and width of a city block in the central zone of Mexico City (as set by 16th-century Spanish urban models) on each of three levels.

Secretaría de Educación Pública, Level I

Court of Labor, ca. March–July 1923, fresco mixed with nopal juice[15]

Labors of the Mexican People

North wall

1. *Weavers*, 4.71 × 3.67 m
   Reclining Tehuana (overdoor)
2. *Dyers*, 4.71 × 2.13 m
   Reclining Tehuana (overdoor)
3. *Tehuanas*, 4.25 × 2.15 m
   Pyramid with Flames (overdoor, exterior of elevator alcove entrance)
   a. *Yucatán Well*, 4.56 × 2.94 m
   b. *Tehuantepec Bathers*, 4.56 × 2.87 m
   c. *Tehuana Woman with Baby*, approx. 2.32 × 1.60 m (not including hammer-and-sickle motif above figures)
   d. *Market Figures with Scales*, 1.05 × 3.00 m (overdoor, interior of elevator alcove entrance)
   e. *Maya Woman with Baby*, 2.32 × 1.23 m (not including hammer-and-sickle motif above figures)
   f. Decorative motif, 4.56 × .83 m
   g. Decorative motif, 4.56 × .90 m

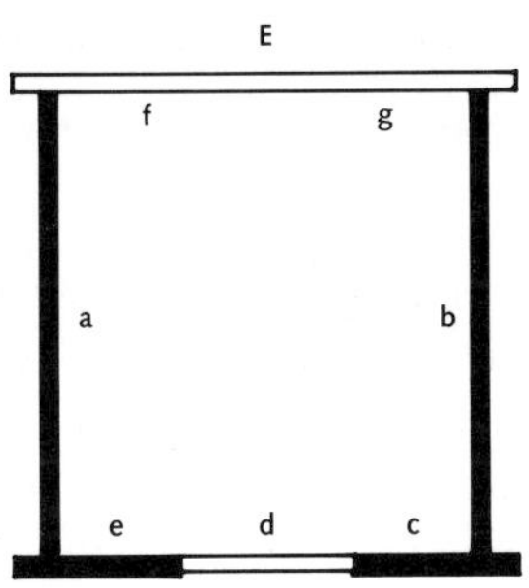

4. *Tehuanas*, 4.76 × 2.14 m
   Reclining Tehuana (overdoor)
5. *Cane Harvest*, 4.25 x 2.13 m
   Tropical Landscape (overdoor)
6. *Sugar Factory*, 4.82 × 3.66 m
   Reclining Tehuana (overdoor)
   Palm Tree (NE corner, both sides of right angle)

East wall

Náhuatl Poem (overdoor)[16]

7. *Entering the Mine*, 4.74 × 3.50 m
   Náhuatl Poem (overdoor)[17]
8. *Leaving the Mine*, 4.78 × 2.15 m
   Northwestern Landscape (overdoor)
9. *Embrace*, 4.78 x 1.83 m
   Northwestern Mountain Mining Town (overdoor)
10. *Peasants*, 4.78 × 2.47 m
    Landscape (overdoor)
11. *Foreman*, 4.78 × 2.13 m
    Náhuatl Poem (overdoor)[18]
12. *Pottery Makers*, 4.78 x 3.22 m[19]
    Náhuatl Poem (overdoor)[20]
    Palm Tree (SE corner, both sides of right angle)

South wall

Reclining Worker and Flaming Sun (overdoor)

13. *Foundry—Opening the Smelter*, 4.26 x 3.36 m
    Symbols (overdoor)
14. *Surface Miners*, 4.26 × 2.10 m
    Northern Landscape (overdoor)
15. *Liberation of the Peon*, 4.38 × 3.48 m
    Northern Landscape Illuminated by the Dawning Light of Revolution (overdoor)
16. *Rural Schoolteacher*, 4.38 × 3.27 m
    Northern Landscape (overdoor)
17. *Shepherd with Sling*, 4.38 × 1.10 m
    Symbols of War and Labor (overdoor)
18. *Foundry—Pouring the Crucible*, 4.38 × 3.16 m

Court of Fiestas, south wall: August 1923–24; west wall: ca. July 1923–early 1924; north wall: 1923–24,[21] fresco

Festivals of the Mexican People

South wall

19. *Deer Dance*, 4.38 × 3.48 m
20. *Corn Harvest*, 4.38 × 2.39 m
    Homage to Corn and Nixtamal (overdoor)[22]
21. *Corn Festival*, 4.38 × 2.39 m
    Melon, Gourd, and Flower with Five-pointed Pistil (overdoor)

22–24. *Distribution of the Land*, three connected panels, 4.15 × 2.38 m; (overdoor); 4.15 × 2.38 m; (overdoor); 4.15 x 2.35 m
Biznaga (fruit of a highland cactus) (overdoor)

25. *Day of the Dead—The Offering*, 4.15 × 2.37 m
    Maguey Cacti (overdoor)
26. *Day of the Dead—The Dinner*, 4.15 x 2.37 m
    Overdoor
27. *Day of the Dead—City Fiesta*, 4.17 × 3.75 m
    Overdoor

West wall

Floating Gardens of Lake Texcoco (overdoor)

28. *Burning Judases*, 4.30 x 3.83 m
    Mountain Landscape (overdoor)

29–32. *May Day Meeting*, four connected panels, 4.43 × 2.14 m; (overdoor); 4.43 × 2.13 m; (overdoor); 4.43 × 2.12 m; (overdoor); 4.43 x 2.11 m
Valley of Mexico Landscape (overdoor)

33. *Friday of Sorrows on the Canal at Santa Anita*, 4.56 × 3.56 m
    Landscape (overdoor)

North wall

Overdoor

34. *Ribbon Dance*, 4.68 × 3.63 m
    Overdoor
35. *Washerwoman*, 4.68 × 2.38 m (artist: Charlot)
    Still Life (budding flowers, tortillas, and sunflowers under bamboo canopy) (overdoor)
36. *The Little Bull*, 4.68 × 2.36 m (artist: de la Cueva)
    Overdoor

37–39. *The Market (El Tianguis)*, three connected panels, 4.68 × 2.39 m; (overdoor); 4.68 × 2.36 m; (overdoor); 4.68 × 2.36 m
Clusters of Fruit and Cactus (overdoor)

40. *Battle Dance (Los Santiagos)*, 4.68 × 2.34 m (artist: de la Cueva)
    Still Life (tropical flowers under bamboo canopy) (overdoor)
41. *Burden Carriers (Los Cargadores)*, 4.68 × 2.32 m (artist: Charlot)
    Cane Bundle (overdoor)
42. *La Zandunga*, 4.68 × 3.60 m[23]
    Overdoor

Secretaría de Educación Pública, Level II

Court of Labor, ca. 1924, fresco grisaille[24]

Intellectual Labor

North wall

1. *Land Measure,* 1.32 × 2.82 m
   Four-man team of surveyors.
2. *Medicine,* 1.33 x .82 m
   Two plants, funnel-shaped vial coiled by a serpent.
3. *Chemistry,* 1.34 × .82 m
   Technician with test tube and vial.
4. *Chemistry,* 1.34 × .83 m
   Technicians with mixing bowl and brazier.
5. *Electric Machine,* 1.34 × .83 m
   Fan connected to wire coils and generator with sparks between poles.
6. *Medicine,* 1.34 × 3.33 m
   Four ancient men kneel over a brazier; one holds a tablet, another a test tube; in front of the others is a vented bottle.
7. *Electric Arc,* 1.34 × .38 m
   Carbon-pointed welding (?) apparatus.

East wall

8. *X-rays,* 1.34 × .60 m
   Radium arc, hand, lens, transparent hand on plate.
9. *Geology,* 1.34 × 3.14 m
   Four ancient men studying rock strata.
10. *Esoteric symbol,* 1.34 × .85 m
    Two hands upholding a table with a money sack that shrinks away from a flaming arrow; in the foreground a star and two hammers.
11. *Esoteric Symbol,* 1.34 × 1.46 m
    Seated female figure with extended arms and open hands; behind her two detached hands holding a hammer and sickle.
12. *Esoteric Symbol,* 1.34 × 2.11 m
    Three seated figures, two at right in profile holding hammer and sickle as though received from figure at left in the pose of an angel *annunciata* under a cloud and sun-ray motif.
13. *Esoteric symbol,* 1.34 × 2.11 m
    Mirror image of number 10, but with sickles instead of hammers.
14. *Operation,* 1.36 × 2.85 m
    Two surgeons and two assistants operate on a geometrically abstracted patient while another figure observes.
15. *Esoteric Symbol*
    Three-quarter-length female figure with the symbol for infinity suspended between her hands.

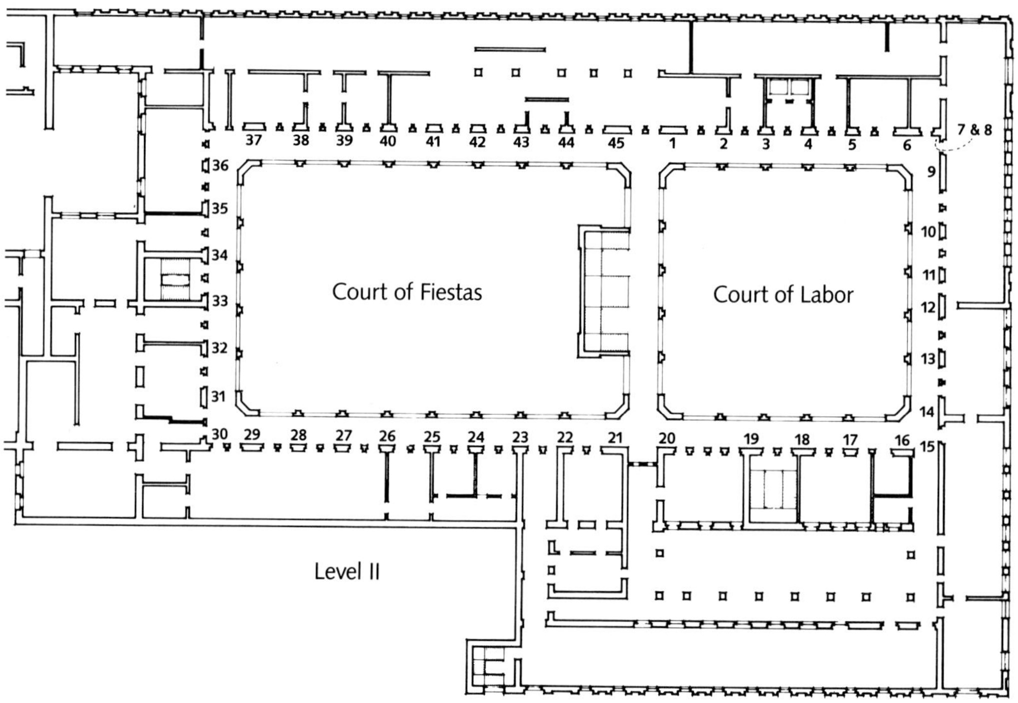

South wall

16. *Investigation,* 1.39 × 2.75 m
    Four scientists (astronomers) in a vaulted room record data.
17. *Cactácea,* 1.40 × .50 m
    Blossoming spiney cactus above burning scrolls.
18. *War,* 1.40 x 2.19 m
    Seated woman, legs extended to the right, holding a sword; behind her an Aztec shield and heavy blocks.
19. *Science,* 1.38 × 1.97 m
    Seated woman, legs extended to the left, holding a tablet; behind her a pedestal on which is a five-pointed star.
20. *Researchers,* 1.40 × 2.44 m
    Four pathologists in a laboratory.

Court of Fiestas, ca. 1924–25, fresco

Escutcheons of the States of Mexico[25]

South wall

21. Sinaloa, Sonora, Nayarit
22. Chihuahua
23. Coahuila
24. Nuevo León
25. Tamaulipas
26. Zacatecas
27. Aguascalientes
28. Guanajuato
29. Durango
30. San Luis Potosí

West wall

31. Morelos, Querétaro
32. Hidalgo
33. México
34. Jalisco
35. Colima
36. Guerrero, Michoacán

North wall

37. Tlaxcala
38. Puebla
39. Veracruz
40. Oaxaca
41. Chiapas
42. Tabasco
43. Campeche
44. Quintana Roo
45. Yucatán

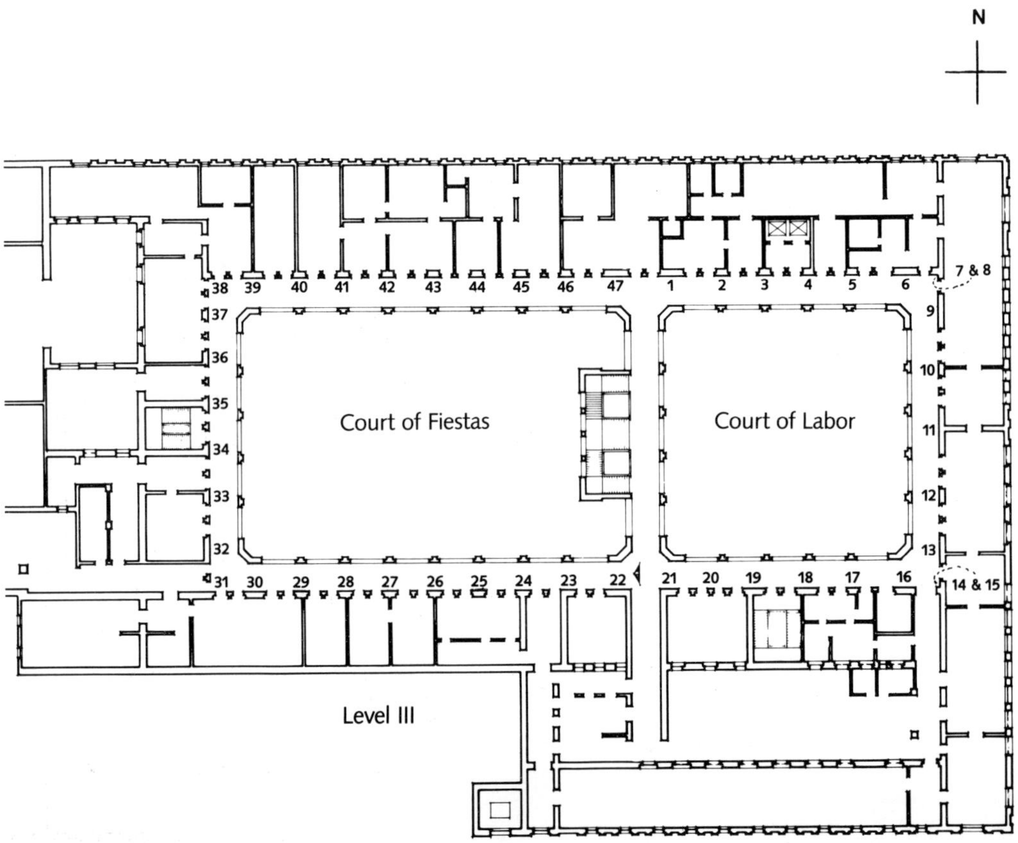

Secretaría de Educación Pública, Level III

Court of Labor, 1928, fresco[26]

Apotheosis of the Mexican Revolution[27]

North wall

1. *Music,* 2.04 x 3.33 m (grisaille)
2. *Martyr David,* 2.04 × 1.34 m
3. *Martyr Felipe Carrillo Puerto,* 2.04 × 1.34 m
4. *Martyr Emiliano Zapata,* 2.04 × 1.32 m
5. *Martyr Otilio Montaño,* 2.04 x 1.32 m
6. *Dance (La Zandunga),* 2.03 × 3.82 m (grisaille)
7. *Three Serpents,* 2.03 × .85 m (grisaille)

East wall

8. *Tambourín Player,* 2.03 × 1.11 m (grisaille)
9. *Deer Dance,* 2.03 x 3.65 m (grisaille)
10. *Women with Vessel and Spoon,* 2.04 × 1.35 m
11. *Fraternity,* 2.04 × 6.46 m
12. *Women with Flowers and Vegetables,* 2.04 × 1.34 m
13. *Painting,* 2.05 × 3.35 m (grisaille)
14. *Writing,* 2.05 × 1.51 m (grisaille)

South wall

15. *Serpents,* 2.07 × .85 (grisaille)
16. *Sculpture,* 2.07 × 3.26 m (grisaille)
17. *The Three Graces,* 2.06 x 1.30 m
18. *The Sciences,* or *The Proclaimer of Tasks,* 2.06 × 2.68 m
19. *The Arts,* or *The Distributor of the Goods of Achievement,* 2.06 × 2.46 m
20. *Shells,* 2.06 × .30 (grisaille)
21. Architecture, 2.01 × 2.95 m (grisaille)

Court of Fiestas, west and north walls: 1926; south wall: completed about November 1928[28]

Corrido of the Proletarian Revolution

South wall

22. *Distributing Arms,* 2.03 × 3.98 m
23. *In the Trenches,* 2.03 × 1.64 m (signed 1928)
24. *The Wounded,* 2.03 × 1.53 m
25. *"Let him work who wants to eat,"* 2.03 x 1.65 m (signed)
26. *The Cooperative,* 2.04 × 1.60 m
27. *Death of the Capitalist,* 2.04 × 1.58 m (signed)
28. *United Front,* 2.04 × 1.61 m (signed, 7 Nov. 1928)
29. *Our Bread,* 2.04 × 1.58 m (signed)
30. *Protest,* 2.04 × 1.68 m
31. *Emiliano Zapata,* 2.05 × 1.46 m (signed)

Corrido of the Agrarian Revolution[29]

West wall

32. *Singing the Corrido,* 2.08 × 2.03 m
33. *To Work,* 2.07 × 1.33 m
34. *Union,* 2.06 × 1.33 m
35. *Learning the ABC's,* 2.06 × 1.33 m
36. *Threshing,* 2.06 × 1.30 m (signed)
37. *Rain,* 2.05 × 2.84 m

North wall

38. *Tractor,* 2.07 × 1.85 m
39. *Capitalist Dinner,* 2.07 × 1.60 m
40. *The Learned,* 2.07 × 1.53 m
41. *Wall Street Banquet,* 2.05 × 1.55 m
42. *Sleep—Night of the Poor,* 2.06 × 1.59 m
43. *Fruits of the Earth,* 2.06 × 1.59 m (signed)
44. *Orgy—Night of the Rich,* 2.05 × 1.54 m
45. *"We want to work,"* 2.05 × 1.57 m
46. *Guarantees—Debris of Capitalism,* 2.05 × 1.51 m
47. *"All the world's wealth comes from the land,"* 2.05 × 2.40 m (signed)

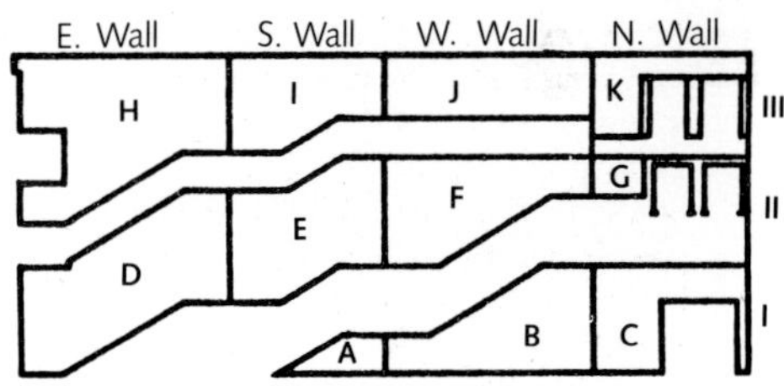

Secretaría de Educación Pública, Stairway

A. *The Sea,* 1.26 × 3.64 m[30]
B. *The Littoral,* 3.71 × 7.70 m
C. *The Diver,* 3.71 x 5.67 m
D. *Tropical Mexico,* 3.83 × 7.78 m
E. *Xochipilli and His Votaries,* 3.84 × 5.67 m
F. *Plantation Serfdom,* 3.84 × 7.70 m
G. *Peon,* 1.38 × 1.94
H. *Highland Landscape,* 6.15 x 7.78 m
I. *Mechanization of the Country,* 3.52 × 5.67 m
J. *New World Schoolteacher,* 2.19 × 7.70 m
K. *Rivera and Associates,* 2.80 × 5.67 m

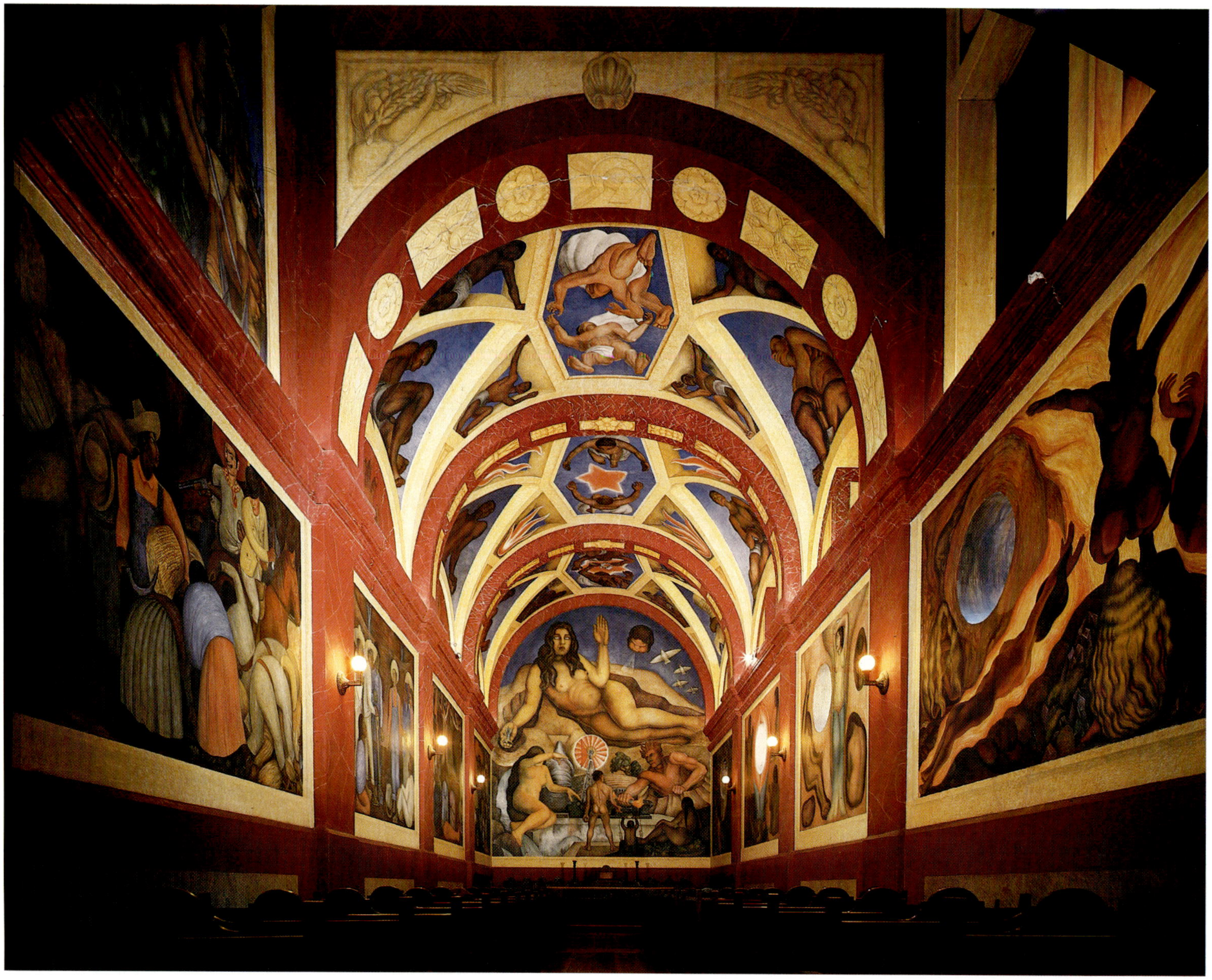

Universidad Autónoma de Chapingo

Figure 378.
View of chapel showing *The Liberated Earth with Natural Forces Controlled by Man* (on end wall), 1926–27, fresco, 6.92 × 5.98 m. Universidad Autónoma de Chapingo, Chapel.

In this chapel . . . Diego Rivera shaped the agrarian ideal of the Mexican Revolution.[1]

Rivera's two mural programs at the Universidad Autónoma de Chapingo (established in 1920 as the Escuela Nacional de Agricultura) are in two separated areas in the central administration building: (1) the entrance corridor, stairwell, and second-floor foyer connecting the rector's office with other administrative departments and (2) the chapel, which has a separate entrance facing the campus grounds, at the southeast corner of the building. This large patioed building (fig. 379) was originally the main house of the Convent of San Jacinto, founded by the Jesuits in the late 17th century as a *reducción* (an economically productive religious community in which Indians worked the land under Jesuit management). When the Jesuit order was expelled from Mexico by the Spanish crown in the late 1760s, the convent and the surrounding land changed hands, eventually becoming the Hacienda of San Jacinto. Between 1880 and 1884, the hacienda served as the residence of Mexican president Manuel González.

Administration Building

Rivera was first commissioned to create decorations in the administrative area flanking the main entrance, and these were probably completed, with the exception of two doorway portraits, before he began work in the chapel. The murals in this area fulfill decorative, textural, architectural, honorary, and narrative functions. Beginning in the second-floor foyer, the first of four main panels (diag. I) depicts the breakup of the Hacienda of San Jacinto by the order of the revolutionary government of President Alvaro Obregón and its distribution to the peasants while the disgruntled former owners look on (one of the new government officials holds a blueprint of the triangular tract of land, which was primarily devoted to the cultivation of the maguey cactus; fig. 380). Two facing panels on the east and west walls (II and IV) treat the complementary themes of good and bad government and clearly reflect Ambrogio Lorenzetti's mid-14th-century frescoes on the same subjects in the Palazzo Publico in Siena, which Rivera undoubtedly saw during his tour of Italy in 1921. The *Bad Government* panel portrays a despoiled coastal landscape under siege by tanks and battleships, an allusion to foreign intervention, while *Good Government* (fig. 381) presents a scene of a thriving industrial harbor (possibly based on a site near the oil fields of Tampico). The final panel (III) shows the coming together of *compesino* and industrial worker in the interest of creating a healthy society based on their common commitment to productive labor as opposed to

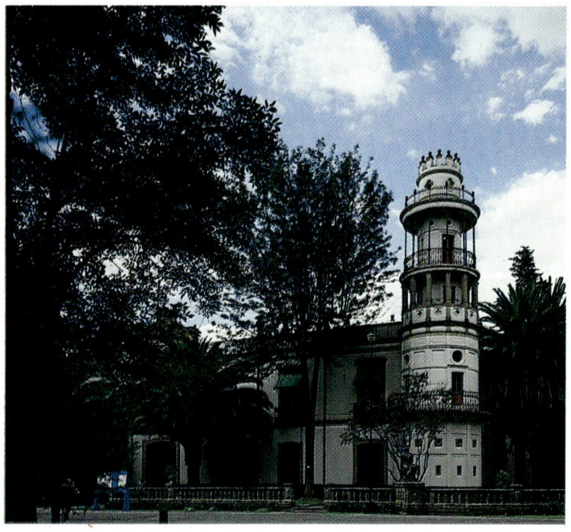

Figure 379.
Exterior view of chapel at Chapingo.

privileged leisure and to political cooperation as a means of achieving that goal; this union is symbolized by the inclusion of the crossed hammer and sickle. The ideal of proletarian solidarity that arose from this occupational, *qua* doctrinal duality was by no one more tenaciously upheld in Mexican art than by Rivera, no doubt as much because of his deep personal feeling for the land and his belief that its protective husbandry was essential to healthy community life as for ideological or political reasons.

Rivera's fresco decorations in the administrative area at Chapingo have always been treated as adjunct and secondary to his acknowledged masterpiece in the adjoining chapel, and none of the former is an acknowledged exemplar of his style. However, they preceded the chapel program by a probable two years (except for the later honorary patron portraits) and, therefore, had importance in preparing his mind, as well as opening the way, for the more important chapel commission. It is even possible that the composition for *Dividing the Land* was the trial theme and design for three connected panels treating a similar theme on the east wall of the Court of Fiestas at the Secretaría de Educación Pública (SEP I, 22–24), painted at about the same time. The panel has the freshness and expressive directness of a first statement. The theme of the meeting of peasant and worker is also repeated at the Secretaría (SEP III, 11), again on a larger scale, but the two versions are too close in treatment on a stylistic basis to put one before the other in time. There can be little doubt, however, that Rivera's first experience in the stately complex at Chapingo and the potential offered by the new school for encouraging the regeneration of Mexican agriculture in the service of the farming and working population of the countryside deeply affected him at the time. The administrative area series was one of the earliest of Rivera's works to assume a directly tutorial role in terms of social revolution, and it prefigured the extensive series of didactic themes at the Secretaría as well as that of the chapel next door, the epitome of this approach in the artist's Mexican work of the 1920s.

Chapel

The fourteen principal and twenty-seven subsidiary themes of Rivera's pictorial program for the chapel constitute a scholastically reasoned curriculum, following the principles of dialectical materialism, aimed at eradicating the people's memory of past subservience and backward ways by substituting images that present Marxist revolutionary doctrines and advanced technology as the assured pathway to social and economic emancipation. The chapel program was intended to function as a catechism, providing inspiration and guidance to a new generation of Mexican farm workers and agricultural planners and exhorting them to uphold a modern, nationally constructive, self-respecting way of life based on the credo "exploitation of the land, not of man," as stated in the rector's dedicatory text in the administrative area (ad. bldg. diagram, 1 and 3).

The panels on the left side of the nave show successive stages in the transformation of society through "Social Revolution," whereas the panels on the right portray symbolically the parallel changes that take place in nature from seedling to flower, in a sequence called "Natural Evolution," with the implication that both processes are natural, related, and inevitable.

The panels of the "Social Revolution" (chapel diag., A–E) sequence begin with three themes, the *Birth of Class Consciousness, Formation of Revolutionary Leadership* (fig. 382), and *Reactionary Forces,* that seek to establish the identification between worker and peasant in support of the revolutionary idea of class struggle. This stage of awakening is followed by portrayals of the struggle itself in

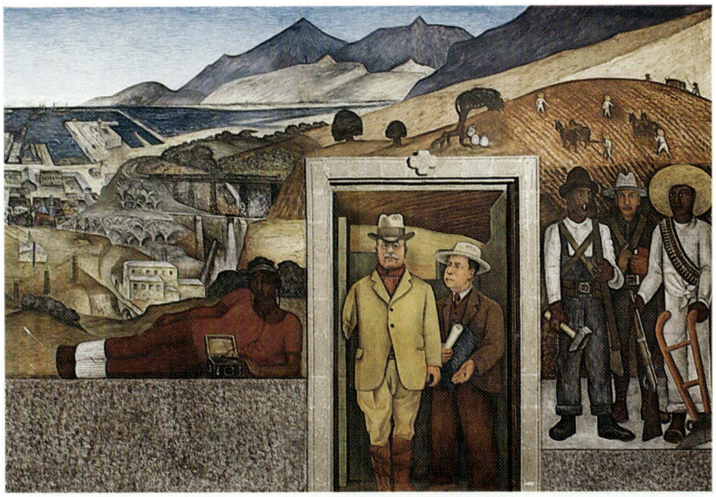

Figure 380.
Good Government (detail), 1924, fresco, 2.98 × 9.46 m. Universidad Autónoma de Chapingo, Administration Building.

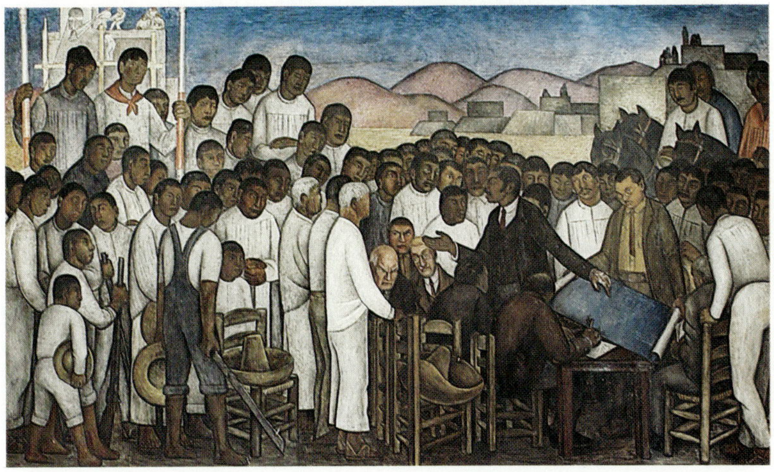

Figure 381.
Dividing the Land, 1924, fresco, 2.99 × 5.12 m. Universidad Autónoma de Chapingo, Administration Building.

the main panels, scenes of uprising, death (D), and triumph, while monumental hands in the arched tympana above are exhortatory symbols with revolutionary significance.

The first panel of the "Natural Evolution" sequence (F–J) symbolizes the correspondence between natural and social forces. The people's historical memory is invoked by reference to the buried martyrs and folk heroes Zapata and Montaño, whose blood is shown fertilizing the soil. This metaphorical device suggests that this event is part of both the natural cycle of life and the revolutionary process of injustice followed by retribution. The confluence of these two ideas in this introductory position in the narthex anticipates the synthesis of the two sequences in the end-wall panel. The second phase of the sequence depicts in metaphorical terms the earth's fiery underground (fig. 383) and the emergence of man as unspoiled expressions of the natural and anthropological order. These three themes representing nature's awakening are similarly followed by further symbols and portrayals of the process of evolution on two levels, in this case the inception and growth of life, with human beings and plant forms being used interchangeably. In the main panels surrounding the circular light openings of the nave are allegorical representations of *Germination* (H), *Maturation* (I), and *The Abundant Earth* (J), while in the narrow windows of the

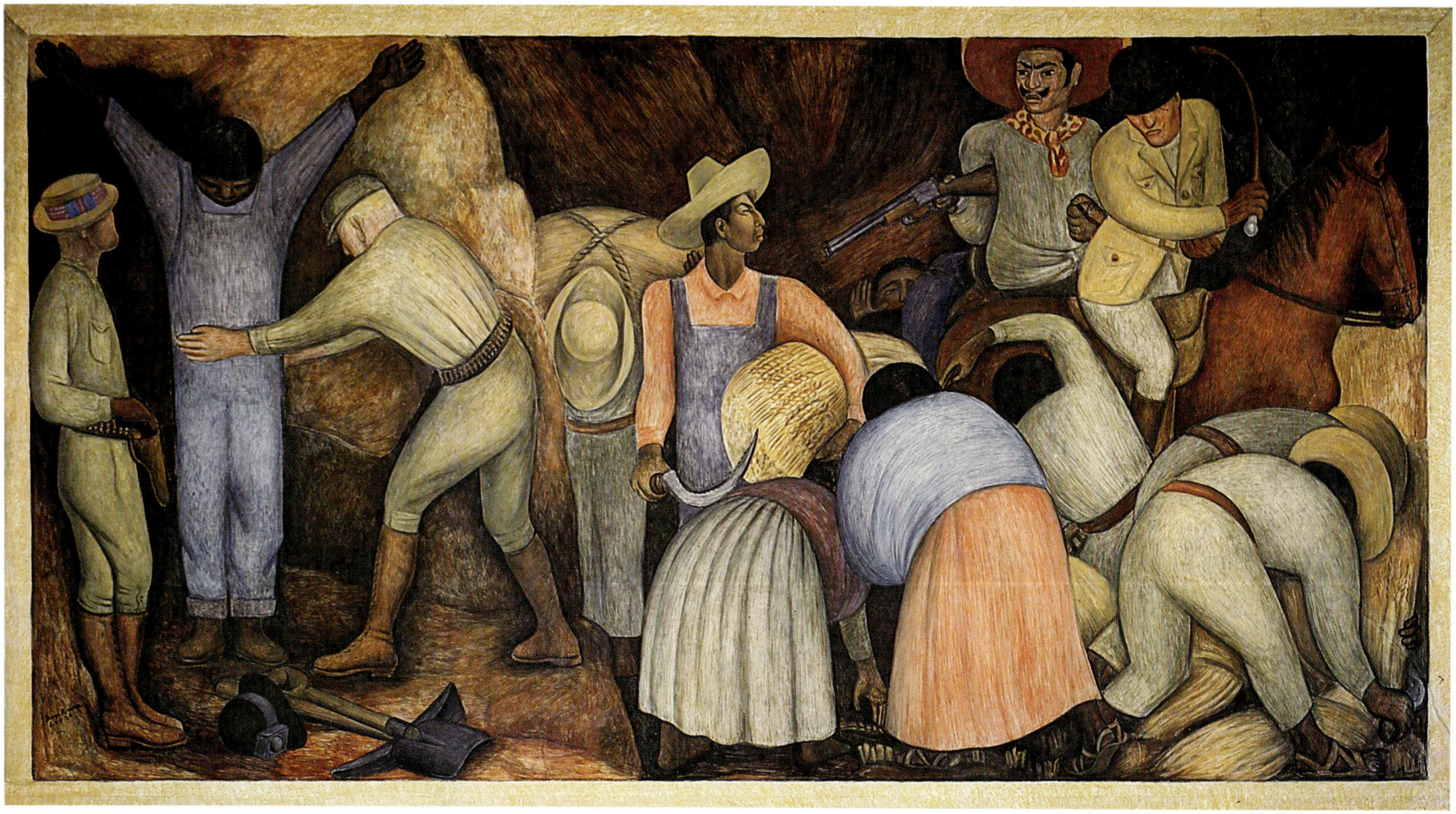

Figure 382.
***Formation of Revolutionary Leadership*, 1926–27, fresco, 3.54 × 5.55 m. Universidad Autónoma de Chapingo, Chapel.**

tympana appear phallic symbols of the biological inception of life (h, i) and the fruits of the harvest (j).

These step-by-step facing progressions are brought to a climax in the end-wall panel, *The Liberated Earth with Natural Forces Controlled by Man* (IV), representing the harmony between man and nature once both have been liberated from the bondage of selfish interests.

Entering the chapel at Chapingo one is immediately struck by the enveloping totality of its painted program. It is a place that engenders both reverence and resolution, one in which to render homage and dedication to an ideal. The artist's marriage of a 17th-century architectural setting conceived as a Christian Jesuit temple with a narrative predicated on a revolutionary belief in human rather than divine control of mankind's destiny produces a mystical effect that brings both together in an implausible but impressive symmetry.

In his first decade of mural painting, Rivera set before his Mexican audience of a new view of human experience, which found its pivotal manifestation, if not its epitome, in the chapel at Chapingo. This view consisted in seeing beyond the accustomed forms of social organization and the accepted interpretations of reality to perceive the disenfranchised Mexican peasants as fully part of humankind and their social evolution as part of the larger order of nature. But even more important

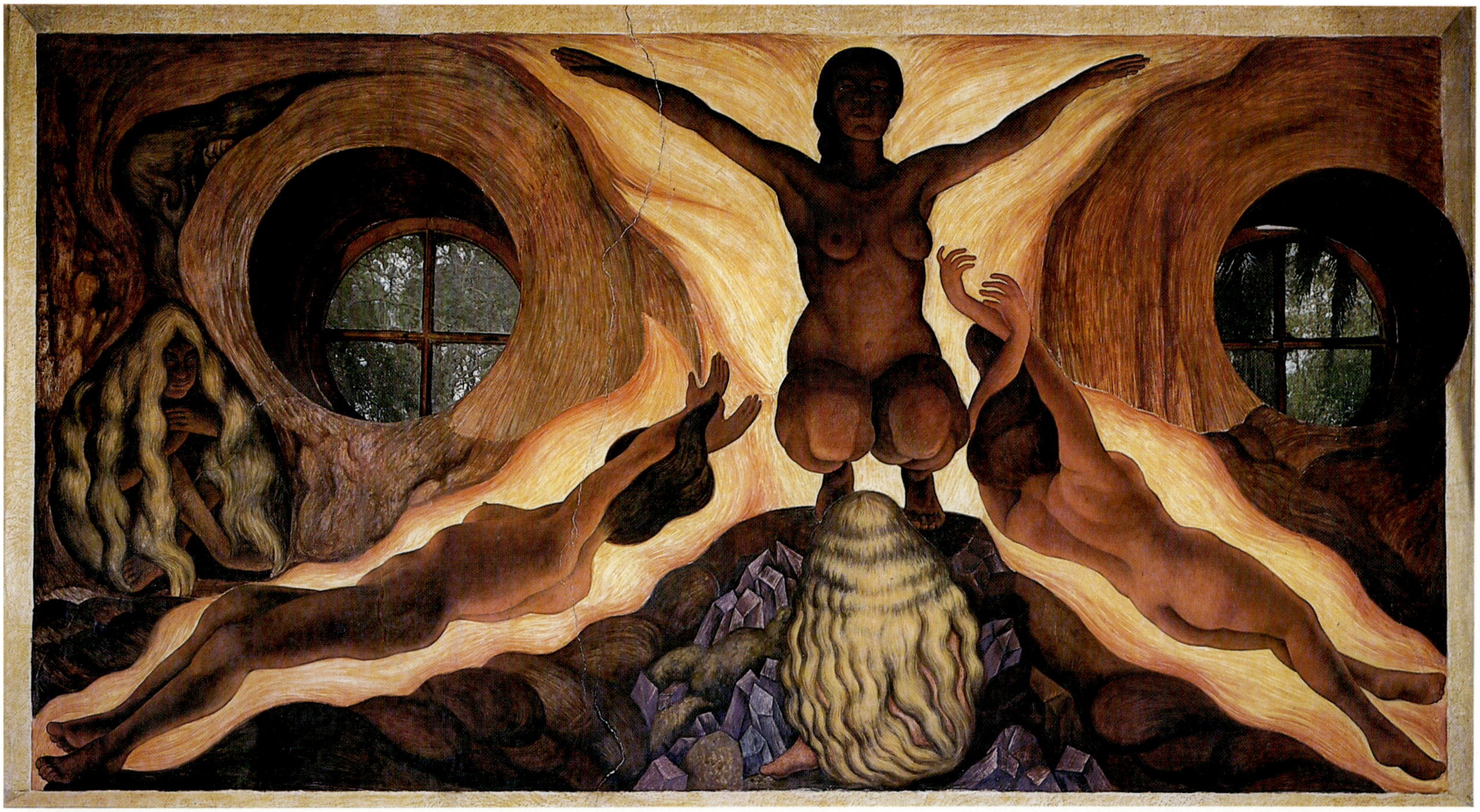

Figure 383.
***Subterranean Forces*, 1926–27, fresco, 3.54 × 5.55 m. Universidad Autónoma de Chapingo, Chapel.**

was his conception, now become theology, that the organized peasantry had the power to generate social forces, and that, through political action, they could bring the realm of nature into harmony with the best interests of the Mexican nation as a whole.

Summary

Location: Universidad Autónoma de Chapingo, state of Mexico, approx. twenty-five miles (forty km.) from Mexico City

Site: Central Administration Building

Theme/Subject: *The Land Liberated (La Tierra Liberada)*

Format: Entrance corridor, stairway, and second-floor foyer: four main panels, four honorary portraits, subsidiary decorations, and fifty-three geometrical decorative motifs
Chapel: fourteen main panels, twenty-seven subsidiary themes, and motifs simulating architectural elements

Date: *Entrance corridor and stairway*: 1924; *second-floor foyer*: 1924 and (portraits) 1940s
Chapel: 1926–27

Medium: True fresco made part of wall except for portraits on doorway panels of second-floor foyer

Dimensions: *Entrance corridor*: 5.10 × 11.95 m
Stairway: 5.62 × 5.71 m
Second-floor foyer: 5.84 × 4.42 m
Chapel: 5.98/6.08 × 24.12 m

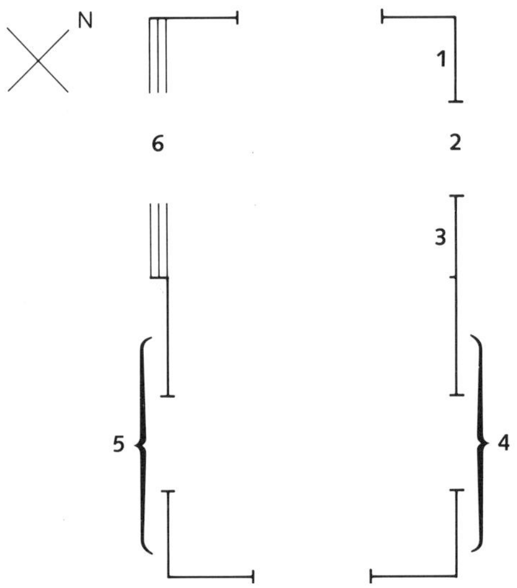

Universidad Autónoma de Chapingo, Administrative Area, Entrance Corridor[2]

1. *Rector's 1924 inaugural address,* 1924
   Earth red on ocher ground, 3.40 × 1.79 m
2. Transom design, 1924
   Earth red on blue ground, approx. 1.80 × 2.05 m
3. *Rector's address* (continued), 1924
   Earth red on ocher ground, 3.40 × 1.75 m
4. *Men and Women of Tehuantepec under Wind and Cloud Symbols,* 1924
   4.31 × 4.81 m
5. *Men and Women of Tehuantepec in Mountain Landscape with Sunburst,* 1924
   4.31 × 4.80 m
6. (Lower stairwell) Geometric decorations simulating architectural details, in earth red on ocher ground: two trapezoids on side walls, four rectangles on landing, and twenty-six square coffers on ceiling

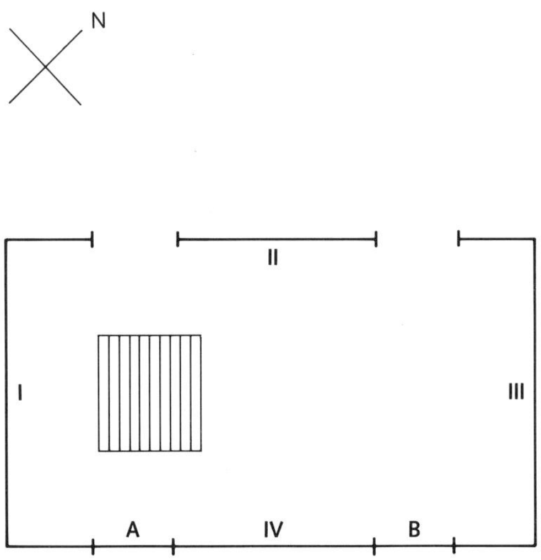

Universidad Autónoma de Chapingo, Administrative Area, Second-floor Foyer

I. *Dividing the Land,* 1924
   2.99 × 5.12 m
   Signed, *DR 1924*
II. *Bad Government,* [1924]
   2.99 × 9.47 m
III. *Meeting of Peasant and Worker,* 1924
   2.99 × 5.12 m
IV. *Good Government,* [1924]
   2.98 × 9.46 m
   A. Official patrons, early 1940s
      2.25 × 1.25 m
      Inscribed, *Pres*[ident] *Avila Camacho / Sec. Ag. y Fomento Marte R. Gómez*
   B. Official patrons, early 1940s
      2.25 × 1.25 m
      Inscribed, *Pres*[ident]A[lvaro] *Obregón 1921–24 / Sec. Ag.* [?] *y Fomento P. Denegro 1940–46*

Universidad Autónoma de Chapingo, Chapel

Left Wall: "Social Revolution"

A. *Birth of Class Consciousness,* 2.44 × 5.53 m
   Farmers and mine workers produce Mexico's wealth.
B. *Formation of Revolutionary Leadership,* 3.54 × 5.55 m
   Mining inspector, armed guard, and white (i.e., foreign) patron oppress mine workers and peasants.
   b. *Reactionary Forces,* 3.54 × 4.95 m
      Caricatures personifying Capital, Militarism, and the Church corral Earth behind spearheads.
C. *Underground Organization of the Agrarian Movement,* 3.54 × 3.48 m
   A young agrarian leader exhorts farmers and their families to rebel.
   c. *Beginning of Warfare,* 1.66 × 3.48 m
      Open left hand, palm forward.
D. *Continuous Renewal of Revolutionary Struggle,* 3.54 × 3.67 m
   Death and burial of the young leader, whose sacrifice causes the tree overhead to flower.
   d. *Resolution,* 1.66 x 3.67 m
      Left hand closed in a fist, palm forward.
E. *Triumph of the Revolution,* 3.54 × 3.53 m
   Distribution of the land and its harvests after the revolution, showing modern machinery in use.
   e. *The Rightness of the New Order,* 1.66 × 3.53 m
      Open left hand with outstretched fingers—an allusion to the Christian sign of benediction.

Right Wall: "Natural Evolution," also known as "Song to the Earth" *(Canción a la Tierra)*

F. *Blood of the Revolutionary Martyrs Fertilizing the Earth,* 2.44 × 4.91 m
   The buried bodies of Emiliano Zapata and Otilio Montaño invigorate the soil of Mexico.
G. *Subterranean Forces,* 3.54 × 5.55 m
   Muscular female nudes representing the volcanic forces of the earth's interior reach upward through flaming crevices. Their abundant hair and an outcrop of multicolored crystals symbolize the earth's riches that await possession.

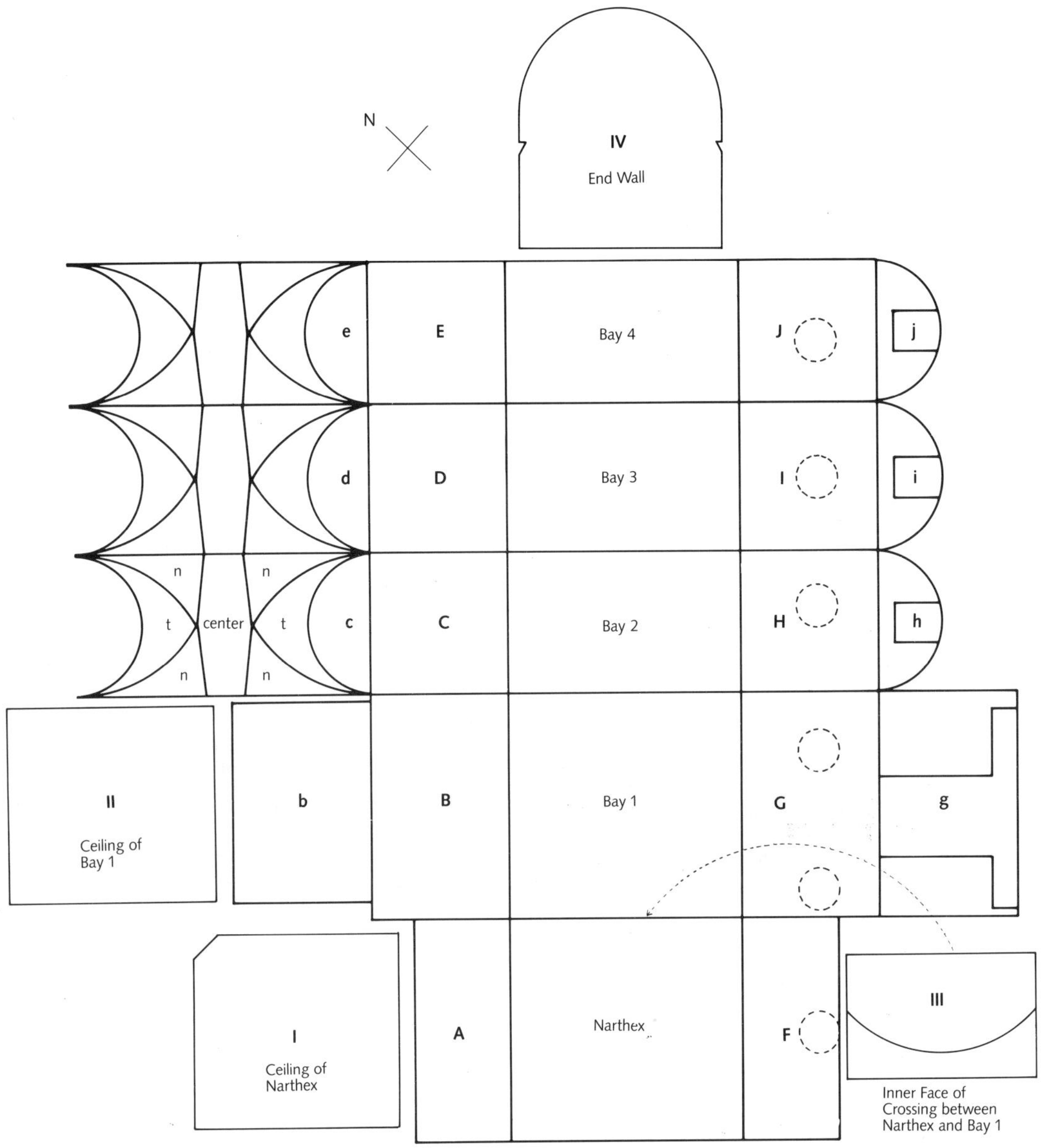

g. *Emergent Man,* 3.54 × 4.95 m³
A nude male figure emerges unspoiled from the elements of the earth.

H. *Germination,* 3.54 × 3.48 m
Nude female figures summarize the various stages of gestation, from conception to near birth.
h. Phallus (in window oculus), diam. 1 m

I. *Maturation,* 3.54 × 3.67 m
Around a budding flower, four female nudes recline, sit, turn and stand to express the burgeoning of natural life.
i. Phallus (in window oculus), diam. 1 m

J. *The Abundant Earth,* 3.54 × 3.53 m
Three nude female figures and a child reflect on nature's prodigal fruitfulness and promise.
j. Fruits of the harvest (in window oculus), diam. 1 m

Ceilings of Narthex and First Bay of Nave

I. *Symbols of the New Order,* 5.53 × 6.08 m
Five-pointed red star against an azure background, two paris of hands extending outward from behind the star; the lower pair clasp a hammer and sickle, the open palms of the upper face the viewer.

II. *The Elements,* 5.60 × 6.03 m
Sun and wind, symbolized by human heads, a rainbow in prismatic colors, and three female figures are grouped around a female nude floating in the sky, holding her breasts in a nourishing gesture toward the world below.

Inner Face of Crossing and End Wall

III. *The Virgin Earth,* 3.54 × 5.88 m
A nude young woman, asleep, reclines on the ground, her face covered by dark hair. In her outstretched hand she cups a seedling, a dream symbol of fertility.

IV. *The Liberated Earth with Natural Forces Controlled by Man,* 6.92 × 5.98 m
A reclining female nude of superhuman proportions gazes serenely outward, her right hand sheltering a budding plant, her left pointed upward with open palm. Around her are nude male and female figures, each manifesting an attribute of nature—water, electricity, fire—with which the earth can endow mankind and sustain human welfare.

Vaulted Bays: *Proletarian Prophets and Guardians*

Bay 2

Center•*Searching for the Way*
Two floating male figures with white skins and drapery, seen from below, grope in the air.

Triangles•Seated male figures with dark bronze skins. One rests his hand on a hammer handle, the other rests his on a sickle.

Niches•Four bronze-skinned male figures push outward against their enclosures.

Bay 3

Center•*Revelation of the Way*
Two floating male figures, seen from above, discover a shimmering red star.

Triangles•*Guardians of Truth*
Seated male figures with bronze skins and set expressions, seen frontally. One holds a heavy bat, the other a machete.

Niches•Flames shaped like the maguey cactus.

Bay 4

Center•*The Land's Bounty Rightfully Possessed*
Two floating male figures with dark bronze skins, seen from below. One holds a hammer, the other a sickle, which they cross against the light of the red star.

Triangles•Seated male figures with dark bronze skins hold wheat sheaves. One holds an earthen jar and a sickle bound into the sheaf; in front of the other a blue hammer lies on the ground.

Niches•Four male figures with dark bronze skins hold corn, sugar cane, [grapes?], and [mangoes?].

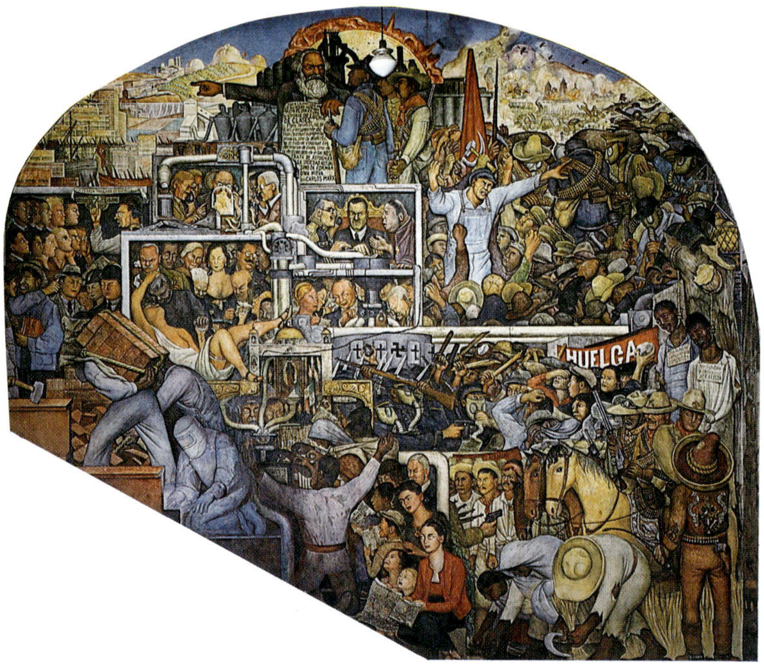
HUELGA

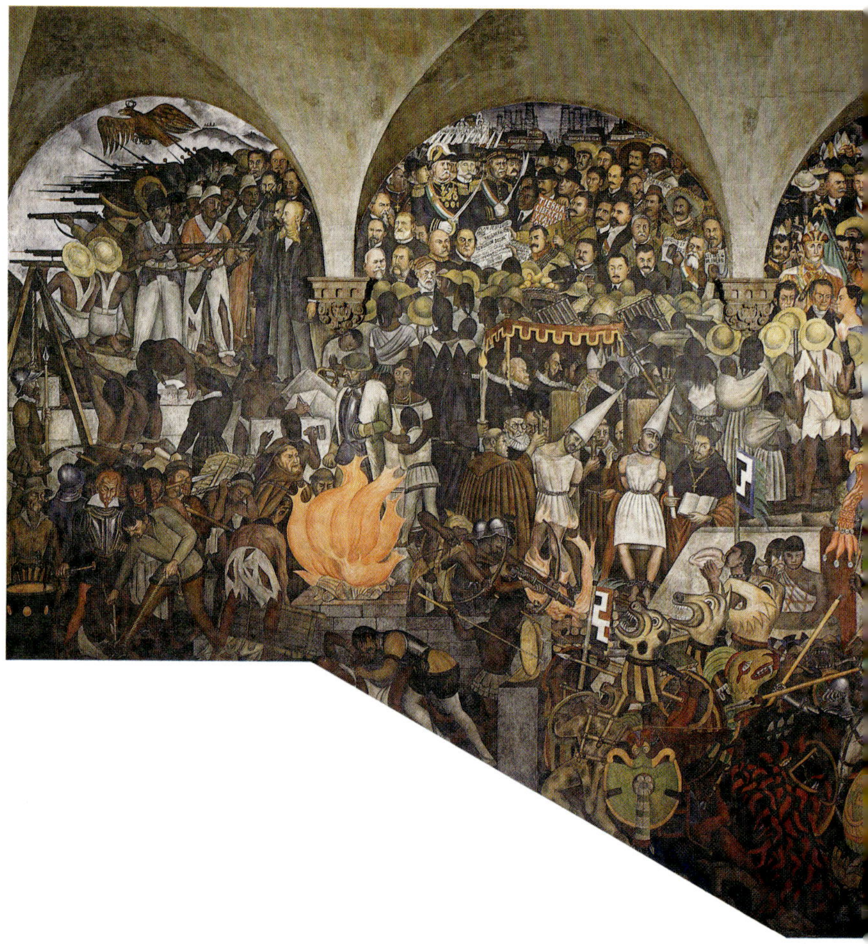

Palacio Nacional

Mexico City

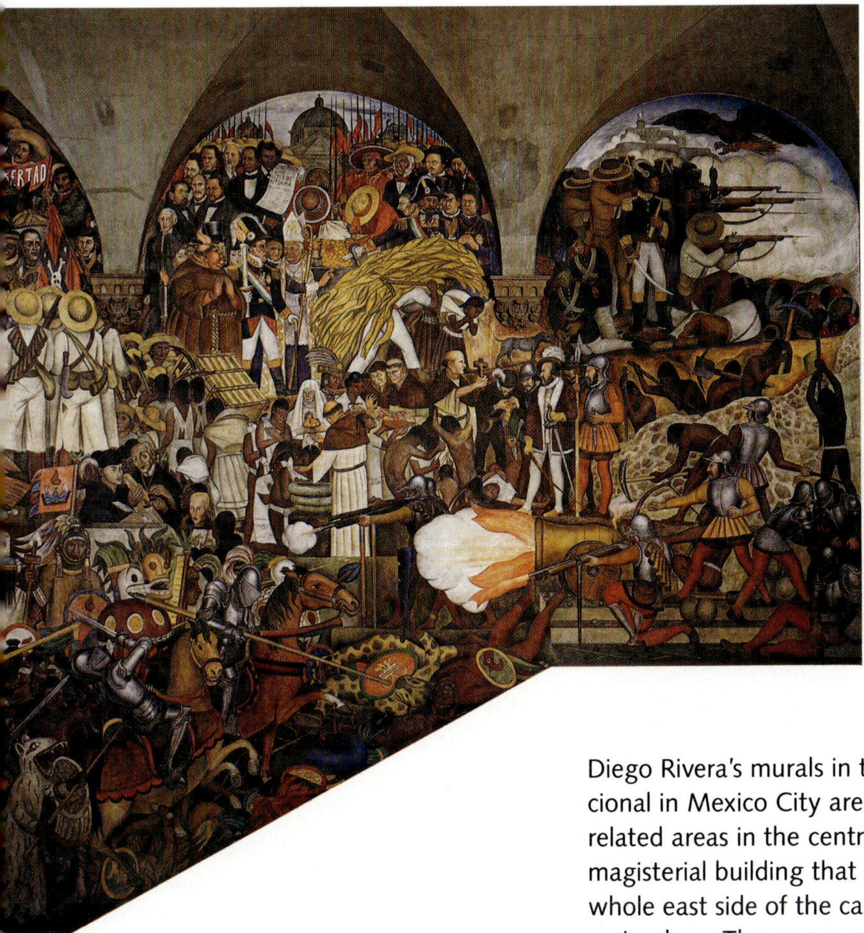

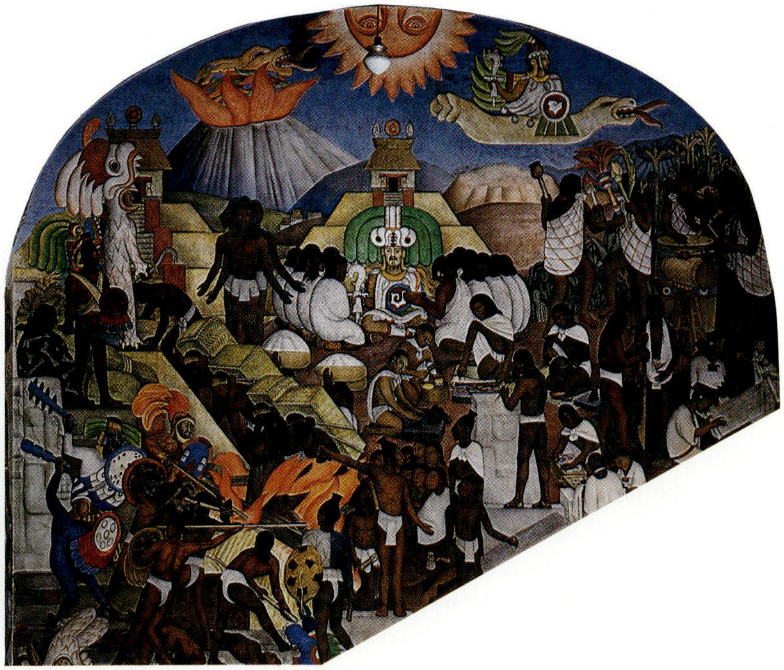

Figure 384
***History of Mexico: From the Conquest to the Future*, 1929–30 (west and north walls), 1935 (south wall), fresco, 7.49 × 8.85 m (north and south walls), 8.59 × 12.87 m (west wall). Mexico City, Palacio Nacional, Stairway.**

Diego Rivera's murals in the Palacio Nacional in Mexico City are in two closely related areas in the central part of the magisterial building that occupies the whole east side of the capital's grandiose main plaza. They were commissioned in 1929 during the two-year interim presidency of Emilio Portes Gil (former president Plutarco Elías Calles actually held the reins of power). The expansive, low-lying edifice has been the seat of Mexico's executive power since the end of the Wars for Independence in 1821. For nearly three hundred years before that, after the fall of Tenochtitlán and the overthrow of the Aztec hegemony in August 1521, it was the headquarters and residence first of Cortés and from 1550 of the Viceroy of New Spain.

The subject matter of the murals is the history of Mexico from the fall of Teotihuacán, presumably about A.D. 900, to the beginning of the presidency of Lázaro Cárdenas in 1935. A massive cavalcade of events and personalities, it is one of the most compendious visual displays of historical material in near human scale in the history of art, inviting comparison in terms of size and comprehensiveness (as related to medium) with Trajan's Column, the Bayeux Tapestry, the biblical history components of Michelangelo's Sistine Ceiling, and Hans Burgkmair's wood engraving *Der Reise von Maximilian* as well as the screen-fold codices of pre-Conquest Mexico (it might be seen as an outstretched muralistic projection of the latter).

This allegorical portrayal of the history of Mexico is organized in two parts: (1) "From the Conquest to the Future" on the main entrance stairway and (2) "From the Pre-Hispanic Civilization to the Conquest" in the covered gallery surrounding the building's central patio on the second floor. Its execution was realized in three stages: in 1929–30, the stairway's main and right side walls were completed; in 1935, the left side wall composition was added, completing the decoration of the stairway area; and in 1943–51, eleven interdoorway panels in the patio corridor on the second level extended the historical program even further into Mexico's ancient past.

Stairway

Over the sweeping expanse of the palace's entrance stairway, Rivera assumed the task of visually defining the progress of Mexican nationhood as it developed in the one hundred years following Independence. In keeping with the modern revolution's constitutional recognition of the Amerindian origins of native Mexicans and the acceptance of their cultural heritage as basic elements of the new national philosophy, he chose to introduce his chronological narrative with a mythologized version of ancient life and religion in the Valley of Mexico, presented from the social revolutionary perspective that is indissociable from Mexico's historical experience and its new consciousness as a self-governing people.

In the first scene, the white-skinned, bearded creator god, Quetzalcóatl (the plumed serpent), beneficent to man, holds court, serenely instructing his votaries.[1] At the right the creative activities of Aztec life are depicted in detail: music, ceremonial dancing, agriculture, weaving, stone carving, pottery making, and painting. To the left a knight of the warrior Order of Eagles wearing a flamboyant headdress commands tribute from a file of heavily burdened porters. This scene is pointed out below by an Indian of plebian station who protests to a group of fellow subjects. At the lower left of the composition is a scene of open battle between ruled and ruling forces. (By giving prominence to the struggle between rulers and the ruled in Aztec society as evidence of aboriginal class struggle, Rivera clearly injected an element of his personal political philosophy into the historical context, an inference that became explicit in his final stairway composition on the opposite wall.) At upper right, Quetzalcóatl, true to prophecy, departs toward the east on a feathered serpent. At the crown of the arched wall an upside-down half-sun bearing a face appears. This inverted head and the erupting volcano to the left have been seen as a combined reference to "the destruction of the Pre-Spanish world."[2] The theme as a whole also symbolizes, as it emblazons, the indigenous origins and revolutionary foundation of modern Mexico, even as it portends future strife.

On the main wall of the stairway is a five-part historical pageant of events connected in space and time, designed to be read both horizontally and vertically. At the center of this panoramic composition stands an eagle, the national symbol of Mexico, an image of strength and self-confidence. In its beak, instead of the traditional serpent, it holds the Aztec symbol of war. On the lower section of this wall, up to the horizontal midpoint of the composition, are described in detail the ferocious encounters of the Conquest, a panorama of hand-to-hand fighting between Indian warriors in ceremonial battle dress and the armored Spanish invaders led by Cortés, followed by the plight of the native population under the colonial regime during and immediately after the Conquest.

The topmost area of the main stairway wall is described by five rounded pictorial areas (formed by the stairway ceiling vaults), four of them painted to represent themes and figures from major periods during the century between the proclamation of independence in 1921 and 1930, the year in which this part of the mural was completed. This arched-panel sequence is not arranged in chronological order and may be read in any order. The outermost panels present the two 19th-century military invasions of Mexico by foreign powers, while the panels flanking the central arch focus on two lengthy periods, the age of the Reform and the era of Porfirio Díaz. The central arched space is occupied by a symbolic montage of historical personalities from the other four periods.

In reference to this panel, Rosa Casanova has pointed out that while Rivera maintained that he painted the history of Mexico in terms of the struggle of the masses, "it is clear this is not so, above all from this moment on, in which a series of personalities are assembled as a means of stitching together the plot of a history which flows out from the government that sponsored the murals. The masses appear only as decorative groupings which divide the scenes and create a certain rhythm and movement."[3]

In the five years between completion of the main stairway wall (1929–30) and the beginning of the adjoining south wall (1935), Rivera had undertaken five fresco programs in he United States: two in San Francisco; one in Detroit; and two in New York, his never completed effort at the RCA building in Rockefeller Center, and a series of twenty-one movable panels at the New Workers School. The artist's experiences with the capitalist power structure of the United States (See RCA section of this census) seem to have moved his already revolutionary thinking as to the political role his art ought to play from a focus that was local and national to one that was international and involved a full and open advocacy of the Marxist-Leninist view of historical process.

The subject of the south wall is *Mexico Today and Tomorrow*. The sequence of themes in this crowded montage follows a rational part-to-part plan, however overwhelming and disconnected to the other parts of the stairway program it may seem to the faraway eye.[4] It proceeds roughly along the line of a reverse S-curve, beginning with a scene of contemporary Mexicans: *campesinos*, teachers and students, devotees of the church, workers, day laborers, Marxist union members ridiculing other doctrines being preached in a university classroom. In the center, four areas compartmented by the pipelines of power isolate the roots of social evil: foreign capitalism;[5] the three-sided base of reaction in Mexico (military, political,[6] ecclesiastical); corrupt journalism; and high society. At the far center right, figures wearing gas masks repress a strike by workers and *campesinos,* and above this is depicted an armed uprising against the existing social order in downtown Mexico City. At the very top Karl Marx points to an ideal industrial, agricultural, and scientific landscape and exhorts an alliance of worker, soldier, and *campesino* to abolish property and class divisions and to form a new society.

Patio Corridor

The eleven related patio corridor frescoes at the Palacio Nacional are arranged in a conventional, panel-to-panel sequence, following the rectangular plan of the building. Mounted between handsome ornamental doorways, the frescoes are panels in the true sense, being measured to fit into wall spaces and being removable. There are nine principal fresco murals, each with a grisaille predella panel underneath, and two introductory panels in grisaille. The first and largest panel depicts Tenochtitlán, the capital and epicenter of the 15th/16th-century Aztec civilization (see fig. 333), while the others are drawn from other, earlier, high points of pre-Columbian civilization that lay to the northeast, east, south, and west of this city in the Valley of Mexico (see figs. 268, 282, 284, and 286). The last shows the arrival of the Spaniards under Cortés, who is denigrated as a deformed victim of syphilis (see fig. 385). The two introductory text panels describe the cultural and agricultural achievements with which Mexican civilization has benefited the world. Originally planned to continue around all four sides of the corridor, the series as completed occupies the full length of the north patio wall and about one third of the east wall.

Opinions differ on the symbolic purpose of this phase of the Palacio Nacional program. Villagómez describes it as a ring that, had all the projected panels been completed, would circle the patio and join with the left side of the stairway decoration, thus not only adding artistic splendor and a symmetrical decorative program to the building housing the presidency but also linking the indigenous soul of the nation to the proletarian social order of the future, this being the logical path for the nation to follow in fulfilling its destiny.[7] (On the north wall of the stairway, where it joins the patio corridor, Quetzalcóatl departs eastward toward the patio "ring," while from his opposite position on the south wall Karl Marx also points to the east. Thus, the idea of their meeting is implicit in a common horizon, perhaps following the concept of Hegelian synthesis as well as the closed "circle" of the patio walls.)

Whatever the symbolic relationship of the patio corridor frescoes to those of the stairway, the former may be seen as part of the artist's intention to make real and memorable to the common people of Mexico the achievements of their native ancestry as a source of pride in race, nation, and way of life.

Three artistic phases, corresponding to the three work periods, are evident in the Palacio Nacional program: (1) the style of the main and north walls of the stairway, which brings into a unified formal idiom the artist's previous seven years in evolving a personal style that would stand as an image of national reality and purpose; (2) a polemical style on the south wall that reflects his sharpened revolutionary resolve following his experiences in the United States in 1930–33, and which he found acceptable under the Cárdenas presidency on his return to Mexico; and (3) the more descriptive style of his illustrations of pre-Columbian civilization, presented as dioramas picturing in ideal terms life as it was lived by present-day Mexico's indigenous ancestors.

It is in the first two of these phases that Rivera shows his mastery—bringing together the experience of his previous undertakings into an epitome of pictorial clarity and expressiveness to convey native Mexican history, cultural values, and horizons. His parallel work in the Palacio de Cortés in Cuernavaca shares the quality, if not the massive visual and historical compass, of the Palacio Nacional stairway frescoes. Together these murals constitute the high point of the artist's command, in the "full tide of his genius," at the end of the first decade of his career as a muralist.[8]

Summary

Location: Mexico City, Plaza de la Constitucion (Zócalo)

Site: Palacio Nacional, seat of the executive power of the United States of Mexico situated on the site of Montezuma's Aztec palace.[9]

Theme/Subject: *History of Mexico.* An allegorical portrayal of the history of Mexico in two parts: "From the Conquest to the Future" on the walls of the building's entrance stairway, leading from the ground to the second level, and "From the Pre-Hispanic Civilization to the Conquest" on the corridor walls of the main patio on the second level.[10]

Format: *Stairway:* Two blind-arched side walls flank a blind-arcaded main wall, forming a U-shaped surface below a five-part vaulted ceiling. This main (west) wall faces a broad observation area and was treated as a continuous panorama. The flanking walls at either end were treated as separate compositions.
Patio Corridor: Eleven fresco panels on movable frames hung between doorways (each contains separate compositions in grisaille, emulating sculptural reliefs, below the main design).[11]

Date: *Stairway:* 1929–30 (main and north walls); 1935 (south wall)
Patio Corridor: 1945–51

Medium: *Stairway:* True fresco made part of wall
Patio Corridor: True fresco on movable steel frames

Dimensions: See diagram keys

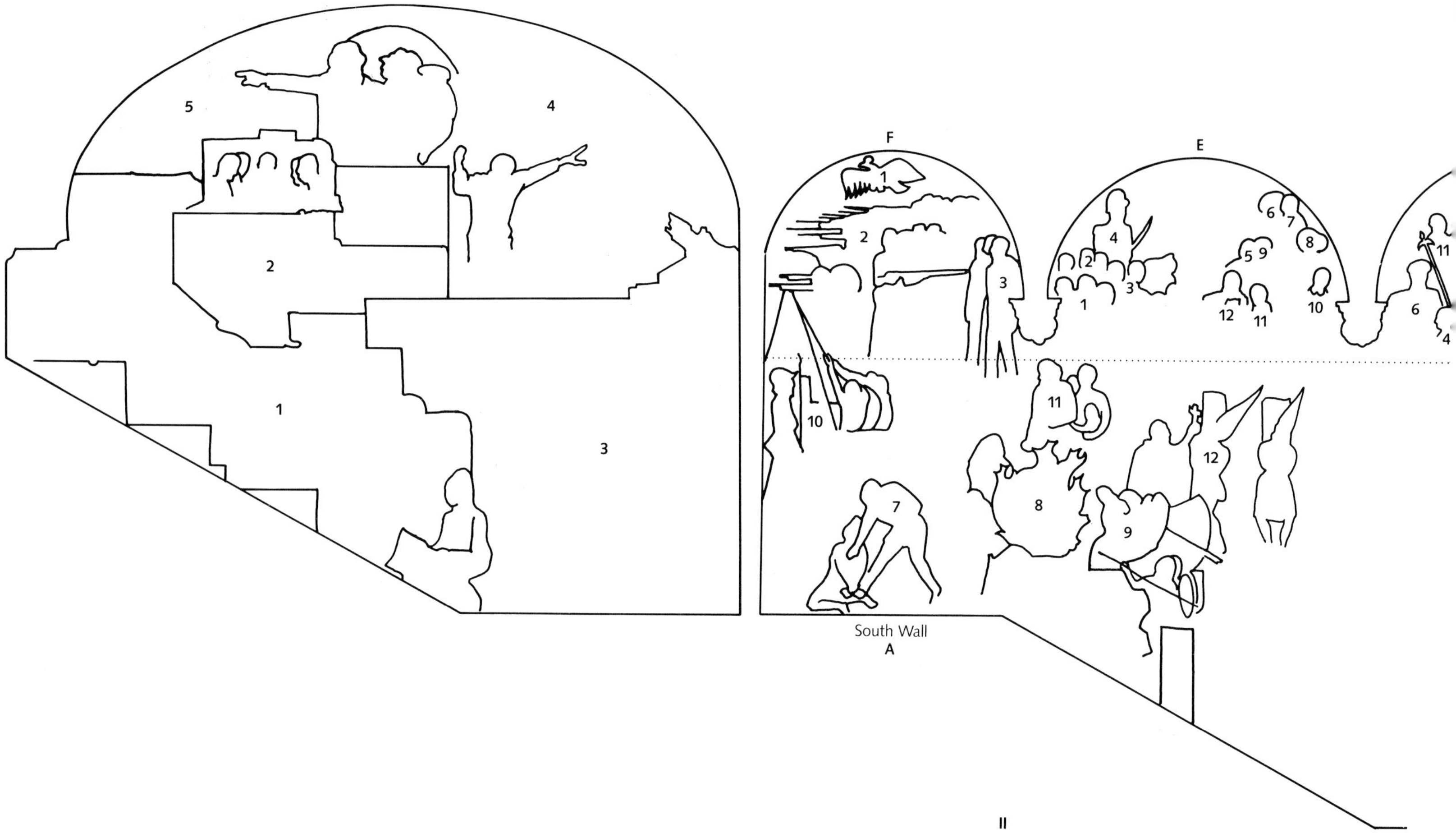

Palacio Nacional, Stairway

I. North Wall: *The Aztec World,* 1929, 7.49 × 8.85 m (h. from crown of arch to dado)

1. Quetzalcóatl instructs his votaries.
2. Productive activities.
3. Commanding tribute.
4. Pre-Hispanic dissent.
5. Class warfare.
6. Quetzalcóatl's departure; the end of the Aztec world foretold.

II. West Wall: *From the Conquest to 1930,* 1929–30, 8.59 × 12.87 m.

A. Spanish Conquest and Colonization

1. The Mexican eagle, symbol of nationality, holds the Aztec emblem of ceremonial war, showing defiance and pride.
2. Cuauhtémoc, last Aztec emperor and defender of Tenochtitlán.
3. Cortés leading the assault of the conquistadores.
4. Invaders attack with cannon and firearms.
5. Slaughter of Aztecs by armed horsemen.
6. Melee of battle at close quarters.
7. Enslavement of the Indian.
8. Destruction of Indian culture, symbolized by flames; Bishop Diego de Landa watches with misgiving.
9. Spaniards aided by Tlaxcalan allies.
10. Indians constructing buildings for the conquerors.
11. Cortés next to Malinche, who embraces a youth, symbolizing racial intermixture *(mestizaje).*
12. Civil and religious authorities participating in an *auto-da-fé* (public punishment) under the Inquisition.
13. Bernardo de Sahgún recording the details of indigenous Mexican life before the Conquest; Vasco de Quiroga, humanitarian first bishop of Guadalajara; Pedro de Gante, Franciscan educator of Indians in the Valley of Mexico.
14. Indoctrination for rule and riches through baptism before an Aztec serpent font.
15. The Franciscan friar Bartolomé de las Casas, who was with Columbus on his first voyage, defending the Mexican Indians before Cortés.

B. United States Invasion (1847)

1. The American eagle arrives at the ramparts of Chapultepec Castle.
2. Defenders of Mexico City.
3. Mexican president Nicolás Bravo, commander of the defense at Chapultepec.

C. Reform and the Era of Benito Juaréz (1855–76)

1. Rich clergy.
2. Antonio López de Santa Anna, several times dictator between 1833–55.
3. Archbishop Labastida, defender of church property and privilege.
4. Miguel Miramón, antireformist general.
5. Juan Álvarez, leader of southern forces against Santa Anna.
6. Benito Juárez, president of Mexico (1856–62 and 1867–72), holding a proclamation announcing the Reform Laws that followed the Constitution of 1857.
7. Leaders of the Reform.

D. Legacy of Independence

1. The priest Hidalgo, holding the chains of slavery, presides over the cause of independence.

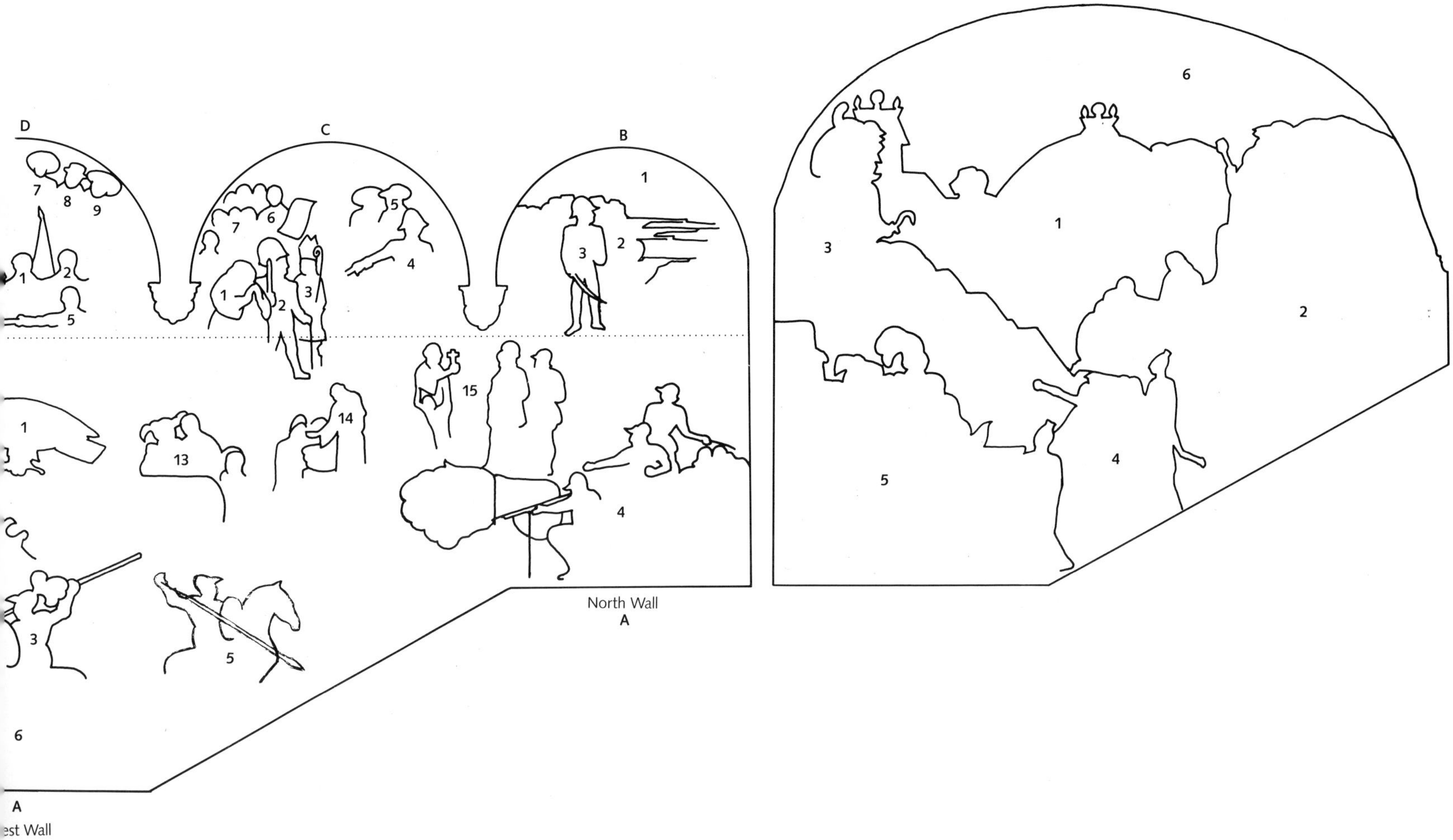

2. José María Morelos, mestizo parish priest and the most formidable general of the popular forces in the Wars of Independence.
3. General Ignacio Allende, aristocratic commander of the Querétaro peasant forces, first army to march against the colonial regime.
4. La Corregidora (Doña Josefa Ortiz de Dominguez, who informed the Querétaro conspirators of the order to arrest them).
5. Vincent Guerrero, southern peasant leader during the Wars of Independence.
6. Emperor Agustín de Iturbide, first head of state after Independence (1821–23).
7. Emiliano Zapata, leader of the 1910–17 peasant revolt in Morelos.
8. Felipe Carillo Puerto, revolutionary governor of Yucatán, assassinated (1923)
9. José G. Rodríguez, assassinated Communist agrarian leader
10. Plutarco Elías Calles, president of Mexico (1924–28)
11. Alvaro Obregón, president of Mexico (1920-24)

E. The Porfirian Era (1876–1910)[12]
   1. Followers of Díaz (Guillermo Prieto, journalist; Gabino Barreda, apostle of positivism; and Justo Sierra, minister of education).
   2. Other positivist members of the Díaz regime, known as *los scientificos*.
   3. Sebastián Lerdo de Tejada, president of Mexico after Juárez.
   4. Porfirio Díaz, president of Mexico (1876–80, 1884–1910); to his left, José Limantour, his finance minister, and Victoriano Huerta, Madero's assassin; to his right, his wife.
   5. Gustavo Madero, leader of the 1910 revolution and first president of the new republic; around him are grouped:
   6. Emiliano Zapata, leader of the peasant revolt in Morelos and southern Mexico.
   7. Otilio Montaño, assassinated author of the Plan of Ayala (1911).
   8. Francisco "Pancho" Villa, leader of the revolt in Chihuahua and northern Mexico.
   9. Luís Cabrera, secretary of the treasury under Carranza and advisor to the 1917 Querétaro Convention.
   10. Venustiano Carranza, de facto president of Mexico (1916–20), holding Article 27 of the 1917 Constitution.
   11. José Vasconcelos, early follower of Madero who became minister of education under Alvaro Obregón.
   12. José Guadalupe Posada, social caricaturist of the Pofiriato and early Revolutionary period.

F. French Intervention and the Empire under Maximilian (1862–67)
   1. The Hapsburg eagle taking flight from Mexico.
   2. Forces of Júarez struggle against Maximilian and the French army of Napoleon III.
   3. Maximilian and his generals arrested and then executed at Querétaro.

III. South Wall: *Mexico Today and Tomorrow,* 1935, 7.49 × 8.85 m. (h. from crown of central arch to dado)

1. Exploited Mexican people.
2. Roots of social evil.
3. Repression of strikers.
4. Armed uprising in downtown Mexico City.
5. Karl Marx pointing to the utopia that awaits the abolition of social classes and private property.

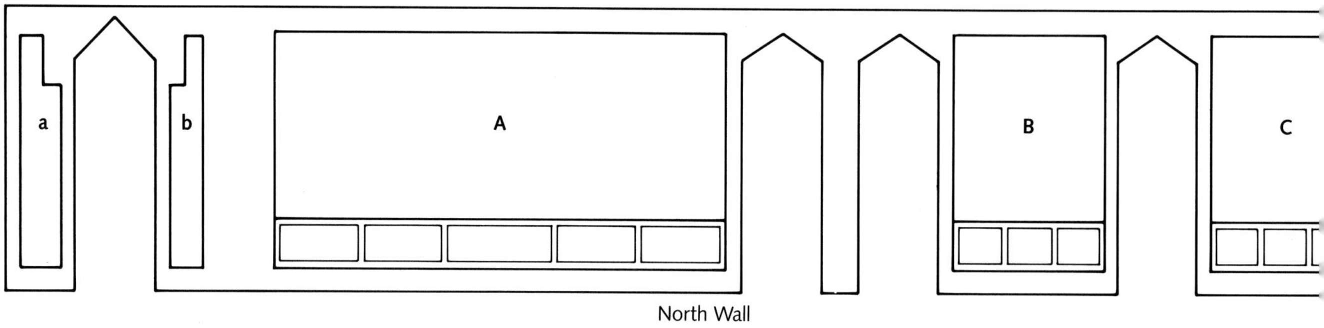

Palacio Nacional, Patio Corridor

- a. *What the World Owes to Mexico*, 1942, approx. 4.80 × .90 m
- b. *The Culture of Ancient Mexico*, 1942, approx. 4.80 × .70 m
- A. *The Great City of Tenochtitlán*, 1945, 4.92 × 9.71 m
- B. *The Tarascan Civilization*, 1942, 4.92 × 3.20 m
- C. *The Zapotec Civilization*, 1942, 4.92 × 3.20 m
- D. *The Totonac Civilization*, 1950, 4.92 × 5.27 m
- E. *Indigenous Rubber Production*, [1950], 4.92 × .64 m
- F. *The Huastec Civilization*, 1950, 4.92 × 2.24 m
- G. *Harvesting Cocoa*, 1951, 4.92 × 1.23 m
- H. *Maguey Industry*, September 21, 1951, 4.92 × 4.02 m
- I. *Disembarkation of the Spanish at Veracruz*, 1951, 4.92 × 5.27m

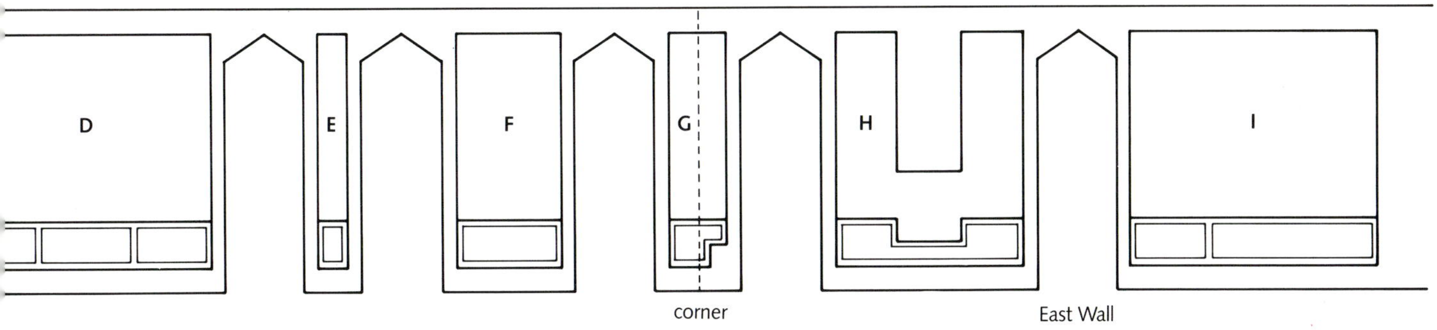

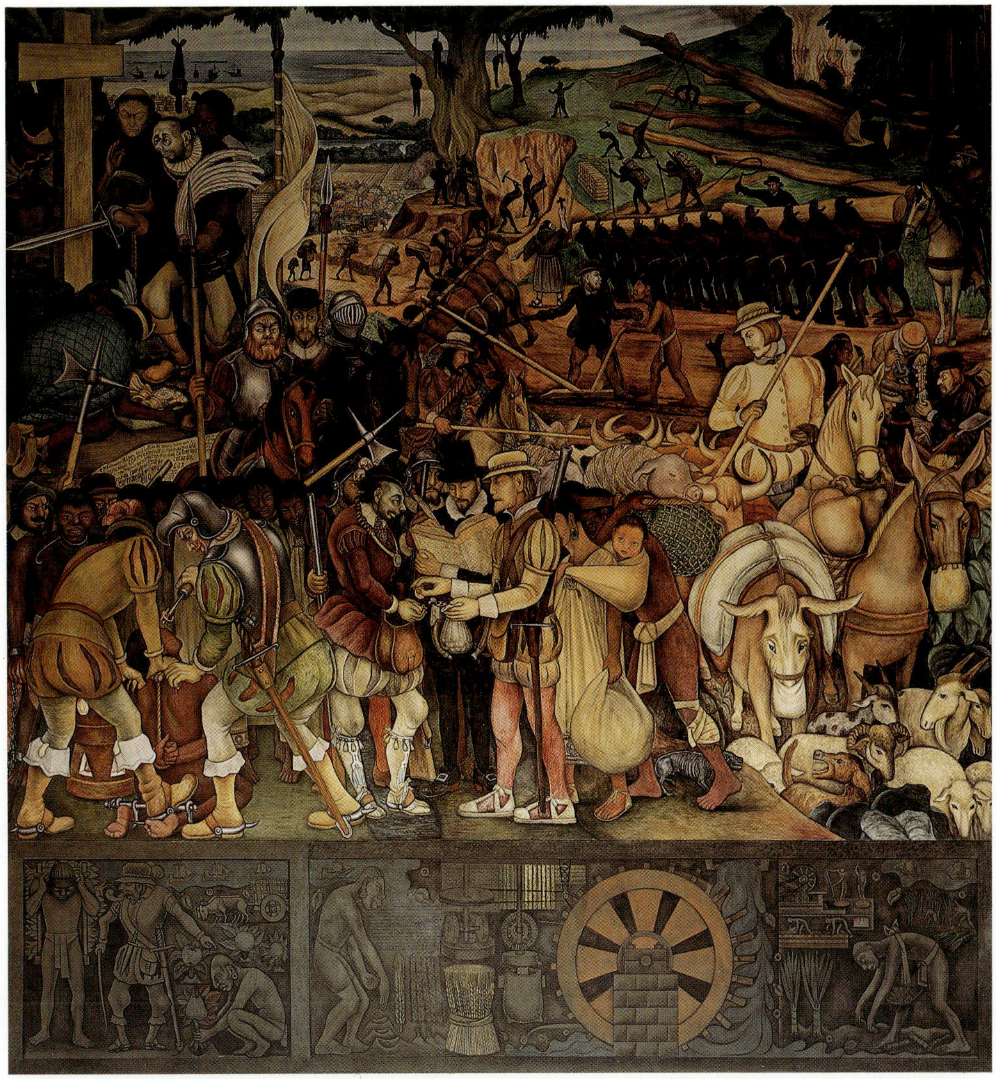

Figure 385.
Disembarkation of the Spanish at Veracruz, 1951, fresco, 4.92 × 5.27 m. Mexico City, Palacio Nacional, Patio Corridor.

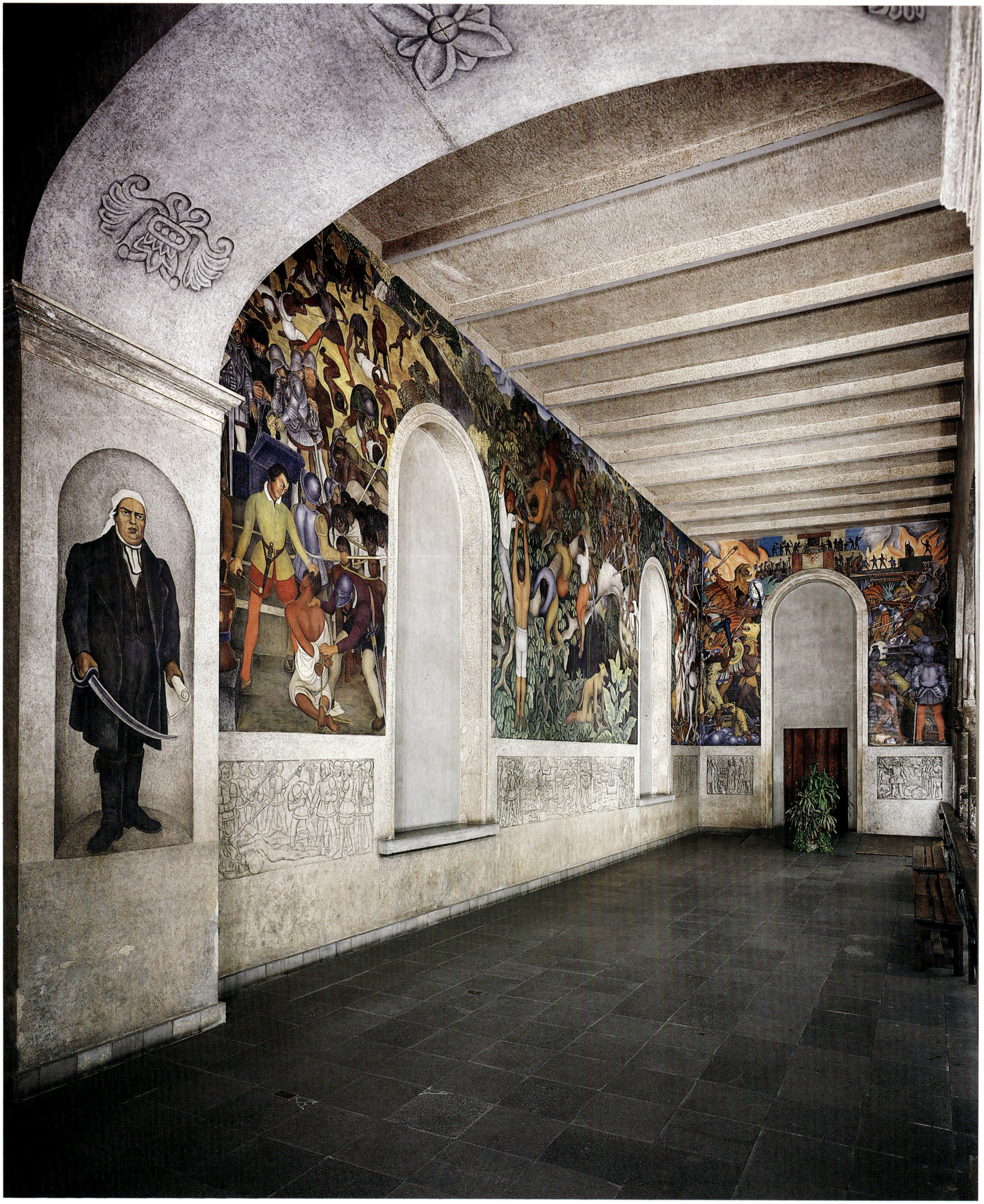

Palacio de Cortés

Cuernavaca

Figure 386.
View of loggia showing *Battle of the Aztecs and Spaniards*, 1930, fresco. Cuernavaca, Palacio de Cortés.

Rivera's murals in the Palacio de Cortés were a gift to the people of Cuernavaca and the state of Morelos from the late Dwight W. Morrow. They were conceived and executed during the last year of Morrow's eventful term as United States Ambassador to Mexico (September 1927–September 1930). The commission originated in the ambassador's desire to make a gift to Mexico that would stand in remembrance of his mission, his liking for the people, and the attachment he had formed to his Cuernavaca home. It was the first and only work of art he gave. He died a year after its completion.

When the commission was given in October of 1929, Morrow had been in Mexico two years. In that time he had, by unprecedented feats of diplomacy, arrested the deterioration of American relations with Mexico that had occurred in the wake of the Mexican Revolution. His outgoing, trusting approach to people, his mastery of historical facts, his acceptance of realities (the Mexican Revolution), and his belief in modifying practices where principles were irreconcilable won the confidence of the Mexican president, Plutarco Elías Calles, and less than two months after his arrival, he was able to arrange a settlement of the embittered struggle between foreign interests and the Mexican government over the question of oil rights that had lasted nearly a decade. In the ensuing months, he also devoted himself to an agonizing, wholly domestic problem: the schism between the government and the church. Through a long series of negotiations, he achieved what had come to be thought impossible: the reconciliation of major differences between the Vatican and the Mexican government, with the result that the churches, which had been closed for a year, were reopened.

According to the late William Spratling, who played a key role in the negotiations, arrangements for the murals were concluded to the satisfaction of both patron and artist. The fee of twelve thousand dollars was by far the largest Rivera had ever received. However, the actual painting, according to Spratling, did not progress as easily. Rivera had already begun his extensive series on the history of Mexico on the stairway of the Palacio Nacional in Mexico City, and he spent a great deal of his working time there. He had recently been appointed director of the Academy of San Carlos and was caught in a storm of controversy over his proposed reforms in its curriculum. He became the target of a variety of attacks, ranging from charges that his paintings were a "desecration" of public buildings to the accusation that Communists, led by him, were trying to involve Mexico in the Sino-Russian dispute and otherwise embarrass the government. The echoes of this battle were heard in the United States. At the time of Rivera's appointment to the academy, the Associated Press, in a dispatch from Mexico City, reported his critics as pointing out that "in recent years, [his] paintings have shown a decided Communist influence and, employed by the government to decorate the walls of public buildings, he has covered them with figures [*monigotes*—ridiculous puppets] which, while not lacking in artistic perfection, nevertheless prove a shock to the conservative tastes of certain classes."[1]

Despite these circumstances and the differences in position, background, and political belief, if not in historical perspective, between the two men, the only problem in this unprecedented relationship arose over the representation of priests in the mural. Somewhere near the middle of the project the ambassador became concerned over their "hard faces" and asked Rivera to put in "at least one kindly priest."[2] Rivera demurred, and after a series of polite exchanges, in which friends and family on both sides became involved, he left unfinished the face of a truly kindly 16th-century Franciscan friend of the Indians, Toribio de Benevente, called Motolinía (the ragged one). The figure remains ambiguous and perplexing to this day in its easily noticed position next to the loggia's entrance doorway.

It may be suggested that Rivera, though out of the Communist Party at the time, still wanted to be known as a Communist, however independently so in his own mind. Furthermore, his acceptance of a commission from Morrow on top of the government sponsored Palacio Nacional commission left little doubt on the part of his colleagues that his expulsion from the party was well deserved. At any rate, he could not have shown himself as being too close to the ambassador, a former partner of J. P. Morgan and Company, without compromising his reputation as an anti-capitalistic spokesman for Mexican farmers and workers.

On September 14, 1930, after nine months of work, the main panels were finished when the Morrows came again to the gallery, shortly before the ambassador left Mexico for the last time. On that day Mrs. Morrow wrote in her diary: "We went to see Diego's frescoes this morning; very wonderful, and *finished*. He was there and we had a few words with him and his wife."[3]

The subject of the murals, which cover the three walls of an outdoor, second-floor loggia that faces eastward across the Valley of Cuernavaca toward the snow-covered peaks of Popocatépetl and Iztaccíhuatl, is the history of Cuernavaca and Morelos, from the Spanish Conquest in 1521 to the agrarian revolt led by Emiliano Zapata in 1911. Rivera saw this regional history as parallel to the history of Mexico on which he was simultaneously at work on the central wall of the Palacio Nacional, and he freely excerpted and refined motifs from the larger work for use in Cuernavaca.

Rivera's eight-part program is arranged chronologically, beginning on the north wall and moving across the west wall to end on the south.

In April 1521, from his winter base at Texcoco, on the eastern shore of the lake surrounding Tenochtitlán, Cortés undertook an expedition to Cuernavaca with a detachment of 330 Spanish footsoldiers and horsemen, supported by a strong complement of Tlaxcalan and Texcocan allies. His purpose was to reconnoiter the regions surrounding the lakes of the Valley of Mexico, preparatory to a final assault on the Aztec capital. Five good-sized battles were fought during this campaign, including the one for Cuernavaca. The beginning of this battle is the subject of Rivera's first theme (diag. I), which covers the north end wall and an adjacent section of the main wall. On the north wall, Spaniards and Aztecs are shown firing at each other across the doorway. In the right foreground (A), a Spanish officer orders two Tlaxcalans to move up a cannon. To the left of the doorway (C), Tlaxcalans engage the Aztecs at close quarters, while one of the defenders, in the garb of a Tiger or Jaguar Knight, appears ready to stab an armored conquistador whom he has pinned to the ground. Over the doorway (B) is a pyramid on which a human sacrifice takes place with a Spaniard as the victim. On the platforms of the pyramid, Aztec chiefs watch the battle below while the flames of war and destruction fill the sky.

The battle continues without an obvious break onto the main wall (D), where the composition is dominated by an Aztec Eagle Knight who battles a mounted Spaniard using a club set with obsidian blades. This central pair of warriors is surrounded by a melee of fighting Indians, while above, a group of Spanish horsemen charges a rank of Aztecs armed with spears. The Aztecs' colorful standards and their ceremonial battle dress contrast with the shining armor of the European invaders, symbolizing both the military and the cultural differences of the two opposing civilizations.

The second theme (II) represents the beginning of the operation against Cuernavaca as Spaniards cross into the village through the branches of a tree felled across a deep *barranca* (ravine). According to Bernal Díaz del Castillo, who accompanied the expedition, the Spaniards could not get into the settlement because all the bridges across the ravine had been destroyed. But farther away a Tlaxcalan guide noticed two trees on opposite sides of the ravine and pointed the way across by climbing from one to the other. Several Spaniards fell in the attempt to follow him, but eventually a group got across and attacked the town from the rear. After repairing the bridges, they joined the other Spaniards who had waited behind and quickly overcame the defender's resistance. Rivera's version has the Spaniards bending a single tree over the ravine instead of climbing up one and down another.

The next panel (III) shows Cortés and his lieutenants taking inventory of the captured settlement's gold supply. Conquistadores in the foreground bring in Indian captives; in the background, aided by their Tlaxcalan allies, they loot the village and kill or shackle those who resist.

In the next panel (IV), Cortés takes possession of certain lands of the region of Cuernavaca as the Marqués del Valle de Oaxaca. He is shown touching the Cross, symbol of the Christian faith, with his sword, symbol of conquest and military supremacy, a juxtaposition used to convey the anomaly of this relationship.

Building the Palace of Cortés (V) gives Rivera's view of the *reparmiento* system, by which tributes in produce and thus, eventually, services were exacted from the Indians in return for religious instruction and material care, as wards of the Spanish crown. In the foreground, Indian women and children are bringing forward the first fruits of the harvest, the tax known as the *primícia*. Above this, Cortés's country palace, the building that houses the murals, is being constructed. Indian *cargadores* (burden carriers) lift heavy blocks of masonry up the scaffolding; stone craftsmen carve capitals and other decorative members; while the *maestro de obras* (field engineer) gauges the lines of the structure with the help of an Indian assistant in the far background.

The next panel (VI) represents the operation of a sugar plantation in Morelos during the colonial period. Cortés imported cane from Santo Domingo and established a huge refinery to the southeast of Cuernavaca in the present village of Atlacomulco. In Rivera's version of this enterprise, a mounted *capataz* (foreman) directs Indian workers with a whip, while in the background, Indians haul a heavily laden cane cart. In the far background, the cruel-faced *encomendero* (a plantation owner assigned Indian wards) reclines on a hammock while an Indian woman brings him refreshment. A statue of the Virgin of Guadalupe stands in a niche above his head.

The *New Religion* (VII), which occupies the southwest corner of the loggia, is given over to Rivera's interpretation of the role of the church in the days following the Conquest. On the right, Motolinía (the ragged one), teaches the Scriptures to an attentive and respectful group of Indians. On the left, two quite different friars, a Franciscan and a Dominican, cynicism and greed on their façes, receive tribute from a local tribe and their *cacique* (chief). Rivera was not trying merely to show opposite extremes of religious practice on the part of representatives of the early church in Mexico. These scenes are rather the beginning and climax of a dialectical argument designed to show that both the purpose and the effect of the new religion was exploitation. In Rivera's interpretation, the altruistic motives of the humane priest, Motolinía, prepare the Indians to submit to that exploitation more docilely, by offering an illusory reward in Heaven. Over the end-wall doorway is an Inquisition scene, showing three women burning at the stake. Its placement directly opposite the human sacrifice scene on the north end wall, was intended to convey that the new religion also engages in human sacrifice and that persecution is an integral part of its belief.

To the left of the doorway on the south end wall is a group of motifs symbolizing the condition of the Indians in the three centuries that followed the establishment of the Spanish colonial system in Mexico (VIII). At the top, the bodies of Indian *campesinos* hang from gallows after their execution for insubordination to owners of the landed estates in Morelos, while below some Indians and their families grieve and others leave their villages following a disaster in their community (probably the abolition of the *ejido* under the Díaz regime). The figure of the revolutionary hero, Emiliano Zapata, provides the climax not only to the scene but also to the entire program.

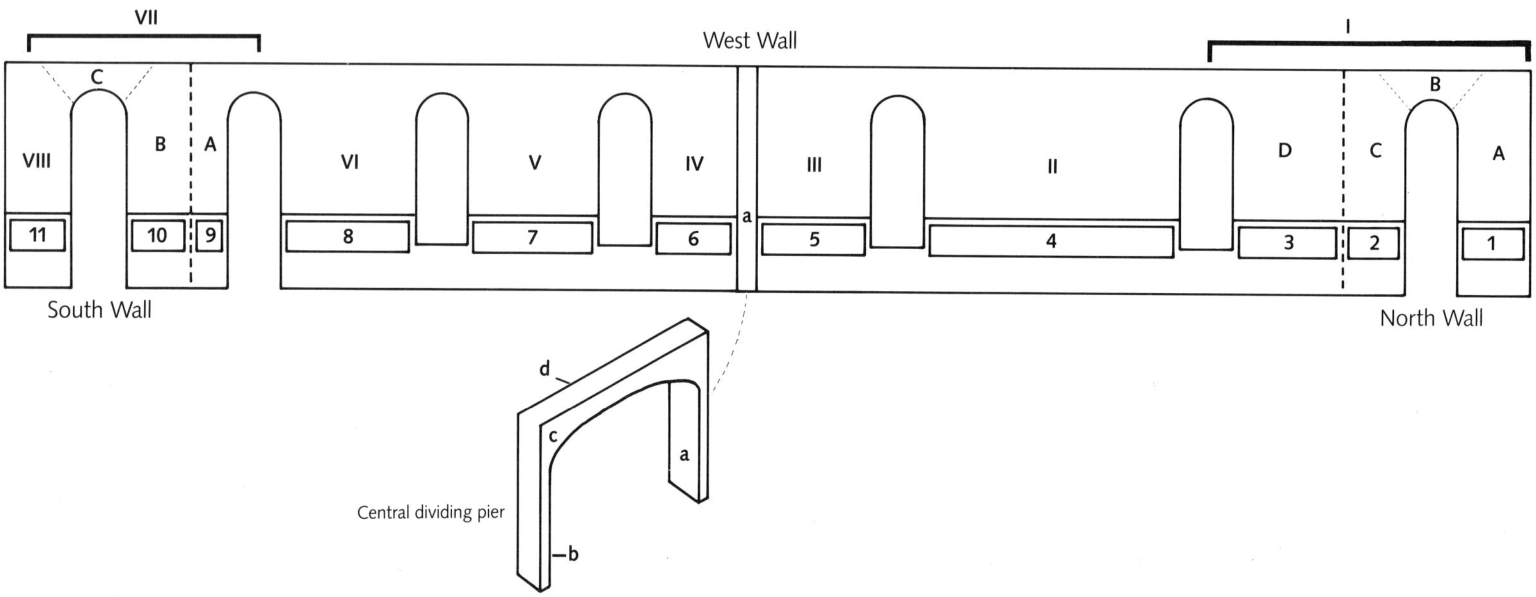

Palacio de Cortés

Main Themes

I. *Battle of the Aztecs and Spaniards*
  A. Approx. 4.25 × 1.47 m
  B. Irregular overdoor panel
  C. Approx. 4.30 × 1.29 m
  D. Approx. 4.35 x 2.26 m
II. *Crossing the Barranca*, 4.35 × 5.24 m
III. *The Taking of Cuernavaca*, 4.35 × 2.36 m
IV. *Possessing the Lands of Cuernavaca*, 4.35 x 1.81 m
V. *Building the Palace of Cortés*, 4.35 × 2.70 m
VI. *Sugar Plantation in Morelos*, 4.35 × 2.82 m
VII. *The New Religion*
  A. Approx. 4.35 × .82 m
  B. Approx. 4.30 × 1.34 m
  C. Irregular overdoor panel
VIII. *Revolt*, Approx. 4.25 × 1.34 m

Grisaille panels

1. *Arrival of Cortés in Mexico*, .81 × 1.12 m
2. *Cortés Receives Moctezuma's Emissaries*, .81 × .94 m
3. *Cortés Wins Support from the Tlaxcalans*, .81 × 1.91 m
4. *Siege of Tenochititlán*, .81 × 4.89 m
5. *Torture of Cuauhtémoc*, .81 x 2.01 m
6. *Death of Cuauhtémoc*, .81 × 1.46 m
7. *Destruction of Indian Culture*, .81 × 2.35 m
8. *Indian Slave Labor in the Silver Mines*, .81 × 2.47 m
9. *Bartolomé de Las Casas Protecting the Indians*, .81 × .47 m
10. *Vasco de Quiroga Teaching the Indians New Crafts*, .81 × .99 m
11. *Assassination of the Indian Leader Roquetilla*, .81 × .99 m

Central piers and connecting arch

a. *Morelos*[4]
b. *Zapata*
c. Reclining figure with slogan "Independencia"
d. Reclining figure with slogan "Tierra y Libertad"

Place glyphs on spandrels between columns of facing arcade (from right to left)

1. Tepoztlán
2. Jiutepec
3. Tlayacápan
4. Yautepec
5. Yecapixtla
6. Oaxtepec

Summary

Location: Museo Quaunahuac, Plaza de la Constitución, Cuernavaca, Morelos

Site: The east-facing second-floor loggia of the former Palacio de Cortés, an early 16th-century building, which is now the historical museum of the state of Morelos

Theme/Subject: *The History of Cuernavaca and Morelos*

Format: A three-sided surface formed by the long main wall and the two end walls of an open gallery, broken at irregular intervals by blind-arched window and door openings; the mural covers the entire wall area and is treated as a single chronologically arranged design except for motifs on a central dividing pier. On the inner spandrels of the arcade facing the main wall are six heraldic designs based on Aztec place glyphs for indigenous communities in the region surrounding Quaunahuac.

Date: Main themes: January 2–September 14, 1930. Grisailles and supplementary decoration probably the next year; the south wall is signed and dated September 16, 1931, beneath the figure of Zapata.

Medium: True fresco

Dimensions: Overall height varies from 4.2 to 4.35 m (end walls slope slightly downward from the inner wall to the outer arcade, following the angle of the ceiling). Overall width including end walls is 31.78 m (excluding central pier, which is 1.27 m wide).

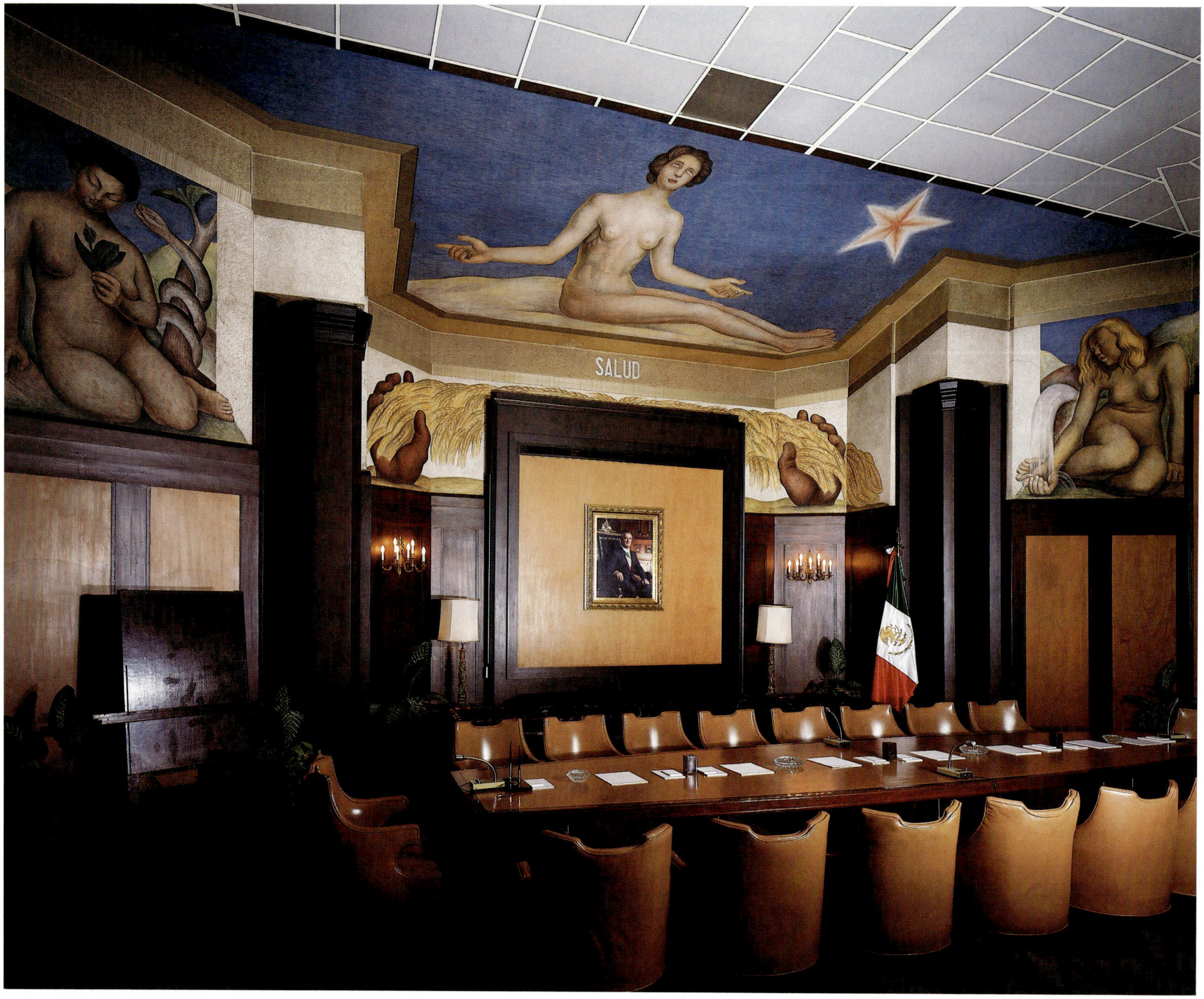
SALUD

Secretaría de Salubridad y Asistencia

Mexico City

Figure 387a
View of conference room showing *Health, Purity, Knowledge,* and *Symbols of Fruition,* 1929, fresco. Mexico City, Secretaría de Salubridad y Asistencia.

Rivera's mural in the Secretaría de Salubridad y Asistencia, in Mexico City, is entitled *Health and Life*.[1] On the main ceiling and wall areas of an eccentrically shaped interior conference room built in early Mexican Art Deco fashion are female nudes representing "Purity, Continence, Health, Life, Strength, and Knowledge."[2] These are supplemented by budding plant forms and large, Chapingo-style hands holding grain and sunflower blossoms in the smaller wall areas. The large nudes in the six main fresco panels are posed in seated or half-reclining positions or floating in the air to fit the polygonal shapes of the ceiling and upper side-wall areas and were plainly conceived to fill a decorative function.

The forms of the figures—not the painting as a whole—are in the tradition of 19th-century French salon painting, of which Cabanel's *Dawn,* allegedly the favorite work of Emperor Napoleon III, is the epitome. Rivera, through the use of fresh colors and simple forms, has transferred the salon nude, with its suggestive salaciousness, from a "palace garden" to more natural backgrounds and skies of pure azure—an obvious parody. As a literary precedent for this transformation, one could think that Homer's story of the Sirens, those omniscient half-birds, half-women, who were turned into exemplars of female beauty by Hellenistic artists, was not beyond the reach of Rivera's roving imagination.

Rivera's commission to decorate the building including not only the walls and ceiling of the conference room but also four stained-glass windows on the subject of the elements, in stairway areas of the Paseo de la Reforma part of this low-lying building complex. According to the architect, Carlos Obregón Santacelia, Rivera also painted "friezes" in the Pavilion of Laboratories on the far side of the central court.[3] Indeed, two horizontal frescoes, each extending around a ninety-degree corner angle, face each other in an area fronting the auditorium entrance at the ground-floor level. The one on the left is called *Microbiology* (.82 x 2.10/1.96 m.); the one on the right, *Education and Prophylaxis* (.82 × 2.12/1.95 m.). They are dedicated "To the memory of Dr. Francis Javier de Balmes and the Mexican children who, with smallpox vaccine in their arms, sailed from Acapulco for the Philippines on February 5, 1805, to provide material necessary to prevent the disease." (The children's names are listed as part of a familiar Riveraesque gesture of recognition, here framed in a frescoed commemorative plaque.)

Obregón Santacelia was undoubtedly responsible for this commission. He was a longtime admirer of Rivera and a proud

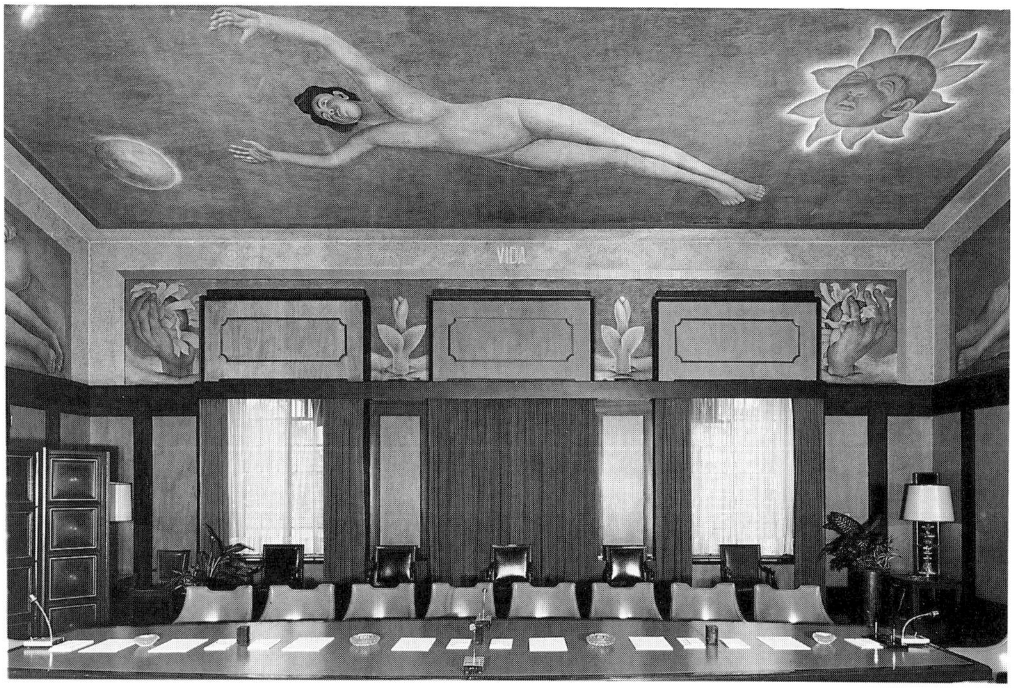

Figure 387b
View of conference room showing *Life* and *Symbols of Germination*.

sponsor of the artist's works in buildings of his own, including the now endangered Hotel del Prado mural (1946). The Salubridad buildings were begun in 1925 under the presidency of Plutarco Elías Calles. Rivera's frescoes, painted in 1929–30, paralleled his work in the Palacio Nacional and at Cuernavaca, during the following two-year interim presidency of Emilio Portes Gil.

Summary

Location: Mexico City, Paseo de la Reforma and Calle Lieja

Site: Conference room of the main building of a neorationalistic, Art Deco complex situated at the entrance to Chapultepec Park (Carlos Santacelia, architect)

Theme/Subject: *Health and Life*

Date: 1929 (signed *Diego Rivera 13 Noviembre 1929*)

Medium: True fresco showing evidence of restoration[4]

Dimensions: See diagram

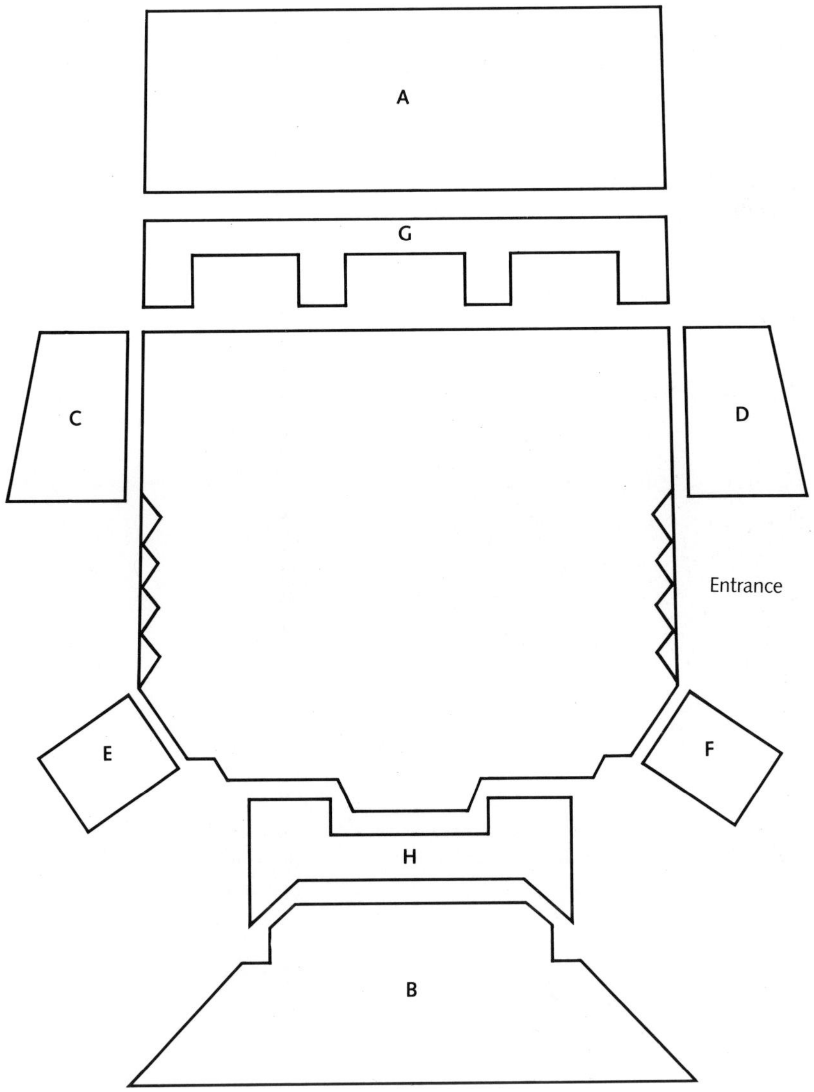

Secretaría de Salubridad y Asistencia[5]

A. *Life*, 2.70 × 10.40 m
B. *Health*, 3.15 × 10.40 m
C. *Continence*, 2.70 × 2.98 m
D. *Strength*, 2.70 × 2.98 m
E. *Purity*, 2.20 × 1.80 m
F. *Knowledge*, 2.20 x 1.80 m
G. *Symbols of Germination*, 1.10 × 10.27 m
H. *Symbols of Fruition*, 1.10 × 4.60 m

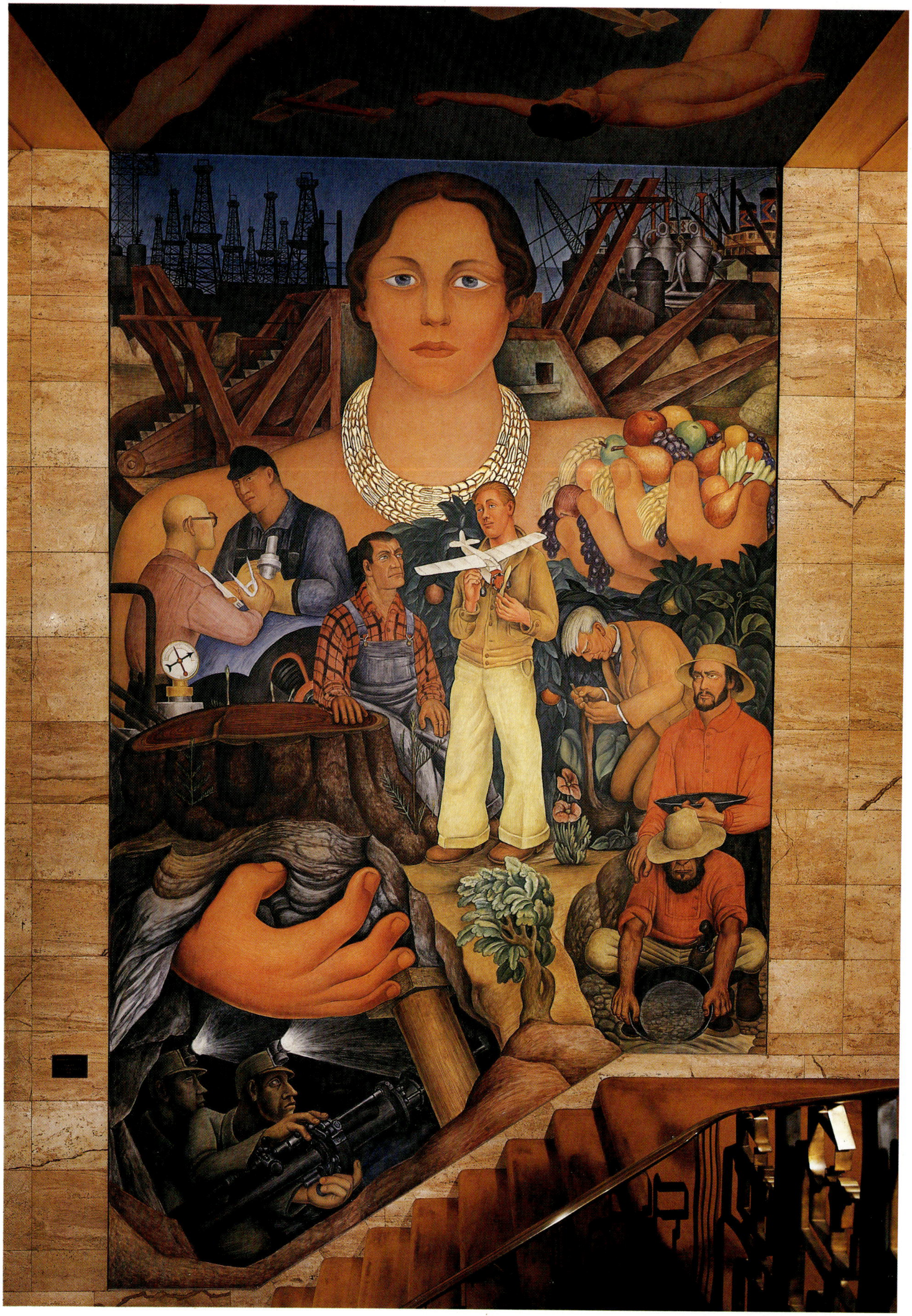

Pacific Stock Exchange

San Francisco

Figure 388.
Allegory of California, 1931, fresco, 43.82 square meters. San Francisco, Pacific Stock Exchange.

Rivera's commission to paint a mural for the Luncheon Club of the Pacific Stock Exchange in San Francisco was, in effect, part of a package that included the mural in the California School of Fine Arts (now the San Francisco Art Institute). Both resulted from Rivera's meeting in Paris, at least a decade earlier, the California sculptor Ralph Stackpole. The two artists subsequently met again in Mexico in 1926, when Rivera was well into his frescoes at the Secretaría de Educación Pública and at Chapingo. Stackpole returned to San Francisco "enormously excited" by Rivera's new work and reported what he had seen to influential friends in art and architectural circles.[1] Soon efforts were begun to create an assignment and put together the financial wherewithal that would bring Rivera to San Francisco for a working visit. Nearly five years were to pass before the right combination of support was achieved and agreement reached between the several parties, undoubtedly much having depended on Rivera's own work commitments and the political situation in Mexico in the meantime. Although the California School of Fine Arts' proposal was put forward first, it was the much more substantial Stock Exchange commission that became the determining factor financially, and it consequently became the first fresco mural executed by Rivera in the United States.

The mural is an allegory depicting the bountiful human and natural resources of California as explored, exploited, and brought to varied fullness by North American inventiveness, industry, and adventurism. California is symbolically cast in the image of a mature woman, undoubtedly inspired by the American champion tennis star of the 1920s and 1930s, Helen Wills Moody. A superscale model of feminine serenity, athletic strength, and maternal warmth, whose hands gather up the fruits and the underground riches of the earth, her steady gaze radiates natural health and confidence. Surrounding her, as if clustered in her embrace, are the attributes of California's enterprise and resulting material progress—its practical, methodical husbandry of nature, its genius for invention and innovative technology, its individualistic drive for quick riches, its industrious harvesting of forests and minerals, its advanced engineering, and its oil, shipping and trading businesses—standing before the Pacific horizon. Every aspect of this scene and the material success of California seems to have attracted the artist like a magnet. On the ceiling is a diagonally placed figure of a nude woman, a recapitulation of the ceiling design of the Secretaría de Salubridad y Asistencia mural in Mexico City, against the background of a sun-and-sky theme carried over from the first bay at Chapingo.

For the first venture into a world once part of Mexico and now developed by a different race in more pragmatic ways, Rivera resorted to the compositional and symbolic method of his end-wall subject at Chapingo, portraying, in a sense, the California earth in the historical process of fulfillment, artistically eclecticizing himself as he assimilated this new environment.

Summary

Location: San Francisco, Stock Exchange Tower[2]

Site: The main stairway connecting the tenth-floor lounge and eleventh-floor dining room of the Stock Exchange's private Luncheon Club (Timothy Pfleuger, architect). The stairway, like the rest of the club's interior, is in high Art Deco style. The mural is set in a marble terrazzo wall and is flanked by two small stone wall reliefs by the California sculptor Ralph Stackpole.

Theme/Subject: *Allegory of California*

Date: 1931 (signed, left center, *Diego Rivera, 1931*) Unveiled March 31, 1931

Medium: True fresco

Dimensions: 43.82 square meters[3]

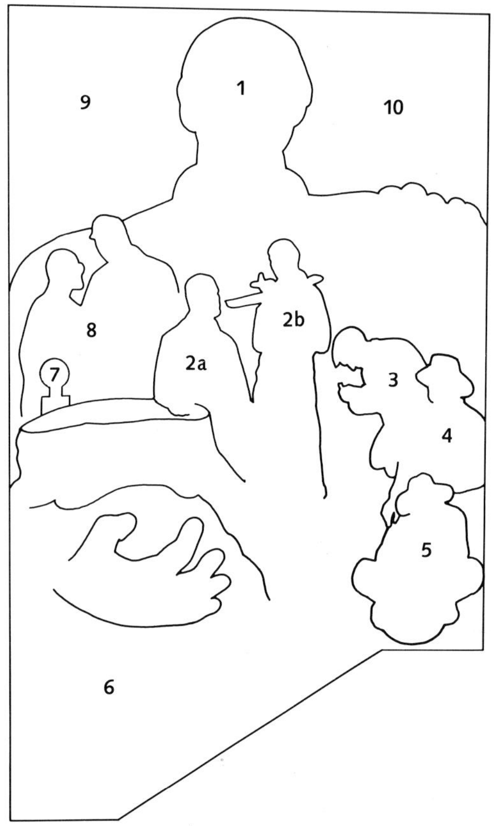

Pacific Stock Exchange

1. Symbol of California (Helen Wills Moody)
2a. Skeptical older generation
2b. Inventive youth (holding model aircraft)
3. Luther Burbank
4. James Wilson Marshall (discoverer of gold in California)
5. Gold prospector
6. Mechanized coal mining
7. Pressure gauge
8. Engineer and tool operators
9. California dredging machine and oil field
10. Ocean shipping, dock loading, and storage

Stern Residence

Atherton, California

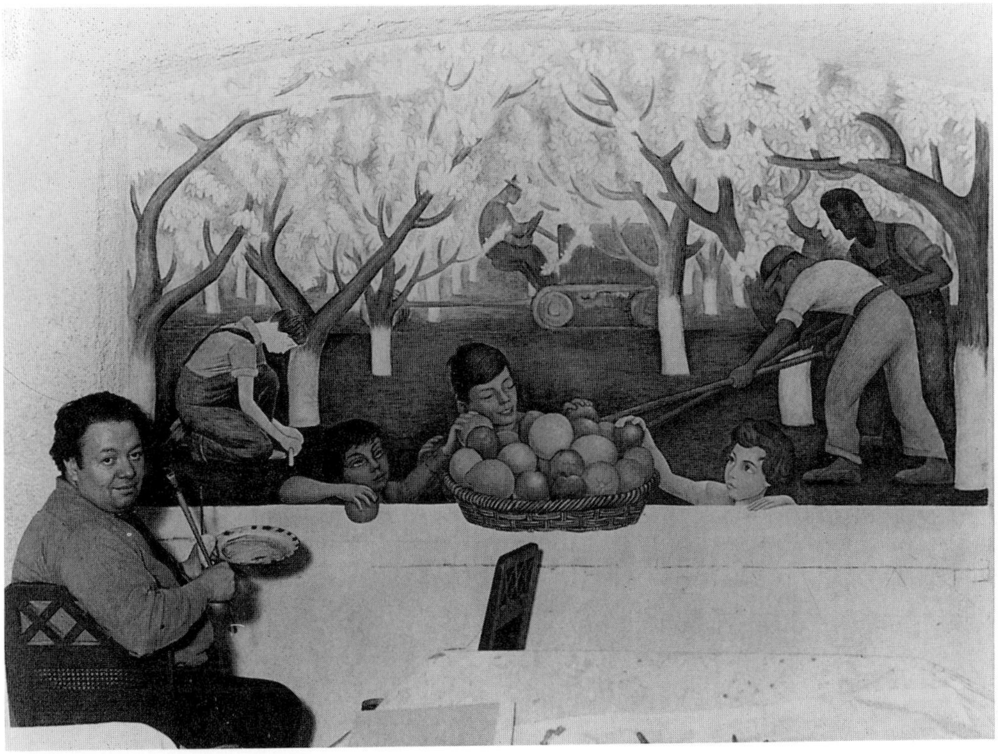

Figure 389.
Rivera painting his mural for the residence of Mrs. Sigmund Stern. Photo by Ansel Adams. Courtesy of the San Francisco Museum of Modern Art.

From all accounts, one of the most relaxed periods that Rivera knew in the United States was his several weeks' stay in the house of Mrs. Sigmund Stern in Atherton, California, south of San Francisco, where he and his wife Frida were invited for a rest after he had finished the Stock Exchange mural. Their visit seems to have lasted considerably longer than originally planned, and while they were there Mrs. Stern engaged her guest to paint a small fresco in a site chosen by the artist: a shallow niche in her outdoor dining area.

In the fresco, three children (from right to left: Mrs. Stern's granddaughter, Rhoda, Rhoda's friend Peter, and Diaga, the child of the estate's gardener) reaching into a basket of fruit are shown against an orchard of blossoming almond trees in which four caretakers are studiously working the soil. Social meaning is discreetly introduced in the figure of the mestizo child who seeks a share of the fruit, and California's Spanish and Mexican past is suggested by the inclusion of the slender Spaniard raking the ground at right. Rivera's admiration for modern methods of cultivation is evidenced by the tractor-drawn harrower. Such socially pointed accents, however, do not lessen the pleasure given by this gentle picture's references to the area's benign climate, the generosity of nature well treated, the hospitality of the patron, and that patron's humane circle of friends, artists, art lovers, and helpers.

Summary

Location: University of California at Berkeley, Stern Hall

Site: Foyer of a student dormitory and dining hall, facing the entrance doorway. The original fresco has been remounted against a cement wall and surrounded by a carefully conceived outbuilt niche, its upper part a canted semiarch, perhaps simulating the painting's original situation (William W. Wurster, architect). Originally commissioned for the residence of Mrs. Sigmund Stern Atherton, California.

Title/Subject: *Still Life and Blossoming Almond Trees*

Date: 1931

Medium: True fresco on steel frame base (Matthew Barnes, plasterer)

Dimensions: 1.58 × 2.64 m

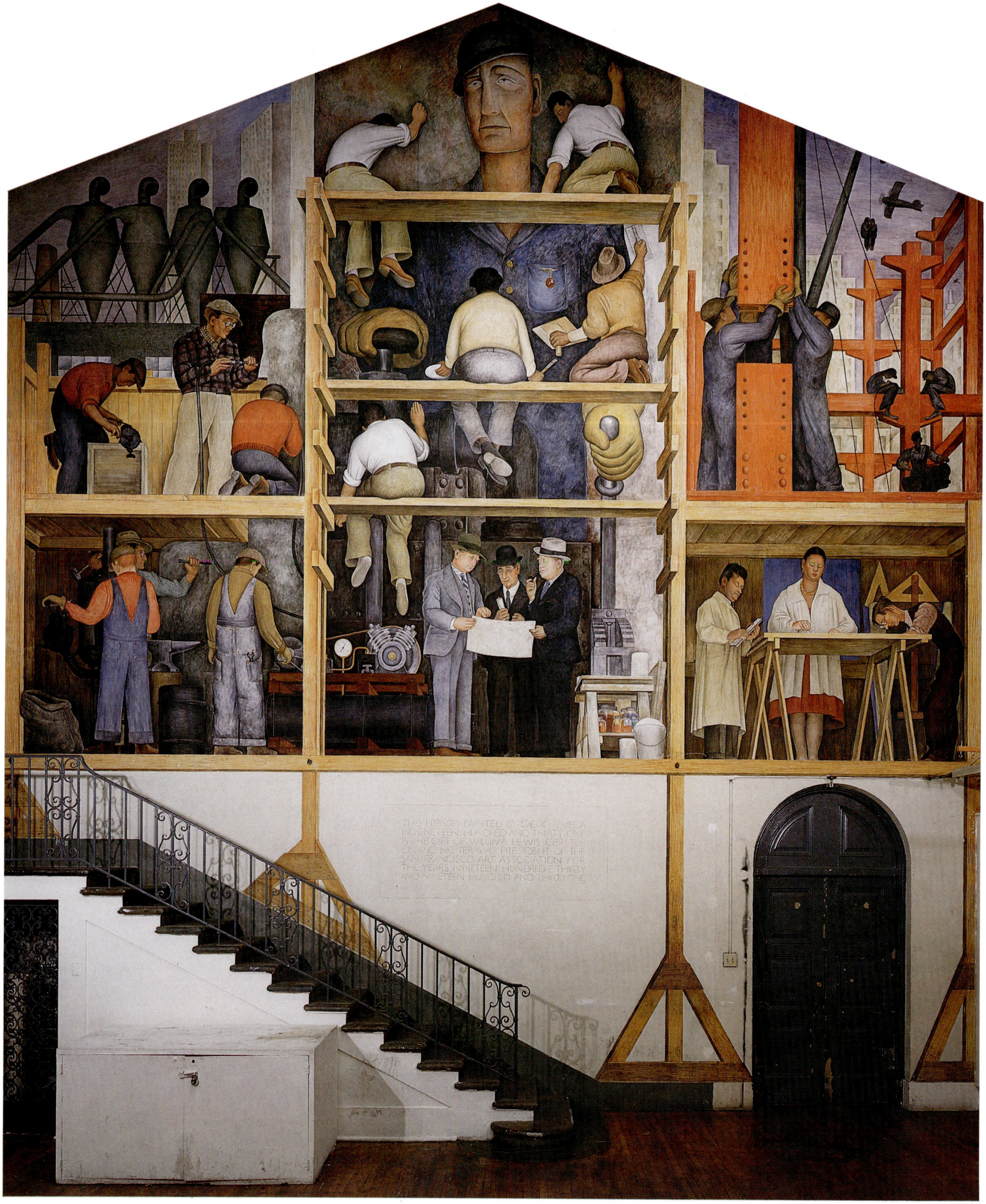

San Francisco Art Institute

Figure 390.
The Making of a Fresco, Showing the Building of a City, April–June 1931, fresco, 5.68 × 9.91 m. San Francisco Art Institute.

According to Bertram Wolfe, the California School of Fine Arts (now the San Francisco Art Institute) originally offered Rivera a very limited wall space, and when he finally arrived in San Francisco the artist was apparently reluctant to undertake the project. In any case, he was soon at work on his commission for the Stock Exchange, and it was not until his visit to San Francisco was drawing to an end that William Gerstle, president of the San Francisco Art Commission, pressed him to fulfill his original commitment. Rivera then sought and was given an awkward but considerably larger wall at the north end of the school's exhibition hall. He set to work and in less than three months completed all but the simulated stilts that extend from its base to the floor. The mural's theme is the design and construction of a modern industrial city in the United States. The coordinated activities of workers and planners, both above and below ground, are seen through a scaffold that supports a fresco painter (Rivera himself) and his assistants, thus representing the events of modern construction from the viewpoint of an art school student. Behind and above towers the monumental figure of a helmeted engineer-worker, symbol of a technologically planned and worker-controlled industrial society.

The regularity of the pedimented wall (the lower part of which is interrupted by the doorway and the curiously placed staircase) may have recalled to the artist the traditional use of this triangle-topped shape, and its division into a compositional triptych, in Italian religious painting from the 13th century onward.[1] Rivera would no doubt have been familiar with such works (e.g., the *Enthroned Madonnas* of both Cimabue and Giotto in the Uffizi, Florence) from his Italian sojourn in 1920–21.

In any case, Rivera conceived his wall space as a triptych further subdivided into eight parts. His elaboration of the triptych format into two parts on the sides and four parts in the central area suggests similar elaborations in both height and depth that developed in Florentine painting of the quattrocento (cf. the murals of Masaccio and Masolino in the Brancacci Chapel, Florence). Another Italian Renaissance compositional derivation is the consistently followed perspective vanishing point taken from near floor level (cf. Masaccio's *Trinity*, Santa Maria Novella, Florence). The combination of elements in Rivera's treatment, however, implies a dynamic simultaneity that is given axis and order by the central authoritative figure of the worker-engineer, an iconic derivation from the Christian belief in a sovereign Lord.

The inclusion of donor portraits is another Renaissance convention. In his typical fashion, Rivera enlarges it to include portraits or identifiable images of his own associates and assistants. The extension of the painted scaffolding toward the actual floor can perhaps be taken as evidence of Rivera's insistence on techtonic as well as decorative consistency in his murals. Here it does not succeed. It is likely that the artist turned the execution of a suggested device over to others.

Obviously, Rivera's sweeping vision of modern progress is not original. The motifs of the skyscrapers, their steel skeletons rising in the background, and the airplane soaring above them echo the positivist philosophy of scientific progress, the influence of which spread far beyond the economic policies of the Díaz regime in late 19th- and early 20th-century Mexico.[2]

The portents of social revolution in this, Rivera's second major mural in the United States, are *sotto voce*. On the blue denim pocket of the giant worker-engineer is a tiny hammer and sickle, and in the bottommost central section, next to the piston pump, is a pressure gauge, the warning arrow of which is close to the red mark, an obvious if inconspicuous reference to a revolutionary denouement.

Summary

Location: San Francisco Art Institute (originally the California School of Fine Arts), 800 Chestnut Street

Site: A high-ceilinged, triangular-roofed room, designed as a studio and exhibition hall, situated in a group of buildings in eclectic Italian Romanesque ("Spanish Revival") style, near the top of San Francisco's Russian Hill (Arthur Brown, Jr., architect)

Title/Subject: *The Making of a Fresco, Showing the Building of a City*

Format: The mural covers the upper two-thirds of a pedimented interior wall (the painted scaffold that divides the composition extends into the lower third.)

Date: April–June 1931

Medium: True fresco

Dimensions: 5.68 m (apex to bottom of painted area) × 9.91 m; vertical dimensions of left and right sides, approx. 5.27 m; angled sides of pediment, approx. 5 m

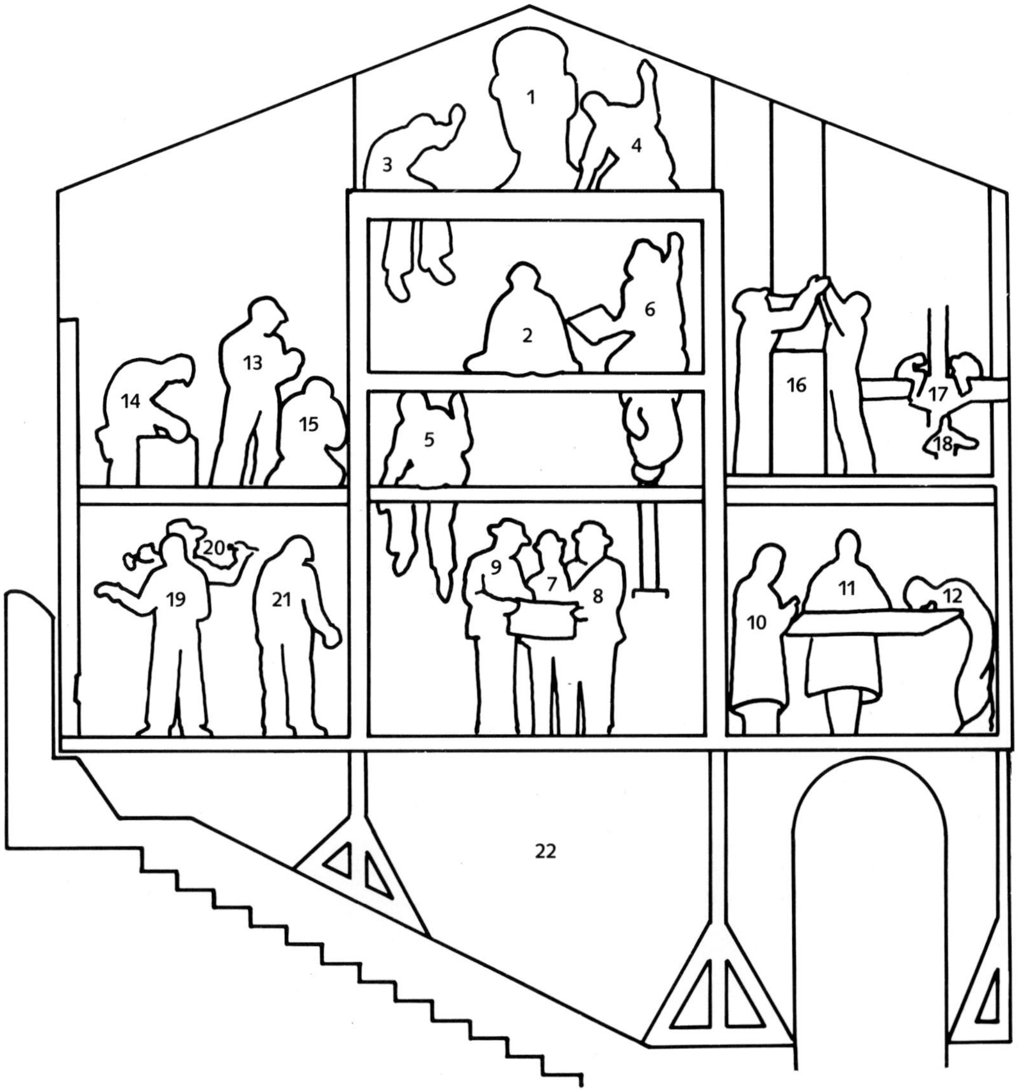

San Francisco Art Institute[3]

1. Engineer-worker coordinating the building of an American city
2. Diego Rivera painting a mural
3. Assistant to the artist (John Viscount Hastings) holding plumb line
4. Assistant to the artist (Clifford Wight) measuring surface distances
5. Assistant to the artist
6. Assistant to the artist (Matthew Barnes) plastering
7. William Gerstle (president of the San Francisco Art Commission, 1930–31)
8. Arthur Brown, Jr. (architect of the California School of Fine Arts main building)
9. Timothy Pfleuger (architect of the San Francisco Stock Exchange)
10. Michael Baltekal-Goodman
11. Mrs. Marion Simpson[4]
12. Alfred Barrows
13. Ralph Stackpole (sculptor)
14. Sculptor's assistant sharpening chisel
15. Sculptor's assistant
16. Steel workers group
17. Steel riveters
18. Heating rivets
19. Operator of forge bellows
20. Sculptor
21. High-pressure belt-machine operator
22. *Inscription:* "This fresco painted by Diego Rivera in nineteen hundred and thirty-one is the gift of William Lewis Gerstle during his term as President of the San Francisco Art Association for the years nineteen hundred and thirty and nineteen hundred and thirty-one."

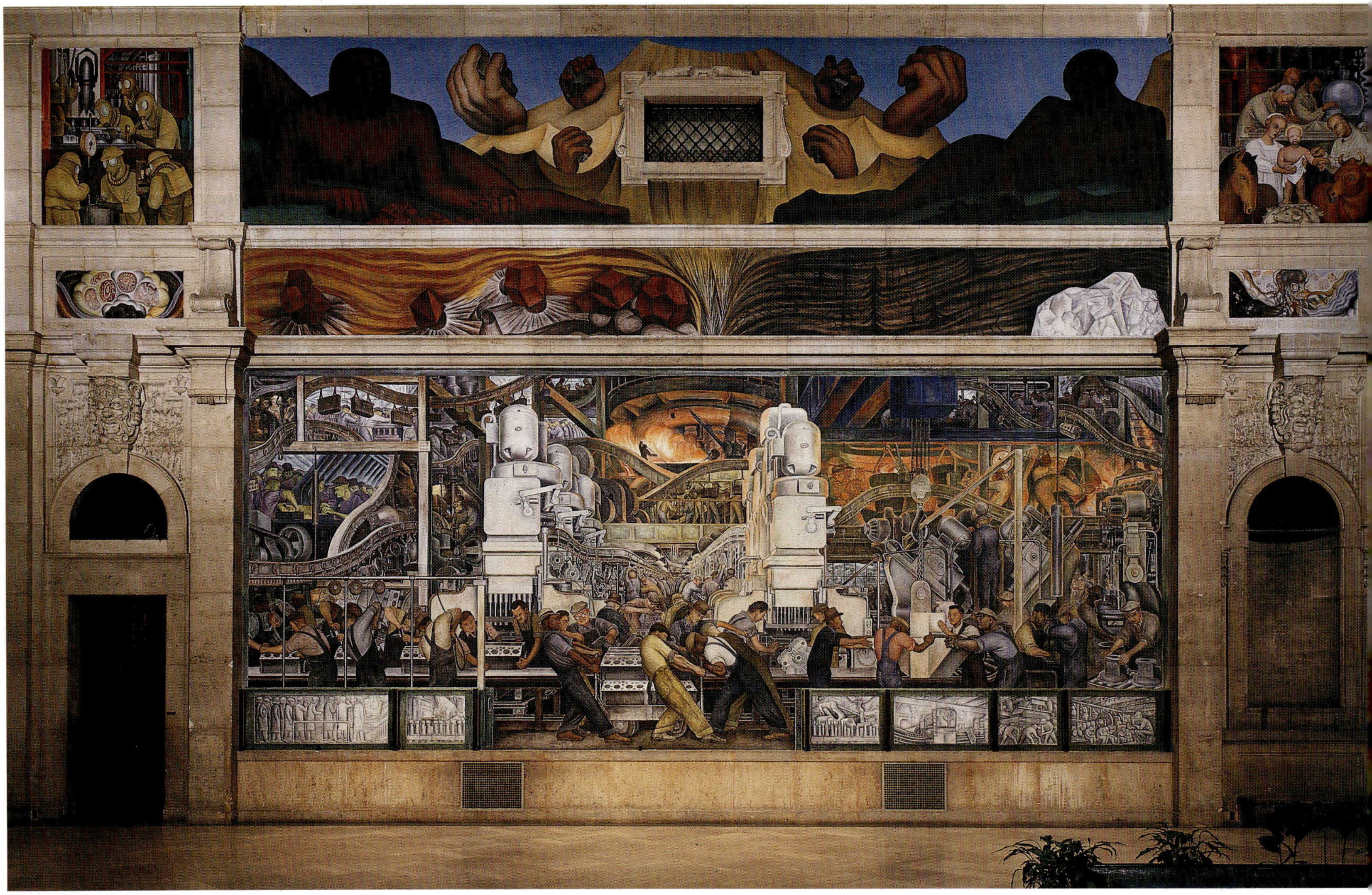

The Detroit Institute of Arts[1]

Figure 391.
North wall, *Detroit Industry*, May 1932–March 13, 1933, fresco. The Detroit Institute of Arts.

In the spring of 1931, Rivera was commissioned to paint two panels in the central court, then known as the "garden court," of the Detroit Institute of Arts. In the initial letter of agreement, Dr. William R. Valentiner, the museum's director, who had met Rivera in San Francisco while he was working on the Stock Exchange mural and whose idea it was for the artist to create a work for Detroit, indicated that the Arts Commission (the museum's governing board) hoped that he would choose a theme related to "the history of Detroit, or some motif suggesting the development of industry in this town."[2] No doubt this suggestion met with Rivera's immediate and complete approval. In San Francisco he had been struck by the beauty of that city's technical accomplishments—its highway systems, skyscrapers, industries, and machines, and he believed that "the best known modern architects of our age are finding their aesthetic and functional inspiration in American industrial buildings, machine-design, and engineering, the greatest expressions of the plastic genius of this New World."[3]

Rivera initially planned to devote the two panels to the automotive industry, specifically to the Ford Motor Company's Rouge complex in Dearborn. He arrived in Detroit in April 1932 and spent over a month at the Rouge, touring, studying, and sketching. He was aided by a Ford staff photographer, W. J. Stettler, who took reference photographs and subsequently documented the mural project with hundreds of photographs and thousands of feet of film.

To Rivera, whose worldview held nature, man, and technology to be inextricably linked, the huge complex must have seemed like a microcosm of the industrial age. At the Rouge, raw materials, aged thousands of years in the earth, were transformed from their primordial state into modern self-propelled machines that seemed to defy time and space. People of all races worked side by side, operating powerful machines whose forms seemed to him comparable to the monumental sculptures of ancient peoples. As he toured the Rouge and other industries around the city, Rivera's enthusiasm for Detroit increased and his involvement with the fresco project deepened. At the end of May, he sought approval to paint all twenty-seven panels in the court.[4] On June 10, the final contract was signed, and after approximately a month spent working on his preliminary designs, Rivera began to paint on July 25, 1932.

The East Wall

Rivera's fresco cycle begins on the east wall, where the origins of human life and of technology are represented (see fig. 393). In the center panel, an infant is cradled in the bulb of a plant. Two steel plowshares appear in the lower corners of this panel, which is flanked by female nudes holding fruit and sheaves of wheat.

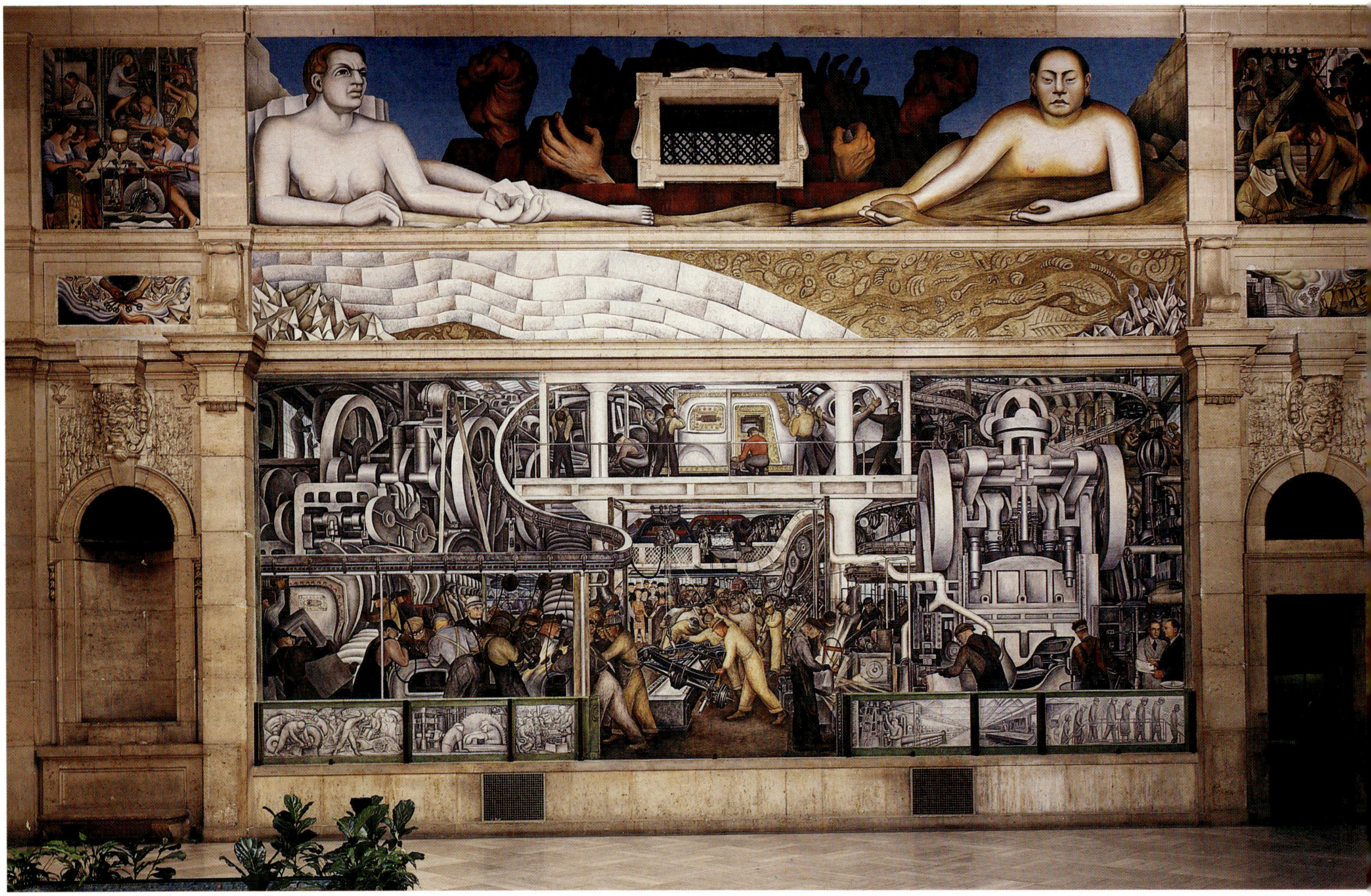

Figure 392.
South wall, *Detroit Industry*, May 1932–March 13, 1933, fresco. The Detroit Institute of Arts.

The child in the plant bulb was referred to as a "germ cell" by Rivera and represents not only life's origin and human dependence on the land but also, by its central position, Rivera's belief that the art museum is the essential organism for the development of the aesthetic culture of the community.[5] The plant takes root in a representation of Michigan's geological strata. The plowshares symbolize agriculture, the first form of technology, and relate to the more advanced automotive technology represented on the north and south walls. The agricultural theme is continued in the female figures, symbols of Michigan's abundant harvest. The fruits, grains, and vegetables represented are all indigenous to Michigan. The themes of dependence on the resources of the land and the evolution of technology are developed throughout the fresco cycle.

The West Wall

The themes established on the east wall are continued on the west wall, where the technologies of the air (aviation) and water (shipping and pleasure boating) are represented (see fig. 294). The half-face/half-skull in the central monochrome panel symbolizes both the coexistence of life and death as well as humanity's spiritual and physical aspects, while the star symbolizes aspirations and hope for civilization. This heraldic image introduces another major theme of the cycle: the dual qualities of human beings, of nature, and of technology. On the same monochrome panel, the city of Detroit and the industrial port of the Rouge are shown opposite a rubber tree plantation, representing the interdependence of the industrial north and agrarian south. In the center ore freighters, pleasure boats, and fish glide through a body of water representing the Detroit River and a South American river, presumably the Amazon. Technology's constructive and destructive uses are shown in the aviation panel where both passenger and war planes are being assembled. This theme is reinforced in the two smaller panels depicting peaceful and predatory birds, the airplane's equivalent in nature.

Vertical panels on each side of the west entrance to the court introduce the automobile industry theme through the representation of Power House No. 1, the energy source for the Rouge complex. The worker depicted in front of the steam engine is a generalized portrait of Rivera, while the engineer in front of the electrical generator is a composite of Henry Ford and Thomas Edison (see west wall diag., 1 and 2). In these panels, Rivera shows two kinds of industrial interdependence: that of raw and transformed power, as coal is burned to create electricity, and that of labor and management, represented by the worker/mechanic at left and the engineer/manager at right.

The North Wall

The north and south walls (see figs. 291 and 292) are devoted to three sets of images: the representation of the races that shape North American culture and make up its work force, the automobile industry, and the other industries of Detroit (medical, pharmaceutical, and chemical). Figures representing the four races hold the raw materials that Rivera saw as analogous to each. Between each pair of figures, gigantic hands grasp materials used in the production of steel, symbolizing both mining in particular and the aggressive drive to capture the riches of the earth in general. At the very bottom of the north and south walls are small panels that depict a day in the life of the workers by incorporating various scenes of daily life at the Rouge.

The center panel at the top of the north wall depicts figures representing the red and the black races holding iron ore and coal, respectively; below are the geological strata from which these materials are mined. In the far right panel, a child is being vaccinated in a medical laboratory surrounded by the animals whose blood is used to make serum and the scientists who make the serum into vaccine. In the far left panel, gas bombs are being made, and in the lower panels, Rivera further contrasts the constructive and destructive results of science—a healthy human embryo is below the vaccination panel, and cells suffocated by poisonous gas are represented beneath the chemical bomb panel.

The largest panel of the north wall represents important operations in the production and manufacture of the engine and transmission of the 1932 Ford V-8. In the upper center of the panel, a blast furnace is being tapped (1). A large ladle beneath the blast furnace pours molten steel into the open-hearth furnace. From left to right in the upper half of the panel are depicted other foundry operations in the sequence in which they occur: the making of mold patterns for the engine block and small engine parts (2); the mixing of the sand for the molds and the packing of the sand into mold cores (3); the hammering of plugs into the molds (4); the securing of tops on the casting boxes (5); casting boxes being loaded on the conveyor (6); and the conveying of casting boxes to the cupola furnace (7), where workmen pour molten steel into the molds (8). Above the furnace, the excess metal is removed from the newly cast engine block (9), followed by the deburring, spindling, and honing of the block (10). Depicted in the lower right corner are foundry and drilling operations in the manufacture of the transmission housing (11). In the center of the panel, flanked by two rows of giant spindles, is the assembly of the engine (12). Below the main section, small monochrome panels represent stages in the steel-making process: the open-hearth operations where workers punch in at the time clock (14); ingots in the foreground and the open-hearth furnace being charged with molten iron in the background (15); the ingot reheating operation (16); ingots being rolled into billets at the billet mill (17); bars being stacked at the bar mill (18); and workers taking a lunch break (19).

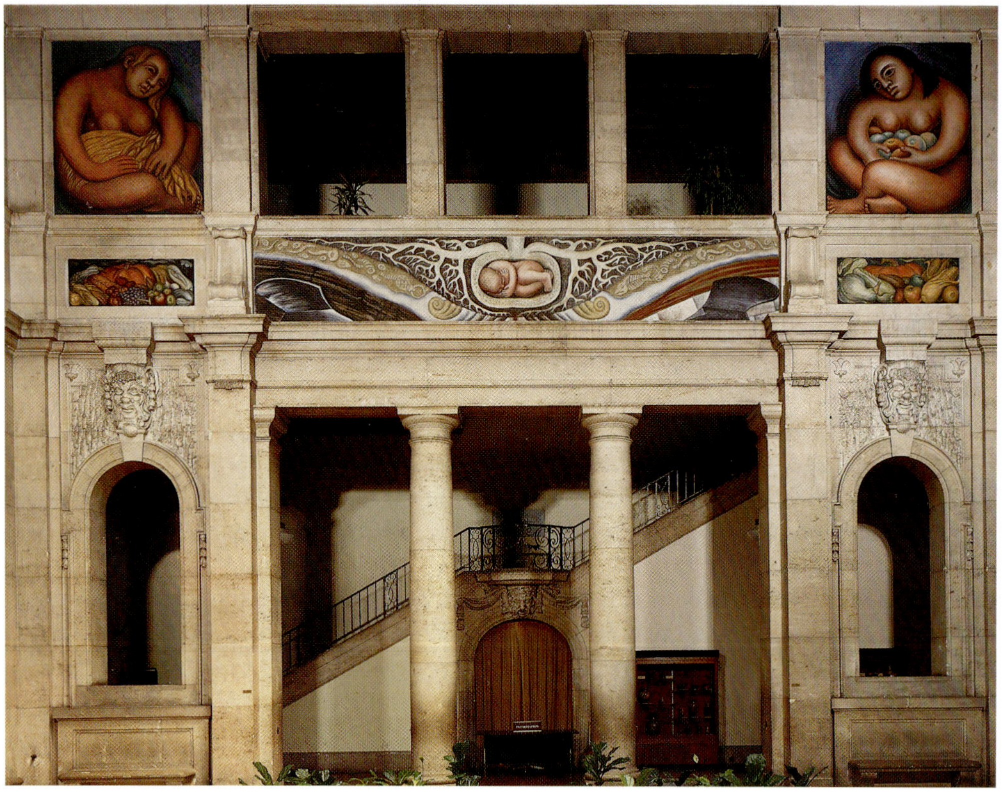

Figure 393.
East wall, *Detroit Industry*, May 1932–March 13, 1933, fresco. The Detroit Institute of Arts.

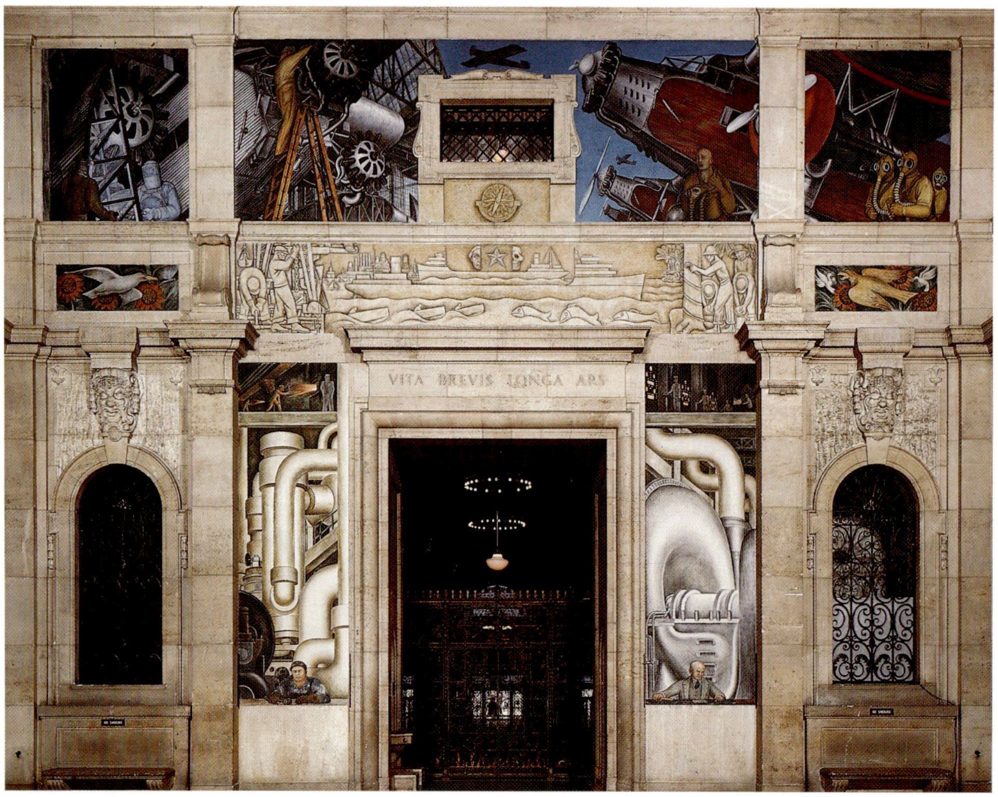

Figure 394.
West wall, *Detroit Industry*, May 1932–March 13, 1933, fresco. The Detroit Institute of Arts.

The workers represented in the foreground of the automotive panel are actually portraits of Rivera's assistants and Detroit acquaintances: Stephen Pope Dimitroff, general assistant (20); Arthur S. Niendorf, general assistant (21 and 25); Alberto T. Lopez, a Mexican friend of Rivera (22); Clifford Wight, chief assistant (23); John Bauer, Henry Ford's schoolmate, and a museum guard (24); Joseph Spinney, museum gardener (26); Ernst Halberstadt, plaster maker (27); Andrés Sánchez Flores, chemist (28); and a Ford engineer (29). Finally, Rivera included a self-portrait (30).

The South Wall

In the central panel at the top of the south wall, figures representing the white and yellow races are depicted holding limestone and sand, respectively; below these reclining figures are geological strata of these materials (see fig. 292). The industries represented in the corner panels of the south wall are pharmaceutics (left) and commercial chemicals (right). The small panels below show a surgical operation and crystallized sulphur and potash.

The major panel of the south wall is devoted to production of the automobile's exterior. Unlike the north wall panel, this panel is not arranged sequentially, though all major operations are included. Creation of the body parts begins at the far right of the panel where the stamping press makes fenders from large sheets of steel with spot and seam welders in the foreground (1). A cluster of stamping presses is shown in the upper left section (2). Large conveyors at the lower left carry body parts to be bumped and ground (3), while a foreman in hat and glasses supervises the procedure (the foreman is a generalized portrait of Charles E. Sorenson, in charge of production at the Rouge and head of Ford's international operations in 1932). In the upper central portion of the panel, major body parts are welded together in the welding buck (4). In the upper left corner, painters are shown next to the oven used to bake the painted finish (5). Directly below the welding buck, an engine is being lowered onto the final assembly line where it will be attached, with the transmission, to the chassis (6). At the end of the assembly line, the finished car can be seen, ready to be taken to the drive-away building for testing. Other scenes include workers testing spark plugs and ignition systems (7), the constant temperature testing room (8), and the heat-treating furnace (9).

The small monochrome panels on this wall represent, from left to right, by-products of the coke oven being made into fertilizer (10); cutting and forging of steel to repair machine parts (11); a trade school engine class being taught by Henry Ford (12 and 18); the glass plant (13 and 14); and workers being paid from the armored truck at gate 4 and crossing the foot bridge over Miller Road to the parking lots (15). Portraits of Dr. William Valentiner, director of the Detroit Institute of Arts (16), and Edsel B. Ford, president of the Arts Commission (17), appear at lower right.

In addition to his primary interest in the production and manufacture of the automobile, Rivera was also greatly interested in the men who worked in the plants. As a Marxist, Rivera believed the hope of civilization rested with the working classes. Thus, not only are the workers prominently represented in the automotive panels, but a special section, the predella panels on the north wall, is devoted to a day in the life of the workers. Rivera's portrayal is neither idealized nor condescending, realistically presenting the seriousness and perseverance that are required to perform a job at the Rouge.

While it is Rivera's depiction of the industrial process that ties the fresco together thematically, it is his use of techniques and devices adopted from historical artistic traditions that adds symbolic meaning to the cycle. Rivera incorporated his study of Cubism, his knowledge of pre-Columbian art and the traditions and techniques of Italian Renaissance art, and his vision of the new aesthetic of the age of steel into the Detroit frescoes. The compression of space, representation of simultaneous operations, and separation of forms into distinct geometrical elements, for example, are analogous to the compositional methods employed by Picasso and Braque, while his representation of two workers in motion in the south wall commercial chemical panel borrows a device developed by the Italian Futurists and subsequently used in the popular art form of cartoons. Rivera used powerful sculptural forms related to pre-Columbian art to evoke the awesomeness of the huge machines. The two rows of multiple spindles on the north wall and the stamping press on the south wall are adapted from ancient Aztec and Mayan sculptures representing deities.

From Italian Renaissance painting, Rivera adopted specific compositional forms (as can be seen in the vaccination panel, a variant of the traditional Nativity scene), the use of predella panels and portraits of contemporaries, and, most importantly, the technique of fresco painting itself. His series of predella panels devoted to the passage of time in the workers' day, all painted in monochrome to simulate relief sculpture, are reminiscent of the tympanum sculpture of medieval Christian churches, where pictographic calendars represent the labors of each month of the year.

Among the many actual portraits of Rivera's assistants and Detroit acquaintances in the murals, only two men are shown not working—Edsel Ford and William Valentiner. They appear in the traditional donor pose in the lower right corner of the south wall automotive panel. Ford and Valentiner's involvement and their appreciation of the artist's work place them within the great tradition of Renaissance patrons, and Rivera paid tribute to them through this placement.

The *Detroit Industry* fresco cycle is not only the most ambitious mural commission Rivera carried out in the United States, but also the best integrated and most cohesive, aesthetically and thematically. It harks back to the complex conception of the chapel at Chapingo and prefigures the technological themes presented in the RCA mural.

Summary

Location: Detroit, Michigan, 5200 Woodward Avenue

Site: An interior court in the main section of the Detroit Institute of Arts, an early 20th-century building in international Beaux-Arts style (Paul Cret, architect).

Theme/Subject: *Detroit Industry*

Format: Twenty-seven panels of varying sizes arranged around the court's four walls and carefully fitted to their classical post and lintel architectural divisions

Date: May 1932–March 13, 1933

Medium: True fresco

Dimensions: See diagram key

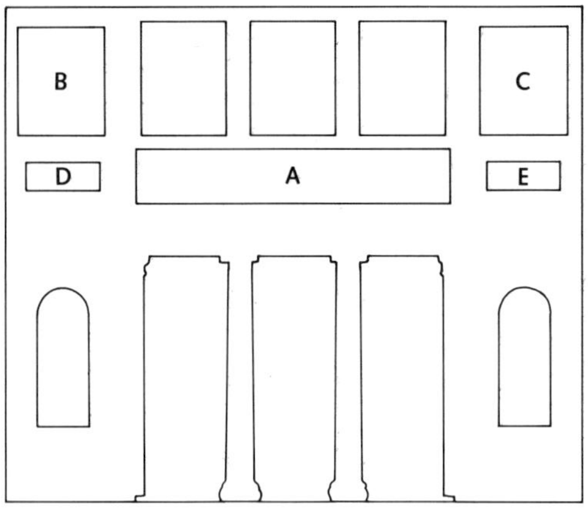

Detroit Institute of Arts, East Wall

A. *Infant in the Bulb of a Plant,* 1.33 × 7.96 m
B. *Woman Holding Grain,* 2.58 × 2.13 m
C. *Woman Holding Fruit,* 2.58 × 2.13 m
D. *Michigan Fruits and Vegetables,* .68 × 1.85 m
E. *Michigan Fruits and Vegetables,* .68 × 1.85 m

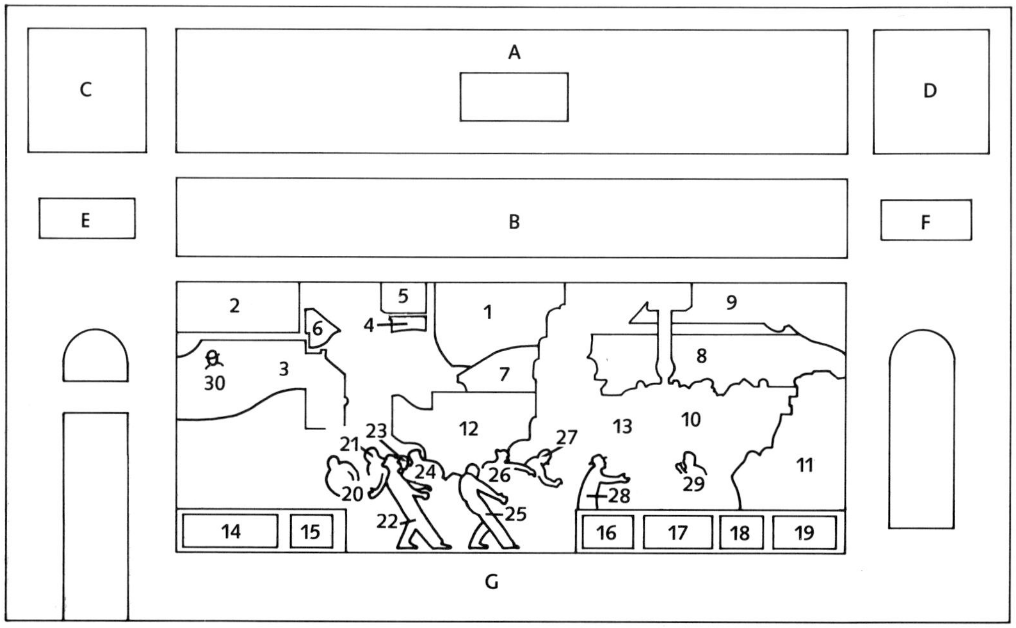

Detroit Institute of Arts, North Wall

A. *The Red and Black Races,* 2.69 x 13.72 m
B. *Geological Strata,* 1.33 × 13.72 m
C. *Manufacture of Poisonous Gas Bombs,* 2.58 × 2.13 m
D. *Vaccination,* 2.58 × 2.13 m
E. *Cells Suffocated by Poisonous Gas,* .68 x 1.85 m
F. *Healthy Human Embryo,* .68 × 1.85 m
G. *Production and Manufacture of Engine and Transmission* (Ford V-8), 5.40 × 13.72 m
1. Blast furnace and open-hearth furnace
2. Making mold patterns
3. Mixing sand for molds (right); packing sand into mold cores (left)
4. Hammering plugs into molds
5. Securing tops on casting boxes
6. Casting boxes put on table-height conveyor
7. Casting boxes put on overhead conveyor to cupola furnaces in foundry
8. Molten steel from cupola being poured into casting boxes from ladles
9. Chippers and sand blasting taking rough edges off newly cast engine blocks
10. Drilling and honing operations of engine block
11. Foundry and drilling operations of transmission housing
12. Motor assembly: men attaching cylinder head covers and smaller parts to engine block
13. Gear silent test, layout, and connecting rod inspections
14. Open-hearth operations entrance: workers punch in at time clock
15. Open-hearth operations: molten metal being poured into ingot molds
16. Rolling mill: ingots being transferred by buggy to reheat furnaces before rolling
17. Billet mill: billets being rolled into bars
18. Bar mill: metal bars being piled and cut
19. Tandem mill: lunch break
20. Stephen Pope Dimitroff
21. Arthur S. Niendorf, assistant to Rivera
22. Mexican friend of Rivera
23. Clifford Wight, chief assistant to Rivera
24. Henry Ford's schoolmate, Ford employee
25. Arthur S. Niendorf (see portrait 21)
26. Museum gardener
27. Ernst Halberstadt, assistant to Rivera
28. Andrés Sánchez Flores, assistant to Rivera
29. Ford engineer
30. Diego Rivera

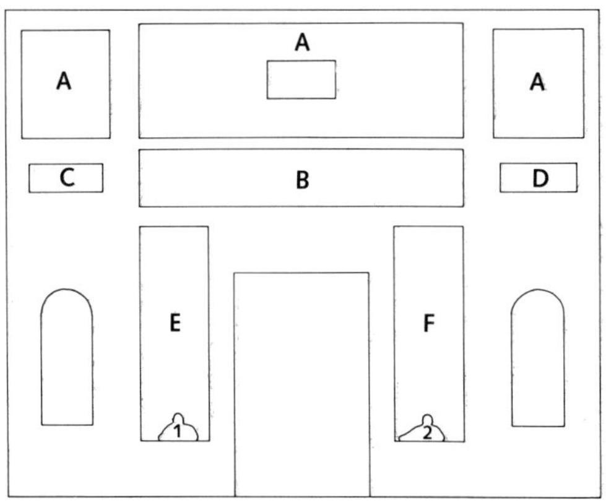

Detroit Institute of Arts, West Wall

A. *Aviation,* left 2.58 x 2.13 m, center 2.58 × 7.96 m, right 2.58 × 2.13 m
B. *Interdependence of North and South,* 1.33 × 7.96 m
C. *The Peaceful Dove,* .68 × 1.85 m
D. *The Predatory Hawk,* .68 × 1.85 m
E. *Steam,* 5.18 x 1.85 m
   1. Worker/mechanic
F. *Electricity,* 5.18 × 1.85 m
   2. Engineer/manager

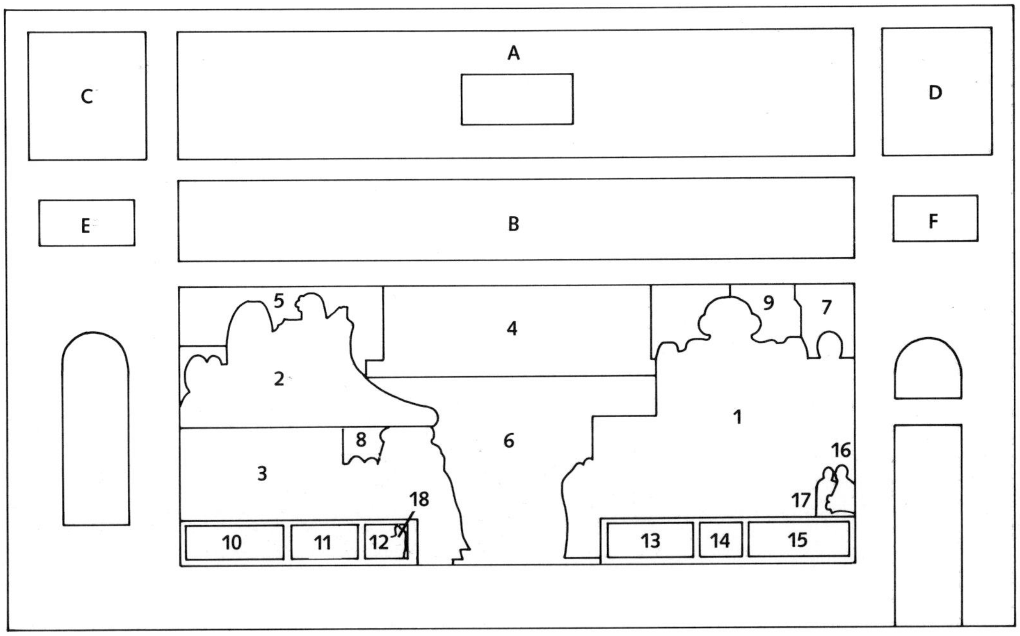

Detroit Institute of Arts, South Wall

A. *The White and Yellow Races*, 2.69 × 13.72 m
B. *Geological Strata*, 1.33 × 13.72 m
C. *Pharmaceutics*, 2.58 x 2.13 m
D. *Commercial Chemical Operations*, 2.58 × 2.13 m
E. *Surgery*, .68 × 1.85 m
F. *Crystals*, .68 × 1.85 m
G. *Production of Automobile Exterior and Final Assembly*, 5.40 x 13.72 m
   1. Fender stamping press (center); spot and seam welders (lower left)
   2. Top portion of stamping press
   3. (Left to right) steam pipe fitter fixing air valve; bumpers and grinders working on body panels
   4. Welding buck
   5. Painters
   6. Final assembly
   7. Women testing spark plugs and ignition systems
   8. Constant temperature testing room
   9. Heat treating furnace where metal bars are heated to be shaped into automobile parts
   10. By-products building: fertilizer operations
   11. Spring and upset building: making parts to repair machines
   12. "B" building: trade school engine class led by Henry Ford
   13. Glass plant: rolling operations
   14. Glass plant: polishing and stacking operations
   15. Gate 4 pedestrian walkway overpass at Miller Road
   16. Dr. William Valentiner
   17. Edsel B. Ford
   18. Henry Ford

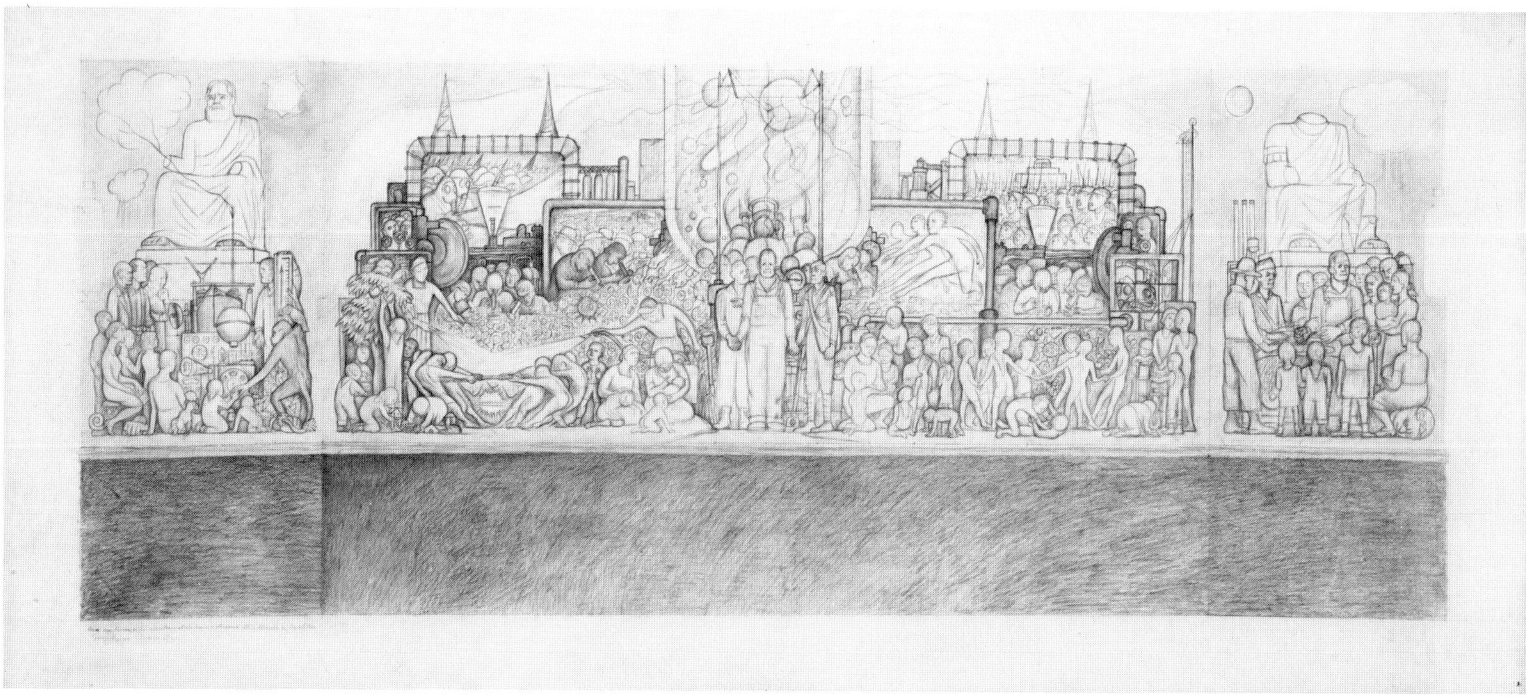

RCA (Radio Corporation of America) Building, Rockefeller Center

New York

Figure 395.
Man at the Crossroads, 1932, pencil on light tan paper, 78.7 × 181 cm. New York, The Museum of Modern Art, Anonymous Gift (138.35). Study for the RCA Building mural.

The RCA Building commission was Rivera's fifth in the United States. It led to the stormiest period of his career and culminated in one of the most notorious scandals in the history of modern art. While the general circumstances are well known and the controversy lingers on in popular legend, the facts and their historical significance have not yet been the subject of a published scholarly analysis.[1] What follows is a review of the events and some suggestions as to the causes and effects of this extraordinary confrontation.

The commission in charge of the decorative program for the Rockefeller Center complex prescribed the subject and content of the mural in a lengthy statement that can be said to be fairly summarized in the mural's proposed title: "Man at the Crossroads Looking with Hope and High Vision to the Choosing of a New and Better Future." The artist, in turn, restated his understanding of this program at considerable length in writing from Detroit. He concluded his elaborate description with the following statement:

In the centre, Man is expressed in his triple aspect—the Peasant who develops from the Earth the products which are the origin and base of all the riches of mankind, the Worker of the cities who transforms and distributes the raw materials given by the Earth, and the Soldier who, under the Ethical Force that produces martyrs in religions and wars, represents Sacrifice. Man, represented by these three figures, looks with uncertainty but with hope towards a future more complete balance between the Technical and Ethical Development of Mankind necessary to a New, more Humane and Logical Order.[2]

In this rationalization of his overall conception with that of the commission, there is a note of reservation, as Man's hope for the future is qualified by uncertainty. In this fine distinction one can hear the first squeak of the horrendous controversy to follow.

Rivera then rendered his conception in an explicit drawing dedicated to Mrs. John D. Rockefeller, Jr. (see fig. 395), in which there is no recognizable evidence of a head of Lenin. Following the sketch's approval by "Mr. Rockefeller" via the architect, on November 7, 1932, and by Mr. Todd of the construction engineers on November 14, Rivera began work in March of 1933.[3] All seems to have proceeded smoothly until early May, when the head of Lenin appeared in the right section of the main wall. In a polite letter to the artist, the young Nelson Rockefeller, who had assumed the role of intermediary between Rivera and the Rockefeller family, who were sponsoring the entire project, took exception to this portrait and asked Rivera to substitute some other figure. In an equally polite reply, in which he had been coached by artist Ben Shahn, Rivera declined this request.[4]

On May 9, the mural was surrounded by guards and an officer of the construction company served Rivera notice that his commission was cancelled and gave him a check for the full amount of his fee. On February 10–11, 1934, the mural, which had been approximately two-thirds finished when work was stopped, was destroyed by hammering its surface.

Of the many aspects of this controversy that have received attention in the explosion of comment and criticism that ensued, the least considered has been the artistic quality of the work itself. But an assessment of this lost masterwork is crucial to any understanding of the nature of Rivera's mural art at this, the high point of his powers as an artist vis-à-vis "modern" art *and* Mexican art.

From surviving photographs (see fig. 396), it is apparent that the finished two-thirds of the painting drew together the many human, scientific, technical, and socio-political parts of the subject into one of the most articulate and integrated units to be found in Rivera's multipanel works up to this date. It also shows a precision and clarity of interconnecting thematic imagery plus an intensity of mood that gives it a power that is both abstract and representational to a degree not exceeded by any of his other multispace, multitime compositions. Furthermore, with the exception of the figure of Lenin, it fulfills the demands of the program he was given to follow, albeit in terms of his own ideology (from which, according to all accounts, he was never precluded). The variations in motif and in the form and arrangement of symbolic groups from those represented in his preliminary sketch are clearly improvements that add to the effectiveness of the overall design and do not substantively alter, in content or in meaning, what he originally proposed and what was accepted.

Perhaps it is in his having reached this level of expressive command that at least a partial answer to the origins of the highly charged public controversy between artist and patron can be found. From any point of view, Rivera's inclusion of Lenin in this context—an inclusion both unforewarned and predictably unwanted—was a public affront to his patrons, and Rivera could not have helped knowing it would be. Why, then, did he pursue such a course? From this perspective, half a century later, it seems possible that the artist, stimulated by the revolutionary yeast of the time, was simply carried away by the progress of his mural. It was certainly one of the best compositions he had yet achieved, and in it he could see his revolutionary outlook becoming ever more manifest as the work developed. Added to this may have been his exasperation, as William Valentiner pointed out, in the face of continuing public harassment over his political beliefs.

Although both of these factors provide plausible reasons for Rivera's course of action, they do not provide any clue as to how the portrait of Lenin came to occupy such an integral place in the overall design and the concept behind it.

By the time he reached New York and began work at the RCA Building, Rivera had undergone an intellectual and artistic experience of the first magnitude. This was his encounter with the overpowering industrial world of machines and workers in the automobile factories of Detroit—the North American capital of mass-production technology under private enterprise. This industrial world was both the dream model and the nemesis of the social revolutionary system he had adopted as the basis for his art as well as for his conception of the future of Mexico. But the dichotomy inherent in the highly organized productive forces that he idealized and the exclusive system of management that he deplored seemed to him to require some broadly encompassing resolution if the rational development of human affairs was to proceed. At this tense moment of history, Rivera clearly believed radical revolutionary political leadership was the logical answer, and no other historical figure could have symbolized for him so fully as Lenin the vision and the way toward the future that he had come to feel. Stalin, with whose policies he had first become disaffected during his Moscow trip in 1927, was temporizing with Nazi Germany; Trotsky had been exiled and the leaders of Communist Party opposition were divided. Capitalism had led the world to the brink of economic collapse, and Europe was falling before Fascist military aggression. In Rivera's mind, Lenin, the patriarch of unified, successful, egalitarian, working-class action as exemplified by the October Revolution that had brought the Soviet Union into being, provided the most viable rallying point in an impending world revolution, and thus in his example as leader lay the world's hope of salvation.

Having always in the past been ready to take active part in radical political campaigns, protest demonstrations, and organized Communist Party activities, Rivera now found himself in a position—the most auspicious seat of capitalist power in the United States—to cross the threshold from the Mexican onto the world political stage by choosing, for the first time, a non-Mexican, internationally controversial figure as his icon, a figure commensurate in significance with the universal scope and power implications of his RCA mural theme.

If one examines the role of the New York patrons, there seems little doubt that the commission was approved without any discussion as to how the artist's Marxist views might surface in the course of its execution. The key person in determining the commission was Abby Aldrich Rockefeller (Mrs. John D. Rockefeller, Jr.). Mrs. Rockefeller was then involved in establishing the artistic and curatorial policies of the fledgling Museum of Modern Art and was working regularly with its director, Alfred H. Barr, Jr. His widow, who knew her well, recently observed that "she was interested in modern art, not politics."[5] Under these circumstances, it is reasonable to assume that Mrs. Rockefeller's personal interest gave the Rivera commission a specially protected status in the councils of the architects, the art planning committee, and the executives of the corporation. But once the Lenin portrait appeared in paint,[6] it could not have been overlooked. If a managerial consensus of disapproval was arrived at (or perhaps seen as inevitable), the Rockefellers could scarcely have been expected to decide in favor of the mural over the objection of contributing partners, who might pull out of the project, and thus risk the collapse of the entire Rockefeller Center enterprise. Much was at stake

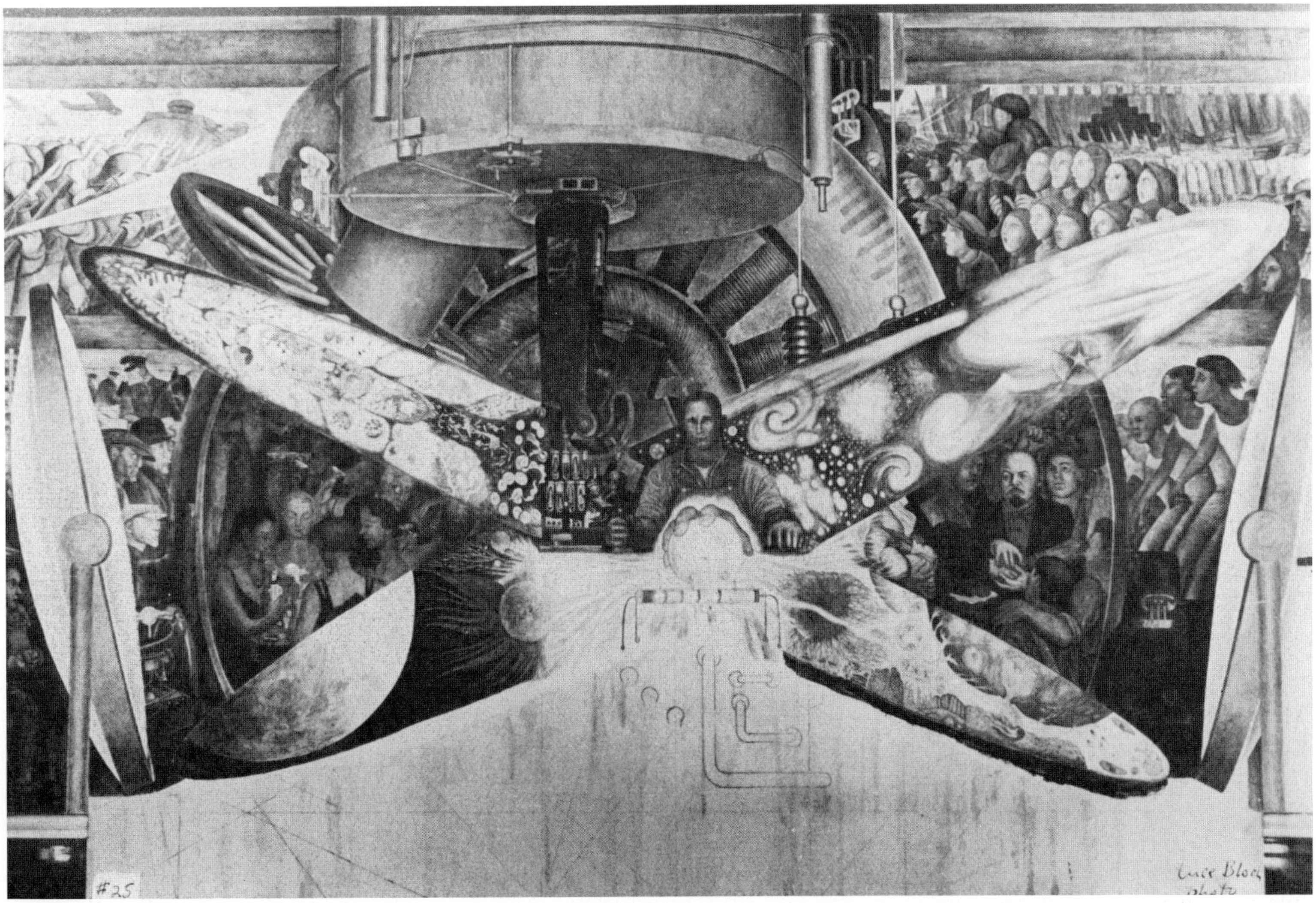

Figure 396.
Photograph of unfinished RCA Building mural, taken by Lucienne Bloch just before all work was stopped in May 1933.

beyond the personal interest of the patrons and therein, in this view, lies the reason for their nonintervention during the controversy.

Summary

Location: New York, 30 Rockefeller Plaza (destroyed 1934)

Site: Front and side walls of the broad bank of elevators facing the main entrance of the principal building of Rockefeller Center, a pioneer inner-city, office complex, privately undertaken to stimulate economic recovery at the beginning of the Depression (Raymond Hood and Associates, architects)

Theme/Subject: *Man at the Crossroads with Hope and High Vision to the Choosing of a New and Better Future*

Format: A three-part composition spread over three walls; a main wall with two side walls turned at right angles away from it

Date: March–May 9, 1933 (unfinished)

Medium: True fresco

Dimensions: Central wall: 5.82 × 12.46 m
Right side wall: 5.06 x 3.21 m
Left side wall: 5.06 × 3.21 m

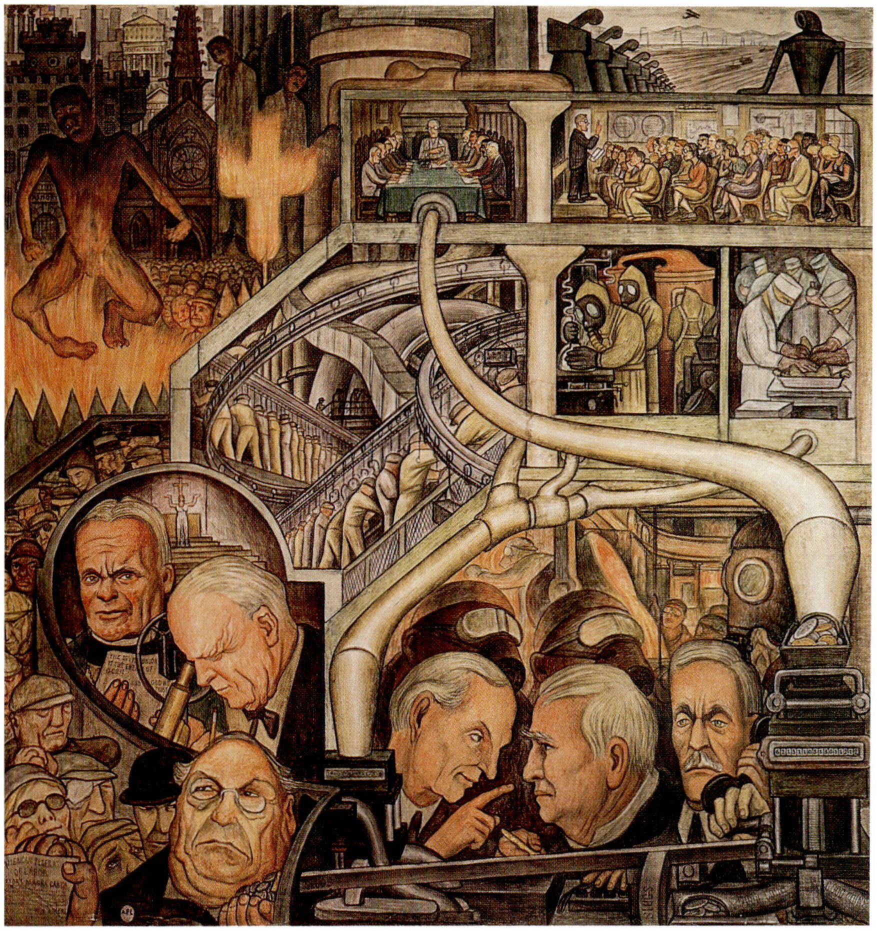

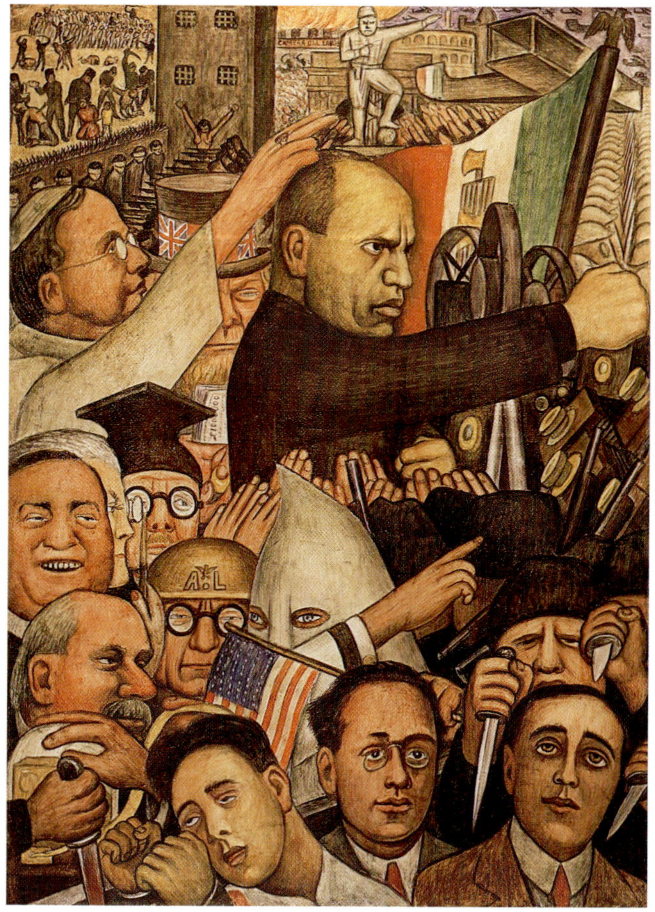

New Workers School

New York

Figure 397.
Modern Industry, July 15–December 8, 1933, fresco, 1.83 × 1.80 m.
Private Collection.

Figure 398.
Mussolini, July 15–December 8, 1933, fresco, 1.83 × 1.52 m.
Private Collection.

Diego Rivera's *Portrait of America* series[1] was originally designed for the New Workers School, then located in the fourth-story loft of a storage building on the north side of Fourteenth Street between Fifth and Sixth avenues, to the west of Union Square. At the time, the area around the square was Manhattan's rallying point for workers' demonstrations and political protest oratory. It was also the location of union headquarters for workers in the garment industry. The New Workers School had been founded by Jay Lovestone, leader of the Communist Party in the United States, which was known as the Opposition since it opposed the dictatorial policies of Stalin and the Comintern (the international revolutionary arm of the Soviet government from 1919 through the 1930s).

As a whole, the mural program is essentially a course in American history, as interpreted by the artist, from the country's beginnings under European colonization to the present day as it faced the rise of Nazism and Fascism. In Rivera's dramatization, this history is seen as a part of a worldwide historical, deterministic revolution that will culminate in "the progressive aspect of American development . . . in proletarian unity and the victory of the new social order."[2]

The historical-ideological theme of the work was developed in a series of twenty-one frescoes on movable frames (see fig. 186), following the precedent of those Rivera created for his exhibition at the Museum of Modern Art in New York in 1931. Each tableau summarized particular historical events or social conditions through the inclusion of historical personalities and symbolic figures as motifs representing the struggles of the proletariat over the course of three centuries.

The series culminated in the central panel on the north wall (diag. S), an emblematic exhortation to proletarian unity in the form of a group portrait of the fathers of Marxist doctrine and the leaders of its 19th- and 20th-century international movements.[3] This panel was flanked by two smaller panels representing opponents (diag. R and T) of the war-threatening movements of National Socialism (Nazism) in Germany, depicted in a panel entitled *Hitler* (diag. U), and Fascism in Italy, in one titled *Mussolini* (diag. Q, see fig. 398).[4] The remaining panels are divided between those showing positive and those showing negative aspects of political and social conduct in the historical rise of the international proletariat. Figures of known and anonymous individuals representing the "forces of good and evil" from America's history are seen to be engaged in a mortal struggle that will finally result in the establishment of a harmonious, classless society, run by the world's workers.

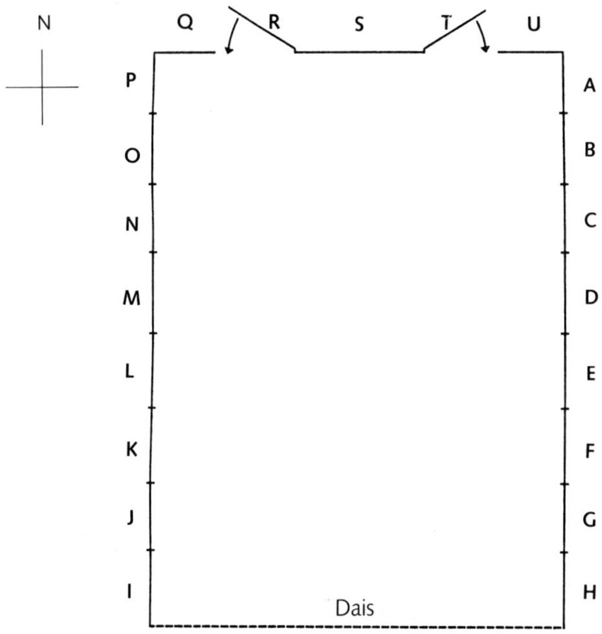

New Workers School

A. *Colonial America*, 1.83 × 1.52 m
B. *The American Revolution*, 1.83 × 1.80 m
C. *Revolution and Reaction: Shay's Rebellion*, 1.83 × 1.80 m
D. *Expansion*, 1.83 × 1.80 m
E. *The Conflict over Slavery*, 1.83 × 1.80 m
F. *The Civil War*, 1.83 × 1.80 m
G. *Reconstruction*, 1.83 × 1.80 m
H. *The Labor Movement*, 1.83 × 1.52 m
I. *Class War*, 1.83 × 1.52 m
J. *Modern Industry*, 1.83 × 1.80 m
K. *World War*, 1.83 × 1.80 m
L. *The New Freedom*, 1.83 × 1.80 m
M. *Imperialism*, 1.83 × 1.80 m
N. *Depression*, 1.83 × 1.80 m
O. *The "New Deal"*, 1.83 × 1.80 m
P. *Division and Depression*, 1.83 × 1.52 m
Q. *Mussolini*, 1.83 × 1.52 m
R. *Opponent of Fascism*, .89 × .81 m (overdoor)
S. *Proletarian Unity*, 1.82 × 2.16 m
T. *Opponent of Nazism*, .89 × .81 m (overdoor)
U. *Hitler*, 1.83 × 1.52 m

Summary

Location: Originally, New York City, the New Workers School, 51 West Fourteenth Street (1933–36). Moved to 131 West Thirty-third Street (1936–41);[5] given to the International Ladies Garment Workers Union (1941); thirteen panels of the twenty-one panels were installed at Unity House, Forest Park, Pennsylvania, and eight placed in storage (1942);[6] the latter eight panels were eventually donated to the International Rescue Committee and then sold (1964);[7] of these, four (J, K, L, Q) are now in a private collection in Mexico; the largest (S) is in a private collection in Venezuela; another (O) is at the Arkiv för Dekorativ Konst in Lund, Sweden; and one (T) was offered for sale by Sotheby's on November 26, 1985, leaving only the *Opponent of Fascism* panel (R) unlocated.[8] The thirteen panels at Unity House were destroyed by fire on February 28, 1969.

Site: A low-ceilinged room, with a skylight, two small doors on the north wall and two windows on the south, on the fourth floor of a building (since destroyed) used for business storage

Theme/Subject: *Portrait of America*

Format: Twenty-one fresco panels covering every inch of the east, west, and north walls above the dado, in a continuous horizontal sequence, similar to a series of comic strip squares, with vertical slats of steel approximately four inches wide separating the individual panels. Conceived as surrounding a seated audience facing a speaker's platform in front of the windowed south wall

Date: July 15–December 8, 1933

Medium: True fresco mounted on movable wood-framed, steel-mesh panels backed by double-thickness composition board (Celotex), which were designed by the artist

Dimensions: Room: Approx. 14 × 6.7 m

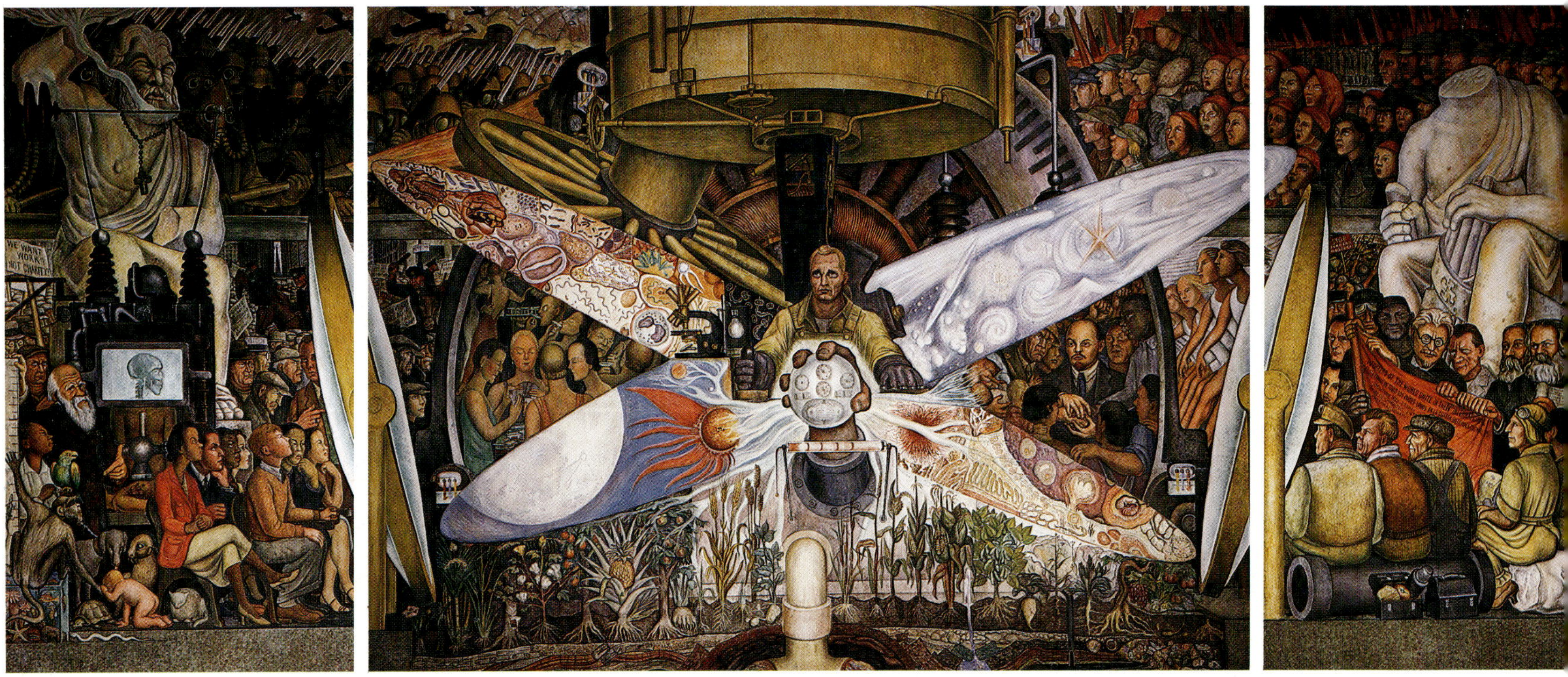
WE WANT
WORK
NOT CHARITY

Palacio de Bellas Artes

Mexico City

Figure 399.
Man, Controller of the Universe, 1934, fresco, 4.85 × 11.45 m. Mexico City, Museo del Palacio de Bellas Artes.

The Palacio de Bellas Artes, which houses a museum, concert hall, and theatre, and until recently was the headquarters of the Instituto Nacional de Bellas Artes, has been the focal point of the official Mexican art world since the latter years of the Díaz regime. According to Bertram Wolfe, following the destruction of the RCA mural in February 1934, when Rivera asked the government of Mexico for a wall on which to duplicate the RCA work,[1] he was given a west wall on the third level of this national cultural center. Whether this action initiated or simply confirmed a decision to use the Palacio's spacious galleries as a showcase for the work of Mexico's most honored artists has not been determined. But in any case Rivera was the first to achieve this superior order of official recognition. Today, the upper two levels of the foyer are also the site of large-scale works by the three other primary mural painters of Mexico's mural renaissance: José Clemente Orozco, David Alfaro Siqueiros, and Rufino Tamayo.

As nearly as one may tell from the fragmentary photographic records of the aborted New York fresco, the composition of the new version does nearly duplicate the earlier work, even to the extent of its stepped baseline.[2] As in New York, a figure in workers' overalls and representing Man occupies the center of the scene.[3] His role as controller of the universe is symbolized by his manipulation of machinery, i.e., his mastery of science and technology; one hand grasps a lever, while the fingers of the other press a series of control buttons. Two great ellipses cross diagonally behind his helmsmanlike form, his role as pilot accentuated by the gigantic wheels in the background. The ellipses represent, respectively, the microcosm, or world of living things, as seen through the microscope shown at Man's right, and the macrocosm, the stellar universe as viewed through the cylindrical telescope that looms above him. Below this scene, Rivera shows the earth sending forth its fruits, using cultivated plants to indicate that this bounty results from Man's efforts. Between the ends of the ellipses to Man's left, the figure of Lenin, the cause of the controversy in New York, joins the hands of several workers of different races. To Man's right in the correlative position is a scene of debauchery among the wealthy (in a departure from the New York original, Rivera has included here a portrait of John D. Rockefeller, the paterfamilias of his former patrons; the disease-causing cells in the ellipse nearby are a further negative implication).

There are changes from the original, however. Both areas on the far sides of the magnifying lenses that flank the central scene are larger in Mexico City than in New York, and because they are on the same plane as the main image, the sense that the composition is arranged as a triptych is restored. The area to Man's left shows the workers of the world embracing socialism, while to his right, appears the capitalist world, accompanied by scenes of repression and war. These areas are crowded with additional portraits. To the right Marx, Engels, Trotsky, Jay Lovestone, and Bertram D. Wolfe are grouped behind a banner proclaiming the establishment of the IV International, which had recently been formed by Communist opponents of the official Soviet party, then dominated by Stalin. On the left side, rather than the full-size standing men and women who had been planned for this area at the RCA Building, Rivera packed in many seated figures, gesturing and staring from around the statue and the machines. This, and the multiplicity of lettered signs and banners, anticipates the churning masses and piled-up montage treatment of the south wall of the stairway at the Palacio Nacional, which he had left unfinished before leaving for San Francisco in 1932, and which he now resumed painting in a more aggressive revolutionary mood.

Summary

Location: Mexico City, at Avenida Júarez and Ruiz de Alarcón

Site: Third level, Museo del Palacio de Bellas Artes, a massive Porfirian building in an Italian Art Nouveau (Floreale) style

Theme/Subject: *Man, Controller of The Universe* (revised version of the RCA Building mural, New York City, reduced in scale, with minor extensions and changes)[4]

Format: A three-part rectangular composition on a single plane[5]

Date: 1934

Medium: True fresco panel (movable?) inset against the wall under a parallel ceiling beam

Dimensions: 4.85 × 11.45 m

Hotel Reforma

Mexico City

In 1939 Rivera had been at home in Mexico City for nearly five years following his time in the United States. He had finished the Palacio Nacional stairway mural and his new version of the RCA Building fresco. But without further mural bids in the wake of his battles in the United States, he had been spending much of his time on easel paintings and portraits of friends and international celebrities, many from the United States.

The national capitol of Mexico was at that time a city of well under one million inhabitants. The atmosphere was more like that of a parochial town than a major metropolis. The peaks of Iztaccíhautl and Popocatepetl could still be clearly seen on the horizon, and there were hardly more than a half dozen bars and restaurants that catered to international visitors. The center of tourist traffic was Sanborn's drugstore and restaurant, which was housed in the splendid 18th-century palace of the Counts of the Valley of Orizaba called the Casa de los Azulejos (the House of Tiles), on Avenida Gustavo I. Madero. The nightlife was largely of the folkloric, "Mexicanista" variety, now become the social fashion following Rivera and his colleagues' success in bringing Mexico's autochthonous popular culture to the center of the national stage.

In this milieu, on a side street off the grand Paseo de la Reforma, the ambitiously chic Hotel Reforma was designed and built in semi-Art-Deco style, its ground story solidly faced with the red pumice stone called *tezontle* in Náhuatl. Situated close to the site of the principal Mexico City art gallery, Galería de Arte Mexicano, which was both internationally minded and dedicated to contemporary Mexican art, the appearance of this pink-faced *hôtel grande* may well have been the origin of the epithet *Zona Rosa* for this fashionable area of the city.

The Rivera murals, commissioned by the Pani family, owners of the Reforma, were planned to decorate the banquet hall of the hotel. Mexican popular festivals are the basic theme for this set of tableaux that flamboyantly satirize four aspects of 19th-century and contemporary Mexican life. The panels are titled *The Dictatorship, Dance of the Huichilobos, Touristic and Folkloric Mexico,* and *Festival of Heujotzingo (Agustín Lorenzo).* Almost all of the figures that appear are caricatures that slyly ridicule, in carnival fashion, some phase of Mexican life: its myths, conventions, sacred political figures, as well as eccentric street personalities, American tourists, and, most prominently, in scenes that are infectiously vitriolic, the connection between national and international political demagoguery.

On completion, the hotel's patrons objected to the inclusion of the biting caricatures of living Mexican personalities, as

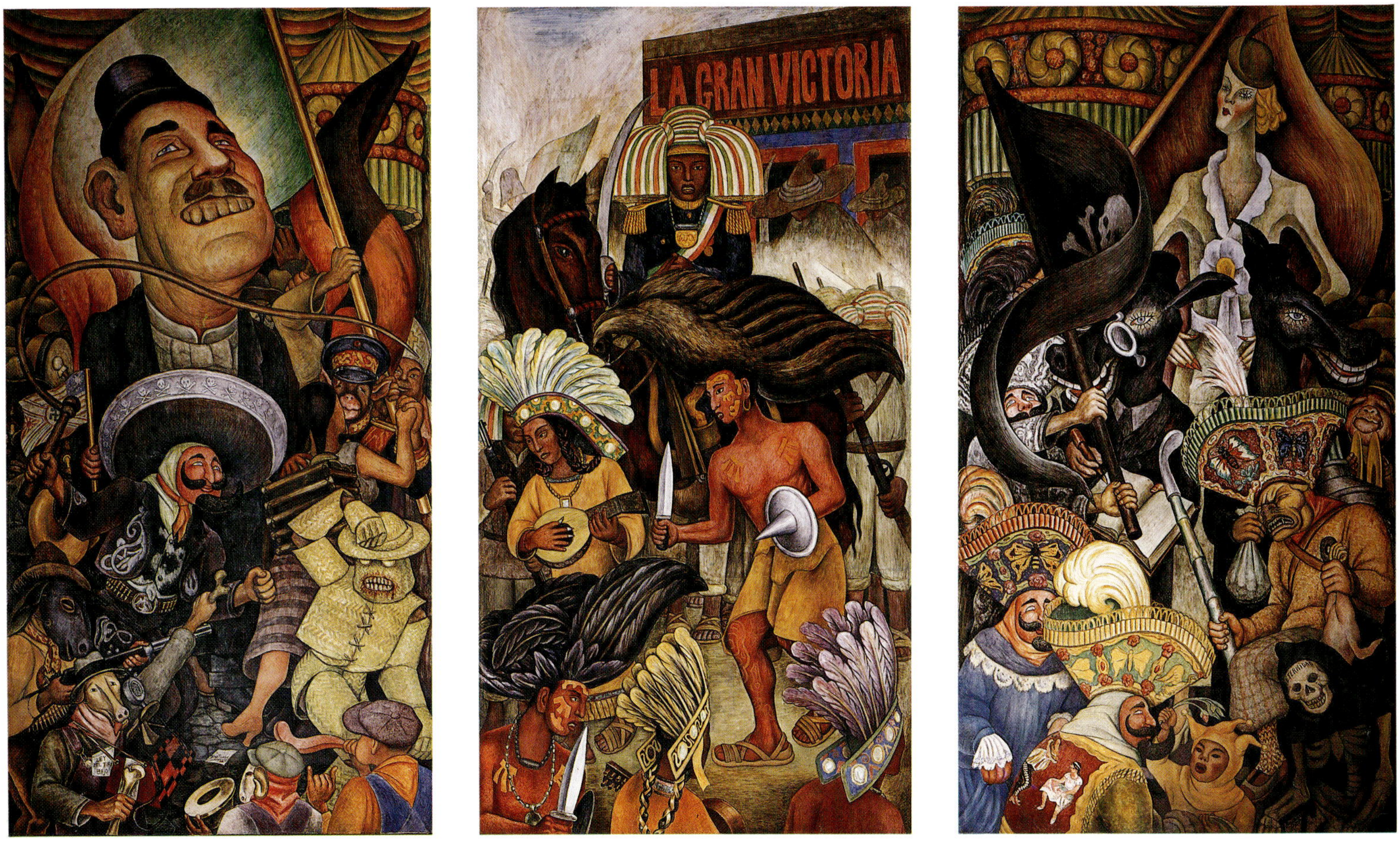
LA GRAN VICTORIA

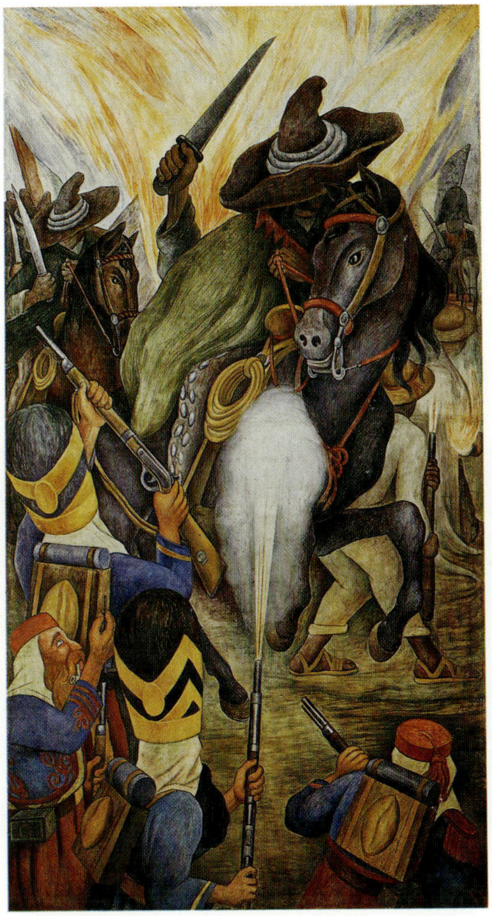

Figure 400.
***A Burlesque of Mexican Folklore and Politics (The Dictatorship, Dance of the Huichilobos, Touristic and Folkloric Mexico,* and *Festival of Huejotzingo),* 1936, fresco, 3.89 × 2.11 m (each panel). Mexico City, Museo del Palacio de Bellas Artes.**

well as leading figures in world affairs. Without consulting Rivera, members of the Pani family doctored the offensive images. The ensuing controversy led to a court case and the eventual vindication of the artist, to whom unprecedentedly heavy damages were awarded. The panels were sold and eventually acquired by the Instituto Nacional de Bellas Artes.

Summary

Location: Mexico City, Avenida Juárez at Ruiz de Alarcón

Site: Third level, Museo del Palacio de Bellas Artes. Originally commissioned for the Hotel Reforma, Paseo de la Reforma, Mexico City.

Theme/Subject: *A Burlesque of Mexican Folklore and Politics (Una parodia del folklórico y política mexicana)*

Format: Four vertical panels of the same rectangular shape and size, intended to decorate opposite ends (two at either end) of the banquet hall of the hotel. In their present installation, a wainscot at their base interrupts the lower extremity of each panel.

Date: 1936

Medium: True fresco mounted on movable steel frames

Dimensions: 3.89 × 2.11 m (each)

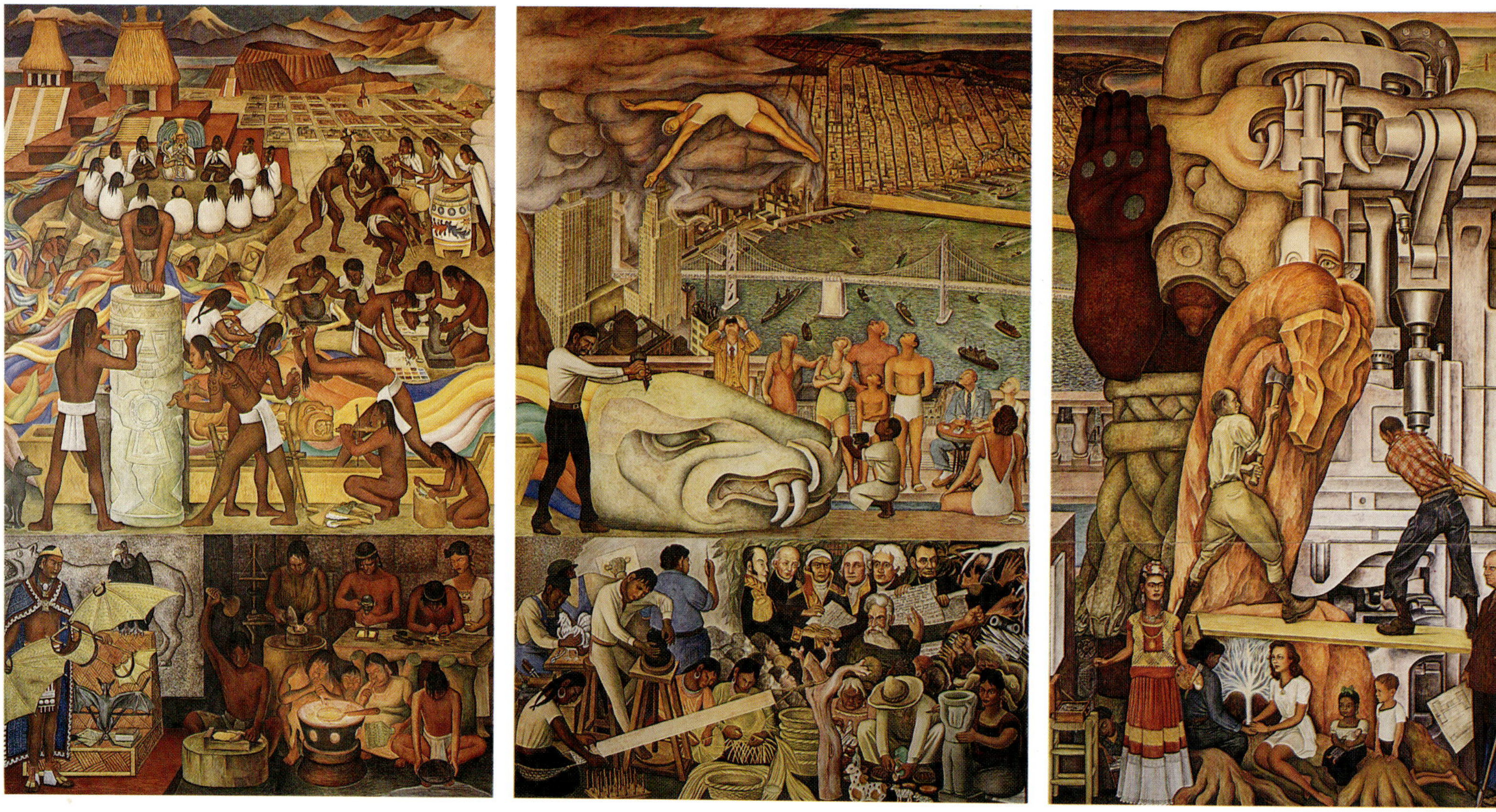

City College of San Francisco

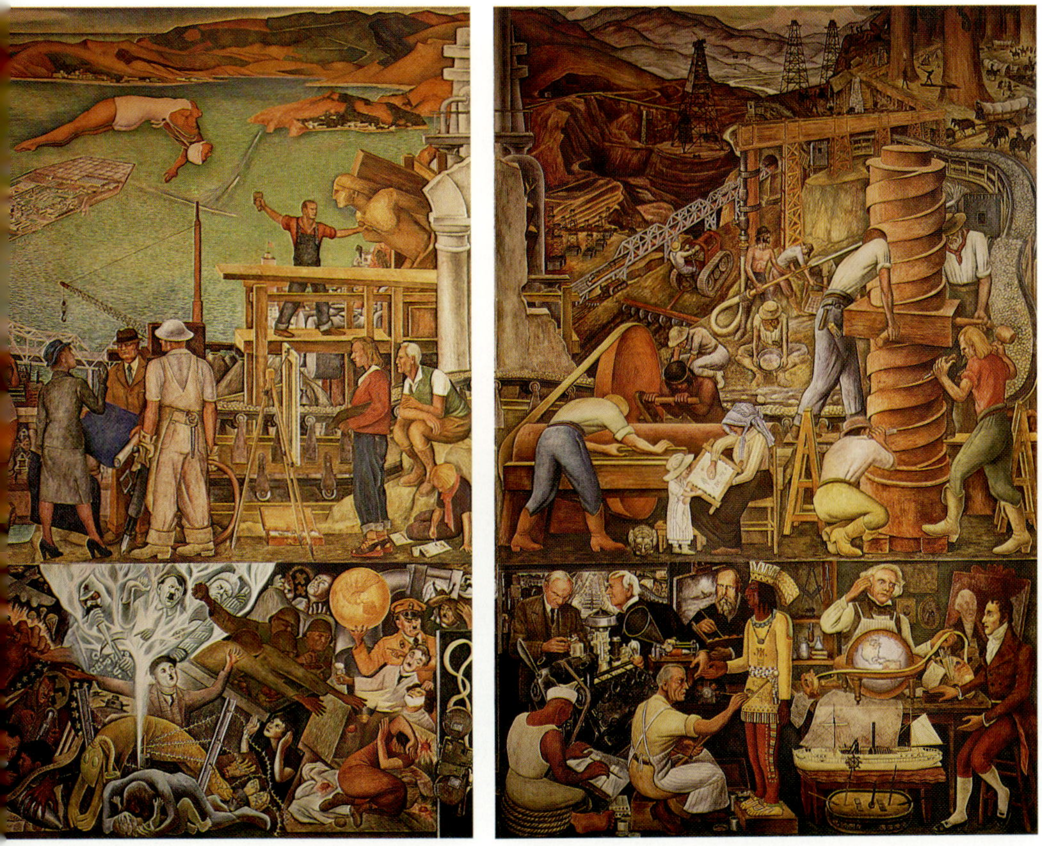

Figure 401.
Pan-American Unity,
1940, fresco, 6.74 ×
22.5 m. City College of
San Francisco.

"In 1939, when the Golden Gate International Exhibition opened on manmade Treasure Island in San Francisco Bay, the planners of the fair envisioned that an art exhibit of European Old Masters would continue for the two years of the Fair. However, World War II was beginning in Europe. Nervous nations recalled the $40,000,000 art collection after the first year, leaving blank the calendar for the second. At that time, local architect Timothy Pfleuger was designing the newly established campus of City College. With clarity of vision, Pfleuger organized an Art in Action exhibit of artists at work at the Fair for spectators to watch daily as a replacement for the Old Masters. The resultant art work was to come to the new college campus as its major adornment."[1]

Such were the circumstances surrounding the largest mural Diego Rivera was ever to paint in the United States. In boldly arranging this spectacle, Pfleuger was plainly influenced by the example of the public art of the Mexican muralists as well as his previous association with Rivera at the San Francisco Stock Exchange.

The sequence of events and course of negotiations between Rivera and Pfleuger are unclear, but the artist seems to have arrived in San Francisco sometime during the summer of 1940. If, as reported, he had gone into hiding at home after the sensational attempt on the life of Leon Trotsky, a guest at his house, in May of that year, he was no doubt ready, if not eager, to accept the invitation.[2]

He agreed to work in the open area on Treasure Island, where the public was invited to watch him and other artists produce "living" art, on the condition that he be permitted to make this work his personal contribution toward the promotion of good will between the two countries, in light of his great affection for the friends in San Francisco who a decade earlier had made his stay in the city such a pleasant one. As this statement reflects, Rivera had tempered his earlier critical stance vis-à-vis the United States. The Stalinist purges and the signing of a pact between the Soviets and the Nazis had led directly to the outbreak of war in Europe.

In the face of the growing threat of Fascism, Rivera began to express himself, strongly and consistently, in terms of inter-American solidarity. The San Francisco City College mural is his paramount statement on this Pan-American political theme.

The theme of the mural is the need for union among the Americas and Americans, in the broad sense of the word. The historical evolution of the arts of North and Latin America is depicted in the context of their ancient and modern civilizations, with emphasis on ancient Mexican and 19th- and 20th-century American aspects, in a geographical setting based on the San Francisco Bay Area and the Valley of Mexico. Constructive, technical, and artistic activities characteristic of each region, with portraits of celebrated personalities, are arranged in graded historical sequence against a sweeping landscape in aerial perspective. The juxtaposition of the two regional creative traditions is symbolized at the center of the composition by a massive, bilaterally divided figure, one-half the Aztec goddess of earth and death, Coatlicue, and one-half a giant industrial stamping press. Before this portentous double image, two full-length figures, based on the Canadian wood-sculptor and engineer Dudley Carter, are shown hewing a giant Rocky Mountain ram from a redwood timber, underscoring the theme of synthesis of the artistic genius of the South with the mechanical expression (technology) of the North.

The upper register of the mural forms a continuous panorama, whereas the lower register consists of a sequence of separately "framed" compositions, in a manner similar to Rivera's earlier use of grisaille panels in this position, that depict epochs from the history and culture of both societies. The lower register of the central section, which lampoons contemporary political personalities and events, is held in close relationship to the upper register.

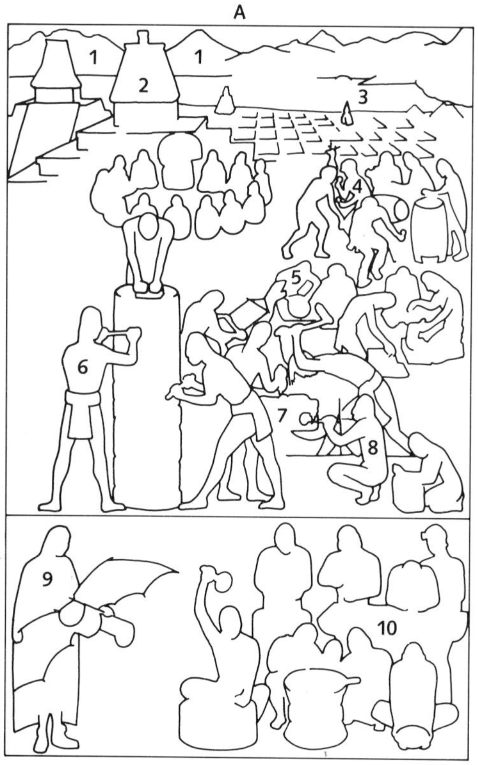

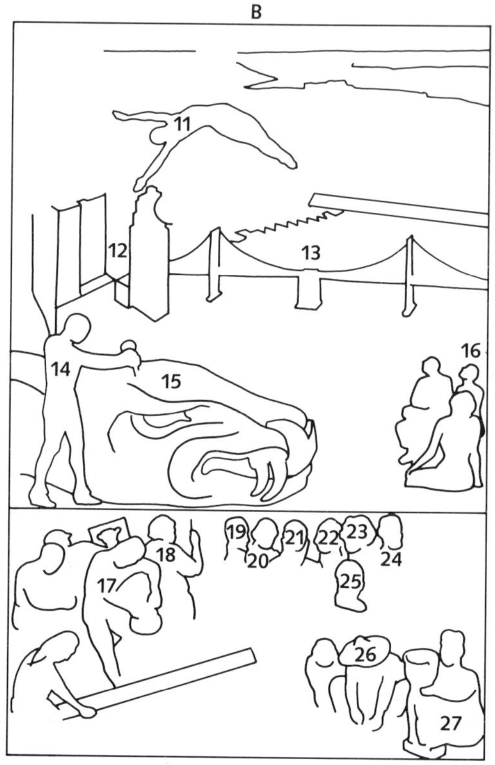

Summary

Location: City College of San Francisco (formerly San Francisco Junior College), at the junction of Ocean and Geneva avenues

Site: The lobby of the college's arts auditorium.[3] Originally painted and installed in the Palace of Fine and Decorative Arts at the 1939–40 Golden Gate International Exposition, San Francisco.

Theme/Subject: *Pan-American Unity (Marriage of the Artistic Expression of the North and South of this Continent)*[4]

Format: Ten connected panels now installed on a slightly convex rectangular wall

Date: 1940

Medium: True fresco mounted on movable steel frames

Dimensions: 6.74 × 22.5 m

City College of San Francisco

A. The Creative Genius of the South Growing from Religious Fervor and a Native Talent for Plastic Expression[5]

1. Iztaccíhuatl and Popocatepetl mountains
2. Náhuatl temples; in front, priest and disciples (Aztec, 15–16th centuries)
3. Teotihuacán, temple complex twenty-five miles NE of Mexico City (A.D. 300–800)
4. Yaqui deer dancers and musicians
5. Ceramic artists
6. Artists with sculptured Toltec column
7. Jaguar effigy
8. Sculptor with bow drill
9. Netzahualcoyotl, Aztec poet king of Texcoco (15th century)
10. Goldsmiths of the "Cloud People" (Mixtec, ca. A.D. 1000)

B. Elements from Past and Present

11. Helen Crienkovich, national A.A.U. indoor diving champion (1939), being admired by sports-conscious Americans at right
12. 450 Sutter Building (left) and Pacific Telephone Building (right), both designed by Timothy Pfleuger
13. Oakland Bay Bridge (completed 1939)

C

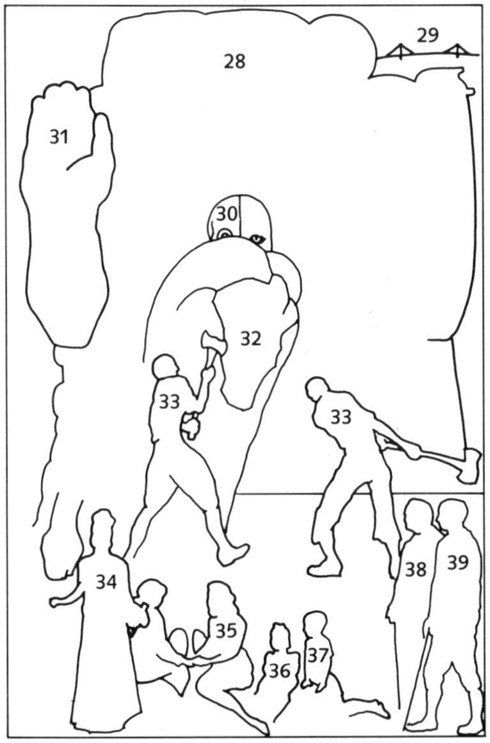

D

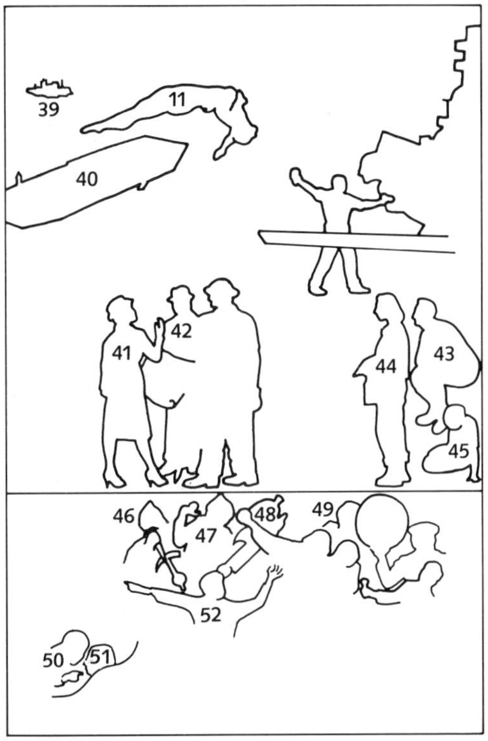

E

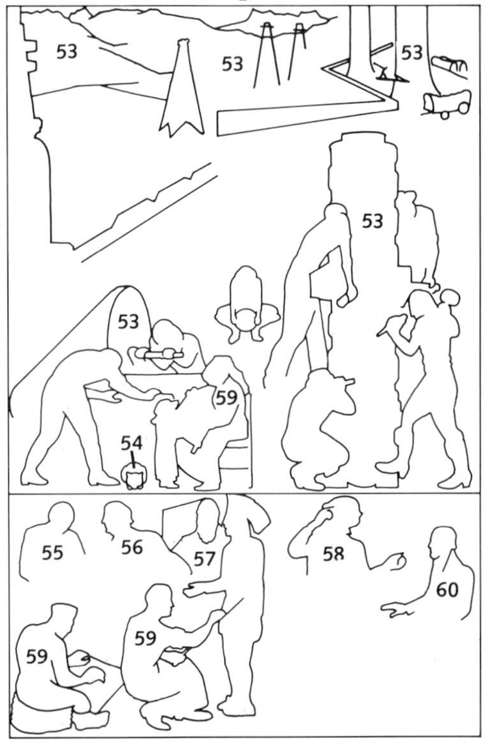

14. Mexican peasant sculptor Mardonio Magaña
15. The feathered-serpent God, Quetzalcóatl
16. Abstract painter Mona Hoffman
17. Modern Mexican artists, including fresco painters, tinsmiths, potters, and weavers
18. Rivera painting the patriots of South American, Mexican, and United States independence:
19. Simón Bolívar
20. Father Hidalgo
21. José María Morelos
22. George Washington
23. Thomas Jefferson
24. Abraham Lincoln
25. John Brown
26. Family of Mexican village woodcarvers
27. Woman sculptor of Tehuantepec, a native matriarchal society in southern Mexico, where women are the leaders and creators

C. The Plastification of the Creative Power of the Northern Mechanism by Union with the Plastic Tradition of the South

28. Earth and death goddess, Coatlicue, with fangs and skirt of snakes
29. Golden Gate Bridge
30. Head of Life and Death
31. Hand warding off tyranny
32. Rocky Mountain ram, emblem of City College of San Francisco
33. Engineer and artist Dudley C. Carter, in three views
34. Frida Kahlo, wife of Rivera
35. Rivera and Paulette Goddard, Ziegfeld girl and film star, holding the tree of Life and Love
36. Cristina Kahlo, sister of Frida
37. Donald Cairns, son of Emmy Lou Packard, Rivera's assistant
38. San Francisco architect Timothy L. Pfleuger

D. Trends of Creative Effort in the United States and the Rise of Woman in Various Fields of Creative Endeavor through Her Use of the Power of Manmade Machinery

39. Alcatraz Island, site of a notorious federal prison from 1933 to 1963
40. Treasure Island, site of Golden Gate Exposition, 1939–40
41. Woman architect (modeled by Mary Anthony, forester and botanist)
42. Architect Otto Deichman
43. Architect Frank Lloyd Wright
44. Emmy Lou Packard, artist and Rivera's primary assistant on the mural[6]
45. Daughter of Mona Hoffman
46. Joseph Stalin
47. Adolf Hitler
48. Benito Mussolini
49. Jack Oakie as "Benzini Napaloni, Dictator of Bacteria"—a takeoff on Mussolini in the 1940 film *The Great Dictator*
50. Edward G. Robinson, actor and noted collector of modern art
51. Francis Lederer in scene (with Robinson) from the film *Confessions of a Nazi Spy*
52. Charlie Chaplin in his film *The Great Dictator*[7]

E. The Creative Culture of the North Developing from the Necessity of Making Life Possible in a New and Empty Land

53. Mount Lassen, prospectors, wagon trains, and oil derricks, symbolizing the richness of the western lands and the pioneer industry of the United States
54. Mona Hoffman's cat
55. Henry Ford
56. Thomas A. Edison
57. Albert P. Ryder
58. Samuel F. B. Morse
59. Embroiderer, figurehead carver, maritime artist, and carver of cigar store Indian, representing the American folk artists who have contributed to the nation's cultural heritage
60. Robert Fulton

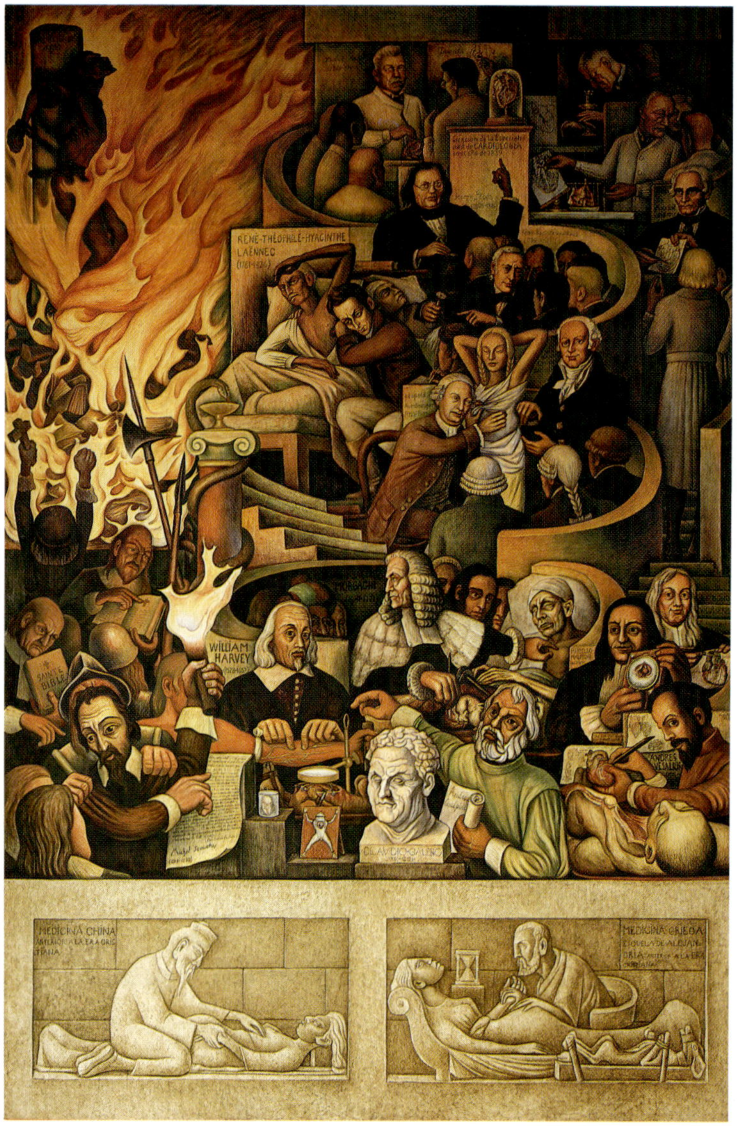
WILLIAM HARVEY
MEDICINA CHINA
MEDICINA GRIEGA

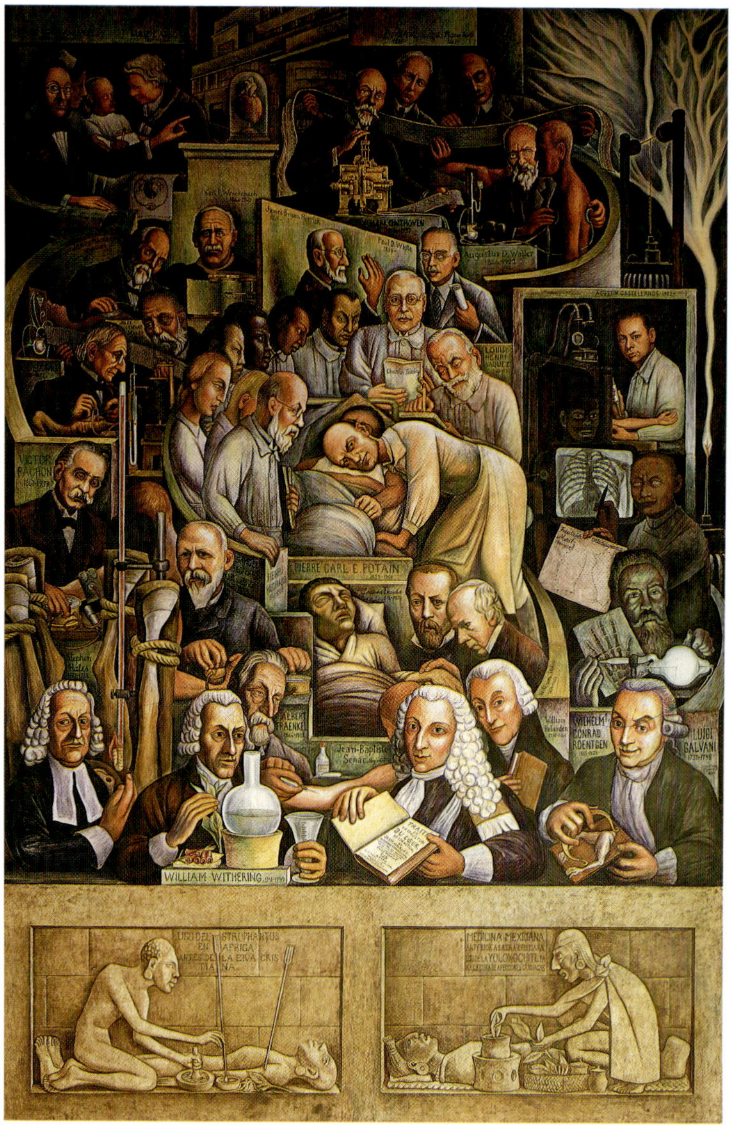
WILLIAM WITHERING
PIERRE CARL E. POTAIN
WILHELM CONRAD ROENTGEN
LUIGI GALVANI
MEDICINA MEXICANA

Instituto Nacional de Cardiología

Mexico City

Figure 402.
The History of Cardiology, 1943–1944, fresco, 6 × 4.05 m (each panel). Tlalpan, Universidad Ibero-Americana, Auditorium.

The murals Rivera painted for the Instituto Nacional de Cardiología present a "historical synthesis"[1] of the study of the human heart and its clinical care, from its beginnings in the pre-Christian era in China, Egypt, Greece, and Rome to the mid-20th century, by means of a kind of genealogical précis—a series of portraits of outstanding international contributors, past and present, to the development of this science. Each of the two vertical rectangular panels presents a "curtain" of bustlike portraits in which famous physicians associated with heart therapy are depicted in period dress, some appearing with attributes symbolic of their specialties. All are clearly identified by name and date. They are assembled in various groups according to discipline and arranged in an ascending order that is roughly chronological.

The composition of the panels—the portraits are arranged along and around a trellislike central structure like so many blossoms on a climbing plant—recalls the familiar family tree found in Victorian-era family albums. This is in distinct contrast to the type of narrative posters, usually showing scenes from the lives of little-known scientists, later popularized by the pharmaceutical industry. Rivera's only concession to a "story" in this illustrative sense is the scene of the execution of the Spanish anatomist and theologian Miguel Servet by fire—a reference to penalties faced by those who attempted to overcome superstition. In all other respects, Rivera's program was intended to remind the younger members of the medical profession of the legacy left to them by their forerunners in the field of cardiology.

Summary

Location: Tlalpan, near Mexico City, Universidad Ibero-Americana, Avenida Rio Churubusco

Site: Foyer of the auditorium in a multi-building complex, consisting of a hospital and research and training centers for advanced study in the treatment of heart disease. Originally commissioned for the Instituto Nacional de Cardiología, Mexico City, which is now part of the Centro Médico Nacional.

Theme/Subject: *The History of Cardiology*

Format: Two vertical rectangular panels

Date: 1943–44

Medium: True fresco on movable frames

Dimensions: 6 × 4.05 m each

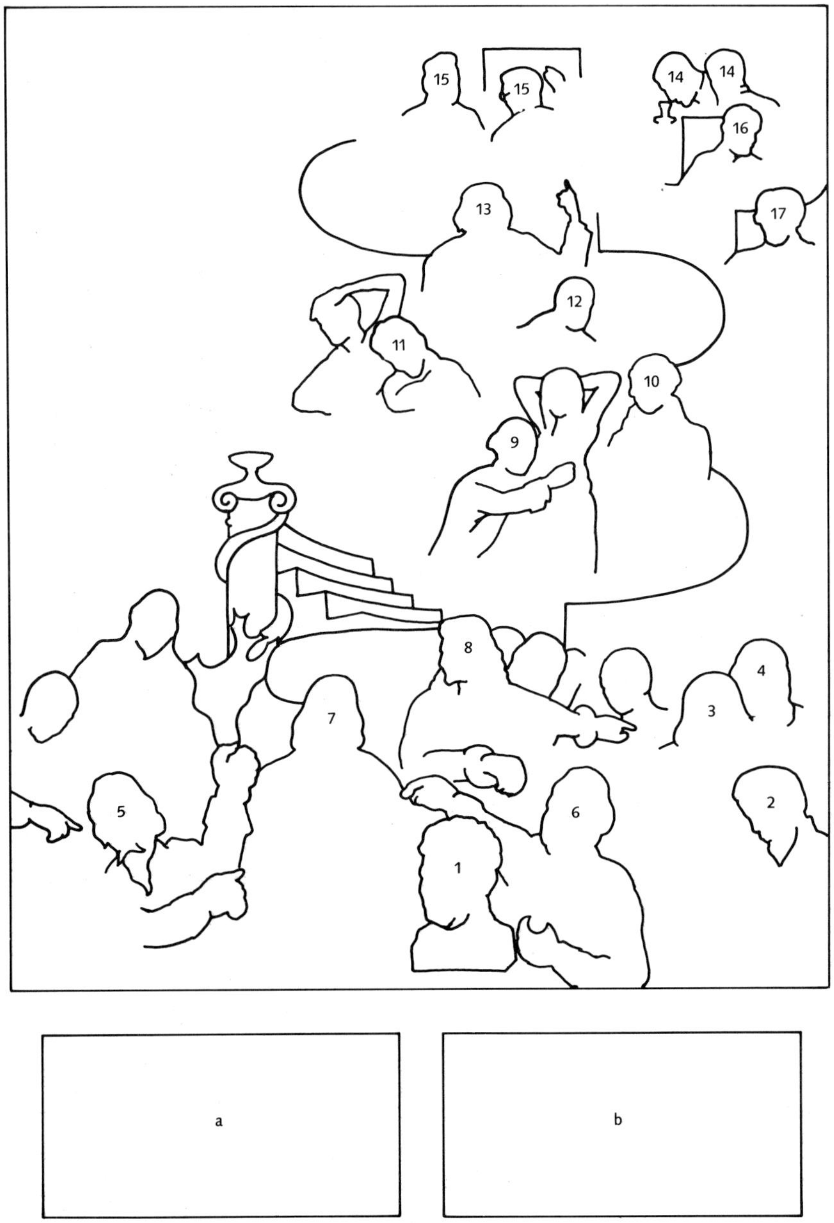

Instituto Nacional de Cardiología

I. Anatomists, Physiologists, Clinicians[2]

Ancient Forerunner

1. Claudio Galen (Greek, 131–201): first rudimentary heart descriptions and pulse studies[3]

Anatomists

2. Andres Vesalius (Belgian, 1514–64): first detailed description of heart structure
3. Marcello Malpighi (Italian, 1628–94): discovered capillary net of the lungs
4. Raymond Vieussens (French, 1641–1716): first description of coronary net

Physiologists

5. Michel Servet (Spanish, 1509–53): first to describe pulmonary circulation; sacrificed at the stake by order of John Calvin (see top left, fig. 402).
6. Andrea Cesalpini (Italian): described general circulation

Experimental Method

7. William Harvey (English, 1578–1657): demonstrated existence of blood circulation

Pathology

8. Giovanni-Battista Morgagni (Italian, 1681–1771): compared clinical signs in life with autopsy evidence

Methods of Exploratory Practice

9. Leopold Auenbrugger (Vienna School, 1722–1809): devised digital percussion
10. Jean Nicolas Corvisart (School of Paris, 1755–1821): made digital percussion a standard practice
11. René-Théophile-Hyacinthe Laënnec (French, 1781–1826): invented mediate auscultation and stethoscope; first describer of cardiac and friction murmurs; beginning of anatomo-clinical era

Clinicians and Teachers

12. Jean-Baptiste Bouillard (French, 1796–1881): classified lesions; described endocarditis and relation to rheumatism
13. Joseph Škoda (Czech, 1805–81): as professor in Vienna, interpreted heart sounds and created the speciality of cardiology

Micro- anatomists

14. Sir Arthur Keith (English, 1866–) and Flack: discovered node named after them
15. Ludwig Aschoff (German, 1866–1942) and Tawara (Japanese): discovered auriculo-ventricular node
16. Wilhelm His (German, 1863–1934): described "connecting bundle" that bears his name
17. Jan E. V. Purkynje (Czech, 1787–1869): first to describe network of heart muscle fibers named after him

Grisaille

a. *Medicine in China before the Christian Era*
b. *Medicine in Egypt before the Christian Era*

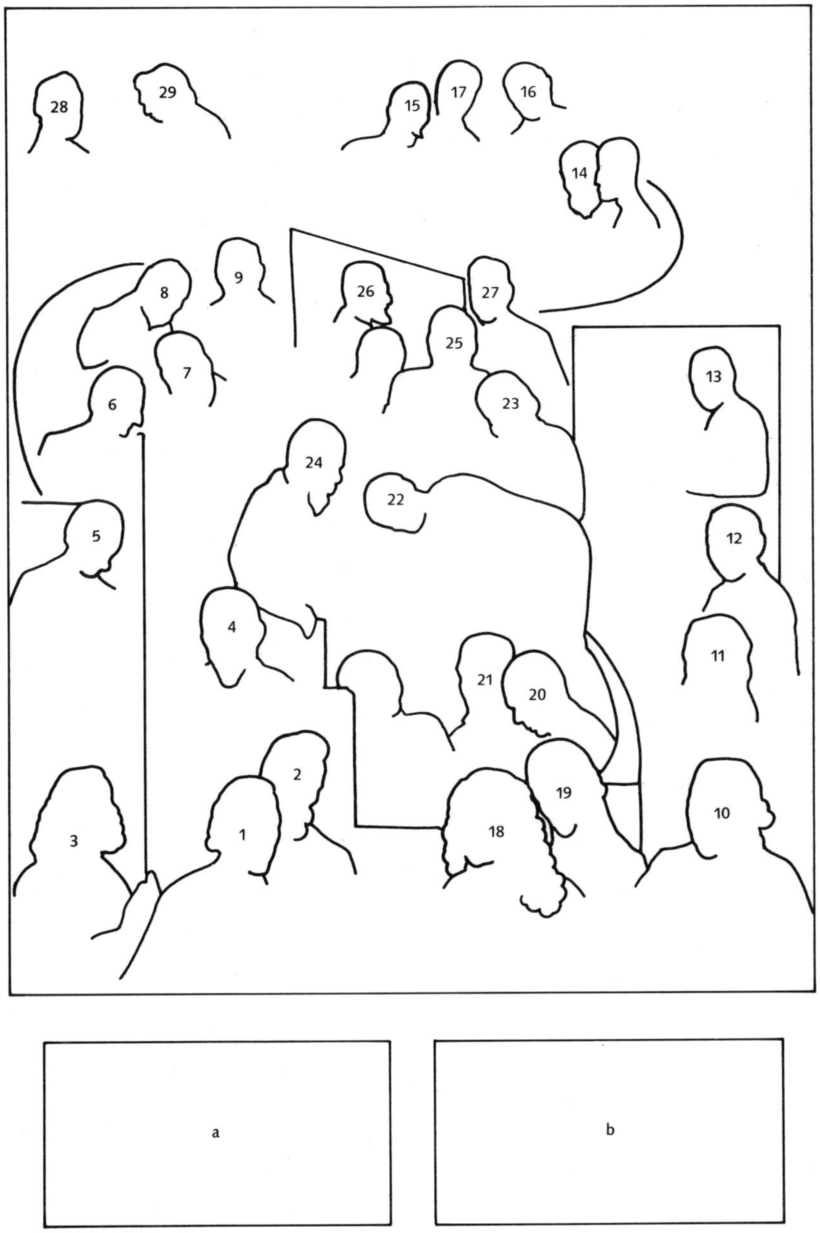

II. Investigators Using Instruments and Apparatus

Therapists

1. William Withering (English, 1741–99): introduced new way of using herbs
2. Albert Fraenckel (German, 1864–1938): used poisonous plant as lifesaving drug source

Experimenters

3. Stephen Hales (English, 1677–1761): first to measure blood pressure, by means of a piezimeter
4. Karl Von Basch (Austrian, 1837–1905): invented first sphygmomanometer, while in Mexico as Maximilian's physician
5. Victor Pachon (French, 1867–1939): invented oscillometric means of measuring blood pressure.

Students of Mechanism of Circulation

6. Carl Ludwig (German, 1816–95): recorded circulatory phenomena in animals
7. Jules Etienne Marey (College de France, 1830–1910): traced circulation in animals and man
8. Sir James MacKenzie (Scotch, 1853–1925): described auricular fibrillation by graphical method
9. Karl F. Wenckebach (Dutch, 1864–1940): developed records of arrhythmia and explanations of blockages

Conquerors of Electric Energy for Penetrating Heart Recesses

10. Luigi Galvani (Italian, 1737–98): discovered electric current in frog muscles
11. Wilhelm Conrad Roentgen (German, 1845–1923): discovered X-rays and measured cardiovascular image
12. Friedrich Moritz (German, 1861–1938): contributed orthodiagraphy for measuring heart and great vessels
13. Agustín Castellanos (Cuban, 1902–): developed living heart opaquing to allow study of congenital malformation

Tracing of Heart Activity through Electrical Means

14. Augustus D. Waller (English, 1856–1922): first electrocardiogram of man
15. Willem Einthoven (Dutch, 1856–1927): first "string galvanometer"
16. Sir Thomas Lewis (English, 1882–): applied electrocardiography to clinical medicine
17. Frank N. Wilson (American, 1890–): developed scientific electrocardiography and concept of the "unipolar" precordial leads

Semeiologists and Clinicians, Men of "Chaste Observation"

18. Jean Baptiste Senac (French, 1693–1770): first systematic treatise on cardiology; contributions on arrhythmias and venous pulse
19. William Heberden (English, 1710–1801): description of angina pectoris
20. William Stokes (Irish, 1804–78): studies of dyspnea (shortness of breath) and other symptoms of heart block
21. Ludwig Traube (German, 1818–76): discovered alternation of pulse and diagnosed arterial hypertension

Clinicians of the French and Anglo-Saxon Schools

22. Pierre Carl Potain (French, Hôpital de la Charité, Paris, 1825–1901): identified gallop rhythms, anorganic murmurs, tricuspid insufficiency, hepatic pulse; Potain's disciples and followers:
23. Louis Henri Vaquez (1860–1936): Potain's professional heir; introduced ouabain into therapy
24. Henri Huchard (1844–1910): discovered relation between angina pectoris and coronary pain
25. Charles Laubry (French): Leader of French cardiological school
26. James Byran Herrick (American, 1861–): studied coronary occlusion and myocardial infarction
27. Paul D. White (American, 1886–): diffusion of American doctrines; White syndrome

Congenital Malformations

28. Carl Rokitansky (Czech, 1804–78): first profound studies of congenital problems
29. Maude Abbott (Canadian, 1869–1940): differentiated and classified formerly obscure mass in congenital patients

Grisailles

a. *Use of the Herbal Cardiac Stimulant Strophanthin in Africa before the Christian Era*
b. *Use of Yoloxochitl for the Cure of "Afliciones Camacas" in Mexico before the Christian Era*

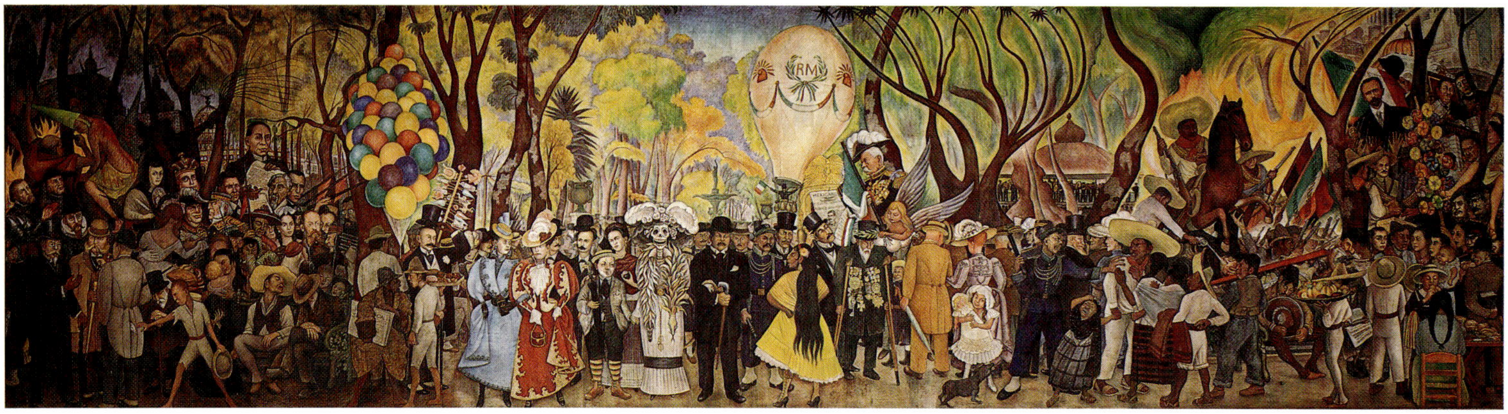
RM

Hotel del Prado

Mexico City

Figure 403.
Dream of a Sunday Afternoon in the Alameda, 1947–48, fresco, 4.8 × 15 m. Mexico City, Hotel del Prado.

Rivera's impressive mural for the Hotel del Prado presents a summation of Mexican history and the artist's personal involvement in it as an uninterrupted stream of reflective consciousness. It is a kind of valedictory in which Rivera reviews his experience as a Mexican artist and his humanist social credo. It is the least systematically doctrinaire work among his major mural programs and the most autobiographical.

This extremely horizontal composition—its width is a little over four times its height – is subtly divided into three more or less equal parts from left to right and three horizontal planes of depth. The historical narrative moves chronologically across the full width of the mural from a tiered assembly of colonial and early 19th-century events and characters on the left through a single rank of late 19th-century full-length figures at the center of the composition and on to another broad tier of early 20th-century figures and activities on the right. The autobiographical nature of the theme is given emphasis, but without diminishing the presence of any other part of the composition, by the placement of the artist as a young boy, next to and held in hand by an ostentatiously dressed lady of fashion (José Guadalupe Posada's celebrated burlesque of vanity—the *calavera,* or cartoon skeleton of the symbolically named "Dead Catrina"), near but not precisely at the center of the composition. The focusing of interest at this central point is subtly reinforced by the downward sloping arc created by the overhead tree branches, toy balloons, building profiles, and flames of revolution at right. Although the figures face the observer as a theatrical mise-en-scène, the sense of the assemblage promenading, or being seen on promenade, is ever present. Any avalanching effect of a massed procession is, however, absent. This dispersal, together with the equal implausibility of presenting such a historical progression seemingly at one moment in time, contributes to the work's aura of illusion or fantasy, especially when the wall in its present setting is lit while the rest of the room remains dark.

The progression of past events and personalities repeats the chronological method and dialectical treatment that Rivera used in his historical murals from the Palacio Nacional onward. However, in the del Prado mural, there is a variation that recalls but goes beyond the confused battlefield of the Conquest that makes up the lower register of the main wall of the Palacio Nacional stairway mural. It consists in an immediate foreground row of full-length figures that intervenes between the viewer and the middleground historical procession and that keeps present time constantly in mind (i.e., the present that is contemporary with Rivera's youth as he portrays himself in the center of the composition). Along the full length of the mural's foreground, everyday Mexicans of the lower classes during the Díaz era are depicted as abandoned or outcast in continuous counterpoint to their class-conscious superiors immediately above. Rivera's daughter has said that these are scenes that Rivera witnessed as a young boy in Mexico city and that influenced his outlook on life and society in general.[1]

The artist's aim seems clearly to be to underscore the causal relationship between the strict and unbridgeable division of Mexican society into classes, inherited from the colonial past, and the rebellion of the Mexican people against inhuman social and economic conditions and the suppression of dissent, which led to the 1910 Revolution. This back-and-forth sequence of interacting motifs is first massed to the top of the upper left side of the composition, descends to the midpoint of the wall, and then rises again toward the right along the line of the arc separating middleground from background. Into this sequence in the front plane are subtly woven the specifics of the artist's childhood memories of his Sunday visits to Alameda Park: the urchin pickpocket, the hustling newsboy, the old people lost in the memory of their past, the flamboyant ladies of fashion (a satiric reference to the stylish wife of the dictator, Carmen Romero Rubio de Díaz, and perhaps also to her imagined companion, Rivera's own aunt, the imposing Tanta Vicenta), the fruit and tortilla vendors, the taunting prostitute, the brutish policeman ejecting the Indian peon and his family, their knife-pulling companion, the *esquincle* dog, defiantly snarling at the cop.[2] That these are personal memories is evident by the artist's presence in a self-portrait as a youth, dressed in short trousers and straw hat with a frog and snake in his pocket. José Guadalupe Posada, the printmaker who invented thousands of images castigating the foibles of late Porfirian society is given the position closest to midpoint in the design—Rivera's ultimate testimony to his indebtedness to this popular artist. Behind this group, Rivera's wife, Frida Kahlo, holds the Chinese spherical symbol of infinity, with its sign of the yin and the yang. To the far right, his whole family by his first Mexican wife, Lupe Marín, appears, thereby bringing out the strong family sentiment that informs this summary reflection on his life.

There are four background portraits that are larger than life-size: those of Juárez, Díaz, Zapata, and Madero. They are part of, but placed above, the curving line of the middleground progression of historical figures. They may be thought of as transcendant figures in the evolution of the artist's intellectual comprehension of the national issues of his time as well as landmarks in the development of Mexico's ideology.

Supplementing these figures in the body of the congregation are portraits of José Martí, the 19th-century spokesman for Cuban independence, and Ignacio Ramírez, the 19th-century scholar and champion of the separation of church and state, who dared to declare "God does not exist" in a lecture at Mexico City's Letrán Academy in 1836. The latter originally held a placard with this slogan, which at the time of the mural's creation caused a great outcry, particularly from Catholic students, who defaced parts of the fresco and stoned Rivera's house, causing the mural to be shielded from public view by a screen for eight years. In the end Rivera removed the heretical words, leaving on the date and the place of Ramírez's declaration.[3]

The principle of visual and thematic counterpoint, which first appeared in the stairway scenes at the Secretaría de Educación Pública and soon thereafter reached a high point in the chapel at Chapingo, attains a subtle and intricate plane of refinement, fraught with social and political meaning, in the del Prado mural. Four interlaced thematic lines traverse the elongated composition from left to right: the primary historical figures from colonial times through the Revolution at the top level; figures symbolizing the constituencies that supported these leaders below them; the historical personalities who contributed to the formation of national consciousness and saw the moral value of social responsibility next; and finally, at the bottom level, the fundamental world of Mexican, and by ideological extension all human, society—figures manifesting the common condition of the poor, the outcast, and the exploited, and the general populace, shown as a *lumpen* proletariat.

Summary

Location: Mexico City, Avenida Juárez 70

Site: Hotel del Prado

Theme/Subject: *Dream of a Sunday Afternoon in the Alameda (El sueño de una trade dominical en la alameda central)*

Format: A single rectangular area, which presents a sequence of images in extended continuous time that flows from left to right in the manner of a Chinese scroll

Date: 1947–48

Medium: Fresco

Dimensions: 4.8 × 15 m[4]

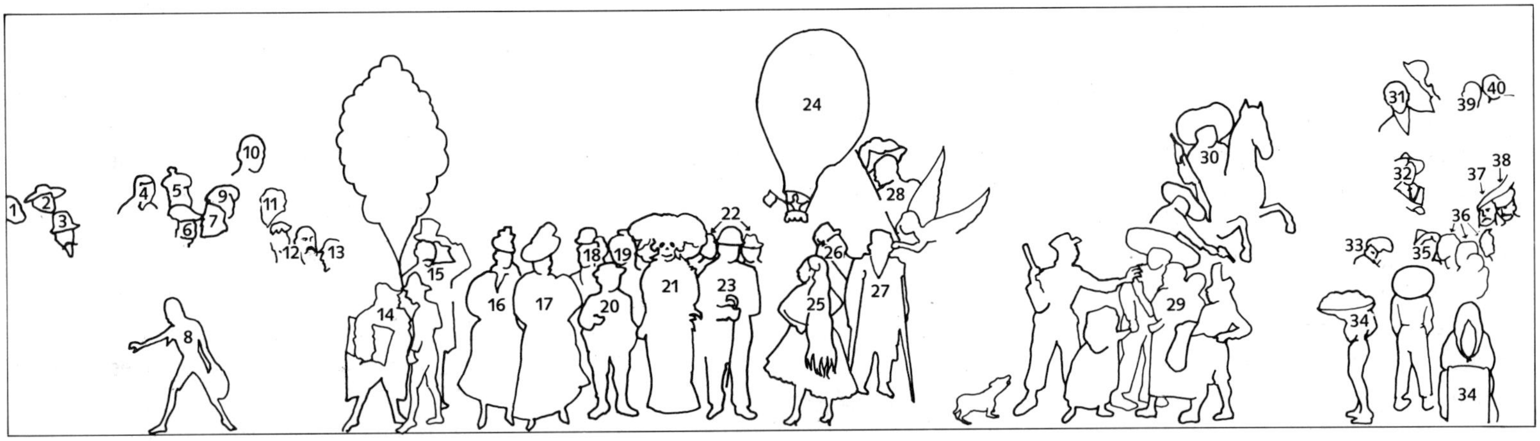

Hotel del Prado

Conquerors, Invading Military Commanders, and Heads of State

Hernan Cortés, conqueror of Mexico (1)
Luís de Velasco, viceroy of Mexico, 1550–64 (3)
Agustín de Iturbide, emperor of Mexico, 1822–23 (5)
Antonio Lopéz de Santa Anna, general and politician, eleven times president of Mexico, 1833–55 (6)
Winfield Scott, American general whose troops occupied Mexico City during the war between Mexico and the U.S., 1846–48 (7)
Benito Júarez, liberal leader and president during the Reform, 1855–72 (10)
Carlotta and Maximilian of Hapsburg, empress and emperor of Mexico, 1864–67 (12)
Porfirio Díaz, president of Mexico, 1876–80 and 1884–1911 (27)
Francisco I. Madero, president of Mexico, 1911–13 (30)
Plutarco Elías Calles, president of Mexico, 1924–28 (38)

Powerful Figures Representing Various Constituencies

Juan de Zumárraga, first bishop of Mexico (2)
Sor Juana Inés de la Cruz (1651–95), poetess and early exponent of women's rights (4)[5]
Achille François Bazine, commander of French army of occupation (13)
Manuel Gutíerrez Nájera, author of Parnassian poetry, tales, and realistic chronicles, founder of the journal *Revista azul* (15)
Tanta Vicenta, Rivera's aunt, who sympathized with the mores of the Porfirian establishment (16)
Carmen Romero Rubio de Díaz, fashionable wife of Porfirio Díaz (17)
Nicolas Zuñiga y Miranda, sham opponent to Díaz in presidential elections (26)
"Lobo" Guerrero, a Mexican hero of the War of French Intervention (27)
Victoriano Huerta, general who turned against, assassinated, and briefly succeeded Madero (31 above) (37)
Manuel Mondragón, general who in league with Huerta, led federal forces against Madero (38)
Luís Martínez Rodríguez, archbishop of Mexico, d. 1956 (40)

Influences in the Formation of Independent Mexico's Social Consciousness

Ignacio Altamirano (1834–95), novelist and radical member of congress (9)
Ignacio Ramírez, 19th-century scholar who declared in a lecture at the Letrán Academy that "God does not exist" (11)
José Martí, father of Cuban independence (18)
Frida Kahlo, artist, wife of Rivera (19)
Diego Rivera (20)
Calavera Catrina (21)
The Brothers Flores Magón, publishers of *Regeneración*, a liberal anti–Díaz weekly, and leaders of the Revolution in Baja California (22)
José Guadalupe Posada, artist who caricatured the political and social foibles of the Porfirian era (23)
Joaquin de Cantolla, disciple of the Montgolfier brothers, first man to go up in a hot-air balloon in Mexico (24)
Emiliano Zapata, leader of the agrarian Revolution in Morelos (30)
General Francisco Múgica, one of the framers of the 1817 Constitution (32)
José Vasconcelos, minister of education under President Alvaro Obregón and official patron of Mexican muralists (33)
Manuel Martinez, Rivera's assistant (35)
Rivera's family, his first Mexican wife Lupe Marín and their daughters (36)

Members of Proletarian Underclass during Porfiriato

Pickpocket (8)
Newsboy (14)
La Lupe, a notorious prostitute (25)
Peon and family, being ejected from the Alameda (29)
Vendors of fruit and tortillas (34)

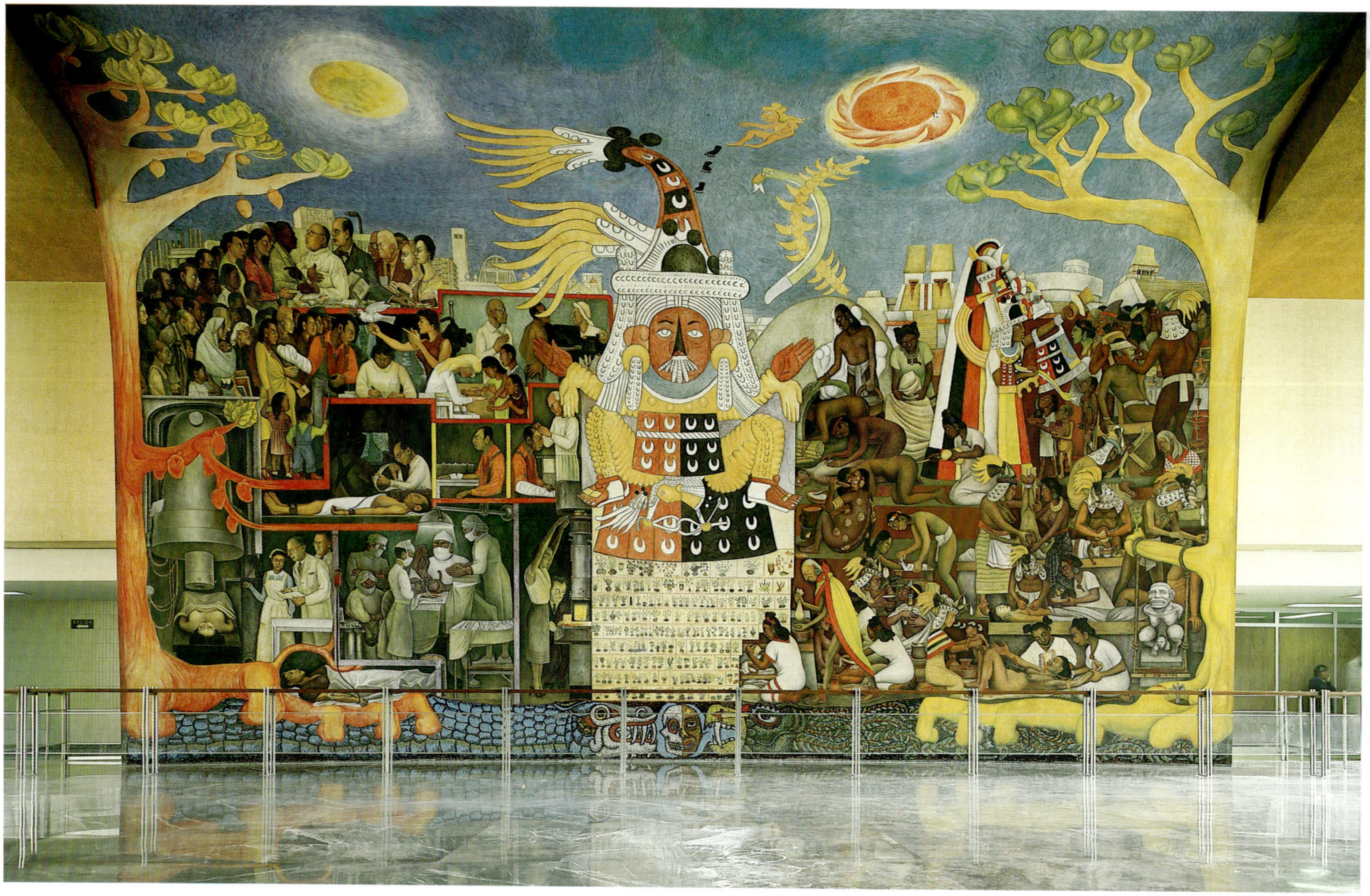

Hospital de la Raza

Mexico City

Figure 404.
The History of Medicine in Mexico: The People's Demand for Better Health, **1953, fresco, approx. 7.4 × 10.8 m. Mexico City, Hospital de la Raza.**

Rivera's mural for the Hospital de la Raza, the foremost national hospital dedicated to the care of Mexico's indigenous population, is a visual homily and celebration of medical science, newly organized as an up-to-date and cost-free service to the Mexican people. The artist divided his theme into two parts: on the one hand, recounting ethnological aspects of native medical history—the methods of pre-Colombian religion, its treatment of disease, curative practices, and the kinds and uses of ancient medicaments—and on the other, presenting scenes of modern medical science and technology, in which members of the Mexican medical profession, from distinguished physicians to hospital assistants, are honored by portraits showing them on the job in working dress.

The dominant motif of this mural is the figure of Tlazoltéotl, or Ixcuina, "goddess of repulsive things," one of the major deities of the earth in the Aztec pantheon.[1] Her purview is removal of, not attachment to, filth, as well as, in some interpretations, the guardianship of childbirth. The two-dimensional figure of the goddess dominates the center of the principal composition, which is flanked by two treelike forms at the junctions of the main wall with the two side-wall extensions. These towering blood red stems, which can be seen as great "arteries," form a massive "vascular" frame for the main wall, which in turn is organized in three parts both horizontally and vertically. In the center, below Tlazoltéotl, is a painted tablet on which eighty-four varieties of medicinal plants are assembled as though lifted from an illustrated herbarium and pasted in place. Their names are given in Náhuatl. Beneath this, at the lowest level a life/death mask is flanked by two serpents, their bodies forming undulating mosaic strips that extend along the base of the composition. In the center sky are peregrination footprints, while to the right and left the sun and moon, with vague features, are poised in the heavens.

To the right are depicted in realistic detail pre-Colombian medical practices in childbirth, vascular and orthopedic surgery, and other curative activities. Surmounting these scenes is a tall, grandly attired figure identified by Crespo de la Serna as the goddess Izcuitl and shown as intercessor for the people's medical concerns.[2] To the left, the instruments and technologies of modern medicine are being applied for the same socially beneficial purposes. The changeover from private to public medicine in Mexico is commemorated by two facing groups of contemporary figures at the top of this section, where the poor, aged, and afflicted are informed by a physician and an official that they no longer need to pay for their treatment. Behind these representatives of the state's protection are the former profit-takers of private medicine, rebuffed and sour-faced.

The figure of Tlazoltéotl is taken directly from a facsimile of an early 16th-century pictorial manuscript, the Codex Borbonicus, now in the Bibliothèque de l'Assemblée National, Paris. The codex shows her with her typical attributes: cotton headdress and ear pendants, flayed human skin as a covering, and blackened nose and mouth. Her central position in the composition is in keeping with Rivera's habit of using human images as axial motifs in many of his other murals. The special prominence given here to an Aztec deity, in a literal transcription of the indigenous pictorial style, reinforced by an itemized graphic catalogue of native plant specimens used for ancient medicinal purposes, is indicative of a new kind of emphasis on native roots in Rivera's art, which invites explanation in the context of contemporary (now historical) events.

Beginning in 1946, the first year of the six-year presidency of Miguel Alemán, Mexico was led vigorously in the direction of full development as a modern nation. Emphasis was placed on rapidly expanding the use of the country's physical resources and the transformation of its economy, following Western capitalist forms of material and cultural progress. In the capital city, transportation and communications networks (surface arteries, subway and telephone systems) were introduced or improved, suburban areas developed, and public services and various social institutions established, including art and archaeological museums and agencies for the conservation of Mexico's cultural heritage. This internationalizing trend brought with it a reversal of the long-held prejudice against Mexico's Spanish colonial tradition in art and architecture. It also marked the beginning of the controversy between indigenism and modernism in art that saw the introduction, despite strong official opposition, of the international modernist interpretation of Mexican values, when Rufino Tamayo was invited to paint a mural in the Palacio Nacional de Bellas Artes in his semiabstract style.

Rivera took no public stand against these developments. But considering his career and political credo, he could not have been sympathetic, ideologically or artistically, to this turn of affairs. As the international modernizing trend developed, it seems altogether probable that he dug in his heels and insistently continued to uphold his traditional indigenist, popular, and anti-capitalist social-revolutionary point of view. This is borne out by his last, stridently anti-imperialist murals, which he put on display in Paris and Tokyo, and his recantation of his past anti-orthodox positions vis-à-vis the Communist Party in order to be reaccepted into the fold of the Soviet-based revolutionary community and the graces of the post-Stalinist order. The archaeologically exact figure of Tlazoltéotl in the Hospital de la Raza mural, made as this new trend gained headway in Mexico, is the sign of his perseverance and loyalty to the old ideals of the Mexican Revolution, as he had defined and committed himself to them thirty years before.

Summary

Location: Mexico City, Calzada del Norte in the Colonia Francisco Villa, intersection of Avenida Rio Consulado and Avenida Insurgentes Norte

Site: Foyer above the main entrance stairway of the Hospital de la Raza, completed in 1953

Theme/Subject: *The History of Medicine in Mexico: The People's Demand for Better Health*[3]

Format: A projecting concave wall, facing the stairway, that rolls gently upward and outward over the foyer floor in a parabolic curve. The main surface is extended by side walls that fold backward at the sides.[4]

Date: Signed and dated, November 30, 1953, on right side extension

Medium: True fresco

Dimensions: Height at center: Approx. 7.4 m
Width of frontal area at floor level: Approx. 10.8 m
Width of side extensions at floor level: 1.1 m

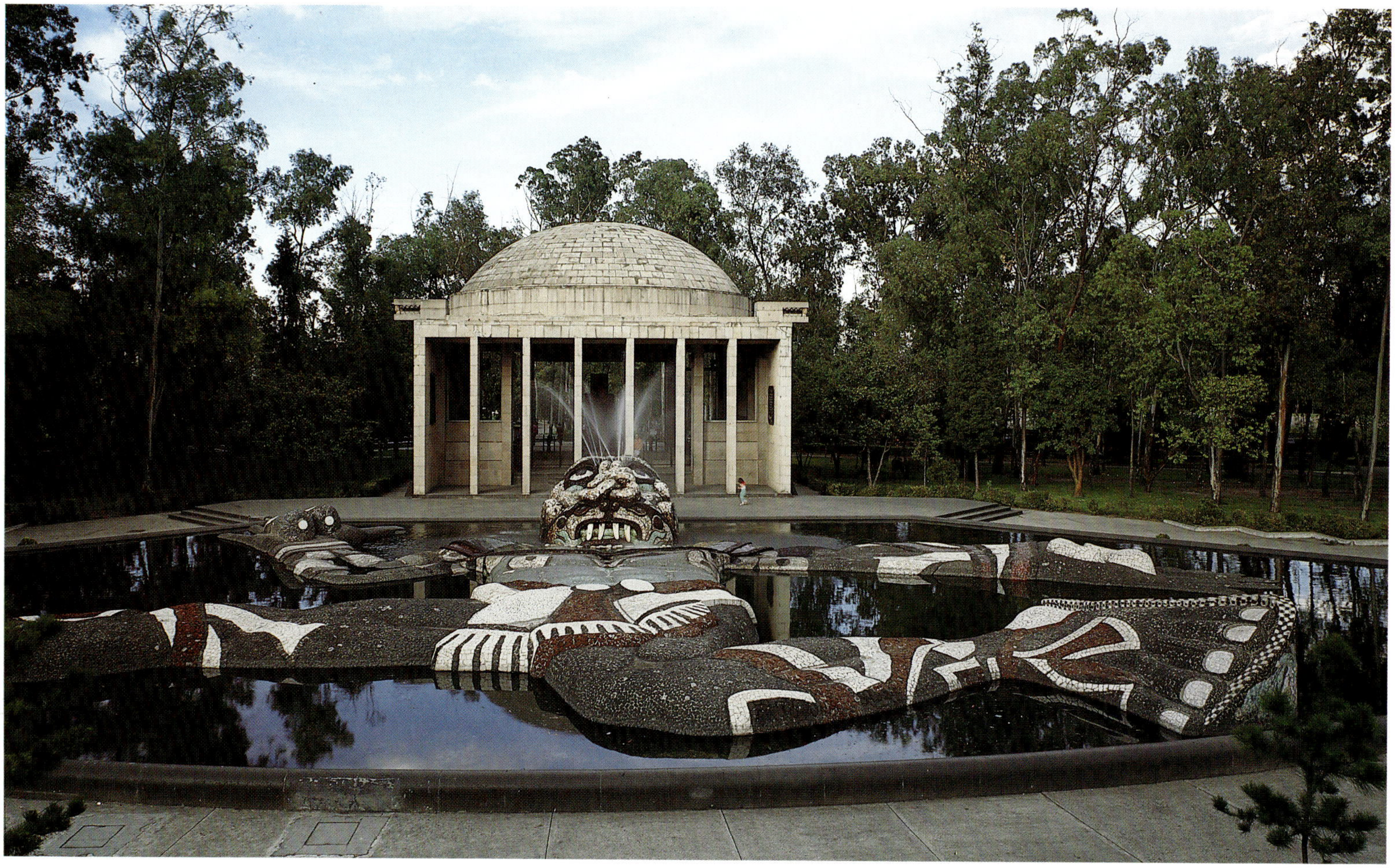

Cárcamo del Río Lerma

Mexico City

Figure 405. Exterior water basin showing Tlaloc, the rain god. Mexico City, Cárcamo del Río Lerma.

The Cárcamo del Río Lerma (Lerma waterworks) is a water distribution system that taps the underground mountain sources of the Lerma River system as it nears the Valley of Mexico to provide water for the fashionable Polanco district of Mexico City. It was begun in 1943 and finished in 1951. Through the cooperation of government authorities, the architect, the engineers, and the artist, the building and its surroundings were constructed to serve not only city water distribution but also educational and artistic functions.

The theme of Rivera's program at the Lerma waterworks is the legacy of water to the human race, its uses by mankind around the world, its primary role in the origin and evolution of life, and its association with deity in ancient Mexican religion and modern popular fantasy. It is divided into two parts: murals that cover the floor and walls of an open cistern within a pavilion and an expansive earth sculpture in the exterior water basin.

The design (no longer visible) on the floor of the cistern emulated the actual flow of Lerma River water as it enters the cistern, through an arched opening in one of its walls, from an underground aqueduct. The design was centered in the painted design of a circular pool that showed many smaller forms of aquatic life from amoebae and starfish to primitive crustaceans as evidence of the beginnings of life. Viewed from above, the painted water appeared to be rhythmically gushing from the giant providential hands, cupped in beneficence, on the wall of the cistern. Still visible on the walls to the right and left are depictions of more advanced forms of water life, which culminate above the waterline in the heads and torsos of two human figures, one representing the African race, the other the Asiatic. The figures, which face each other, are framed by undulant wave forms, representing the water to which, implicitly, they owe their origin. On the wall facing the water inflow are twenty-four portraits of the projects's engineers, directors, planners, and workers, including those who died constructing it.

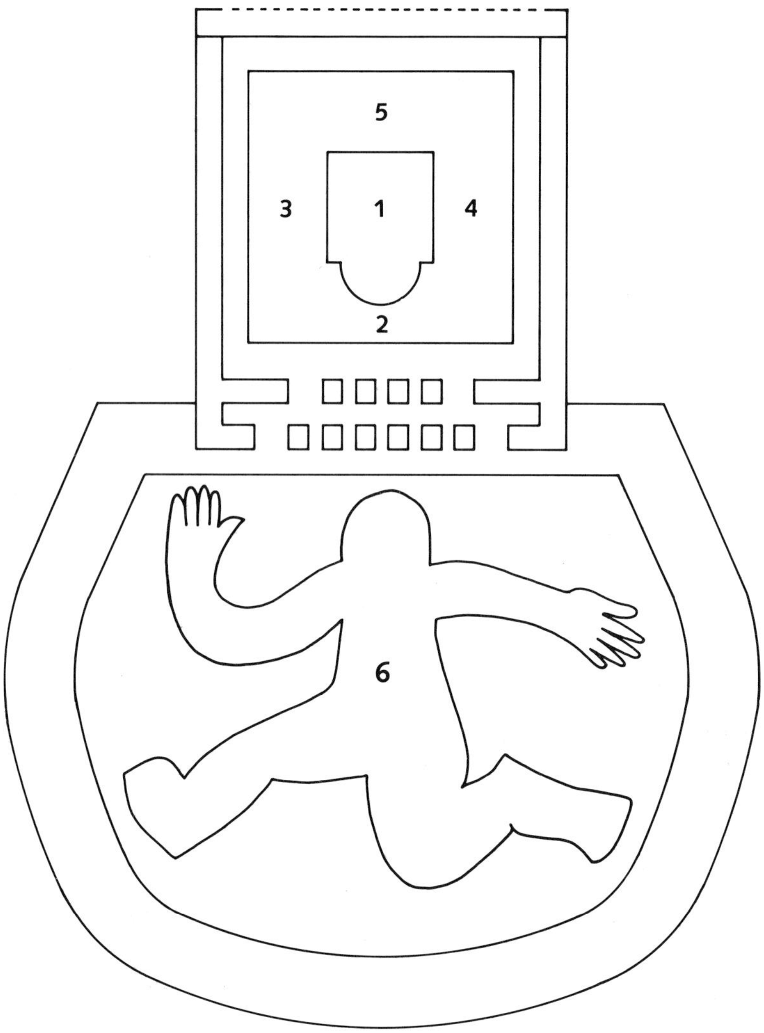

Cárcamo del Río Lerma

1. Water, the Source of Life
2. Beneficent Hands of Nature Bestow the Gift of Water
3. Figure Symbolizing the Asiatic Race
4. Figure Symbolizing the African Race
5. Engineers and Planners of Cárcamo del Río Lerma
6. The Rain God, Tláloc

The crowded commemorative wall is essentially a separate composition that follows the traditional portrayal of the Last Supper. The members of the group, all in work clothes, stand on one side of a long table examining a blueprint. The pictorial treatment of the other wall surfaces is, at the floor level and in the lower side-wall areas, an uninterrupted, closely woven texture of organic forms expressive of the fluid continuum of water and water motion. Halfway up, as the scene emerges into open air, the composition merges into a series of scenes depicting nonaquatic man's dependency on water. These show people of various origins and stations at work, at play, and under the duress of water deprivation.

The mosaic earth sculpture depicting the striding figure of Tláloc in the water basin can only be observed at ground level. The resulting extreme foreshortening gives undue prominence to the huge limbs from the roadside approach and to the two-faced head as one circles toward the pavilion. One may presume that the sculpture was conceived metaphorically as a symbolic intermediary between man and the supernatural forces of the sky that have the power to provide water as a gift to all living creatures. The color of the dress and the features of the god are predominantly black and brown, highlighted by white dividing lines, white and black fret-and-checkerboard designs, and piquant accents of turquoise at the eyes and other points of dress and ornament.

The date of this astonishingly unconventional, indeed for its time almost preposterous, work, which was born out of native Mexican fantasy and the artist's popular sympathies, might seem to put it among the very first of the 20th-century American earth sculptures. However, in all probability it would not be accepted as part of, or even seen as anticipating, this recent North American movement by the British and American critics who have elaborated its precepts. The Tláloc figure has been called, instead, "no more than low relief flopped on its back."[1] The fact cannot be denied, however, that Rivera is probably one of the first artists—Siqueiros's use of massive relief forms turned vertically onto the walls of the Universidad Autónoma de Mexico occurred at about the same time—to return to an inherited tradition of earth forms with any sense of belonging to it, that is, from inside his own tradition rather than acquiring it by adoption from the outside.[2] Rivera's work in this genre, geographically and culturally, is in a direct line of descendance from its pre-Colombian sources, however long this influence may have been carried "underground."

In the three decades since the murals were completed, the chemicals of the water purification process have taken a ruinous toll, an ironic fate for one of Rivera's final works on the theme of man's relation to the forces of nature. (He was quoted in *Life* magazine as saying the experimental polystyrene used as the medium for the frescoes would never be eroded.) In this author's opinion, the fearsome visage of Tláloc, which from inside the pavilion appears to loom over the offering hands, has the ring of exhortation, of a call to human onlookers and the beneficiaries of this gift to awaken to the generosity of nature and of life's natural heritage.

Summary

Location: Mexico City, western border of Chapultepec Park

Site: A domed pavilion facing a man-made water basin to the west and the forested park to the east, which is part of Mexico City's water-distribution system (Ricardo Rivas, architect)[3]

Theme/Subject: *Water, the Source of Life*

Format: An environmental work consisting of two parts: (1) frescoes on the floor and four walls of an open cistern and (2) an earth sculpture in colored-rock mosaic in the adjoining water basin

Date: 1951

Medium: True fresco (cistern); rough stone mosaic (earth sculptures)

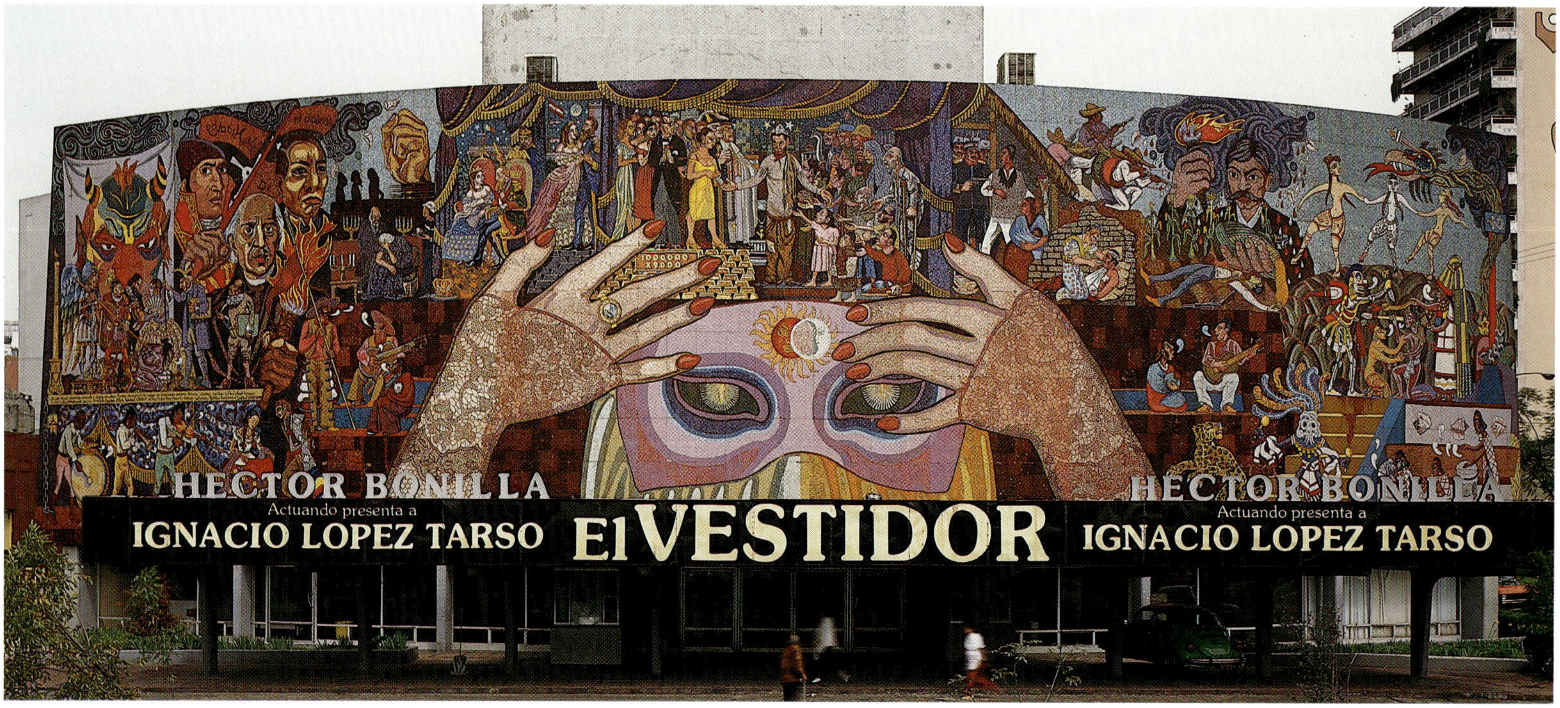
HECTOR BONILLA
Actuando presenta a
IGNACIO LOPEZ TARSO
El VESTIDOR
HECTOR BONILLA
Actuando presenta a
IGNACIO LOPEZ TARSO

Teatro de los Insurgentes

Mexico City

Figure 406.
***A Popular History of Mexico*, 1953, mosaic, 12.85 × 42.79 m. Mexico City, Teatro de los Insurgents.**

Rivera's mosaic façade for the Teatro de los Insurgentes is probably the first major work conceived in his latter-day "pop" style. It evolved without too great a jump from the often grotesquely caricatured figures in his earlier murals (e.g., the "corridos" at the Secretaría de Educación Pública and in the chapel [diag. b] at Chapingo). However, its humor and festive spirit come from the funny papers rather than political cartooning, from his great liking for "the 'comic' sheets so beloved by the masses."[1] Rivera's enthusiastic identification with and elaboration of the Mexican popular imagination and love of buffoonery is in distinct contrast to the ironic attitude toward commercial clichés that was the impetus for the pop-art movement in England and the United States, which began about the same time.

The mural is a "popular" history of Mexico from Cortés to Cantinflas, which elaborates on revolutionary figures and traditions through raucous, vividly colored caricatures, in which the rich are confronted by the poor, and Aztec rituals are juxtaposed with Christian religious symbols, all in keeping with the boisterous, irreverent spirit of Mexican popular humor. This spirit is further enhanced by the use of mosaic, which glitters in the sunlight and lends a dancing effect to everything depicted.

A three-part montage of foreground and background scenes on a single plane, the mural is dominated at the center by the huge seductive hands and star-struck eyes of an exotic masked woman, who has a sun-and-moon mating symbol, the Hindu mark of karma, on her forehead. To her left are scenes of oppression under the Spanish conquerors, who are in turn confronted by the stern-faced fathers of Mexican Independence and the Reform movement. To her right, the old Aztec religious rites and the continuing popular impulse to follow them appear as a bawdy chorus-line skit. This scene is presided over by the more sympathetic visage of the modern revolutionary leader Emiliano Zapata. Centered over the brow of the hands-and-visage symbol of alluring femininity is the figure of the actor Cantinflas, the inimitable bumbling tramp, universally adored by the common people of Mexico. Here, in the role of a Mexican Robin Hood, he takes from the rich to give to the poor and destitute.

Church authorities took exception to Rivera's treatment of Cantinflas, which they felt implied their complicity in taking money from the poor, an issue often raised in the artist's murals and one with wide ramifications and causal importance in Mexico's revolutionary history. In this particular case, Rivera may have seen his critical treatment of the church's role as being the last word in his longstanding confrontation with the archbishop of Mexico over the latter's strenuous objection to the lettered-in quotation "God does not exist" in the Hotel del Prado mural.[2]

Summary

Location: Mexico City, Avenida de los Insurgentes, south of Ciudad de los Deportes

Site: The façade of a motion picture theater, whose entrance faces east-southeast, on one of the city's busiest thoroughfares, near Sport City and the former bullring

Theme/Subject: *A Popular History of Mexico (Historia popular de México)*

Format: A wide, rectangular, slightly convex façade that overlooks a broad area of the street from above and behind an almost equally wide marquee

Date: 1953; signed "Invented, composed and directed by Diego Rivera and worked on by a team of his comrade painters. . . ."[3]

Medium: Mosaic

Dimensions: Approx 12.85 × 42.79 m

Movable Frescoes and Other Large-scale Public Works

Rivera seems to have first employed the idea of movable fresco panels in 1931, when he made several large "hanging" frescoes for his one-man exhibition at the Museum of Modern Art. He was invited to paint seven such works, of which at least three, all Mexican subjects, were included in the display when it opened on December 23, 1931.[1] He devised a technique in which composition board was placed on a skeleton of wood, then overlaid with a coat of concrete (consisting of cement, goats' hair, marble dust, and lime). Before the concrete dried, a wire-mesh grid was placed over the entire surface of the panel, into which it would sink to about half its depth, and the whole allowed to set. Once the panel was dry, it received a first coat of plaster preparatory to the completion of the fresco process. The finished panels were generally mounted in braced steel frames. He next used the technique in his panels for the New Workers School in 1933, and from then until the end of his career, almost all of his frescoes were painted on movable steel frameworks.

The following eight works were created before and during Rivera's stay in New York on the occasion of the Museum of Modern Art exhibition (numbers 1, 3, and 4 were the three exhibited):

1. *Agrarian Leader Zapata,* 1931, fresco, 2.38 × 1.88 m. New York, The Museum of Modern Art, Abby Aldrich Rockefeller Fund (1631.40) (see fig. 334). Variant of the theme *Revolt* (VIII), Palacio de Cortés, Cuernavaca.

2. *Indian Fighting,* 1931, fresco, 1.04 × 1.33 m. Present location unknown.

3. *Liberation of the Peon,* 1931, fresco, 1.88 × 2.38 m. The Philadelphia Museum of Art. Variant of panel of the same name (SEP I, 15), Secretaría de Educación Pública, Mexico City (see fig. 158).

4. *Sugar Cane,* 1931, fresco, 1.45 × 2.39 m. The Philadelphia Museum of Art. Variant of the theme *Sugar Plantation in Morelos* (VI), Palacio de Cortés, Cuernavaca.

5. *The Uprising (Soldiers and Workers)* 1931, fresco, 1.04 × 1.33 m. Collection of Mr. and Mrs. Marcos Micha Levy.

6. *Electric Welding,* 1931, fresco, 1.42 × 2.39 m. Collection of Mr. and Mrs. Marcos Micha Levy (see fig. 265).

7. *Frozen Assets,* 1931, fresco, 2.39 × 1.88 m. Collection of Dolores Olmedo (see fig. 264).

8. *Pneumatic Drilling,* 1931, fresco, 2.39 × 1.88 m. Sotheby Parke Bernet sale, May 26, 1977. Present location unknown.

In 1930–33, Rivera painted two panels based on his frescoes for the Palacio de Cortés, Cuernavaca:

9. *Market Scene,* 1930, fresco, 1.25 × .99 m. Northampton, Massachusetts,

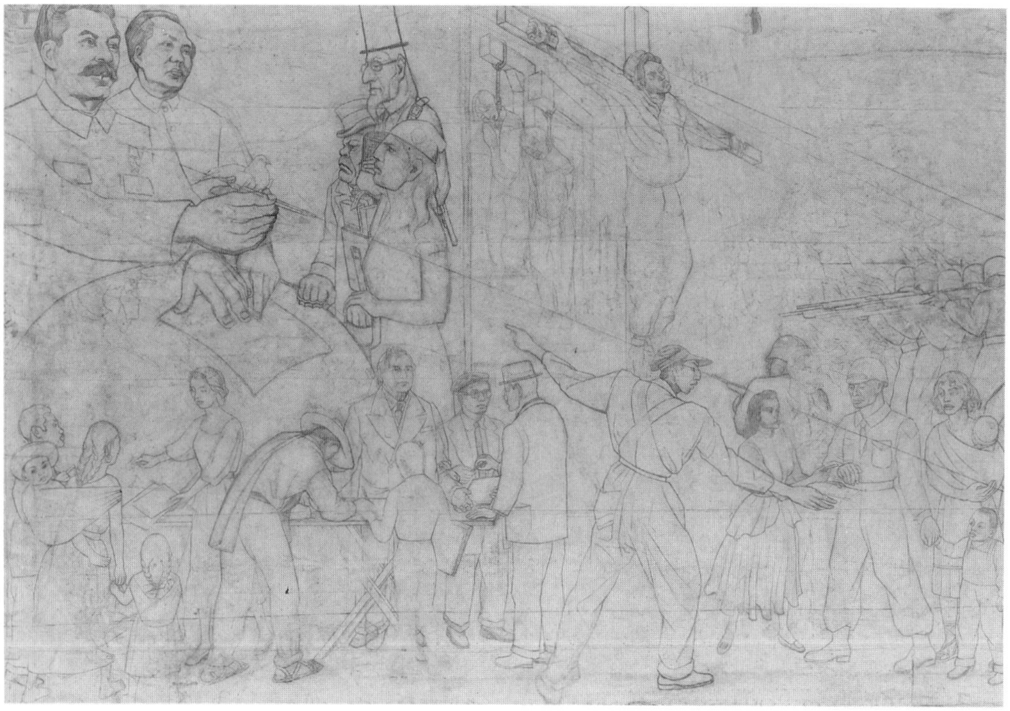

Figure 407.
Sketch for *The Nightmare of War and the Dream of Peace* (detail), 1952, pencil. Mexico City, Museo Anahuacalli.

Smith College Museum of Art, Gift of Mrs. Dwight Morrow '96, 1938 (1938:13–1). Variant of a detail from the theme *Building the Palace of Cortés* (V), Palacio de Cortés, Cuernavaca.

10. *The Knight of the Tiger,* 1931, fresco, 1.04 × 1.34 m. Northampton, Massachusetts, Smith College of Museum of Art, Winthrop Hillyer Fund, 1934 (1934:8–1). Variant of a detail from the theme *Battle of the Aztecs and Spaniards* (I), Palacio de Cortés, Cuernavaca.

In 1933, after completing the New Workers School frescoes, Rivera painted two panels for the headquarters of the Communist League of America, a Trotskyite center, in New York:

11. *The Russian Revolution,* 1933, fresco. Mexico City, Museo del Palacio de Bellas Artes.

12. *The Fourth International,* 1933, fresco. Mexico City, Museo del Palacio de Bellas Artes. Variant of detail from *World War* panel (K) at the New Workers School, New York.

In 1952, Rivera was commissioned by the Instituto Nacional de Bellas Artes to paint the following mural-sized painting for an exhibition of Mexican art intended for a European tour:

13. *The Nightmare of War and the Dream of Peace,* 1952, oil on composition board (?). Present location unknown (see figs. 242 and 407).

In 1951, Rivera began work on what was intended to be an entire series of mosaic decorations for the new stadium (intended for the Olympic Games), at the Universidad Nacional Autónoma de Mexico in Mexico City. Only the front section was completed:

14. *Two Figures Bringing Nourishment to a Child while Mexican Athletes Carry Torches to Light the Olympic Flame,* 1952, multicolored stone tessarae. Mexico City, Universidad Nacional Autónoma de Mexico.

The author would like to thank the following individuals who assisted him in the course of compiling this census: Dirk Bakker; Mrs. Alfred H. Barr, Jr.; Javier Beccaril Mecalco; Mrs. Malu Cabrera de Block; Jorge Hernández Campos; Mickey Carpenter, Photo Archives, and Judith Cousins, Department of Painting and Sculpture (MOMA); Claire Collier (Rockefeller Archives Center); Armando Colina; Mildred Constantine; Rafael Coronel; John D. Diehl, Sidney Thomas, Tim Wilson, and Randy Bond (Syracuse University); Lucienne Bloch Dimitroff; Gordon F. Ekholm (American Museum of Natural History); Ricardo Perez Escamilla; Mrs. Philoine Hillman Fried; Fernando Gamboa; Alejandro Garcia; Alfonso Govela; Manny Greer (Greer Gallery); Carole Krinsky (Washington Square College, New York University); Mrs. Rojo Kuckhoff; Robert Lazar, archivist (ILGWU); Karin Lee; Mary-Anne Martin; Mrs. Ann Moore, director, and the staff (Fayetteville Free Library); Laura Palmas O., public relations (Hotel del Prado); Raúl Santiago Pinelo; Miguel Angelo Sámano Renteria; Mrs. Susana Torruella de Leval; Monroe Wheeler; the Museum of Modern Art Library (New York), and the Tamiment Library and Labor Archives (Bobst Library, New York University).

Stanton L. Catlin

Notes

Anfiteatro Bolívar

1. A skeptical José Clemente Orozco, Rivera's colleague at the Preparatoria, called the work "a peanut" and its recourse to experiments in fourth-dimensional form "pseudo-science." See Charlot 1962a, 149 (IV).

2. See Charlot (note 1), pl. 18a.

3. Charlot (note 1), 291.

4. For a concise explanation of Pythagoreanism and the ideas and beliefs of Pythagoras and his followers, see *Encyclopedia Britannica* (Macropedia) 15: 322–26. For Vasconcelos's interpretation and personal views, see his *Pitágoras* (Havana, 1916).

5. Quoted in Wolfe 1939, 151 (I).

6. Iconography for the Anfiteatro Bolívar mural is based on Alicia Azuela in Acevedo et al. 1984, 14–16 (IV) and Wolfe (note 5), 150–53.

7. Azuela (note 6), 16. Rivera himself referred to "The Pantocrat" following his return from Tehuantepec (see Charlot [note 1], 145).

8. Azuela (note 6), 15.

Secretaría de Educación Pública

1. Vasconcelos as quoted by Olivier Debroise in Acevedo et al. 1984, 131 (IV).

2. Ibid.

3. Susana Gamboa in Mexico City 1949, 297 (III).

4. All correlations between areas of the building, subjects, and compass directions are based on research by Francis V. O'Connor, who has generously shared his discoveries on this subject (see his essay on the *Detroit Industry* murals earlier in this volume).

5. Gamboa (note 3), 298.

6. Debroise (note 1), 134.

7. Bartolomé de las Casas was a Spanish missionary and historian (1474–1566), who was instrumental in the passage of laws to protect the Indian population of New Spain. He wrote several books on America, including *Historia de las Indias* (first published in 1875).

8. Charlot 1962a, 278–79 (IV).

9. The description of this "Corrido" is based in part on Debroise (note 1), 138.

10. The description of this "Corrido" is also based on Debroise (note 1), 137–38.

11. The description of the stairway scenes is based in part on Rodríguez 1984, 85–93 (I).

12. George C. Vaillant, *Aztecs of Mexico: Origin, Rise and Fall of the Aztec Nation* (Garden City, NY.: Doubleday, Doran & Co., 1941), 179.

13. Charlot (note 8), 184.

14. Ibid., 278.

15. Dimensions for Level I (given for main panels only) are based on this author's on-site calculations in conjunction with an architectural survey conducted in September 1985 by Javier Becerril Mecalco. In the elevator alcove, the dimensions for the framed images c, d, and e were interpolated from Gamboa (note 3), 298–99, in conjunction with the survey. English titles are translations of the posted wall labels (1984).

16. This panel is inscribed: NI CON UN MONTON DE TESOROS PODRAS AVIVAR TU VASALLAJE, POR QUE LOS TESOROS HUMO SON; ENSALZA SOLO A LOS CANTARES Y A LAS FLORES QUE CUBREN LA TIERRA POR QUE ELLOS EMBRIAGARAN TU ALMA.

17. This panel is inscribed: TODA LA REDONDEZ DE LA TIERRA ES UN SEPULCRO: NO HAY COSA QUE SUSTENTE QUE CON TITULO DE PIEDAD NO LA ESCONDA Y LA ENTIERRE. =NETZAHUALCOYOTL.

18. This panel is inscribed: NOS INFAMEN Y NOS MENOSCABAN PORQUE SOMOS PLEBEYOS. SOLO NOSOTROS QUE LO HEMOS SENTIDO. SABEMOS LO QUE SON PENAS, LO QUE SON CONGOJAS COMO ES NOTORIO. =HEXOTZIQUENSE.

19. Above the scene of potters is this panel is a small framed sculptural relief, frescoed in grisaille, depicting the biblical story of the Creation.

20. This panel is inscribed: ¡OH! ELLA ES NUESTRA MADRE DIOSA DE LA TIERRA, QUE PROVEE DE ALIMENTO EN EL DESIERTO A LAS BESTIAS SALVAJES Y LAS HACE VIVIR. =ASI, ASI LA VEIS SER UN MODELO FRESCO SIEMPRE DE LIBERALIDAD HACIA TODA CARNE. =HIMNO A LA MADRE DE LOS DIOSES.

21. Work on this series was begun before Rivera completed the stairway at the Secretaría and probably continued throughout the period that he was painting the frescoes in the administration building at Chapingo.

22. *Nixtamal* is the ancient form of cornmeal used for making tortillas.

23. The medium of *La Zandunga*, like that of the first-floor panels of the Court of Labor, may be fresco mixed with nopal juice.

24. All measurements on Level III are to the outside edge of the painted frames that enclose the images and are based on this author's calculations.

25. The order of the shields is based on Gamboa (note 3), 301–2. These frescoed compositions are "floated" within their wall areas, following the Spanish manner of displaying sculptured heraldic motifs on both interior and exterior walls, a convention sometimes called *placage*.

26. All measurements on Level III are to the outside edge of the painted frames that enclose the subjects and are based on the Becerril Mercales survey (see note 15). In both the "Corrido" series some of the subjects overlap the frame, giving the impression that they were conceived as trompe l'oeil representations or as dioramas set into the walls. Rivera used a similar technique in the ceiling niches at Chapingo. In the latter case, the intent may have been to create a metaphor for escape from confining circumstances.

27. The overdoor areas on the third level of the Court of Labor include reclining angels (between the martyrs) and a variety of allegorical symbols. See Rodrígues 1984, 128, 135, 137 (I).

28. The areas above the main panels as well as the connecting overdoors on the third level of the Court of Fiestas are joined by a painted ribbon on which appear the words of the two *corridos* (composed especially for Rivera's program), a device that emphasizes the lyrical rhythm of the pictorial sequence.

29. The "Corrido of the Agrarian Revolution" is close in both style and date to the series on "Social Revolution" at Chapingo.

30. Dimensions given are for greatest height and greatest width and are based on 1985 survey (see note 15).

Universidad Autónoma de Chapingo

1. From the official English-language description of the murals issued by the Universidad Autónoma de Chapingo (Ms. JPRS–260184).

2. Dimensions for Chapingo based on architectural survey (see note 15, SEP, above).

3. Upper horizontal area, .65 × 4.95 m; lower vertical area, 2.85 × 1.95 m

Palacio Nacional

1. Iconography based in part in Rosa Casanova in Acevedo et al. 1984, 119–29 (IV).

2. Ibid., 119.

3. Ibid., 119–20.

4. The size of the figures and the lettered texts is scaled to accommodate the changing sightlines of an observer ascending the south stairway who, reaching the top of the landing, generally moves toward the center of the balcony for an overall view.

5. This section contains portraits, from left to right, of John D. Rockefeller, Jr., Harry Sinclair, William Durant, J. P. Morgan (partial profile), Cornelius Vanderbilt, and Andrew Mellon. Casanova (note 1), 121.

6. Former president Plutarco Elías Calles is the middle figure in this section. His inclusion in this unfavorable context is obviously a politically motivated remonstrance by the artist, considering Calles's portrayal in a positive manner on the stairway's main wall, painted in 1929, while he was still president.

7. Adrián Villagomez in Reyero 1983, 141 (I).

8. Vaillant (note 12, SEP), 270. The late George Vaillant, Curator of Mexican Archaeology, American Museum of Natural History, was referring here to the slightly earlier Secretaría de Educación Públic murals. In this author's view the comment applies equally to those at the Palacio Nacional and Cuernavaca.

9. Casanova (note 1), 117.

10. Ibid., 118–22.

11. The first two (introductory) panels were probably added as afterthoughts. They bracket a doorway leading at right angles away from the patio corridor.

12. In general, it is the direction in which walls face rather than that from which they are seen that

determines associative meanings in Rivera's iconographic system. Thus, in this scene, the personalities arranged on the left side of the arch in ascending order represent the forces of political reaction, while those on the right, in descending order, represent the liberal revolution of 1910.

Palacio de Cortés

1. *New York Times,* August18, 1929.

2. Mrs. Morrow, conversation with author, spring 1950.

3. Mrs. Morrow, letter to author, spring 1950.

4. Rivera used himself as the model for this portrait of Morelos.

Secretaría de Salubridad y Asistencia

1. Mexico City 1977, 199 (III).

2. The figures are labeled on the wall as follows: *Vida, Salud, Continencia, Pureza, Fortaleza,* and *Ciencias.* The last can be translated either as "science" or as "exact and reasoned knowledge."

3. Henestrosa et al. 1960, 71–72 (I).

4. Three sections, *Life, Health,* and *Symbols of Germination,* are set in their ceiling and wall positions as panels, apparently as part of a process of restoration.

5. The outlines in this diagram represent the general configurations of these eccentrically shaped panels. All dimensions are approximate and provide only the greatest height and width. They are based on sight projection (by this author) in situ and later adjusted by proportioning, except for C, D, and H, which are based on Gamboa (note 3, SEP), 307–8.

Pacific Stock Exchange

1. Wolfe 1939, 316 (I).

2. This mural is not available for public viewing.

3. Mexico City 1977, 200 (III).

San Francisco Art Institute

1. Frederick Hartt, *Italian Renaissance Art* (New York: Harry N. Abrams and Prentice-Hall, 1969), 29.

2. See Charlot 1962a, 109–11 (IV).

3. Key based on information from author's site notes and Wolfe 1939 327 (I).

4. Other possible identifications for this figure are Geraldine Colby or Mrs. Fricke (designer).

The Detroit Institute of Arts

1. This section has been adapted from Linda Downs, "The Rouge in 1932: The *Detroit Industry* Frescoes," in *The Rouge of Industry in the Art of Charles Sheeler and Diego Rivera* (Detroit: The Detroit Institute of Arts, exh. cat., 1978), 47–52.

2. Letter from William Valentiner to Diego Rivera, April 27, 1931. Museum Archives, Detroit Institute of Arts.

3. Wolfe 1939, 313–14 (I).

4. Margaret Sterne, "The Museum Director and the Artist: Dr. William Valentiner and Diego Rivera in Detroit," *Detroit in Perspective* 1, 1 (1973): 88–111.

5. Rivera 1933a, 289 (V).

Rockefeller Center

1. A detailed study of this controversy, based on documentary evidence, is being prepared for publication by Dr. Laurance P. Hurlburt.

2. Wolfe 1939, 359 (I).

3. Ibid., 360.

4. Ibid., 363–64.

5. Mrs. Alfred H. Barr, Jr., interview with author, March 1985.

6. According to Lucienne Bloch, Rivera's assistant at the time, the portrait of Lenin was clearly sketched on the plaster undercoat of the wall six weeks before it was painted, in plain view for all to see. Apparently this change in the figuration of his original plan was never presented for approval, but there is no evidence that the earlier acceptance of his original plan required him to submit such changes for approval, and in any case his normal way of working was to improvise as he went. It is hard not to believe that he reflected about this, but that in the end, after the Lenin head had been drawn in without provoking comment, he simply decided to proceed on the basis of the overall, and presumed blanket, understanding.

New Workers School

1. *Portrait of America* is also the title of a book by Rivera and Bertram D. Wolfe (New York: Covici-Friede, 1934), which discusses and illustrates the entire New Workers School series as well as Rivera's other murals in the United States to that date.

2. Ibid., 232.

3. Among the figures pictured in the *Proletarian Unity* panel are Lenin; Marx; Friedrich Engels; Nikolai Bukharin; Rosa Luxemburg; Clara Zetkin; James P. Cannon, secretary of the American Trotskyite group in 1933; William Z. Foster, then chairman of the American Communist Party: Jay Lovestone, then head of the Communist Party (Opposition); Charles E. Ruthenberg, an early leader of the American Communist Party; and Bertram D. Wolfe, spokesman for the Communist Party (Opposition) and Rivera's biographer.

4. The opponent of Fascism is choking an eagle, which represents not only the eagle of "Roman" Fascism but also, since it is painted blue, the New Deal program known as the National Recover Act (NRA), which had as its emblem a blue eagle and which Rivera saw as an expression of Fascism in the United States.

5. Lucienne Bloch Dimitroff, letter to author, March 13, 1985.

6. Lucienne Bloch Dimitroff, the telephone conversation with Linda Downs, November 20, 1985.

7. Before the sale, Ms. Bloch and her husband, Stephen Pope Dimitroff, repaired several of these panels, which were then stored in a building on Seventy-seventh Street in New York City.

8. According to a 1941 letter in the ILGWU archives, one of the two overdoor panels was then in the possession of Jay Lovestone (Lucienne Bloch Dimitroff maintains that this was panel T [telephone conversation with Linda Downs, November 20, 1985]). In 1969 John Canaday stated in the *New York Times* (6 July 1969, section D, 19) that a family in New York City owned one of the overdoor panels.

Bellas Artes

1. Wolfe 1939, 374 (I).

2. This two-level line is still evident in the molded decorative strip beneath the scene that now occupies the site of the destroyed mural.

3. This description is based in part on wall labels installed at the Palacio de Bellas Artes (1978).

4. Title from wall label (1978).

5. The site is not ideal for viewing the mural as a whole. Two rectangular marble-faced piers run from ceiling to floor less than ten feet from the mural's surface, dividing the composition into three parts at the top of each magnifying lens, or approximately where, in the RCA Building, the side walls of the elevator bank would have folded back at right angles to the central composition in the original work.

City College of San Francisco

1. From the statement by Marsha Zakheim Jewitt in the printed program for the opening of the exhibition "Art and Architecture: The Marriage of True Minds" at the Dudley C. Carter Art Gallery, City College of San Francisco, May 3–June 9, 1983 (City College files).

2. See Herrera 1983, 295–96 (IV).

3. Following Rivera's death in 1957, the San Francisco Board of Education approved the reinstallation of Rivera's mural, which had been in storage for seventeen years, in a planned campus theatre. A wall space was specially designed, and the mural was installed in 1961.

4. Rivera stated the theme of this mural as follows: "It is the representation of the union of the technical and industrial genius of North America and the artistic and creative genius of South America. It is a symbol of the friendship and common purpose that binds the Americas together." Unidentified newspaper clipping. (San Francisco Main Library).

5. Iconography and identifications based in part on Puccinelli 1940 (I).

6. Packard is the author of the forthcoming publication *Diego Rivera; the San Francisco Frescoes,* which promises to be the definitive work on this subject.

7. In *The Great Dictator,* Chaplin poked fun at Fascism. He played a dual role as a Jewish barber and as Hitler—a grotesque caricature that upset many pro-German individuals in the United States.

Instituto Nacional de Cardiología

1. Susana Gamboa in Mexico City 1949, 314 (III).

2. Key based in part on Chávez 1946 (I).

3. Names and dates are given as inscribed on murals. Nationalities have been added.

Hotel del Prado

1. From a printed statement by Ruth Rivera and Agustín Yañez. Courtesy of Hotel del Prado.

2. An *esquincle* is a dark-skinned hairless dog known in Mexico since pre-Colombian times. Such dogs were supposedly the models for the animal sculptures created by the Tarascan Indians (see Brown essay earlier in this volume).

3. See Teatro de los Insurgentes, note 2.

4. Dimensions based on Susana Gamboa in Mexico City 1949, 315 (III).

5. Sor Juana, Najera, Lobo Guerrero, and Tanta Vicenta are transitional figures who could be considered appropriate to the following category as well.

Hospital de la Raza

1. Vaillant (see note 12, SEP, above), 180.

2. Crespo de la Serna 1957, 12 (II).

3. Ibid.

4. On the right side extension appears a portrait of a teaching nurse, professor Guadalupe Eguiluz, and on the left side extension, portraits of doctors Manuel Aceves Pérez and Ignacio Millan.

Cárcamo del Río Lerma

1. Eugene Goossen, Professor of Art, Hunter College, City College of New York, conversation with author.

2. In support of this view, there now seems to be little question that the Native American mounds in Louisiana and Alabama, which have been such an inspiration to the present generation of modern sculptors producing earthworks, are part of the religious, civic, and architectural tradition that radiated out from Middle America before Columbus.

3. The condition of the cistern frescoes is very poor. All areas below 1.5 meters form the top molding have been erased by the action of the chlorine (or other chemicals) used in the water purification process. Above this level, the composition and some of the details are recognizable but have been artistically emasculated.

Teatro de los Insurgentes

1. Lucienne Bloch Dimitroff, letter to John Canaday, art critic of the *New York Times*, July 29, 1969.

2. The Insurgentes controversy turned out to be an interim skirmish in the nearly decade long standoff over the Hotel del Prado mural, which finally ended in 1956, the year before Rivera's death and the final year of Archbishop Luís Martínez Rodríguez's life, but only after Rivera removed the offending quotation.

3. Fifteen names follow in different hands, undoubtedly those of the collaborating artists.

Movable Frescoes

1. There is documentary evidence in the Museum of Modern Art, New York, files that Rivera produced at least one more panel than the original seven requested.

Checklist of the Exhibition

Gina Alexander
Alicia Azuela
Karen Cordero
Durdica Segota

Paintings

1. Landscape, 1896/97

Oil on canvas, 70 × 55 cm

Collection of Guadalupe Rivera de Iturbe

2. Landscape with Lake, ca. 1900

Oil on canvas, 53 × 73 cm

Inscriptions: lower right, *D. M. Rivera.*

Provenance: A. DeSilva. Francisco Bernal

Collection of Daniel Yankelewitz B., Costa Rica

3 La Casteñada, also known as *Paseo de los melancólicos,* 1904

Oil on canvas, 85 × 50 cm

Inscriptions: lower left, *Diego Rivera/1904*

Exhibitions: Mexico City 1949, no. 29

References: Arquin 1971, 32 (I)

Mexico City, Museo Franz Mayer

4. La era, 1904

Oil on canvas, 100 × 114.6 cm

Exhibitions: Mexico City 1949, no. 28; Washington/Los Angeles 1978, no. 172

References: Arquin 1971, 32, pl. 28 (I); Reyero 1983, 16 (I); Phoenix 1984, 9 (III)

Guanajuato, Museo Diego Rivera, Marte R. Gómez Collection (INBA)

5. Self-Portrait, 1907

Oil on canvas, 84.5 × 61.5 cm

Exhibitions: Leningrad 1978; Mexico City 1983, no. 29; Mexico City/Monterrey 1983, no. 11

References: Reyero 1983, 20–21 (I)

Collection of Dolores Olmedo

6. Night In Ávila, 1907

Oil on burlap, 97 × 90.5 cm

Inscriptions: lower left, *Raphael Cravioto / Diego M. Rivera / Avila 1907.*

Provenance: Rafael Cravioto. Teodoro A. Dehesa. Diego Rivera.

Exhibitions: Mexico City 1977, no. 11; Mexico City/Monterrey 1983, no. 1

References: Reyero 1983, 22–23, pl. 7 (I)

Collection of Dolores Olmedo

7. La calle de Ávila, 1908

Oil on canvas, 129 × 141 cm

Inscriptions: lower left, *Diego M. Rivera / Avila. 1908.*

Exhibitions: Mexico City 1949, no. 42

References: Arquin 1971, 15, pl. 3 (I); Reyero 1983, pl. 6 (I)

Mexico City, Museo Nacional de Arte (INBA)

8. Nôtre Dame de Paris, 1909

Oil on canvas, 144 × 113 cm

Exhibitions: Mexico City 1949, no. 46; Mexico City 1977, no. 14; Mexico City 1983, no. 1

References: Fernández 1952, 311 (IV); Charlot 1962, 123 (IV); Fernández 1964, 51 (IV); Reyero 1983, 24–25, pl. 12 (I)

Mexico City, Museo Nacional de Arte (INBA)

9. House on the Bridge, 1909

Oil on canvas, 146 × 140 cm

Exhibitions: Paris 1910, no. 4338; Mexico City 1949, no. 43; Mexico City 1958; Washington/Los Angeles 1978, no. 174; Mexico City 1983, no. 9.

References: Fernández 1937, 189 (IV); Fernández 1952, 311, fig. 341 (IV); Charlot 1962, 122 (IV); Wolfe 1963, 57 (I); Fernández 1964, 51 (IV); Arquin 1971, 46, pl. 21 (I), Reyero 1983, 25, pl. 14 (I)

Mexico City, Museo Nacional de Arte (INBA)

10. Breton Girl, 1910

Oil on canvas, 100 × 80 cm

Exhibitions: Mexico City 1949, no. 43; Mexico City 1978, no. 10; Washington/Los Angeles 1978, no. 174

References: Arquin 1971, 58–59 (I); Reyero 1983, 28 (I)

Mexico City, Museo Nacional de Arte (INBA)

11. The Old Ones, also known as *En las afueras de Toledo*, 1912

Oil on canvas, 210 × 184 cm

Inscriptions: lower right, *Diego M. Rivera.*

Provenance: D. Enrique Freyman, Paris. Swiss Private Collection. Parke-Bernet auction, New York, 1959

Exhibitions: Mexico City 1977, no. 97; Leningrad 1978; Mexico City 1983, no. 17; Mexico City/Monterrey 1983, no. 5

References: Wolfe 1963, 80 (I); Reyero 1983, pl. 17 (I); Phoenix 1984, 32–33, pl. 11 (III)

Collection of Dolores Olmedo

12. At the Fountain near Toledo, 1913

Oil on canvas, 166 × 204 cm

Inscriptions: lower left, *Diego M. Rivera 1913 Toledo.*

Provenance: D. Enrique Freyman, Paris, Swiss Private Collection. Parke-Bernet auction, New York, 1959

Exhibitions: Mexico City 1977, no. 18; Mexico City 1983, no. 11; Mexico City/Monterrey 1983, no. 3; Phoenix 1984, no. 2

References: Guzmán 1961, 84 (IV); Taracena et al. 1979, 11, 31, pl. 10 (I); Reyero 1983, 29–32, pl. 20 (I)

Collection of Dolores Olmedo

13. Portrait of Adolfo Best Maugard, 1913

Oil on canvas, 226.8 × 161.6 cm

Inscriptions: lower left, *Diego M. Rivera/1913.*

Provenance: Dr. Arturo Aruaiz y Freq. Christie's London

Exhibitions: Paris 1913a, no. 2605; Phoenix 1984, no. 5

References: Best Maugard 1949, 283 (I); Mexico City 1949, 67 (III); Suárez 1962, 115 (I); Taracena et al. 1979, 34 (I); Reyero 1983, 32–33, pl. 21 (I)

Mexico City, Museo Nacional de Arte (INBA)

14. The Viaduct—Sun Breaking through the Fog, 1913

Oil on canvas, 83.5 × 59 cm

Inscriptions: lower left, *Diego M. Rivera / 1913.*

Provenance: Victoria Marín

Exhibitions: Paris 1914, no. 8; Mexico City 1949, no. 57; Mexico City 1977, no. 98; Mexico City/Monterrey 1983, no. 4; Phoenix 1984, no. 13

References: Fernández 1952, 312 (IV); Fernández 1961, 155 (IV); Debroise 1979, 57 (I); Taracena et al. 1979, 71, pl. 57 (I); Reyero 1983, 32, pl. 29 (I)

Collection of Dolores Olmedo

15. Sailor at Lunch, 1914

Oil on canvas, 114 × 70 cm

Inscriptions: lower left, *D. M. Rivera 14*; on sailor's hat, *Patrie.*

Provenance: Galerie Rosenberg, Paris. Marte R. Gómez

Exhibitions: Mexico City 1949, no. 72; Houston 1951, no. 2

Guanajuato, Museo Diego Rivera (INBA)

16. Two Women, 1914

Oil on canvas, 198.1 × 160 cm

Inscriptions: lower right, *Diego M. Rivera, 14.*

Provenance: Abby Rockefeller Mauze

Exhibitions: Paris 1914; New York 1931, 23–24, no. 3; Mexico City, 1949, no. 75; New Orleans 1968, no. 316; Phoenix 1984, no. 22

References: Wolfe 1939, 88–92, pl. 19 (I); Wolfe 1963, 88, 89, pl. 22 (I) Fernández 1964, 52, (IV); Taracena et al. 1979, 32 (I)

Little Rock, The Arkansas Art Center Foundation Collection, Gift fo Abby Rockefeller Mauze, New York, 1955 (55.10)

17. Young Man with Stylograph—Portrait of Best Maugard, 1914

Oil on canvas, 79.5 × 63.5 cm

Inscriptions: lower right, *D. M. Rivera*

Provenance: D. Enrique Freyman, Paris. Swiss Private Collection. Parke-Bernet auction, New York, 1959

Exhibitions: Paris 1914, no. 18; Mexico City 1977, no. 22; Mexico City/Monterrey 1983, no. 6; Phoenix 1984, no. 24

References: Arquin 1971, 72–73 (I); Taracena et al. 1979, 38 (I); Reyero 1983, 33–34, pl. 35 (I)

Collection of Dolores Olmedo

18. Portrait of Ramón Gómez de la Serna, 1915

Oil on canvas, 109 × 90 cm

Inscriptions: lower left, *DMR/15*; on books, *GRECUERIAS, EL LIBRO MOD°, EL RASTRO POR RAMON GOMEZ D LA SERNA*

Provenance: Ramón Gómez de la Serna, Buenas Aires. Carlos Ortiz, Madrid. Christies sale, London, 1966. Christies sale, New York, 1983

Exhibitions: Phoenix 1984, no. 32

References: Wolfe 1939, 94–98 (I)

The Placido Arango Collection

19. The Architect (Jesús T. Acevedo), 1915

Oil on canvas, 144 × 113.5 cm

Exhibitions: New York 1931, no. 5; Mexico City 1949, no. 90; Houston 1951, no. 3; Phoenix 1984, no. 35

References: Fernández 1964, 52 (IV); Reyero 1983, 33, pl. 43 (I)

Mexico City, Museo de Arte Alvar y Carmen T. Carrillo Gil (INBA)

20. Still Life with Bread Knife, 1915

Oil on canvas, 49.9 × 59.7 cm

Inscriptions: lower center, *D.M.R.*; on reverse, *Diego M. Rivera/1915*

Provenance: Coady Gallery, New York. John Quinn, New York, 1917. American Art Association sale, February 1927. Ferdinand Howald, New York and Columbus, Ohio.

Exhibitions: Columbus Gallery of Fine Arts, Ohio, *Inaugural Exhibition*, 1931, no. 201; Washington 1978, no. 64, 135, 181; Phoenix 1984, no. 38.

Columbus, Ohio, Columbus Museum of Art, Gift of Ferdinand Howald (31.89)

21. Zapatista Landscape—The Guerrilla, 1915

Oil on canvas, 144 × 123 cm (on the reverse of *Woman at the Well*, 1913)

Inscriptions: *D. M. Rivera 15.*

Provenance: Galerie Rosenberg, Paris. Marte R. Gómez

Exhibitions: Mexico City 1949, no. 8; Rome 1962, no. 971; Los Angeles 1963, no. 958; Washington/Los Angeles 1978, no. 175; Phoenix 1984, no. 40

References: Fernández 1952, 312 (IV); Torriente 1959, I; 68 (I); Reed 1960, 75 (IV); Guzmán 1961, 86 (IV), Wolfe 1963, 91, pl. 16 (I); Fernández 1964, 53 (IV); Fernández 1969, 155 (IV); Arquin 1971, 79–81, pl. 8 (I); Mexico City 1977, 37; Debroise 1979, 74–75 (I); Taracena et al. 1979, 40, pl. 64 (I); Reyero 1983, 37, pl. (I)

Mexico City, Museo Nacional de Arte (INBA)

22. Angeline and Baby Diego—Maternity, 1916

Oil on canvas, 132 × 86 cm

Exhibitions: Mexico City 1949, no. 87; Mexico City 1983, no 25; Phoenix 1984, 143, no. 154

References: Mexico City 1977, 87, pl. 39 (III); Debroise 1979, 75 (I); Reyero 1983, pl. 55 (I)

Mexico City, Museo de Arte Alvar y Carmen T. Carrillo Gil (INBA)

23. Portrait of a Poet, 1916

Oil on canvas, 130 × 97 cm

Inscriptions: lower right, *D. M. Rivera.*

Exhibitions: Mexico City 1949, no. 93; Mexico City 1977, no. 52; Washington/Los Angeles 1978, no. 176

References: Debroise 1979, 77 (I); Reyero 1983, pl. 52 (I)

Mexico City, Museo de Arte Alvar y Carmen T. Carrillo Gil (INBA)

24. The Telegraph Pole, 1916

Oil on canvas, with applied sand and other objects, 98 × 79.5 cm

Inscriptions: lower right, *D. M. Rivera / Octobre 1916;* on back, *Diego M. Rivera / Octobre 1916*

Provenance: Léonce Rosenberg, Paris. Guadalupe Marín, 1959

Exhibitions: Mexico City 1982, no. 13; Mexico City/Monterrey 1983, no. 13; Phoenix 1984, 119, pl. 24

References: Mexico City 1977, 65 (III); Debroise 1979, 75 (I); Taracena et al. 1979, 38 (I); Reyero 1983, pl. 51 (I); Favela 1984, 122 (I)

Collection of Dolores Olmedo

25. Composition: Still Life with Green House, 1917

Oil on canvas, 61 × 46 cm

Inscriptions: verso, *Diego M. Rivera / 1917*

Provenance: J. H. Gosschalk, Waasenaar, 1950

Exhibitions: Delft 1951; Eindoven 1951; Utrecht 1961; Phoenix 1984, 135, no. 60

Amsterdam, Stedelijk Museum.

26. Woman with Geese, 1918

Oil on canvas, 62.5 × 81.5 cm

Inscriptions: lower right, *Diego Rivera*

Exhibitions: Mexico City 1965, no. 6; Mexico City 1977, no. 19; Mexico City/Monterrey 1983, no. 69

References: Taracena et al. 1979, 34 (I); Reyero 1983, pl. 63 (I)

Collection of Dolores Olmedo

27. The Mathematician, 1918

Oil on canvas backed by panel, 115.5 × 80.5 cm

Inscriptions: lower left, *D. Rivera.*

Annotations: on back, upper left, *26*, upper right, *19*.

Provenance: Alberto J. Pani, Ramón Beteta

Exhibitions: Mexico City 1949, no. 100; Mexico City 1977, no. 68; Mexico City 1982, 68, no. 19; Mexico City 1983, no. 34; Mexico City/Monterrey 1983, no. 19; Phoenix 1984, no. 74

References: Gorostiza 1939 (IV); Gual 1950 (I); Fernández 1952, 312 (IV); Torriente 1959, II: 72 (I); Fernández 1964, 53 (IV); Arquin 1971, 92, pl. 164 (I); Taracena et al. 1979, 42, pl. 77 (I)

Collection of Dolores Olmedo

28. Portrait of Alberto J. Pani, 1920

Oil on canvas, 79.5 × 99 cm

Inscriptions: lower right, *A Don Alberto Pani, / Mi amigo / Diego Rivera / Paris 1920.*

Provenance: Alberto J. Pani, Marte R. Gómez

Exhibitions: Mexico City 1949, no. 125; Mexico City 1977, 43, no. 81; Mexico City/Monterrey 1983, no. 70

References: Reyero 1983, 40, pl. 71 (I); Wolfe 1963; 112 (I)

Collection of Dolores Olmedo

29. Portrait of Xavier Guerrero, 1921

Oil on canvas, 41.7 × 29.9 cm

Inscriptions: upper right, *Diego Rivera 1921.*

Provenance: Frida Kahlo, 1949. Emma Hurtado de Rovera, Acapulco, 1970/71

Exhibitions: Mexico City 1949, no. 211

References: Reyero 1983, 174 (I)

Collection of Madeleine Blanche Vallier

30. Bather of Tehuantepec, 1923

Oil on canvas, 63.5 × 53.5 cm

Inscriptions: lower right, *Diego Rivera*

Exhibitions: Mexico City 1949, no. 239; Mexico City 1973; Mexico City 1983 (not in cat.)

Guanajuato, Museo Diego Rivera, Marte R. Gómez Collection (INBA)

31. The Grinder, 1924

Encaustic on canvas, 90 × 117 cm

Exhibitions: Paris 1952, no 998; Stockholm 1952, no. 983; London 1953, no. 988; Berlin 1959, no. 1169; Rome 1962, no. 972; Los Angeles 1963, no. 962; Washington/Los Angeles 1978, no. 177

References: Fernández 1952, 323 (IV); Sheldon Chaney, *The Story of Modern Art* (New York: The Viking Press, 1958), 560, fig. 551

Mexico City, Museo de Arte Moderno (INBA)

32. Flower Day, 1925

Encaustic on canvas, 147.4 × 120.6 cm

Inscriptions: lower left, *Diego Rivera.*

Exhibitions: Los Angeles 1925, no. 339; San Francisco 1930, no. 21; New York 1931, no. 20; Mexico City 1949, no. 250; Venice 1950, no. 13; Paris 1952, no. 997; Stockholm 1952, no. 982; London 1953, no. 987; New Orleans 1968, no. 318; Santa Barbara 1970, no. 60; Mexico City 1983, no. 37

References: *Bulletin of the Los Angeles Museum of History, Science, and Art* (January 1926), 203 and 205; Wolfe 1939, 316 (I); Wolfe 1963, 280 (I); Torriente 1959, II; 240 (I); Revero 1983, 174

Los Angeles County Museum of Art, L.A. County Funds (25.7.1)

33. La Siesta, 1926

Oil on canvas, 54.6 × 73.7 cm

Inscriptions: lower right, *Diego Rivera / 1926.*

Provenance: Private Collection. Sotheby Parke-Bernet sale, 1979

Exhibitions: Mexico 1983, no. 38

San Antonio, Texas, San Antonio Museum Association, Purchased with funds provided by Mrs. Vaughan B. Meyer and the Alice Kleberg Reynolds Meyer Foundation in memory of Mr. and Mrs. Richard M. Kleberg Sr., Mary Etta Kleberg Sugden and Richard M. Kleberg, Jr.

34. Waiting for Tortillas, also known as *La tortillera,* 1926

Encaustic on canvas, 107.3 × 89.5 cm

Inscriptions: lower right, *Diego Rivera 26*

Provenance: Dr. Leo Eloesser

Exhibitions: San Francisco 1930, no. 13; Detroit 1931; New York 1931, no. 18; Mexico City 1949, no. 263

References: Richardson 1931, 76 (II); Reyero 1983, 174 (I)

San Francisco, Regents of the University of California

35. Peasant with Sombrero, 1926

Tempera on linen, 69 × 48 cm

Inscriptions: lower left, *Diego Rivera / 26,* verso, *dedicated to Ella Wolfe*

Private Collection

36. Portrait of Guadalupe, 1926

Encaustic on canvas, 67.3 × 56.5 cm

Inscriptions: lower left, *Diego Rivera*

Provenance: Jackson Coles Phillips, New York, 1951

Exhibitions: New York 1931, no. 24; Mexico City 1949, no. 260

References: Wolfe 1963, 183, pl. 67 (I)

Poughkeepsie, New York, The Vassar College Gallery of Art, Anonymous Loan (L82.1)

37. Dance in Tehuantepec, also known as *Fiesta Tehuana,* 1928

Oil on canvas, 199 × 162 cm

Inscriptions: lower right corner, *Diego Rivera*

Provenance: Mrs. James Murphy, New York, 1928–32. Grand Central Art Gallery, New York, 1946

Exhibitions: New York 1931, no. 31; New York 1946, no. 12; Mexico City 1949, no. 346; Venice 1950, no. 16; Dallas 1966; Mexico City 1983, 13, no. 39

References: Secker 1957, 103, pl. 88 (I); Taracena et al. 1979, 49–50, pl. 149 (I); Mexico City 1977, 71 (II); Reyero 1983, pl. 89 (I)

Armonk, New York, IBM Corporation

38. Women Washing Clothes in a River among Zopilotes, 1928

Oil on canvas, 84.8 × 64.8 cm

Provenance: Evaline M. Foley. Sotheby Parke-Bernet auction, 1984

Collection of Frances de Santos

39. Portrait of Caroline Durieux, 1929

Oil on canvas, 66 × 50.8 cm

Inscriptions: lower left, *Diego Rivera. 1929.*

Exhibitions: New York 1931, no. 30

Baton Rouge, Louisiana, Louisiana State University, Anglo-American Museum

40. The Flowered Canoe, 1931

Oil on canvas, 200 × 160 cm

Inscriptions: *1931.*

Provenance: Walter C. Arensberg, Los Angeles; Joseph W. Damman, Los Angeles; Carl Stendahl Gallery, Los Angeles; William H. Wright, Los Angeles; Algus H. Meadows, Dallas; Meadows Museum, Southern Methodist University, Dallas; Sotheby Parke-Bernet sale, 1981

Exhibitions: New York 1931, no. 46; Mexico City 1949, no. 392; Chicago 1959, no. 79; Dallas 1966; Mexico City 1983, no. 42; Mexico City/Monterrey 1983, no. 20

References: Taracena et al. 1979, 50, 163 (I)

Collection of Dolores Olmedo

41. Cactus on the Plains, also known as *Hands,* 1931

Oil on canvas, 69.2 × 84.5 cm

Inscriptions: lower right, *Diego Rivera.*

Provenance: Frida Kahlo. Edsel B. and Eleanor Clay Ford

Exhibitions: New York 1931, no. 52; Mexico City 1949, no. 394; Mexico City 1983, no. 43

References: Reyero 1983, pl. 112 (I)

Grosse Pointe, Michigan, Edsel and Eleanor Ford House

42. Portrait of Edsel B. Ford, 1932

Oil on canvas, 97.8 × 125.1 cm

Inscriptions: *Verdadero retrato / del Señor Edsel B. Ford / ingeniero industrial / y Presidente de la Co / mision de Arte de la / Ciudad de Detroit / Estado de Michigan / E. U. de America / Lopinto Diego Rivera / el mes de Novembre de / 1932.*

Provenance: Commissioned from the artist in 1932

Exhibitions: Detroit 1938; Detroit 1978, 5–6, 51; Berlin 1980, no. 267; Mexico City 1983, no. 46; Los Angeles, 1984, no. 104

References: Downs 1979, 47–52 (II)

The Detroit Institute of Arts, Bequest of Eleanor Clay Ford (77.5)

43. Portrait of Robert H. Tannahill, 1932

Oil on canvas, 88.3 × 69.9 cm

Inscriptions: *Verdadero Retrato de Don ROBERTO HUDSON TANNAHILL natural de DETROIT estado de Michigan y miembro de la Comision de / Bellas Artes en dicha Ciudad.—lo hice yo, Diego Rivera, cuando pintaba los Frescoes en el Museo de Bellas Artes de la Misma Villa, en 1932.*

Provenance: Commissioned from the artist in 1932.

Exhibitions: Detroit 1932, no. 15; Detroit 1938; Mexico City 1949, no. 404; Mexico 1983, no. 45

The Detroit Institute of Arts, Bequest of Robert H. Tannahill (70.187)

44. The Flower Carrier, formerly known as *The Flower Vendor,* 1935

Oil and tempera on masonite, 121.9 × 121.3 cm

Inscriptions: lower left, *Diego Rivera 1935.*

Exhibitions: Boston 1941, no. 31; Toronto 1944, no. 59; San Francisco 1945; Mexico City 1949, no. 525; Venice 1950, no. 17; Paris 1952, no. 1005, Stockholm 1952, no. 990; London 1953, no. 994; Santa Barbara 1958, no. 87; Los Angeles; 1963, no. 964; New Haven 1966, no. 308; New Orleans 1968, no. 319; Flushing 1979, no. 30; Miami 1984, 204–5, no. 179

References: San Francisco 1940, 11 (III); Wolfe 1947, pl. 12 (I); Wolfe 1963, 283–84 (I)

San Francisco Museum of Modern Art, Albert M. Bender Collection, Gift of Albert M. Bender, in memory of Caroline Walter (35.4516)

45. The Pinole Vendor, 1936

Watercolor on canvas, 81.4 × 60.7 cm

Inscriptions: lower right, *Diego Rivera*

Exhibitions: Mexico City 1948; Mexico City 1949, no. 543; Houston 1951, no. 10; Paris 1952, no. 1008; Stockholm 1952, no. 993; London 1953, no. 997; Mexico City 1958; Los Angeles, 1963, no. 965

References: Reyero, pl. 131 (I)

Mexico City, Museo Nacional de Arte (INBA)

46. Indian Spinning, also known as *Indian Weaving,* 1936

Oil on canvas, 59.7 × 81.3 cm

Inscriptions: upper left, *Diego Rivera, 1936.*

Exhibitions: Mexico City 1949, no. 542; Mexico City 1983, no. 49

References: Reyero 1983, pl. 132 (I)

Phoenix Art Museum, Gift of Mrs. Clare Boothe Luce (68/29)

47. Roots, 1937

Watercolor on linen, 45.7 × 61.5 cm

Inscriptions: lower left, *Diego Rivera '37*

Provenance: Ralph Smith, Mexico City. John H. Cohen, Pittsburgh. Sotheby Parke-Bernet auction, New York, 1984

Exhibitions: Mexico City 1938

Private Collection

48. Tecalpexco, 1937

Tempera on board, 58.4 × 80 cm

Amherst, Massachusetts, Amherst College, Mead Art Museum, Bequest of Mrs. Phillip Youtz (1975.93)

49. The Tent, 1937

Oil on canvas, 58.4 × 80 cm

Provenance: Misrachi Gallery, Mexico City, 1946

Collection of the Sollins Family

50. Portrait of Lupe Marín, 1938

Oil on canvas, 171.3 × 122.3 cm

Inscriptions: lower right, *Diego Rivera. 1938*

Provenance: Guadalupe Marín

Exhibitions: San Francisco 1940, no. 952; New York 1942, no. 127; Mexico City 1949, no. 561; Venice 1950, no. 20; Houston 1951, no. 12; Paris 1952, no. 1009; Stockholm 1952, no. 994; London 1953, no. 998; Washington/Los Angeles 1978, no. 182; Mexico City 1983, no. 55

References: Fernández 1952, 342 (IV); Fernández 1964, 69 (IV); Fernández 1969, 161 (IV); Mexico City 1977, 48 (III); Reyero 1983, pl. 140 (I)

Mexico City, Museo de Arte Moderno (INBA)

51. Dancer in Repose, 1939

Oil on canvas, 164 × 94 cm

Inscriptions: lower left, *Diego Rivera. 39.*

Provenance: José Domingo Lavin

Exhibitions: Mexico City 1949, no. 569; Houston 1951, no. 11; Paris 1952, no. 1011; Stockholm 1952, no. 996; London 1953, no. 1000; Mexico City 1977, no. 289; Leningrad 1978; Mexico City 1983, no. 56; Mexico City/Monterrey 1983, no. 22

References: Gual 1950 (I); Fernández 1952, 343, 377 (IV); Fernández 1964, 69 (IV); Fernández 1969, 161 (IV); Reyero 1983, pl. 148 (I)

Collection of Dolores Olmedo

52. Symbolic Landscape, also known as *Tree with Glove and Knife,* 1940

Oil on canvas, 121.6 × 152.7 cm

Exhibitions: San Francisco 1940, no. 951; Mexico City 1940, no. 81; Flushing 1979, no. 29

References: Fernández 1945, 137 (I); Prampolini 1969, 62, fig. 38 (IV); Mexico City 1949, no. 576 (III); Wolfe 1947, pl. 13 (I)

San Francisco Museum of Modern Art, Gift of friends of Diego Rivera, Mrs. Sigmund Stern, Mrs. E. S. Heller, Albert M. Bender, William L. Gerstle, W. W. Crocker, Harry Camp, and Timothy Pflueger (40.6551)

53. Self-Portrait, 1941

Oil on canvas, 61 × 43 cm

Inscriptions: *Pinte mi retrato para la / bella y famosa artista Irene / Rich, y fue en la ciudad de / Santa Barbara, de / en California del Sur / durante el mes de Enero / del ano de 1941 / Diego Rivera.*

Provenance: Irene Rich, Santa Barbara, California

Exhibitions: Boston 1941, no. 32

References: Mexico City 1949, no. 16 (III)

Northampton, Massachusetts, Smith College Museum of Art, Gift of Mrs. Irene Rich Clifford, 1977

54. Day of the Dead, also known as *El Velorio,* 1944

Oil on masonite, 73.5 × 91 cm

Inscriptions: lower right, *Diego Rivera / 1944*

Provenance: Gift of the artist to the Museo Nacional de Artes Plasticas 1951. Museo de Arte Moderno 1966

Exhibitions: Mexico City 1949, no. 680; Mexico City 1983 (not in cat.)

References: Wolfe 1963, 377 (I)

Mexico City, Museo de Arte Moderno (INBA)

55. Carregador—Las ilusiones, 1944

Oil on canvas, 75 × 59 cm

Inscriptions: lower left, *Diego Rivera 1944*

Provenance: Valentin Boujas, Rio de Janeiro, 1948

Museu de Arte de São Paulo

56. The Milliner (Henry de Chatillon), 1944

Oil on masonite, 121 × 152 cm

Exhibitions: Mexico City 1983, no. 69

References: Reyero 1983, pl. 159 (I)

Collection of Mr. and Mrs. Marcos Micha Levy

57. Nude with Calla Lilies, 1944

Oil on masonite, 157 × 124 cm

Provenance: Pedro Guzzy

Exhibitions: Mexico City 1949, no. 685; Houston 1951, no. 14; Mexico City 1977, 45, no. 324; Mexico City 1983, no. 68

References: Taracena et al. 1979, pl. 119 (I); Reyero 1983, pl. 151 (I)

Collection of Emilia Guzzy de Gálvez

58. Portrait of Adalgisa Nery, 1945

Oil on canvas, 122 × 62 cm

Inscriptions: lower right, *1945*

Exhibitions: Mexico City 1977, no. 264; Mexico City 1983, no. 70

References: Reyero 1983, pl. 160 (I)

Collection of Rafael and Dora Mareyna

59. Portrait of the Knight Family, 1946

Oil on canvas, 181 × 202 cm

Inscriptions: lower right, *Retrato de / Dick Knight / Nora Knight / y Dinah Knight / sus hijas / y se comienzo a pin / tar al dia 17 / de Abril del ano / de 1946 y VIII cumpleaños de Dinah Knight*

Provenance: Commissioned from the artist in 1946

Minneapolis Institute of Arts, Gift of Mrs. Dinah Ellingson in memory of Richard Allen Knight

60. Portrait of Irene Estrella, 1946

Oil on canvas, 120.4 × 93 cm

Inscriptions: upper left, *IRENE Estrella / la pinta Diego Rivera / año de MCMXLVI*

Provenance: Alberto Misrachi, Mexico City, 1949. Private Collection, 1959

Exhibitions: Mexico City 1949, no. 787; Paris 1952, no. 1017; Stockholm 1952, no. 1002; London 1953, no. 1006

Exeter, New Hampshire, Phillips Exeter Academy, The Lamont Gallery, Gift of Corliss Lamont '20

61. Nocturnal Landscape, 1947

Oil on canvas, 111 × 91 cm

Inscriptions: lower right, *Diego Rivera 1947.*

Exhibitions: Mexico City 1949, no. 713; Houston 1951, no. 15; Mexico City 1977, no. 318; Mexico City 1983, no. 73

References: Reyero 1983, pl. 164 (I)

Mexico City, Museo de Arte Moderno (INBA)

62. The Temptations of Saint Anthony, 1947

Oil on canvas, 90 × 110 cm

Provenance: José Maria Dávila

Exhibitions: Mexico City 1949, no. 712; Houston 1951, no. 16; Mexico City 1977, no. 229; Mexico City 1983, no. 74

References: Reyero 1983, pl. 162

Mexico City, Museo de Arte Moderno (INBA)

63. Self-Portrait, 1949

Tempera on linen, 31.1 × 25.1 cm

References: Mexico City 1977, 19 (III)

Collection of Burt B. Holmes

64. Portrait of Ruth Rivera, 1949

Oil on canvas, 199 × 100.5 cm

Inscriptions: upper right, *Diego Rivera / 1949*

Provenance: Ruth Rivera, 1969

Exhibitions: Mexico City 1949, 198; Mexico City 1977, no. 314; Leningrad 1978; Mexico City 1983, 53

References: Taracena et al. 1979, 97 (I); Reyero 1983, 234 (I)

Collection of Rafael Coronel

65. Portrait of Señorita Matilda Palou, 1951

Oil on canvas, 200.5 × 123 cm

Inscriptions: upper left: *Diego Rivera, 1951*

Provenance: Commissioned from the artist by Osceola Heard Davenport, 1950

Collection of the family of Osceola Heard Davenport

66. The Painter's Studio, 1954

Oil on canvas, 178 × 150 cm

Exhibitions: Mexico City 1977, no. 276

References: Reyero, pl. 172 (I)

Mexico City, Secretaria de Hacienda y Crédito Público

67. Portrait of Dolores Olmedo, 1955

Oil on canvas, 200 × 152 cm

Inscriptions: bottom left/right, *Retrato De Lolita Olmedo Diego Rivera 1955*

Exhibitions: Berlin 1959, no. 1172; Mexico City 1977, no. 321; Leningrad 1978; Mexico City 1983, no. 90; Mexico City/Monterrey 1983, no. 26; Miami 1984

References: Reyero 1983, pl. 169 (I)

Collection of Dolores Olmedo

68. Hitler's Refuge—Ruins of Berlin's Chancellery, 1956

Oil and tempera on canvas, 105 × 135 cm

Inscriptions: lower right, *Diego Rivera 1956.*

References: Taracena et al. 1979, 86 (I)

Private Collection

69. Containing the Ice on the Danube, 1956

Oil on canvas, 90 × 116 cm

Inscriptions: lower left, *Diego Rivera 1956.*

Exhibitions: Mexico City 1965; Washington/Los Angeles 1978, no. 183; Mexico City 1983, no. 96

Mexico City, Secretaria de Hacienda y Crédito Público

70. Sunsets (series of twenty), 1956

Oil and tempera on canvas, 313.5 × 204 cm overall (average size 30 × 40 cm)

Inscriptions: *Diego Rivera, 1956.*

Exhibitions: Mexico City 1977, nos. 334–53; Mexico City/Monterrey 1983, no. 74

References: Taracena et al. 1979, pl. 118 (I)

Collection of Dolores Olmedo

71. The Watermelons, 1957

Oil on canvas, 67 × 91 cm

Inscriptions: upper left, *Diego Rivera / 1957.*

Exhibitions: Leningrad 1978; Mexico city/Monterrey 1983, no. 25

Collection of Dolores Olmedo

Graphics

72. Portrait of Maria Barrientos de Rivera (Mother of the Artist), 1986

Pencil on tan paper, 31 × 22 cm

Inscriptions: center right, *D. Rivera*

Provenance: Maria Rivera Barrientos

Exhibitions: Mexico City 1977, no. 33; Leningrad 1978; Mexico City 1983, no. 125; Mexico City/Monterrey 1983, 7, no. 36

References: Taracena et al. 1979, 9, pl. 17 (I)

Collection of Dolores Olmedo

73. Head of a Woman, 1898

Pencil on greenish blue paper, 36.2 × 28.3 cm

Inscriptions: lower center, *Diego Rivera*

Annotations: lower right, *1900*; on mat, *copy after French 19th-Century lithograph after C. Gleyre / lith. (#642798)*

Exhibitions: Mexico City 1949, no. 21; Mexico City 1977, no. 32

References: Arquin 1971, 10 (I)

Mexico City, UNAM, Escuela Nacional de Artes Plásticas

74. Classical Standing Figure Leaning on an Urn, 1899

Pencil, 50.7 × 35.2 cm

Inscriptions: lower left, *Diego Rivera / 1899*

Mexico City, UNAM, Escuela Nacional de Artes Plásticas

75. Swag, 1900

Pencil on gray paper, 60.6 × 44.1 cm

Inscriptions: lower right, *Diego Rivera 1900*

Exhibitions: Mexico City 1977, no. 29 (as *Guirnalda*)

Mexico City, UNAM, Escuela Nacional de Artes Plásticas

76. Dead Horse, 1906

Charcoal, gouache, and brush in black ink on greige paper, 32.6 × 39.7 cm

Inscriptions: lower right, *D.M. Rivera. 1906*

Provenance: Piccadilly Gallery, London

New York, The Museum of Modern Art, New York Inter-American Fund (1586.68)

77. Béguinage à Bruges, also know as *Night Scene*, 1909

Charcoal, 27.8 × 46 cm

Inscriptions: upper left, *A. Mlle. Angeline Beloff / para que se acuerde de me afecto / Brujes 9 de Octobre de 1909. / Diego M. Rivera*

Provenance: Angeline Beloff, Marte R. Gómez

Exhibitions: Mexico City 1973, no. 46

Guanajuato, Museo Diego Rivera (INBA)

78. Tree, 1913

Watercolor, 33.8 × 26 cm

Inscriptions: lower right, *Diego M. Rivera / 13*

Provenance: Marte R. Gómez

Exhibitions: Mexico City 1949, no. 63; Mexico City 1973, no. 38; Phoenix 1984, 46, no. 14

Guanajuato, Museo Diego Rivera (INBA)

79. Still Life with Teapot, 1913

Pencil, 25.8 × 35 cm

Inscriptions: lower right, *Diego M. Rivera / 13*

Provenance: Marte R. Gómez

Exhibitions: Phoenix 1984, no. 16

Guanajuato, Museo Diego Rivera (INBA)

80. Landscape (Majorca), 1914

Watercolor and pencil, 50.8 × 32.5 cm

Inscriptions: lower right, *Diego M. Rivera / 14*

Provenance: Marte R. Gómez

Exhibitions: Mexico City 1973, no. 39; Phoenix 1984; 88, no. 30

Guanajuato, Museo Diego Rivera (INBA)

81. Spanish Still Life, 1914

Pencil, 41.8 × 25 cm

Inscriptions: lower right, *D.M.R.*

Provenance: Marte R. Gómez

Exhibitions: Mexico City 1973, no. 22; Phoenix 1984, no. 20

Guanajuato, Museo Diego Rivera (INBA)

82. Sailor's Head (second version), 1914

Pencil, 42.8 × 26 cm

Provenance: Marte R. Gómez

Exhibitions: Mexico City 1973, no. 25; Mexico City 1977, no. 26; Phoenix 1984, no. 27

Guanajuato, Museo Diego Rivera (INBA)

83. Paris Cityscape—"Foll", ca. 1913

Pencil, 33.4 × 25.8 cm

Provenance: Marte R. Gómez

Exhibitions: Mexico City 1973, no. 17 (dated 1913); Phoenix 1984, no. 4

Guanajuato, Museo Diego Rivera (INBA)

84. Portrait of Angeline Beloff, 1917

Pencil, 33.7 × 25.7 cm

Inscriptions: lower left, *D. M. Rivera / 12–17*

Provenance: E. Weyhe, Inc., New York, 1927. Lewis B. Williams, Cleveland. Lewis C. Williams, Chagrin Falls, Ohio. Sotheby Parke-Bernet, New York, 1974. Achim Moeller, Ltd., London

Exhibitions: Cleveland 1927; Mexico City 1977, no. 249

References: Taracena et al. 1979, 42 (I)

New York, The Museum of Modern Art, Gift of Mr. and Mrs. Wolfgang Schoenborn in honor of René d'Harnoncourt

85. Portrait of the Engraver Lebedeff, 1918

Pencil, 31.1 × 23.8 cm

Inscriptions: lower left, *Lebedeff graveur / Rivera-IIII-18*

Provenance: John S. Newberry, Jr., Grosse Pointe Farms, Michigan. Parke-Bernet sale, New York, 1961. Private Collection, Sotheby Parke-Bernet sale, New York, 1980. Private Collection. Christie, Manson and Woods sale, New York, 1982.

Exhibitions: Cambridge 1948, 19; New York 1948, no. 43; Detroit 1949, 28

Collection of Burt B. Holmes

86. Still Life with Petit Dejeuner and Wine Bottle, 1918

Pencil, 48.9 × 40.9 cm

Inscriptions: lower left, *Rivera IV–18*
Provenance: E. Weyhe, Inc., New York

Amherst, Massachusetts, Amherst College, Mead Art Museum, Museum Purchase (1957.37)

87. Still Life with Carafe, Knife, and Chestnuts, 1918

Pencil, 31.4 × 23.3 cm

Inscriptions: lower right, *Rivera-18*

Exhibitions: New York 1928, no. 34

The Detroit Institute of Arts, Bequest of Robert H. Tannahill (70.333)

88. Man with Pipe (Alberto J. Pani), 1919

Pencil, 31.4 × 23.5 cm

Inscriptions: lower right, *1919 D.R.*

Provenance: Marte R. Gómez

Exhibitions: Mexico City 1949, no. 125; Mexico City 1973, no. 31

Guanajuato, Museo Diego Rivera (INBA)

89. Bound volume of thirty-one sketches made in Italy, 1920–21
Pencil, red chalk, and ink, page size varies from 21 × 13.3 cm to 11.5 × 12.7 cm

Annotations: on righthand sheet of first spread after endpapers, *Angelina Beloff / amicalement a / Jean Charlot / pour la meilleur con- / cervation [sic] de ces dessins.*

Provenance: Angeline Beloff, Jean Charlot

Exhibitions: Mexico City 1949, no. 192

References: Charlot 1953 (II)

Collection of Mrs. Jean Charlot

90. Self-Portrait, 1921

Charcoal and red chalk on tan paper, 38 × 24 cm

Provenance: Angeline Beloff, Oscar Morineau

Exhibitions: Mexico City 1949, no. 13; Mexico City 1977, no. 79; Leningrad 1978; Mexico City 1983, no. 130; Mexico City/Monterrey 1983, 11, no. 37

References: Reyero 1983, 272, no. 218 (I)

Collection of Dolores Olmedo

91. Portrait of David Alfaro Siqueiros, 1921

Charcoal and red chalk on tan paper, 38.8 × 24.4 cm

Inscriptions: upper right, *Diego Rivera / 1921*

Provenance: Marte R. Gómez

Exhibitions: Mexico City 1949, no. 138; Mexico City 1973, no. 48; Mexico City 1977, no. 78; Mexico City 1983, no. 131

References: Reyero 1983, 255, no. 189 (I)

Guanajuato, Museo Diego Rivera (INBA)

92. Study of Anthropomorphic Etruscan Vase, 1921

Pencil, 32 × 22.2 cm

Inscriptions: lower left, *Diego Rivera, 21*

Philadelphia Museum of Art, Purchase, Lola Downin Peck Fund from the estate of Carl Zigrosser (1976–97–98)

93. Head, 1921–22

Study for the figure of *Music,* Anfiteatro Bolivar, Escuela Nacional Preparatoria

Red and black chalk heightened with white on blue-gray paper, 61.6 × 47.5 cm

Inscriptions: lower right, *D. Rivera*

Exhibitions: San Francisco 1930, no. 73; San Francisco 1939, no. 10; Mexico City 1949, no. 831; San Francisco 1982, no. 11; San Francisco 1984, no. 8

San Francisco Museum of Modern Art, Albert M. Bender Collection, Gift of Albert M. Bender through the San Francisco Art Institute (64.29)

94. Hand, 1921–22

Study for the figure of *Science,* Anfiteatro Bolivar, Escuela Nacional Preparatoria

Red and black chalk on light gray paper, 47.3 × 61.3 cm

Inscriptions: lower right, *D. Rivera*

Exhibitions: San Francisco 1930, no. 73; New York 1931, no. 89; San Francisco 1939; San Francisco 1978, no. 18; Flushing 1979, no. 42; San Francisco 1982, no. 10

San Francisco Museum of Modern Art, Albert M. Bender Collection, Gift of Albert M. Bender through the San Francisco Art Institute (64.26)

95. Two Hands (palms up), 1922

Study for the figure of *Wisdom,* Anfiteatro Bolivar, Escuela Nacional Preparatoria

Red and black chalk, 48.9 × 66.1 cm

Inscriptions: lower right, *D. Rivera. 22*

Exhibitions: San Francisco 1930, no. 73; New York 1931, no. 89; San Francisco 1939; Mexico City 1949, no. 833; San Francisco 1978, no. 17; San Francisco 1982, no. 9; Mexico City 1983, no 135

San Francisco Museum of Modern Art, Albert M. Bender Collection, Gift of Albert M. Bender through the San Francisco Art Institute (64.25)

96. Spinners, 1923

Study for *Weavers,* Court of Labor (first floor), Secretaría de Educación Pública

Charcoal and pencil, 45.7 × 30.5 cm

Inscriptions: lower left, *Diego Rivera. 23*

Provenance: Ralph Stackpole. Albert M. Bender, 1940. San Francisco Museum of Art. San Francisco Art Institute. Sotheby Parke-Bernet sale, New York, 1979

Mexico City, Galerías A. Cristóbal

97. Man at Spinning Wheel, 1923

Study for *Weavers,* Court of Labor (first floor), Secretaría de Educación Pública

Pencil, 30.2 × 44.5 cm

Inscriptions: lower right, *D. Rivera. 23*

Philadelphia Museum of Art, Purchase, Lola Downin Peck Fund from the estate of Carl Zigrosser (1976–97–81)

98. Horse with Bridle and Saddle, 1923

Study for horse at left in *Liberation of the Peon,* Court of Labor (first floor), Secretaría de Educación Pública

Pencil, 48.1 × 29.2 cm

Inscriptions: lower right, *D. Rivera. 23*

Philadephia Museum of Art, Purchase, Lola Downin Peck Fund from the estate of Carl Zigrosser (1976–97–77)

99. Flower Vendor Resting, Tehuantepec, 1923

Pencil, 27.3 × 21.2 cm

Inscriptions: lower left, *D. Rivera 23*

Exhibitions: San Francisco 1939, no. 5; Muskegon 1943; Mexico City 1949, no. 235; San Francisco 1982, no. 6; San Francisco 1984, no. 9

San Francisco Museum of Modern Art, Albert M. Bender Collection, Gift of Albert M. Bender (35.2702)

100. Two Standing Women Conversing, Tehuantepec, 1923

Preliminary study for mural, *Cane Harvest,* Court of Labor (first floor), Secretaría Educación Pública

Pencil, 33 × 21.6 cm

Inscriptions: lower right, *D. Rivera 23*

Exhibitions: San Francisco 1939, no. 13; Muskegon 1943; Mexico City 1949, no. 232; San Francisco 1984, no. 10

San Francisco Museum of Modern Art, Albert M. Bender Collection, Gift of Albert M. Bender (35.2705)

101. Head of a Tehuantepec Woman, 1923

Watercolor over black chalk, 42.8 × 31.7 cm

Inscriptions: lower left, *Diego Rivera / 23*

Provenance: Palma Guillén de Nicolan D'Oliver, Mexico 1949

Exhibitions: Mexico City 1949, no. 236

Philadelphia Museum of Art, Purchase, Lola Downin Peck Fund from the estate of Carl Zigrosser (1976–97–76)

102. Woman Bather, Tehuantepec, formerly *Woman Bending Over,* ca. 1923

Study for the oil painting *Bather of Tehuantepec* (figure 92)

Charcoal on tan paper, 62.6 × 46.5 cm

Inscriptions: lower right, *D. Rivera*

Exhibitions: San Francisco 1930, no. 76

San Francisco Museum of Modern Art, Bequest of Harriet Lane Levy (50.6110)

103. Day of the Dead in the Country, 1925

Study for*The Offering,* Court of Fiestas (first floor), Secretaría de Educación Pública

Charcoal, colored chalk, and pencil, 46.4 × 29.8 cm

Inscriptions: lower right, *D. Rivera / 25*

Exhibitions: New York 1931, no. 102A; Cambridge 1942; Worcester 1944; New Haven/Austin 1966, no. 307

New York, The Museum of Modern Art, Anonymous Gift

104. Blessed Fruit of Knowledge, 1925

Study for *Fruits of the Earth,* Court of Fiestas (third floor), Secretaría de Educación Púbica

Pencil, 48.3 × 53.5 cm

Inscriptions: lower right margin, center, *Diego Rivera 1925*

Provenance: Ruth Rivera

Collection of Rafael Coronel

105. False Learning, 1925

Study for *The Learned,* Court of Fiestas (third floor), Secretaría de Educación Pública

Pencil, 48.3 × 53.3 cm

Inscriptions: lower right margin, center, *Diego Rivera 1925*

Provenance: Ruth Rivera

Collection of Rafael Coronel

106. Reclining Nude, 1925

Study for the figure of *The Virgin Earth,* Chapel, Universidad Autónoma de Chapingo

Pencil, 45.1 × 63 cm

Inscriptions: lower left, *Diego Rivera. 25*

Exhibitions: New York 1931, no. 103

References: Wolfe 1963, 188, pl. 65 (I)

Philadelphia Museum of Art, Purchase, Lola Downin Peck Fund from the estate of Carl Zigrosser

107. Seated Nude with Braided Hair, 1925

Study for figure in *The Liberated Earth,* Chapel, Universidad Autónoma de Chapingo

Pencil, 35.8 × 50.9 cm

Inscriptions: lower right, *Diego Rivera. 25*

Exhibitions: Cambridge 1942

New York: The Museum of Modern Art, Anonymous Gift (206.40)

108. Male Nude Holding a Stalk of Sugar Cane, 1925

Study for fourth ceiling vault, Chapel, Universidad Autónoma de Chapingo

Pencil, 40.6 × 30.8 cm (top) 21.8 cm (bottom)

Inscriptions: lower right, *Diego Rivera, 25*

Philadelphia Museum of Art, Purchase, Lola Downin Peck Fund from the estate of Carl Zigrosser (1976–97–83)

109. Night of the Poor, ca. 1925

Study for the panel of the same title, Court of Fiestas (third floor), Secretaría de Educación Pública

Pencil, 31.8 × 29.8 cm

Inscriptions: left of center, *D. Rivera 2*[?]

Philadelphia Museum of Art, Purchase, Lola Downin Peck Fund from the estate of Carl Zigrosser (1976–97–72)

110. Miner Being Searched, ca. 1925

Illustration for Alfons Goldschmidt, *Mexiko* (Berlin: Ernst Rowohlt, 1925), opposite page 188

Brush and black ink heightened with white over pencil on paper, 31 × 22.5 cm

Provenance: Eric Cohn, New York, 1945. New Arts Center Gallery, New York, 1965. Sotheby Parke-Bernet sale, New York, 1981.

Mexico City, Galerias A. Cristóbal

111. Liquidation of the Feudal Order, 1926

Study for *Guarantees—Debris of Capitalism,* Court of Fiestas (third floor), Secretaría de Educación Publica

Pencil, 33 × 43.4 cm

Inscriptions: lower center, *D. Rivera 26*

Philadelphia Museum of Art, Purchase, Lola Downin Peck Fund from the estate of Carl Zigrosser (1976–97–71)

112. Fire, 1926

Study for figure in *The Liberated Earth,* Chapel, Universidad Autónoma de Chapingo

Charcoal, 30.5 × 45.7 cm (sight)

Inscriptions: lower right, *Diego Rivera / 26*

Collection of Dr. and Mrs. David R. Sacks

113. Crouching Nude with Arms Outstretched, 1926

Study for the central figure in *Subterranean Forces,* Chapel, Universidad Autónoma de Chapingo

Charcoal, 48.2 × 62 cm

Inscriptions: lower left, *A Tina Modotti / Diego Rivera. 26*

The Baltimore Museum of Art, Gift of Blanche Adler (1931.41.2)

114. Back of a Seated Nude, 1926

Study for figure at right in *Germination,* Chapel, Escuela Nacional de Agricultura, Chapingo

Red chalk and charcoal, 63.2 × 48.5 cm

Inscriptions: lower left, *Diego Rivera 1926*

Exhibitions: Muskegon 1943; Mexico City 1983, no. 141.

References: Reyero 1983, pl. 85 (I)

San Francisco Museum of Modern Art, Albert M. Bender Collection, Gift of Albert M. Bender (35.1655)

115. Seated Nude with Long Hair, 1926

Study for the figure at lower center in *Subterranean Forces,* Chapel, Universidad Autónoma de Champingo

Black chalk and watercolor, 62.2 × 48.2 cm

Inscriptions: lower left, *Diego Rivera, 26*

Provenance: Private Collection, Chicago. Private Collection, Mexico City

The Detroit Institute of Arts, Founders Society Purchase, Matilda R. Wilson and Mr. and Mrs. Walter B. Ford Funds (F1984.27)

116. Blossoming, 1926

Study for *Maturation,* Chapel, Universidad Autónoma de Chapingo

Pencil, 48.1 × 38.5 cm

Inscriptions: lower left, *Diego Rivera, 26*

Philadelphia Museum of Art, Purchase, Lola Downin Peck Fund from the estate of Carl Zigrosser (1976–97–75)

117. Reclining Nude, 1926

Study for the central figure in *Reactionary Forces,* Chapel, Universidad Autónoma de Chapingo

Pencil, 31 × 48.1 cm

San Francisco, California Palace of the Legion of Honor, Achenbach Foundation for Graphic Arts, Gift of Miss Bea L. Habeil (1985.2.18)

118. Drunken Women, 1926

Charcoal, 27 × 37.8 cm

Inscriptions: lower right, *D. Rivera, 26*

Exhibitions: San Francisco 1939, 8, no. 18, Muskegon 1943; Mexico City 1949, no. 256, San Francisco 1978, no. 2; Flushing 1979, no. 56, Mexico City 1983, no. 142

San Francisco Museum of Modern Art, Albert M. Bender Collection, Gift of Albert M. Bender (35.2690)

119. The Eating Place, 1926

Charcoal and pencil, 37.8 × 27.3 cm

Inscriptions: lower right, *Diego Rivera, 26*

Exhibitions: San Francisco 1939, no. 19; Muskegon 1943; Mexico City 1949, no. 253; San Francisco 1978, no. 6; Flushing 1979, no. 54

References: Crespo de la Serna 1949 (II)

San Francisco Museum of Modern Art, Albert M. Bender Collection, Gift of Albert M. Bender (35.2700)

120. Indian Woman with Corn, 1926

Black chalk, 63.2 × 48.3 cm

Inscriptions: lower right, *Diego Rivera, 26*

Exhibitions: San Francisco 1930, no. 75

San Francisco, California Palace of the Legion of Honor, Achenbach Foundation for Graphic Arts, Gift of Albert M. Bender (1927.55)

121. Woman Kneeling over Sleeping Child, 1926

Brush and black ink over pencil, 60 × 46.8 cm

Inscriptions: lower right, *D. Rivera / 1926*

Philadelphia Museum of Art, Gift of an Anonymous Donor (1945–66–2)

122. Landscape, Tlalnepantla, formerly known as *Tehauntepec Pass No. 13*, 1926

Conté crayon, 27.3 × 38.8 cm

Inscriptions: lower left, *D. Rivera, 26*

Exhibitions: San Francisco 1939, no. 24; Muskegon 1943; Mexico City 1949, no. 254

San Francisco Museum of Modern Art, Albert M. Bender Collection, Gift of Albert M. Bender (35.2707)

123. Portrait of Tina Modotti, 1926

Black chalk, 48.5 × 31.5 cm

Inscriptions: lower left, *Para Tina Modotti / Diego Rivera, 26*

References: Wolfe 1939, 213, pl. 67 (I); Tarcena et al. 1979, 51 (I)

Philadelphia Museum of Art, Purchase, Lola Downin Peck Fund from the estate of Carl Zigrosser (1976–97–89)

124. Portrait of Mr. and Mrs. Ralph Stackpole, ca. 1926

Pencil, 64.8 × 54 cm

Inscriptions: lower left, *A. Madame et Mon / sieur Ralph Stack / Pole comme cadeau / de mariage. / Diego Rivera*

Exhibitions: San Francisco 1930, no. 105

References: Villaurrutia 1928, 30 (II); Wolfe 1939, 316 (I); Wolfe 1963, 280 (I)

Collection of Mr. and Mrs. Fred H. Altshuler

125. Germination, 1927

Study for panel of same title, Chapel, Universidad Autónoma de Chapino

Pencil, 50.5 × 75.6 cm

Inscriptions: lower right in pencil, *Diego Rivera, 27*

Honolulu Academy of Arts, Gift of Miss Bea L. Haberl, 1971 &15.707)

126. Cover design for *Mexican Folkways,* 1927

Black ink, 31.1 × 23.5 cm

Inscriptions: lower left, *D., lower right, R.*, uppe rright, *Dos Colores*

Provenance: Rafael Coronel. Juan Coronel Rivera

Palm Springs, California, B. Lewin Galleries

127. Adobe Hut with Pumpkins on the Roof, 1927

Charcoal with red pigment, 63.5 × 48.9 cm

Inscriptions: lower left, *Diego Rivera 27*

Provenance: E. Weyhe, Inc., New York, 1928

References: Richardson 1931, 75–76 (II)

The Detroit Institute of Arts, Museum Purchase (29.338)

128. Portrait of Mariano Azuela, ca. 1927

Pen and black ink over pencil, 31 × 24 cm

Inscriptions: lower right, *Diego Rivera. 2 [?];* lower left, *Don Mariano Azuela autor de "Los de Abajo."*

Philadelphia Museum of Art, Purchase, Lola Downin Peck Fund from the estate of Carl Zigrosser (1976–97–85)

129.–130. Convenciones de la liga de Communidades Agrarias y Sindicatos Compesinos del Estado de Tamaulipas (album of 42 sketches), 1927, (album of 39 sketches), 1928

Brush in black ink, album, 41 × 34 cm; sketches, 31.1 × 23.5 cm

Provenance: Marte R. Gómez

Exhibitions: Mexico City 1949, nos, 365–67;Mexico City 1973, no. 63; Mexico City 1977, no. 239

References: Taracena et al. 1979, 50 (I)

Guanajuato, Museo Diego Rivera, Marte R. Gómez Collection (INBA)

131.–135. May Day, Moscow (five from a series of forty-five watercolors), 1928

Watercolor, each sketch approx. 10.5 × 16.2 cm

Exhibitions: Mexico City 1949

References: Fernández 1952, 322 (IV); cf, Reyero 1983, nos. 194–97 (I)

New York, The Museum of Modern Art, Gift of Abby Aldrich Rockefeller (137.35.13, 137.35.21, 137.35.23, 137.35.27, 1137.35.30)

136. Reclining Nude with Snake, ca. 1929

Study for the figure of *Continence,* Secretaría de Salubridad y Asistencia

Pencil, 45.5 × 61.2 cm

Inscriptions: lower left, *Diego Rivera*

Philadelphia Museum of Art, Purchase, Lola Downin Peck Fund from the estate of Carl Zigrosser (1976–97–101)

137. Harvesting Sugar Cane, 1930

Study for *Sugar Plantation in Morelos,* Palacio de Cortés, Cuernavaca

Pencil, 46.4 × 29.7 cm

Inscriptions: lower left, *A.C. Zigrosser, Diego Rivera 30*

Philadelphia Museum of Art, Purchase, Lola Downin Peck Fund from the estate of Carl Zigrosser (1976–97–82)

138. Cortés's Soldiers Torturing and Plundering, 1930

Study for *The Taking of Cuernavaca,* Palacio de Cortés, Cuernavaca

Pencil, 41.6 × 43.8 cm

Inscriptions: lower center, *Diego Rivera, 30*

Provenance: E. Weyhe, Inc., New York

Amherst, Massachusetts, Amherst College, Mead Art Museum, Museum Purchase (1952.16)

139. Building the Palace of Cortés, 1930

Study for panel of the same title, Palacio de Cortés, Cuernavaca

Pencil on brownish paper, 47.9 × 31.8 cm

Inscriptions: lower right, *Diego Rivera 30*

Exhibitions: Cambridge 1942; Worcester 1944; Mexico City 1949, no. 965; New Haven 1966, no. 305

New York, The Museum of Modern Art, Anonymous Gift (207.40)

140. Mesa and Cacti, 1930

Watercolor, 31.8 × 48.3 cm

Inscriptions: lower right, *Diego Rivera, 30*

Exhibitions: San Francisco 1930, no. 35; Detroit 1936; Detroit 1976, no. 236

References: Richardson 1931, 76 (II)

The Detroit Institute of Arts, City Purchase (31.24)

141. Vultures on Cactus, 1930

Watercolor over black chalk, 42.9 × 32.2 cm

Inscriptions: lower right, *Diego Rivera 30*

Exhibitions: San Francisco 1930, no. 39; Detroit 1932, no. 19; Detroit 1936; Detroit 1938a, no. 115; Detroit 1976, no. 237

The Detroit Institute of Arts, Bequest of Robert H. Tannahill (70.331)

142. Untitled (Energy), 1930

Study for *Allegory of California,* Luncheon Club, Pacific Stock Exchange, San Francisco

Pencil, 63.5 × 48.3 cm

Inscriptions: lower left, *Diego Rivera, 1930*

Annotations: lower left, *"Energy"*

Exhibitions: New York 1931, no. 113; San Francisco 1939, no. 12; Flushing 1979, no. 46; San Francisco 1982, no. 1

San Francisco Museum of Modern Art, William L. Gerstle Collection, Gift of William L. Gerstle through the San Francisco Art Institute (64.10)

143. Miners Panning Gold (Marshall's Discovery of Gold in California), 1930

Study for *Allegory of California,* Luncheon Club, Pacific Stock Exchange, San Franscisco

Pencil, 61.6 × 47.9 cm

Inscriptions: lower left, *Diego Rivera, 30*

Exhibitions: New York 1931, no. 114; San Francisco 1939, no. 15; San Francisco 1982, no. 3; San Francisco 1984, no. 19

San Francisco Museum of Modern Art, William L. Gerstle Collection, Gift of William L. Gerstle through the San Francisco Art Institute (64.15)

144. Head of a Woman, 1931

Red and black Chalk, 62.3 × 48 cm

Inscriptions: lower right, *Diego Rivera*

Exhibitions: New York 1931, no. 115

San Francisco Museum of Modern Art, William L. Gerstle Collection, Gift of William L. Gerstle through the San Francisco Art Institute (64.12)

145. Ducks, 1931

Pastel, 61.9 × 48 cm

Inscriptions: lower left, *A mon cher ami Monsieur Gerstle / en souvenir des models dont il / me fit cadeau et qui furent / tres savoureux. Diego Rivera*

Exhibitions: San Francisco 1939, no. 45

San Francisco Museum of Modern Art, Collection of William L. Gerstle, Gift of William L. Gerstle (39.179)

146. Portrait of Arthur Brown, 1931

Study for *The Making of a Fresco,* San Francisco Art Institute

Red chalk and charcoal, 58.4 × 48.2 cm

Inscriptions: lower right, *Diego Rivera 1931*

Provenance: William L. Gerstle. San Francisco Art Institute. San Francisco Museum of Art. Sotheby's sale, [Los Angeles], 1979

Exhibitions: San Francisco 1939, no. 31; Mexico City 1949, no. 1027; San Francisco 1984, no. 21

San Francisco, California Palace of the Legion of Honor, Achenbach Foundation for Graphic Arts, Gift of Drs. Daniel and Hilary Goldstine and Mr. and Mrs. C. David Robinson through the San Francisco Art Institute (1981.2.26)

147. Ralph Stackpole Cutting Stone, 1931

Study for *the Making of a Fresco,* San Francisco Art Institute

Charcoal, 60.9 × 45.7 cm

Inscriptions: lower right, *Diego Rivera, 31*

Provenance: William L. Gerstle, San Francisco Art Institute. San Francisco Museum of Art. Sotheby's sale, [Los Angeles], 1979

Exhibitions: San Francisco 1939, no. 40

Palm Springs, California, B. Lewin Galleries

148. Clifford Wight Measuring, 1931

Study for *The Making of a Fresco,* San Francisco Art Institute

Charcoal, 60.9 × 45.7 cm

Inscriptions: lower left, *Diego Rivera, 1931*

Provenance: William Gerstle. San Francisco Art Institute. San Francisco Museum of Art. Sotheby's sale, [Los Angeles], 1979

Exhibitions: San Francisco 1939, no. 41

Mexico City, Galerías A. Cristóbal

149. Mexican Highway, 1931

Illustration in Stuart Chase, *Mexico: A Study of Two Americas* (New York: The MacMillan Company, 1937), opposite page 258

Brush and black ink, 48 × 31.6 cm

Inscriptions: lower right, *Diego Rivera, 31*

Philadelphia Museum of Art, Gift of Carl Zigrosser (1976–97–69)

150. Flower Sellers, 1931

Illustration in Stuart Chase, *Mexico: A Study of Two Americas* (New York: The MacMillan Company, 1937), opposite page 232

Brush and black ink, 48 × 31.5 cm

Exhibitions: Mexico City 1949, no. 385

Mexico City, Museo Franz Mayer

151. Market Scene, 1931

Illustration in Stuart Chase, *Mexico: A Study of Two Americas* (New York: The MacMillan Company, 1937), opposite page 134

Brush and black ink, 48 × 31 cm

Exhibitions: Mexico City 1949, no. 387

Mexico City: Museo Franz Mayer

152. Production and Manufacture of Automobile Motors, 1931

Sketch for north wall automotive panel, *Detroit Industry,* Detroit Institute of Arts

Charcoal, 45.7 × 83.3 cm

Provenance: Contemporary Art Society, 1938

Exhibitions: Detroit 1978, 49, no. 74

Leeds City Art Galleries

153. Manufacture of Automobile Bodies and Final Assembly, 1932

Sketch for south wall automative panel, *Detroit Industry,* Detroit Institute of Arts

Charcoal, 45.7 × 83.8 cm

Provenance: Contemporary Art Society, 1938

Exhibitions: Detroit 1978, 49, 82, no. 106

Leeds City Art Galleries

154. Electricity, 1932

Sketch for west wall panel, *Detroit Industry,* Detroit Institute of Arts

Charcoal and wash, 51.7 × 14.5 cm

Provenance: Contemporary Art Society, 1938

Exhibitions: *Cityscape 1910–1939,* Arts Council Touring Exhibition, 1977–78, no. 117; Detroit 1978, no. 57

Leeds City Art Galleries

155. Steam, 1932

Sketch for west wall panel, *Detroit Industry,* Detroit Institute of Arts

Pencil, 51.6 × 14.5 cm

Provenance: Contemporary Art Society, 1938

Exhibitions: *Cityscape 1910–1939,* Arts Council Touring Exhibition, 1977–78, no. 118; Detroit 1978, no. 56

Leeds City Art Galleries

156. Portrait of Robert H. Tannahill, 132

Red and black chalk, 73 × 57.9 cm

Inscriptions: lower right, *Diego Rivera, 1932.*

Exhibitions: Detroit 1932, no. 23; Mexico City 1949, no. 404

The Detroit Institute of Arts, Bequest of Robert H. Tannahill (70.332)

157. Zapata, ca. 1932

Study for a lithograph

Red chalk, 45.7 × 37.7 cm

Philadelphia Museum of Art, Purchase, Lola Downin Peck Fund from the estate of Carl Zigrosser (1976.97.103)

158. Man at the Crossroads, 1932

Study for mural, Rockefeller Center, New York

Pencil on light tan paper, 78.7 × 181 cm

Inscriptions: lower left, *Diego Rivera, Novembre 1, 32 avec mes hommages tres respectueux et afectueus [sic] a Madame Abby Aldrich de Rockefeller*

Exhibitions: New Haven/Austin 1966, no. 309; Berlin 1980, no. 268

New York, The Museum of Modern Art, Anonymous Gift (138.35)

159. Maternidad Mecánica, 1933

Watercolor, 47 × 25 cm

Inscriptions: upper right, *NUEVA YORK / 1933 / Diego Rivera.*

Provenance: Carlos Gutierrez Cruz

Exhibitions: Leningrad 1978; Mexico City/ Monterrey 1983, 51, no. 35

Collection of Dolores Olmedo

160. Zandunga, Tehuantepec Dance, ca. 1935

Charcoal and watercolor, 48.1 × 60.6 cm

Inscriptions: lower right, *Diego Rivera*

Los Angeles Country Museum of Art, Gift of Mr. and Mrs. Milton W. Lipper from the Milton W. Lipper Estate (M. 74.22.4)

161. Mexican Woman with Basket, 1935

Red and black chalk, 55.9 × 42.9 cm

Inscriptions: lower right, *Diego Rivera*

Exhibitions: San Francisco 1939, no. 46; Mexico City 1949, no. 428; San Francisco 1972; San Francisco 1978; Flushing 1979, no. 49

San Francisco Museum of Modern Art, Albert M. Bender Collection, Gift of Albert M. Bender (35.3400)

162. Huarache Sale, 1936

Brush in black ink and watercolor, 26 × 37.5 cm

Inscriptions: lower left, *Diego Rivera*

Los Angeles County Museum of Art, Gift of Mrs. Ewing Seligman (M.63.73)

163. Profile of an Indian Woman with Calla Lilies, 1938

Pastel and charcoal, 62.9 × 47.5 cm

Inscriptions: upper left, *Diego Rivera / 38*

Provenance: Private Collection, Beverly Hills, California. Dalzell Hatfield Galleries, Los Angeles

Collection of Mr. and Mrs. Kenneth E. Hill

164. Indian Woman with Marigolds, 1938

Pastel and charcoal, 63 × 48.5 cm

Inscriptions: upper right, *Diego Rivera / 38*

Annotations: on verso of frame, *appartient a S.A. le Maharaja Holker / 21.4 '39 H. P. Roché*

Provenance: The Maharaja of Holkor

Exhibitions: Mexico City 1977, no. 371; Leningrad 1978; Mexico City/Monterrey 1983, 35, no. 30

References: Taracena et al. 1979, 165, no. 144 (I)

Collection of Dolores Olmedo

165. Frida Kahlo, Diego Rivera and Paulette Goddard Holding the Tree of Life and Love, 1940

Study for *Pan American Unity.* City College of San Francisco

Pencil, 51.2 × 85.4 cm

Exhibitions: San Francisco 1982, no. 13; San Francisco 1984, no. 26

San Francisco Museum of Modern Art, Gift of Emmy Lou Packard (49.141 A–C)

166. Volcano Erupting (from the album "El Paricutín"), 1943

Watercolor, 44 × 31 cm

Inscriptions: lower right, *Diego Rivera 43*

Provenance: Marte R. Gómez

Exhibitions: Mexico City 1949, no. 676; Mexico City 1973, no. 43; Mexico City 1977, no. 413

Guanajuato, Museo Diego Rivera (INBA)

167. Tree Branches against the Sky (from the album "El Paricutín"), 1943

Watercolor, 47.5 × 31.3 cm

Inscriptions: lower right, *Diego Rivera 43*

Provenance: Marte R. Gómez

Exhibitions: Mexico City 1949, no. 678; Mexico City 1973, no. 43; Mexico City 1977, no. 414

Guanajuato, Museo Diego Rivera (INBA)

168. Palm Sunday in Xochimilco, 1948

Pencil and charcoal, 38.7 × 28 cm

Inscriptions: lower left, *Diego Rivera 1948*

Exhibitions: Mexico City 1965, no. 46; Mexico City 1977, no. 150; Leningrad 1978; Mexico City/Monterrey 1983, 58, no. 50

Collection of Dolores Olmedo

169. Self-Portrait, 1949

Black chalk, 36.2 × 28.6 cm

Inscriptions: lower left, *Diego Rivera 1949 / Para la vida de mi vida / Lolita Olmedo al dia de las / madres de 1957, Diego Rivera*

Exhibitions: Mexico City 1983, no. 149; Mexico City/Monterrey 1983, 59, no. 52

References: Taracena et al. 1979, 24, pl. 22 (I); Reyero 1983, no. 221, pl. 272 (I)

Collection of Dolores Olmedo

170. Four Ball Players and Battle Scene with Tiger and Eagle Knights, 1950/57

Study for mural, Olympic Stadium

Pencil, 46 × 62 cm

Exhibitions: Mexico City 1977, no. 455; Mexico City 1983, no. 157

Mexico City, UNAM, Museo Universitario de Ciencias y Arte

171. Dancer, Dancer with Rattles, Three Seated Persons, Archer, and Lancer, 1950/57

Study for mural, Olympic Stadium

Pencil, 46 × 62 cm

Exhibitions: Mexico City 1977 no. 444(?)

Mexico City, UNAM, Museo Universitario de Ciencias y Arte

172. Tiger Knight Offering Heart to Quetzalcóatl, 1950/57

Study for mural, Olympic Stadium

Pencil, 46 × 62 cm

Exhibitions: Mexico City 1977, no. 446

Mexico City, UNAM, Museo Universitario de Ciencias y Arte

173. Woman Struggling with Death, 1950/57

Study for mural, Olympic Stadium

Pencil, 46 × 62 cm

Exhibitions: Mexico City 1977, no. 448

Mexico City, UNAM, Museo Universitario de Ciencias y Arte

174. Coat-of-Arms of the University, 1950/57

Study for mural, Olympic Stadium

Pencil, 46 × 62 cm

Exhibitions: Mexico City 1977, no. 454

Mexico City, UNAM, Museo Universitario de Ciencias y Arte

175. Portrait of Cantinflas, 1953

Study for mural, Teatro de los Insurgentes

Pencil, 48.3 × 63.5 cm

Inscriptions: lower right, *Diego Rivera 53*

Collection of Dr. and Mrs. David R. Sacks

176. The Offering I, 1954

Black chalk or charcoal, 39.4 × 27.3 cm

Inscriptions: lower left, *Diego Rivera 1954*

Exhibitions: Mexico City 1965, no. 53; Mexico City 1977, no. 151; Leningrad 1978; Mexico City/Monterrey 1983, no. 55

Collection of Dolores Olmedo

177. The Offering II, 1954

Black chalk or charcoal, 39.4 × 27.7 cm

Inscriptions: lower left in pencil, *Diego Rivera / 1954*

Exhibitions: Mexico City 1965, nos. 54 and 55; Mexico City 1977, no. 152; Leningrad 1978; Mexico City/Monterrey 1983, no. 56

Collection of Dolores Olmedo

178. Portrait of Pita Amor, 1957

Pencil, 39 × 28 cm

Inscriptions: lower left, *para Pita. Amor / da Diego Rivera / 1957*

Provenance: Inés Amor, 1959

Exhibitions: Mexico City 1965, no. 91; Mexico City 1977, no. 235; Leningrad 1978; Mexico City/Monterrey 1983, 65, no. 62

References: Reyero 1983, 271, no. 217 (I)

Collection of Dolores Olmedo

Bibliography

I. Books, Monographs, and Pamphlets on Diego Rivera

Abbott 1933
Abbott, Jere. *The Frescoes of Diego Rivera*. New York: Plandome, 1933.

Acevedo 1920
Acevedo, Jesús T. *Los pintores Gonzalo Arquelles Bringas y Diego Rivera*. Mexico City: México Moderno, 1920.

Arquin 1971
Arquin, Florence. *Diego Rivera: The Shaping of an Artist, 1889–1921*.
Norman: University of Oklahoma Press, 1971.

Azuela 1974
Azuela, Alicia. "La obra mural de Diego Rivera y los cambios socioeconómicos, 1930–1934." Unpub. diss., Universidad Iberoamericana, 1974.

Cardona Peña 1975
Cardona Peña, Alfredo. *El monstruo en su laberinto: conversaciones con Diego Rivera, 1945–1950*. Mexico City: Coata-Amic, 1975.

Cardoza y Aragón 1980
Cardoza y Aragón, Luís. *Diego Rivera: los frescos en la Secretaría de Educación Pública*. Mexico City: Secretaría de Educación Pública, 1980.

Castro Leal 1959
Castro Leal, Antonio. *Obras de Diego Rivera*. Mexico City: Museo Nacional de Arte Moderno, 1959.

Chávez 1946
Chávez, Ignacio. *Diego Rivera: sus frescos en el Instituto Nacional de Cardiología*. Text in English and Spanish. Mexico City: Sociedad Mexicana de Cardiología, 1946.

Civita 1967
Civita, Victor, ed. *Diego Rivera*. Sao Paulo: Abril Cultural, 1967.

Crespo de la Serna 1962
Crespo de la Serna, Jorge Juan. *Diego Rivera: pintura mural*. Mexico City: Artes de Mexico, 1962.

Das Werk 1928
Das Werk des Malers Diego Rivera. Berlin: Neuer Duetscher Verlag, 1928.

Debroise 1979
Debroise, Oliver. *Diego de Montparnasse*. Mexico City: Fondo de Cultura Económica, 1979.

Díaz del Castillo 1958
Díaz del Castillo, Bernal. *Diego Rivera: sus frescos en el Palacio Nacional de México*. Mexico City, 1958.

Diego Rivera 1957
Diego Rivera: sus frescos en el Palacio Nacional de Mexico. Mexico City: Editorial Fotocolor, 1957.

Diego Rivera 1964
Diego Rivera Arquitecto. Museo Anahuacalli. Mexico City: INBA, 1964.

Edwards 1932
Edwards, Emily. *The Frescoes by Diego Rivera in Cuernavaca*. Mexico City: Editorial Cultura, 1932.

Evans 1929
Evans, Ernestine. *The Frescoes of Diego Rivera*. New York: Harcourt Brace, 1929.

Favela 1984
Favela, Ramón. "Rivera Cubista: A Critical Study of the Early Career of Diego Rivera, 1898–1921." Unpub. diss., University of Texas at Austin, 1984.

Fernández n.d.
Fernández, Justino. *Diego Rivera: Artist of the New World*. Mexico City: Editorial Fischgrund, n.d.

Flores Arauz 1965
Flores Arauz, María Cristina. "La obra cubista de Diego Rivera." Unpub. diss., UNAM, 1965.

Fuentes Rojas 1980
Fuentes Rojas de Cadena, Elisabeth. "The San Francisco Murals of Diego Rivera: A Documentary and Artistic History." Unpub. master's thesis, University of California at Davis, 1980.

Gual 1949
Gual, Enrique F. *Cien dibujos de Diego Rivera*. Mexico City: Ediciones de Arte, 1949.

Gual 1950
Gual, Enrique F. *Fifty Years of the Work of Diego Rivera: Oils and Watercolors, 1900–1950*. Mexico City: Editorial Fischgrund, 1950.

Gual and Reyes 1965
Gual, Enrique F., and Victor M. Reyes. *Diego Rivera: pinacoteca de los genios*. Buenos Aires: Editorial Codex S.A., 1965.

Guido 1941
Guido, Angel. *Diego Rivera: los dos Diegos*. Rosario, Argentina: Universidad del Litoral, 1941.

Gurria Lacroix 1971
Gurria Lacroix, Jorge. *Hernán Cortés y Diego Rivera*. Mexico City: UNAM, 1971.

Guzmán 1921
Guzmán, Martín Luís. *Diego Rivera y la filosophia del Cubismo*. Mexico City, 1921.

Hanson and Rue 1932
Hanson, Anton, and Harald Rue. *Arbeiderkunst: Diego Rivera*. Copenhagen: Kultur og Politik, 1932.

Henestrosa et al. 1960
Henestrosa, Andrés, et al. *Testimonios sobre Diego Rivera*. Mexico City: Imprenta Universitaria, 1960.

Homenaje 1960
Homenaje del Colegio Nacional al pintor Diego Rivera. Mexico City: Colegio Nacional, 1960.

Karetnikova 1966
Karetnikova, Inga Abramovna. *Diego Rivera*. Moscow: Iskustvo, 1966.

Maceo y Arbeu 1921
Maceo y Arbeu, Eduardo. *Diego Rivera y el pristinismo*. Mexico City, 1921.

March 1960
March, Gladys. *Diego Rivera: My Art, My Life*. New York: The Citadel Press, 1960. Published in Spanish as *Diego Rivera; mi arte, mi vida*. Translated by H. González Casanova. Mexico City: Editorial Herrero, 1963.

Micheli 1973
Micheli, Mario de. *Rivera*. Mexico City: Editores Anesa-Noguer-Rizzoli, Intermex, 1973.

Mittler 1965
Mitler, Max, ed. *Diego Rivera: Wort und Bekenntnis*. Zurich: Verlag der Arche, 1965.

Morosini 1966
Morosini, Dulio. *Diego Rivera*. Milan: Fratelli Fabri Editori, 1966.

O'Gorman 1954
O'Gorman, Juan. *La técnica de Diego Rivera en la pintura mural*. Mexico City: Frente nacional de artes plásticas, 1954.

Olachea 1946
Olachea, Elena A. *Diego Rivera*. Mexico City: Universidad Nacional, 1946.

Olivares 1957
Olivares, Armando. *Diego de Guanajuato*. Guanajuato, Mexico: Universidad de Guanajuato, 1957.

Ospovat 1969
Ospovat, Lev Samoilovich. *Diego Rivera*. Moscow: Molodar Guardir, 1969.

Page 1956
Page, Addison Franklin. *The Detroit Frescoes by Diego Rivera*. The Detroit Institute of Arts, 1956.

Pierrot and Richardson 1934
Pierrot, George F., and Edgar P. Richardson. *An Illustrated Guide to The Diego Rivera Frescoes*. The Detroit Institute of Arts, 1934.

Pierrot and Richardson 1934a
Pierrot, George F., and Edgar P. Richardson. *Diego Rivera and His Frescoes of Detroit*. The Detroit Institute of Arts, 1934. Previously published as *The Diego Rivera Frescoes: A Guide to the Murals of the Garden Court*. Detroit: People's Museum Association, 1933.

Poniatowska 1978
Poniatowska, Elena. *Querido Diego te abraza Quela*. Mexico City: Ed. Era, 1978.

Puccinelli 1940
Puccinelli, Dorothy. *Diego Rivera: The Story of His Mural at the 1940 Golden Gate Exposition*. San Francisco, 1940.

Ramos 1935
Ramos, Samuel. *Diego Rivera*. Mexico City: Imprenta Mundial, 1935.

Ramos 1948
Ramos, Samuel. *Diego Rivera: acuarelas (1935–1945)* (*Colección Frida Kahlo*). Mexico City: Editorial Atlante, 1948. Published in English as *Diego Rivera Watercolors (1935–1945)*. New York and London: The Studio Publications, 1949.

Ramos 1958
Ramos, Samuel. *Diego Rivera*. Mexico City: UNAM, Direccion General de Publicaciones, 1958.

Reyero 1983
Reyero, Manuel, ed. *Diego Rivera*. Essays by Ramón Favela, Adrian Villagómez, and Salvador Elizondo. Mexico City: Fundación Cultural Televisa A.C., 1983.

Rodríguez 1948
Rodríguez, Antonio. *Diego Rivera*. (*Colección Anáhuac de arte Mexicano*). Mexico City: Ediciones de Arte, 1948.

Rodriguez 1984
Rodriquez, Antonio. *Guia de los murales de Diego Rivera en la Secretaría de Educación Pública*. Mexico City: Secretaria de Educación Pública, 1984.

Secker 1957
Secker, Hans F. *Diego Rivera*. Dresden: Verlag der Kunst, 1957.

Silva E. 1963
Silva E., R. S. *Mexican History: Diego Rivera's Frescoes in the National Palace and Elsewhere in Mexico City*. Mexico City: Secretaría de Educación Pública, 1963.

Spilimbergo 1954
Spilimbergo, Jorge Enea. *Diego Rivera y el arte en la revolución mejicana*. Buenos Aires: Editorial Indoamérica, 1954.

Suárez 1962
Suárez, Luís. *Confesiones de Diego Rivera*. Mexico City: Ediciones E. R.A., S.A, 1962.

Taracena 1976
Taracena, Berta. *Palacio Nacional*. Mexico City: Secretaría de Obras Pública/Secretaría de Hacienda y Crédito Público, 1976.

Taracena et al. 1979
Taracena, Berta, Xavier Villaurrutia, Samuel Ramos, and Gloria Taracena. *Diego Rivera: pintura de caballete y dibujos*. Mexico City: Fondo Editorial de la Plástica Mexicana, 1979.

Taracena 1981
Taracena, Berta. *Diego Rivera: su obra mural en la Ciudad de México*. Mexico City: Ediciones Galería de Arte Misrachi, 1981.

Thiele 1976
Thiele, Eva-Maria. *Diego Rivera*. Dresden: Verlag der Kunst, 1976.

Tibol 1979
Tibol, Raquel, ed. *Arte y politica/Diego Rivera*. Mexico City: Editorial Grijalbo, 1979.

Torriente 1959
Torriente, Loló de la. *Memoria y razón de Diego Rivera*. 2 vols. Mexico City: Ed. Renacimiento, 1959.

Wolfe 1939
Wolfe, Bertram D. *Diego Rivera: His Life and Times*. New York and London: Alfred A. Knopf, 1939. Published in Spanish as *Diego Rivera: su vida, su obra, y su epoca*. Santiago de Chile: Ercilla, 1941.

Wolfe 1947
Wolfe, Bertram D. *Diego Rivera*. Washington, D.C.: Pan-American Union, 1947.

Wolfe 1963
Wolfe, Bertram D. *The Fabulous Life of Diego Rivera*. New York: Stein and Day, 1963. Published in Spanish as *La fabulosa vida de Diego Rivera*. Mexico City: Editorial Diana, 1972.

II. Selected Articles on Diego Rivera

Acha, Rodríguez, and Belkin 1978
Acha, Juan, Antonio Rodríguez, and Arnold Belkin. "Conferencia sobre Diego Rivera." *El nacional*, 21 January 1978.

Alden 1933
Alden, S. "Further Query: Reply to Men, Machines and Murals." *American Magazine of Art* (June 1933): 254–55.

Amabilis 1935
Amabilis, Manuel. "Diego Rivera y su obra." *El arquitecto* (September 1935).

American Magazine of Art 1935
"Rivera at the New Workers School." *American Magazine of Art* 27, 2 (February 1935): 97–98.

Architectural Forum 1934
Architectural Forum (Special edition on the murals at the New Workers School) 60 (January 1934).

Arenol 1950
Arenol, Angelica. "La bienal de Venecia. Una lección sin precedente." *Hoy*, 26 August 1950, 37–38.

Arnaiz y Freq 1949
Arnaiz y Freq, Arturo. "Diego Rivera en Bellas Artes." *El nacional*, 14 December 1949, 3.

Art Digest 1932
"Rivera's New Sociological Frescoes." *Art Digest* 6, 8 (15 January 1932): 6–8.

Art News 1930
"Mexican Art Group Formed." *Art News*, 12 December 1930, 15.

Art Review 1922
Diego Rivera: Mexican Post-Impressionist." *Art Review* (October 1922): 5.

Atl 1923
Atl, Dr. [Gerardo Murillo]. "Colaboración artistica. Renacimiento artistico?" *El universal*, 13 July 1923.

Atl 1923a
Atl, Dr. [Gerardo Murillo]. "El renacimiento artistico en México." *El universal*, 17 August 1923.

Atl 1933
Atl, Dr. [Gerardo Murillo]. "Le Salon des Indepéndants." *L'action d'art* 4 (1 April 1933): 3–4.

Atl 1956
Atl, Dr. [Gerardo Murillo]. "Como arte el mar." *México en la cultura*. Supplement to *Novedades*, 9 December 1956.

Atl 1957
Atl, Dr. [Gerardo Murillo]. "Se puede decir un poco paradójicamente que el arte sovíetico es mexicano." *México en la cultura*. Supplement to *Novedades*, 15 December 1957.

Azuela 1979
Azuela, Alicia. "El maximato y los muralistos." *Revista Mexicana de cultura*. Supplement to *El nacional*, 27 May 1979.

Azuela 1983
Azuela, Alicia. "Diego Rivera: cambios en una ideología." *Plural*, no. 145 (October 1983): 33–40.

Azuela 1984
Azuela, Alicia. "El escandalo de Diego Rivera en Detroit." *La palabra y el hombre* (Universidad Veracruzana) (January–March 1984).

Barragan Lomeli 1983
Barragan Lomeli, Maria Antonieta. "Diego Rivera y los ciencias médicas." *Tiempo libre*. Supplement to *Uno mas uno*, 15 April 1983.

Barrios 1914
Barrios, Roberto. "Diego Rivera." *La semana ilustrada*, 30 June 1914.

Barrios 1921
Barrios, Roberto. "Diego Rivera pintor." *El universal ilustrado*, 28 July 1921.

Barry 1931
Barry, John D. "Characteristics of Rivera." *Stained Glass Association of America Bulletin* (1931): 247–52.

Basurto 1939
Basurto, Luís G. "Diego Rivera ante los ojos de un iguaro." *Excelsior*, 5 January 1939.

Bayón 1983
Bayón, Damian. "Diego Rivera o las cuentas claras." *Vuelta* 8, 85 (December 1983).

Benitez 1952
Benitez, Fernando. "En Paris existe expectación por el arte mexicano." *Novedades*, 20 May 1952, 1–5.

Best Maugard 1949
Best Maugard, Adolfo. "Diego Rivera, su ética y estética." *Cuadernos americanos* 47, 5 (September–October 1949): 282–89.

Blunt 1935
Blunt, Anthony. "The Art of Diego Rivera." *Listener*, 17 April 1935.

Boynton 1926
Boynton, Ray. "Rivera." *Mexican Folkways* 2, 8 (August–September 1926): 24–31.

California Arts and Architecture 1932
"Evolution of a Rivera Fresco." Interview with Mrs. Sigmund Stern concerning the fresco in her home. *California Arts and Architecture* 41 (June 1932): 34–35.

Cap 1944
Cap, A. R. "Diego Rivera autor de las epopeyas mexicanas." *Así*, 24 June 1944, 27–32.

Cardiel Reyes 1977
Cardiel Reyes, Raul. "La pintura cubista de Diego Rivera." *México en la cultura*. Supplement to *El sol de México*, 11 December 1977.

Cardona Peña 1949–50
Cardona Peña, Alfredo. "Fotocharlos." *El nacional*. Series of 52 articles on Rivera published weekly between 14 August 1949 and 6 August 1950.

Cardoza y Aragón 1957
Cardoza y Aragón, Luís. "Su creación y su ejemplo." *México en la cultura*. Supplement to *Novedades*, 15 December 1957.

Carillo Puerto 1926
Carillo Puerto, Felipe. "From a mural by Diego Rivera." *Mexican Folkways* (February–March 1926).

Catlin 1948
Catlin, Stanton L. "Rivera's Cuernavaca Series." Excerpt from an unpub. manuscript in the Museum of Modern Art library. 1948.

Catlin 1964
Catlin, Stanton L. "Some Sources and Uses of Pre-Columbian Art in the Cuernavaca Frescoes." *Proceedings of the 35th International Congress of Americanists* (Mexico, 1962): 439–49.

Catlin 1978
Catlin, Stanton L. "Political Iconography in the Diego Rivera Frescoes at Cuernavaca, Mexico." In *Art and Architecture in the Service of Politics*, edited by Henry A. Millon and Linda Nochlin, 439–49. Cambridge, Massachusetts: MIT Press, 1978.

Charlot 1950
Charlot, Jean. "Diego Rivera at the Academy of San Carlos." *College Art Journal* 10, 1 (Fall 1950): 10–17.

Charlot 1953
Charlot, Jean. "Diego Rivera in Italy." *Magazine of Art* 46, 1 (January 1953): 3–10.

Climent 1957
Climent, B. Juan. "La evolución artistica de Diego Rivera." *Excelsior*, 14 December 1957.

Colín 1977
Colín, José Luís. "Diego Rivera ante la historia." *El nacional* 7 (continued in volumes 9 and 10) (December 1977).

Cosío Villegas 1923
Cosío Villegas, Daniel. "La pintura en México." *El universal*, 19–20 July 1923, 3–9.

Cosío Villegas 1925
Cosío Villegas, Daniel. "La pintura en México." *Revista de revistas*, 29 March 1925, 23–44.

Cosío Villegas 1953
Cosío Villegas, Daniel. "Nuestra historia." *México en la cultura*. Supplement to *Novedades*, 11 January 1953.

Coss 1935
Coss, Arnulfo. "El contenildo revoluciónarios de la pintura de Diego Rivera." *Octobre* 1 (Mexico City, 1935).

Covarrubias 1949
Covarrubias, Miguel. "Arte moderno en México." *Novedades*, 5 June 1949.

Crespo de la Serna 1949
Crespo de la Serna, Jorge Juan. "Diego Rivera y su evolución artística." *Excelsior,* 24 July 1949.

Crespo de la Serna 1951
Crespo de la Serna, Jorge Juan. "Colore di Diego Rivera." *La biennale* 3 (1951): 6–7.

Crespo de la Serna 1953
Crespo de la Serna, Jorge Juan. "Circunstancias y evolución de las artes plásticas en México en el período 1900–1950." *México en el arte* 10–11 (1953).

Crespo de la Serna 1957
Crespo de la Serna, Jorge Juan. "Diego Rivera obra mural." *Artes de México* 4, 15 (January–February 1957): 64; and 4, 19–20 (September–December 1957): 5–17.

Crespo de la Serna 1967
Crespo de la Serna, Jorge Juan. "El taller de Diego Rivera." *Novedades,* 26 December 1967.

Cruden 1932
Cruden, Robert L. "Open Letter to Edsel Ford." *New Masses* (April 1932): 23.

Cruz 1953
Cruz, Rául de la. "Siqueiros enjuicia a Diego." *Hoy,* 1 August 1953, 43.

Debroise 1977
Debroise, Olivier. "Diego Rivera y la representación del espacio." *Artes visuales* 16 (Winter 1977): 1–16.

Debroise 1977a
Debroise, Olivier. "Rivera y los vanguardios de Paris." *El nacional,* 20 December 1977.

Del Rio 1977
Del Rio, Salvador. "Rivera y la arqûitectura." *Mexico en la cultura.* Supplement to *El sol de México,* 11 December 1977.

Demócrata 1923
"Críticas a las pinturas de Diego Rivera en el Anfiteatro Bolívar y en la Secretaría de Educación Pública." *Demócrata,* 5 July 1923.

Demócrata 1923a
"El movimiento actual de la pintura en México." *Democrata,* 2 August 1923.

Design 1933
"Diego Rivera." *Design* 34 (April 1933): 262–70.

d'Harnoncourt 1930
d'Harnoncourt, René. "Loan Exhibition of Mexican Arts." *Bulletin of the Metropolitan Museum of Art* (October 1930): 210–17.

d'Harnoncourt 1942
d'Harnoncourt, René. "Diego Rivera y José Clemente Orozco." *Tiempo,* 13 November 1942.

Dos Passos 1927
Dos Passos, John. "Diego Rivera Murals." *New Masses* (March 1927).

Douglass 1931
Douglass, Walter H. "Desde el renacimiento, nadie ha igualado la obra pictórica del gran Diego Rivera." *Excelsior,* 24 December 1931, 2–7.

Downs 1979
Downs, Linda. "Diego Rivera's Portrait of Edsel Ford." *Bulletin of the Detroit Institute of Arts* 57, 1 (1979): 47–52.

Driben 1983
Driben, Julia. "Diego Rivera y su legado a la historia de México." *Revista de la Universidad de México,* n.s. 31 (November 1983).

El arquitecto 1926
El arquitecto (Issue devoted to Rivera) 2, 8 (March–April 1926).

Elitzik 1980
Elitzik, Paul. "Discovery in Detroit: The Lost Rivera Drawings." *Americas* 3, 9 (September 1980): 22–27.

Evans 1927
Evans, Ernestine. "Diego Rivera." *Art Work* 3 (June–August 1927): 80–87.

R. Evans 1932
Evans, Robert. "Painting and Politics: The Case of Diego Rivera." *New Masses* (January 1932): 22–25.

Faure 1934
Faure, Elie. "La peinture murale mexicaine." *Art et medécine* (April 1934): Also published in *El universal,* 1 January 1935.

Favela 1979
Favela, Ramón. "Jean Cocteau: An Unpublished Portrait by Diego Rivera." *The Library Chronicle* (University of Texas at Austin) 12 (1979): 10–12.

Fernández 1950
Fernández, Justino. "Diego Rivera: antes y después." *Anales del Instituto de Investigaciones Estéticas* (UNAM) 18 (1950): 63–82.

Fernández 1953
Fernández, Justino. "Tres décadas de la pintura mural en México." *México en el arte* 10–11 (1953): 27–42.

Fernández 1956
Fernández, Justino. "Un retrato excepcional de Diego Rivera." *México en la cultura.* Supplement to *Novedades,* 22 July 1956.

Frías 1920
Frías, José D. "Los pintores mexicanos en Paris." *Zig-zag,* 5 August 1920, 32–34.

Frías 1921
Frías, José D. "El fabuloso pintor Diego Rivera." *Revista de revistas,* 27 November 1921.

García Calderón 1914
García Calderón, Francisco. "La obra del pintor mexicano Diego Ma. Rivera." *El mundo ilustrado,* 19 May 1914.

García Maroto 1928
García Marota, Gabriel. "La obra de Diego Rivera." *Contemporáneos* 1, 1 (June 1928): 43–75.

García Naranjo 1929
García Naranjo, Alfredo. "Repercuciones estéticas." *El universal,* 16 July 1929.

Garcia Naranjo 1956
García Naranjo, Nemesio. "Los setenta años de Diego Rivera." *Novedades,* 5 December 1956.

Gelber 1979
Gelber, Steven M. "Working to Prosperity: California's New Deal Murals." *California History* 58, 2 (Summer 1979): 98–127.

Goldman 1982
Goldman, S. M. "Mexican Muralism: Its Social-Educative Roles in Latin America and the United States." *Aztlan* 13, 1–2 (1982): 111–33.

Gómez de la Serna 1930
Gómez de la Serna, Ramón. "Modigliani et Diego Rivera." *Paris Montparnasse* 13 (February 1930).

Gómez de la Serna 1931
Gómez de la Serna, Ramón. "Riverismo." *Sur* 1, 2 (October 1931): 59–85.

Gómez Morin 1925
Gómez Morin, Manuel. "Los frescos de Diego Rivera." *Antorcha* 1, 20 (14 February 1925): 13–14.

Gual 1949
Gual, Enrique. "El dibujante Diego Rivera." *Novedades,* 5 June 1949.

Guillén 1957
Guillén, Fedro. "Diego Rivera y el mundo de nosotros." *Excelsior,* 8 December 1957.

Guzmán 1961
Guzmán, Martin Luís. "Diego Rivera y la filosofia del Cubismo." In *Obras completas de Martin Luís Guzmán.* 2 vols. Mexico City: Compania General de Educaciones, 1961.

Henríquez Urena 1921
Henríquez Urena, Pedro. "En la orilla: notas sobre Diego Rivera." *Azulejos* 1, 2 (September 1921): 22–23.

Hoy 1952
"De Carlos Chávez a Diego Rivera." *Hoy,* 22 March 1952.

Hoy 1957
Hoy (Entire issue devoted to Rivera), 28 December 1957.

Huerta 1977
Huerta, Efrain. "Cuando digo Diego." *Diario de México,* 14–15 December 1977, 1 and 3.

Hurtado 1951
Hurtado, Emma. "Murales de Diego Rivera en Lerma." *Mexico en la cultura.* Supplement to *Novedades,* 1 July 1951.

Icaza 1948
Icaza, Xavier. "Anticipo a 'El México de Diego.' " *México en el arte* (July 1948): 69–70.

Kahlo 1949
Kahlo, Frida. "Retrato de Diego." *Hoy,* 22 January 1949, 18–21.

Kahn 1918
Kahn, Gustav. "MM. Diego Rivera, André Lhote, et al." *Mercure de France,* 1 December 1918, 518–19.

Kozloff 1978
Kozloff, Max. "The Rivera Frescoes of Modern Industry at the Detroit Institute of Arts: Proletarian Art under Capitalist Patronage." In *Art and Architecture in the Service of Politics,* edited by Henry A. Millon and Linda Nochlin, 216–29. Cambridge, Massachusetts: MIT Press, 1978.

Kupchenko 1977
Kupchenko, Vladimir. "Maximilian Voloshin i Diego Rivera." *Latinskaia Amerika* 2 (1977): 66–182.

Life 1940
"Artists in Action Steal the Show at San Francisco Fair." *Life,* 29 July 1940, 44–49.

Life 1941
"Diego Rivera: His Amazing Mural Depicts Pan-American Unity." *Life,* March 1941, 52–57.

Magdaleno 1949
Magdaleno, Mauricio. "La exposición de Rivera." *El universal,* 9 August 1949.

Malraux 1938
Malraux, André. "Los fresquistas revolucionarios de México." *Todo,* 7 July 1938, 38–39.

Maza 1946
Maza, Francisco de la. "Diego Rivera, historiador." *Excelsior,* 25 January 1946.

Mérida 1924
Mérida, Carlos. "Los nuevos valores en la pintura mexicana." *Revista de revistas,* 18 May 1924, 2 and 30.

Mexican Folkways 1927
"Frescoes in the Ministry of Education." *Mexican Folkways* 3 (April–May 1927): 70 ff.

Mexican Folkways 1928
"Frescoes by Diego Rivera." *Mexican Folkways* (January–March 1928): 167–72.

Mexican Folkways 1930
Issue in homage to Diego Rivera. *Mexican Folkways* 4 (June–August 1930): 160–204.

Micheli 1976
Micheli, Mario. "Le revoluzioni si dipingono sui menti." *Bolaffiarte* 7, 64 (November 1976).

Molina Enriquez 1923
Molina Enriquez, Renato. "La decoración de Diego Rivera en la Preparatoria." *El universal ilustrado,* 22 March 1923.

Moreno Sánchez 1938
Moreno Sánchez, Manuel. "El retrato y la pintura mexicana actual." *Cuadernos de arte* (Universidad de México) 5 (1938): 10.

Moyssen 1976
Moyssen, Xavier. "Leonardo da Vinci y Diego Rivera en Chapingo." *Cuadernos de Culhuacan* 1, 2 (September 1976): 51–55.

Moyssen 1977
Moyssen, Xavier. "El 'Retrato de Detroit' por Diego Rivera." *Anales del Instituto de Investigaciones Estéticas* 13, 47 (1977): 45–58.

Moyssen 1978
Moyssen, Xavier. " 'Vida Nocturna': un cuadro desconocido de Diego Rivera." In *Homenaje al Dr. Arturo Aruaiz y Freq.* Mexico City, 1978.

Moyssen 1982
Moyssen, Xavier. "El 'Heroe' en la obra de Diego Rivera." In *La iconografía en al arte contemporáneo,* 195–206. Instituto de Investigaciones Estéticas, 1982.

Moyssen 1983
Moyssen, Xavier. "El periodo formativo de David Alfonso Siqueiros, Roberto Montenegro, Diego Rivera y José Clemente Orozco." *Historia del arte mexicano* 91–92 (September–November 1983): 21–25.

Nelken 1949
Nelken, Margarita. "La exposición de Diego Rivera." *Hoy,* 6 August 1949.

Novedades 1949
"Obra y estilo de Diego Rivera." *México en la cultura.* Supplement to Novedades, 5 June 1949.

Novo 1924
Novo, Salvador. "Diego Rivera." *El universal ilustrado,* 3 July 1924.

Novo 1957
Novo, Salvador. "Cartas a un amigo." *Hoy,* 14 December 1957, 28–30.

O'Gorman 1956
O'Gorman, Juan. "Diego apostol de la mexicana." *México en la cultura.* Supplement to *Novedades,* 9 December 1956.

O'Higgins 1976
O'Higgins, Pablo. "Homenaje a Diego Rivera—en el Anahuacalli." *El nacional,* 1 November 1976.

Ortega 1922
Ortega, [?]. "La pintura y la escultura en 1922." *El universal ilustrado,* 28 December 1922.

Ortega 1923
Ortega, [?]. "La obra admirable de Diego Rivera." *El universal ilustrado,* 15 March 1923.

Ortega 1924
Ortega, [?]. "Diego Rivera, 'íntimo.' " *El universal ilustrado,* 10 January 1924.

Pach 1929
Pach, Walter. "The Evolution of Diego Rivera." *Creative Art* 4, 1 (January 1929): 17–39.

Palacios 1926
Palacios, Enrique. "Paisajes y gentes de México." *Mexican Folkways* 10 (December 1926–January 1927): 23–29.

Palencia 1949
Palencia, Ceferino "La etape cubista de Diego Rivera." *México en la cultura.* Supplement to *Novedades,* 17 August 1949.

Palencia 1949a
Palencia, Ceferino. "La obra pictórica de desnudo de Diego Rivera." *México en la cultura.* Supplement to *Novedades,* 20 August 1949.

Palencia 1949b
Palencia, Ceferino. "La población infantil y los alcatraces en la pintura de Diego Rivera." *México en la cultura.* Supplement to *Novedades,* 27 August 1949.

Palencia 1949c
Palencia, Ceferino. "El retrato en la exposición de Diego Rivera." *México en la cultura.* Supplement to *Novedades,* 31 August 1949.

Palencia 1950
Palencia, Ceferino. "El pintor ante la historia." *México en la cultura.* Supplement to *Novedades,* 10 September 1950.

Palencia 1957
Palencia, Ceferino. "Las horas de España de Diego Rivera." *México en la cultura.* Supplement to *Novedades,* 15 December 1957.

Palomino 1949
Palomino, Pablo. "El artepopulismo y Diego Rivera." *Excélsior,* 21 August 1949.

Parker 1932
Parker, Howard. "El nuevo Diego Rivera." *Mexican Folkways* 7, 1 (January–March 1932): 31–49.

Paz 1979–80
Paz, Octavio. "Social Realism in Mexico: The Murals of Rivera, Orozco and Siqueiros." *Artscanada* 36 (December 1979–January 1980): 55–65.

Paz 1983
Paz, Octavio. "Re/visiones: Orozco, Rivera, Siqueiros." *Vuelta* 8, 85 (December 1983).

Pellicer 1923
Pellicer, Carlos. "El pintor Diego Rivera." *Azulejos* (December 1923).

Pellicer 1948
Pellicer, Carlos. "Sueño dominical en la Alameda Central de la ciudad de México." *México en el arte* 1 (July 1948): 28–38.

Pellicer and Fernández 1957
Pellicer, Carlos, and Justino Fernández. "México en la pintura mural." *México en la cultura.* Supplement to *Novedades,* 12 May 1957.

Poniatowska 1956
Poniatowska, Elena. "Diego Rivera." *México en la cultura.* Supplement to *Novedades,* 13 November 1956.

Poniatowska 1957
Poniatowska, Elena. "Diego Rivera." *México en la cultura.* Supplement to *Novedades,* 6 January 1957.

Poniatowska 1957a
Poniatowska, Elena. "Sandoval Vallarta." *México en la cultura*. Supplement to *Novedades*, 8 December 1957.

Poniatowska 1957b
Poniatowska, Elena. "El desconocido Diego Rivera." *México en la cultura*. Supplement to *Novedades*, 15 December 1957.

Ramos 1952
Ramos, Samuel. "L'esthétique de Diego Rivera." *México en el arte* (1952): 221–34.

Reyes 1955
Reyes, Alfonso. "Historia documental de mis libros: de las conferencias del Centenario e los cartones de Madrid." *Revista de la Universidad de México* 9, 7 (March 1955): 1–16.

Reyes 1956
Reyes, Alfonso. "Los recuerdos de Diego." *México en la cultura*. Supplement to *Novedades*, 9 December 1956.

Reyes et al. 1957
Reyes, Alfonso, A. Rodríguez, and C. Pellicer. "Diego Rivera." *México in la cultura*. Supplement to *Novedades*, 18 August 1957.

Richardson 1931
Richardson, Edgar P. "Diego Rivera." *Bulletin of the Detroit Institute of Arts* 12, 6 (March 1931): 74–76.

Rodríguez 1944
Rodríguez, Antonio. "Diego Rivera, su vida, obra y accion." *Hoy*, 10 and 17 June 1944.

Rodríguez 1944a
Rodríguez, Antonio. "México ciudad de arte." *Así*, 14 October 1944, 51–54.

Rodríguez 1944b
Rodríguez, Antonio. "Panorama de la pintura mexicana." *Así*, 14 April 1945, 38–45.

Rodríguez 1949
Rodríguez, Antonio. "Yo fui el autor del primer fresco en México." *Hoy*, 5 February 1949, 14–17.

Rodríguez 1949a
Rodríguez, Antonio. "Diego bailó al son del toque! dice Vasconcelos." *Hoy*, 19 February 1949, 20–23.

Rodríguez 1949b
Rodríguez, Antonio. "La novela de un genio." *Hoy*, 9 July 1949, 20–23.

Rodríguez 1949c
Rodríguez, Antonio. "Diego Rivera en la vida y en la leyenda." *Hoy*, 13 and 20 August 1949, 32–37.

Rodríguez 1949d
Rodríguez, Antonio. "Exposición de Diego Rivera." Sunday supplement. *El nacional*, 14 August 1949.

Rodríguez 1949e
Rodríguez, Antonio. "Diego a través de su magna obra." Sunday supplement. *El nacional*, 21 August 1949.

Rodríguez 1949f
Rodríguez, Antonio. "Memorias de Diego Rivera." *Así*, 27 August 1949, 23–25.

Rodrıguez 1949g
Rodríguez, Antonio. " 'Censuran mi pintura porque no han podido triunfar como yo'—dice Diego Rivera." *Hoy*, 24 September 1949, 22–24.

Rodríguez 1949h
Rodríguez, Antonio. "Diego Rivera a través de su magna exposición." Sunday supplement. *El nacional*, 11 September 1949.

Rodríguez 1950
Rodríguez, Antonio. "Exposición de Rivera." Series in Sunday supplements to *El nacional*, 1, 5, 8, and 22 January 1950.

Rodríguez 1950a
Rodríguez, Antonio. "Y así fue el impacto de la pintura mexicana en Europa." *Hoy*, 22 July 1950, 18–21.

Rodríguez 1952
Rodríguez, Antonio. "El Cortés de Diego, monstruo pictórico." *Hoy*, 12 January 1952, 18–21.

Rodríguez 1957
Rodríguez, Antonio. "D. R. en su contacto en Europa." *Siempre*, 18 December 1957.

Rodríguez 1963
Rodríguez, Antonio. "Diego Rivera en la obra del escritor. Ilia Erenburg [*sic*]." *El nacional*, 31 March 1963.

Rodríguez 1978
Rodríguez, Antonio. "Pintor de la revolución que no se hizo." *El universal*, 31 January 1978.

Ross 1942
Ross, Betty. "Posando para Rivera." *Excélsior*, 6 November 1942.

Ross 1942a
Ross, Betty. "Lo cobrado por los murales de Ford sirvió para repatriar a obreros mexicanos." *Excélsior*, 9 November 1942.

Ross 1942b
Ross, Betty. "Posando para Diego Rivera. América no debe vivir ya a merced de la cultura del arte y la filosofía europea." *Excélsior*, 30 November 1942.

Ross 1942c
Ross, Betty. "Posando para Diego Rivera. Los murals de Detroit fueron objeto de controversia." *Excelsior*, 18 December 1942.

Ross 1942d
Ross, Betty. "Posando para Diego Rivera. El arte para los trabajadores debe expresarse en los murales." *Excélsior*, 22 December 1942.

Salazar Mallen 1948
Salazar Mallen, Rubén. "Diego Rivera." *Excélsior*, 11 June 1948.

Sánchez Vásquez 1977
Sánchez Vásquez, Adolfo. "Diego Rivera: pintura y militancia." *El universal*, 12 December 1977.

Silva 1977
Silva, Federico. "Carta a un jóven pintor guanajuatense." *Proceso*, 19 December 1977.

Siqueiros 1921
Siqueiros, David Alfaro. "Diego Rivera pintor de América." *El universal ilustrado*, 7 July 1921.

Siqueiros 1934
Siqueiros, David Alfaro. "El camino contra revolucionario del pintor Rivera." *El universal ilustrado*, 13 September 1934. Originally published in *New Masses* (May 1934): 16–17, 38.

Siqueiros 1935
Siqueiros, David Alfaro. "Hacia la derrota final del Riverismo." *Revista de revistas*, 20 October 1935.

Siqueiros 1944
Siqueiros, David Alfaro. "La obra de Diego Rivera." *Hoy*, 22 July 1944, 24–26.

Siqueiros 1945
Siqueiros, David Alfaro. "Rectificaciones sobre las artes plásticas." *Así*, 27 October 1945, 36–37.

Siqueiros 1949
Siqueiros, David Alfaro. "Ten respuestas de Siqueiros." *Hoy*, 19 November 1949, 22–23.

Souza 1959
Souza, Antonio. "Los niños mexicanos, pintados por Diego Rivera." *Artes de México*, 5, 27 (1959): 3–11.

Souza 1983
Souza, Antonio. "Niños de Diego Rivera." *Revista de la Universidad de México* 31 (November 1983).

Sterne 1973
Sterne, Margaret. "The Museum Director and the Artist: Dr. William Valentiner and Diego Rivera in Detroit." *Detroit In Perspective* 1, 1 (1973): 88–111.

Suárez 1956
Suárez, Luís. "Siqueiros rectifica a Diego Rivera." *Mañana*, 28 April 1956.

Los sucesos 1904
"La exposición de pintura y de apreciación del certamen y de los llamados discípulos de Fabrés." *Los sucesos*, 27 November 1904.

Los sucesos 1904a
"Con toda la oficiosa solemnidad de rigor, asistiendo el señor presidente de la Republica y el señor subsecretario de instrucción, quedo inaugurada el domingo la exposición annual." *Los sucesos*, 27 November 1904.

Tablada 1904
Tablada, José Juan. "El Salón de Alumnos de Bellas Artes." *Revista moderna de México* (December 1904).

Tablada 1911
Tablada, José Juan. "Desde Paris: el Salón de Otoño." *Revista de revistas*, 10 December 1911, 1–9.

Tablada 1920
Tablada, José Juan. "Triunfo de los pintores mexicanos." *Revista de revistas*, 1 August 1920.

Tablada 1923
Tablada, José Juan. "Mexican Painting of Today." *International Studio* 76 (January 1923): 267–76.

Tablada 1923a
Tablada, José Juan. "Diego Rivera, Mexican Painter." *The Arts* 4, 4 (October 1923): 221–33.

Tablada 1930
Tablada, José Juan. "La exposición mexicana en Nueva York." *El universal*, 7 November 1930.

Taracena 1949
Taracena, Berta. "El arte mural de Diego Rivera." *Novedades*, 5 June 1949.

Taracena 1975
Taracena, Berta. "Diego Rivera y su aportación al cubismo." Cultural supplement to *El nacional*, 15 June 1975.

Taracena 1977
Taracena, Berta. "Pintura mural." *México en la cultura*. Supplement to *El sol de México*, 11 December 1977.

Tibol 1954
Tibol, Raquel. "El último fresco de Diego Rivera." *México en la cultura*. Supplement to *Novedades*, 3 January 1954.

Tibol 1957
Tibol, Raquel. "Última entrevista con Diego Rivera." *México en la cultura*. Supplement to *Novedades*, 15 December 1957.

Tibol 1978
Tibol, Raquel. "Diego Rivera en la contradicción ideológica." *El nacional*, 28 January 1978.

Tibol 1983
Tibol, Raquel. "Rivera en el Tamayo: como y porque." *Procesco*, 19 September 1983.

Tibol et al. 1974
Tibol, Raquel, Jorge Alberto Manrique, and Berta Taracena. "Como entender un mural." *Revista de revistas*, 2 January 1974.

Toor 1930
Toor, Francis. "Homenaje a Diego Rivera." *Mexican Folkways* 6, 4 (July–August 1930).

Toor 1935
Toor, Francis. "New Frescoes by Two Mexican Masters." *Three Americas* (April 1935): 7–9.

Torres Bodet 1956
Torres Bodet, Jaime. "Profunda impresión." *México en la cultura*. Supplement to *Novedades*, 9 December 1956.

Torriente 1947
Torriente, Loló de la. "Conversación de David Alfaro Siqueiros, sobre la pintura mural mexicana." *Cuadernos Americanos* (November–December 1947): 4.

Toscano 1949
Toscano, Salvador. "El historicismo en la pintura de Diego Rivera." *Novedades*, 5 June 1949.

El universal grafico 1924
"Diego Rivera habla sobre los enemigos de sus obras." *El universal grafico*, 30 June 1924.

El universal ilustrado 1924
"Diego Rivera y sus discípulos." *El universal ilustrado*, 3 July 1924.

Usita 1925
Usita, Jorge. "Don Rafael Nieto y las pinturas de Rivera." *Demócrata*, 30 June 1925.

Usigli 1955
Usigli, Rodolfo. "Los pintores pintados porsi mismo." *Excélsior*, 13 February 1955.

Vasconcelos 1924
Vasconcelos, José. "Los pintores y la arquitectura." *El universal*, 3 May 1924, 3–4.

Vera de Córdova 1922
Vera de Córdova, Rafael. "Nuestras criticas de arte. El éxito de la exposición de Bellas Artes." *El universal*, 16 November 1922.

Villa Moreno 1950
Villa Moreno, J. "La imaginación y la muerte." *Novedades*, 29 October 1950.

Villaurrutia 1927
Villaurrutia, Xavier. "Historia de Diego Rivera." *Forma* 1, 5 (1927): 29–52.

Villaurrutia 1928
Villaurrutia, Xavier. "The Story of Diego Rivera." *Mexican Life* (April 1928).

Villaurrutia 1938
Villaurrutia, Xavier. "La pintura mexicana moderna." *Hoy*, 23 April 1938.

Villaurrutia 1940
Villaurrutia, Xavier. "Los niños en la pintura de Diego Rivera." *Hoy*, 16 November 1940.

Vlady 1983
Vlady, [?]. "Diego." *Vuelta* 8, 85 (December 1983).

Werner 1960
Werner, Alfred. "The Contradictory Señor Rivera." *The Painter and Sculptor* 3, 1 (Spring 1960): 21–26.

Wiessing 1929
Wiessing, H. P. L. "Diego Rivera." *Wendingen* (Amsterdam) 10, 3 (1929): 2–24.

Wolfe 1924
Wolfe, Bertram D. "Art and Revolution in México." *The Nation* 119 (27 August 1924): 207–8.

Wolfe 1934
Wolfe, Bertram D. "Diego Rivera on Trial." *Modern Monthly* 8, 6 (July 1934): 337–40.

Wolfe 1934a
Wolfe, Bertram D. "Diego Rivera en el banquillo." *El universal ilustrado*, 2 August 1934.

Wolfe 1955
Wolfe, Bertram D. "The Strange Case of Diego Rivera." *Arts Digest* (1 January 1955): 6–8.

Worker's Age 1933
Worker's Age (Rivera supplement) 2, 15 (June 15, 1933).

Ziffren 1933
Ziffren, Lester. "Diego Rivera pintara otra obra monumental." *El nacional*, 4 May 1933.

Zigrosser 1936
Zigrosser, Carl. "Mexican graphic art." *Print Collector's Quarterly* 23, 1 (1936): 64–78.

III. Selected Exhibitions of Diego Rivera's Work

Paris 1910
Paris, Société des Artistes Indépendants. *Catalogue de la 26me Exposition*. 1910.

Paris 1911
Paris, Grand Palais des Champs-Elysées. *Salon d'Automne 9me exposition*. 1911.

Paris 1912
Paris, Societe des Artistes Indépendants. *Catalogue de la 28me exposition*. 1912.

Paris 1912a
Paris, Grand Palais des Champs-Eyesées. *Salon d' Automne 10me exposition*. 1912.

Paris 1913
Paris, Galerie Bernheim-Jeune. *IVe exposition du 'Groupe Libre.'* Preface by Camille Mauclair. 1913.

Paris 1913a
Paris, Société des Artistes Indépendants. *Catalogue de la 29me exposition*. 1913.

Paris 1913b
Paris, Grand Palais des Champs-Elysées. *Salon d'Automne 11me exposition*. 1914.

Munich 1913
Munich, Königliche Kunstausstellungs-gebäude. *Secession: Fruhjahr-Ausstellung*. 1913.

Vienna 1913
Vienna, Opernring 19. *International Schwarz-Weiss Ausstellung*. 1913.

Paris 1914
Paris, Galerie Weill. *Exhibition de Diego H. Riviera* [sic]. Text by B. [Berthe Weill]. 1914.

Paris 1914a
Paris, Société des Artistes Indépendants. *Catalogue de la 30me exposition*. 1914.

Prague 1914
Prague, S.V.U. Mánes. *Moderni Umeni, XXXXV Vystava*. Preface by Alexandre Mercereau. 1914.

Brussels 1914
Brussels, Galerie Georges Giroux. *Artistes indépendants*. 1914.

Amsterdam 1914
Amsterdam, De Onafhankelijken. *3de International Jury-Vrije Tentoonstellung*. 1914.

Madrid 1915
Madrid, Salon de Exposición Arte Moderno. *Los pintores integros*. Text by Ramón Gómez de la Serna. 1915.

New York 1916
New York, Modern Gallery. *Paintings by Cézanne, Van Gogh, Picasso, Picabia, Braque, and Rivera*. 1916.

New York 1916a
New York, Modern Gallery. *Paintings by Cézanne, Van Gogh, Picasso, Picabia, and Rivera*. 1916.

New York 1916b
New York, Modern Gallery. *Exhibition of Paintings by Diego M. Rivera and Mexican Pre-Conquest Art*. 1916.

New York 1917
New York, Society of Independent Artists. *First Annual Exhibition*. 1917.

Paris 1918
Paris, Galerie Eugène Blot. *Exhibition de peinture . . . de Eugène Corneau, André Favory, Gabriel Fournier, André L'hote et Diego Rivera; Sculptures de Paul Cornet et Adam Fischer*. Preface by Louis Vauxcelles. 1918.

Barcelona 1920
Barcelona, Galerie Dalmau. *Exposicion de arte francés de avantaguarda*. Preface by Maurice Reynal. 1920.

New York 1920
New York, 19 E. Forty-seventh Street. *Société anonyme*. 1920.

Los Angeles 1925
Los Angeles Museum. *First Pan-American Exhibition of Oil Paintings*. Text by William Alanson-Bryan. 1925.

Cleveland 1927
Cleveland Museum of Art. *Drawings by Old and Modern Masters*. 1927.

Worcester 1927
Worcester, Massachusetts, Worcester Art Museum. *Exhibition of Sketches by the Mexican Artist Diego M. Rivera*. 1927.

New York 1928
New York, Weyhe Gallery. *Diego Rivera*. Introduction by George W. Eggers. 1928.

New York 1928a
New York, The Art Center. *Mexican Art*. Introductory note by Frank Crowninshield. 1928.

New York 1930
New York, American Federation of the Arts. *Mexican Art* (circulated to New York; Boston; Pittsburgh; Cleveland, Ohio; Washington, D.C.; Milwaukee, Wisconsin; Louisville, Kentucky; and San Antonio, Texas). 1930–31.

San Francisco 1930
San Francisco, California Palace of the Legion of Honor. *Diego Rivera*. Foreword by Katharine Field Caldwell. 1930.

Detroit 1931
The Detroit Institute of Arts. *Exhibition of Paintings and Drawings by Diego Rivera*. No cat. 1931.

New York 1931
New York, The Museum of Modern Art. *Diego Rivera*. Essay by Francis Flynn Paine, notes by Jere Abbott. 1931.

Detroit 1932
Detroit, Galleries of the Society of Arts and Crafts. *Diego Rivera*. 1932.

New York 1933
New York, College Art Association of America. *Mexican Art*. Text by Jorge Crespo de la Serna. 1933.

Chicago 1934
The Art Institute of Chicago. *International Exhibition of Contemporary Prints for A Century of Progress*. 1934.

Detroit 1936
Detroit, Alger House. *Modern Watercolors, Drawings, and Prints*. No cat. 1936.

Detroit 1937
The Detroit Institute of Arts. *Selected Exhibition of the Walter P. Chrysler, Jr., Collection*. Foreword by Walter P. Chrysler, Jr. 1937.

Mexico City 1937
Mexico City, Galería de Arte Moderno. *La pintura mexicana*. Text by Agustín Velázquez Chávez. 1937.

Detroit 1938
Detroit, Alger House. *Exhibition of Portraits of Prominent Detroiters*. No. cat. 1938

Detroit 1983a
The Detroit Institute of Arts. International Watercolor Exhibition. 1938.

Mexico City 1938
Mexico City, Galería de Arte Mexicano. Diego Rivera. 1938.

San Francisco 1939
San Francisco Museum of Art. *Diego Rivera. Drawings and Watercolors from the Collection of the San Francisco Museum of Art and the Collection of the San Francisco Art Association in Custody of the Museum*. Foreword by Grace L. McCann Morley, essay by Heinz Berggruen. 1939 (catalogue published 1940).

San Francisco 1940
San Francisco, Treasure Island, Palace of Fine Arts. *Golden Gate International Exhibition*. Text by Thomas Carr Howe, Jr. 1940.

New York 1940
New York, Riverside Museum. *Latin American Exhibition of Fine Arts*. Introduction by Henry A. Wallace, foreword by L. S. Rowe. 1940.

New York 1940a
New York, The Museum of Modern Art. *Twenty Centuries of Mexican Art*. Essays by Antonio Castro Leal, Alfonso Caso, Manuel Toussaint, Roberto Montenegro, and Miguel Covarrubias. 1940.

Mexico City 1940
Mexico City, Galería de Arte Mexicano. *Exposición internacional de Surrealismo*. Text by André Breton, Wolfgang Paalen, and Cesar Moro. 1940.

Boston 1941
Boston, The Institute of Modern Art. *Modern Mexican Painters* (circulated to Washington, D.C.; Cleveland, Ohio; Portland, Oregon; San Francisco; and Santa Barbara, California). Essay by MacKinley Helm. 1941.

Forest Park/New York 1942
Forest Park, Pennsylvania, Unity House, and New York, International Ladies Garment Workers Union. *Rivera Murals* (New Workers School). Text by Will Herberg. 1942.

New York 1942
New York, The Museum of Modern Art. *Twentieth-Century Portraits*. Essay by Monroe Wheeler. 1942.

Cambridge 1942
Cambridge, Massachusetts, Fogg Museum of Art. *Drawings and Prints by Mexican Artists and by Pablo Picasso*. Text by Justino Fernández. 1942.

New York 1943
New York, The Museum of Modern Art. *Romantic Painting in America* 1943.

Muskegon, 1943
Muskegon, Michigan, The Hackley Art Gallery. *Drawings by Diego Rivera*. (lent by the San Francisco Museum of Art). 1943.

Philadelphia 1943
Philadelphia Museum of Art. *Mexican Art Today*. Introduction by Henry Clifford, essay by Luís Cardoza y Aragón. 1943.

New York 1944
New York, The Museum of Modern Art. *Modern Drawings*. Foreword by Monroe Wheeler, essay by Monroe Wheeler and John Rewald. 1944.

Toronto 1944
Art Gallery of Toronto. *Loan Exhibition of Great Paintings in Aid of Allied Merchant Seamen*. 1944.

Worcester 1944
Worcester, Massachusetts, Worcester Art Museum. *Mexican Art Today*. 1944.

San Francisco 1945
San Francisco Museum of Art. *Art of Our Time*. 1945.

Chicago 1946
The Art Institute of Chicago. *Drawings Old and New*. Text by Carl Schniewind. 1946.

New York 1946
New York, Grand Central Art Galleries. *From Market Place to Museum* (Exhibition of Mexican Arts). 1946.

Mexico City 1947
Mexico City, Museo Nacional de Artes Plásticas. *45 autoretratos de pintores mexicanos*. INBA, 1947.

Cambridge 1948
Cambridge, Massachusetts, Fogg Museum of Art. *Drawings and Watercolors XIX and XX Centuries from the Collection of John S. Newberry, Jr*. Prefatory note by Paul J. Sachs. 1948.

Dallas 1948
Dallas Museum of Fine Arts. *Three Contemporary Mexican Painters*. 1948.

New York 1948
New York, Buchholz Gallery. *Drawings and Watercolors* from *the collections of John S. Newberry, Jr*. (also circulated to Ann Arbor). 1948.

Mexico City 1948
Mexico City, Museo Nacional de Artes Plásticas. *Arte mexicano antiguo y moderno*. 1948.

Detroit 1949
The Detroit Institute of Arts. *Fifty Drawings from the Collection of John S. Newberry, Jr*. Introduction by John S. Newberry, Jr. 1949.

Mexico City 1949
Mexico City, Museo Nacional de Artes Plásticas. *Diego Rivera: 50 años de su labor artística. Exposición de homenaje nacional*. Text by Carlos Chávez, Fernando Gamboa, Frida Kahlo, Samuel Ramos, Germaine Wenziner, Jorge Juan Crespo de la Serna, Ceferino Palencia, Walter Pach, Xavier Villaurrutia, Fernando Benitez, Antonio Rodríguez, Juan O'Gorman, and Susana Gamboa. 1949 (catalogue published 1951).

Venice 1950
Venice. *XXV Biennale di Venezia*. 1950.

Delft 1951
Delft, The Netherlands, Delftse Studenten Kunststichting. *De-schil-der-kunst*. No cat. 1951.

Eindoven 1951
Eindoven, The Netherlands, Stedelijk Van Abbemuseum. *Zomertentoonstelling*. No cat. 1951.

Houston 1951
Houston, Museum of Fine Arts. *Diego Rivera*. 1951.

Paris 1952
Paris. Musée National d'Art Moderne. *Art mexicain du precolombien á nos jours* (an exhibition organized by the Instituto Nacional de Bellas Artes under the direction of F. Gamboa; also circulated to Stockholm and London [see below]). 2 vols. Preface by Fernando Gamboa. 1952.

Stockholm 1952
Stockholm, Liljevalchs Konsthall. *Mexikanst Konst Fran Forntid Till Nutid*. Preface by Fernando Gamboa, essays by Tage Evlander, Carl Albert, and Otte Skold. 1952.

London 1953
London, The Tate Gallery. *Exhibition of Mexican Art from Pre-Columbian Times to the Present*. 2 vols. Introduction by Fernando Gamboa, essay by L. Linné. 1953.

Berlin 1955
Berlin, Akademieder Künste. *Mexikanische Malerei und Graphik*. Introduction by Ignacio Marquez Rodiles. 1955.

Havana 1958
Havana, Museo Nacional de Cuba. *Exposición Rivera*. 1958.

Ann Arbor 1958
Ann Arbor, University of Michigan. *Mexican Art: Pre-Columbian to Modern Times* (circulated to Omaha, Nebraska; Bloomington, Indiana; Syracuse, New York; and Dallas, Texas). Text by James B. Griffin, Harold E. Wethey, and Charles H. Sawyer. 1958.

Brussels 1958
Brussels. *Exposición universal e internacional de Bruselas*. 1958.

Mexico City 1958
Mexico City, Museo Nacional de Arte Moderno. *Obras de Diego Rivera*. Various texts excerpted from essays in Mexico City 1949. 1958.

Santa Barbara 1958
Santa Barbara, California, The Santa Barbara Museum of Art. *Fruits and Flowers in Painting*. 1958.

Zurich 1959
Zurich, Kunsthaus. *Masterworks of Mexican Art from Pre-Columbian Times to the Present* (an exhibition organized by the Instituto Nacional de Bellas Artes under the direction of Fernando Gamboa; also circulated to Cologne, The Hague, Berlin [see below], Vienna, Moscow, Leningrad, Warsaw [see below], Paris, Rome [see below], Copenhagen, and Los Angeles [see below]). 1959–63.

Berlin 1959
Berlin, Akademie der Künste. *Kunst aus Mexiko und Mittelamerika*. Text by Fernando Gamboa, Samuel K. Lothrup, and Gerdt Kutscher. 1959.

Chicago 1959
The Art Institute of Chicago. *The United States Collects Pan-American Art*. Text by Joseph R. Shapiro. 1959.

Mexico City 1959
Mexico City, Museo Nacional de Arte Moderno. *Exposicion de obras de Diego Rivera*. Introduction by Antonio Castro Leal. 1959.

Mexico City 1960
Mexico City, Museo Nacional de Arte Moderno. *El retrato mexicano contemporaneo*. Essays by Paul Westerheim and Justino Fernández. 1960.

Warsaw 1961
Warsaw, National Museum. *Skarby sztuki meksykanskiej od czasów prekolunbyskich do nasych dni*. 1961.

Rome 1962
Rome, Palazzo delle Esposizioni. *Arte messicana dall' antichtà nostri giorni*. Introductory essay by Fernando Gamboa, 1962.

Los Angeles 1963
Los Angeles County Museum of Art. *Master Works of Mexican Art from Pre-Columbian Times to the Present*. Foreword by Richard F. Brown, introduction by Fernando Gamboa. 1963.

Mexico City 1965
Mexico City, Museo de Arte Moderno. *Diego Rivera/ The Collection of Mrs. Dolores Olmedo de Olvera*. Introduction by Antonio Rodríguez. 1965.

Mexico City 1965a
Mexico City, UNAM, Escuela Nacional de Artes Plásticas. *Homenaje al maestro Diego Rivera*. 1965.

New York 1965
New York, The Rockefeller University. *Contemporary Mexican Art*. 1965.

Dallas 1966
Dallas, Southern Methodist University, Meadows Museum. *The Bold Tradition*. No cat. 1966.

Ghent 1966
Ghent, Musée des Beaux-Arts. *Art contemporain du Mexique*. Text by Rodolfo Usigli, Fernando Castro Pacheco, and Samuel Marti. 1966.

Mexico City 1966
Mexico City, Galería de Artes Plásticas, Direccion General de Accion Social, and Departamento del Distrito Federal. *Homenaje a Diego Rivera*. 1966.

New Haven/Austin 1966
New Haven, Connecticut, Yale University Art Gallery, University of Texas Art Museum. *Art of Latin America since Independence* (circulated to San Francisco; La Jolla, California; New Orleans, Louisiana; Tucson, Arizona; Mexico City). Text by Stanton L. Catlin and Terence Grieden. 1966.

Rome 1966
Rome, Palazzo Barberini. *Arte messicana contemporanea*. 1966.

San Diego 1966
San Diego, Fine Arts Gallery. *Latin American Art*. 1966.

Mexico City 1967
Mexico City, Gallerias de la Cuidad de México. *El taller de Diego Rivera*. 1967.

Palm Springs 1967
Palm Springs, California. *The Thirty-Five*. 1967.

New Orleans 1968
New Orleans, The Isaac Delgado Museum of Art. *The Art of Ancient and Modern Latin America*. Text by James B. Byrnes, Marjorie Smith-Zengel, and Hugh J. Smith. 1968.

Los Angeles/New York 1970
Los Angeles County Museum of Art, and New York, The Metropolitan Museum of Art. *The Cubist Epoch.* Text by Douglas Cooper. 1970.

Santa Barbara 1970
Santa Barbara, California, The Santa Barbara Museum of Art. *El arte moderno de Mexico, 1920–1970.* 1970.

New York 1971
New York, Greer Gallery. *Diego Rivera: Guanajuato 1886–Mexico City 1957.* 1971.

Riverside 1971
University of California at Riverside, The Art Gallery. *The Cubist Circle.* Text by Shirly N. Blum. 1971.

San Francisco 1972
San Francisco, Galeria de la Raza. *Drawings and Graphics from the Collection of the San Francisco Museum of Art by Diego Rivera, José Clemente Orozco, and David Alfaro Siqueiros.* No cat. 1972.

Mexico City 1973
Mexico City, Museo de Arte Moderno. *Colección Marte R. Gómez: Obras de Diego Rivera, 1886–1957.* Text by Enrique F. Gual. 1973.

Santiago 1973
Santiago de Chile, Museo Nacional de Bellas Artes. *Orozco, Rivera, Siqueiros.* Essay by Pablo Neruda. 1973.

Mexico City 1974
Mexico City, Museo de Arte Alvar y Carmen T. de Carillo Gil. *Orozco, Rivera, Siqueiros, Paalen Gerzso.* Text by Luís Echevarría Álvarez.

Worcester 1974
Worcester, Massachusetts, Worcester Art Museum. *Mexican Prints and Drawings.* 1974.

Detroit 1976
The Detroit Institute of Arts. *Art and Crafts in Detroit, 1907–1976.* Essays by Joy H. Colby, Thomas Holleman, Sheila Tabakoff, Thom Brunk, Mary Jane Jacob, Dennis Barrie, and Susan Rossen. 1976.

Bradford 1977
Bradford, England, Bradford City Art Galleries *Cityscape, 1910–39: Urban Themes in American, German and British Art* (organized by the Arts Council of Great Britain; circulated to Newcastle-upon-Tyne, Portsmouth, and London). Preface by Joanne Drews, essays by Ian Jeffrey and David Mellor. 1977–78.

Mexico City 1977
Mexico City, Palacio de Bellas Artes. *Exposición nacional de homenaje a Diego Rivera.* Essays by Frida Kahlo, Berta Taracena, Rita Eder, Raquel tibol, Antonio Rodríguez, and Fernando Gamboa. 1977–78.

Detroit 1978
The Detroit Institute of Arts. *The Rouge: The Image of Industry in the Art of Charles Sheeler and Diego Rivera.* Foreword by Frederick J. Cummings, essays by Linda Downs and Mary Jane Jacob. 1978.

Leningrad 1978
Leningrad, The Hermitage. *Diego Rivera and His Master José Maria Velasco.* 1978.

Washington 1978
Washington, D.C., Hirshhorn Museum and Sculpture Garden. *The Noble Buyer: John Quinn, Patron of the Avant-Garde.* Text by Judith K. Zilcer. 1978.

Washington 1978a
Washington, D.C., Hirshhorn Museum and Sculpture Garden. *Orozco/Rivera/Siqueiros: A Selection from Mexican National Collections.* 1978.

Washington/Los Angeles 1978
Washington, D.C., Smithsonian Institution, National Museum of Natural History, and the Los Angeles County Museum of Art. *Treasures of Mexico from the Mexican National Museums (An Exhibition Presented by the Armand Hammer Foundation).* Introduction by Octavio Paz. 1978.

San Francisco 1978
San Francisco, Western Association of Art Museums. *Drawings and Prints by Orozco and Rivera* (circulated to twelve sites in the United States and Canada). No cat. 1978–81.

Flushing 1979
Flushing, New York, The Queens Museum. *José Clemento Orozco and Diego Rivera* (includes San Francisco 1978). Text by Carlos Gutíerrez Solava. 1979.

San Diego 1980
University of California at San Diego, Mandeville Art Gallery. *Images of Mexico from the Pre-Columbian Era to Modernism* (selected works from the collection of Banco Nacional de Mexico and its affiliates presented by Fomento Cultural Banamex). 1980.

Berlin 1980
Berlin, Neue Gesellschaft für bildende Kunst. *Amerika—Traum und Depressions (Malerei und Fotografie 1920/40).* Edited by Eckhart Gillen and Yvonne Leonard. 1980.

Mexico City 1981
Mexico City, Banamex. *250 joyas de Diego Rivera.* Text by Fernando Gamboa. 1981.

Berlin 1982
Nationalgalerie Berlin. *Wand Bild Mexico.* Edited by Horst Kurnitzky and Barbara Beck. 1982.

Mexico City 1982
Mexico City, Edificio del Arzobispado. *Patrimonio cultural de la Secretaría de Hacienda y Credito Público.* 1982.

San Francisco 1982
San Francisco Museum of Modern Art. *Diego Rivera: Mural Studies.* Text by Melissa Broaddus. 1982.

Mexico City/Monterrey 1983
Mexico City, UNAM, Universitaria Facultad de Medicina, and Monterrey, Museo de Monterrey. *Diego Rivera* (colleción Dolores Olmedo). 1983. (Also traveled to Puebla, Museo de Arqueología. 1984).

Mexico City 1983
Mexico City, Museo Rufino Tamayo. *Diego Rivera.* Coordinated by Dolores Olmedo. Text by Charles Pellicer, Xavier Moyssen, Antonio Rodríguez, and José Juárez. 1983.

Mexico City 1983a
Mexico City, Pinacoteca Marques de Jaral de Berrio. *Obras maestras de la coleccion del Banco Nacional de Mexico.* 1983–84.

Holland 1984
Holland, Michigan, Hope College, DuPree Art Center and Gallery. *Art-Mexico: Pre-Columbian–Twentieth Century.* Text by Mary Anne Martin. 1984.

Houston 1984
Houston, The Museum of Fine Arts. *Works on Paper: Mexican Prints and Drawings of the Twentieth Century.* 1984.

Miami 1984
Miami, Center for the Fine Arts. *In Quest of Excellence.* 1984.

Phoenix 1984
Phoenix Art Museum. *Diego Rivera: The Cubist Years* (circulated to New York, San Francisco, and Mexico City). Text by Ramón Favela. 1984.

San Francisco 1984
San Francisco, The Mexican Museum. *Diego Rivera: Selected Works, 1918–1949.* Foreword by Tomás Ybarra-Fausto, essay by Terri Cohn. 1984.

Santa Fe 1984
Santa Fe, New Mexico, Santa Fe Museum of Fine Arts. *A Spirit Shared: Twentieth-Century Art in Mexico and New Mexico.* 1984.

Los Angeles 1984
Los Angles, Museum of Contemporary Art. *The Automobile and Culture.* Essays by Gerald Silk, Henry Flood Robert, Jr., Strother McMinn, and Angelo Tito Anselmi. 1984.

IV. Books Containing Information on Rivera's Life and Art

Abreu Gómez 1946
Abreu Gómez, Ermilo. *Sala de retratos.* Mexico City: Editorial Leyenda, 1946.

Acevedo et al. 1984
Acevedo, Esther, et al. *Guía de murales del centro histórico de la Ciudad de Mexico.* Mexico City: Consejo Nacional de Fomento Educativo, 1984.

Acha 1979
Acha, Juan. *Arte y sociedad en América Latina: el producto artístico y su estructura.* Mexico City: Fondo de Cultura Económica, 1979.

Bayón 1974
Bayón, Damian. *América Latina en sus artes.* Mexico City: Siglo XXI/UNESCO, 1974.

Brenner 1929
Brenner, Anita. *Idols behind Altars.* New York: Payson and Clarke, 1929.

Bufala and Paredes 1979
Bufala, Enzo del, and Edgar Paredes. *El pensamiento critico latinoamericano.* Mexico City: Nueva Sociologia, 1979.

Burchwood 1971
Burchwood, Katharine Tyler. *The Origin and Legacy of Mexican Art*. New York: A. S. Barnes, 1971.

Cabanne 1963
Cabanne, Pierre. *L'epopée du Cubismo*. Paris: La Table Ronde, 1963.

Cardoza y Aragón 1940
Cardoza y Aragón, Luís. *La nube y el reloj: pintura mexicana contemporánea*. Mexico City: UNAM, 1940.

Cardoza y Aragón 1953
Cardoza y Aragón, Luís. *Pintura mexicana contemporánea*. Mexico City: Imprenta Universitaria, 1953.

Cardoza y Aragón 1961
Cardoza y Aragón, Luís. *México: pintura actual*. Mexico City: Ediciones Era, 1961.

Cardoza y Aragón 1964
Cardoza y Aragón, Luís. *México: pintura de hoy*. Mexico City and Buenos Aires: Fondo de Cultura Económico, 1964.

Catlin 1951
Catlin, Stanton L. *Art moderne mexicain*. Paris: Braun, 1951.

Charlot 1962
Charlot, Jean. *Mexican Art and the Academy of San Carlos, 1785–1915*. Austin: University of Texas Press, 1962.

Charlot 1962a
Charlot, Jean. *The Mexican Mural Renaissance, 1920–1925*. New Haven, Connecticut: Yale University Press, 1962.

Cimet 1979
Cimet, Esther. "El muralismo mexicano: una nueva forma de la producion artistica." Unpub. diss., Universidad Iberoamericana, 1979.

Coquiot 1920
Coquiot, Gustave. *Les indépendants, 1884–1920*. Paris: Librairie Ollendorff, 1920.

Cortés Juárez 1951
Cortés Juárez, Erasto. *El grabado contemporaneo*. Mexico City: Ediciones Mexicanas, 1951.

Cossio del Pomar 1939
Cossio del Pomar, Felipe. *Neuvo arte*. 2nd ed. Mexico City: Editorial América, 1939.

Cossio del Pomar 1945
Cossio del Pomar, Felipe. *La rebelión de los pintores*. Mexico City: Editorial Leyenda, 1945.

Craven 1931
Craven, Thomas, *Men of Art*. New York: Simon and Schuster, 1931.

Craven 1940
Craven, Thomas. *Modern Art*. New York: Simon and Schuster, 1940.

Crespo de la Serna 1949
Crespo de la Serna, Jorge Juan. *Cinco interpretes de la Ciudad de México*. Mexico City: Ediciones Mexicanos, 1949.

Debroise 1983
Debroise, Olivier. *Figuras en el tropico plastica mexicana, 1920–1940*. Barcelona: Ediciones Océano, 1983.

de Zayas 1980
de Zayas, Marius. *How, When and Why Modern Art Came to New York*. New York: F. M. Naumann, 1980.

Diehl 1966
Diehl, Gaston. *La peinture moderne dans le monde*. Paris: Flammarion, 1966. Published in English as *The Moderns: A Treasury of Painting throughout the World*. Translated by Edward Lucie Smith.

DuPont et al. 1984
DuPont, Diana C., Katherine Church Holland, Garna Garren Muller, and Laura L. Sueoka. *The Painting and Sculpture Collection, San Francisco Museum of Modern Art*, 249–50. New York: Hudson Hills Press in association with the San Francisco Museum of Modern Art, 1984.

Edwards 1934
Edwards, Emily. *Modern Mexican Frescoes*. Mexico City: Central News Agency, 1934.

Edwards 1966
Edwards, Emily. *Painted Walls of Mexico, from Prehistoric Times until Today*. Photographs by Manuel Álvarez Bravo, foreword by Jean Charlot. Austin: University of Texas Press, 1966.

Ehrenburg 1962
Ehrenburg, Ilya. *People and Life, 1891–1921*. New York: Alfred A. Knopf, 1962. First published in French as *Souvenirs, les années et les hommes*. 2 vols. Paris: Gallimard/L'air du temps, 1962.

Estampas 1947
Estampas de la Revolución Mexicana. Edited by [?] La Estampa Mexicana. Mexico City: La Estampa Mexicana[?], 1947.

Fauchereau, 1982
Fauchereau, Serge. *La révolution cubiste*. Paris: Denoël, 1982

Fauchereau 1985
Fauchereau, Serge. *Peintres revolutionnaires mexicains*. Paris: Messidor, 1985.

Fernández 1937
Fernández, Justino. *El arte moderno en México*. Mexico City: Intituto de Investigaciones Estéticas, Antigua Libreria Robredo José Porrú e Hijos, 1937.

Fernández 1945
Fernández, Justino. *Prometeo*. Mexico City: Editorial Porrúa, S.A., 1945.

Fernández 1949
Fernández, Justino. *Sobre pintura mexicana contemporánea*. Mexico City: Andhra Research University, 1949.

Fernández 1952
Fernández, Justino. *Arte Moderno Contemporáneo de Mexico*. Mexico City: Imprenta Universitaria, 1952.

Fernández 1962
Fernández, Justino. *El hombre: estética del arte moderno y contemporáneo*. Mexico City: Instituto de Invesigaciones Estéticas/UNAM, 1962.

Fernández 1964
Fernández, Justino. *La pintura moderna mexicana*. Mexico City: Ed. Promaca, 1964.

Fernández 1965
Fernández, Justino. *Mexican Art*. Middlesex, England, The Hamlyn Publishing Group Limited, 1965.

Fernández 1969
Fernández, Justino. *A Guide to Mexican Art from Its Beginnings to the Present*. Translated from the Spanish by Joshua C. Taylor. Chicago and London: University of Chicago Press, 1969.

García Granados 1937
García Granados, Rafael. *Filias y fobias: opúsculos historicos*. Mexico City: Polis, 1937.

Goldman 1977
Goldman, Shifra. *Contemporary Mexican Painting in a Time of Change*. Austin: University of Texas Press, 1977.

Gómez de la Serna 1943
Gómez de la Serna, Ramón. *Ismos*. Buenos Aires: Editorial Poseidon, 1943.

Gorostiza [1939]
Gorostiza, José. *Thirteen Mexican Painters*. Mexico City: José Segu, [1939].

Gruening 1928
Gruening, Ernst. *Mexico and Its Heritage*. New York: Century, 1928.

Guerrero 1958
Guerrero, Rául Flores. *Antología de pintores mexicanos del siglo XX*. Prologue by Justino Fernández. Mexico City: Buro Interamericano de Arte, 1958.

Guido 1942
Guido, Angel. *Redescubrimiento de América en el arte*, 245–68. Rosario, Argentina: La Universidad del Litorel, 1942.

Haab 1957
Haab, Armin. *Mexican Graphic Art*. New York: G. Wittenborn, 1957.

Handbook 1935
Handbook of the American Artists Group, 63–66. New York: American Artists Group, 1935.

Helm 1941
Helm, MacKinley. *Modern Mexican Painters*, 37–61. New York: Harper and Brothers, 1941.

Henderson 1983
Henderson, Linda. *The Fourth Dimension and Non-Euclidean Geometry in Modern Art*, 300–310. Princeton, N.J.: Princeton University Press, 1983.

Herrera 1983
Herrera, Hayden. *Frida: A Biography of Frida Kahlo.* New York: Harper and Row, 1983.

Jean 1967
Jean, Marcel, in collaboration with Arpad Mezei. *The History of Surrealist Painting,* 290–91. Translated from the French by Simon Watson. New York: Taylor Grove Press, 1967.

Kirstein 1943
Kirstein, Lincoln. *The Latin-American Collection of the Museum of Modern Art.* New York: The Museum of Modern Art, 1943.

Lewisohn 1937
Lewisohn, Samuel A. *Painters and Personality,* 157–64. New York: Harper and Brothers, 1937.

Luna Arroyo 1972
Luna Arroyo, Antonio. *Juan O'Gorman.* Mexico City: Cuadernos Populares de Pintura Mexicana Moderna, 1972.

Maugard 1923
Maugard, Adolpho Best. *Método de dibujo, tradición, resurgimiento y evolución del arte mexicano.* Mexico City: Departamento Editorial de la Secretariad Educación Pública, 1923.

Maples Arce 1944
Mapels Arce, Manuel. *Modern Mexican Art (El arte mexicano moderno).* London: A. Zwemmer, 1944.

Marques 1975
Marques, René. *Esa mosaico fresco sobre aquel mosaico antiquo.* Rios Piedras, *Puerto Rico: Editorial Cultural,* 1975.

Mérida 1937
Mérida, Carlos. *Modern Mexican Artists.* Mexico City: Frances Toor Studios, 1937.

Mérida 1937a
Mérida, Carlos, ed. *Mexican Art Series.* 10 vols. Mexico City: Frances Toor Studios, 1937.

Michel 1929
Michel, André. *Histoire de l'art.* Paris: Colin, 1929.

Monteforte Toledo 1965
Monteforte Toledo, Mario. *Las piedras vivas: escultura y sociedad en México.* Mexico City: UNAM and Instituto de Investigaciones Sociales, 1965.

Moreno Villa 1948
Moreno Villa, José. *Lo mexicano en las artes plásticas.* Mexico City: Colegio de Mexico, 1948.

Myers 1956
Myers, Bernard. *Mexican Painting in Our Time.* New York: Oxford University Press, 1956.

Nelken 1964
Nelken, Margarita. *El expresionismo en la plástica mexicana de hoy.* Mexico City: Artes Plásticas, INBA-SEP, 1964.

Neuvillate Ortiz 1966
Neuvillate Ortiz, Alfonso. *Pintura actual México,* Mexico City: D.F., 1966.

Neuvillate Ortiz 1977
Neuvillate Ortiz, Alfonso. *La pintura moderna de México,* II. Mexico City: Galeria Misrachi, 1977.

Palencia 1951
Palencia, Ceferino. *Arte contemporáneo de México.* Mexico City: Editorial Patria, 1951.

Payro 1942
Payro, Julio E. *Pintura moderna.* Buenos Aires: Poseidon, 1942.

Paz 1960
Paz, Octavio. *La pintura mural de la revolución mexicana, 1921–1960.* Mexico City: Fondo Editorial de la Plastica Mexicana, 1960.

Portuondo n.d.
Portuondo, José A. *Estética y revolución.* Havana, Cuba: Empresa consolidada de Artes Graficas, n.d.

Reed 1960
Reed, Alma. *The Mexican Muralists.* New York: Crown Publishers, 1960.

Reyes 1963
Reyes, Alfonso. *Frente a la pantalla.* Mexico City: Direccion General de Difusion, UNAM, 1963.

Robinson 1946
Robinson, Ione. *A Wall to Paint On.* New York: E. P. Dutton, 1946.

Rodríguez 1969
Rodríguez, Antonio. *A History of Mexican Mural Painting.* London: Thames and Hudson, 1969.

Rodríguez 1970
Rodríguez, Antonio. *El hombre en llamas: historia de la pintura mural en México.* London: Thames and Hudson, 1970.

Rodríguez Prampolini 1969
Rodríguez Prampolini, Ida. *El Surrealismo y el arte fantastico de Mexico.* Mexico City: UNAM, 1969.

Rojas 1968
Rojas, Pedro. *The Art and Architecture of Mexico from 10,000 B.C. to the Present Day.* Translated by J. M. Cohen. Middlesex, England: The Hamlyn Publishing Group limited, 1968.

Salazar 1926
Salazar, Rosendo. *Mexico en pensamiento y acción.* Mexico City: Avante, 1926.

Schmeckebier 1939
Schmeckebier, Laurence E. *Modern Mexican Art.* Minneapolis: University of Minnesota Press, 1939.

Shapiro 1973
Shapiro, D., ed. *Social Realism: Art as a Weapon.* New York: Frederick Ungar, 1973.

Stewart 1951
Stewart, Virginia. *Forty-five Contemporary Mexican Artists: A Twentieth-Century Renaissance.* Palo Alto, California: Stanford University Press, 1951.

Suárez 1972
Suárez, Orlando S. *Inventario del muralismo mexicano.* Mexico City: UNAM, 1972.

Tablada 1927
Tablada, José Juan. *Historia del arte en México.* Mexico City: Aguilar, 1927.

Teja Zabre 1935
Teja Zabre, Alfonso. *Guía de la historia de Mexico: una interpretación moderna.* Mexico City: Imprenta del Ministerio de Relaciones Exteriores, 1935.

Tibol 1964
Tibol, Raquel. *Arte mexicano—epoca moderna y contemporanea.* Mexico City and Buenos Aires: Editorial Hermes, 1964.

Tibol 1966
Tibol, Raquel. *Historia general del arte mexicano.* 2 vols. Mexico City: Editoral Hermes, 1966.

Tibol 1974
Tibol, Raquel. *Orozco, Rivera, Siqueiros, Tamayo.* Mexico City: Cuadernos del Fondo de Cultura Económica, 1974.

Vela 1936
Vela, Arqueles. *Historia materialistica del arte.* Mexico City: Secretaría de Educación Pública, 1936.

Velázquez Chávez 1935
Velázquez Chávez, Agustín. *Indice de la pintura mexicana contemporanea.* Mexico City: Arte Mexicano, 1935.

Velázquez Chávez 1937
Velázquez Chávez, Agustín. *Contemporary Mexican Artists.* New York: Covici-Friede, 1937.

Villaurrutia 1936
Villaurrutia, Xavier. *La pintura mexicana.* Barcelona: Salvá Editores, 1936.

Vorobëv 1962
Vorobëv, Marevna. *Life in Two Worlds.* Translated by Bennett Nash. New York: Abelard-Schuman, 1962.

Vorobëv 1972
[Vorobëv], Marevna. *Life with the Painters of La Ruche.* New York: MacMillan, 1974.

Zabludowsky 1966
Zabludowsky, Jacobo. *Charlos con pintores.* Prologue by D. A. Siqueiros. Mexico City: Costa-Amic, 1966.

V. A Selected List of Rivera's Writings on Art

Rivera 1921
"La exposicion de la Escuela Nacional de Bellas Artes." *Azulejos* 1, 3 (October 1921): 21–26 (ill.).

Rivera 1921a
"La conferencia del pintor Diego Rivera." *Excelsior,* 21 October 1921.

Rivera 1923
"Las pinturas decorativas del Anfiteatro de la Preparatoria." *El universal ilustrado*, 1 January 1923, 363.

Rivera 1923a
"Manifesto de los pintores mexicanos." *Mundo*, 26 June 1923, 434.

Rivera 1923b
"Dos años." *Azulejos* (December 1923): 26 and 41.

Rivera 1923c
La accion de los ricos yanquis y la servidumbre del obrero mexicano. Mexico City: Biblioteca Defensor del Pueblo, 1923.

Rivera 1924
"Diego Rivera habla sobre la arquitectura." *El universal*, 28 April 1924, 3 and 6.

Rivera 1924a
"The Guild Spirit in Mexican Art." (As related to Katherine Anne Porter.) *Survey Graphic* 5, 2 (1 May 1924): 174–78.

Rivera 1924b
Abraham Angel. Mexico City: Talleres Graficos de la Nacion, 1924.

Rivera 1925
"From a Mexican Painter's Notebook." *The Arts* 7, 1 (January 1925): 21–24.

Rivera 1925a
"Art Interpretations." *Mexican Art and Life* 1, 10 (27 January 1925).

Rivera 1925b
[Note on Anfiteatro Bolívar]. *El arquitecto* 2, 5 (September 1925).

Rivera 1925c
"Los retablos." *Mexican Folkways* 1, 3 (October–November 1925): 7–12.

Rivera 1926
"La pintura mexicana: el retrato." *Mexican Folkways* 1, 5 (February–March 1926): 5–8.

Rivera 1926a
"Autobiografía." *El arquitecto* 2, 8 (March–April 1926): 1–36 (ill.).

Rivera 1926b
"Edward Weston y Tina Modotti." *Mexican Folkways* 2, 6 (April–May 1926): 27–28, trans. 16–17.

Rivera 1926c
"Pintura de pulquerías." *Mexican Folkways* 2, 7 (June–July 1926): 10–15, trans. 16–17.

Rivera 1926d
"La nueva arquitectura mexicana." *Mexican Folkways* 2, 9 (October–November 1926): 24–27, trans. 18–19.

Rivera 1926e
"Pintores modernos de México." *Social* [Havana] (November 1926).

Rivera 1926–27
"Children's Drawings in Mexico." *Mexican Folkways* 2, 10 (December 1926–January 1927): 6–7.

Rivera 1927
"Verdadero, actual y unica expresion pictorica del pueblo mexicano." *La sierra* 1, 9 (September 1927).

Rivera 1927a
"Talla directa." *Forma* 1, 3 (1927): 1–3.

Rivera 1928
"Conferencias sobre arte y cultura sovieticos" (in *Gacetilla* by Eugene Lyons of the *United Press*?), dated Moscow, 17 April 1928.

Rivera 1928a
"Del trabajo de Cristina Durieux." *Mexican Folkways* 5, 3 (July–September 1928): 158.

Rivera 1929
"The Revolution in Painting." *Creative Art* 4, 1 (January 1929): 17–18, 23–30.

Rivera 1929a
"Conferencia sobre la modalidad de la obra de los artistas franceses contemporaneos." *El universal*, 10 August 1929.

Rivera 1929b
"Maria Izquierda." *El universal*, 6 October 1929. Also published in *Mexican Life* 5, 12 (December 1929): 33–38.

Rivera 1930
"Mardonio Magana." *Mexican Folkways* 6, 2 (March–April 1930): 66–71. Also published in Sunday supplement to *El universal*, 30 November 1930.

Rivera 1930a
Introduction to *José Guadalupe Posada*, edited by Frances Toor. Mexico City, 1930.

Rivera 1931
The Genius of America, 88-94. New York: Committee on Cultural Relations with Latin America, 1931.

Rivera 1931a
"Scaffoldings." *Hesperian* (Spring 1931).

Rivera 1932
"Mickey Mouse and American Art." *Contact* 1, 1 (1932): 37–39.

Rivera 1932a
"Children's Drawings in Mexico." *School Arts* 31, 6 (February 1932): 378–81.

Rivera 1932b
"Position of the Artist in Russia Today." *Arts Weekly* 1, 1 (March 1932).

Rivera 1932c
"The Revolutionary Spirit in Modern Art." *The Modern Quarterly* 6, 3 (Autumn 1932): 51–57.

Rivera 1933
"El arte de un revolucionario." *Excelsior*, 1 April 1933.

Rivera 1933a
"Dynamic Detroit—An Interpretation." *Creative Art* 12, 4 (April 1933): 289–95.

Rivera 1933b
"Sobre el arte en el municipio de New York." *Excelsior*, 14 May 1933.

Rivera 1933c
"Art and the Worker." *The Modern Monthly*, (June 1933).

Rivera 1933d
Various articles in *Worker's Age* (Rivera Supplement), 2, 15 (15 June 1933): 1, 7–8, 9.

Rivera 1933e
"What is Art For?" *The Modern Monthly* 8 (June 1933): 275–78.

Rivera 1933f
"The Stormy Petrel of American Art on His Art." *London Studio* 6, 28 (July 1933): 23–26.

Rivera 1933g
"Diego Rivera Exposes the Lies of *Daily Worker*." *Worker's Age* (August 1933).

Rivera 1933h
"I Paint What I See." *Worker's Age* (December 1933).

Rivera 1934
"Architecture and Mural Painting." *Architectural Forum* 60 (January 1934): 3–6.

Rivera 1934a
"La perspectiva curvilinea." *El universal grafico*, 1 December 1934.

Rivera 1934b
Renascent Mexico. New York: Covici-Friede, 1934.

Rivera 1934c
"Trés pinturas murales en el Palacio Nacional." *Mexico Antiguo* (1934).

Rivera 1934d
Introduction to *Portrait of America*. Text by Bertram Wolfe. New York: Covici-Friede, 1934.

Rivera 1935
"Lo que opina Diego Rivera sobre la pintura revolucionaria." *Octobre* [Mexico City] (October 1935): 1. Also published in *Claridad* [Buenos Aires] 15, 298 (February 1936.

Rivera 1935a
Raices politicos y motivos personales de la controversia Siqueiros-Rivera. Mexico City: Imprenta Mundial, 1935.

Rivera 1938
"Desfile del primero de mayo." *Novedades*, 6 May 1938.

Rivera 1938a
"Cardenas agarra el toro por los cuernos." *Novedades*, 20 May 1938.

Rivera 1938b
"Marchar separados pero pagar juntos." *Novedades*, 27 May 1938.

Rivera 1938c
"Rivera on Trade Union Congress." *Socialist Appeal,* 10 September 1938.

Rivera 1938d
"Protesta contra el vandalismo en la destruccion de la pinturas de Juan O'Gorman." *Clave* (December 1938).

Rivera 1938e
"Haya de la torre." *Clave* (December 1938).

Rivera 1939
"Los paises del Caribe." *Clave* 4 (1 January 1939): 33–41.

Rivera 1939a
"Pintura mural y arquitectura." *Arquitectura* 7, 74 (September 1939): 345–46.

Rivera and Breton 1938
Rivera, Diego, and André Breton. "Manifesto: Towards a Free Revolutionary Art." *Partisan Review* 6, 1 (Autumn 1938): 49–53.

Rivera 1942
"La pintura mexicana." *Excelsior,* 18 March 1942.

Rivera 1943
"México y Posada." *Novedades,* 4 June 1943, 4.

Rivera 1943a
"El arte base del Panamericanismo." *Así,* 14 August 1943, 8–9 and 54, and *Así,* 23 October 1943, 16 and 58.

Rivera 1943b
"Cuidemos nuestro prestigio." *Mañana,* 25 September 1943, 56–58.

Rivera 1943c
"Frida Kahlo y el arte mexicano." *Boletín del Seminario de Cultura Mexicana* 1, 2 (October 1943): 89–101.

Rivera 1945
"¿Hay crisis en la pintura mexicana?" *Así,* 6 January 1945, 66–67.

Rivera 1945a
"Papel de la escuelas al aire libre." *Así,* 27 January 1945, 60–61.

Rivera 1945b
"Sobre el 'gusto' durante la revolucion." *Excelsior,* 28 January 1945.

Rivera 1945c
Pages 18–19 in *Manuel Álvaréz Bravo Fotografias* (exh. cat.). Mexico City: Sociedad de Arte Moderno, 1945.

Rivera 1946
"El movimiento en la escultura." *Novedades,* 30 May 1946, 7.

Rivera 1947
Introduction to *45 autoretratos de pintores mexicanos* (exh. cat.). Mexico City: Museo Nacional de Artes Plásticas, 1947.

Rivera 1949
"Diego relata a los que afirman ser los autores del primer fresco en Mexico." *Hoy,* 12 February 1949, 17–19.

Rivera 1949a
"Los Judas." *Espacios* 3 (Spring 1949).

Rivera 1949b
"Diego Rivera narra sus memorias a Antonio Rodríguez." *Hoy,* 2 July 1949; 6 August 1949; 13 August 1949; 27 August 1949; and 1 October 1949.

Rivera 1950
"La escultura de Francisco Arturo Marin." *Espacios* 6 (January 1950).

Rivera 1952
"Integración plástica en la cámara de distribición del agua del Lerma, Tema Medular: el agua origin de la vida en la tierra." *Espacios* 9 (February 1952).

Rivera 1956
Text for the catalogue of an exhibition of works by Pablo O'Higgins, 3 July 1956.

Rivera 1956a
"Homenaje a Frances Toor." *Mexico en la cultura.* Supplement to *Novedades,* July 1956.

Rivera 1956–57
"Mis confesiones." *Mañana,* 8 and 29 December 1956; 5, 12, 19, and 26 January 1957; 2, 9, 16, and 23 February 1957; and 2 March 1957.

VI. Books and Periodicals Illustrated by Rivera

1912
Dario, Ruben. "Cabezas: Angel Zarraga (con dibujos de Diego Maria Ribera [*sic*])." *Mundial Magazine* 2, 19 (November 1912).

1925
Méndez Rivas, Joaquin. *Cuauhtémoc, tragedia.* Mexico City, 1925.
Goldschmidt, Alfons. *Mexiko.* Berlin: Ernst Rowohlt, 1925.

1927
Velázquez Andrade, Manuel. *Fermín.* Mexico City: Textos Modernos, 1927.
Velázquez Andrade, Manuel. *Fermín Lee.* Mexico City: Textos Modernos, 1927.

1928
Cover for *Krasnaya Niva* (Moscow), 17 March 1928.
Cover for *Le Monde* (Paris), 20 October 1928.
Marín, Guadalupe. *La unica.* Mexico City: Editorial Jalisco, 1928.

1931
Cover and illustrations in *Fortune* (January 1931).

1932
Ludwig, Emil. "Joseph Stalin." *Cosmopolitan Magazine* (September 1932).
Cover for *Fortune* (November 1932).

1933
Beals, Carleton. *Mexican Maze.* Philadelphia: J. B. Lippincott, 1933.
Cover for *Fortune* (February 1933).

1935
Chase, Stuart. *Mexico: A Study of Two Americas.* New York and Mexico City: MacMillan, 1935.
Mediz Bolio, Antonio. *La tierra del venado y el faisán.* Mexico City: Editorial Cultura, 1935. Published in English as *The Land of the Deer and the Pheasant.* Translated by Enid Eder Perkins. Mexico City: Editorial Cultura, 1935.

1936
Berliner, Isaac. *La ciudad de los palacios.* Mexico City, 1936.

1937
López y Fuentes, Gregorio. *El Indio.* Indianapolis: Bobbs-Merril, 1937.

1938
Cover for *Fortune* (October 1938).

1943
Brenner, Leah, Diego Rivera, and W. L. White. "Two Reports on Mexico at War." *Town and Country* (March 1943): 48–49 ff.

1945
Brenner, Leah. "Moon Magic: A Story Based on the Boyhood of Diego Rivera." *Virginia Quarterly* (Winter 1945): 68–81.
Brenner, Leah. "The Drunken Lizard: A Story of the Boyhood of Diego Rivera." *Asia and the Americas* 45 (August and October 1945): 382–87 and 485–90.

1949
Frontispiece (*Retrato de Benito Juárez*) in *Tiempo* 14, 360 (25 March 1949).

1950
Neruda, Pablo. *Canto general.* Mexico City, 1950 (with David Alfaro Siqueiros; limited edition of 500 copies).

1953
Brenner, Leah. *An Artist Grows Up in Mexico.* New York: Beechhurst Press, 1953.

1964
Brenner, Leah. *The Boyhood of Diego Rivera.* New York: A. S. Barnes, 1964.

Index to Works by Rivera

Photo Credits

Photographs of works of art by Diego Rivera have been supplied, in the majority of cases, by the owners or custodians of the works, as cited in the captions and in the checklist of the exhibition. Individual photographers are acknowledged below, as are the sources for documentary photographs and comparative illustrations.

Akademische Druck-und-Verlagsanstalt, Graz, Austria: figs. 273, 283, 364
Alinari/Art Resource: fig. 363
Archivo Mérida, Mexico City: fig. 121
Artcetera (Earl Hudnall, photographer): fig. 324
Dirk Bakker: figs. 2, 4, 7–10, 13–15, 20–23, 25–27, 31–32, 37–40, 42–43, 45–47, 52–56, 66, 68–69, 70–71, 73, 76–77, 81, 92–93, 99, 103, 109, 115, 140–41, 145, 156, 161, 173, 185, 198–99, 210, 212, 227, 229, 230, 233–35, 238, 243–44, 250–51, 253, 255, 257, 261–65, 268–69, 284, 295, 336, 338, 340–41, 343–46, 349–51, 353, 355, 357, 359, 361–62, 365–66, 368, 373–88, 390–94, 397–406
Don Beatty: figs. 292, 310–15
Ben Blackwell: figs. 82, 190
Irving Bloomstram: fig. 301
Lola Alvarez Bravo: figs. 237, 242
Manuel Alvarez Bravo: fig. 271
Joan Broderick: figs. 74, 88, 90, 101, 105, 114, 117, 136, 157
Betty Brown: figs. 276–77
Art Carter: fig. 221
Mildred Constantine: figs. 87, 122, 132
Swain Edens: fig. 245
Dick Eels: fig. 209
Miguel Primo Rivera Estrada: figs. 95, 240
Fototeca del INAH (Instituto Nacional de Antropología e Historia), Mexico: figs. 30, 41, 78, 86, 96, 133, 138, 236, 241, 246, 248, 252, 259, 270, 272, 274, 278–79, 281, 285, 287–88, 290, 337, 372
Ford Archives, Henry Ford Museum, Dearborn, Michigan (W. J. Stettler, photographer): figs. 177, 370–71
Galería de Arte Mexicano, Mexico City: fig. 215
Phillip Galgiani: figs. 89, 104, 120, 144, 146
Bob Hawks: fig. 62
R. H. Hensleigh: fig. 153
Hoover Institution, Bertram Wolfe Archives, Stanford, California: figs. 160, 188, 224
INBA, Centro de Informacion y Documentation de Artes Plasticas, Mexico: figs. 1, 3, 5, 19, 28–29, 79, 95, 240, 242, 291
Eric Mitchell: figs. 100, 129
Gabriel Moulin: fig. 222
Museum of Fine Arts, Boston: fig. 231
Don Myer: figs. 85, 108, 155
Francis V. O'Connor: figs. 305–7, 316–19, 321–22
Dolores Olmedo: fig. 247
Alexander Piaget: fig. 191
Emmy Lou Packard: fig 222
Francis Rich: fig. 221
San Francisco Museum of Modern Art: fig. 389
Bob Schalwijk: figs. 11, 12, 34, 36, 44, 91, 97, 154, 189, 256, 258, 282, 333, 352, 360, 407
Robert Sengstacke: fig. 326
Smithsonian Institution, National Museum of American Art, Peter A. Juley and Son Collection, Washington, D.C.: figs. 134 (J00033259) and 304 (J0081016)
Smith College, Sophia Smith Collection, Northampton, Massachusetts: fig. 137
Victor A. Sorell: fig. 331
Sotheby's, New York: figs. 17, 75, 128, 192, 226, 342
Peter Stackpole: fig. 218
Tagliarini: fig. 33
UPI/Bettmann Newsphotos, New York: page 12, figs. 179, 180, 181, 214, 253, 260
Crispin Vázquez: fig. 247
John P. Weber: figs. 327–28
Yale University, Beinecke Library, Yale Collection of American Literature, New Haven, Connecticut: fig. 178